The Complete Illustrated Book of

HERBS

The Complete Illustrated Book of
HERBS

Gardening • Health • Beauty • Crafts • Cooking

Reader's
digest

New York | Montreal

A READER'S DIGEST BOOK

Copyright © 2016 Trusted Media Brands, Inc.

All rights reserved. Unauthorized reproduction, in any manner, is prohibited.
Reader's Digest is a registered trademark of Trusted Media Brands, Inc.

ISBN 978-1-62145-314-7

Library of Congress Cataloging-in-Publication Data
The complete illustrated book of herbs : growing, health & beauty, cooking, crafts.
        p. cm.
    Includes index.
1. Herbs. 2. Herb gardening. 3. Herbs--Therapeutic use. 4. Cookery (Herbs) I. Reader's Digest
Association.
    SB351.H5C65 2009
    635'.7--dc22

                                    2008046082

We are committed to both the quality of our products and the service we provide to our customers.
We value your comments, so please feel free to contact us.

    Reader's Digest Adult Trade Publishing
    44 South Broadway
    White Plains, NY 10601

For more Reader's Digest products and information, visit our website:
    www.rd.com (in the United States)
    www.readersdigest.ca (in Canada)

Printed in China

1 3 5 7 9 10 8 6 4 2

Contents

Introduction

Herbs have been used for thousands of years to flavor and preserve food, treat ailments, ward off pests and diseases, freshen the air, and decorate and enhance our lives. Over the centuries they have also become associated with fascinating myths, legends, and folklore.

In general terms, an herb is a plant that is valued for its flavor, aroma, or medicinal properties, and different parts of an herb — such as the stalks, flowers, fruits, seeds, roots, or leaves — may have important applications. From small herbs growing beside our highways to bushy shrubs in mountain areas to tall trees in lush tropical rain forests, there are literally thousands of plants all over the world that belong to the herb family.

In *The Complete Illustrated Book of Herbs* we have combined traditional knowledge and herbal wisdom with up-to-date advice from gardening experts, herbalists, natural therapists, cleaning specialists, craft experts, and cooks to show you how to grow herbs successfully and make the best use of them in your daily life. The comprehensive information on more than 100 herbs in the A-to-Z directory, together with the chapters on how to use them, will enable you to improve your health, save money, and use fewer chemicals in your home.

With gardening know-how, safe herbal remedies, natural beauty products, innovative craft ideas, herbal cleaning items, and delicious recipes, this practical reference guide to herbs is packed with information and illustrated with beautiful photographs. We hope you will find it a source of inspiration.

> **IMPORTANT NOTE FOR OUR READERS**
>
> **Growing herbs** Some herbs can become invasive and may be toxic to livestock. This information has been given where possible, but regulations do change from time to time. Readers are advised to consult local plant services if they have any concerns.
>
> **Herbal medicine** While the creators of this book have made every effort to be as accurate and up to date as possible, medical and pharmacological knowledge is constantly changing. Readers are advised to consult a qualified medical specialist for individual advice. Moreover, even though they are natural, herbs contain chemical substances that can sometimes have marked side effects. If used unwisely, they can be toxic. The writers, researchers, editors, and publishers of this book cannot be held liable for any errors, omissions, or actions that may be taken as a consequence of information contained in this book.

Top row, left: Sacred lotus (*Nelumbo nucifera*). Right: Sweet marjoram (*Origanum marjorana*). Bottom row, left: Garden thyme (*Thymus vulgaris* 'Silver Posie'). Right: Echinacea (*Echinacea* sp.)

Herb directory

The history of herbs, their uses, and methods of cultivation are fascinating, rewarding topics. This practical guide to more than 100 herbs, most of which can be grown in a home garden, tells you how to cultivate, use and store herbs.

Top row, left to right: Common thyme (*Thymus vulgaris*), feverfew (*Tanacetum cinerariifolium*), *Ocimum basilicum* 'Thai Basil' and *Ocimum basilicum* 'Dark Opal'

Middle row, left to right: Common sage (*Salvia officinalis*), pink-flowering rosemary (a variety of *Rosmarinus officinalis*), hawthorn (*Crataegus* sp.)

Bottom row, left to right: Marsh mallow (*Althaea officinalis*), rau ram or Vietnamese mint (*Persicaria odorata* syn. *Polygonum odoratum*)

Herb directory

Aloe vera

Aloe vera syn. *A. barbadensis, A. vulgaris* Aloeaceae

The ancient Egyptians called it the "plant of immortality," and Cleopatra used its juices to help preserve her beauty. The clear gel from the cut leaves has soothing and healing properties. Aloe vera is suitable for large pots and rockeries and as an indoor plant.

Other common names Barbados aloe, bitter aloe, Curacao aloe
Part used Leaves

■ Gardening

Aloe vera is a succulent plant with very fleshy light green leaves that create a fan from the stemless base. In warm climates it produces narrow tubular yellow flowers. Cape aloe (*A. ferox*) is a tall single-stemmed species that has long, grayish, spiny succulent leaves and tall, handsome spikes of tawny orange flowers.

• **Position** Aloe requires a sunny position and a very well-drained soil.

• **Propagation** *Aloe vera* can be raised from seed, but it rarely sets seed in other than warm climates. Propagate it from offsets that form at the base of the plant. Allow these plantlets to dry for two days before planting them into small pots filled

Plant the dried-out plantlets into small pots filled with gritty free-draining potting mix.

with a gritty free-draining potting mix. Once they are well established, transfer them to their permanent position.

• **Maintenance** Aloe is affected by even light frosts, and in areas where winter temperatures fall below 40°F (5°C), it is best grown in pots and brought indoors in cool weather. It makes an excellent indoor plant in good light.

• **Pests and diseases** Mealybug may prove a problem for plants grown indoors, although it rarely occurs on those grown in the garden. Spray with insecticidal soap, which is nontoxic to animals and leaves no residue. Apply it late in the afternoon, because it can burn sensitive plants in full sun or at high temperatures.

• **Harvesting and storing** Harvest leaves as needed, using only as much of the leaf as required. Cut the used end back to undamaged tissue, then wrap in plastic wrap and store in the refrigerator for further use.

■ Herbal medicine

Aloe sp., including *Aloe vera* syn. *A. barbadensis* and *A. ferox*. Part used: leaves. The clear mucilaginous gel from the center of the aloe vera leaf has anti-inflammatory and healing properties. Probably best known for its ability to encourage the healing of burns, aloe vera gel can also be applied to wounds, abrasions, eczema, psoriasis, and ulcers.

The exudate from the cut aloe vera leaf acts as an extremely cathartic laxative, and consequently, homemade preparations

Aloe vera

of aloe vera should not be consumed. Commercial preparations (without the laxative constituents) are available, and preliminary research indicates that they may be beneficial in a range of conditions, including non-insulin-dependent diabetes mellitus and high blood lipid levels.

For the safe and appropriate use of aloe vera, see First aid, *page 220*. Do not take aloe vera internally if you are pregnant or breastfeeding. Topical application is considered safe during these times.

■ Natural beauty

Ultra-soothing and nourishing for even the most parched and dehydrated skin, aloe vera is also a mild exfoliant, gently removing dead skin cells and stimulating cell regeneration, helping to prevent scarring and diminish wrinkles. For specific treatments, see Sunburn, *page 255*, and Hands and nails, *page 258*. To treat your cat or dog, see Herbal pet care, *page 297*.

Angelica

Angelica archangelica Apiaceae

A showy, aromatic herb, angelica has both medicinal and culinary uses. Angelica's name honors the archangel Raphael, who is said to have revealed to a monk that the plant could cure the plague.

Angelica (*Angelica archangelica*)

Other common name Archangel
Parts used Leaves, stems, seeds, roots

■ Gardening

Native to northern Europe, *Angelica archangelica* grows to 4 ft. (1.2 m) and has ribbed hollow stems, compound leaves and a flowering stem that can reach 6 ft. (1.8 m), although it often does not appear until the third year.

Ornamental angelica (*A. pachycarpa*) grows to about 3.5 ft. (1 m) high and has shiny dark green leaves. It is mostly grown for its ornamental value. Purple-stem angelica (*A. atropurpurea*) has similar uses to *A. archangelica*. It grows to about 6 ft. (1.8 m), has stems suffused with purple, and pale green to white flowers. The most striking species is the beautiful *A. gigas*, which grows to 6 ft. (1.8 m), with deep garnet buds opening to large wine red to rich purple flowers.

• **Position** Angelica requires a shady position in well-drained but moist and slightly acidic soil that has been enriched with compost. Allow a distance of 3.5 ft. (1 m) between plants.

• **Propagation** Plant angelica seed soon after collection. Mix the seed with damp, but not wet, vermiculite and place the mixture in a sealed plastic bag (see also *page 44*). Store in the crisper section of the refrigerator for six to eight weeks before planting into seed trays. Barely cover the seed, and keep the soil moist. Transplant seedlings when around 4 in. (10 cm) high or when the fifth and sixth leaves emerge.

• **Maintenance** Plants die once the seed has matured, but you can delay this by removing the emerging flower stem. First-year plants will die back in winter but will grow readily in spring. Water regularly.

• **Pests and diseases** This plant is virtually pest- and disease-free. The flowers are attractive to many beneficial insects, including parasitoid wasps and lacewings.

• **Harvesting and storing** Harvest the leaves and flowering stalks in the second year. Dig the roots at the end of the second year, then wash and dry them. Gather the seed when brown and dry.

■ Herbal medicine

Angelica archangelica. Part used: roots. Angelica is an important digestive tonic in European herbal medicine. It stimulates the production of gastric juices and can relieve symptoms of poor appetite, dyspepsia and nausea. Angelica can also reduce the discomfort of flatulence, stomach cramps and bloating. It is a warming herb and suited to individuals who suffer from the effects of cold weather.

For the safe and appropriate use of angelica and dong quai (see box below), consult your healthcare professional. Do not use angelica in greater than culinary quantities. Do not use dong quai if you are pregnant or breastfeeding.

■ Cooking

Angelica is a popular boiled or steamed vegetable dish in some Scandinavian countries; it has a musky, bittersweet taste. The dried seeds and stems are used (in maceration or via the essential oil) in vermouth and liqueurs such as Chartreuse and Benedictine. Crystallized leaves and young stems are a popular decoration for cakes and sweets.

Blanch young shoots for use in salads. Use leaves and stalks in marinades and in poaching liquids for seafood. Add leaves to recipes for tart fruits, such as rhubarb. They cut the acidity, and their sweetness allows you to reduce the amount of sugar.

Dong quai

Angelica polymorpha var. *sinensis.* Part used: roots. Indigenous to China, dong quai is found in damp meadows, moist valleys, and on riverbanks. It grows to about 6 ft. (1.9 m) and has greenish white flowers. Worldwide, dong quai is one of the most commonly used women's herbs. In traditional Chinese medicine it is considered a valuable tonic for the female reproductive system and is used to treat many menstrual and menopausal symptoms.

Anise

Pimpinella anisum Apiaceae

Anise is responsible for much of the "licorice" flavoring in baked goods, liqueurs, teas, and chewing gum. Chinese star anise and aniseed myrtle, although unrelated to anise, have a similar flavor.

Other common names Aniseed, common anise
Parts used Roots (anise only), leaves, seeds, dried fruits (star anise only)

Anise (*Pimpinella anisum*)

■ Gardening

Anise is an aromatic annual with stalked, toothed leaves that may be simple or lobed. The slender flowering stems bear compound umbels of white flowers followed by ridged gray seeds.

Chinese star anise (*Illicium verum*, Family Illiciaceae), an evergreen tree, bears fruits that open to an eight-pointed star. Do not confuse it with the neurotoxic Japanese star anise (*Illicium anisatum*) or the inedible Florida anise (*I. floridanum*).

Aniseed myrtle (*Backhousia anisata*, Family Myrtaceae) is a beautiful small tree from the rain forests of northern New South Wales, Australia. The leaves are strongly aromatic, with a sweet anise scent.

• **Position** Anise prefers an enriched, light, well-drained and fairly neutral soil.
• **Propagation** Sow anise seed directly in spring. Propagate Chinese star anise by semi-ripe cuttings; they will grow in well-drained but moist, acidic soil in light shade. Propagate aniseed myrtle from semi-hardwood cuttings. It is quite hardy, will grow in full sunlight, and prefers a deep, rich, moist acidic soil.
• **Maintenance** Keep anise free of weeds.
• **Pests and diseases** Anise repels aphids and attracts beneficial insects, such as parasitoid wasps.
• **Harvesting and storing** Cut anise when the seeds are fully developed. Tie bunches inside paper bags and hang them upside down to dry and catch the seed. Harvest leaves as required, and dig up roots in autumn. Harvest star anise fruits just before ripening, and harvest firm leaves of aniseed myrtle at any time.

■ Herbal medicine

Pimpinella anisum, Illicium verum. Part used: dried ripe fruits. Anise and its Chinese equivalent, star anise, are used medicinally for similar purposes. Despite belonging to different plant families, the essential oils derived from the seeds of each plant both contain a high percentage of a compound called anethole, which imparts the licorice-like flavor. They both possess calming and antispasmodic properties, making them ideal remedies for alleviating flatulence, intestinal colic, and bloating. Do not use star anise in infants and young children, as it has produced serious side-effects. *Backhousia anisata*. Part used: leaves. The essential oil of aniseed myrtle is believed to be similar to that of anise, although little is known of its medicinal use. Some studies suggest it may have important antimicrobial properties.

For the safe and appropriate use of anise and star anise, see Indigestion, *page 204*, and Wind, bloating and flatulence, *page 206*. For aniseed myrtle consult your healthcare professional. Do not use these herbs in greater than culinary quantities if you are pregnant or breastfeeding.

■ Cooking

Anise seeds and oil are used throughout Europe in drinks such as the French pastis, the Greek ouzo, and Turkish raki. Use the seeds whole or crushed, but for the best flavor grind them as you need them. Use them in bakery goods, confectionery, tomato-based dishes, vegetable and seafood dishes, curries, pickles, soups, and stews. Add the young leaves sparingly to green salads, fish dishes, fruit salads, and cooked vegetables.

The leaves of aniseed myrtle are a major Australian bush-food spice. Use dried or fresh to flavor desserts, preserves, sweet or savory sauces, and marinades.

A culinary star

Star anise is an essential ingredient in many Asian cuisines. In Vietnamese cooking it is used to flavor the noodle soup known as pho. Along with Sichuan pepper, cloves, cassia and fennel seeds, it is a component in Chinese five-spice mix (ingredients pictured below) and in Indian garam masala.

You can use star anise whole, broken, or ground. Add it to pork, chicken, or duck stews. Insert a whole star anise into the cavity of a chicken or duck before roasting.

1. Sichuan pepper 2. Cassia 3. Cloves
4. Star anise 5. Fennel seeds

Anise hyssop

Agastache foeniculum syn. *A. anethiodora* Lamiaceae

Many agastaches have fragrant foliage, their scents ranging from anise to mint and citrus. The leaves are used to make herbal tea, for flavoring, and in medicines, while the ornamental flower spikes, which attract beneficial insects, make a pretty addition to salads.

Other common names Anise mint, giant blue hyssop, licorice mint
Parts used Leaves, flowers

■ Gardening

Anise hyssop (*A. foeniculum*) is a hardy perennial with a sweet anise scent. Both balsamic and peppermint–pennyroyal scented forms are available.

• **Varieties** Two varieties are 'Golden Jubilee', with its golden foliage, and white-flowered 'Alabaster', while fragrant varieties and hybrids include 'Heather Queen' and 'Just Peachy'.

Korean mint (*A. rugosa*), similar to anise hyssop, is a short-lived perennial, slightly more frost-tender, with a flower that ranges in color from rose to violet.

Licorice mint (*A. rupestris*) is a perennial with small licorice-scented leaves and spikes of nectar-rich apricot flowers.

Hummingbird mint (*A. cana*) is a spectacular perennial species growing to 3 ft. (90 cm) with long, dense spikes of large rosy pink flowers and aromatic foliage.

Agastache is from the Greek words for "very much" and "ear of wheat," referring to the flower spikes.

• **Position** *A. foeniculum, A. rugosa,* and *A. urticifolia* prefer light shade and a slightly acid to neutral soil. Most other species are from areas with a dry climate, are water-thrifty, prefer a light well-drained soil and sunny position, and are well-suited to pot culture.

• **Propagation** Sow agastache seed in spring; just cover the seed with soil. It takes 6 to 8 weeks to germinate. Plant in pots when large enough. Established plants produce many basal shoots in spring. Propagate these as softwood cuttings and plant outside in summer, or multiply plants by root division.

• **Maintenance** Agastaches are generally hardy. In cool-climate areas keep plants in a greenhouse and transfer to the garden in their second spring; in warm-climate areas do so in the first summer.

• **Pests and diseases** Leaf-chewing insects can be a minor problem.

• **Harvesting and storing** Use the leaves and flowers freshly picked, or dry them by hanging them upside down in small bunches away from direct sunlight. They will retain their color and scent.

Anise hyssop (*Agastache foeniculum* syn. *A. anethiodora*)

Korean mint (*A. rugosa*), with its lavender blue flowers, is also known as wrinkled giant hyssop.

■ Cooking

The flowers of anise hyssop yield large quantities of nectar, which was popular with North American beekeepers in the 19th century for producing a faintly aniseed-flavored honey. Native American Indians used it as a tea and a sweetener.

Infuse the dried leaves to make a hot or cold drink. Also, use them to season lamb, chicken or salmon. Add the seeds to cakes and muffins. Use the flowers or fresh leaves of anise hyssop or Korean mint in salads. Korean mint has a peppermint and aniseed flavor and aroma and is a good substitute for mint.

Arnica

Arnica montana Asteraceae

There are about 30 species of *Arnica*, and all of them are perennials that spread by rhizomes. With its cheerful golden flowers, arnica has long been used for sprains and bruises as well as homeopathic treatments.

Other common names Leopard's bane, mountain tobacco
Part used Flowers

Gardening

Arnica montana is an aromatic hardy perennial that forms a basal rosette of leaves. From late spring to late summer, it produces flowering stems up to 2 ft. (60 cm) high, and each terminates in a single, golden, daisy flower.
- **Varieties** Most varieties are native to subalpine areas. European arnica (*A. montana*) is also known as mountain tobacco and leopard's bane (not to be confused with the ornamental perennial leopard's bane, *Doronicum orientale*, which is also poisonous, from the family Asteraceae). Native to the northern Iberian peninsula northward to Scandinavia, its natural habitat is low, ferte meadows to an altitude of about 1,000 ft. (3,000 m). *Arnica montana* is becoming rare, due to over-collection and the inroads of agriculture, and wild collection is being curtailed.

Consequently, the American species *A. chamissonis* is sometimes used in its place in herbal treatment.
- **Position** Arnica requires a cool climate and full sun as well as slightly acid to slightly alkaline free-draining soil. In areas with wet winters, grow it in raised beds to prevent fungal attack.
- **Propagation** You can raise arnica from seed but you'll need a period of moist cold. In climates with cold winters, sow the seed outside in autumn. In milder winter areas, stratify the seed by mixing it with a little damp vermiculite or sterile sand. Seal it in a plastic bag, and place it in the crisper tray of the refrigerator for about 12 weeks before sowing (see also *page 44*). Propagate mature plants by division in spring.
- **Maintenance** Arnica is a slow grower and resents competition from pasture weeds such as white clover. Mulch well and weed regularly, or grow plants in weed mat.
- **Pests and diseases** Fungal rots occur in wet winters.
- **Harvesting and storing** Gather the flowers when fully open and dry them.

Arnica is toxic in all but the tiniest doses. In some countries, it is restricted to external use only.

Arnica (*Arnica montana*)

Herbal medicine

Arnica montana, A. chamissonis. Part used: flowers. Arnica flowers have significant anti-inflammatory and mild analgesic properties. They are applied topically in the form of infused oils, ointments and creams to bruises, sprains and strains to encourage healing and to reduce the discomfort of pain and swelling. The pain-relieving effects of arnica also make this a suitable topical remedy for the treatment of sore and aching muscles and rheumatic joint problems.

Internally, *Arnica montana* is taken as a homeopathic remedy, in a very dilute preparation of the herb. It may help with the emotional effects of trauma as well as shock resulting from injury. It may also help to alleviate the physical complaints described above.

Arnica has been ruled unsafe in some countries. For the safe and appropriate use of arnica, see First aid, *page 220*. Do not use arnica if you are pregnant or breastfeeding.

The name "arnica" probably derives from the Greek "arnakis," meaning "lamb's skin," due to the soft texture of the leaves.

Artemisia

Artemisia sp. Asteraceae

Named for the Greek goddess Artemis, *Artemisia* is a genus containing about 300 species, although few are grown in gardens. A number of species inhibit other plants, sometimes to the point of death.

Other common names *Artemisia absinthium*: wormwood, old woman. *A. pontica*: Roman wormwood, old warrior. *A. abrotanum*: southernwood, lad's love, maiden's ruin, old man. *A. afra*: wilde als
Parts used Aerial parts, roots

■ Gardening

Wormwood (*A. absinthium*) forms a woody shrub to about 2.5 ft. (80 cm) with a bittersweet smell. Its deeply incised gray-green leaves are densely covered in fine hairs.
Tree wormwood (*A. arborescens*) resembles wormwood but grows upright to about 5 to 6 ft. (1.5 to 1.8 m), with narrower leaf segments; it smells less strongly.
Roman wormwood (*A. pontica*) is a low-growing plant to about 1.5 ft. (40 cm), with finely cut, scented leaves. It spreads by rhizomes.
White sage or native wormwood (*A. ludoviciana*) has silvered foliage. An aromatic upright subshrub to 4 ft. (1.2 m) that spreads by stolons, it is used as ornamental ('Silver King' is popular).
Mugwort (*A. vulgaris*) is a perennial that spreads via rhizomes. It grows to about 3 ft. (90 cm), with deeply incised leaves that are deep green above and grayish white below.
Southernwood (*A. abrotanum*) forms an upward-growing bush to about 3 ft. (90 cm) with threadlike, finely divided leaves with a "lemon and camphor" smell.
Wilde als (*A. afra*) is indigenous to Africa, from the Western Cape up to Ethiopia. A popular garden plant, it forms clumpy bushes from 1.5 to 6.5 ft. (0.5 to 2 m).
• **Varieties** Some excellent ornamental forms of *A. absinthium* include "Lambrook Silver" and aromatic "Powis Castle," a hybrid.
• **Position** Most species prefer full sun, good drainage and almost neutral soil, (although mugwort tolerates partial shade).

As it is strongly insecticidal, use it as a companion plant in the edge of gardens.
• **Propagation** Propagate all perennial artemisias by semi-hardwood cuttings taken from midsummer to autumn, or raise from seed. Propagate rhizomatous species by root division in autumn. Directly sow the annual species *A. annua* into the garden in spring, or raise as seedlings and transplant at 6 weeks.
• **Maintenance** Lightly prune and shape perennial bushy artemisias in spring. Prune southernwood heavily in spring. Artemisias are a drought-tolerant group once they are established, and perennial forms have good frost tolerance.
• **Pests and diseases** Wormwoods are very rarely troubled by pests and diseases.
• **Harvesting and storing** Harvest the leaves as required to use fresh or dried.

■ Herbal medicine

A. absinthium. Parts used: aerial parts.

Wormwood (*Artemisia absinthium*)

Tree wormwood
(*Artemisia aborescens*)

Wormwood is used to treat symptoms associated with poor digestion, including wind. In many cultures it is regarded as a valuable remedy for worm infestations and other parasitic infections of the gut. It is also used as a nerve tonic and to treat fever and menstrual complaints.

A. vulgaris. Parts used: aerial parts. Mugwort is used as a digestive stimulant and nerve tonic, and is also used to treat menstrual problems.

A. annua. Parts used: aerial parts. According to traditional Chinese medicine, Chinese wormwood (qing hao) is a cold remedy and is used for treating fevers, rashes and nosebleeds. It is the subject of intense scientific research. See Herbs in the future, *page 187*, for more information.

A. afra. Parts used: leaves, stems, roots. Wilde als is used as a traditional medicine by many African cultures, and like wormwood and mugwort, is sometimes taken as a digestive tonic. Other traditional applications include respiratory problems, such as colds, flu, sore throats and nasal congestion, for which it is sometimes applied topically.

For the safe and appropriate use of these herbs, consult your healthcare professional. Do not use these herbs if you are pregnant or breastfeeding.

Basil

Ocimum sp. Lamiaceae

While sweet basil, with its savory clove fragrance, is the quintessential Italian culinary herb, basils are available in an amazing range of forms and fragrances—from lemon, lime, anise, spice, cinnamon and thyme to incense and sweet camphor.

Parts used Leaves, flower spikes

■ Gardening

There are 64 basil species, all native to the subtropics and tropics, but generally speaking, they are annuals, or evergreen perennials and shrubs, with simple aromatic leaves and spikes of lipped flowers arranged in whorls.

• **Varieties** Many varieties of sweet basil (*O. basilicum*) have been developed, particularly in the Mediterranean region.

Compact small-leafed forms of sweet basil are popular in Greece and for pot and windowsill culture. They include 'Greek Bush' and 'Green Globe'.

Lemon basil (*Ocimum americanum*) has a fresh lemon scent with sweet basil undertones.

Large-leafed sweet basils include 'Lettuce Leaf' and 'Mammoth' (both have leaves that are large enough to use as food wraps); the very ornamental 'Magical Michael'; and 'Medinette', a large-leafed dwarf form suitable for pot culture.

Colored-leaf forms are widely used as modern ornamental plantings, as well as for culinary purposes. They include 'Red Rubin' and the frilly leafed 'Purple Ruffles'. The variety 'Ararat' is green, deeply suffused with purple, and has a licorice-and-clove fragrance.

Citrus-flavored varieties include lemon basil (*O. americanum*). Hybrid varieties (*O. x citriodorum*) include 'Sweet Dani' and 'Mrs Burn's Lemon', which are richly lemon-scented and ideal for culinary use. The variety 'Lesbos' or 'Greek Column' contains heady spice, floral and citrus notes. A similar variety, known as 'Greek' or 'Aussie Sweetie' in Australia, is a separate introduction from Greece. 'Lime' basil (*O. americanum*) has a fresh lime and sweet basil scent.

Strongly spice-scented varieties of *O. basilicum* include 'Oriental Breeze', a purple-flowered form much used for ornamental and culinary purposes; 'Cinnamon'; 'Spice' (often incorrectly sold as 'Holy Basil'), with its heady, almost incenselike fragrance; and 'Blue Spice', which contains additional vanilla notes.

'Peruvian Basil' (*O. campechianum* syn. *O. micranthum*) is a spice-scented species. 'Sacred Basil' or 'Holy Basil'

Sweet basil
(*Ocimum basilicum*)

"A man taking basil from a woman will love her always."

Sir Thomas More
Tudor statesman and philosopher,
1478–1535

(*O. tenuiflorum* syn. *O. sanctum*), which is available in both green- and purple-leafed strains, has a mild spice scent and is widely planted in India around temples and in gardens.

'Anise Basil' (*O. basilicum*), also sold as 'Licorice Basil', has a sweet anise scent and purple-suffused leaves. The basil encountered in the cooking of Thailand and Vietnam, 'Thai Basil' (*O. basilicum*), has a light, sweet anise scent, glossy green foliage and ornamental lavender flowers. Several selections have been made, including the very aromatic 'Queenette' and 'Siam Queen', with a spicy anise fragrance.

Some handsome perennial basils are the result of hybridization between *O. basilicum* and *O. kilimandscharicum*, the camphor-scented perennial species. They have a spicy clove fragrance, with a hint of balsam. They include white-flowered, green-leafed 'All Year' basil, and the beautiful purple-suffused 'African Blue'.

Tree basil or East Indian basil (*O. gratissimum*) is native to tropical Africa but widely grown in India and South America. The plant is pleasantly thyme- and clove-scented and makes a substantial bush to about 1.5 m. Another strain of this species, sold as 'Mosquito Plant' or 'Fever Plant', has a strong thyme scent.

• **Position** Basils require a protected, warm, sunny site with a well-drained soil.

• **Propagation** With the exception of the perennial basils mentioned above, basils are generally treated as annuals and propagated from seed. Do not plant seeds directly in the garden until the soil warms. For an early start, plant into seed

'Dark Opal', a variety of *O. basilicum*, bears long cerise flowers and has a delicate scent.

trays kept in a warm and protected environment. Grow seedlings of smaller varieties in pots or spaced about 1 ft. (30 cm) apart, larger bush types about 1.5 ft. (45 cm) apart. Basils cross very readily between varieties, so seeds saved in a mixed planting will not grow true to type in the following year unless you prevent cross-pollination by bees. You can also take cuttings from side shoots.

• **Maintenance** Water regularly. Being a tropical plant, basil grows rapidly at temperatures in excess of 60°F (16°C) and is frost-sensitive. Pinch out flower heads to promote bushy plant growth and to prolong the plant's productive life.

• **Pests and diseases** A fungal disease called fusarium wilt can attack plants, causing sudden wilting. Remove and destroy affected plants (do not compost them), and do not replant basil in the contaminated soil. Consider planting basils among other plants, rather than en masse. They make a fashionable addition to the ornamental garden.

• **Harvesting and storing** Harvest mature leaves and flower spikes for fresh use at any time. To dry the leaves, cut bushes at the base and hang out of direct light, then store in an airtight container in a cool place.

'Thai Basil', another variety of *O. basilicum*, has a sweet aroma that combines anise and licorice.

Classically Italian

Insalata Caprese ("salad in the style of Capri"), in the colors of the Italian flag, is a light, summery salad that showcases the flavor of basil and ripe tomatoes. Arrange tomato slices on a plate. Intersperse with slices of fresh bocconcini (baby mozzarella). Season well. Add a dash of olive oil and a scattering of fresh basil leaves.

Aromatic basil oil

Preserve basil the Italian way. Layer the leaves in a jar and sprinkle each layer with salt. Then at the top add a good-quality olive oil. Seal the jar securely and store in the refrigerator, allowing several days for the oil to be infused with the flavor of the basil. Use the leaves and the oil for making pesto (see recipe, *page 340*). Drizzle a little oil over pizzas or salads. Also, try adding a dash to a marinade.

Basil *Continued*

■ Herbal medicine

Ocimum basilicum. Part used: leaves. Sweet basil is known more for its pleasant taste than for its medicinal effects. Due to its mild sedative properties, herbalists traditionally prescribed basil as a tea for easing nervous irritability.

Ocimum tenuiflorum syn. *O. sanctum.* Part used: leaves. Holy basil, an important herb in Ayurvedic medicine, is used for a range of complaints. Scientific research supports its role in the management of diabetes (due to a hypoglycaemic effect) and as a supportive herb during times of stress. It may also improve concentration and memory and, due to an antiallergic effect, may be beneficial in treating hay fever and asthma.

For the safe and appropriate use of basils, consult a professionally trained medical herbalist. Do not use these herbs in greater than culinary quantities if you are pregnant or breastfeeding.

■ Around the home

Basil is a natural disinfectant. Use the essential oil in combination with other antiseptic herbal oils to make disinfectant sprays for cleaning household surfaces. Plant basil in a pot close to the back door to deter flies. Cut a bunch of basil as an aromatic table centerpiece when you eat outdoors. The dried flower heads add a sweet and spicy note to a pot-pourri.

■ Cooking

Basil is one of the great culinary herbs; different varieties are used extensively in both European and Asian cooking. If a recipe specifies simply "basil," sweet or common basil (*Ocimum basilicum*) is the type generally meant. Fresh sweet basil is highly aromatic, with a distinctive scent and flavor reminiscent of aniseed, and tends to be either loved or loathed. Dried basil tastes more of curry, and is a poor substitute for the fresh herb and should be avoided.

Sweet basil is sometimes called the Royal Herb.

Herb of contradictions

Basil has both positive and negative associations that include love and fear, danger and protection, and life and death. The negative connotations probably come from basil's Latin epithet *basilicum*, which links it to the basilisk (left), the mythical serpent with the deadly gaze. The ancient Greeks and Romans believed that uttering a curse when sowing basil would ensure its germination.

In Greece, Greek basil (*Ocimum minimum* 'Greek') is placed on tables to deter flies.

Using a knife to cut basil can bruise and darken the leaves. For salads and pasta sauces where appearance matters, shred the leaves with your fingers. Young leaves have the best flavor, while old ones have a coarser, stronger taste.

In cooked dishes, basil quickly loses its aroma and the leaves tend to darken, so add it to give depth of flavor during cooking and then, for fragrance and visual appeal, stir in a little more just before serving. Tomato dishes, chicken, egg and rice dishes, spaghetti sauces, fish and vegetables — especially beans, capsicum and eggplants — all go well with basil. See Vegetarian spring rolls recipe, *page 354*. Basil is a good addition to stuffings. The most famous use of basil is in pesto (or pistou in French). Citrus-scented and spice-flavored varieties of basil work well in a range of Asian recipes.

The heart-shaped leaves caused basil to be adopted as a symbol of love.

Bay

Laurus nobilis Lauraceae

The bay is a long-lived and slow-growing, pyramid-shaped evergreen tree. According to folklore, a bay tree in the garden or at the front door keeps away evil as well as thunder and lightning.

Other common names Bay laurel, Grecian bay, sweet bay
Parts used Leaves, flower buds, fruits, bark, roots

■ Gardening

While a bay tree can reach about 50 ft. (15 m) over a long period, its slow, dense upright growth habit makes it an ideal specimen for a large pot, whether it is allowed to grow into its natural form or is shaped into an ornamental topiary or standard. In this form, a small garden can accommodate a bay without concern; its growth is even slower when cultivated in a pot. Bay generally flowers only in warm climates, and the small, very fragrant flower buds open to tiny cream flowers, after which come blue-black berries.

• **Varieties** There are two species of bay, *L. nobilis* and *L. azorica*; the latter is used ornamentally. There is a gold-leafed form of *L. nobilis* called 'Aurea', as well as a willow-leaf form, 'Angustifolia'.

Bay (*Laurus nobilis*)

Several other species are known as bay or laurel, and some are also classified as herbs or spices. The northern bayberry (*Myrica pensylvanica*), which is the source of bayberry candles; the bay rum tree (*Pimenta racemosa*), used in men's colognes; and Indonesian bay (*Eugenia polyantha*) have all been used for cooking.

The ornamental plants cherry laurel (*Prunus laurocerasus*) and mountain laurel (*Kalmia latifolia*) are easily confused with sweet bay due to a similar leaf shape. However, the leaves of these species are very poisonous if ingested, and even the honey harvested by bees can be toxic.

History and myth

The bay tree was considered sacred to the sun god Apollo, and later to his son Asclepius, the Greek god of medicine. According to myth, Apollo fell in love with Daphne, a beautiful nymph who, rather than returning his affection, appealed to the gods to rescue her from him. She was duly changed into a bay tree, the perfect disguise. Apollo declared the tree sacred and thereafter wore a bay laurel wreath in Daphne's honor.

The gods turned the nymph Daphne into a bay tree so Apollo would stop pursuing her.

Bay has long been considered an herb of strong magic, able to attract good fortune and wealth, and to keep away evil. The death of bay trees was considered a portent of evil times; when the city of Rome fell to invasion from the north in the 4th century, all the bay trees are reputed to have died.

During outbreaks of the plague, Roman citizens burned bay leaves in the public squares, and the herb was still used for this purpose into the 16th century.

The leaves are mildly narcotic in quantity; it is said that the Oracle of Delphi in Greece chewed bay leaves before she entered a prophetic trance. The temple at Delphi was roofed with protective branches of bay.

Bay *Continued*

- **Position** Bay trees prefer a deep soil, so if you are growing one in a pot, plant it in one of generous depth, in a compost-enriched potting mix. Provide full sun and good air circulation. Bay prefers a moist, rich, well-drained soil.
- **Propagation** Seed may take 6 months to germinate. Cuttings, best made from semi-ripe wood, may take 3 or more months to form roots, and must never be allowed to dry out.
- **Maintenance** In areas with cold winters, sweet bay is best grown in pots and brought inside during the winter months or if the temperature is likely to drop below 5°F (–15°C). Check plants regularly for both scale and fungal infestations. Re-pot potted specimens into larger containers with fresh additional soil as required; when transplanting, disturb the root system as little as possible.
- **Pests and diseases** Bay is generally trouble-free but can suffer from scale insects, which may infest the underneath of leaves and stems. To remove these, blend 2 cloves of garlic with a cup of water, filter, and add a little liquid soap. Apply to the insects with cotton buds. Alternatively, apply horticultural oil in the same manner. Plants grown without adequate ventilation and light can develop disfiguring gray mildew, which should be treated with sulphur while the plant is wet with morning dew.
- **Harvesting and storing** Pick green leaves for use at any time. Dry leaves out of direct sunshine and store in an airtight bottle. Also see Harvesting, preserving and storing, *page 172*.

■ Cooking

Sweet bay is indispensable in French and other Mediterranean cookery. The tough leaves withstand long cooking, so use them in soups and stews. Apart from meat and fish, they go well in dishes that contain lentils or beans. Two leaves are sufficient in a dish that serves six people.

Bay is essential in a bouquet garni, which is made with fresh herbs or dried herbs wrapped in muslin. Bay is also used in pickling spice and garam masala.

Fresh leaves tend to be bitter, but the taste will diminish if they are left to wilt for a few days. Fresh sprigs stripped of a few leaves make aromatic skewers for meat or fish cooked on the barbecue.

Dried leaves retain their flavor for about a year. Remove dried leaves from dishes before serving.

Bouquet garni, a bundle of classic herbs, usually includes bay, thyme, parsley and peppercorns.

Vanilla bay custard

Bay complements fish, meat and poultry dishes, sauces such as béarnaise (see recipe, *page 339*), and, surprisingly, perhaps, sweet custards such as this, where it imparts a slightly spicy taste.

Place 5 fl. oz. (150 ml) milk, 5 fl. oz. (150 ml) thick cream, 1 split vanilla pod and 1 bay leaf in a saucepan. Bring to a simmer, remove from heat and leave to infuse for 15 minutes. Remove pod and leaf. Beat 3 egg yolks and 1 tablespoon soft brown sugar in a bowl. Add infused milk, mixing thoroughly. Return mixture to a clean saucepan. Cook over a low heat, stirring, until custard thickens; do not let it boil. Serve warm with hot fruit pies and steamed puddings.

To deter weevils in your pantry, add bay leaves to jars of flour and rice.

Crowning glory

Bay's botanical name, *Laurus*, stems from the Latin word, *laus*, or "praise," in reference to the crown of bay leaves worn by the ancient Romans to celebrate victory. Other herbs were often incorporated into wreaths. The Roman emperor Tiberius always wore a wreath of bay laurel when thunderstorms were raging, because he believed that it would provide protection from the gods of thunder and lightning.

Bergamot

Monarda sp. Laminaceae

Native Americans used *Monarda* to make medicinal tisanes. After the Boston Tea Party, in 1773, when American colonists dumped tea shipped by the British East India Company, in protest against British rule, the bergamot tea of the Oswego Indians became a popular substitute.

Other common names Bee balm, Monarda, Oswego tea
Part used Leaves

Wild bergamot (*Monarda fistulosa*)

■ Gardening

Monarda obtained its common name in Europe because the scent of its foliage resembled that of bergamot orange (*Citrus bergamia* syn. *C. aurantium* var. *bergamia*), a small tree that resembles Seville orange (*C. aurantium*). Bergamot's leaf fragrances range from oregano to lemon. This herb's spectacular flowers attract bees and also honey-seeking birds.

Oswego tea (*M. didyma*) is a perennial growing to 4ft. (1.2 m), with several stems terminating in heads surrounded by dense whorls of long-tubed, scarlet flowers. The leaves have a very pleasant citrus scent.

Wild bergamot (*M. fistulosa*) is found on well-drained hillsides and in light woodland. Two botanical varieties to 4ft. (1.2 m) are grown, both with lance-shaped leaves. *M. fistulosa* usually has whorled heads of lavender flowers (occasionally pink), and different strains have thyme- or rose geranium-scented leaves.

The cold-hardy *M. menthifolia*, known as oregano de la Sierra, has a true oregano scent and flavor. Spectacular spotted bergamot (*M. punctata*) has densely whorled heads of cream flowers speckled purple and showy lavender bracts. Lemon bergamot (*M. citriodora*) is a tall annual species with heads of large, lipped, pink or lavender flowers.

• **Varieties** Most garden bergamots are hybrids (*M. x media*), and include varieties such as 'Blue Stocking' and 'Mohawk.'
• **Position** With the exception of *M. fistulosa*, which is drought-resistant, bergamots prefer a sunny position and an enriched, moist but well-drained soil.
• **Propagation** Propagate by seed, or by dividing perennials in early spring. You can also take stem cuttings in summer.
• **Maintenance** Clear dead material from plants in winter. Divide plants every 3 years.

• **Pests and diseases** Some of the garden varieties are susceptible to powdery mildew, which, although it is disfiguring, does not appear to cause any permanent damage.
• **Harvesting and storing** Harvest the edible flowers as required. Collect leaves in late spring and dry them.

■ Herbal medicine

Monarda didyma, M. fistulosa. Part used: leaves. *M. didyma* has been used medicinally to ease flatulence and colic and reduce fevers. It is reputed to contain thymol, an essential oil compound that is also found in thyme and marjoram, and may explain the calming effect that the plant has on the digestive system.

Do not confuse this herb with bergamot essential oil. For the safe and appropriate use of *M. didyma* and *C. bergamia*, consult your healthcare professional. Do not use these herbs if you are pregnant or breastfeeding.

Bergamot is an ingredient in the eau de cologne 4711, which dates from the late 18th century.

The versatile bergamot orange

The intensely fragrant waxy white flowers of the bergamot orange (*Citrus bergamia* syn. *C. aurantium* var. *bergamia*), borne in clusters in spring, are the source of the essential oil of neroli, used widely in the perfumery trade, and also orange flower water. The bitter but highly aromatic yellow peel is used to flavor Earl Gray tea, and also yields bergamot essential oil, which is used for aromatherapy purposes. It can be beneficial for a range of skin conditions, including an oily complexion and acne, but take care when applying skin creams and oils containing the essential oil: one of its compounds, bergapten, has a known photosensitizing effect.

Borage

Borago officinalis Boraginaceae

Considered a cure for "melancholia" in ancient times, borage is a hardy annual herb and an excellent companion plant, helping to deter tomato hornworm and Japanese beetles, and stimulating the growth of strawberries.

Other common name Starflower
Parts used Leaves, flowers

In the first century CE, Pliny declared that borage made men merry and glad.

Gardening

Borage forms a rosette of large ovate leaves before sending up hollow flowering stems to 3 ft. (90 cm). The whole plant has a cucumber scent, is coarsely hairy and can irritate sensitive skin. The flower is five-petaled with a white ring in the center and a cone of black stamens.

• **Varieties** There are three species of borage, but only *B. officinalis* is used as an herb. There are three color variants. The common form has intense blue flowers, but some plants have flowers suffused with pink. There is also a rare white form.

• **Position** Borage requires a sunny, well-drained position and prefers a well-dug and composted soil.

• **Propagation** Sow plants directly into the ground in spring and in autumn. You can sow them in pots, but you should transplant them while they are young, because they develop a large taproot. Borage germinates readily, in 3 to 5 days. Thin the plants to a spacing of 1.5 ft. (45 cm).

• **Maintenance** Keep the soil moist, and fertilize in spring.

• **Pests and diseases** Generally pest- and disease-free.

• **Harvesting and storing** Harvest borage year-round as required. Dry the leaves in a very cool oven or in a well-aired place, out of direct sunlight.

Herbal medicine

Borago officinalis. Part used: seed oil. Borage seed oil is a rich source of gamma-linolenic acid (GLA), an omega-6 fatty acid that is also found in evening primrose oil. GLA exhibits anti-inflammatory activity; some research suggests that it may be of therapeutic value in the treatment of dry and itching skin conditions, including eczema and psoriasis. The latest evidence suggests that better therapeutic results may be achieved when GLA and other omega-6 oils are taken in combination with omega-3 essential fatty acids, such as those found in flax seed and fish.

The leaves are used as a poultice for sprains, bruises and inflammation, and in facial steams for dry skin.

For the safe and appropriate use of borage seed oil, consult your healthcare professional. Do not use borage seed oil if you are pregnant or breastfeeding.

Cooking

Remove the sepals from flowers and use them in salads, or crystallize (see *page 380*) for use as cake decorations.

The age of chivalry

During the Crusades, borage was infused in stirrup cups and offered to Crusaders mounted on their horses in readiness for departure for the Holy Land. Also, ladies traditionally embroidered its starlike flowers onto scarves, which they gave to their chosen knights before they went into combat.

Borage (*Borago officinalis*)

Boxwood

Buxus sempervirens Buxaceae

Although there are some 70 species of boxwood, it is the slow-growing and long-lived common box, with its neat foliage and dense wood, that is used in formal gardening. It is also used in homeopathy but not in modern herbal medicine, due to its toxicity.

Parts used Leaves, bark (note that the plant can cause allergic reactions in susceptible individuals, and that all parts are toxic if ingested)

▇ Gardening

Common boxwood is a hardy evergreen shrub to small tree, attaining full height over a long period of time. The small, oval glossy leaves are deep green to yellowish green. Borne in spring, the nectar-rich flowers are pale green with very reduced petals, while the fruits are three-horned.

• **Varieties** Some garden varieties selected for their form include 'Elegantissima', a very compact type with white-edged leaves; 'Aureomarginata', also known as 'Marginata', with gold-edged leaves; 'Suffruticosa', which is dwarf, dense, and very slow-growing, making it particularly popular for edging herb gardens and creating topiary; and 'Kingsville Dwarf', which is favored by bonsai growers.

• **Position** Boxwood prefers full sun but is tolerant of shade, and prefers a well-drained neutral-to-alkaline soil.

• **Propagation** Take semi-ripe tip cuttings with a little hardened wood at the base, preferably in autumn.

• **Maintenance** To encourage dense, compact growth, trim boxwood toward the end of spring. Carry out light shaping of topiary and hedges in summer.

• **Pests and diseases** This plant is not susceptible to many pests and diseases, although the young spring leaves may be damaged occasionally by sucking insects, and rust can occur on leaves. It is natural for boxwood to appear bronzed in winter.

• **Harvesting and storing** Harvest and dry leaves in spring, before flowering.

The wood of box was traditionally used in engraving blocks, marquetry and instruments.

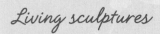

Living sculptures

The art of topiary — sculpting compact, small-leafed plants into various shapes (see also Parterre gardens, *page 144*) — dates back to Roman times, when topiary animals and obelisks were sculpted to adorn gardens and atriums.

Topiary reached its peak in the grand European formal gardens of the 17th and 18th centuries, but declined when fashion declared a return to more natural landscapes. In 1713, the poet Alexander Pope wrote a satirical essay for *The Guardian* newspaper in which he described an unfinished boxwood topiary of St George that would not slay the dragon until it was completed — six months hence.

Today, topiary is once again a feature of grand country homes, particularly in the UK and Europe, but it is also popular in container gardens where herbs, such as boxwood, are sculpted into simple shapes. In Japan, cloud-pruning – the art of creating cloudlike forms – and bonsai are both forms of topiary.

The small leaves and compact growth habit of boxwood (*Buxus sempervirens*) make it ideal for topiary.

Brahmi

Bacopa monnieri Scrophulaceae

This tropical herb is reputed to improve both brain function and memory, and the dried plant is used in many traditional Ayurvedic formulations. Brahmi makes an attractive hanging basket. You can also grow it in an ornamental pond.

Other common names Bacopa, thyme-leafed gratiola, water hyssop

Parts used Whole plant above ground

Brahmi (*Bacopa monnieri*)

■ Gardening

Bright green brahmi is a modest ground-hugging perennial plant that grows in wetland environments. The leaves are simple, oval, arranged in opposite pairs, smooth-edged and bitter-tasting. It is slightly succulent and bears small five-petaled flowers that are white, which faintly turn blue on the petal backs, over many months. The fruits are small, flat capsules.

• **Position** Brahmi requires a moist soil and preferably light shade. It grows well in a pot, preferably with a diameter of 1 ft. (30 cm) or more, and makes an attractive hanging basket if grown in the shade. It is frost tender, so grow brahmi under protection in winter.

• **Propagation** You can grow brahmi from seed, but it forms adventitious roots

The name 'brahmi' comes from Brahma, the Hindu god of creation.

on creeping shoots, and the detached shoots quickly grow into new plants when potted. Unrooted tip cuttings also strike quickly.

• **Maintenance** As brahmi has very shallow roots, water it regularly, especially if exposed to direct hot sunshine. Promote rapid growth with liquid seaweed fertilizer diluted to the recommended strength.

• **Pests and diseases** None of note.

• **Harvesting and storing** Harvest stems and leaves when plant is 5 months old, leaving 2-in. (5-cm) stems so that plant can regenerate for further harvesting. Dry leaves in the shade at room temperature and store in airtight containers.

■ Herbal medicine

Bacopa monnieri. Parts used: whole herb. In Ayurvedic medicine, brahmi is prescribed by herbalists to improve memory, learning and concentration. Scientific research has provided encouraging evidence for some of these effects, but suggests improvements

Food for the brain

Keeping our brains healthy is as important as keeping our bodies in shape. Brahmi has been used as a "brain workout" herb in the Ayurvedic tradition of medicine for about 500 years. Researchers hypothesize that it may help by improving the way the nervous system transmits messages in the brain. Gotu kola (*Centella asiatica* syn. *Hydrocotyle asiatica*) is also sometimes confusingly referred to by the common name brahmi and is a "brain" herb in its own right. However, the two plants are easily distinguished by their different leaf shapes (see Gotu kola, *page 61*).

take around 3 months to occur. Brahmi is also renowned as an exceptional nerve tonic, so it is notable that a reduction in anxiety levels was also observed in some clinical studies, supporting its use during times of anxiety and nervous exhaustion.

For the safe and appropriate use of brahmi, see Memory and concentration, *page 213*. Do not use brahmi if you are pregnant or breastfeeding.

Brahmi is an aquatic herb, ideal for growing in damp places in the garden or even in a pond.

Burdock

Arctium lappa Asteraceae

Burdock is enjoying a resurgence in popularity, both as a vegetable and as a traditional medicinal plant. It is regarded as a weed in the Northern Hemisphere, where it grows well on rough ground in a sunny position.

Other common names Beggar's buttons, great burdock
Parts used Leaves, roots, seeds

Burdock (*Arctium lappa*)

◼ Gardening

Burdock is a strong-growing biennial. The fairly bitter but tender young foliage of spring regrowth is used as a green vegetable. The leaves are large and oval, and the numerous purple thistlelike flowers are quite remarkable in their perfect symmetry. Burdock can grow as high as 8 ft. (2.4 m).

• **Varieties** Some named varieties are grown as a vegetable for their slender, crisp, textured taproots, which can grow as long as 4.5 ft. (1.3 m). These include two Japanese varieties — 'Takinogawa Long' and 'Watanabe Early'. Both have a flavor between that of parsnip and Jerusalem artichoke. *Arctium minus* is a very bitter weedy species that is found all over North America.

• **Position** Burdock requires a moist humus-rich soil and full sun, although it will tolerate some light shade. It is also fully cold-hardy, and dies down in winter.

• **Propagation** Propagate from seed in spring or late autumn. Although the seed usually germinates easily, soak the seed overnight in warm water before sowing, then lightly cover it with soil and firm down. Thin seedlings to about 6 in. (15 cm) apart. To produce high-quality, long straight roots, dig the soil to a depth of 2 ft. (60 cm) and incorporate well-rotted compost before sowing.

• **Maintenance** Keep the soil moist and weed the crop regularly, particularly when the plants are young. Remove the flowers and burrs to promote root growth.

• **Pests and diseases** Burdock is rarely seriously affected by pests and diseases.

• **Harvesting and storing** For cooking, collect young shoots and leaves in spring. Lift the roots in autumn, about 100 days after planting, when they are at least 1 ft. (30 cm) long. For medicinal purposes, dry the grayish brown roots, which are white on the inside.

◼ Herbal medicine

Arctium lappa. Part used: roots. In Western herbal medicine, burdock root is used as an alterative or blood purifier. These terms describe its gentle detoxifying effect on the body and stimulation of the body's eliminatory channels, namely the lymphatic, digestive and urinary systems. It is commonly prescribed for chronic inflammatory skin and joint conditions, which traditional herbalists regard as the result of a buildup of unwanted toxins in the body. When used over a long period of time, burdock root can be particularly effective in clearing dry, scaly skin complaints, such as eczema and psoriasis, and improving rheumatic joint conditions.

For the safe and appropriate use of burdock, consult your healthcare professional. Do not use burdock if you are pregnant or breastfeeding.

◼ Cooking

Burdock is not an important edible plant, although the cultivated Japanese form, gobo, is used as a vegetable and also in various pickles and a miso-based condiment. It is also eaten as a vegetable in Korea. Scrape the young leaf stalks and cook them as you would celery. Use the roots raw as a salad vegetable, or cooked in stir-fries like carrots.

Making it stick

The evenly distributed hooks on the burdock burrs, which kept sticking to his clothes on walks in the countryside, inspired George de Mestral to invent Velcro in 1945. The name comes from the French words *velour*, meaning "velvet" and *crochet* or "hook." The invention has been applied to a wide range of items, from fasteners on clothes, bags and shoes to stainless-steel hook and loop fasteners that are used to attach car parts.

Calendula

Calendula officinalis Asteraceae

Calendula has large daisylike flowers in golden yellow or orange. In ancient Rome, the herb was used to make a broth that was said to uplift the spirits. In India, the bright flowers decorated the altars in Hindu temples.

Other common names Golds, marigold, pot marigold, ruddles
Part used Petals

Calendula (*Calendula officinalis*)

◼ Gardening

Native to the Mediterranean, calendula forms a dense clump of simple lance-shaped aromatic leaves. The flowers resemble large daisies.

• **Varieties** The original calendula of the herb garden was the single form; however, in the 20th century, double-flowered forms were extensively bred, yielding much larger harvests of petals. Two notable choices are 'Pacific Beauty' and the dwarf 'Fiesta Gitana'. 'Erfurter Orangefarbigen' from Germany is used for commercial medicinal flower production in Europe. A remarkable heirloom single variety from the Elizabethan period, *C. officinalis* 'Prolifera', is still grown. This is the quaint 'Hen and Chickens', which has a central flower encircled by a number of miniature flowers.

• **Position** Plants need full sun but will tolerate partial light shade. They prefer a moderately fertile, well-drained soil.

• **Propagation** Calendula is an annual that is very easy to grow from seed.

In the Middle Ages, many plants were renamed 'Mary's gold' in honor of the Virgin Mary.

• **Maintenance** In hot summers, calendulas usually cease flowering. Regular deadheading will help to prolong flowering.

• **Pests and diseases** Plants are prone to mildew in autumn. The variety 'Orange King' has good resistance. Spider mite can be a problem in midsummer, although reducing water stress lessens the severity of attack.

• **Harvesting and storing** Gather petals after the dew has dried and spread them very thinly over paper on racks, out of direct sunlight, in a well-ventilated place. When they are dried, store them in airtight containers.

◼ Herbal medicine

Calendula officinalis. Part used: flowers. Brightly colored calendula flowers possess significant wound-healing and local anti-inflammatory properties. To aid the healing of wounds, cuts and burns, apply them topically in the form of an ointment, cream or infused oil.

Calendula's slight astringency may help to staunch bleeding, while its antimicrobial effects help to keep the site of injury free from infection. Use a calendula tincture as an effective mouthwash against gum infections and mouth ulcers and also as a topical antifungal agent for some skin conditions.

Traditionally, calendula flowers are taken internally for infections and inflammation of the gut, including stomach and duodenal ulcers, and also as a lymphatic remedy for the treatment of swollen lymph nodes.

For the safe and appropriate external use of calendula, see First aid, *page 220.* For internal use, consult your healthcare professional. Do not take calendula internally if you are pregnant or breast-feeding. Topical application is considered safe at these times.

Globetrotting

Pot marigold should not be confused with the Mexican genus (*Tagetes*), which includes the so-called African and French marigolds (right) as well as the coriander-tasting Andean herb huacatay or Peruvian black mint (*Tagetes terniflora*), and the closely related *T. minuta*.

Caraway

Carum carvi Apiaceae

Caraway was a popular Middle Eastern herb before being introduced into Western Europe in the 12th century. Its seeds are used as an anise-scented spice in cooking. The herb also has medicinal and cosmetic uses.

Other common name Persian cumin
Parts used Leaves, roots, dried ripe fruits (known as seeds) and their essential oil

■ Gardening

Caraway is a biennial with divided fernlike leaves and a parsley–dill fragrance. It has a spindle-shaped taproot, which can be cooked as a root vegetable, like carrot. The flowering stem, about 2 ft. (60 cm) tall, bears tiny white flowers touched with pink that are followed by crescent-shaped ridged 'seeds.' *C. roxburghianum*, known as ajmud, is a popular Indian spice.

• **Varieties** 'Sprinter' is high-yielding and the seeds don't shatter, making it easier to save the seeds.
• **Position** Caraway requires a well-drained fertile soil and a warm sunny position. Thin plants to 6 in. (15 cm) apart.
• **Propagation** Sow caraway seed directly into the soil in either spring or autumn (the latter crop will seed the following summer).

• **Maintenance** Regularly weed and water the crop, because the seed is often slow to germinate.
• **Pests and diseases** Caraway is rarely troubled by pests. To prevent fungal diseases of foliage, water in the morning; try not to water from above.
• **Harvesting and storing** Gather leaves at any time. Lift roots after harvesting seed. Cut flowering stems when the seeds begin to darken and ripen. Secure stems in small bunches to allow air movement, and hang the bunches upside down until dry. Then shake bunches over sheets. The seeds often contain insects, such as weevils, so freeze to kill the eggs before storage.

■ Herbal medicine

Carum carvi. Part used: dried ripe fruits. Caraway's ability to dispel wind and exert a calming, antispasmodic effect on the gastrointestinal tract makes it a reliable remedy in cases of flatulence, intestinal colic and bloating. As a result of its slightly drying nature, it is also prescribed with other appropriate herbs to assist in the relief of diarrhea.

For the safe and appropriate use of caraway, see Wind, bloating and flatulence, *page 206.* Do not use caraway in greater than culinary quantities if you are pregnant or breastfeeding.

■ Cooking

Caraway seeds are used to flavor rye bread, sausages, cabbage dishes, cheeses, soups, pork dishes, goulash and cooked apples, as well as liqueurs and spirits such as schnapps. A digestive known as "sugar plums" is made from sugar-coated seeds. Use the feathery caraway leaves in salads and soups. Their taste resembles a mixture of parsley and dill.

Caraway (*Carum carvi*)

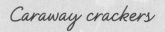

Caraway crackers

Roll out ready-made pizza dough or puff pastry on a lightly floured work surface. Whisk 1 egg yolk with 2 tablespoons water until combined and brush lightly over dough. Cut dough into squares. Combine 2 tablespoons each of poppy seeds, caraway seeds, sunflower seeds and chopped almonds. Sprinkle over squares. Cook in preheated 400°F oven for 10–15 minutes, or until pastry is golden. Serve warm. Makes 36.

Catnip

Nepeta cataria Lamiaceae

Many cats that encounter this velvety, curiously scented perennial react by rolling in it, rubbing against it and generally behaving as though the aroma is irresistible. Catnip is used to relieve fevers, colic and teething pain in young children.

Part used Leaves

■ Gardening

Catnip is a short-lived perennial native to Europe that resembles its relative, mint. It has soft, hairy, aromatic gray-green leaves and small, white, lipped flowers. The chemicals responsible for the amazing response of many cats are nepetalactones. A lemon-scented variety, *N. cataria* var. *citriodora*, has a similar effect. Not all cats exhibit such reactions: young kittens and older cats show almost no response.

• **Varieties** There are some 250 species of *Nepeta*, many of which contain nepetalactones and attract cats. These include two common garden perennials that are both called catmints, namely *N. mussinii* and *N. x faassenii*.

• **Position** Catnip needs a well-drained soil, and preferably full sun.

• **Propagation** Grow catnip from seed, if possible in seed trays; seeds germinate best between 68 and 86°F (20 and 30°C). You can also propagate it easily by tip cuttings, and by root division in early spring.

• **Maintenance** Cover young transplants in wire netting to protect them from felines. Plants grow rapidly in summer to form quite large, floppy bushes, so you'll need to stake them. Water regularly.

• **Pests and diseases** In warm humid climates, septoria leaf spot may cause spotting, followed by yellowing of mature leaves. The nepetalactones effectively repel insect pests.

Catnip (*Nepeta cataria*)

• **Harvesting and storing** Once the bush is well grown, harvest catnip at any time after the dew has dried. Secure small bunches of stems with string and hang them upside down in a well-aired place. When perfectly dry, strip the foliage and store it in an airtight container.

■ Herbal medicine

Nepeta cataria. Parts used: leaves, flowers. An excellent remedy for children, catnip helps to resolve feverish conditions, and its antispasmodic properties alleviate flatulence and colic. It is a mild sedative and can reduce sensitivity to the pain of teething and improve irritability.

Catnip can also be used to treat the symptoms of colds, flu, digestive bloating, nausea and cramping in adults, and it is particularly effective when stress is a contributing factor.

For the safe and appropriate use of catnip, consult a healthcare professional. Do not use catnip if you are pregnant or breastfeeding.

■ Around the home

Catnip is a useful herb to have on hand in the home. Nepetalactones are a very powerful mosquito repellent and cockroaches don't like them much, either.

Catnip cat toy

You will need

☐ thin cardboard

☐ soft pencil

☐ two 5 x 6½ in. rectangles fabric

☐ sewing thread

☐ dried catnip

☐ small bell

1 Trace a fish outline onto some thin cardboard and cut out a template. Place the fabric rectangles right sides together. Trace the fish onto the wrong side of one rectangle, remembering to add ¼-in. seam allowance all round.

2 Stitch the two shapes together, leaving a small opening for turning. Trim seam, clip curves and turn right side out. Fill with dried catnip and stitch opening closed. Stitch a small bell to the head of the fish.

Celery

Apium graveolens Apiaceae

Rich in vitamins and minerals, wild celery has been used as a food and flavoring since ancient Egyptian times. The Greeks crowned the victors in the Nemean Games with garlands of its leaves, and also made funeral wreaths from them.

Other common names Cutting leaf celery, smallage
Parts used Leaves, seeds, roots

■ Gardening

The deep green leaves of wild celery may reach 2.5 ft. (80 cm), while the flowering stem bears compound umbels of inconspicuous white-tinged green flowers. The whole plant, including the tiny brown seeds, is very aromatic. Chinese celery or kin tsai (*A. graveolens*) is strongly flavored, with thin stalks that can be dark green to white in color. *A. prostratum* is a creeping, shiny-leaved, somewhat succulent Australian coastal plant with a strong celery flavor. It is now used as a flavoring in commercial bush foods.

• **Varieties** Excellent selections include 'French Dinant' and the Dutch 'Soup Celery d'Amsterdam'.
• **Position** Celery prefers a well-drained soil enriched with rotted compost and a sunny but protected position, and is tolerant of saline soils.

• **Propagation** Grow wild celery from seed in spring. Space plants about 1.5 ft. (40 cm) apart.
• **Maintenance** Keep the soil moist with regular watering.
• **Pests and diseases** Celery has good disease tolerance, although septoria leaf spot can occur.
• **Harvesting and storing** Harvest leaves from midsummer to autumn, as required. Pick ripe seeds, then dry, deep-freeze for several days to kill any insect eggs, and store in an airtight container.

■ Herbal medicine

Apium graveolens. Part used: dried ripe fruits (seeds). Celery seed has a strong diuretic effect and enhances elimination of uric acid and other toxins from the body via the urinary system. This action may help to explain its use as a specific remedy for the treatment of painful joint conditions, such as gout and arthritis, in which an accumulation of toxins in the joint area may be partly responsible for the characteristic symptoms of pain and swelling.

As a result of its diuretic properties, celery seed can also be used to treat fluid retention. Due to its slightly antiseptic nature, it can be of assistance in treating urinary tract infections.

For the safe and appropriate use of celery seed, see Arthritis and gout, *page 225*. Do not use celery seed in greater than culinary quantities if you are pregnant or breastfeeding.

■ Cooking

Celery's tiny edible seeds are aromatic and slightly bitter, tasting of celery. The whole seeds retain their flavor well; crush as needed and use to complement fish and seafood dishes, pickles and relishes, soups, stews, egg dishes, salad dressings, breads and savory biscuits.

Celeriac

Celeriac is a selected form of *Apium graveolens* with a very large taproot, which is grown as a root vegetable. Slice off the rough, tough outer skin rather than peel it, then use it raw or cooked, in soups and baked dishes. The root and hollow stems have a celery flavor; slice the stems and use them as straws for drinking Bloody Marys.

Celery (*Apium graveolens*)

Chamomile

Chamaemelum nobile syn. *Anthemis nobilis* and *Matricaria recutita* Asteraceae

Roman or perennial chamomile or manzanilla (*C. nobile*), the annual German chamomile (*M. recutita*) and dyer's chamomile (*Anthemis tinctoria*) share the same common name. The flowers of both Roman and German chamomile are used medicinally, while the flowers of dyer's chamomile yield a golden brown dye.

Roman chamomile (*Chamaemelum nobile*), foreground; German chamomile (*Matricaria recutita*), background

----

Parts used Flowers, leaves

■ Gardening

Roman chamomile is a densely carpeting and low-growing, cold-hardy plant. Its feathery green leaves have a ripe apple scent and the flowers of the species are single white daisies. It is often confused with German chamomile, an upright growing annual with fine ferny leaves and white daisy flowers. Another annual species, pineapple weed *(Matricaria matricarioides)*, has greenish yellow flowers and foliage with a pineapple scent.

• **Varieties** A non-flowering variety, *C. nobile* 'Treneague', is popular for lawns. An attractive fully double variety, *C. nobile* 'Flore Plena', is grown commercially for its essential oil in many countries. Varieties of dyer's chamomile include the golden-flowered 'Kelwayi'.

• **Position** All these chamomiles require a sunny position and well-drained soil.

• **Propagation** Raise each species from seed in spring. Propagate perennial varieties by cuttings or root division.

• **Maintenance** Weed regularly, especially if you are establishing a chamomile lawn.

• **Pests and diseases** There are no significant problems.

• **Harvesting and storing** Gather the flowers when fully open. German chamomile will reflower if harvested in summer. Dry the flowers and store them in an airtight container.

■ Herbal medicine

Matricaria recutita. Part used: flowers. Chamomile has a mild sedative effect on the nervous system. Chamomile's relaxing effects extend to the gut, helping to ease colic, and also to the female reproductive system, alleviating the pain of menstrual cramps. Chamomile's bitter-tasting compounds can help to stimulate the digestion and relieve the discomfort of nausea. Chamomile is a gently acting herb, making it especially suitable for children.

Topically, the soothing and anti-inflammatory effects of chamomile are excellent for treating itchy and inflamed skin conditions; it has also been shown to promote wound healing.

Chamaemelum nobile syn. *Anthemis nobilis.* Part used: flowers. Roman chamomile is commonly used in essential oil form and the dried flowers can be hard to obtain. Some herbalists suggest that the Roman variety has a more pronounced relaxing effect on the gut and uterus, and can be used in a similar way to German.

For the safe and appropriate use of these herbs, see Nausea, *page 205*. Do not use these herbs in greater than culinary quantities if you are pregnant or breastfeeding.

A multipurpose herb

For a relaxing sleep, try combining the essential oils of both chamomile and lavender in an oil burner. Chamomile is also antifungal and antibacterial. Next time you make chamomile tea, brew a second cup that's extra strong and use the liquid to wipe down the kitchen sink and table, or to wipe out a cabinet to rid it of a musty smell. Also, spray it onto plants and vegetables to deter fungal diseases such as mildew in the yard.

Chervil

Anthriscus cerefolium Apiaceae

This delicious culinary herb, used since Roman times, has a delicate flavor between tarragon and parsley that is indispensable in French cuisine. Either use it raw or add it at the last minute, after the dish has been taken off the heat and is ready to serve.

Other common name Garden chervil
Parts used Leaves, stems

■ Gardening

Apicius, the renowned gourmet of 1st-century Rome, set his seal of approval on chervil, which is an annual plant with delicate and lacy, fernlike foliage that forms a low-growing rosette. The tiny white flowers, borne in umbels on slender stems, are followed by thin black seeds.

• **Varieties** There are flat-leafed and lightly curled forms as well as a strain called 'Brussels Winter' that is tolerant of colder conditions.

• **Position** Chervil requires good drainage and a moist soil that is close to neutral, preferably enriched with compost. Grow chervil in a lightly shaded position, because excessive sun exposure will cause the leaves to burn and turn rose pink. In warm climates, grow chervil in spring, autumn and even winter, as it has some cold tolerance and will withstand light frosts.

• **Propagation** Scatter seed over the soil, press down lightly and water regularly. Seedlings usually emerge in about 10 to 14 days. Plants are ready for harvesting about 8 to 10 weeks after planting. Chervil has a long taproot and bare-rooted seedlings do not easily transplant. It will not germinate in soil that is too warm. In cool-climate areas with mild summers, grow chervil for a continuous supply during the growing season, although light shade promotes lush growth, and the season can be further extended with the use of protective covers.

• **Maintenance** Water regularly to promote lush growth.

• **Pests and diseases** There are no significant problems.

• **Harvesting and storing** As with parsley, harvest leaves from the outside, preferably with scissors, because the plant is delicate. Leaves can also be deep frozen in sealed plastic bags.

■ Cooking

Chervil flowers, leaves and roots are all edible, although it is the faintly anise-flavored leaves that are most frequently used. There are various types, including curly leafed varieties that make a pretty garnish. Use fresh chervil in cooking, because its delicate flavor is destroyed by heat or drying. It goes well with glazed carrots and in butter sauces and cream-based soups. Chervil frozen into ice cubes adds a refreshing taste to summery fruit drinks.

Chervil butter (see Herb butters, *page 336*), makes a delicious spread for savory biscuits or bread. Also, use it as a flavorsome topping for barbecued fish, meat or poultry.

Chervil (*Anthriscus cerefolium*)

Fines herbes

Chervil is especially popular in French cooking, and essential (along with parsley, chives and tarragon) in the classic herb blend called fines herbes, which is used fresh with poached fish, shellfish and chicken and in green salads and egg dishes such as omelettes.

Grow chervil to lure slugs away from nearby vegetable crops.

Chili

Capsicum sp. Solanaceae

Part of the South American diet for at least 7,000 years, chili varieties are the world's most frequently used culinary spice. The heat is mostly concentrated in the seeds and the white pith, so remove either or both for a milder hit.

Part used Fruits

■ Gardening

All *Capsicum* species are indigenous to South America. The most commonly grown is *C. annuum*, which contains many chili varieties as well as the bell peppers, pimentos and other sweet capsicum varieties, such as 'Banana' and 'Cubanelle'. Chilies and bell peppers differ from each other by a single gene that produces the fiery-flavored compound capsaicin.

C. baccatum, a species less known outside South America, requires a long growing season.

The rocoto pepper (*C. pubescens*), from the Andes and upland Mexico, forms a perennial bush that is tolerant of cooler weather and that produces purple flowers

Some chili varieties make an attractive landscaping feature.

and thick-walled, fruity-flavored hot fruits with black seeds.

• **Varieties** There are possibly hundreds of named varieties of *C. annuum*, and these have been selected worldwide for climate tolerance, color, size, shape, degree of heat and flavor, which may vary from citrus and prune to smoky, coffee, raisin, almond and tobacco. They are all divided into groups by shape: cherry-shaped (Cerasiform), cone-shaped (Coniodes), clustered elongated cones (Fasciculatum), sweet peppers (Grossum) and long hot peppers (Longum).

Among the best-known varieties of *C. baccatum* are 'Anaheim', with large, long, tapering, mildly pungent fruit; 'Poblano', which has large, medium-hot, heart-shaped fruits (and is known as 'Ancho' in its dried form); 'Pasilla', a large raisin-flavored tapering variety; 'Jalapeño', a thick-walled variety that is used in salsas or smoked (when it is known as chipotle); 'Guajillo', a leathery, dark reddish brown variety that is moderately hot; and 'Mirasol', a reselection of a pre-Columbian Mexican variety.

Some — such as 'Purple Tiger', 'Filius Blue', 'Variegata' syn. 'Bellingrath Gardens' — are very ornamental and widely grown for landscape purposes. They are all edible.

Tiny bird peppers (var. *aviculare*)

The tiny bird peppers — including the wild pepper of New Mexico, the 'Chiltepin' or 'Tepin' — all belong to *C. annuum* var. *aviculare*. 'Tabasco' is the most widely known variety of the species *C. frutescens*.

The species *C. chinense* contains some of the hottest chili varieties, including the 'Habañero' and its variants, the 'Scotch Bonnet' or 'Jamaican Hot', and the somewhat milder Puerto Rican 'Rocatillo'. All three types are excellent for culinary use and widely grown in the Caribbean. The best-known variety, 'Aji Amarillo' or 'Kellu-Uchu', is widely used in the cuisine of Peru.

• **Position** All chili varieties require good drainage, full sunshine and an enriched soil. Do not grow chilies where related species of the family Solanaceae, such as tomatoes and eggplants, have recently been grown.

'New Mexico', a variety of *C. annuum*, has a sweet flavor and can be either green or red.

The dark purple fruits of Thai chili (*C. annuum* var. *fasciculatum*) turn red when ripe.

Chili 'Ebony Fire' is one of many chili varieties whose name indicates the intensity of its heat.

• **Propagation** Even the fastest-maturing chili varieties of *C. annuum* require a minimum growing season of 3 months. In cooler areas, grow seedlings under protection before planting them out after the last frost. Although the flowers are self-pollinating, they also readily cross-pollinate, so carefully isolate plants intended for seed saving with fine netting.

• **Maintenance** You may need to protect your plants from birds. Control aphids to prevent the spread of viral diseases; destroy any plants that have mottled or distorted leaves.

• **Pests and diseases** Plant rotation will minimize verticillium wilt and other soil-borne diseases. Vegetable bugs may damage leaves.

• **Harvesting and storing** Pick peppers at any time, but remember that they reach peak heat when they turn red.

■ Cooking

Some cuisines — Indian, West Indian, African and Asian cuisines in general — are almost unthinkable without chilies, yet they were unknown in those regions until after 1492, when Columbus introduced them from the New World.

1. Cherry-shaped chilies 2. Red and yellow capsicums 3. Banana chili
4. Olive chilies 5. Bird chilies
6. Long hot peppers 7. Bird chilies

Too hot to handle!

Most of the capsaicin that's responsible for the heat in peppers is stored in the seeds and the white septae within the fruit. To reduce the heat in a dish, you need to remove these before cooking. Capsaicin is not water-soluble, and neither water nor beer will neutralize the heat. It is, however, fat-soluble, and a glass of milk or yogurt, or the Indian yogurt-based drink lassi are effectively soothing.

Wear protective gloves when chopping quantities of chili peppers, because they can numb your fingertips for many hours. Also, avoid touching your face, eyes or genitals after preparing them. Do not feed pets food containing chili, because it is fatal for some breeds.

Chili heat is commonly measured in Scoville Heat Units (SHU), with the 'Habañero' equating to between 200,000 and 300,000 SHU. Until recently, the world's hottest chili was an infamous variety of *C. chinense* known as the 'Red Savina Habañero,' which measured 577,000 SHU. Far less lethal for the tastebuds, 'Tabasco' is a mere 30,000 to 50,000. In 2007, a new record was established by a variety from Assam in India known as 'Bhut Jolokia,' which reached a very dangerous 1,000,000 SHU.

High-pressure liquid chromatography (HPLC) is now used to measure SHU. A relative heat scale, based on a simple 0 to 10 rating, has also been developed, with bell peppers rating 0 and 'Habañero' 10.

Habañero, a *C. chinese* variety, is among the hottest chilies in common use.

Chili *Continued*

Chilies are always green when unripe; when ripe, they may be red, yellow, purple or almost black. Their heat level varies from negligible to incendiary. Generally, the smaller the chili, the hotter it will be.

Varieties lacking the capsaicin gene produce sweet fruits that taste more like capsicum (to which they are related) and have a fruity flavor but little or no heat. The heat level may vary considerably even among chilies of the same variety, so the stated quantity in a recipe should always be adjusted to taste.

To check the heat level of your chilies, cut the end off one and give it the tiniest, tentative lick. A remedy for chili burn on the palate is dairy foods, such as milk or yogurt.

To minimize irritation from the fumes when grinding chilies, use a spice grinder rather than a mortar and pestle.

Choose firm, shiny fresh chilies; avoid those that are wrinkled. Green chilies are

These colorful strings of chilies include only a fraction of the varieties available.

Dried chilies: 1. Thai chilies 2. Pasilla 3. Guajillo 4. Habañero 5. Chipotle (dried, smoked jalapeño) 6. Pimentos 7. Ancho (dried poblano)

always used fresh; red chilies can be used fresh or dried. Dried chilies differ in flavor to fresh, being fruitier and sweeter, although still retaining their heat. Buy dried chilies whole, crushed or powdered, and fresh chilies whole, or chopped and preserved in vinegar in jars; these are a good substitute for fresh.

In one of those transatlantic differences in spelling, "chili" — together with the less often used "chilie" — are both used in the UK, while the Spanish-originated 'chile' is commonly used in the United States and Mexico. The term "chili" is reserved for a regional hot and spicy stew, originally from Mexico, which the United States subsequently made its own.

Chili and lime sauce

This Caribbean sauce recipe is delicious with barbecued or baked fish or vegetables. Baste the food with it, or serve it separately.

- **2 fresh red chilies**
- **1 tablespoon sea salt**
- **1 cup (250 ml) fresh lime juice**

Remove the seeds and white pith from the chilies if you do not want too much heat. Slice chilies finely and pack into a jar. Dissolve the salt in the juice and pour over the chilies. Seal and store in a cool place to let the flavors develop. It is ready for use after 4 days and keeps for up to 4 weeks.

Chili condiments

There is a range of chili condiments to choose from.

- **Paprika** is a mildly hot, sweet, bright red chili powder that is produced by drying and grinding suitable varieties. Spain and Hungary are the world's largest producers. Suitable varieties, which must be intensely red when fully ripened, include 'Hungarian,' 'Paprika Supreme' and 'NuMex Conquistador.'

- **Cayenne** is a spice powder that is derived from dried hot red chilies. 'Cayenne' is a pre-Columbian variety from French Guiana. A number of cayenne-type varieties have been developed from it, including 'Hot Portugal,' 'Long Red,' 'Ring of Fire' and 'Hades Hot.' Dried chilies and chili flakes are also used.

Cayenne pepper

- **Tabasco**, the most famous chili sauce, is made in Louisiana, according to a 3-year process invented in 1868 by Edmund McIlhenny.

- **Peri Peri** is a sauce developed by the Portuguese from the tiny but powerfully hot Southern African variety 'Peri Peri'; it includes lemons, spices and herbs.

- **Mole poblano** — compounded of chili (such as pasilla), chocolate, spices and seeds or peanuts — is a popular sauce in Mexico, and increasingly abroad.

Clove pinks

Dianthus caryophyllus and *D. plumarius* Caryophyllaceae

With an intoxicating spicy fragrance, the pretty flowers of clove pinks resemble small carnations. The fresh petals are edible and are used in mulled wines, cordial nerve tonics, salads and desserts, while the essential oil is used in perfumery.

Other common name Gillyflower
Parts used Petals, whole flowers

■ Gardening

Clove pinks were bred from the grass pink or cottage pink (*D. plumarius*) and *D. caryophyllus* (which also gave rise to the carnation). They form a dense, low, spreading cushion of grasslike foliage, from which emerge many flower stems in early summer. All are perennial.

• **Varieties** A remarkable number have survived the centuries, including 'Sops in Wine', used in Elizabethan times to flavor mulled wines. 'Bridal Veil', 'Queen of Sheba', 'Ursula le Grove' and 'Pheasant's Eye' date from the 17th century. Eighteenth-century heirlooms include the Paisley Pinks, such as 'Dad's Favorite' and 'Paisley Gem', which were bred to resemble intricate Paisley fabric patterning, as well as 'Inchmery' and 'Cockenzie'. Nineteenth-century large

The Greeks and Romans regarded the clove pink as the flower of the gods.

double-flowered forms include 'Mrs Sinkins', 'Earl of Essex', 'Rose de Mai' and 'Mrs Gullen'. 'Napoléon III' is a historic variety that involves a cross with sweet william (*D. barbatus*). The Carthusian pink (*D. carthusianorum*) was used in medicinal liqueurs by the Carthusian monks.

The famed Allwoodii 20th-century pinks include 'Arthur', 'Kestor', 'Doris' and 'Fusilier'. Other very fragrant modern

pinks include 'Kim Brown', 'Tuscan Lace', 'Highland Fraser', 'Pretty', 'Tudor Manor', 'Jean d'Arc', 'May Queen', 'Falstaff' and 'Gloire Lyonnaise'.

• **Position** These plants require a well-drained, sunny position. They grow well in pots, and are both drought- and cold-tolerant once established. Pinks thrive in alkaline soil; if gardening on acid soil, add dolomite or garden lime. Alternatively, tuck small pieces of concrete rubble under the plant. These will leak lime into the soil during watering.

• **Propagation** Mixed seed of perennial pinks are available. Named varieties must be propagated by cuttings.

• **Maintenance** Clove pinks are hardy and easily grown. Do not let these plants be overshadowed.

• **Pests and diseases** There are no significant problems.

• **Harvesting and storing** Harvest flowers as required. To use fresh, remove the bitter white heels of the petals.

Clove pinks (*Dianthus caryophyllus*)

Comfrey

Symphytum officinale Boraginaceae

Comfrey's other common name, knitbone, is a clue to its traditional use in poultices to encourage the healing of broken bones. Comfrey is also a fabric dye and dynamic compost accelerator.

Other common name Knitbone
Parts used Leaves, roots (high in toxic alkaloids)

Comfrey *(Symphytum officinale)*

■ Gardening

Common comfrey is a vigorous perennial, with mauve bell-shaped flowers, that grows to about 80 cm. Varieties are not commonly available. Comfrey is also an "accumulator," a deep-rooted plant that taps into minerals in the subsoil. A "soup" made from rotting comfrey leaves in water makes a great organic liquid feed for crops. Other species are the ornamental cream-flowered groundcover *S. grandiflorum*, and *S. asperum*, which has bright blue flowers.

• **Position** Comfrey grows readily from segments of root and, once established, is difficult to remove.

• **Propagation** Dig the site deeply, incorporating ample compost or rotted manure. Space plants 3.5 ft. (1 m) apart. Lay out segments of root horizontally and cover with about 2 in. (5 cm) of soil.

• **Maintenance** Comfrey requires ample nitrogen; an annual top dressing of rotted manure is recommended. Water regularly in the first season.

• **Pests and diseases** Comfrey is generally trouble-free. Some strains are prone to rust, usually when the plants are water-stressed.

• **Harvesting and storing** Harvest mature plants up to 5 times a year. Cut with shears and wear gloves, because the hairs on the leaves are an irritant. Leaves can be dried. Do not harvest in the first year or after early autumn.

■ Herbal medicine

Symphytum officinale. Parts used: leaves, roots. Traditionally, comfrey has been used as a topical application for bruises, fractures and wounds. It has a remarkable reputation for hastening the repair and renewal of damaged tissue as well as reducing inflammation. One of the compounds found in comfrey, called allantoin and thought to be responsible for many of the healing effects of this herb, has been shown to have a regenerative action on connective tissue.

While traditionally comfrey was also prescribed for internal use, these days such practice is strongly discouraged because comfrey contains pyrrolizidine alkaloids that have been shown to have toxic effects.

For the safe and appropriate topical use of comfrey, refer to Sports injuries, *page 222*. Do not use comfrey if you are pregnant or breastfeeding.

Comfrey comes in many color variations, including pink, lavender or white.

The dyer's art

For centuries, dyes have been made from herbs and other plants. Comfrey leaves produce a golden yellow dye, while dandelion roots create a reddish one. Until indigo from the Far East was traded with Europe, woad *(Isatis tinctoria)* was used to produce a blue dye, and the characteristic war paint of the ancient Britons and Celts was made from it. In today's commercial world, synthetic dyes are favored over natural ones because they are resistant to fading from exposure to light. To make your own herbal dyes, consult the Internet or craft books.

Coriander

Coriandrum sativum Apiaceae

For more than three millennia, coriander has been cultivated for its aromatic foliage, roots and seeds, all found in the tombs of the pharaohs. It is mentioned in the Bible and is one of the bitter herbs traditionally eaten at Passover.

Other common names Chinese parsley, cilantro
Parts used Leaves, seeds, roots

■ Gardening

Coriander resembles flat-leaf parsley, although it is more tender in texture, forming rosettes of long, thinly stalked leaves arising from a crown. The leaves are dissected into wedge-shaped segments, developing a fernlike appearance. Vietnamese coriander or rau ram (*Polygonum odoratum*) is a leafy perennial used in tropical areas. The leaves of Mexican coriander or cilantro (*Eryngium foetidum*) are strongly aromatic.

• **Varieties** 'Spice' is popular for its seeds, while 'Santo' is a variety in which premature flowering is delayed and profuse deep green foliage develops.
• **Position** Good air circulation, a sunny position and adequate fertilizing will minimize disease problems.
• **Propagation** Sow this annual directly in the garden in spring after the last frost. Assist germination by rubbing the seed, separating it into halves and then

presoaking the halved seeds for 48 hours.
• **Maintenance** Weed the crop regularly. To stop premature bolting of varieties grown for foliage, protect the plants from water stress. Apply seaweed liquid fertilizer to promote leaf growth over flowering.
• **Pests and diseases** Late crops may be susceptible to mildew and fungal leaf spot.
• **Harvesting and storing** Harvest the seed crop when half the seeds on the plant have turned brown. Tie harvested stems into bunches and then hang them upside down inside paper bags to trap the falling seed. Once the plant is full-size, harvest foliage to use fresh at any time.

■ Herbal medicine

Coriandrum sativum. Part used: dried ripe fruits (seeds). Seeds have antispasmodic properties and a stimulating effect on the appetite. Traditionally, coriander is often used in conjunction with caraway, fennel, cardamom and anise to ease symptoms of indigestion, including spasm, flatulence, and abdominal distension.

For the safe and appropriate medicinal use of coriander, consult your healthcare professional. Do not use coriander in greater than culinary quantities if you are pregnant or breastfeeding.

■ Cooking

The pungent leaves and stalks are popular in Southeast Asian, Middle Eastern, South American and Mexican cooking, in salads, soups, legume dishes, curries and stir-

Coriander (*Coriandrum sativum*)

fries. In India, the leaf is used in types of fresh chutneys. Long cooking destroys the flavor of the leaves, so add them just before serving.

Roast the seeds to enhance their flavor. Used whole or ground, their mild, slightly sweet taste works well in sweet and savory dishes and in sauces such as harissa (see recipe *page 338*). The fiber in ground seeds absorbs liquid and helps to thicken curries and stews.

The root has a more intense flavor than leaves. It is used in Thai cooking, especially pounded into curry pastes.

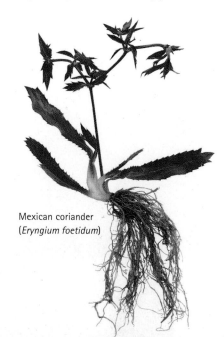

Mexican coriander
(*Eryngium foetidum*)

Coriander and figs

Palathai, or fig cakes, date from Roman times. They are popular in Egypt and Turkey. Remove stalks from 400 g dried figs (select soft ones). Process figs to a paste in food processor. Shape into an oval cake with your hands. Combine 1 teaspoon freshly ground coriander seeds and 1 teaspoon flour. Dust cake with mixture. Serve wedges for dessert.

Curry plant

Helichrysum italicum syn. *H. angustifolium* Asteraceae

The intensely silvered needlelike foliage of this plant releases a mouthwatering fragrance of curry. The flowers can be dried and included in floral arrangements or used in craft work, while the essential oil is used in perfumery.

Other common names Strawflower Italian everlasting
Parts used Leaves, flowers

■ Gardening

The common form of curry plant found in herb gardens is *H. italicum* subsp. *italicum*, a form widely sold in the nursery trade as *H. angustifolium*. It is an upright but eventually semi-sprawling shrub to about 2 ft. (60 cm), with densely arrayed, needle-shaped leaves covered in very fine hairs, which give the plant a silvered appearance.

• **Varieties** Other forms that are less commonly grown include the dwarf curry plant (*H. italicum* subsp. *microphyllum*), which is popular for edging herb gardens.

H. stoechas is also used as a source of essential oil for the fragrance industry. The oil of both species is known as 'immortelle' or 'helichrysum.'

• **Position** Curry plant requires an open sunny position and a very well-drained soil. Plants may suffer temporary dieback after light frosts. In areas where the temperature can drop below 23°F (–5°C), grow plants under protection in winter.

• **Propagation** Take tip cuttings in spring and autumn.

• **Maintenance** Curry plants respond well to a light pruning and shaping.

Curry plant
(*Helichrysum italicum*)

Curry tree

Curry plant is sometimes confused with the curry tree (*Murraya koenigii*), which is used in Ayurvedic medicine. This small tree with pinnate leaves is also intensely curry-scented and may eventually reach 10 to 13 ft. (3 to 4 m). Use fresh leaves in Indian dishes, adding them just before serving. The curry tree makes an attractive container plant, preferring a warm climate in full sun to partial shade.

• **Pests and diseases** Pests are rarely a problem but curry plant is affected by prolonged rain, often developing fungus on the foliage. To avoid this, mulch around the plant with gravel and ensure that the plant has excellent air circulation.

• **Harvesting and storing** As an herb, curry plant is only used fresh. Pick sprigs as required.

■ Cooking

The entire plant is strongly aromatic of curry, particularly after rain. Add sprigs to egg, rice and vegetable dishes to impart a mild curry flavor, but cook only briefly.

To enhance fruit flavors, the oil and the extract are used commercially in food and beverage processing.

Curry plant responds well to trimming, so consider using it in a low-growing, aromatic hedge.

Dandelion

Taraxacum officinale Asteraceae

Dandelions are the plant world's equivalent of the pig: Almost all of it is eaten. The flowers make a delicious wine, the vitamin-rich, slightly bitter young leaves are used in cooking and the roots are used to make herbal coffee.

Other common names Clocks and watches, fairy clocks
Parts used Leaves, roots, flowers

Dandelion
(*Taraxacum officinale*)

◼ Gardening

Dandelion is a perennial with a thick, fleshy, deep taproot and a rosette of coarsely toothed leaves. From the leaves emerge many unbranched flower stalks, each terminating in a double golden yellow flower. The flowers are followed by spherical balls of seed, or 'clocks', which are dispersed by the wind.

• **Varieties** Improved forms were developed in France in the 19th century. 'Thick Leaved' has tender, broad, thick leaves. 'Improved Full Heart' has profuse foliage that is easily blanched.

• **Position** Despite its weedy reputation, dandelion crops will thrive if you dig the soil deeply and enrich it with rotted compost. It requires a sunny situation and prefers a neutral to slightly alkaline soil.

• **Propagation** Sow the seed directly into the soil in spring. The plants die down in winter.

• **Maintenance** Cut spent flowers to prevent reseeding.

• **Pests and diseases** The leaves are prone to mildew, particularly late in the season. Root rot can occur in poorly drained soil.

• **Harvesting and storing** Blanch the leaves for culinary purposes by covering them from the light for 2 to 3 weeks before harvesting in late spring and before flowering occurs. Lift roots at the end of the second season. Both leaves and roots can be dried for herbal use.

A good garden may have some weeds.

A proverb

◼ Herbal medicine

Taraxacum officinale. Parts used: leaves, roots. Dandelion is well known for its therapeutic effects on both the kidneys and liver, hence its traditional reputation as a cleansing cure in the spring months. The leaf exerts a powerful diuretic action on the urinary system and may reduce fluid retention and assist the removal of toxins from the body. It also contains high levels of potassium and helps to replenish potassium that would otherwise be lost as a result of increased urination.

The root, which has a bitter taste, is utilized when a stimulating action on the digestive system is required. It promotes bile secretion and is a valuable remedy for many liver and gallbladder conditions.

Dandelion root can improve a sluggish digestion and provide a laxative effect.

For the safe and appropriate use of dandelion, see Liver support, *page 208*. Do not use dandelion in greater than culinary quantities if you are pregnant or breastfeeding.

◼ Cooking

The variety 'Thick Leaved' has leaves that can be used fresh in salads, or cooked in a similar way to spinach.

Dandelion and burdock is a traditional British, naturally fizzy soft drink made from fermented dandelion and burdock roots — in much the same way as root beer and sarsaparilla.

Clock flower

Dandelion has acquired a number of names, including *piss en lit* (French for 'wet the bed'), a reference to its diuretic effect. Its common names include fairy clocks and clocks and watches, both of which refer to the children's game of telling time by the number of seeds left after blowing a 'clock.' Another name, *caput monachi*, refers to the tonsured head of a medieval monk.

Dandelion flowers are rich in pollen and nectar, attracting beneficial insects such as bees.

Dill

Anethum graveolens Apiaceae

Traditionally, if you suffered from hiccups, insomnia or indigestion, dill was an ideal remedy. Its name comes from the old Norse word "dylla," meaning to soothe or lull. With its slight caraway taste, dill has a long history of use in Indian cooking and medicine.

Other common name Dillweed
Parts used Leaves, seeds

Dill seed is used in the spice mix, ras el hanout. See Moroccan lamb recipe, *page 368*.

■ Gardening

Dill is an annual plant with feathery, aromatic, blue-green foliage and attractive flat-headed compound umbels of yellow flowers, which are followed by small elliptical flat seeds.

- **Varieties** Dill varieties suited to dillweed harvesting that are also slow to bolt include 'Hercules', 'Tetra Leaf' and 'Dukat', which is strongly flavored. Dwarf varieties suited to pot culture include 'Fernleaf' and 'Bouquet'. If you are growing dill for seed, 'Long Island Mammoth' is a good dual-purpose heirloom variety.
- **Position** Dill requires full sun and a well-drained, moist soil.
- **Propagation** Sow seeds directly into the soil in spring after the last frost, lightly cover them with soil and keep them moist until they germinate, or plant seedlings with the potting soil attached. In frost-free areas, plant it in late autumn.
- **Maintenance** You may need to stake some tall varieties. Thin plants to about 1.5 ft. (45 cm) apart.
- **Pests and diseases** Dill has no noteworthy pests or diseases.
- **Harvesting and storing** Harvest leaves as required. Spread them thinly on paper, then microwave them to retain good color and fragrance. Store in an airtight container in a cool, dry place. Store fresh leaves in a plastic bag in the refrigerator, or chop them finely, put into ice-cube trays, top with water and freeze. Harvest the seeds after the heads have dried on the plant.

■ Herbal medicine

Anethum graveolens. Part used: dried ripe fruits (seeds). The essential oil found in dill seed is a key ingredient in the preparation of dill water, a popular treatment for flatulence and intestinal colic in infants and children. Dill seeds have been used to improve the flow of breast milk in breast-feeding mothers. Used in this way, even culinary quantities of dill seeds can allow the herb's medicinal properties to be passed on to the child.

Dill seeds can be used in adults for gastrointestinal conditions characterized by wind, bloating and cramping as a result of its antispasmodic effects.

For the safe and effective medicinal use of dill, see Wind, bloating and

flatulence, *page 206*. Do not use dill in greater than culinary quantities if you are pregnant or breastfeeding except under professional supervision.

■ Cooking

With a taste reminiscent of anise and parsley, the fresh leaves complement soft cheeses, white sauces, egg dishes, seafood and chicken, salads, soups and vegetables dishes, especially potatoes. Dill is famously used in gravlax, a Scandinavian dish of salmon cured with salt and dill. Add fresh dill to hot dishes just before serving, because cooking diminishes its flavor.

Dill seeds are used in pickling spice mixtures, in breads (especially rye bread), and in commercial seasonings for meat.

Dill (*Anethum graveolens*)

Echinacea

Echinacea sp. Asteraceae

Echinaceas are not only strikingly beautiful, butterfly-attracting plants, they are also among the most significant medicinal herbs, widely used as an immune-system stimulant, with antiviral, fungicidal, bactericidal, anti-inflammatory and detoxifying properties.

Other common name Coneflower
Parts used Roots, leaves, flowers, seed

Echinacea (*Echinacea* sp.)

■ Gardening

There are nine species of echinacea, all North American, of which three are commonly used medicinally. *Echinacea purpurea* syn. *Rudbeckia purpurea* is the best known and the most widely grown species. Its roots are the most potent part of the plant, but the leaves and seeds are also used in herbal medicine.

• **Varieties** A number of varieties are valued as ornamentals and as cut flowers while retaining their herbal potency. They include 'Magnus', with rose-purple flowers; 'White Swan', which is believed to have a similar potency to the pink forms; and the large-flowered 'Primadonna' series, available in deep rose and pure white. The extraordinary 'Doppelganger' has a crownlike second tier of petals emerging from the top of the cone. 'Fancy Frills' resembles a fragrant pink sunflower.

Narrowleaf echinacea (*E. angustifolia*) and pale purple echinacea (*E. pallida*) are more potent medicinally than *E. purpurea*. Yellow echinacea or yellow coneflower (*E. paradoxa*) is a handsome species that has large flowers with narrow yellow petals and a chocolate center. Its roots have similar properties to those of *E. pallida*.

• **Position** Echinaceas require a well-drained, sunny position. The plants are deep-rooted and, if grown in areas with shallow soil, should be planted into raised beds. They are drought resistant once they are established.

• **Propagation** Echinaceas are perennials, and can be divided in autumn and spring or propagated by root cuttings. However, most propagation is by seed, which will germinate more readily after stratification (see box above).

• **Maintenance** Plants require little except watering and weeding.

• **Pests and diseases** No serious pests or diseases are likely to occur.

• **Harvesting and storing** Dig up the roots of mature plants in autumn, then clean and dry them. Gather flowers and foliage from mature plants as required.

■ Herbal medicine

Echinacea angustifolia, E. purpurea, E. pallida. Parts used: roots, aerial parts. Echinacea's reputation as an effective treatment for the common cold, flu and acute upper respiratory infections has been the focus of extensive scientific research. The results of many clinical trials indicate that echinacea can indeed reduce the symptoms and duration of such conditions.

Traditionally, echinacea has been used as a popular and valuable herbal remedy for the treatment of many contagious illnesses and skin infections. It has a significant immune-stimulating effect, enhancing the body's ability to fight off bacteria, viruses and other disease-causing microorganisms.

Consequently, individuals who have weakened immune systems due to prolonged ill health or drug therapy may also benefit from using echinacea.

For the safe and appropriate use of echinacea, see Immune support, *page 202*. Do not use echinacea if you are pregnant or breastfeeding.

Elder

Sambucus nigra Caprifoliaceae

There is a continuing belief in the mystical and magical powers of the elder, so many people ask the tree's permission before harvesting its flowers or berries. The flowers are used to brew elderflower champagne and to flavor desserts while the berries are the nutritional equal of grapes.

Other common names Bore tree, devil's wood, Frau Holle, Judas tree, pipe tree
Parts used Flowers, ripe berries, leaves (insecticidal only)

■ Gardening

The European elder is a multi-stemmed shrub–tree with deep green compound leaves that repel flies, mosquitoes and midgets. The large lacy inflorescences bear tiny, creamy white, fragrant flowers. The leaves, bark, green berries and roots are poisonous if consumed.

- **Varieties** Ornamental varieties of elder include 'Black Lace' syn. 'Eva', with finely cut purple-black foliage and pink flowers; 'Black Beauty' syn. 'Gerda', with similar coloring; and the bronze-purple semi-dwarf 'Guincho Purple' syn. 'Purpurea'. European red elder *(S. racemosa)*, which has large bunches of red berries, is also used herbally, while the 'Sutherland Gold' and 'Plumosa Aurea' varieties both have golden foliage.

- **Position** These cold-hardy plants prefer a moist but well-drained, humus-rich soil and full sun to partial shade.
- **Propagation** Collect fresh seed in autumn or stratify older seed for 4 weeks (see *page 44*). Alternatively, propagate by suckers, by semi-ripe wood cuttings taken in late summer or by cuttings of ripe wood in autumn.
- **Pests and diseases** Elder is resistant to honey fungus. To repel aphids, mites, leafhoppers, whitefly and cabbage loopers from the garden, make a strong infusion of the leaves.
- **Harvesting and storing** Harvest the berries when they are black. Pick flowers early on a dewless morning, spread the heads on clean kitchen paper and leave in a warm, dark, dry place for several days.

Elder (*Sambucus nigra*)

■ Herbal medicine

Sambucus nigra. Parts used: flowers, berries. Elder flowers and berries have a long history of use for alleviating the symptoms of colds and flu, in particular fever and congestion of the nose and sinuses. Elder flowers have also been used to reduce mucus production in hay fever, sinusitis and middle-ear infections.

Recently, clinical trials found that a commercial elderberry syrup reduced both the symptoms and duration of flu in sufferers. Laboratory studies suggest that constituents in the berries may activate certain immune cells and act directly on viruses to reduce their infectivity.

For the safe and appropriate use of elder, see Sore throats, colds and flu, *page 200*. Do not use elder if you are pregnant or breastfeeding.

■ Cooking

Use the fresh flowers to make elderflower wine or cordial or an herbal infusion; such processing results in a pleasant floral-tasting beverage. High in vitamins A and C, the berry juice is fermented to produce elderberry wine. Freeze the berries for later use, but cook them for a few minutes first and use them in baked goods.

The dark side

In many parts of Europe, elder was used in magic and medicine, acquiring names such as Frau Holle (Hulda) for its association with the goddess of death, transformation and Halloween, and devil's wood and Judas tree for its medieval association with Christ's cross; Judas was said to have been hanged from the bough of an elder.

The young stems, with the poisonous pith removed, were once used to make flutes.

Eucalyptus

Eucalyptus sp., *Corymbia* sp. Myrtaceae

Largely indigenous to Australia, the eucalypts are rich in essential oils that are valued for both their medicinal applications and their fragrance, which ranges from lemon to peppermint and turpentine.

Eucalyptus seeds or "gum nuts" (*Eucalyptus* sp.)

Other common name Gum tree
Parts used Leaves, gum (kino)

◼ Gardening

The genus *Eucalyptus* has undergone taxonomic revision and a number of botanical names have been changed, although older names still prevail in much of the literature. Kino, a gum produced as a response to wounding of the tree, is gathered commercially from species such as scribbly gum, also known as white gum kino (*E. haemostoma*), and the red blood-wood (*E. gummifera*). Some eucalyptus species have shown weedy tendencies in parts of the world, such as South Africa, so consult local plant services before growing them.

Use a little eucalyptus oil on a cotton pad to remove a stubborn label and glue from a jar. See also Caring for clothing, *pages 286-7*.

• **Varieties** Many species are steam-distilled for their essential oil. These include the lemon-scented gum (*Corymbia citriodora* syn. *Eucalyptus citriodora*) and lemon ironbark (*E. staigeriana*), which has a fragrance of lemon and rosemary, and *E. globulus*, the most significant species. Narrow-leafed peppermint (*E. radiata*) yields a sweet, fruity essential oil with some camphor. The commercial chemotype of broad-leafed peppermint (*E. dives*) produces a pepperminty essential oil with sweet balsamic notes; it is used in toiletries and aromatherapy. Gully gum (*E. smithii*) essential oil is used in aromatherapy.
• **Position** Most species require a sunny position and do not tolerate low temperatures. In general, eucalypts require a well-drained soil and are quite drought-tolerant once established. When mature, they are able to regenerate after fire.
• **Propagation** Raise from seed.
• **Maintenance** Water regularly during the establishment phase. Plantation-grown crops are usually coppiced for ease of harvesting and to improve yields.

• **Pests and diseases** The oils in eucalypt leaves render them distasteful to most insects; they are not susceptible to fungal diseases of the leaves. Heavy beetle infestation, particularly during droughts, will cause dieback and eventually the death of the whole tree.
• **Harvesting and storing** The foliage of mature or regenerated coppiced trees is harvested for steam distillation.

◼ Herbal medicine

Eucalyptus globulus. Part used: leaves. The essential oil from eucalyptus leaves possesses significant antibacterial and antiviral effects.

Eucalyptus essential oil is used today as a popular remedy for upper respiratory tract infections, predominantly as a decongestant for catarrhal conditions. It is commonly used as an external preparation in the form of a chest rub or as an inhalant with a few drops added to a vaporizer or put on a handkerchief. Internal use of the essential oil is not recommended except in commercial preparations, such as cough lozenges and cough mixes, in which the oil is present in a diluted form.

The oil can also be used topically, especially for as a cold sore treatment. It is also common in a number of ointments used to relieve muscle aches and joint pain.

For the safe and appropriate use of eucalyptus, consult your healthcare professional. Do not use eucalyptus if you are pregnant or breastfeeding.

Opposite: Eucalyptus globulus. It takes 11 lb. (5 kg) of leaves to produce 1.5 fl. oz (50 ml) of pure oil.

Chewing gum

Contrary to popular belief, the long-sleeping koala is not permanently intoxicated from ingesting eucalyptus oil — koalas sleep for up to 20 hours a day because the low-nutrient gum leaves that form the major part of their diet require a great deal of digesting and give them little energy.

Evening primrose

Oenothera sp. Onagraceae

The beautiful evening primroses gain their name from the many species that are pollinated by moths, opening their flowers at night and pouring forth exquisite fragrance. Evening primrose oil has applications in the beauty and health industries.

Other common names Suncups, sundrops
Parts used Seeds, roots, leaves

Evening primrose (*Oenothera biennis*)

◼ Gardening

The principal species cultivated for evening primrose oil extraction is *O. biennis*, a biennial forming a basal rosette of leaves from which emerges a central flowering stalk. This terminates in a cluster of buds that open during successive nights. The large, circular, faintly phosphorescent lemon-colored flowers mimic the moon and, together with their sweet lemon and tuberose fragrance, draw the attention of moths, which are their chief pollinators. By the following morning, the flowers begin to wither and turn reddish orange, later developing slender pods, which are filled with tiny seed.

• **Varieties** Other *Oenothera* species used as sources of evening primrose oil include *O. lamarckiana* (sometimes considered a synonym of *O. glazioviana*) and *O. parviflora*.

• **Position** Wild *Oenothera* species require a sunny position. They are, however, very tolerant of freely draining, poorer, sandy loam soils and are also fairly drought-tolerant and frost-hardy.
• **Propagation** Propagate plants by seed sown in spring to early summer. Extreme heat in summer reduces the gamma-linolenic content.
• **Maintenance** Keep free of weeds. *O. lamarckiana* is a much better competitor than the other species mentioned above.
• **Pests and diseases** Where plants are overcrowded, powdery mildew may affect the foliage. In inadequately drained soils, root rot may also occur.
• **Harvesting and storing** Gather the fresh young leaves as required. Lift roots at the end of the second season and use them as a vegetable. Gather the seed when ripe; shattering can be a problem.

◼ Herbal medicine

Oenothera biennis. Part used: seed oil. Evening primrose oil (EPO) contains significant levels of omega-6 essential fatty acids, especially gamma-linolenic acid (GLA), thought to be involved in many of the oil's therapeutic effects. GLA has notable anti-inflammatory activity and several clinical studies suggest that this effect may be of benefit in alleviating the symptoms of rheumatoid arthritis, diabetic neuropathy, eczema and dermatitis.

Further research also indicates that EPO supplementation may help to reduce high blood pressure and improve some of the symptoms of PMS. However, results of

other trials have been negative. The latest research suggests that a greater therapeutic effect may be achieved if EPO or GLA supplements are taken in combination with omega-3 essential fatty acids, found in flax seeds and fish.

For the safe and effective use of EPO, consult your healthcare professional. Do not use EPO if you are pregnant or breastfeeding.

◼ Natural beauty

Evening primrose oil is widely used in cosmetics. To make your own skincare treatment, see Three roses moisturizer, *page 247*.

Evening primrose oil tends to be taken in high doses, so capsules are the most convenient.

Taming the beast

Theophrastus (371–c. 287 BCE) wrote two influential botanical volumes, *On the Causes of Plants* and *Enquiry into Plants*; this led to him being regarded by some as the Father of Taxonomy. He named evening primrose *Oenothera*, possibly from the Greek words *oinos*, meaning wine, and *thera*, meaning hunt. It is thought that Theophrastus recommended using evening primrose for taming wild beasts.

Eyebright

Euphrasia officinalis Orobanchaceae

Eyebright is a European alpine wildflower that takes its common name from its use in various eye ailments, including conjunctivitis, styes and the inflammation and congestion caused by hay fever and colds.

Parts used Whole plant

■ Gardening

The use of eyebright dates back to the Middle Ages when it was cultivated in Northern European monastic herb gardens. All *Euphrasia* species are semi-parasitic on the roots of host plants, namely grasses, plantain (*Plantago* sp.) and clover (*Trifolium* sp.). The genus is widely distributed around the world.

• **Varieties** The principal species used herbally as eyebright are *E. officinalis, E. brevipila* and *E. rostkoviana*, all annual herbs with small, toothed, rounded leaves and yellow-throated white flowers, striped or spotted with purple. The lower flower lip is three-lobed, and each lobe is incised.

• **Position** These particular species, which will not thrive under hot summer conditions, require a moist soil. Eyebright's native habitat is meadowland with alkaline soil and a cool climate.

Euphrasia comes from a Greek word meaning "good cheer."

• **Propagation** If you have these conditions in your garden, you can establish these three species by scattering seed around host grasses during spring. Alternatively, grow seedlings in pots, but add generous amounts of dolomite or lime to the soil and also some established soft meadow grasses.

• **Maintenance** Ensure that the soil remains moist.

• **Pests and diseases** No problems of significance has been noted.

• **Harvesting and storing** Harvest the whole plant when in flower, and dry it for use in herbal preparations.

Eyebright (*Euphrasia officinalis*)

■ Herbal medicine

Euphrasia officinalis. Parts used: leaves, flowers. Eyebright, as noted above, has traditionally been used as a specific remedy for irritated or inflamed conditions of the eye. The combined astringent and anti-inflammatory effects of eyebright also make it well suited to the treatment of catarrhal conditions of the upper respiratory tract. It can also help to clear up postnasal drip, middle-ear infections and sinus congestion.

Eyebright is regarded as an effective hay fever remedy and can ease many of the symptoms experienced by hay fever sufferers, including itchy, weeping eyes, watery secretions of the nose and also sinus headaches.

For the safe and appropriate use of eyebright, see Hay fever and sinusitis, *page 203*. Do not use eyebright if you are pregnant or breastfeeding.

■ Natural beauty

The pretty flowers of this plant have a toning, cooling and mildly astringent effect on the eye. Eyebright may be used as a compress or topical lotion to relieve common eye disorders and infections. To make a compress, see Eyebright compress, *page 256*.

Fennel

Foeniculum vulgare Apiaceae

Some varieties of fennel have a particular sweetness and some
ornamental qualities, while others are eaten as a vegetable or
used to flavor pickles and baked goods. No wonder Charlemagne
demanded in 812 that fennel be planted in every monastery garden.

Parts used Leaves, flowers, seeds, stems, roots

■ Gardening

Fennel plants are annual or perennial and
can reach 5 ft. (1.5 m) or more, with one
to several erect, hollow stems coming from
the base and bearing fine, glossy aromatic
pinnate foliage. The tiny yellow flowers,
borne in umbels, are used in pickling and
the small seeds are very aromatic.

• **Varieties** There are two subspecies:
a large group classified under *F. vulgare*
subsp. *vulgare*, with the second, *F. vulgare*
subsp. *piperitum*, containing only the
pepper or Italian fennel. *F. vulgare* subsp.
vulgare is further divided into three
botanical varieties: var. *vulgare*, which
contains perennial fennel; var. *azoricum*,
which contains the annual Florence
fennel, with its enlarged bulbous leaf
bases grown as a vegetable; and var.
dulce, known as sweet or Roman fennel.
Many superb Italian regional varieties of
Florence fennel include 'Romanesco' and
'Fennel di Firenze'.

The bulbous leaf bases of Florence fennel are
delicious sliced raw in salads or roasted.

• **Position** It prefers a light, well-drained,
slightly alkaline soil in a sunny position but
is adaptable and tolerates the cold well.
• **Propagation** Raise all fennel varieties
by seed sown in spring. Propagate
perennial forms by division in spring.
• **Maintenance** Cut down and remove
old stems.
• **Pests and diseases** Fennel rarely
has any problems.
• **Harvesting and storing** Harvest
foliage and flowers as required. Harvest
seeds when ripe, then dry and freeze for
a few days to kill any insects. Lift roots
in autumn and dry them.

■ Herbal medicine

Foeniculum vulgare. Part used: dried
ripe fruits (seeds). Fennel has calming
effects on the digestive system, relieving
flatulence, bloating and abdominal
discomfort, and its pleasant taste and
gentle action make it popular for such
conditions in children. Fennel has also
been taken by breastfeeding mothers as
a remedy for improving breast milk flow;
used in this way, the therapeutic effects
of fennel can be passed on to young
infants experiencing colic and griping.

Fennel has long been used to treat
respiratory complaints with catarrh and
coughing, and is suitable for treating
these conditions in adults and children.

For the safe and appropriate medicinal
use of fennel, consult your healthcare
professional. Do not use fennel in greater
than culinary doses if you are pregnant
or breastfeeding except on the advice of
a healthcare professional.

Fennel (*Foeniculum vulgare*)

■ Around the home

Fennel is a natural flea repellent. Crush
a handful of fresh fronds and rub them
all over your dog or cat. Put handfuls of
fennel fronds under your pet's bedding.

■ Cooking

Slice the raw bulb thinly and add to
salads, or cut in half and roast as a
vegetable to bring out its sweetness.
Use fresh fennel leaves in salads, salad
dressings and vinegars (see Fennel and
saffron vinegar, *page 332*), with fish,
pork and seafood dishes, or as a garnish.
The dried seeds are used in cakes and
breads, Italian sausages, salads, pickles,
curries and pasta and tomato dishes.

Field of Marathon

The ancient Greek name for fennel,
marathon, was also the name of
the battlefield to the north of Athens
where, in 490 BCE, a Greek army
defeated the invading Persian force.
Word of the Greek victory was carried
the 26 mi. (42 km) to Athens from the
battle-field by a runner, who died on
the spot after delivering his message.

Feverfew

Tanacetum parthenium syn. *Chrysanthemum parthenium, Matricaria parthenium* Asteraceae

With a long history in European herbal medicine, the name feverfew is derived from "febrifuge," because it was said to dispel fevers. Its excellent ornamental flower is as fresh-looking as checked gingham. Feverfew is used as an insect repellent and a companion plant.

Part used Leaves

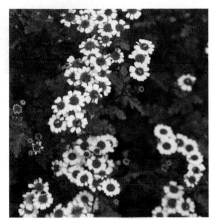

Daisy-like feverfew. Varieties can be confused with pyrethrum (*Tanacetum cinerariifolium*).

■ Gardening

Feverfew is a perennial, forming a clump of deeply incised compound leaves to about 1.5 ft. (50 cm). The tall branched inflorescence contains many small, white-petaled, yellow-centered daisy flowers.

• **Varieties** In addition to the species, several varieties are commonly grown. 'Golden Feather' has golden yellow foliage, and there is also a compact form called 'Golden Ball' and a dwarf form, 'Golden Moss'. Double-flowered forms include 'Flore Pleno' and the ivory-flowered 'Snowball', 'White Bonnet' and 'Tom Thumb'.

• **Position** It is a very easygoing plant, which responds to a sunny position, good soil, regular watering in summer and good drainage. The plants remain evergreen in winter and are frost-hardy.

• **Propagation** Feverfew self-seeds readily, but you can also grow it from seed, by cuttings or by root division.

• **Maintenance** After flowering is finished, cut back the tall flowering stalks.

• **Pests and diseases** The leaves of feverfew are bitter and highly aromatic, and act as an insect repellent. No fungal diseases are of significance.

• **Harvesting and storing** Harvest the fresh leaves at any time. (Take note that handling plants can cause dermatitis in some sensitive individuals.)

■ Herbal medicine

Tanacetum parthenium. Part used: leaves. Feverfew is used as a valuable remedy for the treatment and prevention of migraine headaches. Clinical trials have shown that the herb can reduce the severity of symptoms, including visual disturbances and nausea. Laboratory studies suggest that the therapeutic effects of feverfew are a result of its anti-inflammatory and pain-relieving properties as well as a muscle relaxant action.

Feverfew (*Tanacetum parthenium*)

Migraine medicine

In 1973 Anne Jenkins of Wales took three fresh leaves of feverfew a day to cure herself of migraines. After 10 months, as long as she kept taking the leaves, Anne no longer suffered from migraines, which prompted a London migraine specialist to conduct a survey. The clinical trial which followed found that there was a benefit in taking feverfew to prevent migraine.

Fresh leaves of feverfew are sometimes chewed for medicinal purposes. However, feverfew is more likely to cause adverse effects if taken this way, so the use of commercially produced feverfew extracts may be preferable.

For the safe and appropriate use of feverfew, see Headaches and migraine, *page 215*. Do not use feverfew if you are pregnant or breastfeeding.

■ Around the home

Feverfew is noted for its moth-repellent qualities. For information on using moth-repellent herbs, see Herbs for your clothes, *page 288*, and also Scented coat hangers, *page 290*.

Flax

Linum usitatissimum Linaceae

Beautiful blue-flowered flax is one of the oldest-known crop plants. It produces a fiber that's used to make linen, and flaxseed oil, also known as linseed oil, which is a source of linolenic acid (omega-3). Seeds, whole or cold-milled, are used in cooking.

- -

Parts used Whole plant, seeds, stems

Flax (*Linum usitatissimum*)

◼ Gardening

Linum usitatissimum is a crop species developed by humans that has been cultivated for at least six millenia. The species has been developed as two distinct types: the taller forms known generically as long-stalked flax (for fiber); the shorter, more floriferous types known as crown flax (for seed production). The plants are slender, erect, narrow-leafed annuals, with multiple stems from the base. In summer, they bear single, upward-facing, sky-blue flowers, followed by round capsules, about .4 in. (1 cm) in diameter, filled with glossy, flattened oval seeds. The seed is milled and extracted for flaxseed oil, also known as linseed oil. The industrial-grade oil is used in a range of products, from printing inks, paints and varnishes to linoleum; the residual linseed cake is used as feed for cattle. The cold-extracted oil is used for quality human nutritional supplements.

Linola is a new crop specifically bred for the production of a cooking oil that is comparable to that of sunflower and corn oil. Flaxseed is also used in bakery and cereal products.

- **Position** It requires a sunny position and a well-drained, open soil.
- **Propagation** Sow the seed directly into prepared ground in spring.
- **Maintenance** Keep flax weeded so it does not compete against weeds.
- **Pests and diseases** A 3-year crop rotation is recommended. Flax may be vulnerable to fungal problems.

Traditionally, freshly laundered linen was laid out on grass or even lavender bushes to dry.

- **Harvesting and storing** When mature, cut plants for fiber. Harvest the seed when ripe. Store the seed whole in the refrigerator, or preserve in oil.

◼ Herbal medicine

Linum usitatissimum. Parts used: seeds, oil. Taken whole or crushed with a little water, the seeds of flax have a gentle laxative effect and are a popular remedy for constipation. The mucilage content of the seed produces a soothing effect on many irritable and inflamed conditions of the gut.

The seed oil is the most concentrated plant source of the omega-3 essential fatty acid, alpha-linolenic acid (ALA), which is often deficient in the Western diet, especially for vegetarians.

Supplementing the diet with flaxseed oil or alpha-linolenic acid may have numerous health benefits. Human studies indicate that ALA has positive effects on cholesterol levels and a potential role in the treatment of other cardiovascular diseases. The anti-inflammatory omega-3 oils can also be useful for treating inflammatory skin conditions such as eczema and psoriasis.

For the safe and appropriate use of flaxseed, see Eczema and psoriasis, *page 217*. Do not use flaxseed if you are pregnant or breastfeeding.

New Zealand flax

Native to New Zealand, *Phormium tenax* (from the Family Agavaceae) has been widely adopted for landscaping purposes, because it forms handsome architectural clumps of long, strap-like leaves that have been used in traditional basketry (right). As a Maori herb, known as harakeke, it is used similarly to aloe vera, being applied topically to wounds and sores, burns and abscesses, ringworm, varicose ulcers, chilblains and rheumatic joints. It has also been used to normalize digestive disorders.

Galangal

Alpinia galanga Zingiberaceae

There are two types of galangal — greater galangal, which is native to Java, and lesser galangal, which can be found in the coastal regions of southern China. They are both grown throughout Southeast Asia, Indonesia and India.

Galangal (*Alpinia galanga*)

Other common names Blue ginger, Siamese ginger, Thai ginger
Part used Rhizomes

◼ Gardening

Greater galangal (*Alpinia galanga*) is a rhizomatous perennial producing several 6.5-ft. (2-m) stalks with alternate sheathing leaves. The flowers are followed by red three-valved fruits. The white-fleshed rhizomes have a characteristic spice and pine fragrance, and are widely used in Asian cooking. The flowers, flower buds and cardamom-scented red fruits are all edible. Lesser galangal (*A. officinarum*), native to Vietnam and China, is a smaller plant with aromatic reddish brown rhizomes that are used medicinally.

The related low-growing *Kaempferia galanga* is also known as lesser galangal and resurrection lily, and it flowers at ground level. It is used as a spice and medicinally. Fingerroot (*Kaempferia pandurata*), also called Chinese keys, grows to 1.5 ft. (50 cm) and has long, slender fingerlike storage roots attached to the rhizome, which is crisp, with a fresh lemony

Chewing John

In the United States, galangal was traditionally chewed, just like chewing tobacco, to calm the stomach and sweeten the breath, but it is also associated with good luck: it is said that if you spit the juice onto the floor of a courtroom before the judge enters, you'll win your case. Other names for this root are Little John and Little John to Chew.

taste. The Australian *Alpinia caerulea* has ginger-scented rhizomes. The red fruits of *A. oxyphylla* from southern China, known as black cardamom or sharp-leaf galangal or yi zhi, are used in Chinese medicine.

- **Position** Galangal requires warm-temperate to subtropical conditions, and grows best in rich, moist, well-drained soils.
- **Propagation** Galangal is an annual crop, grown by seed or from rhizome segments; cut them so that each segment contains one or two buds.
- **Maintenance** Keep the soil moist.
- **Pests and diseases** Rhizome rot is the principal problem.
- **Harvesting and storing** For fresh culinary use, dig up the rhizomes in late summer or early autumn. Store fresh galangal in a cool, dark place for up to 2 weeks. Dry the root about 10 months

after planting. Store dried slices in an airtight container in a dry, dark place for 2 to 3 years.

◼ Herbal medicine

Alpinia officinarum. Part used: rhizomes. In the past, galangal's calming effects on the gut were often used to relieve symptoms of indigestion, including flatulence and nausea. Like ginger, it was reputed to be helpful in alleviating seasickness.

For the safe and appropriate medicinal use of galangal, consult your healthcare professional. Do not use galangal in greater than culinary quantities if you are pregnant or breastfeeding.

◼ Cooking

Galangal's flavor is similar to ginger's but is not as strong. Greater galangal (*Alpinia galanga*) is the type more often used in cooking, especially in Thailand, but also in Malaysia, Singapore, India and China.

Use the rhizome fresh, or in dried slices, with fish and in soups (especially the hot-and-sour ones of Southeast Asia). It features in spicy condiments such as sambals and in the Moroccan spice blend ras el hanout (see *page 364*). If galangal is not available, substitute half the quantity of grated fresh ginger.

Before using dried slices, soak them in hot water for 30 minutes.

1. Fingerroot 2. Grated fresh root 3. Whole root 4. Dried ground root 5. Sliced fresh root 6. Sliced dried root 7. Peeled fresh root

Garlic and onions

Allium sp. Liliaceae

The Sumerians planted onions more than 5,000 years ago, while the ancient Egyptians had about 8,000 medicinal uses for them, and often placed them in their tombs. In culinary terms, however, onions are said to be the poor man's truffle.

Garlic
(*Allium sativum*)

Parts used Leaves, bulbs, bulbils, seed, flowers

■ Gardening

The alliums — approximately 700 species of them — include not only globe onions, eschallots, leeks, garlic, wild garlic and chives of various kinds, but also exotic forms, such as walking onions and potato onions. Many are so attractive they long ago made their way into the ornamental garden. Alliums are all either bulbous or rhizomatous in habit, characteristically with straplike or hollow leaves and simple umbels of star-shaped flowers emerging from a papery sheathing bract.

Garlic

Garlic (*A. sativum*) is divided into two groups: 'softnecks' (*A. sativum* var. *sativum*), which contain all the common garlic varieties, and 'hardnecks' (*A. sativum* var. *ophioscorodon*), which contain the remarkable rocambole (serpent garlic or Spanish garlic). It produces tall, sinuously looping stems with a head of bulbils (secondary bulbs that can grow into new plants) mixed with miniature plants. Belowground it forms a bulb of 4 to 14 cloves.
Ramsons or **bear's garlic** (*A. ursinum*) is an intensely garlic-scented species, and both the leaves and bulbils are used.
Russian garlic or giant garlic or sand leek (*A. scorodoprasum*) develops a large basal bulb comprising several huge cloves.
Wild garlic or three-cornered leek (*A. triquetrum*) has garlic-flavored foliage, small garlic-flavored bulbs and nodding umbels of attractive starry white flowers.

Chives

Four culinary species of chives are widely grown for their foliage: fragrant garlic chives (*A. odorum*) from central Asia, with red-striped white petals; onion chives (*A. schoenoprasum*), with umbels of pink flowers; garlic or Chinese chives (*A. tuberosum*), with white flowers and deliciously garlic-scented, straplike foliage; and mauve-flowered, garlic-flavored society garlic (*Tulbaghia violacea*) in both a green and variegated leaf form.

Onions

Common globe onion (*Allium cepa*) is the best known of this aromatic tribe. Spring onions are any variety of onion that is pulled when just beginning to bulb.
Tree onion or Egyptian onion or walking onion (*A. cepa*, Proliferum Group) forms a basal bulb, while the flowers are replaced by a cluster of small bulbils that weigh the stalk to the ground, allowing the bulbils to take root.
Potato onion (*A. cepa*, Aggregatum Group) forms a large cluster of plump smallish onions at the base.
Shallots — or eschallots or scallions (*A. cepa*, Aggregatum Group) — form an aboveground bulb that splits to form a cluster of bulbs with a delicate flavor.
Chinese onion or rakkyo (*A. chinensis*) is an Asian species cultivated for its crisp textured bulbs, which are popularly used raw, pickled or cooked.

Wild garlic (*A. triquetrum*) bears umbels of pretty white flowers.

During World War I, garlic juice was used in field dressings to prevent gangrene.

Nodding onion or lady's leek (*A. cernuum*), a North American perennial, has an intense onion flavor in all parts.

Canada onion (*A. canadense*) forms crisp white bulbs and has deliciously onion-scented foliage.

Milder-flavored leeks (*A. porrum*) originate from the Mediterranean. Some excellent varieties include 'Musselburgh', 'Giant Carentan' and 'Bleu Solaise'.

Garlic leek, sweet leek or Levant garlic (*A. ampeloprasum*) is perennial and develops a large basal bulb, which splits into several cloves.

Poor man's leek or Welsh onion (*A. fistulosum*) grows in the same manner as leeks but has hollow leaves. The plant divides at the base, forming a perennial clump.

Ramps or wood leeks (*A. tricoccum*) form scallionlike, onion and garlic-tasting bulbs.

• **Position** All the principal *Allium* species require a well-tilled and weed-free soil, good drainage and a sunny position.

• **Propagation** Plant onions by seed. In areas with a short growing season, grow them to the size of bulbils, or sets, in their first season, then plant them out to mature in the second season. Raise chives, cold-tolerant leeks and their relatives by seed. Propagate garlic by planting cloves vertically, with the pointed tip covered by about 2.5 cm of soil.

• **Maintenance** Regular weeding is essential, particularly in the earlier stages of growth. Do not overwater.

• **Pests and diseases** The main problems are downy mildew and black aphid. Garlic is susceptible to nematode (eelworm) attack. As it is an accumulator, do not use chemicals. To clear the soil of nematodes, plant a prior crop of dwarf orange marigolds (*Tagetes patula*).

• **Harvesting and storing** If growing species for their aromatic foliage, use them fresh. Harvest globe onions at any stage. When they've stopped growing, the tops of both onions and garlic fall over and wither. Choose a sunny day to pull the bulbs of both types, then leave them for a few days to dry out. Store in a dry, well-ventilated area to prevent fungal rots.

■ Herbal medicine

Allium sativum. Part used: bulbs. Regular consumption of garlic, a potent natural antibiotic, can help to prevent and treat infections of the lungs and Is a traditional cure for coughs and colds. Garlic's antimicrobial effects also extend to the gut, and it can be helpful in the treatment of gastrointestinal infections. Furthermore, inclusion of garlic in the diet has also been shown to have a preventative effect against stomach and colorectal cancers.

Garlic produces a number of beneficial effects on the cardiovascular system, many of which have been confirmed by clinical trials. Garlic supplementation has been shown to lower cholesterol levels, prevent the hardening of arteries and lessen the risk of blood-clot formation. It can also help to reduce blood pressure as well as improve general circulation.

For the safe and effective medicinal use of garlic, see Sore throats, colds and flu, *page 200*, and High blood pressure and cholesterol, *page 228*. Do not use garlic in greater than culinary quantities if you are pregnant or breastfeeding.

1. Green onions 2. Brown onions
3. Green onions with their tops
4. Red onion 5. Spring onions

How to peel garlic

Peeling large quantities of garlic is rather tedious. If you're peeling garlic that is to be sliced or chopped, first thump the clove with the flat blade of a large knife. This will distort and crack the skin, making it easier to remove. If you want to use the cloves whole, use a commercially available gadget consisting of a small flexible rubber tube; place the unpeeled cloves in this and roll the tube on a work surface for a few seconds. When you tip out the contents, the cloves should be neatly separated from their husks.

Elephant garlic

Native to the Mediterranean and the Middle East, the giant cloves of elephant garlic (*A. ampeloprasum* 'Elephant') have a sweet flavor that is much less pungent than the garlic commonly used in cooking. The plant is actually a member of the leek family (one of its common names is perennial sweet leek). Eat the cloves raw or cook them like onions.

Garlic and onions *Continued*

■ Cooking

Garlic complements almost any savory dish, and goes well with most culinary herbs and spices. It is an essential ingredient in many cuisines, especially Asian, Mexican, Mediterranean, Middle Eastern and Caribbean. Even if you don't like the taste of garlic itself, a small amount will enhance the flavor of many dishes.

Garlic comes in white-, pink- and purple-skinned varieties, and in a range of sizes. Choose firm bulbs that are not sprouting, and that are tightly encased in their husks. Peeled cloves should be creamy white, not gray or yellow. Remove any areas of discoloration before using, as these will impart a rank taste to the dish.

When peeled, then sliced or chopped, the enzymes within a clove of garlic react on exposure to air to produce a strong, lingering, sulphurous aroma. The flavor of garlic is similarly strong and sharp, and gives the impression of heat on the palate. The more finely it is crushed or chopped, the stronger its aroma becomes.

When cooked properly, the flavor is mellow and sweet. Try baking a whole head in foil, then squeeze out the contents of the cloves. This mellow, creamy paste is delicious spread on bread or cooked meats or stirred through mashed vegetables such as potato. Take care when cooking garlic; if it is cooked over too high a heat, it will burn, become bitter and taste unpleasant. Even a tiny amount of burned garlic will permeate and spoil a whole dish.

Garlic is used raw in aïoli (a French garlic mayonnaise) and tapenade (olive paste). Crushed garlic mashed into butter is a delicious and simple sauce for cooked meats, or it can be spread on a sliced loaf or baguette, wrapped in foil and baked in a medium-hot oven for 10 minutes or so. Push slivers of garlic into slits in a joint of lamb or pork, or put a few cloves inside the cavity of a chicken before roasting.

Various processed forms of garlic are commercially available, including crushed pastes and dehydrated flakes, powders and granules. If you are using commercial garlic pastes in a recipe, you may need to make adjustments for the flavor of the salt and vinegar that are often added as preservatives. Garlic is also used in many commercial spice blends, including herb salt, garlic salt and pizza seasoning.

Above: Chives (*Allium schoenoprasum*)
Opposite: In a Cambodian village, garlic heads are separated and the cloves set out to dry.

Chives

Depending on the variety, chives (*A. schoenoprasum*) have a mild onion or garlic flavor that goes well with sauces, stews, mashed vegetables such as potatoes, fish, poultry and egg dishes (especially scrambled eggs), and cream cheeses and salad dressings. The delicate flavor is easily destroyed by heat, so add chives during the last few minutes of cooking time, or scatter them on a finished dish to garnish.

Snip chives with scissors, rather than chop them with a knife. They are essential (along with chervil, parsley and tarragon) in the French herb blend called fines herbes (see Herb guide, *page 356*). Snip chives finely and freeze them in ice-cube trays to preserve. The flowers make a pretty garnish.

Chives bear pale purple to pale pink bell-shaped umbels of flowers in summer.

Remove any small green shoots from the center of a cut garlic clove, because these tend to make food taste bitter.

Ginger

Zingiber officinale Zingiberaceae

Ginger was highly recommended by none other than Confucius, who is reputed to have flavored all his food with it. It has many medicinal uses, including treating motion sickness and nausea.

Ginger root
(*Zingiber officinale*)

Part used Rhizomes

■ Gardening

Native to tropical Asia, ginger is a rhizomatous perennial to about 90 cm high, producing many fibrous leaf stalks sheathed in alternating lanceolate leaves. The plump rhizomes, known as 'hands', are pale yellow when freshly dug. The yellow flowers, with purple lips and green bracts, are arranged in dense, club-like spikes. They are followed by fleshy, three-valved capsules.

The spring shoots and flower buds of Japanese or myoga ginger (*Z. mioga*) are popular in Japanese cuisine, and cassumar ginger (*Z. cassumar*) is used in Southeast Asia.

- **Position** It grows best in rich, moist, well-drained soil and requires warm temperate to subtropical conditions.
- **Propagation** Grow ginger by seed or from rhizome segments, cut so that each segment contains one or two buds.
- **Maintenance** Keep the soil moist.

Cured in salt, vinegar and sugar, ginger is used in the Japanese raw fish dish, sashimi.

- **Pests and diseases** Rhizome rot is the principal problem.
- **Harvesting and storing** For fresh culinary use, dig up the rhizomes in late summer or early autumn. If drying, do so about 10 months after planting.

■ Herbal medicine

Zingiber officinale. Part used: rhizomes. Ginger has been clinically proven as a safe, effective remedy for the prevention and treatment of nausea. It can also benefit other digestive symptoms such as indigestion, colic and flatulence.

It is traditionally used to relieve various conditions associated with 'cold' symptoms as well as period pain, cold hands and feet, arthritis and rheumatism. It may also help protect the heart and blood vessels by preventing the formation of blood clots and lowering cholesterol levels.

■ Cooking

Young ginger is tender and sweet, with a spicy, tangy, warm to hot flavor. Older ginger is stronger, hotter and more fibrous. Japanese ginger (*Z. mioga*), known as gari, is widely used as a sushi condiment.

In Asian, Caribbean and African cuisine, ginger is an essential ingredient in curries, stews, soups, salads, pickles, chutneys, marinades, stir-fries and meat, fish and vegetable dishes. Fresh ginger's uses are mostly savory; crystallized ginger is used in baked goods, or eaten on its own as confectionery, often sugar-coated.

Dried ginger is hotter than fresh ginger. Ground dried ginger is used in baking and in commercial spice mixtures. Both ground dried ginger and ginger essential oil are used in commercial food flavoring, while ginger extracts are used in cordials, ginger beer and ginger ale.

Storing and preserving ginger

Select clean, plump, firm rhizomes, then wrap them tightly in foil and store in the vegetable crisper of the refrigerator for several weeks. For long-term storage, ginger may be pickled, preserved in sherry or other strong spirit, or crystallized. Store crystallized ginger or ginger in syrup in an airtight container in a cool, dry place. They will keep for up to 1 year.

1. Whole ginger root 2. Pickled ginger
3. Ground dried ginger 4. Sliced dried ginger
5. Crystallized ginger 6. Glacé ginger

Ginkgo

Ginkgo biloba Ginkgoaceae

The ginkgo dates back to the time of the dinosaurs, before the evolution of flowering plants. It may now be extinct in the wild, but is one of the most frequently prescribed herbs in Western herbal medicine.

Other common name Maidenhair tree
Parts used Fruits, leaves

▣ Gardening

The sole remaining species of the once abundant and widely distributed plant order Ginkgoales, which dates back to the Jurassic and Triassic periods, ginkgo has long been cultivated in Japan and China as a sacred tree. The plant has fan-shaped notched leaves resembling those of the maidenhair fern, and makes an attractive ornamental tree. The species is dioecious, so the unpleasant smelling plum-like fruit are formed only where male and female trees are grown together.

The 'fruits' are naked seeds, as true fruits only developed with the rise of the flowering plants. Within is a seed resembling an almond, prized in both China and Japan, which is boiled, roasted or baked before being cracked open. The tree is deciduous, coloring a clear gold in autumn.

• **Varieties** Most varieties of ginkgo were selected for ornamental purposes.

These include the fastigiate 'Princeton Sentry', the dwarf 'Chi Chi' and 'Jade Butterfly', and the excellent male clone, 'Autumn Gold'.

• **Position** Ginkgo is fully hardy, suited to a cool climate, and prefers a sunny position and well-drained, fertile soil. It is very slow-growing.

• **Propagation** You can propagate ginkgo by seed, and if you require fruit, plant a male with a female. Grow named varieties by grafting or by cuttings of semi-ripe wood in summer.

• **Maintenance** These trees require little pruning.

• **Pests and diseases** Ginkgo is virtually pest-free.

• **Harvesting and storing** Harvest ripe fruits when they fall from the tree and extract the almond-like seed. Harvest the leaves and dry them as they begin to change color in autumn.

▣ Herbal medicine

Ginkgo biloba. Part used: leaves. Extensive laboratory research has identified many pharmacological actions associated with ginkgo leaf, including potent anti-oxidant and anti-inflammatory effects, an ability to enhance blood flow through arteries, veins and capillaries, as well as a protective effect on many cells of the body against toxin damage. These properties explain the therapeutic application of ginkgo to a range of health conditions, many of them verified by human trials. (See A seed of promise, left.)

Clinical studies in patients have shown ginkgo to be beneficial for the treatment of some circulatory disorders, including intermittent claudication, where poor blood flow to the legs results in symptoms of numbness, pain and cramping, and Raynaud's syndrome, where there is poor circulation to the hands and feet. Further clinical trials also indicate its use in the treatment of vertigo, tinnitus, asthma and premenstrual syndrome.

For the safe and appropriate use of ginkgo, see Memory and concentration, *page 213*, and Circulation, *page 226*. Do not use ginkgo if you are pregnant or breastfeeding.

Ginkgo (*Ginkgo biloba*)

A seed of promise

Ginkgo has a longstanding association with improvement in brain function and mood, especially in older people. Human trials have shown positive effects on memory impairment and poor concentration as well as the treatment and prevention of symptoms of some types of dementia, including Alzheimer's disease.

During the Jurassic period, ginkgo trees were part of the landscape in which brachiosaurs roamed.

Ginseng

Panax sp. and *Eleutherococcus senticosus* Araliaceae

Ginseng has been used in Chinese medicine for at least 5,000 years. Today it is widely recognized in Western medicine as an adaptogen, reducing the body's reaction to trauma and stress. The closely related Siberian ginseng and American ginseng have similar uses.

Ginseng root
(*Panax ginseng*)

Part used Roots

■ Gardening

Chinese (Asian or Korean) ginseng (*Panax ginseng*) is a long-lived deciduous perennial with branched taproots, from which spring long-stalked, divided leaves. Siberian ginseng (*Eleutherococcus senticosus*), which is part of the same plant family, is a deciduous shrub with thick roots, divided leaves and umbels of black berries.
• **Varieties** American ginseng (*Panax quinquefolius*) is close in appearance and activity to Chinese ginseng, while Japanese ginseng (*P. japonicus*) is widely used in tonic drinks in Japan. Notoginseng (*P. pseudoginseng*) is a hemostatic herb.
• **Position** Plants grow in full sun to light shade, and need a moist, rich, well-drained soil. *Panax* species require mild summers and cold winters, deep shade and a slightly acidic soil.
• **Propagation** Plants are seed grown, germinating rather erratically, so that seed is often stratified (see box, *page 44*). Propagate *Eleutherococcus* by seed, by softwood or hardwood cuttings, and by root cuttings.
• **Maintenance** With forest-floor crops, little is required other than patience.

• **Pests and diseases** Field-grown crops can attract a range of pests and diseases.
• **Harvesting and storing** Harvest ginseng roots in autumn from plants that are usually 6 years or older. Use them fresh or peeled and dried.

■ Herbal medicine

Korean ginseng (*Panax ginseng*), American ginseng (*P. quinquefolius*), Siberian ginseng (*Eleutherococcus senticosus*). Part used: roots. Modern research has shown that these herbs improve the body's capacity to cope with stress, so they have become popular remedies for enhancing mental function and physical performance during times of overwork, fatigue, exhaustion or convalescence.

American ginseng has recently been successfully trialled as a treatment for reducing the incidence of upper respiratory infections. All three ginsengs have also been shown to lower blood sugar, and may be of benefit in the treatment of diabetes. Although the ginsengs appear to be of benefit in a wide range of chronic illnesses, many clinical trials investigating these herbs have produced mixed results, perhaps due to the large variations in the quality, dose, preparation and duration of the different ginsengs used.

For the safe and appropriate use of Korean ginseng, see Tension and stress, *page 210*. For the safe and appropriate use of Siberian ginseng and withania, see Tiredness and fatigue, *page 212*. Do not use these herbs if you are pregnant or breastfeeding.

Withania

Although not related to the ginsengs, withania (*Withania somnifera*) is sometimes called Indian ginseng as a result of its ability to improve mood, mental capacity and physical strength during recovery from illness and times of stress. Withania also appears to have an adaptogenic-type effect on the body as well as positive effects on immune function. However, in contrast to the ginsengs, withania has a mild sedative action and has traditionally been prescribed for some cases of insomnia. It is also high in iron, and can be a valuable remedy for treating anemia.

Ginseng (*Panax ginseng*)

Gotu kola

Centella asiatica syn. *Hydrocotyle asiatica* Apiaceae

The reputed extraordinary longevity of Professor Li Chung Yon, who is said to have died at the age of 256, outliving 24 successive wives, is attributed to drinking tea made with this Chinese "long-life herb," which is also an important Ayurvedic plant.

Other common names Arthritis herb, Asiatic pennywort
Parts used Whole plant, leaves

Gotu kola (*Centella asiatica*)

■ Gardening

Gotu kola is closely related to the pennywort (*Hydrocotyle* sp.) and more remotely to celery and parsley. The plant is a small, creeping, subtropical to tropical groundcover that spreads by stolons, in a similar manner to strawberries and violets, forming plantlets that root into the ground and eventually form a dense mat. Individual plants have basal rosettes of shiny, kidney-shaped, slightly fleshy, serrated, long-stalked leaves. The modest flowers are borne in umbels below the leaves. Its natural habitat is in damp places and along stream and pond margins.

• **Position** Gotu kola is easily grown in a large pot or a dedicated garden bed filled with free-draining, sandy soil enriched with compost and kept moist. It can be grown in full sun or light shade. In cool-climate areas it should be grown under cover in winter. It tends to die back, but will reshoot in spring.

• **Propagation** It can be propagated by seed, but is most easily grown from rooted sections of stolon with at least one plantlet attached.

• **Maintenance** Regularly water and weed gotu kola as necessary.

• **Pests and diseases** There are no significant problems.

• **Harvesting and storing** Harvest the leaves and use them fresh as required. Dry the leaves out of direct sunlight: Spread them out in a single layer or dry them under warm fan-forced air, then store them in an airtight container for medicinal use and for tea. You can also juice the leaves and add them sparingly to tonics.

■ Herbal medicine

Centella asiatica. Parts used: whole plant, leaves. Gotu kola has been used therapeutically for centuries. Ayurvedic

Used in various skin rejuvenation products, gotu kola stimulates collagen production.

herbalists regard gotu kola as an effective nerve tonic that exerts a calming and strengthening effect on nerve and brain cells, helping to improve memory and reduce anxiety.

According to traditional Chinese medicine, gotu kola is believed to slow senility, act as a promoter of longevity and improve rheumatic problems.

Studies investigating the topical and internal use of gotu kola have confirmed an impressive burn- and wound-healing capacity, and a strengthening effect on veins, with notable improvement in varicose veins and other vein disorders.

For the safe and appropriate use of gotu kola, consult your healthcare professional. Do not use gotu kola if you are pregnant or breastfeeding.

The elixir of youth

According to official records of the Chinese government, Professor Li Chung Yon, a renowned scholar and herbalist, was born in 1677. The story goes that he was a vegetarian who used gotu kola and ginseng and took brisk daily walks while cultivating a calm and serene attitude to life (walking like a pigeon, sitting like a tortoise and sleeping like a dog). When he died in 1933, as reported by *The New York Times*, he apparently looked like a man in his prime, with his hair and teeth intact. He spent the first 100 years of his life studying and gathering wild herbs, and the latter part lecturing and educating people about herbs and longevity.

Heartsease

Viola tricolor Violaceae

This pretty European wildflower, which has acquired an extraordinary number of names, is associated with thought in the language of flowers. Although it may not heal broken hearts, as once reputed, it does have a wide variety of herbal uses.

Other common names Johnny-jump-up, love-lies-bleeding, wild pansy
Parts used Flowers (culinary), aerial parts (medicinally)

◼ Gardening

Heartsease is an annual or short-lived perennial forming a spreading, low-growing herb, which flowers profusely in spring and summer with tiny pansylike flowers. It was one of the progenitors of the modern pansy, and the flowers vary considerably in their color patterns. They usually have a purple spur and upper petals, while the remaining three petals are variously colored purple, white and yellow with characteristic "pussy whisker" markings created by fine purple veins. The leaves are oval and coarsely toothed. The flowers are followed by three-valved capsules, which burst open to reveal densely packed, round brown seeds.

• **Varieties** The variety 'Helen Mount' is a short-lived perennial with richly colored flowers of purple, lavender and yellow.

• **Position** Heartsease prefers a moist, cool location in light dappled shade and slightly acidic soil. In the right position, it will reseed generously.

• **Propagation** Raise plants from seed, then plant the seedlings in autumn and lightly cover with soil. They can also be successfully sown directly into the garden.

• **Maintenance** A gentle clipping over the whole plant in summer will encourage it to bloom through autumn. The plants are fully cold-hardy.

• **Pests and diseases** Heartsease encounters few problems.

• **Harvesting and storing** For culinary purposes, harvest the fresh flowers at any time. The aerial parts of the plant are harvested for medicinal use, usually when in full flower. To dry the plants, hang them upside down in a well-ventilated place away from direct sunshine.

Heartsease (*Viola tricolor*)

◼ Herbal medicine

Viola tricolor. Parts used: aerial parts. Heartsease may have acquired its name from its traditional reputation as a beneficial remedy for heart conditions or a belief that it acted as a love potion.

However, these days heartsease is regarded as a remedy for the skin and is used to treat eczema and other skin conditions. It is commonly prescribed for such conditions in both infants and adults, and is administered either as an infusion or topically to the area in the form of a compress on the affected area.

When taken internally, the soothing and anti-inflammatory properties of heartsease are also useful for conditions of the lungs and urinary system, helping to alleviate the symptoms of bronchitis and cystitis.

For the safe and appropriate use of heartsease, consult your healthcare professional. Do not use heartsease if you are pregnant or breastfeeding.

Hops

Humulus lupulus Moraceae

Malted grains used for brewing beer are very sweet and do not keep well, so many bitter herbs, like hops, have been used to improve its flavor and help preserve it. Hops also has sedative properties, and can be used to make a relaxing decoction for the bath.

Hops
(*Humulus lupulus*)

Parts used Strobiles (cones), shoots, flowers, leaves, vines

▇ Gardening

Hops forms a perennial vine that reaches 33 ft. (10 m) each season. Only female plants produce the required small, conelike inflorescences called strobiles. The leaves resemble those of a grape vine and are used as a brown dye, while the vines are used for papermaking and basketry.

• **Varieties** 'Aureus' is a popular ornamental variety, with light golden leaves that can be used for similar purposes. Early maturing 'Fuggle' is popular with home brewers in England.

• **Position** Hops is very adaptable but prefers an open, sunny position and a moist, humus-rich soil.

• **Propagation** Hops can be raised from seed. Only the female plants are required, so propagate either by root division in spring or from cuttings taken in summer.

• **Maintenance** For the home garden, train hops on a tall tripod or pyramid support. In hop fields, vines traditionally are trained on tall poles. Clean away all dead material in winter.

• **Pests and diseases** The major problems are downy mildew on leaves, and *Verticillium* wilt.

• **Harvesting and storing** Young shoots are harvested in spring for culinary use. Strobiles are harvested in autumn and dried. Both the pollen and leaves can cause allergic responses.

▇ Herbal medicine

Humulus lupulus. Part used: female flowers (strobiles). Hops is well known for its mild sedative properties and is commonly prescribed with other relaxing herbs for insomnia, particularly when there is difficulty falling asleep.

The heavily scented essential oil is believed to be responsible for the plant's relaxing effects on the nervous system; the flowers can be used in pillows placed by the bed to induce sleep. Hops' calming effects can also help in reducing anxiety.

Hops has a gently stimulating effect on sluggish digestion due to the presence of bitter compounds, and it is a useful remedy for gastrointestinal complaints, particularly when they are exacerbated by tension and stress. Hops also contains estrogen-like substances and is being investigated for its use in menstrual and menopausal problems.

For the safe and appropriate use of hops, see Insomnia, *page 214*. Do not use hops if you are pregnant or breastfeeding.

Hopped beer

Brewed in ancient Egypt, hopped beer was mentioned by the Roman writer Pliny, who relished eating the plant's spring growth when it was prepared like asparagus. Hops became widely used in Europe, but in England other bitter herbs were preferred until the 16th century, in part because there was a belief that hops could cause melancholia. Some herbal authorities still advise that patients suffering from depression should avoid hops.

It is said George III cured his insomnia by sleeping on a pillow of dried hops.

Horseradish and wasabi

Armoracia rusticana and *Wasabia japonica* syn. *Cochlearia wasabi* Brassicaceae

The grated root of horseradish, cultivated in the eastern Mediterranean region for more than 3,500 years, is used as a pungent condiment and in medicinal preparations. Wasabi, native to Japan, has been cultivated since the 10th century and possesses a similar, very hot taste.

Parts used Root and leaves (horseradish); rhizomes (wasabi)

■ Gardening

Horseradish and wasabi both belong to the same botanical family, Brassicaceae.

Horseradish

Horseradish (*Armoracia rusticana*) is a hardy perennial that forms a rosette of long leaves. The 30 or more strains in cultivation include 'Bohemian', 'Swiss' and 'Sass', and almost all of them are sterile. There are two ornamental forms — one is variegated with white, the other has purple-suffused leaves. Belowground, horseradish forms a taproot that expands in diameter in the second and third year.

Wasabi

Native to Japan, wasabi or Japanese horseradish (*Wasabia japonica*) is a semi-aquatic perennial with long-stemmed,

Lift the young leaves of horseradish in spring and eat them fresh.

heart-shaped leaves. Its inflorescences of white cruciform flowers reach 16 in. (40 cm). There are a number of varieties, including 'Tainon No. 1' and 'Daruma', but all form thick, knobbly rhizomes.

• **Position** Horseradish requires a sunny position and a well-dug soil enriched with rotted compost. Grow wasabi in very clean, cool, slightly alkaline running water, with plenty of shade. The temperature should be between 50 and 55°F (10°C and 13°C).

• **Propagation** In spring, plant pencil-thin sections of lateral horseradish roots horizontally, or up to an angle of 30° from the horizontal. Cover with soil, and firm down. Propagate wasabi from offsets of the rhizome.

• **Maintenance** Don't let horseradish dry out, or the roots will become bitter. Keep wasabi well-shaded, cool and watered.

• **Pests and diseases** A number of leaf-eating insects can be a problem for horseradish. White rust, *Alternaria* and bacterial leaf spot may occur.

• **Harvesting and storing** Dig up horseradish roots and use them fresh at any time in the second and third year; they are at their peak in flavor after the first frost. Store clean roots in sealed plastic bags in the refrigerator for up to 2 months.

■ Herbal medicine

Armoracia rusticana, Wasabia japonica. Part used: roots or rhizomes. The hot and pungent nature of these roots is due to

Horseradish (left) and wasabi

the presence of compounds responsible for many of their medicinal properties.

Horseradish is antimicrobial and acts as a nasal, sinus and bronchial decongestant, making it a popular remedy for colds and respiratory tract infections. Its antiseptic properties and a diuretic effect have also been used to treat urinary tract infections. Wasabi is believed to have therapeutic effects similar to those of horseradish.

For the safe and appropriate medicinal use of horseradish, see Hay fever and sinusitis, *page 203*. Do not use these herbs in greater than culinary quantities if you are pregnant or breastfeeding.

■ Cooking

Young horseradish leaves can be eaten as a vegetable, but the root is the part most often used. Peel and grate it as needed, as it loses its pungency soon after grating, or when heated. Alternatively, grate the root (in a well-aired place to avoid the fumes), adding ½ cup (125 ml) white wine vinegar and ¼ teaspoon salt to each cup (250 ml) of pulp. Store, covered, in the refrigerator. Use as a condiment for beef or fresh or smoked fish. Wasabi, often in paste form, is served with sushi, sashimi, soba noodles and other Japanese dishes.

Horsetail

Equisetum arvense, E. hyemale Equisetaceae

The forests where dinosaurs once roamed were full of giant horsetails, some the height of large trees, but the few that remain 350 million years later are small by comparison. An excellent source of silica, they were once used to scrub pots.

Other common names Pewterwort, scouring rush
Part used Sterile stems

■ Gardening

Horsetails have slender, hollow, jointed stems with leaves that are reduced to scales. The plants have a deep root system and can spread by rhizomes. Horsetail produces spores in clublike terminal structures, reproducing by cell division of the fallen spores. Occasionally, livestock are poisoned after long-term grazing on horsetail, a condition known as equisetosis.

Horsetails are divided botanically into two major groups: the horsetails, which have whorled branches, and the scouring rushes, which are unbranched.

• **Varieties** The field horsetail, bottle-brush or shave grass (*E. arvense*) grows to about 2.5 ft. (80 cm) and the sterile stems have whorled branches. The rough horsetail or Dutch rush (*E. hyemale*) produces upright unbranched stems to waist height.

• **Position** Horsetails are primarily located around water sources, but the rhizomes allow them to move into drier areas. They prefer full sun to part shade and are fully cold-hardy.
• **Propagation** You can grow horsetails in moist soil from small pieces of rhizome or divisions in spring; however, it can be a very invasive weed that Is both difficult to control and resistant to herbicides. It is a prohibited weed in Australia where it is under statutory control.
• **Maintenance** None required.
• **Pests and diseases** None of note.
• **Harvesting and storing** Harvest the sterile stems in mid- to late summer and dry them.

■ Herbal medicine

Equisetum arvense. Part used: stems. Horsetail has notable astringent and tissue-healing properties due to its exceptionally high silica content. This herb has a particular affinity for the urinary tract and male reproductive system. Combined with its gentle diuretic action, horsetail is a favored remedy for treating mild inflammatory and infectious conditions of the urinary tract, bladder and prostate gland. Perhaps surprisingly considering its diuretic effects, it is also used in the management of incontinence and bedwetting in children.

Horsetail
(*Equisetum hyemale*)

Horsetail has long been regarded as an excellent herb for removing waste material from the body, and was used for arthritic and skin disorders where the presence of toxins was believed to exacerbate these conditions. Externally, a poultice of horsetail was used to staunch bleeding and promote the repair of slow-healing wounds.

For the safe and appropriate use of horsetail, consult your healthcare professional. Do not use horsetail if you are pregnant or breastfeeding.

Equisetum arvense has whorled branches.

Scouring rush

Rich in silica, horsetails were once every cook's blessing. The hardened longitudinal siliceous ridges on the stems were utilized in ancient Roman times through to the 18th century for scrubbing pots and pans. Horsetail stems were found to be particularly effective for cleaning and polishing pewterware, hence one of the plant's common names — pewterwort. Silica also provided a natural type of non-stick coating for cookware.

Concentrations of gold have been found in some horsetails — a good indicator for gold prospectors.

Hyssop

Hyssopus officinalis Lamiaceae

Grown as much for its beauty and ability to attract bees and butterflies as for its culinary and medicinal uses, hyssop is an ancient herb that was attributed with cleansing properties in biblical times, and for this reason was even used against leprosy.

Other common name Gratiola
Parts used Flowering spikes, leaves

Hyssop (*Hyssopus officinalis*)

■ Gardening

A semi-evergreen perennial subshrub to 2 ft. (60 cm), hyssop is multistemmed from the base, and has small linear leaves borne in whorls up the stems. In summer, the plant bears long slender spikes of lipped, rich blue, nectar-filled flowers borne to one side of the stem only.

• **Varieties** A white-flowered variety called 'Alba' and a pink-flowered variety called 'Rosea' are also available. The dried flowers and leaves are used to make a tea for sore throats and bronchitis. Rock hyssop (*H. officinalis* 'Aristatus') is a dwarf compact form with purple-blue flowers.

• **Position** Hyssop requires a sunny, well-drained position, and is not fussy about the soil.

• **Propagation** You can easily propagate hyssop by seed sown in spring, or you can grow it from cuttings taken either in spring or autumn. The plants require a minimum spacing of 2 ft. (60 cm), although the distance can be halved if you are using hyssop for hedging.

• **Maintenance** To prevent plants from becoming "leggy," lightly prune after flowering and again in spring. Hyssop makes an excellent hedge that is comparable to that of lavender.

• **Pests and diseases** Hyssop has few problems. It is used as a trap plant for cabbage white butterfly around brassicas and as a companion plant for grapes.

• **Harvesting and storing** Harvest the leaves at any time and use them fresh, or dry them out of sunlight before storing them in airtight containers. When flowering starts, pick the inflorescences to use fresh, or dry them.

■ Herbal medicine

Hyssopus officinalis. Parts used: aerial parts. Hyssop possesses a remarkable range of medicinal properties. It is particularly suited to alleviating conditions of the respiratory tract and is associated with antibacterial and antiviral activity, assisting the removal of catarrh and alleviating fevers. Hyssop is therefore often prescribed for colds, flu, feverish conditions, bronchitis and coughs.

Hyssop is also reputed to have a calming effect on the nerves and can assist with reducing anxiety. It has been used to help bring on delayed periods, particularly when the cause is due to tension and stress.

Modern research indicates that as a topical agent, hyssop may help combat herpes infections such as cold sores.

For the safe and appropriate use of hyssop, consult your healthcare professional. Do not use hyssop if you are pregnant or breastfeeding.

The bitter mint-tasting leaves are used to flavor rich foods such as wild game and pâté.

Hyssop (*Hyssopus officinalis*)

Iris

Iris sp. Iridaceae

The beautiful irises include several herbal species with rhizomes, known as orris root, which are used for a multitude of purposes, from perfumery (as a fixative) and herbal medicine to flavoring gin and chewing gum.

Part used Rhizomes

■ Gardening

Iris x *germanica* 'Florentina' and the Dalmatian iris (*I. pallida* 'Dalmatica') are used for commercial orris production. The early flowering 'Florentina' is a tall bearded iris with white, sweetly scented flowers. The species form of *I.* x *germanica*, which has also been used for orris, is known by names such as 'Old Purple Flag', 'Germanica Ancien' and 'Florentina Blue'. The beautiful ceremonial white-flowered *I.* x *germanica* 'Albicans' is still planted on Muslim graves in the eastern Mediterranean.

• **Varieties** *Iris pallida* has grape-scented flowers, but its variety, 'Dalmatica', has tall-stemmed, pale lilac flowers. The blue flag (*I. versicolor*) has purple to violet flowers and tall, swordlike deciduous leaves; the plant can cause allergic responses. The yellow flag (*I. pseudacorus*) has tall, sword-like deciduous foliage and tall, stemmed yellow flowers.

• **Position** *Iris pallida* 'Dalmatica' and *I.* x *germanica* 'Florentina' are hardy, easily grown plants if provided with a well-drained soil and full sun. Grow both *I. versicolor* and *I. pseudacorus* in moist soil.

• **Propagation** Grow *I. pallida* 'Dalmatica' and *I.* x *germanica* 'Florentina' from divisions of rhizomes that have at least one leaf fan attached. Cut back the fans to about 6 in. (15 cm), and plant the rhizomes horizontally so that only the lower half is buried in the soil.

• **Maintenance** Control weeds.

• **Pests and diseases** Rhizome rots occur in poorly drained or shaded plants.

• **Harvesting and storing** In late summer, dig rhizomes, clean and dry them, and cure for 2 years to intensify the violet fragrance.

Iris (*Iris* sp.)

■ Herbal medicine

Iris versicolor. Part used: rhizomes. A close relative of the popular garden irises, blue flag has a long history of medicinal use in the treatment of skin problems such as acne and eczema. Traditionally these conditions are believed to be the result of an accumulation of toxins in the body, and blue flag appears to work by encouraging the liver, bowel and lymphatic system to remove waste material from the body more effectively.

Blue flag is often used in combination with other cleansing herbs, such as yellow dock and burdock, for these purposes.

For the safe and appropriate use of blue flag, consult your healthcare professional. Do not use blue flag if you are pregnant or breastfeeding.

■ Around the home

Orris root, a grayish powder with the aroma of violets, is derived from the root of the Florentine iris. It is used less for its scent than for its fixative ability — that is, it slows the evaporation of essential oils and prolongs the life of pot-pourris. Orris root can be sprinkled around the edges of areas of carpet or under rugs to deter, although not kill, moths and destructive carpet beetles.

Dried orris root is used in homemade toothpastes and in pot-pourri (see *pages 284–5*).

Heraldic emblem

The yellow flag (*I. pseudacorus*) is the *fleur de lis* of heraldry. In the 12th century, the French kings were the first to use an image of the flower on their shields and later, English kings used it to emphasize their claims to the French throne. Its resemblance to a spearhead is seen as an appropriate symbol of martial power and strength.

Jasmine

Jasminum sp. Oleaceae

Many species of jasmine — the delicate floral emblem of Indonesia, Pakistan and the Philippines — are renowned for their superb sensuous scent, and the very valuable essential oil is produced in several countries for perfumery and aromatherapy.

Other common name Jessamine
Parts used Flowers, roots

Common jasmine (*Jasminum officinale*)

Angel wing jasmine (*Jasminum nitidum*)

■ Gardening

Common jasmine (*J. officinale*) is a frost-hardy, tall twining climber with compound leaves and five-petaled, intensely fragrant flowers fused into a tube at the base. Brought to Europe in the 16th century, it is now extensively cultivated commercially for its flowers in southern France, Spain, India, Egypt, China, Algeria and Morocco.

• **Varieties** Fancy leaf forms include 'Argenteovariegatum', 'Aureum' and 'Frojas'. Fragrant *J. x stepanense* is a pink-flowered hybrid. The large-flowered Catalonian jasmine, also known as royal jasmine, poet's jasmine or Spanish jasmine, is variously regarded as a variety of *J. officinale* 'Grandiflora', or as the separate species, *J. grandiflora*.

Arabian jasmine (*J. sambac*) is used to make a fragrant tisane in China, the blossoms being hand-picked early in the morning and mixed with dried green or Oolong tea. Native to India, it forms an arching bush.

Double-flowered forms of *J. sambac*, favored for garlands and religious ceremonies, include the very double, miniature rose-like 'Duke of Tuscany' (syn. *kudda-mulla*), the semi-double 'Maid of Orléans' and the smaller-flowered double 'Belle of India'.

Other common fragrant, white-flowered species include angel wing jasmine (*J. nitidum*), the pink-budded *J. polyanthemum*, Azores jasmine (*J. azoricum*), Canary Island jasmine (*J. odoratissimum*), *J. multiflorum* and *J. floribundum*. There are a number of yellow-flowered species, some fragrant, but they are not used herbally.

• **Position** Plants prefer a well-drained soil enriched with rotted compost. Most species require warm to tropical climates but in colder areas can make excellent glasshouse plants.

• **Propagation** Propagate jasmine from semi-ripened wood cuttings.

• **Maintenance** In cold areas *J. sambac* and its varieties should be overwintered under protection, because they are unlikely to survive frost exposure. Trim *J. officinale* immediately after flowering.

• **Pests and diseases** Jasmine plants grown in the open have few problems; however, those grown under glass can be attacked by whitefly, mealy bugs and spider mites.

• **Harvesting and storing** Gather fully developed buds in the early morning and add the opening flowers to tea. You can dry them for herbal use. Lift the roots of *J. sambac* in autumn and dry them for medicinal use.

Jasmine essential oil

The delicate, star-shaped flowers of this evergreen vine are distilled to form an essential oil with a rich, warm floral scent that is important in perfumery. It blends well with other "floral"-style oils, such as rose, and is particularly helpful in preparations for dry, irritated or sensitive skin. The oil is also used in aromatherapy as an antidepressant and relaxant.

The name "jasmine" comes from the Persian "yasmin", which means "gift from God."

Opposite: Women in India display their baskets of harvested jasmine flowers.

Lavender

Lavandula sp. Lamiaceae

Popular around the world, fragrant lavender is becoming one of the most important botanicals with a wide range of medicinal uses, earning it the title of "the Swiss Army knife of herbal medicine." Fresh or dried, lavender also has many applications around the home and the essential oil is used in homemade air fresheners and cleaning products.

Part used Flowers

■ Gardening

There are about 30 species of lavender, which can be found from the Canary Islands eastward into western India, and they are divided into six sections, of which four are significant as herbs: Lavandula, containing true lavender (*L. angustifolia*) and its subspecies — woolly lavender (*L. lanata*), spike lavender (*L. latifolia*) and hybrid lavender (*L. x intermedia*); Stoechas, containing *L. stoechas* together with its various subspecies and green lavender (*L. viridis*); Dentata, containing French or fringed lavender (*L. dentata*) and its varieties and hybrids; and Pterostachys species, characterized by branched inflorescences and pinnate or bipinnate leaves. All have fragrant foliage.

Propagate varieties of lavender by cuttings taken in summer (see Stem cuttings, *page 163*).

True lavender

L. angustifolia syn. *L. vera, L. officinalis*, or 'English' lavender, occurs in the wild on dolamitic soils at altitudes of 1,500 to 5,000 ft. (500 to 1,500 m). Like all lavenders, it is a woody-based subshrub and will rarely exceed 2.5 ft. (70 cm) in height. It has unbranched flowering stems.

Excellent dwarf varieties include 'Rosea', 'Compacta' syn. 'Nana Compacta', 'Folgate' and 'Munstead'. Medium-height varieties include 'Hidcote', 'Miss Katherine', 'Pacific Blue', 'Sarah', 'Summerland Supreme', 'Melissa', 'Twickel Purple', 'Tucker's Early Purple' and 'Ashdown Forest'. The taller varieties include 'Alba' and the twice-flowering 'Irene Doyle'.

Essential oil gathered from wild harvested lavender in France is greatly prized, particularly therapeutically. The very fragrant camphor-free essential oil from high-altitude grown seedling or clonal (single variety) lavender is highly valued in the perfumery industry, herbal medicine and aromatherapy. Lavender has been grown in France on a large scale for the perfume trade since the 17th century.

The varieties grown for essential oil production include the great 'Maillette', 'Matheronne', 'Fring', 'Heacham Blue', 'No. 9' and 'Norfolk J2'.

Both fresh and dried flowers are used in cooking (including herb mixtures such as herbes de Provence) and craftwork, for which the finest variety is 'Super-Blue'. Make sure that any flowers you use for culinary purposes have not been sprayed with garden chemicals.

Lavender (*Lavandula angustifolia*)

Spike lavender

Sometimes called *Nardus italica*, spike lavender (*L. latifolia* syn. *L. spica*) is endemic to Spain, France, Italy and the Balkans, and grows in the wild at much lower altitudes than *L. angustifolia*.

To deter bugs, crumble dried leaves into boxes of documents or drop crushed leaves behind shelved books.

The plant has a lavender and camphor scent, and the flowering stems have paired lateral branches. It is the source of oil of aspic (*oleum spicae*).

Intermedia lavenders

In the overlap zone on mountainsides where both *L. angustifolia* and *L. latifolia* grow, natural hybridization occurs, resulting in plants with intermediate characteristics. They are larger and stronger-growing than true lavender, more tolerant of humidity and yield twice the volume of essential oil compared with true lavender.

Selected hybrids of *L. x intermedia* are the major producers of lavender essential oil worldwide. The oil contains perceptible camphor and is valued at approximately half that of true lavender. It is widely used for personal and household toiletries. Intermedia lavenders may be identified by their paired flowering side branches.

The most popular variety for essential oil production is 'Grosso', although 'Abrialii', 'Super', 'Sumian' and 'Provence' are used, too. The flowers are also dried. Many fine landscape varieties found among the Intermedias include 'Alba', 'Dutch White', 'Grappenhall', 'Hidcote Giant', 'Impress Purple', 'Seal', 'Silver Edge' and the double-duty 'Provence'.

Woolly lavender

L. lanata has leaves that are heavily felted with hairs, and long spikes of scented flowers. It is very resentful of rain and will not tolerate wet feet. It is best grown in large pots in full sun.

Several hybrids are popular for gardens, including 'Richard Gray', 'Silver Frost' and 'Sawyers', which is stronger than the species, with long spikes of bright violet flowers and silver foliage.

L. dentata, one of the Stoechas lavenders

In Europe lavender is harvested from July to September, often by hand.

Stoechas lavenders

These lavenders have compressed flower spikes shaped rather like a pineapple surmounted by flag-like sterile bracts. All of them are suited to low-altitude warm-climate gardens, including those near the sea. The Italian or Spanish lavender (*L. stoechas*) has short flowering stems (peduncles), while Portuguese lavender (*L. stoechas* subsp. *pedunculata*) is distinguished by long stems.

Excellent varieties include 'Major', 'Kew Red', 'Marshwood', 'Somerset Mist', 'Avonview' and 'Butterfly' syn. 'James Compton'. The 'Bee' and 'Bella' series developed by Bob Cherry in New South Wales in Australia and sold worldwide are remarkable breeding breakthroughs.

Green lavender (*L. viridis*) has green foliage, and green inflorescences with cream flowers and green sterile bracts. 'Beverley' differs in having white sterile bracts. Fringed lavender (*L. dentata*) has fragrant inflorescences similar to *L. stoechas*, but the narrow linear leaves are evenly rounded-dentate. Varieties include 'Ploughman's Blue', the green and cream variegated 'Linda Ligon' and the hybrid 'Goodwin Creek Gray'.

Pterostachys lavenders

These include a number of desirable landscape species, including *L. buchii*, Canary Islands lavender (*L. canariensis*), jagged lavender (*L. pinnata*), fernleaf lavender (*L. multifida*) and the electric blue-flowered *L. maroccana*.

- **Position** All lavenders require excellent drainage and full sun. They are better grown fairly hard, and a slow-release fertilizer or a light application of organic compost is recommended. They are all suited to being grown in large pots.
- **Propagation** Varieties are propagated by cuttings, but species are seed sown in spring.
- **Maintenance** Prune lavenders annually, preferably in early spring. True and Intermedia lavenders can be shaped during harvesting. Never cut back hard into old wood, or the plants may die.
- **Pests and diseases** Lavenders are generally free of pests as well as diseases.
- **Harvesting and storing** Harvest True and Intermedia lavenders in midsummer when spikes are one- to two-thirds open. Tie lavender stems in bunches and hang them upside down to dry; strip them of their flowers. The oil is steam distilled.

Cotton lavender

Also known as santolina, cotton lavender (*Santolina chamaecyparissus*) has a compact habit that makes it ideal for a low hedge or edging a path. Its gray, toothed aromatic leaves have a similar scent to lavender and are very useful for repelling moths. Add the dried leaves to moth-repellent sachets and place dried bunches with stored blankets and other woollens. Silverfish also hate santolina.

Lavender *Continued*

■ Herbal medicine

Lavandula angustifolia. Part used: flowers. An age-old remedy for calming and soothing the nerves, improving mood and relaxing muscles, beautifully scented lavender and its essential oil are commonly used for inducing a restful sleep, relieving depression and anxiety and for other disorders relating to a nervous or tense state, including stomach upsets.

Lavender flowers can be taken as an infusion or added to a bath to soothe and aid in relaxation. Apply undiluted essential oil to relieve the sting of insect bites or to prevent cuts and grazes from becoming infected. You can add essential oil to massage oil to help relieve muscle tension and headaches.

For the safe and appropriate internal use of lavender, consult your healthcare professional. For its topical uses, see Depression and anxiety, *page 211*, and First aid, *page 220*. Do not use lavender if you are pregnant or breastfeeding, except under professional supervision.

A history of epic proportions

Reputed to have been brought from the Garden of Eden by Adam and Eve, lavender has a history that is almost as old as humankind itself. The ancient Egyptians dipped shrouds in lavender water, while the Romans scented their public baths with it – hence its name, from the Latin word *lavare*, meaning 'to wash.' Under its biblical name 'spikenard,' it was popularly supposed to have been used by the Virgin Mary to perfume Jesus's swaddling clothes, by Mary Magdalene to anoint Jesus's feet, and was also favoured in the Middle Ages by apothecary monks, who used it to treat everything from labour pains to demonic possession.

Spritz still-damp washing with Lavender linen water (see *page 288*) and hang it out to dry.

■ Around the home

If you could choose only one herb for household use, lavender would have to be at the top of the list. Apart from its pretty flower and much loved scent, lavender is antibacterial, antibiotic, antiviral, antiseptic, deodorizing and insect repelling, which means that you can use it in the living room, kitchen, bathroom, laundry, nursery and patio, as well as in your wardrobes and drawers, on your pets and on your skin.

- Use both the dried flowers and leaves to make moth-repellent sachets and lavender bags (see *Craft, pages 302–5*) – they both contain the aromatic oil that insects hate.
- Infuse distilled white vinegar with the flowers and leaves, fresh or dried, for an inexpensive and very effective spray for cleaning and disinfecting a variety of surfaces.
- Add drops of lavender essential oil to environmentally friendly unscented kitchen and laundry cleaning products for a fresh, natural scent.

Lavender essential oil is antiseptic and antibacterial, ideal for blemished skin.

- Dampen a cotton-wool ball and add a few drops of lavender essential oil. Drop it into your kitchen pantry, or your vacuum cleaner bag, to eliminate stale odors.

■ Cooking

Lavender's culinary applications are limited, although the flowers are edible. They are used in the Moroccan spice blend ras el hanout and in the French herbes de Provence. Lavender goes well in sweet dishes containing cream, such as ice cream. It can be added to shortbread and icings and used in jams and jellies. Crystallize the flowers as edible cake decorations (see *page 380*).

These racks of commercially grown lavender will be dried out of direct sunlight in a dry place.

Lemon balm

Melissa officinalis Lamiaceae

Lemon balm smells like sweet lemon and is used in herbal teas, wines and liqueurs as well as in many eau-de-cologne formulations, including Carmelite water. Handfuls of the leaves, which contain a lemon-scented oil, were once used to polish wooden furniture.

Other common names Bee balm, common balm, melissa, sweet balm
Part used Leaves

Lemon balm (*Melissa officinalis*)

Gardening

Lemon balm is a hardy perennial that bears some resemblance to its close relations, the mints. It is multi-stemmed, growing to about 2.5 ft. (80 cm), with ovate, regularly toothed green leaves. The insignificant lipped flowers are lemon yellow, and borne in clusters on the upper parts of the stems.

• **Varieties** While the common form of balm has a fresh lemon fragrance, there are varieties with related but different scents, including 'Lime', with a true lime fragrance; 'Liqueur'; and 'Citronella', which mimics the scent of citronella oil and is said to act as an insect repellent. Two attractive color variations are available: 'Variegata' is a gold-splashed form, and 'All Gold' has pure golden foliage in spring.

• **Position** Lemon balm is an unfussy plant, but prefers full sun to partial shade and a well-drained but moist soil. It also grows well in pots.

• **Propagation** Lemon balm is a perennial usually grown from seed, although it is easy to raise from cuttings taken in spring and autumn, or from rooted divisions. Grow named varieties from tip cuttings, which will root easily, or by layering.

• **Maintenance** If you do not want seedlings, or you desire a new flush of foliage, cut back the whole plant, including the flowering heads. Cut back 'All Gold' regularly to maintain its color. Remove any plain green shoots from both 'All Gold' and 'Variegata'.

• **Pests and diseases** Lemon balm is prone to powdery mildew, particularly in areas with little air circulation.

• **Harvesting and storing** Harvest the fresh foliage as required. To dry, cut the plant down to about 3 in. (7.5 cm) in mid- to late afternoon, secure the stems in small bunches with rubber bands, and hang upside down in a well-ventilated area out of direct sunlight. Strip off the dried leaves and store them in airtight containers in a cool place.

Herbal medicine

Melissa officinalis. Part used: leaves. Lemon balm's mild sedative and mood-enhancing effects are commonly used to treat sleep disorders, restlessness, anxiety and depression.

It is also suited to afflictions of the gastrointestinal tract and can help with flatulence, spasm and nausea, particularly when these are aggravated by periods of stress and tension.

Recent scientific studies have shown that lemon balm has antiviral effects, and topical preparations of the herb have been used to relieve the symptoms of cold sores, which are caused by the herpes virus.

For the safe and appropriate use of lemon balm, see Tension and stress, *page 210.* Don't use lemon balm if you're pregnant or breastfeeding, except under professional supervision.

Cooking

Lemon balm's lemon scent and lemon-and-mint flavor go with most foods complemented by either of those flavors. Use the leaves in tea, salads, cordials, fruit dishes, wine and chilled summer drinks or in stuffings for poultry or fish.

From nymph to bee

Lemon balm's association with bees goes back to ancient times. According to Greek mythology, Melissa was one of the nymphs who hid Zeus from his father Cronus, feeding him milk and honey. Once Zeus ruled Olympus, he changed her into a queen bee.

Lemon grass

Cymbopogon citratus Poaceae

Lemon grass, a tall tropical grass with a powerful lemon fragrance, is widely used for cooking in Thailand, Vietnam and other Southeast Asian countries. It makes a vitamin A–rich tea, and the essential oil is used in many commercial toiletries.

Harvested lemon grass

Part used Stems

■ Gardening

A number of the 56 *Cymbopogon* species are fragrant, but the herb most commonly called lemon grass is West Indian lemon grass (*C. citratus*), one of several species that share this scent. Its narrow, leafy stalks grow in large clumps that reach 3.5 ft (1 m) or more.

East Indian lemon grass or Cochin lemon grass (*C. flexuosus*) is also widely grown for its essential oil. Ceylon citronella (*C. nardus*) and Java citronella (*C. winterianus*) share the lemon-related scent of citronella.

Palmarosa, geranium grass or rosha grass (*C. martinii*) smells delightfully of rose geranium when crushed. The closely related ginger grass (*C. martinii* var. *sofia*) has a harsher scent.

• **Position** This herb is best suited to a sunny position, well-drained soil, warm growing conditions — ideally between 69°F and 100°F 18°C and 38°C — and high humidity. In cooler areas it is best grown in a large pot and overwintered indoors.

• **Propagation** To propagate, carefully divide the clump. Raise other species, mentioned above, by seed. Feed with seaweed fertilizer.

• **Maintenance** Water plants regularly.

• **Pests and diseases** Crown rot can occur in plants grown in poorly drained or flooded soils.

• **Harvesting and storing** Harvest stems as required. Cut the upper green part into segments and dry it out of direct sunlight, then store it in airtight containers and use it for tea. For cooking, wrap the white bulbous lower portion in plastic wrap and store in the refrigerator for several weeks.

■ Herbal medicine

Cymbopogon citratus. Part used: stems. Lemon-grass tea was traditionally used to treat digestive upsets and to alleviate stomach ache, cramping and vomiting. It was also used for a number of other disorders, including cough, fevers, high blood pressure and exhaustion.

Lemon grass has also traditionally been regarded as having pain-relieving effects and has been used internally as an infusion for nerve and rheumatic pain. Applied as a topical remedy, lemon grass and its essential oil can ease the pain and discomfort of headaches, abdominal pain, aching joints and muscles and neuralgia.

For the safe and appropriate medicinal use of this herb, consult your healthcare professional. Do not use lemon grass in greater than culinary quantities if you are pregnant or breastfeeding.

Natural protection

A natural insect repellent, lemon grass offers some protection from fleas, ticks, lice and mosquitoes. The essential oil can be used in an oil burner. Alternatively, combine a few drops with equal amounts of eucalyptus oil in a water spray and lightly spritz over outdoor furniture on summer evenings. Or, light a candle made with citronella (above), a close relative of lemon grass.

■ Cooking

The strong citrus flavor of lemon grass goes well in Southeast Asian cooking and is often teamed with chillies and coconut milk. Lemon grass is also an excellent addition to Western cooking, particularly in fish and seafood dishes. Use the lower white part of the fresh stems and slice finely crosswise to avoid a fibrous texture in the finished dish. If using a whole stem or large pieces, bruise first to release the flavor and remove before serving.

Lemon grass (*Cymbopogon citratus*)

Lemon verbena

Aloysia citriodora syn. *Lippia citriodora*, syn. *A. triphylla* Verbenaceae

The deliciously fresh, refined and intense lemon fragrance of this herb, which is native to Peru and Argentina, has long been prized for use in tisanes, liqueurs, cooking, pot-pourri and perfumery.

Other common names Herb Louisa, lemon beebrush
Parts used Leaves, flowers

■ Gardening

Lemon verbena is a shrub with arching branches and pointed leaves arranged in whorls of three around the stems. In summer the bush produces large terminal panicles of tiny, four-petaled, white or pale lavender flowers.

• **Position** It requires full sun, and a free-draining loam with nearly neutral pH.
• **Propagation** Propagate by semi-ripe tip cuttings.
• **Maintenance** Lemon verbena is cut back by frost, so it should be winter mulched in cool climates. In heavy frost areas grow it in a pot and bring it under protection during winter dormancy. Trim to shape. Bushes often leaf out very late in spring; don't discard them prematurely.
• **Pests and diseases** Under greenhouse conditions, lemon verbena is prone to whitefly and spider mites.
• **Harvesting and storing** Leaves can be harvested at any time to use fresh or for air-drying.

■ Herbal medicine

Aloysia citriodora syn. *Lippia citriodora* syn. *A. triphylla*. Parts used: aerial parts. Lemon verbena is used as a digestive aid for symptoms of flatulence and colic. It is thought to help with insomnia and nervous agitation. Lemon verbena is also prescribed for feverish conditions.

For the safe and appropriate use of these herbs, consult your healthcare professional. Do not use these herbs if you are pregnant or breastfeeding.

■ Cooking

The leaves are best used fresh and young. Use sparingly, otherwise the flavor can overwhelm the food and be reminiscent of lemon-scented soap. Lemon verbena is a common ingredient in many herbal teas, imparting a wonderfully fragrant flavor, and can be substituted for lemon grass in Asian recipes.

Lemon verbena (*Aloysia citriodora*)

The leaves are used to give a lemon flavor to fruit salads and other fruit dishes, desserts and drinks. Infuse them in custard-based sauces for desserts, or finely chop and add to Asian dishes, poultry and stuffings.

Add whole leaves to apple jelly, and chopped young leaves to fruit salads. With its digestive and relaxant properties, the tea is ideal for drinking after dinner.

In mild climates, lemon verbena can grow to 5 m high, topped with tiny flowers in summer.

Sweet relation

The herb world offers some extraordinary sweeter-than-sugar plants, one of which is, like lemon verbena, a member of the Verbenaceae family. Aztec sweet herb (*Phyla scaberrima* syn. *Lippia dulcis*) is a frost-tender, semi-prostrate perennial with short, compressed spikes of white flowers and oval leaves that suffuse red in the sun. It contains hernandulcin, which is more than 1000 times sweeter than sugar. Strains high in camphor should be avoided, although the Cuban chemotype has only a trace of camphor.

Paraguay sweet herb (*Stevia rebaudiana*) is a tall perennial in the Asteraceae family. It was the *yerbe dulce* of the Guarani Indians, who used it to sweeten yerba maté, a traditional tea made from a species of holly (*Ilex paraguariensis*). Stevia contains stevioside, which is up to 300 times sweeter than sugar.

Licorice

Glycyrrhiza glabra Papilionaceae

In 1305, Edward I of England taxed imports of continental licorice to pay for repairs to London Bridge: Domestic crops became concentrated around Pontefract, where Dominican monks planted licorice in the 14th century.

Parts used Taproot, rhizomes

◼ Gardening

Licorice is a graceful, arching, deciduous perennial to about 5 ft. (1.5 m). It has a thick, deep taproot and spreads underground via extensive stolons. Aboveground, it has pinnately compound leaves and loose spikes of purple flowers. Licorice grows particularly well on the rich alluvial plains of Turkey which, together with Spain and Greece, is still a leading world supplier.

- **Varieties** There are three recognized botanical varieties: Spanish or Italian licorice (*G. glabra* var. *glabra*), Russian licorice (*G. glabra* var. *glandulifera*) and *G. glabra* var. *violacea*. Other species used in a similar way are Chinese or Mongolian licorice (*G. uralensis*) and Manchurian licorice (*G. pallidiflora*).
- **Position** Licorice prefers a rich, deep, sandy loam and a sunny position.
- **Propagation** New crops are propagated by rhizome segments planted in spring, but can also be propagated by seed. Portions of rhizome left in the soil at harvest time will generate new plants.

Slices of dried licorice root

- **Maintenance** Keep weeds at bay.
- **Pests and diseases** There are no significant problems.
- **Harvesting and storing** Both the taproot and the rhizomes can be used. They are usually dug when 3 years old and air-dried before being ground and then processed.

◼ Herbal medicine

Glycyrrhiza glabra. Part used: roots. Licorice root is one of the most scientifically researched herbal medicines of our time and investigations are confirming many of its traditional uses, which date back to ancient times. A common ingredient in many respiratory remedies for its soothing

Licorice (*Glycyrrhiza glabra*)

effects and ability to expel mucus, licorice is used to treat coughs, bronchitis and catarrhal lung conditions.

A compound called glycyrrhizin, which is responsible for the herb's licorice taste, is known to be responsible for the healing effects of licorice on gastrointestinal ulcers and inflammatory conditions of the digestive system. It also acts as a tonic for the adrenal glands, so licorice is often prescribed as a supportive remedy in times of stress and exhaustion.

For the safe and appropriate use of licorice, consult a healthcare professional. Do not use licorice if you are pregnant or breastfeeding.

◼ Natural beauty

This herb is considered an effective natural lightener for brown age spots. For the best result, use it for mild discoloration and pair it with a natural fruit peel containing vitamin C and alpha hydroxy acids to slough off dead skin.

◼ Cooking

Licorice root is one of many spices and herbs used in Chinese master stocks, adding to their intensity and depth of flavor. Add the chopped root sparingly (it can be bitter) when stewing fruit.

Fit for an emperor

Pontefract, or pomfret, cakes became a popular sweet in England in the 16th century. These soft, flat disks made with licorice, gum arabic and sugar were stamped with a stylized image of Pontefract Castle. They are still made and loved, along with another English favorite, the distinctive multicolored licorice allsorts. It is said that Napoléon Bonaparte always carried licorice lozenges, which were based on pontefract cakes.

Lime

Tilia cordata syn. *T. parvifolia, T.* x *europaea* Tiliaceae

Called the "tree of life" due to its many medicinal uses, in the medieval period lime was associated with the Virgin Mary, and was planted for its fragrant healing flowers and to provide shade in monastery gardens.

Other common names Linden, tilia
Part used Flowers

■ Gardening

Small-leafed lime (*T. cordata*) is a small-to-medium deciduous tree (to 33 ft.)(10 m) with glossy, dark green, heart-shaped leaves. In midsummer, it bears clusters of pale yellow flowers, heavy with fragrance, which attract bees to their copious nectar. Hives placed around flowering trees yield a prized fragrant honey. While *T. cordata* is the principal species harvested, other species used herbally include *T.* x *europaea* and *T. platyphyllos. Tilia* is occasionally confused with the citrus fruit species known as lime (*Citrus aurantiifolia*).

Lime (*Tilia cordata*)

Lime is also known as the linden tree in Germany and *tilleul* in France.
- **Position** *Tilia* prefers a moist neutral to alkaline soil and a sunny open position.
- **Propagation** It can be propagated by fresh ripe seed or by stratification of stored seed planted in spring (*see page 44*) and also by suckers.
- **Maintenance** *Tilia* species tend to sucker. Either remove these, or pot them and, when established, plant elsewhere.
- **Pests and diseases** Aphids and caterpillars on leaves can be a problem, although rarely so in Mediterranean areas. Look out for gall mite, too.
- **Harvesting and storing** The petals drop rapidly to allow the fruits to swell so, over a short time interval, harvest flower clusters together with a few attendant young leaves at the peak of flowering. Spread out the flowers and thoroughly air-dry them before storing.

■ Herbal medicine

Tilia cordata, T. platyphyllos. Parts used: flowers, bracts. Lime flowers are a common ingredient of many herbal teas that are prescribed to help induce a restful sleep, especially in children. The plant has a sedative and calming effect on the nerves and muscles, and can help to reduce restlessness, tension and anxiety.

Celebrating lime blossom

Linden trees are popular ornamentals in Europe, where the flowering tips are harvested at their peak and air-dried for use in lime blossom tea, a particularly popular tisane in France. The center of production is Buis les Baronnies (below), a medieval town that each July celebrates an annual lime blossom festival, together with their annual harvest sales.

Lime flowers are a specific remedy for certain circulatory disorders. They have both relaxing and restorative effects on the blood vessel walls, and have been used to counteract high blood pressure, especially when it is associated with nervous tension. The flowers can also be helpful in the treatment and prevention of atherosclerosis (hardening of the arteries).

Regarded as one of the most important diaphoretic herbs in European medicine, lime flowers are beneficial in feverish conditions such as colds, influenza and other respiratory infections.

For the safe and appropriate use of lime flowers, see High blood pressure and cholesterol, *page 228*. Do not use lime flowers if you are pregnant or breastfeeding.

The dense light wood is valued for carving and musical instruments.

Lovage

Levisticum officinale Apiaceae

Lovage has an intense celery flavor that's perfect for winter dishes, but it is far easier to grow than celery. Traditionally used in aphrodisiacs and love potions, these tall plants provide generous harvests and have a wide range of medicinal uses.

Other common names Bladder seed, Cornish lovage, garden lovage, Italian lovage, love parsley
Parts used Leaves, seeds, roots

Lovage (*Levisticum officinale*)

■ Gardening

Lovage is native to the eastern Mediterranean and is the only species in its genus, although it is closely related to both angelica and celery. This hardy perennial plant, with large, frondlike, glossy compound leaves divided into diamond-shaped leaflets, can grow to 6 ft. (1.8 m). The tiny yellow flowers, borne in umbels, are followed by oval seeds (fruits), which can be used like celery seeds in cooking. The plant dies down completely in winter, emerging early in spring.

• **Position** Lovage requires a rich, moist but well-drained soil, and light shade where summers are hot.

• **Propagation** It is propagated by seed, which remains viable for 3 years, or by division in spring. The plants benefit from generous quantities of compost.

• **Maintenance** Remove older, yellowing leaves, and consider cutting back older plants to about 1 ft. (30 cm) high to encourage fresh foliage growth in midsummer. In a mixed herb garden, mark the position of lovage, because it is fully deciduous.

• **Pests and diseases** Lovage is rarely affected, but young leaves may be damaged by leaf miner or slugs.

• **Harvesting and storing** For cooking, pick the leaves as required, but if you intend to use them for essential oil extraction or medicinal preparations, pick them before flowering. Harvest when ripe. Dig the roots after the plant dies down, usually in the third year. You can dry all parts of the plant and also freeze the leaves in sealed plastic bags.

■ Cooking

Called *céleri bâtard*, or false celery, by the French, lovage is used as an ingredient in many commercial bouillons, sauces, stocks and condiments; its seeds are added to liqueurs and cordials as well as to breads and sweet pastries. Blanch the stems in the same manner as rhubarb, or eat them raw in salads. You can also candy the stems and eat them as confectionery, or use the leaves in cooking to provide an intense, celery-like flavoring.

Lovage is sometimes called 'Maggi plant' because its flavor is reminiscent of Maggi bouillon cubes.

Love ache

As its common name indicates, lovage, or love ache as it was once called, was traditionally used as an aphrodisiac and an ingredient in love potions and charms. On a more practical note, however, medieval travelers once lined their boots with lovage leaves to absorb foot odors, while a decoction of lovage root and foliage makes an effective body deodorant. Perhaps lovage was less a love potion than a deodorant, making close physical contact more appealing in a period when people rarely washed.

Mallow and hollyhock

Althaea officinalis, Malva sp. and *Alcea* sp. Malvaceae

Hollyhock reportedly reached Europe from China via the Holy Land, hence its original name of holy mallow or holyoke. The mucilaginous marsh mallow is widely used medicinally, while the ornamental musk mallow was once used for magical protection.

Other common name Hollyhock (cheeses)
Parts used Roots, leaves, flowers, seeds

◼ Gardening

Mallow and hollyhock contain similar mucilaginous compounds.

Mallow

A perennial with finely hairy, gray-green, coarsely toothed leaves, marsh mallow (*Althaea officinalis*) has small, five-petaled pink flowers on stems to 4 ft. (1.2 m). Musk mallow (*Malva moschata*) is a European perennial with kidney-shaped basal leaves and contrasting, much-divided leaves on the upper stems. The leaves and profuse pink (pure white in the variety 'Alba') flowers are musk-scented.

Hollyhock

Hollyhock (*Alcea rosea*) forms a large basal rosette of large, long-stalked, rough-textured leaves, which may be broad and palmately lobed or, in the ancient yellow-flowered Antwerp holly-hock (*A. ficifolia*), fig leaf–shaped. The

tall flowering stems can reach 3 m, and the single or double flowers — in shades of lemon, apricot, white, pink, red or purple — are borne in racemes.

• **Varieties** The black hollyhock 'Nigra' is the darkest maroon single. All mallows have disk-shaped, nutty-flavored seeds.
• **Position** All species prefer a well-drained, moist soil and a sunny position; hollyhocks will thrive in an alkaline soil.
• **Propagation** All species are propagated by seed sown in spring.
• **Maintenance** Stake both hollyhocks and musk mallow in summer. Cut plants down in late autumn.
• **Pests and diseases** All members of the Malvaceae family are prone to rust (*Puccinia malvacearum*) and are also a food source for some butterfly larvae.
• **Harvesting and storing** Gather flowers and leaves as required to use fresh or dried. Dig up and dry marsh mallow roots when they are 2 years old.

◼ Herbal medicine

Althaea officinalis. Parts used: leaves, roots. Rich in mucilaginous compounds, the leaves and roots of the marsh mallow have a soothing effect and are both used to treat irritated and inflamed conditions of the respiratory tract, including irritable cough, bronchitis and sore throat.

With a higher amount of mucilage, the root is regarded as the more effective remedy for inflammatory conditions of the gut, such as stomach and intestinal ulcers, gastroenteritis and ulcerative colitis. The root is also used as a topical agent in

mouthwashes for inflammation of the mouth and throat and as an ointment to soothe eczematous skin conditions.

Malva sylvestris. Parts used: leaf, flower. Due to similar mucilaginous compounds, mallow has been used for similar purposes to marsh mallow, although it is considered less potent. Like marsh mallow, it is used for respiratory and gastrointestinal conditions, characterized by inflammation and irritation, that benefit from the plant's soothing properties.

For the safe and appropriate use of marsh mallow, see Sore throats, colds and flu, *page 200*. Don't use these herbs if you are pregnant or breastfeeding.

Marsh mallow (*Althaea officinalis*)

Confectionery marshmallow was once made from the mucilage in the roots of marsh mallow.

Hollyhock (*Alcea rosea*)

Marjoram and oregano

Origanum sp. Lamiaceae

The Greeks called these fragrant-leafed herbs "Brightness of the Mountain," and it is impossible to imagine the cuisines of the Mediterranean and Aegean without their strong, warm aromatic taste.

Parts used Leaves, flowers

Sweet marjoram
(*Origanum marjorana*, left) and
common oregano (*Origanum vulgare*)

■ Gardening

Origanum is a genus that is fraught with taxonomic difficulties, and there are more than 30 species from the Mediterranean and the Middle East. Confusingly, marjoram and oregano are common names that are often used interchangeably.

Sweet or knot marjoram (*O. marjorana* syn. *Marjorana hortensis*) has gray-green leaves with a mouthwatering fragrance. Although usually treated as an annual, it is a short-lived perennial in mild climates. A hardier hybrid, *O.* x *marjoricum*, may be sold incorrectly as 'Italian Oregano'.

Spartan oregano (*O. minutiflorum*) is frequently included in dried oregano mixes from Turkey. It resembles a diminutive gray-leafed sweet marjoram that has undergone relaxation therapy.

Pot marjoram or Turkish oregano (*O. onites*) is a quite cold-tender, strongly aromatic species from Greece. Selections of *O. vulgare* are often incorrectly sold under this name.

Common oregano (*O. vulgare*) contains six subspecies. *O. vulgare* subsp. *vulgare* is the mild-flavored wild marjoram with clustered heads of pink flowers and deep burgundy bracts that attract bees, but lacks any appreciable flavor. It is often sold as oregano. Cultivars of *O. vulgare* subsp. *vulgare* include the very attractive golden oregano, 'Aureum', sometimes sold as 'golden marjoram', which makes a superb aromatic groundcover for full sun,

and 'Jim Best', which is a vigorous gold and green variegated variety. *O. pulchellum* is a name attached to forms of *O. vulgare* with purple bracts.

Greek oregano (*O. vulgare* subsp. *hirtum*) has a deliciously strong fragrance. The very mildly aromatic *O. vulgare* subsp. *virens* and *O. vulgare* subsp. *viridulum* are both called wild marjoram.

Lebanese oregano, Syrian hyssop or white oregano (*O. syriacum*) forms a tender perennial subshrub with gray-green foliage. Ezov, the biblical hyssop, was almost certainly *O. syriacum*. A hybrid with *O. vulgare*, sold as *O. maru*, has greater cold resistance.

Russian oregano (*O. vulgare* subsp. *gracile*) has an aroma that is similar to Greek oregano.

Algerian oregano (*O. vulgare* subsp. *glandulosum*) is rarely seen outside its native land but is a good culinary herb.

Ornamental origanums Many species and hybrids of *Origanum* are grown simply for their beauty and fragrance. They include 'Herrenhausen', 'Country Cream', the aromatic and strangely beautiful Dittany of Crete (*O. dictamnus*) and *O. creticum*, a very aromatic species, the source of the essential oil *oleum origani*.

Za'atar

Za'atar is an Arabic term for a number of aromatic herbs, often varying according to the region and also the local flora. While the term most often refers to origanums, za'atar species also include conehead thyme (*Thymbra capitata*), za'atar hommar (*T. spicata*), true thyme (*Thymus* sp.) and *Satureja* species such as *S. cuneifolia* and *S. thymbra*. The seasoning mixture called 'za'atar' usually includes toasted sesame seeds and coarse salt, and is used on vegetable and meat dishes and also sprinkled on bread before baking.

- **Position** *Origanum* species are found in the wild in sunny, well-drained and often stony places. They thrive in full sun and are stronger flavored if grown with tough love.
- **Propagation** Raise the species from seed in spring, and ornamental varieties by cuttings.
- **Maintenance** Once the plants are established, do not overwater them. Cut back old growth in spring.
- **Pests and diseases** Origanums are very resistant to both.
- **Harvesting and storing** You can harvest the foliage fresh but the flavor is enhanced if you dry it in bunches in a dark, dry, warm, well-ventilated place for several days. When dry and crisp, rub the leaves off the stems and store in an airtight container.

■ Herbal medicine

Origanum vulgare. Parts used: leaves, flowers. An infusion of the herb is a useful remedy for feverish conditions and also for treating coughs, colds and influenza due to its ability to improve the removal of phlegm from the lungs and relax the bronchial muscles. Traditionally, oregano is also regarded as an herb for the gut; it relieves flatulence and improves digestion as well as treats intestinal infections due to a strong antiseptic effect.

The essential oil of oregano has been shown to possess potent antimicrobial and antioxidant properties, primarily due to the presence of the constituents thymol and carvacrol. Some commercial oregano oil products have been used to treat a range of conditions, including respiratory and gastrointestinal infections, although substantial clinical evidence proving its efficacy is lacking.

Origanum marjorana syn. *Marjorana hortensis*. Parts used: leaves and flowers.

Common oregano (*O. vulgare*) in flower

Medicinally, sweet marjoram is used predominantly in the form of its essential oil, which is applied topically to ease headaches, sore muscles and rheumatic pain. As an external remedy it can also relieve catarrhal conditions of the lung, digestive colic, flatulence and period pain.

For the safe and appropriate medicinal use of these two herbs, consult a health-care professional. Do not use these herbs in greater than culinary quantities or the essential oils of these herbs internally or externally if you are pregnant or breastfeeding.

■ Cooking

Oregano has a more pungent scent than marjoram, with a stronger flavor. The hotter and drier the climate, the more aroma and flavor a variety will have.

Sweet marjoram is the type used in cooking. Its aroma is damaged by heat, so use it in uncooked or lightly cooked dishes, or add it at the end. Oregano is a more robust herb and can withstand longer cooking.

Both herbs go well with lemon, garlic, wine, meats, fish, salads, Greek and Italian dishes, beans, eggplant, capsicum and tomato-based dishes and sauces. They are also used in commercial mixed herbs.

Marjoram and sausage pasta

10.5 oz. (300 g) rigatoni
9 oz. (250) g sausages
2 tablespoons olive oil
1 large red onion, roughly chopped
3 cloves garlic, finely chopped
1 small eggplant, diced
3 small zucchini, diced
2 cups (500 g) tomato pasta sauce
1 tablespoon chopped fresh marjoram or oregano
1.5 oz. (40 g) black olives
9 oz. (250 g) cherry tomatoes
2 tablespoons chopped fresh parsley
fresh marjoram leaves, for garnish
grated parmesan, to serve

Cook pasta in boiling water until al dente, about 10 minutes. Drain. Grill sausages until brown. Cool slightly; cut into thick slices. Heat oil in saucepan over moderate heat. Fry onion until starting to color, about 3 minutes. Add garlic and sausages; cook a few minutes. Increase heat; add eggplant and zucchini; cook, stirring, 5 minutes, until eggplant begins to soften. Add tomato pasta sauce, stir in marjoram and season to taste. Cover and simmer, stirring occasionally, 15 minutes, or until eggplant is tender. Stir in olives and tomatoes. Cover and cook a further 5 minutes. Combine pasta and sauce in a large bowl. Stir in parsley. Sprinkle with marjoram leaves and parmesan. Serves 4.

For a relaxing soak, tie a tablespoonful each of dried sweet marjoram and oatmeal into a piece of cheesecloth and drop into the bathwater.

Meadowsweet

Filipendula ulmaria syn. *Spiraea ulmaria* Rosaceae

With its fragrant and beautiful flowers, meadowsweet was considered one of the most powerful and sacred herbs of the Druids. In medieval times, it was a very popular strewing herb, a favorite of Elizabeth I, who ordered it used in her bedchamber.

Other common names Bridewort, lady of the meadow, meadow queen, queen of the meadow
Parts used Flowers, leaves

▧ Gardening

Meadowsweet forms a basal clump of pinnate leaves, and bears dense, frothy, tall corymbs of almond-scented, creamy white flowers to 1.2 m in summer. (Corymbs are flower clusters with the appearance of a flat or rounded top.) The leaves smell like wintergreen when crushed. The plant occurs in moist meadows and around fresh water, and is widely distributed across Asia and Europe.

• **Varieties** Ornamental but herbally active varieties include the particularly desirable double-flowered 'Flore Pleno'; 'Grandiflora', with large flowers; 'Aurea', with golden foliage; and 'Variegata', with cream-variegated leaves. Dropwort (*F. vulgaris*) is a closely related plant, once employed as a diuretic. It has similar flowers, although the individual leaflets are re-pinnately divided. The beautiful

North American species *F. rubra* is larger, with pink- to rose-colored flowers.

• **Position** Hardy meadowsweet will grow in full sun, provided the soil is very moist. It prefers a well-enriched, alkaline soil.

• **Propagation** Propagate the species by seed in autumn, or by stratified seed (see *page 44*) and plant in spring. Both the species and named varieties can be propagated by division in spring.

• **Maintenance** Every 3 or 4 years, lift and divide meadowsweet in autumn.

• **Pests and diseases** Check for mildew toward the end of the growing season.

• **Harvesting and storing** Cut and dry flowers when in full bloom and use fresh for culinary use, or dried for herbal use. Harvest and dry leaves at the same time.

▧ Herbal medicine

Filipendula ulmaria syn. *Spiraea ulmaria*. Parts used: flowers, leaves. Meadowsweet is considered one of the most important digestive remedies, indicated for many conditions of the gut, particularly those associated with inflammation and excess acidity. Meadowsweet has a balancing effect on acid production in the stomach as well as a soothing and healing effect on the upper digestive tract. It is prescribed commonly for acid reflux, indigestion, gastritis and stomach ulcers.

Meadowsweet contains aspirin-like compounds that are responsible for its pain-relieving and anti-inflammatory properties. These compounds can also

Meadowsweet (Filipendula ulmaria)

help to bring down fevers, so this herb is often recommended for the treatment of colds and flu. The plant's medicinal effects make it an effective remedy for helping to alleviate joint and muscle pain.

For the safe and appropriate medicinal use of meadowsweet, see Indigestion, *page 204*. Do not use meadowsweet if you are pregnant or breastfeeding.

▧ Cooking

The flowers are used to flavor jams, stewed fruits and wine as well as mead and the non-alcoholic Norfolk Punch.

The source of aspirin

In 1827, salicin was isolated from meadowsweet's salicylates-containing leaves, then synthesized to acetyl salicylic acid (aspirin) by Felix Hoffman in Germany in 1899. His employer, Bayer A G, named the drug aspirin after an old botanical name for meadowsweet, *Spirea ulmaria*. The herb is considered less irritating to the stomach than the purified drug.

Meadowsweet was once used in garlands for brides and as a strewing herb at weddings.

Mint

Mentha sp. Lamiaceae

True mints come in an amazing range of flavors and fragrances. While everyone is familiar with spearmint and common mint, there are many more mouth-watering varieties, including apple, chocolate, lime, grapefruit, lemon and ginger.

Spearmint
(*Mentha spicata*)

Part used Leaves

■ Gardening

Spearmint (*Mentha spicata*) has terminal spikes of lavender-colored flowers. There are many named clones, some with typical spearmint fragrance, such as the very sweet 'Provence Spearmint'. Others have a peppermint, fruit-and-mint or even lavender fragrance.

Curly spearmint (*M. spicata* var. *crispa*) has ornamental fluted and curled foliage with a true spearmint scent. The large and slightly crinkly leafed variety, 'Kentucky Colonel', is very close to the common garden mint of Australia and England. 'Moroccan' mint is a neat form with a very sweet flavor.

Peppermint (*M.* x *piperita*) is a virtually sterile natural hybrid of water mint (*M. aquatica*) and spearmint (*M. spicata*). The most commonly cultivated clones are 'Black' (var. *piperita*), with an inflorescence

resembling water mint; 'Mitcham', the best selection of black peppermint; and white peppermint (var. *officinalis*), with a spearmint-like inflorescence. Other varieties include the quite delicious 'Chocolate' mint and 'Grapefruit'.

Water mint (*M. aquatica*) has a strong peppermintlike scent. The best-known variety is 'Eau de Cologne' or 'Bergamot', with a strong and delightful true scent of eau-de-cologne. The whole plant is deep green suffused with purple.

A natural hybrid between corn mint (*M. arvensis*) and spearmint (*M. spicata*), *Mentha* x *gentilis* has a long inflorescence with clusters of lavender-colored flowers in the axils of the lanceolate leaves. Two varieties are 'Red-stemmed Applemint' ('Madalene Hill') and 'Ginger'.

Apple or pineapple mint (*M. suaveolens*) is a sweetly fruit-scented species with

finely hairy leaves. Commercially they are sold as 'Apple' mint or 'Pineapple' mint (the variegated form).

Woolly or Bowle's mint (*M.* x *villosa* var. *alopecuroides*) is a vigorous, tall-growing species with broadly oval furred leaves, often sold as 'Apple' mint, but it is distinguished by the dense, pointed terminal clusters of lavender flowers.

Japanese peppermint or North American cornmint (*M. canadensis*) is piercingly peppermint-scented.

Pennyroyal (*M. pulegium*) is a creeping mint that forms dense mats. Its small smooth leaves are powerfully hot mint-scented and the inflorescences have clusters of lavender flowers. The American pennyroyal is *Hedeoma pulegioides*.

Corsican mint (*M. requinii*) is a strongly mint-scented ornamental that forms a very dense groundcover of tiny emerald green leaves, well-suited to moist areas or cultivation in large pots.

Rau ram (*Persicaria odorata* syn. *Polygonum odoratum*) is an easily grown perennial, ideal for pot culture in a lightly shaded position. Although not of the mint family, it is also called Vietnamese mint and is used in Asian cooking. Its pointed, lance-shaped opposing leaves are green marked with deep brown and burgundy.

Variegated apple mint (*M. suaveolens* 'Variegata')

Pennyroyal (*M. pulegium*)

Mint Continued

Rau ram or Vietnamese mint (*Persicaria odorata*)

- **Position** The ideal conditions are moist, rich soil and half to full sun.
- **Propagation** You can easily propagate mints from cuttings or by dividing clumps.
- **Maintenance** If your mint is proving invasive, grow it in large pots.
- **Pests and diseases** Some mints, mainly varieties of *M. spicata*, are prone to a rust disease, *Puccinea menthae*. The mint flea beetle can cause leaf fall and browning; caterpillars are also a problem.
- **Harvesting and storing** Mints dry well in a warm, airy place away from direct sunlight. Store crumbled leaves in an airtight container. Harvest foliage to use fresh as required.

■ Herbal medicine

Mentha x piperita. Part used: leaves. Peppermint produces notable relaxing effects on the gut and can help to relieve indigestion, nausea, gas and cramping. Clinical trials have verified a therapeutic effect of the herb on many of the symptoms of irritable bowel syndrome, including diarrhea, constipation, bloating and abdominal pain, especially when taken in the form of enteric-coated peppermint oil capsules.

Topically, peppermint essential oil has a pain-relieving effect, which can be valuable in alleviating the discomfort of joint and muscle pain and headaches. When it is inhaled, it can also help to reduce feelings of nausea and act as a nasal decongestant.

For the safe and appropriate medicinal use of peppermint, see Wind, bloating and flatulence, *page 206*; Nausea, *page 205*. Do not use peppermint in greater than culinary quantities, and do not use the essential oil if you are pregnant or breastfeeding.

■ Around the home

Peppermint and pennyroyal (*M. pulegium*) are both natural insect repellents that are easy to grow.

Peppermint (*Mentha x piperita*)

- Sprinkle cotton balls with peppermint essential oil and leave them where rodents enter.
- Add a few drops of peppermint essential oil to a damp rag and wipe on cabinet interiors to deter ants and cockroaches.
- To make a personal insect repellent, mix 1 part lavender, 1 part eucalyptus, 1 part peppermint essential oils with 3 parts unscented moisturizer or sweet almond oil, and rub into the skin.
- To deter fleas, sprinkle dried pennyroyal under your dog's bedding or put a spot of oil on its collar. Don't use pennyroyal on cats or pregnant dogs, because it is toxic.

■ Cooking

Lovely though its flavor is, fresh mint can overwhelm milder flavors and is best used with a light hand. Dried mint is less assertive and is favored in eastern Mediterranean and Arab countries.

In general, mint does not complement other herbs well, except parsley, thyme, marjoram, sage, oregano and coriander. It goes well with yogurt, and is used in Vietnamese food and in some Indian dishes. The coriander and lemon taste of Vietnamese mint is refreshing in salads.

Spearmint is the ordinary garden mint, and the most common culinary type. It is a classic flavoring for roast lamb and its accompaniments, and also goes well with potatoes, peas and salads.

Peppermint has a particularly strong flavor and aroma. It makes a pleasant digestive tea. The oil is used in ice cream, confectionery and liqueurs.

Mint jelly

- 1 lb. (500 g) green apples, cored and roughly chopped
- ½ oz. (15 g) roughly chopped fresh mint leaves
- 1½ cups (375 ml) white wine vinegar
- 1 lb. (500 g) jam-setting sugar
- ½ oz. (15 g) finely chopped fresh mint leaves, extra

Place apples, mint and vinegar in medium saucepan; cook, uncovered, until apples are very tender. Purée apples; drain through a sieve (don't push them through, but allow the liquid to run through so jelly doesn't become cloudy). Return liquid to saucepan; add sugar. Return to the boil,

boiling for 10 minutes. Remove from heat, stir through extra mint. Pour into clean container; refrigerate 6 hours, or until set. Makes about 2 cups (600 g).

Nettle

Urtica dioica Lamiaceae

While the famous 17th-century herbalist Culpeper noted with unusual levity that nettles "may be found by feeling, in the darkest night," arthritis sufferers once whipped themselves with stinging nettles to relieve their pain — not a treatment for the faint-hearted.

Nettle (*Urtica dioica*)

Parts used Leaves, roots

◾ Gardening

The stinging nettle (*Urtica dioica*) is a cold-tolerant herbaceous perennial growing to 4 ft. (1.2 m), with coarsely toothed, oval leaves armed with stinging hairs. Tiny green male and female flowers are borne on separate plants, the pendulous branched inflorescences emerging directly from the upper nodes of the square stems. The spreading roots are yellow. The young leaves are rich in minerals (particularly potassium, calcium, silicon and iron) and also contain vitamin C. Roman nettle (*U. pilulifera*) finds similar uses.

Classified into five subspecies, all of which have similar uses, *U. dioica* is indigenous to much of the temperate Northern Hemisphere. As an introduced plant, it is widespread in the temperate Southern Hemisphere.

• **Position** Nettles prefer full sun to light shade and thrive in a rich, moist soil that is high in nitrogen.

• **Propagation** Plant seed in spring or, if you are brave, by division of plants in spring.

• **Maintenance** Nettles can become invasive plants.

• **Pests and diseases** While nettles are quite disease-free, they are a valuable food supply for the caterpillar stage of a number of butterfly species.

• **Harvesting and storing** In addition to spring picking, harvest in midsummer and again in autumn, and always wear gloves to protect your hands. Dig up the roots in autumn and air-dry them with the tops out of direct sunlight.

Relieve the discomfort of nettle stings by rubbing area with ice or the leaves of dock.

◾ Herbal medicine

Urtica dioica. Parts used: Leaves, roots. Nettle leaf is a traditional blood-purifying remedy. It has a gentle diuretic effect and encourages the removal of toxins from the body. It is used medicinally to treat arthritic conditions and certain skin disorders such as eczema, which some herbalists believe can benefit from a detoxifying action.

The leaf is also associated with anti-allergic properties, and herbalists often prescribe it for symptoms of hay fever and skin rashes.

Modern research has shown that nettle root may inhibit overgrowth of prostate tissue, and clinical trials have provided some compelling evidence that therapeutic use of the root may improve the urinary symptoms associated with disorders of the prostate gland, such as frequent urination and weak flow.

For the safe and appropriate use of nettle, consult a healthcare professional. Do not use nettle in greater than culinary doses if you are pregnant or breastfeeding.

◾ Cooking

The young leaves were once widely used in the spring diet to revitalize the body after winter. For culinary purposes, use leaf tips from plants less than 4 in. (10 cm) high, since these have yet to develop the stinging compounds. Nettle leaves may be cooked as a vegetable, in similar ways to spinach, or added to soups or to vegetable, egg or meat dishes. A tisane can be made from the leaves. Do not eat nettles raw; also note that older leaves are high in calcium oxalate and should not be eaten at all.

Cornish yarg

A handmade semi-hard cheese with a creamy taste, Cornish yarg is wrapped in nettle leaves after pressing and brining. The leaves are carefully arranged by hand to form a pleasing pattern and also to attract natural molds in various colors that aid in the ripening process, adding a subtle mushroom taste. Remove yarg from the refrigerator about an hour before serving.

Parsley

Petroselinum sp. Apiaceae/Umbelliferae

Parsley has widespread culinary, medicinal and cosmetic uses, and is also used as a dye plant. It was once used as fodder for the chariot horses of the Ancient Greeks. Native to the south-eastern Mediterranean, parsley is now cultivated in temperate climates throughout the world, and is one of the most popular herbs for growing at home, both in gardens and containers.

Parts used Leaves, stalks, roots, seeds; root of Hamburg parsley

■ Gardening

Parsley is a biennial crop, forming a dense rosette of leaves in the first year and flowering in its second summer, when the foliage becomes bitter.

Curly parsley (*Petroselinum crispum* var. *crispum*, pot) and flat-leaf parsley (*Petroselinum crispum* var. *neapolitanum*)

There are three distinct types of parsley. Probably the most familiar is curly parsley (*P. crispum* var. *crispum*). The many excellent varieties include 'Triple Curl' and 'Green River'. The plain-leaf types, known as Italian or French or flat-leaf parsley (*P. crispum* var. *neapolitanum*), have flat leaf segments. In Italy, the true Italian parsley is considered to be 'Catalagno', which is usually listed elsewhere as 'Giant Italian'. Hamburg or turnip-rooted parsley (*P. crispum* var. *tuberosum*) is grown more for its delicately flavored tap root than its leaves, although they can also be used. Japanese parsley or mitsuba (*Cryptotaenia japonica*) is in the same family. Its flavor is a mixture of celery, angelica and parsley.

• **Position** Parsley prefers full morning sun to partial shade, and well-composted, well-drained but moist soil. It tolerates fairly acidic to alkaline soil, but if the soil is very acidic, incorporate lime before planting.

• **Propagation** This herb is grown only from seed and takes 3 to 8 weeks to germinate. You can speed up this process by soaking the seed in warm water overnight before planting into trays or pots. Alternatively, pour freshly boiled water along seed drills just before planting. Cover seed very lightly with soil. Transplant seedlings into the garden (or thin seedlings sown directly into the garden) to around 10 in. (25 cm) apart. Parsley self-seeds under suitable conditions. In cold climates, a cloche will warm the soil and allow for earlier planting of seedlings, or even protect a winter crop.

• **Maintenance** Water regularly or parsley will flower ('bolt') in its first season. Cutting out the emerging flowering stalks will frustrate this process to some extent.

Emerald risotto

For a delicious-tasting and attractive emerald-green herb risotto, cook a classic risotto recipe using arborio rice, chicken or vegetable stock and white wine, but add a handful of chopped baby spinach leaves when the rice is almost cooked. Once the rice is fully cooked (it should be a creamy, dropping consistency), stir in a generous amount of finely chopped fresh parsley and coriander. Season to taste.

Country folk once said that only people who were wicked were able to grow lush parsley.

- **Pests and diseases** Generally easy to grow, parsley can be attacked by pests of closely related members of the same family — for instance, celery fly and carrot weevil. Septoria leaf spot can also be a problem. In Hamburg parsley, crown rot can occur after prolonged rain.
- **Harvesting and storing** New growth comes from the center of the stem, so harvest leaves from around the outside of plants. Wrap in a plastic bag and store in the freezer. Parsley is not a good herb for drying, as it loses much of its flavor. Collect seeds when pale brown. They ripen progressively from the outside of the inflorescence inward. Hang bunches of ripening seed heads upside down inside paper bags. Harvest the roots at the end of the second season and air dry them.

Hamburg parsley (*P. crispum* var. *tuberosum*), grown for its roots rather than its leaves, has a mild taste. It can be grown in containers as well as in the ground.

Herbal medicine

Petroselinum crispum var. *crispum*. Parts used: leaves, roots, seeds. The leaves are a good source of vitamin C, and both the leaf and root are well-known for eliciting considerable diuretic effects in the body. Parsley has been used to treat fluid retention, urinary tract disorders and arthritic conditions of the joints, including gout, an inflammatory condition usually affecting a single joint, such as a big toe.

Parsley has a calming effect on the gut, alleviating flatulence and colic, and also a gentle stimulatory action, encouraging appetite and improving digestion. It can also have a notable stimulating effect on the uterus and has been used to encourage menstruation — but should not be used for this purpose if pregnancy is a possibility.

For the safe and appropriate medicinal use of parsley, consult your healthcare professional. Do not use parsley in greater than culinary quantities if you're pregnant or breastfeeding.

Cooking

Flat-leaf parsley is generally considered to have the best flavor, while curly parsley has a pleasing crunchy texture. Use either one as a garnish or in salads, vegetable and egg dishes and sauces (see Frankfurt green sauce recipe, *page 338*).

Parsley is essential to many traditional flavoring mixtures, particularly in French cooking. Bouquet garni, a small bunch of pungent fresh herbs for slow cooking, is most often comprised of a bay leaf, sprigs of parsley and sprigs of thyme. Other mixes include persillade (finely chopped parsley and garlic, see recipe, *page 352*). Sprinkle them on a dish near the end of its preparation to retain its flavor.

The edible root of Hamburg parsley (left) is used in soups and stews and can be roasted or boiled in the same way as other root vegetables.

Mitsuba is used in Japanese cooking, in soups, salads, slow-cooked dishes and fried foods. Blanch the leaves briefly to tenderize them or add to food at the last moment to preserve the delicate flavor.

Rabbit's remedy

According to Greek myth, parsley sprang from the blood of a Greek hero, Archemorus, the forerunner of death, while English folklore has it that parsley seeds go to the Devil and back seven times before they germinate, referring to the fact that they can be slow to sprout. It is also claimed that only witches can grow it. On a more lighthearted note, however, parsley is traditionally a curative, a fact that Beatrix Potter weaves into *The Tale of Peter Rabbit* when Peter eats too much in Farmer McGregor's vegetable patch: 'First he ate some lettuce and some broad beans, then some radishes, and then, feeling rather sick, he went to look for some parsley.'

"An honest laborious Country-man, with good Bread, Salt and a little Parsley, will make a contented Meal with a roasted Onion."

John Evelyn, herbalist, 1620–1706

Chimichurri sauce

Parsley is used in many herb and spice mixes around the world (see Chermoula and Persillade recipes, *page 352*). Try this Argentinian sauce with meat hot off the barbecue.

In a jar, combine 6 cloves garlic, 2 tablespoons fresh oregano leaves and a handful of parsley leaves, all finely chopped. Add 1 tablespoon red onion, chopped, a pinch of dried chilli flakes, 1 teaspoon ground black pepper, 5 fl. oz. (150 ml) olive oil, 6 tablespoons red wine and salt, to taste. Seal jar, shake well. Leave 4 hours for flavors to develop.

Passionflower

Passiflora incarnata Passifloraceae

To Spanish missionaries in South America, the passionflower represented the Passion of Christ: the three stigmas symbolized the nails, the corona the crown of thorns, the five stamens the wounds, and the ten petals the Apostles (except Judas Iscariot and Peter).

Passionfruit (*Passiflora edulis*)

Other common names Maypops, purple passionflower, wild apricot, wild passionflower
Parts used Dried aerial parts (especially leaves), ripe fruits, flowers

■ Gardening

There are about 400 species of passion-fruit. Many are ornamental, tendrilled climbers; some produce delicious fruit. Most require warm-temperate to tropical conditions, although *P. incarnata* is one of the most tolerant of cooler conditions. Deciduous in colder areas, it can survive occasional winter freezes.

A common wildflower in the southern United States, it was used as a tonic by Native Americans, and was first noted by a Western doctor in 1783. The leaves are palmately divided with 3 to 5 smooth, textured, pointed lobes with serrated margins. The fragrant large flowers are lavender-colored, with a white center and a deeper purple, threadlike corona. The fruits, ovoid yellow berries when ripe, are about 2 in. (5 cm) long.

• **Position** It prefers a light, acidic soil and a warm, sunny position. In cooler areas, it is an excellent greenhouse plant.
• **Propagation** Sow passionflower seed in spring when the soil has warmed. Or propagate by semi-ripe stem cuttings in summer, or by layering.
• **Maintenance** Provide a trellis or other support, and mulch plants well. Shape and prune the vine as necessary in spring.
• **Pests and diseases** Passionflower vines are mainly pest-free and, although *Passiflora* is an important food source for the caterpillar stage of some butterflies, they cause no permanent damage.
• **Harvesting and storing** Harvest the aerial parts in mid- to late summer and air-dry for medicinal preparations. For culinary use, pick the fruits at the "dropping" stage.

■ Herbal medicine

Passiflora incarnata. Part used: leaves. Medicinally, passionflower can be of immense benefit in conditions in which nervous tension and stress are prominent factors. This herb has a calming effect on the mind and body, and is commonly prescribed for insomnia in adults and children, especially when there is difficulty falling asleep.

Results of preliminary human trials have provided supportive evidence for the traditional use of passionflower for treating anxiety disorders. It's also interesting to note that further research has elucidated a potential role as a supportive remedy during withdrawal from addiction to narcotic drugs.

The relaxing and antispasmodic effects of passionflower can also be applied in the treatment of digestive symptoms, nervous headaches and neuralgic pain that are exacerbated by stress and tension.

For the safe and appropriate medicinal use of passionflower, refer to *Insomnia, page 214.* Do not use passionflower if you are pregnant or breastfeeding.

■ Cooking

The seeds and pulp of ripe fruits have a tangy flavor, and are eaten raw or used in fruit salads and other desserts, curds, jams, jellies and fruit drinks. The popular cocktail called the Hurricane is made with passionfruit syrup, rum and lime juice.

Opposite: Passionflower (*Passiflora incarnata*)

Passionfruit cordial

Spoon the pulp of 8 passionfruit into a mixing bowl. You need about ¾ cup (180 ml) pulp. Add 1 teaspoon vanilla extract, 1 cup (230 g) sugar and ¼ cup (60 ml) freshly squeezed lemon juice. Stir well. Pour into a clip-lock bottle and refrigerate. Keeps for 1 week. Pour into a jug. Add 4 cups (1 l) chilled club soda. Serves 8.

Passionfruit from the *P. edulis* vine

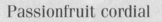

Peony

Paeonia lactiflora syn. *P. albiflora*, *P. officinalis*,
P. suffruticosa syn. *P. moutan* Paeoniaceae

Once the favored flower of Chinese emperors, peonies were first
mentioned as a medicinal herb in about 500 CE. However, the medicinal
use of all three of these peonies is restricted to qualified practitioners.

Other common name Bai shao, Chinese peony, white peony (*P. lactiflora*)
Parts used Roots, flowers

■ Gardening

The Chinese peony (*P. lactiflora*) is a
herbaceous perennial. It has erect stems
with lobed leaves and very large, scented
flowers, which in the wild are white and
single. Cultivated plants grow to 3.5 ft.
(1 m), are fully hardy, can be red, pink or
purple and are usually double.

The tree peony (*P. suffruticosa*), found
from Western China to Bhutan, forms a
branched upright shrub to 6.5 ft. (2 m) with
slash-cut and lobed leaves. The terminal
flowers are very large and slightly fragrant.

Common peony (*P. officinalis*) is a
herbaceous perennial with many erect
stems to 2.5 ft. (75 cm), bipinnate leaves
composed of ovate-lanceolate segments,
and large terminal flowers that are single,
fragrant, usually purple-crimson and
hermaphroditic.

• **Varieties** Common peony varieties
include 'Alba Plena' and 'Rosea Plena'.
• **Position** Peonies prefer cold winters
and a deep, rich, moist (and in the case
of *P. officinalis*, slightly alkaline) soil.

A sculpture in Wangcheng Park, Luoyang, China,
where the beauty of the peony is celebrated.

*The peony is named
after Paeon, physician
to the Greek gods.*

• **Propagation** Plant fresh seed in
autumn, or stratify older seed (*see
page 44*), then plant it in spring. You
can also divide plants in late autumn
or spring, take root cuttings in winter
or semi-ripe stem cuttings.
• **Maintenance** Peonies require heavy
feeding, and their roots resent disturbance.
Remove dead wood in spring.
• **Pests and diseases** These plants are
susceptible to *Botrytis*, peony wilt (caused
by a blight fungus), leaf spot, nematodes
(eel worm) and honey fungus.

■ Herbal medicine

Paeonia lactiflora. Part used: roots. In
traditional Chinese medicine, white peony
root nourishes the blood and is a key
remedy for the treatment of conditions
of the female reproductive system.

Laboratory studies have shown white
peony possesses moderate hormonal
activity. Herbalists prescribe this herb,
often with licorice, to regulate the
menstrual cycle and relieve pain. This
combination is used to treat irregular,
heavy, delayed or absent bleeding, period
pain, premenstrual syndrome, fibroids and
polycystic ovarian syndrome.

White peony can also have a relaxing
effect on muscles, and it may lower

Peony (*Paeonia lactiflora*)

blood pressure due to its ability to dilate
blood vessels and improve circulation.
Traditionally and in combination with
other herbs, white peony has also been
used to ease muscle cramps and reduce
intestinal griping, enhance memory and
concentration, relieve night sweats and
treat angina.

For the safe and appropriate use of
white peony, consult your healthcare
professional. Do not take white peony
if you are pregnant or breastfeeding.

■ Cooking

The flowers of *P. officinalis* are used to
scent tea, and the seeds were once used
as a spice.

Gender bias

The old herbalists recognized two
different leaf forms of *P. officinalis*
as "male" and "female" peonies,
which were used for male and
female complaints, respectively.
The "female" peony had leafier
foliage, scented dark purple flowers
and black seeds, while the "male"
peony had purple-red flowers and
black and crimson seeds.

Perilla

Perilla frutescens syn. *P. ocimoides* Lamiaceae

Perilla is a popular, spicily aromatic culinary herb that is used fresh in salads and for pickling and flavoring. The colorful and curly leafed forms are increasingly popular as an ornamental bedding annual.

Other common names Beafsteak plant, Chinese basil, shiso
Parts used Leaves, flower spikes, seed

◼ Gardening

Perilla is a hardy, branched annual to 4 ft. (1.2 m) with broadly ovate, serrated leaves, which vary in color from green to red and purple. The leaf edges may be curled (a form previously called *P. crispum*), while the tiny white to purple flowers are borne in dense spikes about 4 in. (10 cm) long.

• **Varieties** 'Green Cumin' and 'Purple Cumin', both readily available, have cumin- and cinnamon-scented leaves. 'Aojiso' has green ginger-scented leaves, often used with sashimi. 'Red' or 'Akajiso' has rich, deep red to purple leaves. The large-leafed 'Kkaennip' or Korean perilla is used in salads, as a food wrap and preserve, and the seeds for culinary flavoring. 'Thai' perilla has a strong, delicious flavor.

• **Position** Perilla flourishes in moist, well-drained soils enriched with compost.
• **Propagation** Plant seed in spring when the soil has warmed.
• **Maintenance** Pinch out the initial flower spikes to encourage bushy growth.
• **Pests and diseases** This herb has few problems.
• **Harvesting and storing** Harvest the leaves in summer and use them fresh or dried. Harvest flower spikes when they are fully developed, and the seed in autumn.

◼ Herbal medicine

Perilla frutescens. Parts used: leaves, seeds. Both the leaves and seeds of perilla have been used for centuries in traditional Japanese medicine (a system known as Kampo), and also by Chinese herbalists for similar therapeutic purposes. Perilla is commonly prescribed with other herbs for the treatment of respiratory conditions, including colds, flu and coughs, and to ease symptoms caused by poor digestive function, such as lack of appetite, nausea and bloating. Perilla is also used successfully for the management of hay fever and dermatitis. It is a key ingredient in the Kampo herbal formula known as Saibokuto, a popular remedy that is used for a number of allergic conditions.

Perilla (*Perilla frutescens*)

Japanese cuisine

In Japan the fresh red leaves of perilla are used in salads or as a garnish or wrapping for dishes such as sushi. The leaves are also used to color and flavor pickled plums (pictured) and ginger, while the seeds are sprouted for use in salads, or pickled as a condiment for Japanese dishes. Different varieties of perilla are also used in Indonesian, Vietnamese and Korean cuisine.

Laboratory research has confirmed substantial anti-allergic as well as anti-inflammatory effects of perilla extracts. Clinical trials have produced promising results for the use of oral preparations of perilla for the relief of hay fever symptoms, including watery, itching eyes. Additional studies have also recorded improvements in the symptoms of allergic dermatitis with the use of a topical perilla cream.

For the safe and appropriate medicinal use of perilla, see Hay fever and sinusitis, *page 203*. Don't use perilla in greater than culinary quantities if you are pregnant or breastfeeding.

◼ Cooking

The red variety of perilla is more often used for culinary purposes than the green. (Be aware that excessive handling of the leaves can cause dermatitis.) A volatile oil in the leaves of *P. frutescens* contains a compound that is 2,000 times sweeter than sugar and is used as an artificial sweetener in Japan.

Plantain

Plantago major, P. lanceolata, P. asiatica syn. *P. major* var. *asiatica*,
P. psyllium Plantaginaceae

Common plantain is considered a weed by many gardeners,
but it has long been valued in folk medicine, and continues to
find herbal uses. There are also some equally useful and very
ornamental varieties for the garden.

Other common names Greater plantain, rat-tail plantain (*P. major*)
Parts used Leaves (*P. major, P. lanceolata*); seeds, seed husks (*P. psyllium, P. ovata*)

Rose plantain (*Plantago major* 'Rosularis')

■ Gardening

Common plantain (*P. major*) is an
evergreen perennial that forms a basal
rosette of stalked, broadly ovate leaves
to 15 cm, from which emerge cylindrical
spikes of tiny green flowers to 20 cm.
Ribwort plantain (*P. lanceolata*), with
ribbed lanceolate leaves, is used interchangeably with *P. major* in herbal medicine.
Asian plantain (*P. asiatica* syn. *P. major* var.
asiatica) bears flower spikes to 50 cm.

Psyllium (*P. psyllium*) is an annual with
inflorescences that release tiny seeds.
Blond psyllium (*P. ovata*) is also widely
used; black psyllium (*P. indica*) and golden
psyllium (*P. arenaria*) to a lesser degree.
• **Varieties** The inflorescences of rose
plantain (*P. major* 'Rosularis') resemble
double green roses. 'Rubrifolia' has purple
leaves, and 'Variegata' is marbled white.

• **Position** *P. psyllium, P. ovata* and
P. asiatica prefer full sun and a well-
drained soil. *P. major* prefers a moist
situation with light shade.
• **Propagation** Plant seed directly
in spring after the soil has warmed.
• **Maintenance** Weed regularly.
• **Pests and diseases** In dry weather,
powdery mildew is a problem for *P. major*.
• **Harvesting and storing** Cut the
leaves and dry them for herbal use, as
required. Collect seed when ripe, as soon
as the dew has dried, and dry them also.

■ Herbal medicine

Plantago lanceolata, P. major. Part used:
leaves. Due to plantain's mucilaginous
compounds, it has a soothing effect on
the lungs, reducing inflammation and
irritation, and helping to remove catarrh.
Plantain is also used for its healing effect
on peptic and intestinal ulcers, gastritis
and colitis.

Plantain can be used as a mouthwash
or gargle for inflammatory conditions of
the mouth and throat, and as an ointment
it can be applied to haemorrhoids, cuts
and bruises to aid healing.

Plantago psyllium, P. ovata. Parts used:
seeds, husks. Psyllium is an excellent bulk
laxative. The soluble fiber contained
in the seeds absorbs water, making bowel
movements easier and more regular.

Clinical trials have confirmed its benefit
in the treatment of chronic constipation
and irritable bowel syndrome. Psyllium
can also be used in cases of anal fissures,

recovery from anal/rectal surgery and
haemorrhoids where a softer stool is
needed to ease the passing of stools.

Its content of soluble fiber also makes
psyllium a valuable part of any cholesterol-
lowering program. The fiber binds to
cholesterol in the gut, enabling it to be
excreted from the body.

For the safe and appropriate use of
plantain, consult a healthcare professional.
For the use of psyllium, see Constipation
and haemorrhoids, *page 207*, and Detox,
page 209. Do not use these herbs if you
are pregnant or breastfeeding, except
under medical supervision.

Plantago psyllium seed has commercial worth as
a high-fiber ingredient in breakfast cereals.

A sacred herb

One of the Nine Sacred Herbs of the
Anglo-Saxons, plantain was believed
to cure headaches. The *Lacnunga*, a
collection of medical texts written in
the 11th or 12th century, relates this
story of the god Woden: '...out of the
worm sprang nine poisons. So Woden
took his sword and changed it into nine
herbs. These herbs did the wise lord
create and sent them into the world
for rich and poor, a remedy for all...'

Poppy

Papaver rhoeas, P. somniferum; Eschscholzia californica Papaveraceae

Cultivated for 5,000 years, poppies were once symbolic both of the earth goddess and of Ceres, the goddess of cereals. Opium poppy is the source of some of our most important pain killers, morphine and codeine, but also of dangerously addictive heroin.

Parts used Aerial parts (Californian poppy only); latex (opium poppy only)

■ Gardening

The opium poppy (*P. somniferum*) is a hardy annual that grows to about 4 ft. (1.2 m) with large, coarse, toothed, silvery green foliage and tall flowering stems bearing four-petaled flowers that may be white, pink, lavender or red, followed by a globose capsule with an operculum that opens to scatter the ripe seed. The wall of the green capsule oozes bitter white latex when wounded.

Opium poppy cultivation is strictly controlled in many countries; however, a number of ornamental forms are widely grown, including the 19th century red and white 'Danish Flag', double 'peony' forms and the very old 'Hen and Chickens', which has a ring of tiny flowers encircling each large flower.

> *The species name for the opium poppy, 'somniferum,' means 'sleep-inducing.'*

The European annual red or field poppy (*P. rhoeas*) has four silken, bright red petals, sometimes with a black blotch in the center. It was used to breed ornamental Shirley poppies.

Californian poppy (*Eschscholzia californica*), which is related to true poppies, is a heat- and drought-resistant annual, native to the western United States, with the subspecies *mexicana* extending south into the Sonoran Desert.

Opium poppy

Opium derived from the latex of the unripe seed capsules of the opium poppy (*P. somniferum*) was once a traditional herbal medicine as well as a legal recreational drug, but we now know that opiates are addictive and associated with serious adverse effects. In the Western world, opium is a heavily regulated and licensed product used to produce morphine and codeine. Morphine and codeine provide exceptional pain relief as pharmaceutical drugs, but still carry a risk of dependency with overuse.

Californian poppy (*Eschscholzia californica*)

The blue-green, finely divided leaves form a basal rosette and the many flower stalks bear single silken, four-petaled flowers in lemon to orange.

- **Position** All poppies, including Californian poppy, require a well-drained soil and sunny position.
- **Propagation** To sow poppy seeds evenly during spring, mix them with dry sand.
- **Maintenance** Weed regularly.
- **Pests and diseases** Powdery mildew can be a problem.
- **Harvesting and storing** Harvest and dry the petals immediately after the flowers fully open. Collect seed from ripe capsules and dry them.

■ Herbal medicine

Eschscholzia californica. Parts used: aerial parts. The aerial parts of Californian poppy were used by Native Americans as a pain killer, and have been incorporated into Western herbal medicine as a valuable pain-relieving and relaxing herb. It is used for treating insomnia, anxiety and over-excitability, and may be a useful remedy for aiding relaxation during times of tension and stress.

Californian poppy alleviates many types of pain, including headaches, nervous cramping of the bowel, and rheumatic and nerve pain.

Poppy *Continued*

Substances known as alkaloids are responsible for the plant's sedating and pain-killing properties, and are similar to those found in opium poppy, from which morphine and codeine are derived. However, the alkaloids that are found in Californian poppy have a far gentler therapeutic effect and are also regarded as non-habit forming.

Papaver rhoeas. Part used: petals. Despite being closely related to the opium poppy, the red or field poppy possesses none of its counterpart's potent narcotic effects. Instead, it is used as a reliable traditional remedy for soothing respiratory conditions that are associated with irritable coughing and the presence of catarrh. Red poppy is regarded as mildly sedating and can be useful for alleviating poor or disturbed sleep.

Poppy seeds, the source of poppy oil, are harmless flavorings for baked goods.

For the safe and appropriate use of Californian and red poppy, consult your healthcare professional. Do not use these herbs if you are pregnant or breastfeeding.

◼ Cooking

Poppy seeds are not narcotic and are widely liked for their flavor and crunchy texture. They are popular in baked goods, such as breads, cakes, pastries, muffins and bagels. In India, the seeds are ground and used to thicken sauces. The seeds also feature in Jewish and German cooking.

Red or field poppy (*Papaver rhoeas*)

Remembrance Day

In the World War I battlefields around Flanders in northern Europe, red or field poppies bloomed everywhere in the ravaged earth. Since then, they have become a symbol of Armistice or Remembrance Day on 11 November each year. John McCrae wrote the following poem in 1915, the day after he witnessed the death of a friend.

On November11, Remembrance Day, wreaths of artificial field poppies are placed on war memorials in memory of the fallen.

In Flanders Fields

In Flanders fields the poppies blow
Between the crosses, row on row,
That mark our place; and in the sky
The larks, still bravely singing, fly
Scarce heard amid the guns below.

We are the dead. Short days ago
We lived, felt dawn, saw sunset glow,
Loved, and were loved, and now we lie
In Flanders fields.

Take up our quarrel with the foe
To you from failing hands we throw
The torch; be yours to hold it high.
If ye break faith with us who die
We shall not sleep, though poppies grow
In Flanders fields.

Major John McCrae, 1872–1918

Primrose and cowslip

Primula vulgaris, P. veris Primulaceae

Cowslips were once known as "cowsloppes," in the belief that they grew in cow droppings, or as the "keys of St Peter," who supposedly dropped the keys from heaven, causing cowslips to spring up where they fell.

Other common name Paigle (cowslip)
Parts used Leaves, flowers, roots

■ Gardening

Primrose (*P. vulgaris*) is a perennial forming a basal rosette of oblong, rugose leaves, from which spring a number of stalked, solitary flowers with a sweet, fresh fragrance. The flowers are five-petaled and pale golden yellow (rarely white), with a central cleft in each petal. The foliage of cowslips closely resembles that of primroses, but the smaller, golden yellow, sweetly scented flowers are borne in clusters at the top of each flowering stem, well above the leaves. According to the English herbalist John Gerard, writing in the 16th century, a tisane made from the flowers was drunk in the month of May to cure the "frenzie."

• **Varieties** Primrose varieties that are mentioned in Tudor and Elizabethan herbals, and are still available, include 'Jack in the Green', with a much enlarged persistent rufflike calyx; 'Hose in Hose', with a second flower emerging from the first; and the very attractive fully double varieties such as 'Alba Plena', 'Double Sulphur' and 'Miss Indigo'.

• **Position** Primroses require a moist, rich soil and light shade, while cowslips prefer a well-drained drier site in full sun or light shade.

• **Propagation** Propagate cowslips and primroses by seed or by division. Stratify the seed for 10 weeks to break dormancy (see *page 44*). Because of habitat loss and over-harvesting of these plants, do not gather them in the wild.

• **Maintenance** Mulch the plants. Break up any clumps and replant well-rooted divisions every 2 years.

• **Pests and diseases** Leaf-eating insects can damage plants. Rust may infect leaves, and *Botrytis* can kill plants.

• **Harvesting and storing** Gather leaves and flowers in spring to use fresh, and for use in preserves and wine. Before storing, air-dry flowers, leaves and roots (lifted in autumn).

■ Herbal medicine

Primula veris, P. officinalis. Parts used: flowers, roots. Both the flowers and roots of cowslip have been used medicinally over time. The flowers are more commonly associated with relaxing and sedative properties and are used to treat insomnia and restlessness. They can also act as a valuable supportive remedy in times of stress and tension.

Cowslip is also traditionally used to alleviate catarrhal congestion and irritable

Traditionally, it was believed that if you nibbled on cowslips you would see fairies.

coughs associated with some respiratory disorders, such as bronchitis.

For the safe and appropriate use of cowslip, consult a healthcare professional. Do not use cowslip if you are pregnant or breastfeeding.

Primrose (*Primula vulgaris*)

Purslane

Portulaca oleracea Portulacaceae

In centuries past, purslane was held up as a cure for "blastings by lightning or planets." Like a number of "weeds" condemned in modern gardens, this succulent herb was once appreciated as a salad, pickle and sautéed vegetable. It is now coming back into culinary fashion.

Parts used Leaves, stems

■ Gardening

Purslane is an annual that grows to about 3 in. (7 cm) high and up to 1.5 ft. (45 cm) wide, with soft trailing branches and wedge- to spoon-shaped, succulent green leaves. The ephemeral flowers are inconspicuous, five-petaled and yellow, while the seeds are tiny, spherical and black. Cultivated purslane is sometimes sold as var. *sativa*. The leaves are tender and fleshy, with a slight crunchy texture. Purslane has been used both as a food and a medicine in the Mediterranean basin, India and China for thousands of years.

• **Varieties** There is a golden-leafed variety (var. *aurea*) with reddish stems.

• **Position** Purslane is found very widely in well-drained soils, growing in full sun to light shade.

• **Propagation** Plant the seeds after the soil warms in spring. Barely press

Purslane strewn around a bed was once believed to ward off evil spirits.

them into the soil, which should be kept moist. Left uncovered, they will germinate rapidly. During the growing season, trailing branches will root where they touch the ground; detach the rooted tips and plant them out. In an area with a long growing season, you can sow monthly.

• **Maintenance** For a tender, abundant crop, keep the soil moist at all times. An occasional light application of liquid seaweed fertilizer at the recommended rate is also helpful.

• **Pests and diseases** Slugs may be a problem.

• **Harvesting and storing** Harvest fresh plants before flowering, or the flavor will deteriorate. Dry them for decoctions.

■ Cooking

Purslane has a slightly sour, salty, lemony spinach flavor and has been eaten for thousands of years in India, where it grows wild. It is the leaves that are most commonly used, but the roots, flowers and seeds are also edible.

The plant contains mucilage, giving the palate a glutinous sensation and also serving to thicken such dishes as soups and sauces. Blanching reduces both the mucilage and the jellylike leaf texture.

Purslane (*Portulaca oleracea*)

Purslane was popular in England in the Elizabethan era and is once again finding favor as a culinary herb. You can cook it in a similar manner to spinach. In French cooking, the fleshy leaves are used raw in salads, or cooked in equal amounts with sorrel to make the classic soup bonne femme. They are sometimes included in fattoush, a Middle Eastern salad. Add a few leaves to the version of this dish featured on *page 351*. In Asia, purslane is used in stir-fries. Aboriginal Australians used the seeds to make seed cakes.

Purslane makes an excellent pickle, using wine or apple cider vinegar spiced with garlic, chili and whole peppercorns.

Rich in vitamins A, C and E, purslane is considered one of the future 'power foods.'

Purslane soup

½ lb. (250 g) purslane, chopped
3.5 lb. (50 g) butter
4 cups (1 l) stock
½ lb. (250 g) potatoes, peeled and sliced
3 tablespoons cream
fresh purslane, to garnish

Cook purslane with butter in covered pan. Add stock, cook until potato is tender, then purée in a blender. Stir in cream, then garnish with fresh purslane.

Red clover

Trifolium pratense Fabaceae

Red clover has been an important agricultural forage and fertility-improving crop since the Middle Ages. The plant contains phytoestrogens and is increasingly important as a medicinal herb, particularly for menopausal symptoms.

- -

Other common names Meadow honeysuckle, meadow trefoil, purple clover, wild clover
Parts used Flowers, young leaves

■ Gardening

Red clover is a short-lived European perennial now widely grown as a valuable forage crop. In common with other clovers, nitrogen-fixing bacteria in its root nodules assimilate atmospheric nitrogen into the plant and significantly improve soil fertility. The plants form a creeping groundcover with stalked trifoliate leaves, each leaflet marked with a central pale arrowhead. The stalked inflorescences are dense and club-shaped, composed of many pink to purple pea flowers, which are rich in nectar.

Closely related species include lucerne or alfalfa (*Medicago sativa*), and fenugreek (*Trigonella foenum-graecum*). The latter is an important spice, particularly in Indian curry powders. Medicinally, it is used under professional supervision to help manage blood sugar in patients with diabetes, and as a cholesterol-lowering agent. See Spices, *page 138*.

- **Varieties** There are about 300 species of clover, including the beautiful crimson clover (*T. incarnatum*), an important forage crop that is also used in herbal crafts and planted for roadside erosion control, and white clover (*T. repens*), which is likewise an excellent fodder crop. It also has similar culinary uses to red clover, and is used as a tisane (flowers only).
- **Position** Red clover prefers a light soil, good drainage, a cool to mild spring and full sunlight.
- **Propagation** Sow seed in spring.
- **Maintenance** Keep plants weed-free.
- **Pests and diseases** Powdery mildew can be a problem during dry weather.
- **Harvesting and storing** Harvest red clover up to 3 times in a growing season. Harvest the leaves when young; use the flowers fresh or dried.

■ Herbal medicine

Trifolium pratense. Parts used: flowers, isolated isoflavone compounds. Red clover flowers have been used traditionally, both internally and externally, as a remedy for the treatment of chronic skin conditions such as eczema and psoriasis, particularly in children. Taken as an infusion or syrup of the flowers, red clover also alleviates the coughing associated with some respiratory conditions, such as bronchitis.

White clover
(*Trifolium repens*)

These days, the most common medicinal application for red clover centers around the use of isolated compounds known as isoflavones that come from the leaves and flowers. These compounds have been shown to possess mild oestrogenic activity, and clinical studies suggest that they can alleviate many of the symptoms associated with menopause.

For the safe and appropriate use of red clover, consult a healthcare professional. Do not use red clover if you are pregnant or breastfeeding.

Red clover (*Trifolium pratense*)

The shamrock

In the teachings of St. Patrick, the clover's trifoliate leaves (from the Latin *tri*, meaning "three," and *folium*, "leaf") symbolised the Holy Trinity — the doctrine that God is the Father, Son and Holy Spirit — and became the shamrock of Ireland. Although the Celtic harp is the official symbol of Ireland, the shamrock is the popular symbol of St Patrick's Day.

The four-leafed clover is an aberration of *T. repens*.

Rocket or arugula

Eruca sativa syn. *Eruca vesicaria* subsp. *sativa* Brassicaceae

Native to the Mediterranean basin and eastward to Turkey and Jordan, rocket has been popular as a salad green since ancient Roman times for its peppery, smoky, meaty flavor. Even now, it is still sometimes known as Roman rocket.

Other common names Italian cress, Roman rocket, rucola, rugula
Parts used Leaves, flowers, seeds

Rocket or arugula (*Eruca sativa*)

Wild rocket (*Diplotaxis tenuifolia*)

■ Gardening

Rocket (*Eruca sativa*) is an annual plant resembling an open lettuce, with deeply pinnately lobed (occasionally entire) leaves that are aromatic and peppery, and contain similiar isothiocyanate compounds to horseradish (*Armoracia rusticana*) and wasabi (*Wasabia japonica*); see *page 64*. The leaves add considerable flavor to other salad greens, while the piquantly flavored, four-petaled white flowers can be added to salads. The small round seeds are borne in siliquas (which are seed capsules that separate when ripe).

Tall rocket or tumbling mustard (*Sisymbrium altissimum*), London rocket (*S. irio*) and Mediterranean rocket or smooth mustard (*S. erysimoides*) all have a peppery flavor. Sweet rocket or dame's violet (*Hesperis matronalis*), sometimes confused with rocket, is a popular old-fashioned garden flower that resembles a tall single stock with purple or white evening-scented flowers.

Plants that are sold as wild rocket or wild arugula or *Ruchetta selvatica* or roquette sauvage are usually *Diplotaxis tenuifolia* syn. *Brassica tenuifolia*, a species with yellow flowers and leaves that resemble a more slender version of rocket. The flavor is more intense.

• **Position** Plant rocket in full sun in the cooler months, but in midsummer provide some light shade. Rocket is quite unfussy otherwise, thriving in average garden soil, while wild arugula requires similar conditions.

• **Propagation** Sow rocket in successive plantings each month, from spring to autumn, because it tends to run to flower

Grown in the Mediterranean area since Roman times, rocket has only been cultivated commercially since the 1990s.

Rocket or arugula
(*Eruca sativa*)

fairly easily. If it doesn't self-seed in your garden, carry out monthly plantings to maintain your supplies.

• **Maintenance** Weeding, providing shade protection in midsummer and regular watering are required.

• **Pests and diseases** Flea beetles can be a problem, and some butterfly larvae may eat leaves.

• **Harvesting and storing** Pick rocket leaves before flowering. Harvest the flowers as required for fresh use, and collect seeds when ripe.

Plant rocket in spring and autumn. In summer, you'll need to provide some shade.

High in vitamin C and iron, rocket stimulates the appetite and assists digestion.

■ Cooking

A member of the same plant family as cabbage and broccoli, rocket has a tangy, peppery flavor when grown during the cool spring and autumn months, but a stronger, mustardlike taste if harvested during summer.

The leaves are best gathered before flowering, after which they become more bitter. Wash rocket well and store it in the refrigerator in the same way you would lettuce.

This salad herb goes well with other salad leaves to make a mixed salad or mesclun (see Salad greens in the box, right); the younger leaves tend to have a milder flavor, but old leaves can be bitter.

Rapidly sauté or steam rocket for use in pasta and risotto dishes, stir-fries, soups and sauces, or to replace basil in pesto. Rocket needs only the briefest cooking. Add a scattering of the fresh herb as a traditional topping for pizzas at the end of baking.

The Ancient Romans used rocket seeds to flavor oil and to concoct aphrodisiacs. The seeds make excellent sprouts and are also pressed for oil.

Roman salad

The Romans considered rocket an aphrodisiac but their recipe for a mixed salad of rocket, witlof, cos lettuce, lavender and tender mallow leaves with cheese and dressing is sufficiently seductive in its own right. A modern take on this salad is rocket simply dressed with good olive oil, balsamic vinegar and some shavings of parmesan cheese.

Salad greens

For a salad with more color, flavor and nutritional value, try combining a selection of salad greens. Rocket, mizuna, watercress and curly endive are all more nutritious than lettuce. In combination, they have a slightly bitter taste.

Rose

Rosa sp. Rosaceae

The edible petals of herbal roses make delicious conserves and are used in salads and desserts, while the petals of some varieties yield the fabulously expensive and richly fragrant attar of roses used in perfumery. Both the rosehips and petals find many uses in cosmetics.

Parts used Petals, rosehips

Rosa rugosa 'Frau Dagmar Hastrup'

■ Gardening

Herbal roses, not modern ones — fragrant and beautiful though they are — are the roses of choice for cooking, fragrance and herbal medicines.

'Apothecary Rose'

The most famous herbal rose is *R. gallica* 'Officinalis', sometimes called the 'Rose of Miletus', the 'Rose of Provins', the 'Red Rose of Lancaster' and 'Champagne Rose'; (see also The Wars of the Roses and 'Rosa Mundi' features, opposite page).

The 'Apothecary Rose' was cultivated in vast fields around the famous town of Provins, 30 mi. (50 km) southeast of Paris, from the 13th to the 19th century. Unlike other roses, the fragrance in the petals is strongly retained after drying. The petals are tonic and astringent, and were used by many physicians, including the great Arab doctor Avicenna.

In Provins, the petals of 'Officinalis' were manufactured into conserves, jellies, syrups, cordials, pastilles, fragrant perfumes, salves, creams and candles, all products still favored today.

'Officinalis' was grown in monastery gardens throughout Europe. The petals, either administered as a tea or a syrup, were used to treat the common cold, inflammation of the digestive tract and hysteria. A decoction was used to treat sprains, chapped lips and sore throats.

Other long-favored roses for the herb garden include the Gallica roses 'Tuscany' ('Old Velvet'), 'Belle Isis', 'Duchesse de Montebello' and 'Belle de Crécy', together with the Centifolia rose 'Reine des Centfeuilles'.

Attar of roses

Today, the major producers of rose products and the extremely expensive perfume concentrate attar (otto) of roses are Iran and Bulgaria. Both regions grow the Damask rose (*R. x damascena*), 'Ispahan' and 'Gloire de Guilan' being favored in Iran and 'Kazanlik' syn. 'Trigintipetala' in Bulgaria. The area around Grasse in France still produces

Rosehips of *Rosa rugosa*

Rosehips

The single-flowered varieties of Rugosa rose (*R. rugosa*), with their abundant, repeat-flowering habit, and tolerance of cold and seaside locations, bear clusters of plum-size hips that are excellent for use in syrups and teas. Rosehip oil, also known as rose mosqueta, is very rich in essential fatty acids and has multiple benefits for the skin. This oil, an antioxidant and astringent that contains flavonoids and carotenoids, is prepared from the hips of both *R. canina* and *R. eglanteria*.

Rosa gallica 'Tuscany'

attar, which is derived mainly from the very fragrant 'Old Cabbage Rose' (*R. centifolia*). A small amount comes from the Alba rose and the Damask rose 'Quatre Saisons.'

• **Position** The herbal roses prefer full sun, although the Alba roses are the most shade tolerant of all roses.

• **Propagation** Most of the herbal roses flower only once a year but extremely abundantly over a month. 'Quatre Saisons' is repeat flowering. Rugosa roses are highly repeat flowering over a long season. All respond to the incorporation of well-rotted compost, but avoid using modern fast-release fertilizers.

• **Maintenance** Old roses are very tough and need not be pruned or sprayed. If you wish to prune them for shaping, do so immediately after flowering ceases because they flower on ripe wood. Apply mulch in summer.

• **Pests and diseases** The varieties mentioned above recover rapidly from any attack and can be grown without sprays, while rugosa roses such as 'Frau Dagmar Hastrup' and 'Alba' are remarkably disease-resistant.

• **Harvesting and storing** Harvest herbal roses when they have just opened, on sunny mornings as soon as the dew has dried. To dry, spread the flowers on flyscreen-covered frames out of direct sunlight. Harvest the hips when fully colored and dry in the same way as the flowers.

In Britain, during World War II, wild rosehips were harvested to make a vitamin C supplement for children.

Rosa x damascena 'Kazanlik,' a Damask rose

The Wars of the Roses

The 'Apothecary Rose,' *Rosa gallica* 'Officinalis,' may have been introduced from the Middle East into Western Europe by the Crusaders. In England, it became the symbol of the House of Lancaster in the Wars of the Roses (1455–1487). The opposing House of York adopted the ancient semi-double Alba rose, 'The White Rose of York' (*R. alba* 'Semi-plena'), while the Jacobites chose the fully double form, which became known as the Jacobite Rose (*R. alba* 'Plena'). At the end of the wars, Henry VII, the father of Henry VIII, combined them into the Tudor Rose, usually depicted as a double rose with white on red, one of the symbols of the House of Tudor.

This portrait of Edward VI of England (1537–1553), the son of Henry VIII, shows the Lancaster and York roses combining to form the Tudor rose.

'Rosa mundi'

The charming *Rosa gallica* 'Versicolor' or 'Rosa mundi' ('rose of the world'), is named for Rosamund Clifford, the reluctant mistress of Henry II, King of England in the 12th century. An ancient sport of 'Officinalis,' It bears semi-double deep pink blooms up to 3.5 in. (9 cm) across, with pale pink to white irregular stripes.

Rose *Continued*

◼ Herbal medicine

Rosa canina. Part used: Rosehips. The hips of dog rose contain notable levels of vitamin C, and can be taken as a tea or syrup in winter to help fight off common colds and flus. Because of their slightly drying nature, rosehips have also been used to reduce symptoms of diarrhoea.

Medicinal preparations of rosehip, mainly in powdered form, have been the focus of recent scientific research for the treatment of osteoarthritic conditions. The results of clinical trials suggest that it may reduce symptoms of pain and stiffness.

For the safe and appropriate medicinal use of rosehips, consult your healthcare professional, and also see Pregnancy, *page 236*. Do not use rosehips in greater than culinary quantities if you're pregnant or breastfeeding, except under the supervision of a professional.

◼ Natural beauty

Rosewater distilled from the petals is a fragrant and mildly astringent tonic for

'Reine des Centfeuilles,' a Centifolia rose

the skin; it is especially useful for chapped skin and may also be used in soothing preparations for eye infections, such as conjunctivitis.

The essential oil has anti-aging effects and may be used in preparations for dry and sensitive skins as well as to reduce the appearance of fine wrinkles.

To make beauty products using the rose, see Three roses moisturizer, *page 247*, and Rose-petal bath bags, *page 268*.

◼ Around the home

Place Rose and lavender pot-pourri (see *page 284*) in bowls around your home.

◼ Cooking

The hips (fruits) and petals of some varieties of roses — including *R. canina*, *R.* x *damascena* and *R. gallica* — are edible. The petals can be crystallized and used for decoration, to make rose petal jam, or (with the bitter 'heel' at the base of the petals removed) added to salads. See recipe for Rose-petal jelly, *page 376*.

Rosehips are high in vitamin C and can be made into jams, jellies or a syrup that serves as a dietary supplement for babies.

Ras el hanout, the Moroccan spice blend (see *page 368*), has many variations, some of which contain dried rose petals and flower buds.

Rose oil was traditionally used to anoint British monarchs during the coronation ceremony.

Turkish delight

Rosewater, a by-product of the distilling process that makes rose oil from rose petals, is an important flavoring in Middle Eastern cooking. It is used for some Asian and Middle Eastern sweets, including Turkish delight, and the rasgullas and gulab jamuns of Indian cooking. Turkish delight is a sticky, jelly-like but firm sweet, made from starch and sugar. It is traditionally flavored with rose-water and generously dusted with icing sugar; other flavors include lemon and mint. The sweet was introduced to the West in the 19th century, when a British man, who was fond of it, shipped some home.

Opposite: The beautiful *Rosa canina* is a source of rosehip oil, which has benefits for the skin.

Rosemary

Rosmarinus officinalis Lamiaceae

Few herbs are as universally grown and loved as rosemary. There are a number of varieties available and rosemary has many garden uses, from hedging, spillovers and pots to groundcovers and topiary. The refreshing resinous scent and flavor of its evergreen foliage is indispensable in cooking.

Other common names Compass plant, dew of the sea, incensier, Mary's mantle
Parts used Leaves, flowering tops

▪ Gardening

Rosmarinus means "dew of the sea," and in the wild this herb is most commonly found growing on sea cliffs around the Mediterranean. Despite their different forms and colors, all the rosemary varieties offered in nurseries belong to one species, *R. officinalis*. There are two other species that are both rare — *R. eriocalyx* and *R. tomentosus*, from southern Spain and north-western Africa, which have not entered general cultivation. Rosemary flowers vary from pale to rich blue, violet, mauve, pink or white. The form varies, from rounded bushes and prostrate varieties to columnar varieties up to 10 ft. (3 m) tall. The majority are well suited to culinary uses. All are evergreen with small, dense, narrow, pointed leaves.

• **Varieties** Recommended tall varieties include 'Tuscan Blue' syn. 'Erectus', with large leaves; the delightfully scented 'Portuguese Pink', with pink flowers; and 'Sawyer's Selection'.

Among the most intensely blue-flowered bush forms are 'Collingwood Ingram' syn. 'Majorca' and 'Benenden Blue', 'Salem', 'Blue Lagoon', 'Severn Sea', 'Corsican Blue', the violet blue-flowered 'Miss Jessup's Upright', 'Suffolk Blue', the excellent 'Herb Cottage' and the strong-growing, superbly fragrant 'Gorizia', introduced into general cultivation by Tom DeBaggio from the city of Gorizia in northern Italy.

Pink-flowered bush forms include 'Pink',

Rosemary (*Rosmarinus officinalis*)

Scholars in ancient times wore rosemary garlands during exams to improve their concentration.

In World War II, rosemary leaves and juniper berries were burned in French hospitals to kill germs.

'Majorca Pink' and 'Provence Pink', while white-flowered forms include 'Wendy's White' syn. 'Upright White', 'Sissinghurst White' syn. 'Albus' and 'Nancy Howard'. Semi-prostrate forms ideal for trailing over walls include the glossy-leafed, mid-blue 'Lockwood de Forest', 'Fota Blue', the very fine-leafed 'Mason's Finest', sky-blue-flowered 'Prostratus', 'Santa Barbara', 'Huntington Carpet' and the beautiful 'Shimmering Stars', with pink buds and blue flowers.

Variegated leaf forms currently available include 'Genges Gold', 'Gilded' syn. 'Aureus' and the white-margined 'Silver Spires'. The varieties 'Arp', 'Severn Sea' and 'Madeleine Hill' syn. 'Hill Hardy' are more cold-resistant than most.

• **Position** This plant requires full sunshine and excellent drainage. Rosemary is tolerant of a range of pH, from moderately acid to moderately alkaline soil, although the latter results in more compact growth and intense fragrance. In colder areas, grow plants in pots outdoors, then take them into the greenhouse in winter. Rosemary is excellent for seaside plantings.

• **Propagation** Propagate rosemary by tip cuttings taken in early autumn or spring. Rosemary seed germinates poorly, and plants do not come true to variety.

• **Maintenance** Regular light pruning helps to shape plants. Bushes respond well to clipping and shaping, and make excellent topiaries. Correct mulching is essential, because organic mulches tend to hold moisture near the main stem as well as the lower foliage, encouraging a number of fungal rots. For this reason, gravel, coarse gritty sand or small pebbles are the most suitable mulch.

• **Pests and diseases** Overwatered potted rosemary is very prone to root rot,

often first seen as browning of the leaf tips. Porous clay pots are preferable to plastic because they allow the soil to drain properly. Regular light trimming allows good aeration of the foliage and inhibits fungal wilts. Other problems, largely associated with overwintering plants in greenhouses, include spider mites, white flies and mealybugs (see *page 170*).

• **Harvesting and storing** In milder climates, take clippings of rosemary any time of the year, then air-dry in a well-ventilated place. When completely dry, strip the whole leaves from the stems and store in airtight bottles. Major harvesting should be done before flowering. Gather fresh flowers to use as a garnish on salads and desserts.

▉ Herbal medicine

Rosmarinus officinalis. Parts used: leaves, flowering tops. The medicinal properties of rosemary as a tonic and stimulant to the nerves and circulation make it a popular remedy for combating general fatigue and depression, and for improving poor circulation. Rosemary also enhances memory and concentration by increasing blood flow to the head.

While rosemary can be taken as an infusion, the essential oil is commonly used for these conditions. A few drops can be added to a vaporizer or diluted in a little vegetable oil and applied topically for its beneficial effects.

Prostrate rosemary is ideal for hanging baskets.

Hungary water

Until the invention of eau-de-cologne, this recipe was Europe's favorite fragrance, but it also became popular as a cure-all remedy for everything from dizziness, rheumatism, stomach cramps and headaches to indigestion and lack of appetite. The story of its invention is unclear, but it is thought that, in the 13th century, a hermit gave the recipe to Queen Isabella of Hungary, whose legs were crippled with rheumatism. Daily bathing in this water was said to have restored her legs and also her youthful beauty. Later additions to the formula included thyme, sage, mint and marjoram.

The basic formula uses lavender, rosemary and myrtle, but other herbs can be added.

In this Hungary water recipe, a "handful" is the number of 1-ft. (30-cm) lengths of herb stems that can be encircled by the hand.

> 5 qt. (4.5 l) brandy or clear spirit
> 1 handful flowering rosemary tops
> 1 handful lavender
> 1 handful myrtle

Cut the herbs into 1-in. (2.5-cm) lengths and leave to macerate for a minimum of 2 weeks before filtering.

Rosemary *Continued*

Used externally, rosemary essential oil can be applied in a diluted form to relieve muscle cramps and arthritic joint pain. It also has a reputation for preventing premature baldness and stimulating hair growth.

Rosemary is regarded as a traditional digestive remedy and, when taken as an infusion, it can help to ease cramping, bloating and gas, and may ease "liverish" symptoms, such as headaches and poor digestion of fats.

For the safe and appropriate medicinal use of rosemary, consult your healthcare professional. Also, see Memory and concentration, *page 213*, for external use. Do not use rosemary in greater than culinary quantities if you are pregnant or breastfeeding.

■ Around the home

Rosemary is one of the main ingredients in the famous antiseptic Vinegar of the Four Thieves, *page 110*, and can be used in a number of ways around the home.

- Make a simple rosemary disinfectant by simmering a handful of leaves and small stems in water for 30 minutes. Strain and pour into a spray bottle.
- Disinfect and deodorize hairbrushes and combs by soaking them in a solution of 1 cup (250 ml) hot water,

Rosemary stems, stripped of most of their leaves and used as skewers for fish, meat or vegetables cooked on the barbecue, will impart their flavor.

Rosemary tea makes a fragrant final rinse for darkening brunette hair.

1 tablespoon bicarbonate of soda and 5 drops rosemary essential oil.

- Use dried rosemary in moth-repellent sachets and in pot-pourri.
- Use a rosemary rinse on your dog after washing to deter fleas.
- Wash your pet's bedding, then add a few drops of rosemary essential oil to the final rinse. Or, spritz your pets with rosemary disinfectant as they dry themselves in the sun after a bath.

■ Cooking

The bruised leaves of rosemary have a cooling pinelike scent, with mint and eucalyptus overtones, and the strong taste can overwhelm other flavors if used too generously. It complements similarly strong flavors such as wine and garlic; starchy foods (bread, scones, potatoes); rich meats such as lamb, pork, duck and game; vegetables such as eggplants, zucchini and brassicas; and is also used in sausages, stuffings, soups

An herb of goodness

Rosemary has a strong association with the Virgin Mary. It is said that, when the Holy family was fleeing from Herod's soldiers, Mary spread her blue cloak over a white-flowering rosemary bush to dry, but when she removed the cloak, the white flowers had turned blue in her honor. Also associated with ancient magical lore, rosemary was often called 'Elf Leaf,' and bunches of it were hung around houses to keep thieves and witches out and to prevent fairies from entering and stealing infants.

and stews, or steeped in vinegar or olive oil to flavor them.

The leaves have a rather woody texture, so use them finely chopped. Alternatively, use whole sprigs, or tie leaves in a square of muslin, and remove just before serving. Dried rosemary has a flavor similar to that of fresh, but its very hard texture may not soften, even on long cooking.

Rosemary is popular in Italian cookery. Make a simple and delicious pizza topping with thinly sliced potatoes, crushed garlic and chopped fresh rosemary leaves.

You can crystallize the flowers of rosemary with egg white and caster sugar (see *page 380*).

St. John's wort

Hypericum perforatum Clusiaceae (Guttiferae)

Traditionally, golden-flowered St. John's wort was hung over entrances and cast on midsummer fires as an herb of great protection and purification. Today, it is still the symbol of midsummer solstice celebrations in Europe.

Part used Flowering tops

Gardening

Hypericum is a very large genus of about 400 species. *H. perforatum* is a hardy, partially woody perennial, an upright growing, unpleasant smelling, clumping plant that can reach 1 m high. Its small, smooth, oval leaves have numerous tiny oil glands, borne in opposite pairs along the stems. The small golden yellow flowers are borne in large dense cymes in midsummer. The small, ovoid seed capsule contains round black seed. The crushed flowers ooze a red, bloodlike pigment containing hypericin. Do not confuse St. John's wort with the many ornamental *Hypericum* varieties grown in gardens.

• **Position** This plant is easy to grow in a well-drained, moist to fairly dry soil in full sun to light shade. It's recommended for ornamental meadows, but considered a weed toxic to livestock; it's under statutory control in Australia and New Zealand.

• **Propagation** Sow seed as soon as it is ripe in autumn (under protection in colder areas), or in the following spring. Germination can take up to 3 months. You can also divide the runners either in autumn or spring.

• **Maintenance** It is a strong grower requiring little tending.

• **Pests and diseases** None worth noting.

• **Harvesting and storing** Harvest the flowering heads in early summer, when buds commence opening, and dry them.

Herbal medicine

Hypericum perforatum. Part used: flowering tops. Traditionally used for treating nerve pain, including neuralgia and sciatica as well as psychological disorders such as anxiety and depression, St. John's wort continues to be used for these conditions but these days is best known for its antidepressant activity.

St. John's wort has been proven to be effective against mild to moderate depression in a large number of clinical trials. It was found to have similar effectiveness to other antidepressant medication but with fewer side effects. Two compounds, hypericin and hyperforin, are believed to work in a similar manner to pharmaceutical antidepressants, and many preparations using St. John's wort are produced to contain a fixed level of these constituents.

Clinical trials of St. John's wort also suggest a beneficial use for treating mood symptoms of menopause and premenstrual syndrome, for obsessive compulsive disorder and also for seasonal affective disorder.

Laboratory studies have shown that St. John's wort possesses anti-inflammatory, pain-relieving and antiviral activity. A tea or extract taken internally as well as the external use of the red oil prepared from the flowers can relieve sciatica, shingles, cold sores, genital herpes and rheumatic pain. Topically, the oil is also a valuable wound- and burn-healing remedy.

For the safe and appropriate use of St. John's wort, see Depression and anxiety, *page 211*. Do not use St. John's wort if you are pregnant or breastfeeding.

page 211

St. John's wort (*Hypericum perforatum*)

Sage

Salvia sp. Lamiaceae

There are more than 700 species of salvias, many of them spectacular when in flower, and a number with leaves that are variously scented with pineapple, grapes, tangerine, grapefruit, anise, honey melon or fruit salad. Salvia flowers attract butterflies and nectar-sipping birds.

Parts used Leaves, roots, seeds, flowers

■ Gardening

Common or garden sage (*S. officinalis*) is one of the best-known culinary herbs, but there are also many ornamental species, all with small, lipped flowers in delightful shades, from white to dark purple.

A subshrub native to the Dalmatian Coast, common sage has silver-gray elliptical leaves and spikes of attractive lavender, pink or white flowers. It is a pleasantly pungent culinary herb, which also aids digestion.

In addition to the common form of garden sage, there are handsome broad-leaf varieties, such as 'Berggarten', and colored-leaf forms, such as the purple-leafed 'Purpurea'; the cream-, pink- and purple-variegated 'Tricolor'; and gold- and green-variegated 'Icterina'.
Three-leafed sage (*S. fruticosa*), native to Greece and Turkey, closely resembles garden sage except that most leaves are subtended by a basal pair of leaflets. The dried leaves are often sold as 'garden sage'. A hybrid between this species and garden sage, known as 'Newe Ya'ar', is cultivated commercially in Israel.
Spanish sage (*S. lavandulifolia*), also known as lavender sage, resembles a narrow-leafed garden sage. It has a lavender-and-sage fragrance, and its oil is extracted for toiletries.
Clary sage or muscatel sage (*S. sclarea*), a biennial, is one of the most beautiful sages, forming a large rosette of broadly ovate, pebble-textured leaves and sending up tall dense spikes of large pink flowers. The leaves add a muscatel flavor to a diverse range of liqueurs, vermouths and wines, while the essential oil is used in perfumery. In water, the seeds become mucilaginous, and were once used to remove specks from the eyes.
White sage (*S. apiana*) is a silver-leafed, rosette-shaped subshrub native to south-western North America. The leaves are

Use the pineapple-scented leaves of pineapple sage (*S. elegans* syn. *S. rutilans*) to flavor drinks.

used by Native Americans as a flavoring, medicinally to reduce mucous formation and salivation, and for smudge sticks in purification ceremonies.
The golden chia (*S. columbariae*), an annual, is native to the southwestern United States. Like chia (*S. hispanica*),

Common sage (*Salvia officinalis*)

Dan shen

The root of red root sage or dan shen (*S. miltiorrhiza*) is used for many purposes in Chinese medicine. The leaves are divided into paired leaflets and the flowers are blue.

which was cultivated as an important staple crop by the Aztecs until colonization by the Spanish, it produces tiny oily seeds that are gluten-free, very rich in omega-3 fatty acids (alpha-linolenic acid), and high in anti-oxidants, vitamins, minerals and fiber. A third chia, *S. polystachya*, is also nutritionally valuable.

Diviner's sage (*S. divinorum*) exists only in cultivation and has been used for many centuries by Mazatec shamans in Oaxaca, Mexico, to create visionary experiences and promote spiritual healing. Despite sensationalized media reports, it is neither LSD-like in action nor a "party drug."

It is generally understood to be non-addictive, and toxicological studies have shown it to be non-toxic. The plant is a prohibited substance in Australia, South Korea, Belgium, Italy and Denmark.

Fragrant-leafed species Some of these species find culinary uses. Pineapple sage (*S. elegans* syn. *S. rutilans*) has slender spikes of red flowers and pineapple-scented leaves used to flavor drinks and garnish desserts.

Others include its variety 'Honey Melon'; fruit salad or peach sage (*S. dorisiana*), with large, lush spikes of rose-pink flowers and broad fruit-scented leaves; and the very fragrant

In France, clary sage (*S. sclarea*) is cultivated and the essential oil extracted for perfumery.

California species, Cleveland sage (*S. clevelandii*).

Found on several Greek islands, apple sage (*S. pomifera*) forms fruit-like semi-transparent galls that are candied and eaten as delicacies.

• **Position** With few exceptions, the *Salvia* genus, particularly the gray-leafed species, requires a sunny, well-drained position. Salvias generally make poor indoor plants and become easily infested with white fly and scale. *S. officinalis* prefers alkaline conditions.

• **Propagation** Sages are propagated from seed, or by tip cuttings or division for named varieties.

• **Maintenance** Most shrubby salvias respond well to gentle pruning or pinching back, particularly after flowering. Do not heavily fertilize these plants.

• **Pests and diseases** Pick caterpillars off by hand. Sudden wilting indicates poor drainage and root rot.

• **Harvesting and storing** Harvest fresh leaves and flowers for culinary use at any time. Dry individual leaves and sprigs before flowering; spread them out in a well-aired place, then store in airtight containers.

Potted salvias in flower make a pretty display, but are not suited to long-term indoor life.

Sage and thyme stuffing

Gently heat 1 tablespoon olive oil and 25 g butter in large frying pan over moderate heat. Add 1 finely chopped onion and 2 finely chopped celery stalks. Cook about 10 minutes, until soft. Remove from heat and transfer to a bowl. Stir in 1¼ cups (100 g) fresh white breadcrumbs, 1 tablespoon each chopped fresh sage and fresh thyme and 1 lightly beaten egg. Mix well to bind the mixture; season generously with salt and pepper. Allow stuffing to cool completely. Use it to stuff a turkey. Alternatively, use mixture to loosely stuff a large chicken and cook remaining stuffing in a buttered baking dish, putting it in the oven for the last 30 minutes of the chicken cooking time. To avoid the risk of food poisoning, do not stuff poultry until you are ready to cook it. To vary the recipe, try using 1 tablespoon each finely chopped fresh lemon grass and parsley in place of sage and thyme.

"The desire of sage is to render man immortal."

From a medieval manuscript

Sage Continued

■ Herbal medicine

Salvia officinalis. Part used: leaves. Sage is an anti-inflammatory and antimicrobial remedy, and is frequently used as a mouthwash and gargle for sore throats, gum infections, tonsillitis and mouth ulcers. It appears to have a drying effect on excessive sweating and is a popular herb for the treatment of night sweats associated with menopause. Sage also has a beneficial effect on the mind, improving memory, concentration and mood; results of a recent clinical trial suggest that it may have a positive effect on the symptoms of Alzheimer's disease.

Salvia miltiorrhiza. Part used: roots. In traditional Chinese medicine, dan shen (see also *page 108*) is described as a remedy that "moves blood." Modern research has mostly focused on its beneficial effects on the circulatory system and the heart. The results of some clinical trials indicate potential use for the treatment of angina and high blood pressure. Laboratory studies have shown liver-protective effects and may explain dan shen's traditional use in treating acute and chronic liver conditions.

Variegated sage (*S. officinalis* 'Tricolor') makes a striking addition to the herb garden.

"He who would live for aye, Must eat sage in May."

Old English proverb

For the safe and appropriate medicinal use of sage, see Menopause, *page 235*. For the safe and appropriate use of dan shen, consult your healthcare professional. Do not use dan shen if you are pregnant or breastfeeding. Do not use sage in greater than culinary quantities if you're pregnant or breastfeeding.

■ Around the home

Sage, like so many herbs, is rich in essential oils, antiviral, antibacterial, deodorizing and antifungal, and this is reflected by its old French name, *toute bonne*, or "all is well." Use the leaves to make Herb vinegar spray (see *page 292)* and insect-repellent sprays (see box, right). Alternatively, simply put a few drops of essential oil on a damp cloth when you're wiping down bathroom and kitchen surfaces.

Sage is also a moth-repellent — use it in dried herb or essential oil form to repel clothes moths and pantry moths. In the garden, plant sage to repel cabbage moth.

■ Cooking

Of the many types, which all differ widely in flavor, common sage (*S. officinalis*) is the one most often used for cooking. The aroma is highly pungent, while the flavor, which intensifies on drying, is savory, with camphorous overtones.

Sage goes with starchy, rich and fatty foods such as duck, with poultry and pork (and stuffings for them), red meats, beans, eggplant, tomato-based sauces, casseroles and soups, and also in commercially prepared stuffing mixes and Italian dried mixed herbs. You can also use deep-fried leaves as a garnish.

Best used with a light hand in long-cooked dishes, sage is popular in Italy,

Golden variegated sage (*S. officinalis* 'Icterina') can be used instead of common sage in cooking.

less so in France. In the Middle East, it is used in salads. Sage tea is popular in many European countries. In Dalmatia, where sage grows wild, the flowers are used to make honey.

Vinegar of the Four Thieves

This herbal vinegar is a strong insect repellent that can be used on your skin as well as on socks and shoes to discourage ticks and mites. Dilute it 50:50 with water if you are spraying it onto your skin and test it on a small patch of skin before using. In a glass jar, combine 8.5 cups (2 liters) apple cider vinegar and 2 tablespoons chopped garlic with 2 tablespoons each of the following herbs: rosemary, rue, sage, lavender, wormwood and peppermint. Steep the mixture in a sunny spot for about 2 weeks, shaking the jar daily. Strain out the herbs, and retain the liquid. Add several cloves of crushed garlic, and seal again. Leave to soak for 3 days. Strain out the garlic fiber and discard. Label the jar and store it in a cool place. Do not use this vinegar if you are pregnant, and do not use it on small children.

Salad burnet

Sanguisorba minor syn. *Poterium sanguisorba, Pimpinella sanguisorba* Rosaceae

The ferny leaves of salad burnet have a scent reminiscent of fresh cucumber. The plant is sufficiently pretty to have been recommended by Sir Francis Bacon, the 16th-Century English philosopher, for growing along alleys (paths) with thyme "to perfume the air most delightfully."

Other common names Burnet bloodwort, Di Yu, pimpernel (greater burnet)
Parts used Leaves, roots

Salad burnet (*Sanguisorba minor*)

■ Gardening

Salad burnet (*S. minor*), a dainty, hardy, evergreen perennial to 1.5 ft. (45 cm), forms a low basal rosette of pinnate leaves with many paired, toothed, oval leaflets. Borne on tall, slender stalks, the tiny green, wind-pollinated flowers with deep red anthers are borne in dense globose heads.

Salad burnet's close relative, greater burnet (*S. officinalis* syn. *Poterium officinalis*), is similar to salad burnet in form but larger in all respects. The tiny, deep red flowers are borne in dense club-shaped spikes to 3.5 ft. (1 m).
• **Position** These plants prefer full sun to partial shade, and a well-drained, moist, slightly acid to alkaline soil that contains compost.
• **Propagation** Propagate both species by sowing seed in either spring or autumn. Plants that are allowed to flower will self-seed, producing particularly healthy plants.

Space seedlings about 1 ft. (30 cm) apart for salad burnet, and about 1.5 ft. (45 cm) apart for greater burnet.
• **Maintenance** Cut emerging flower stems for increased leaf production.
• **Pests and diseases** No pests or diseases worth noting.
• **Harvesting and storing** Harvest leaves for medicinal use before flowering. For fresh use, harvest leaves as required. Lift roots in autumn for drying.

■ Herbal medicine

Sanguisorba officinalis syn. *Poterium officinalis.* Parts used: leaves, roots. Greater burnet has a very long tradition of use in Western and Chinese medicine. The plant is astringent due to the presence of some unusual tanins, together with gums and glycosides. It is used externally in treating minor burns and scalds, sores and skin infections, and to staunch bleeding.

In traditional Chinese medicine, the dried root is also sometimes applied internally for the treatment of bleeding hemorrhoids.

■ Cooking

Salad burnet is an ingredient in several sauces, including ravigote, which is used in French cooking and goes well with cold roast chicken or seafood. Add young leaves of salad burnet to salads, chilled summer soups and to soft cheeses. Also use as a garnish or infused in vinegar. This herb does not dry well, but the leaves can be frozen in ice-cube trays.

Add the fresh leaves of salad burnet to salads and drinks.

Savory

Satureja sp. Lamiaceae

Satureja is reputed to have been the source of the mythical satyrs' enormous sexual stamina. Species such as summer savory and winter savory are mainly used to flavor food, while yerba buena and Jamaican mint bush are largely used medicinally.

Part used Leaves

Summer savory
(*Satureja hortensis*)

◼ Gardening

Summer savory (*S. hortensis*), an annual growing to 1.5 ft. (45 cm), has slender dark green leaves, pink flowers and an aroma of thyme and oregano. Winter savory (*S. montana*) is a perennial subshrub with dark green, narrow-leafed foliage and white flowers. Creeping savory (*S. montana* subsp. *montana* var. *prostata*) is semi-prostrate, very ornamental and resembles white heather when in flower.

Lemon or African savory (*S. biflora* syn. *Micromeria biflora*) is an excellent culinary perennial herb with creeping branches, attractive mauve flowers and bright green, fine leaves that are strongly lemon- and oregano-scented.

Thyme-leafed savory or za'atar rumi or savory of Crete or pink savory (*S. thymbra*) is a low-growing, stiffly branched perennial with whorls of small grayish leaves that have an intense oregano and thyme fragrance. Yerba buena (*S. douglasii*) is a perennial herb

Savory's essential oil is used in soaps and toothpaste.

with trailing branches of fragrant round leaves. Jamaican mint bush (*S. viminea*) is an intensely mint-scented plant with small, oval, glossy bright green foliage.

• **Position** Except for yerba buena, which grows well in a hanging basket out of direct sunlight, all species should be grown in full sun in well-drained neutral to alkaline soil. In cold areas, give plants winter protection.

• **Propagation** All species can be propagated by seed sown shallowly in spring. Perennial species are also propagated by cuttings in spring and early autumn.

• **Maintenance** Plants should be regularly weeded.

• **Pests and diseases** No significant pest or disease problems.

• **Harvesting and storing** You can cut down whole plants of *S. hortensis* before flowering and dry them. Harvest the leaves of other species fresh as required, and dry or freeze them in sealed containers.

◼ Cooking

Both summer and winter savory have a similar aroma — fragrant, with a hint of thyme, and a peppery, distinctive taste,

although the flavor of summer savory is stronger. The flavor is better before the plant flowers. Savory retains its flavor when dried; in this form it is preferred for cooking.

Savory goes well with lentils and peas, slow-cooked soups, stews, meatloaf and egg dishes. Use it in coatings for delicate meats, such as veal, and for fish. Add to sauces, pâtés and homemade sausages. It is a key herb in herbes de Provence (see below). Use summer savory in marinades, especially for olives. In Croatian cooking, a lemon-scented strain of savory is used with fish and seafood.

Winter savory (*Satureja montana*) can be used for similar culinary purposes as summer savory.

Herbes de Provence

Use this classic herb mix to season vegetables, chicken and red meat.

  4 tablespoons dried rosemary leaves
  3 tablespoons dried sweet marjoram
    leaves
  2 tablespoons dried thyme leaves
  3 tablespoons dried savory leaves
  2 tablespoons dried lavender flowers
  1 teaspoon dried sage leaves

1 Combine the dried herbs. Place in an airtight jar.

2 Store in a cool, dark place for up to 4 months. If using the mix with fish, add a pinch of fennel seeds.

Scented geranium

Pelargonium sp. Geraniaceae

Scented geraniums are the great mimics of the plant world. At the slightest touch they release intense true-to-name fragrances, from lemon sherbet and ripe apples to peppermint and red roses, making watering a collection a blissful experience.

Parts used Leaves, roots, flowers

Rose geranium (*Pelargonium graveolens*)

Pelargonium hybrid, 'Gooseberry'

◼ Gardening

The species used to create the scented geraniums originated mainly from the Cape of Good Hope area in South Africa. They were introduced into England as a curiosity in the 1630s, but by the 1840s the French realized their potential as an essential oil source.

Steam distillation of rose geranium (*P. graveolens*) yields an essential oil with an enlivening true rose fragrance that is added to perfumes and toiletries. It is produced on the island of Réunion and also in Algeria, China, Egypt, India and Morocco.

The scented geraniums are soft to semi-hard wooded shrubs or subshrubs with a very wide range of leaf shapes. *P. graveolens* is an upright multi-stemmed small shrub to 3 ft. (90 cm), with bright green, much indented leaves that create a lacy shape. The small flowers are mid-pink rouged with bright ruby on the upper petals, and are borne in terminal umbels.

The seed head somewhat resembles that of a stork's head.

Other rose-scented species distilled for oil are *P. capitatum* and its variety 'Attar of Roses', together with *P. radens*. The oil is valued in aromatherapy, and is used in massage oils to relieve tension and soothe the symptoms of dermatitis and eczema. Antifungal and antibacterial in activity, the oil is currently used in the United States as a tick repellent for dogs, and is considered both mosquito- and lice-repellent. The oil of apple geranium (*P. odoratissimum*) is astringent and antiseptic, and repels insects.

Hybridization led to a proliferation of varieties, and scented geraniums became great favorites with 19th-century gardeners, particularly as they proved adaptable to cultivation in greenhouses and on sunny kitchen windowsills during the winter months. They are fashionable once again, but fewer than 100 varieties have survived.

Those suited to cultivation in pots include the following plants:
- 'Nutmeg' and its variegated form, together with 'Old Spice', 'Apple Cider' syn. 'Cody' and 'Tutti Frutti' (all derived from *P.* x *fragrans*)
- *P. odoratissimum* 'Apple'
- *P. nervosum* 'Lime' and its hybrid 'Ginger' syn. 'Toronto'
- varieties of *P. crispum* such as 'Fingerbowl', 'Prince Rupert' and 'French Lace' (all with an intense lemon fragrance)
- cream-variegated *P.* x *asperum* 'Lady Plymouth'
- *P.* x *citronellum* 'Lemon Tart'
- carrot-scented 'Scarlet Pet' syn. 'Moore's Victory'
- hazelnut-scented *P.* x *concolor* 'Concolor Lace' and 'Strawberry' syn. 'Countess of Scarborough'
- *P.* x *scarboroviae* 'Gooseberry' (lemon-, clove- and mint-scented)

Plants better suited to large pots or garden beds include these pelargoniums:
- the darkly handsome, velvety-leafed, semi-prostrate *P. tomentosum* 'Peppermint' and its hybrid 'Dark Lady'
- white-speckled 'Snowflake'
- *P.* x *graveolens* 'Robert's Lemon Rose'
- *P.* x *capitatum* 'Dr Livingstone' syn. 'Skeleton Rose'

Pelargonium quercifolium 'Fair Ellen'

Scented geranium *Continued*

- *P. x asperum* 'Mint Rose'
- *P. graveolens* var. 'Camphor Rose'
- *P. x asperum*, the 18th-century 'M. Ninon' (apricot)
- *P. x scabrum* 'Mabel Gray' (intense lemon sherbet)
- the pungently woodsy-scented hybrids of *P. quercifolium*, such as 'Staghorn Oak', 'Clorinda', 'Chocolate Mint', 'Fair Ellen', 'Endsleigh' and 'Pretty Polly'
- *P. citrosum* 'True Lemon'
- the reputedly insect-repelling 'Citronella' syn. 'Citrosa', a derivative of *P. x asperum*

- **Position** Pelargoniums are drought-resistant, and, where space is limited, a collection can be kept in well-drained pots in a sunny position.
- **Propagation** Propagate scented geraniums from 4-in. (10-cm) cuttings taken in late summer and inserted into a sterilized mix. Make sure to protect them from frost.

Peppermint geranium leaves make an instant poultice for sprains and bruises.

- **Maintenance** Regular harvesting restricts the size of larger specimens. They should be only lightly fertilized, preferably in spring. Water thoroughly when the upper soil dries out.
- **Pests and diseases** They cannot tolerate poorly drained soil and will suffer root rot and death from soil fungi, such as *Pythium*, *Verticillium* and *Fusarium*.
- **Harvesting and storing** Harvest and dry leaves at any time for pot-pourri (see *Around the Home, page 284*) and for sleep pillows (see *Craft, page 300*). Harvesting for distillation occurs around midsummer.

Natural beauty

Rose geranium (*Pelargonium graveolens*) is the classic beauty pick-me-up. Its toning effect revives tired skin and the fresh, pungent smell revives body and mind. Its toning and balancing properties leave hair and scalp clean and fresh. It is a mild anti-irritant, making it helpful for any inflammation, including minor wounds and insect bites. It also helps control stress-triggered oil production, which can result in pimple breakouts.

■ Herbal medicine

Pelargonium sidoides, P. reniforme. Part used: root. In their native South Africa, where these two *Pelargonium* species have been used medicinally for centuries, a preparation of their roots is called umckaloabo. It is traditionally prescribed for digestive complaints, such as diarrhoea and dysentery, and for infections of the respiratory tract, including colds, coughs and tuberculosis. The name is derived from Zulu words meaning "symptoms of lung disease" and "breast pain."

Umckaloabo is widely used today by Southern Africa traditional healers for treating tuberculosis; in the early 1900s, it enjoyed a rather controversial success as a remedy for this condition in Europe.

In more recent times, it has become popular in Europe for treating acute bronchitis, tonsillitis and sore throat; a number of clinical trials have shown that *P. sidoides* reduces symptoms of acute bronchitis by the seventh day of treatment. Laboratory studies suggest that compounds contained in the root may reduce the ability of bacteria to adhere to the lining of the respiratory tract and thus prevent infection as well as improve immune function.

For the safe and appropriate use of these herbs, consult your healthcare professional. Do not use these herbs if you are pregnant or breastfeeding.

Cooking with scented geraniums

Scented geraniums, with their attractive leaves in a wide range of heavenly scents, are a culinary treat. Try using them in the following ways.

- Add dried leaves of rose or lemon varieties to the tea caddy.

- Finely chop fresh leaves. Infuse in warmed liquid such as cream or milk. Strain, and use liquid to make ice creams, sweet custards and sauces for desserts.

- Infuse red wine vinegar with rose geranium and fresh raspberries. Strain after a week for a summer salad vinegar.

- Place a cake still warm from the oven on top of leaves to absorb the fragrance. Try rose geranium with vanilla pound cake or peppermint geranium with a chocolate sponge. Remove the leaves when the cake has cooled.

- Line Jell-o molds with leaves (left) and pour a jelly on top to set.

Sorrel

Rumex acetosa, R. scutatus, R. acetosella Polygonaceae

Sorrel is easily grown, and its fresh lemony flavor is very versatile in dishes such as salads, soups and frittatas. Water dock, Pliny's *herba brittanica*, may not be a gourmet's delight, but Julius Caesar cured his troops of scurvy with its help.

Sorrel
(*Rumex acetosa*)

Parts used Leaves (sorrel); roots (yellow dock)

■ Gardening

Three species of sorrel are commonly grown for culinary purposes — broad leaf, garden or sheep's sorrel, or sour grass (*R. acetosa*); French or buckler-leaf sorrel (*R. scutatus*); and sheep's sorrel (*R. acetosella*).

Broad-leaf sorrel is a perennial forming a basal rosette of leaves up to 6 in. (15 cm) long. In early summer the slender flowering stems, to about 4 ft. (1.2 m), produce spikes of tiny reddish flowers, followed by hard nutlets. French sorrel has smaller ovate to hastate leaves, tiny green flowers and grows to about 1 ft. (30 cm).

• **Varieties** *R. acetosa* 'Blond de Lyon,' with large succulent leaves, is used for classic sorrel soup and to produce blue and green dyes. A pretty silver-leafed variety of *R. scutatus* is 'Silver Shield.'

• **Position** Sorrel requires a rich, moist soil and a sunny to partly shaded position.

• **Propagation** Sow sorrel seed in situ when the soil has warmed in spring, or start it indoors and transplant it. Seeds germinate within 14 days. Thin plants to 1 ft. (30 cm) apart. Considered weedy, *R. crispus* is under statutory control in Australia.

• **Maintenance** Regularly trim plants of all three culinary sorrels to keep up the supply of fresh, tender young leaves. Remove the flowering heads whenever they appear.

• **Pests and diseases** There are none of significance.

• **Harvesting and storing** Pick sorrel fresh throughout the growing season. It does not dry well but, like spinach, it can be frozen. Lift the roots in autumn and dry them for herbal preparations.

■ Cooking

This spinachlike leaf is quite delicious if picked when young and tender. Cook it briefly to retain the flavor; do not use aluminium or iron pots or utensils, because they will make sorrel go black and cause a disagreeable metallic taste. If using raw, select the young, tender leaves. A purée of cooked sorrel is a good accompaniment to fish, eggs, pork and veal. Sorrel's acidity also acts as a meat tenderizer.

Sorrel sauce (see *page 338*) is a French classic that goes well with poached fish.

French sorrel (*Rumex scutatus*)

Sorrels and docks

Sheep's sorrel (*Rumex acetosella*) and other members of the sorrel family have been associated with a marked diuretic effect, and were often taken as a traditional spring tonic. A juice or infusion of fresh leaves was used to reduce fevers.

Sheep's sorrel is commonly found as an ingredient in an herbal formula called Essiac Tea, said to be based on a traditional Native American remedy. While there's no scientific evidence to confirm its immune-stimulating properties, the tea has been used since the 1920s by cancer patients and more recently by those with HIV and diabetes.

Yellow dock (*Rumex crispus*) is a close relative of the sorrels. It is commonly used for chronic skin conditions and for arthritic complaints. Herbalists believe that many of these conditions are related to a toxin buildup in the body; yellow dock root may alleviate them by enhancing the detoxifying capacity of the liver as well as encouraging more efficient removal of toxins from the bowel as a result of a gentle laxative action.

Sweet cicely

Myrrhis odorata Apiaceae

This delightfully ornamental herb has leaves with a sugary anise scent. It is one of the important ingredients in Chartreuse liqueur, and is also included in Scandinavian aquavit, which is used as a digestive and an aperitif.

Other common name English myrrh
Parts used Young leaves and stalks, young roots

Gardening

Native to cool, moist mountainous areas of Europe, sweet cicely is the lone species in its genus. It is a fully hardy perennial, forming a clump of delicate, fern-like and very sweet-tasting leaves. The large handsome umbelliferous heads of white flowers are followed by slender, 1-in. (2.5-cm) seeds, which are technically fruits. They are aromatic and deliciously nutty when eaten raw and green. Both the leaves and green fruits are very high in anethole, which gives them their sweet anise scent. Mature seed are a shiny dark brown.

If you're gathering sweet cicely in the wild, do not to mistake *Myrrhis* for highly toxic hemlock (*Conium maculatum*), which has dark stems spotted red-purple.

• **Position** It requires a humus-rich moist soil, a cool climate and a shady location.

The cooked young roots are considered beneficial for those who are "dull and without courage."

• **Propagation** Allow the seed to fall around the parent plants, where they will germinate in spring. Alternatively, stratify the seed by placing it in moist, sterile sand or vermiculite inside a sealed plastic bag, and store in the refrigerator crisper tray for 8 weeks before sowing in spring (see also *page 44*).

• **Maintenance** Remove flowering stalks to prolong leaf production.

Sweet cicely (*Myrrhis odorata*)

• **Pests and diseases** None of any significance.

• **Harvesting and storing** Harvest young leaves for fresh use. They retain little fragrance after drying. Pickle the unripe seeds, and clean and store the young roots in brandy.

Cooking

Boil the roots as a vegetable; they can also be candied like angelica and used as a decoration for desserts. Use the crisp, celery-tasting stems in salads.

The leaves of sweet cicely have a warm, anise aroma and a pleasantly sweet taste. Use them fresh in salads or add them when cooking sharp fruits such as gooseberries and rhubarb and some varieties of apples, because their natural sweetness will counteract the tartness. They are a safe sweetener for diabetics. The green seeds can be used for the same purpose.

Sweet cicely leaves add a lovely flavor to cream, yogurt, rice pudding, fruit and wine, soups, stews and dressings. Use leaves in omelettes, too. They also make a very pretty garnish.

American sweet cicely

Osmorhiza longistylis, a native North American species of Apiaceae, also known as sweet cicely (or aniseroot, licoriceroot or longstyle sweetroot), is a perennial with small, white umbelliferous inflorescences and coarse, rather celery-like leaves. It is found in rich woodland in eastern North America. The sweet-tasting root, with its strong anise scent, was used by Native Americans as a digestive and antiseptic.

Sweet myrtle

Myrtus communis Myrtaceae

Myrtle was sacred to Venus in ancient times, and groves of fragrant myrtles were grown around her temples. Myrtle also symbolised honorable victory and was woven into bay wreaths at the early Olympic Games. Brides still tuck sprigs of myrtle into their bouquets.

Other common name Greek myrtle
Parts used Leaves, buds, flowers, fruits

■ Gardening

Sweet myrtle is native to the south-eastern Mediterranean. The sweetly spicy essential oil, also known as *eau d'anges* (angel's water), is used in perfumes and for medicinal purposes. The plant varies from a shrub to a small tree with oval, shiny, fragrant green leaves and small white flowers with a central "powder puff" of stamens.

• **Varieties** Varieties of myrtle include the double-flowered 'Flore Plena'; the box-leafed myrtle, 'Tarentina', which is useful for topiary; 'Variegata', a variety with white-edged leaves; a white-fruited variety called 'Leucocarpa'; and the broad-leafed or Roman myrtle, 'Romana'.

• **Position** Sweet myrtle requires sunshine and good drainage.

• **Propagation** You can propagate myrtle by seed, although the resulting

This gold wreath of sweet myrtle, a Greek symbol of victory, dates from the 2nd century BCE.

plants can be quite variable. Propagate named varieties by tip cuttings in mid- to late summer.

• **Maintenance** In frost-prone areas, grow sweet myrtle in pots and bring it under cover in winter.

• **Pests and diseases** There are none of significance.

• **Harvesting and storing** You can air-dry the buds, flowers, fruits and leaves.

Other myrtles

Lemon myrtle (*Backhousia citriodora*), anise myrtle (*B. anisata*) and cinnamon myrtle (*B. myrtifolia*) are rain forest trees from eastern Australia that are rapidly gaining prominence for their culinary and perfumery uses; they are now plantation grown. Lemon myrtle is a broad-leafed evergreen tree with panicles of small, scented white flowers. The leaves have an intensely fresh lemon fragrance, and the essential oil is typically very high in citral. Anise myrtle (see Anise, *page 14*) is used in teas and also as a culinary flavoring. Cinnamon myrtle or carrol forms a shrub–tree with spicy cinnamon-scented ovate leaves that can be used in cooking. Bog myrtle or sweet gale (*Myrica gale*) of the family Myricaceae has sweetly resinous leaves that repel insects. They are used in perfumery, as a condiment, and also in treating skin problems.

■ Cooking

Although of limited culinary use, the leaves, flower buds and fruits of sweet myrtle feature in Mediterranean cooking, especially Corsican and Sardinian recipes, to flavor pork, lamb and small game birds. They are also used in sauces and some liqueurs. The berries have a mild juniper flavor, and both the dried flowers and dried fruits are ground into a spice that has the same flavor. The infused oil is used in teas, salad dressings, fish and chicken dishes, desserts and bakery items.

Lay sprigs over barbecued or roast meats toward the end of cooking to add a spicy flavor.

Sweet myrtle (*Myrtus communis*)

Sweet violet

Viola odorata Violaceae

The sweet fragrance of violets is often detected on early spring breezes long before the flowers are seen, leading inevitably to sayings such as "shy violet" and "modest as a violet." But sweet violets hold a proud place in history, associating freely with gods, kings, and emperors.

Parts used Leaves, flowers

■ Gardening

Of the 250 or so species of *Viola*, two are used medicinally: *V. odorata* (sweet violet) and *V. tricolor* (heartsease, *page 62*). There are single, semi-double and fully double forms of *V. odorata* occurring naturally in a number of different colors.

Among recommended garden varieties of sweet violets are 'Victoria', which is the foundation of the French Riviera industry; 'Princess of Wales' (grown commercially in Australia); sky-blue 'John Raddenbury'; red-purple 'Admiral Avellan'; pink 'Rosina'; the richly colored 'Queen of Burgundy'; white 'Alba'; apricot-colored 'Crépuscule'; and the large purple- and white-striped 'King of the Doubles'.

The very double Parma violets have shiny heart-shaped leaves and profuse, large, intensely fragrant flowers that resemble rosebuds. Excellent varieties include white 'Comte de Brazza', deep lavender 'D'Udine', pale lavender 'Neapolitan' and 'Parme de Toulouse'.

• **Position** Sweet violets thrive in a well-composted, moist soil. Flowering is reduced in shaded locations, so a position under deciduous trees is ideal. Mulching ensures good summer growth.

• **Propagation** Propagate plants by runners formed in autumn.

• **Maintenance** Remove old plants when they become woody. Apply a liquid seaweed fertilizer once or twice annually; overfeeding encourages foliage rather than flowers.

• **Pests and diseases** Check for red spider mite, which thrives under dry conditions. Water under foliage and spray with a seaweed solution.

'D'Udine', one of the Parma violets

• **Harvesting and storing** Gather flowers and leaves fresh when in season.

■ Herbal medicine

Viola odorata. Parts used: leaves, flowers. The medicinal properties of sweet violet closely resemble those attributed to its relative, heartsease (*V. tricolor*). Sweet violet is used for skin conditions such as eczema and psoriasis as well as catarrhal conditions of the respiratory tract, where it can help remove mucus from the lungs.

In traditional herbal practice, sweet violet has a longstanding reputation as an adjunctive remedy in the treatment of certain types of cancer, including those of the breast and lung. Recent laboratory studies have elucidated the presence of specific compounds in the plant that show an inhibitory effect on tumor growth; further investigations need to be undertaken before this traditional use can be substantiated.

For the safe and appropriate use of sweet violet, consult your healthcare professional. Do not use sweet violet if you are pregnant or breastfeeding.

Sweet woodruff

Galium odoratum syn. *Asperula odorata* Rubiaceae

Sweet woodruff and its close relatives, ladies' bedstraw, madder and cleavers, have all been used since medieval times. Known in Germany as master of the woods for its groundcovering habit, sweet woodruff is used to flavor traditional May wine.

Parts used Leaves (*G. odoratum, G. verum*), flowers (*G. odoratum*), roots (*Rubia tinctorium*), whole plant (*G. aparine*)

Sweet woodruff (*Galium odoratum*)

◼ Gardening

Sweet woodruff (*G. odoratum*) is a stoloniferous perennial growing to about 9 in. (23 cm). The ascending stems have whorls of 6 to 8 shiny leaves borne at each node, while the starry white flowers are borne in loose clusters. In 1954, the U.S. Food and Drug Administration banned the use of sweet woodruff in food and non-alcoholic drinks as a suspected carcinogen. The ban remains in place but it is controversial because the evidence is contradictory.

Ladies' bedstraw (*G. verum*), also known as yellow bedstraw and Our Lady's bedstraw, resembles a slender form of sweet woodruff. 'Bedstraw' refers to the plant's former use as mattress stuffing.

Cleavers or goosegrass (*G. aparine*), an annual resembling a coarse version of sweet woodruff, has white flowers and stems and leaves that are covered with hooked bristles. Cleavers has been used as a potted herb, and its seed roasted as a good coffee substitute.

Madder (*Rubia tinctorium*), a scrambling perennial with starry yellow flowers, resembles a larger and coarser version of sweet woodruff. The roots can reach 3.5 ft. (1 m) long and are the source of a valuable pigment, red madder, which is used to make fabric dye, inks and paints.

• **Position** Sweet woodruff and its close relatives all prefer a moist, compost-enriched soil. Woodruff and cleavers prefer a partly shaded position, while bedstraw requires full sun.

• **Propagation** Grow sweet woodruff, ladies' bedstraw and madder by seed or by division; grow cleavers by seed.

• **Maintenance** Weed as required.

• **Pests and diseases** None of any significance.

• **Harvesting and storing** Harvest sweet woodruff and bedstraw, then air-dry as required. Once dried, sweet woodruff develops a pleasing scent of fresh-mown hay. When madder roots are 2 years old, strip them of bark and dry them. They are used to make dye.

◼ Herbal medicine

Galium aparine. Parts used: whole plant. Cleavers is an important medicinal herb in the Western herbal tradition. Essentially, it is regarded as an exceptional lymphatic-system cleanser, helping to remove toxins from the body. It is a valuable remedy for chronic skin conditions such as eczema and psoriasis and, due to its diuretic and detoxifying effect, can also be of use for fluid retention. In addition, it is prescribed for conditions presenting with swollen lymph nodes, including tonsillitis.

For the safe and appropriate use of cleavers, see Detox, *page 209*. Do not use cleavers if you are pregnant or breastfeeding.

Traditional uses

Woodruff was once used as a strewing herb because it produces a fresh hay-like scent as it dries. Traditionally, it was used as a flavoring for jellies, jams and ice-creams as well as beer and sausages in Germany, where it is now replaced with synthetic flavorings and aromas. Woodruff is still in use as a flavoring for tobacco.

Ladies' bedstraw (pictured) has long been used to curdle milk for making cheeses, especially vegetarian types, while its roots were used to dye tartans in Scotland until 1695, when the erosion of native grasslands resulted in the practice being banned.

Ladies' bedstraw (*Galium verum*) produces panicles of honey-scented flowers in summer.

Tansy

Tanacetum vulgare syn. *Chrysanthemum vulgare* Asteraceae

A bitter herb included in liqueurs, in medieval times tansy was eaten in dishes as a penance at Eastertide. The name is derived from the Greek word for "immortality," reflecting the fact that tansy stays in flower for a long period. The plant produces a yellow dye.

Other common name Golden buttons
Parts used Aerial parts

Tansy (*Tanacetum vulgare*)

■ Gardening

A very hardy rhizomatous perennial herb, tansy grows to about 4 ft. (1.2 m), with pinnate leaves, which typically have a camphor scent. There are a number of chemotypes, with the scent of rosemary, artemisia, chrysanthemum or eucalyptus. Tansy bears flat-topped ornamental inflorescences of golden button flowers that dry well.

Crisp-leafed or fern-leafed or curly tansy is a more compact ornamental form with ferny leaves. Costmary or alecost or bible leaf (*T. balsamita*) is a rhizomatous perennial with clusters of white daisy flowers and silvery green, sweetly mint-scented leaves.

Camphor plant (*T. balsamita* subsp. *tomentosum*) has camphor-scented foliage and is used in moth-repellent herb mixtures. *T. cinerariifolium* syn. *Pyrethrum cinerariifolium* is an aromatic, white daisy-flowered perennial, the source of Dalmatian insect powder. The pink-flowered *T. coccineum* is the source of the less-effective Persian insect powder.

• **Varieties** 'Silver Lace' is a variegated variety of *T. vulgare*.
• **Position** All *Tanacetum* species listed prefer a well-drained, sunny position.
• **Propagation** Propagate the species and its varieties by seed, root division in spring or semi-ripe tip cuttings in summer.
• **Maintenance** Tansy can become invasive, so in garden beds take care to keep the rhizomes under control.
• **Pests and diseases** There are none of significance.
• **Harvesting and storing** Harvest tansy foliage during flowering for drying or oil extraction. Harvest the leaves of costmary and camphor plant as required, and the flowers of pyrethrum when they open, then dry and grind them.

■ Herbal medicine

Tanacetum vulgare. Parts used: aerial parts. Tansy was once used as a short-term remedy for the treatment of worm infestations of the gut. Today this herb is no longer used medicinally, because we now know that thujone, a component of the essential oil of the plant, is associated with significant toxic effects.

Thujone also has a strongly stimulating effect on the uterus and can have serious negative side effects in pregnant women or those attempting to become pregnant.

Bible leaf

Costmary once had the common name of bible leaf, in reference to its use as a Bible bookmark — its mintlike scent was perfect for reviving the faint-hearted during interminable Sunday sermons. The word *tanacetum* is from *athanasia*, Greek for "immortality," and in ancient Greece, corpses were packed with tansy leaves to preserve them and ward off insects until burial took place.

Do not use tansy or its essential oil, and take extra care with this plant if you are pregnant or breastfeeding.

■ Around the home

A natural insect repellent, tansy can be grown outside in pots around outdoor entertaining areas to deter flies and mosquitoes. Indoors, use dried tansy to deter ants, clothes moths or fleas in your pet's bedding. A strong tansy tea can be spritzed over the carpet to keep flea populations under control, but do not spray it directly onto your pet or its bedding. Also, do not use it if you are pregnant or breastfeeding.

Plant tansy with potato crops to deter the highly destructive Colorado beetle.

Tarragon

Artemisia dracunculus, A. dracunculoides Asteraceae

Dracunculus is Latin for "little dragon," and once tarragon was reputed to cure the bites of not only diminutive dragons but also all serpents. Today its unique, delicious and piquant flavor is indispensable to the classic cuisine of France.

Part used Leaves

■ Gardening

French tarragon (*A. dracunculus*) is a selected form of exceptional flavor. It rarely sets seed, especially in cool climates, although it may produce tiny, greenish, ball-shaped inflorescences. Its slender linear leaves are warmly aromatic, with a complex fragrance and taste that blends sweet anise, basil and resinous undertones.

Russian tarragon (*A. dracunculoides*) regularly flowers and sets viable seeds. It often improves in flavor the longer it is grown, but seed-grown Russian tarragon has an earthy balsamic scent.

Winter tarragon, or Mexican mint marigold or Mexican tarragon or sweet mace (*Tagetes lucida*), is a true mimic of

French tarragon. A half-hardy perennial with finely toothed, linear, deep green aromatic leaves, it produces a lavish display of small, bright golden flowers, borne in clusters in autumn to 2.5 ft. (75 cm).
• **Position** Winter tarragon thrives in hot, humid climates. French tarragon is cold-hardy and drought-resistant, and can grow in high summer temperatures. It is, however, very susceptible to high humidity and easily infected with fungal diseases. Avoid overhead watering.
• **Propagation** Propagate French tarragon by tip cuttings in spring and early autumn, or by root division.
• **Maintenance** Regularly thin plants of French tarragon by harvesting. Remove any diseased branches.
• **Pests and diseases** Tarragon is susceptible to nematodes (eel worms) and leaf fungal diseases, particularly rust.
• **Harvesting and storing** Harvest foliage until mid-autumn.

■ Herbal medicine

Artemisia dracunculus, A. dracunculoides. Part used: leaves. These days, tarragon is more likely to be used for culinary than therapeutic purposes. Tarragon contains an essential oil component that is reputed to have similar properties to that of anise, which is often used to treat digestive symptoms. Russian tarragon has been used for stimulating the appetite.

In some countries, tarragon is traditionally used to treat the symptoms of diabetes; recent scientific research appears to support this. Preliminary studies in diabetic animals found that

Following the Doctrine of Signatures (see *page 49*), tarragon was used against venomous bites.

an alcoholic extract of French tarragon lowered the levels of both insulin and sugar in the blood.

For the safe and appropriate medicinal use of tarragon, consult your healthcare professional. Do not use tarragon in greater than culinary quantities if you are pregnant or breastfeeding.

■ Cooking

French tarragon's flavor diffuses rapidly through cooked dishes, so use it carefully. Use it fresh with fish and shellfish, turkey, chicken, game, veal and egg dishes. Use chopped leaves in salad dressings, fines herbes (see *page 356*), mustard, ravigote and béchamel sauces, sauce verte and mayonnaise.

Oil of tarragon is used in commercial salad dressings, beverages, confections, perfumes and mustards.

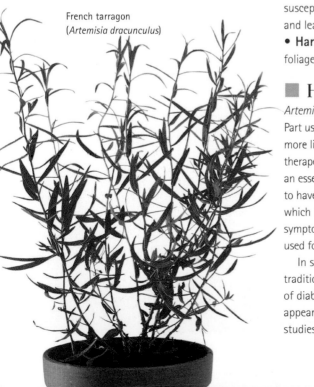

French tarragon
(*Artemisia dracunculus*)

Winter tarragon (*Tagetes lucida*)

Tea

Camellia sinensis syn. *Thea sinensis* Theaceae

Tea has been the favored beverage of China for 3,000 years. While Western palates favored the more robust flavor of black tea, green tea has been shown to be richer in antioxidants and is credited with a number of uses in traditional medicine.

Parts used Leaf tips, leaves, seeds

■ Gardening

There are some 350 varieties of *Camellia sinensis*, and they vary considerably in form. The smooth, leathery leaves are oval, pointed and faintly scented. The small white flowers are single, with a boss of gold stamens, and are borne in the leaf axils.

Tea contains polyphenol antioxidants, the levels being higher in green tea, which has undergone minimal oxidation. An essential oil is distilled from the mature leaves, which is used both in perfumery and as a commercial flavoring. The seeds are pressed for a fixed oil that is processed to remove saponins. Other species that are used for oil production include *C. crapnelliana*, *C. oleifera*, *C. octapetala* and *C. sasanqua*.

- **Position** *Camellia sinensis* is frost-hardy and requires full sun to partial shade, and a rich, moist, but well-drained soil.
- **Propagation** It is propagated from freshly harvested seed, and by semi-ripe wood cuttings for named varieties.
- **Maintenance** Maintain bushes to a height of about 3⅓ ft. (1 m).
- **Pests and diseases** There are none of significance.
- **Harvesting and storing** Harvest leaf tips for tea once bushes are 3 years old.

■ Herbal medicine

Camellia sinensis. Part used: leaves. Leaves picked from the tea plant are subjected to various processing methods to produce green, black, white and oolong varieties of tea: For instance, leaves are fermented and dried for black tea, but steamed and dried for green tea. Each type of tea contains different levels of important compounds, known as polyphenols, which are primarily responsible for the plant's medicinal properties. Green tea contains the highest levels of polyphenols and is regarded as having the greatest therapeutic activity of all these teas.

Green tea polyphenols possess a potent antioxidant capacity that is far greater than that of vitamin C or E, and which may

Tea (*Camellia sinensis*)

help in the prevention and treatment of numerous chronic diseases of our time. Studies of large populations of regular green-tea drinkers report lower rates of some cancers and reduced risk of cardio-vascular disease.

Further human trials have reported a protective effect of green tea against sunburn when applied topically, and regular consumption of chewable green-tea tablets has been shown to reduce gum inflammation and plaque formation.

Due to its caffeine content, green tea continues to be a popular aid for improving mental alertness and concentration, and it has also been investigated for its use as a potential weight-loss agent. New studies also suggest a potential role for green tea in the treatment of diabetes as a result of a blood sugar-lowering effect in addition to its antioxidant properties.

For the safe and appropriate medicinal use of green tea, consult your healthcare professional. Do not use green tea in greater than culinary quantities if you are pregnant or breastfeeding. Caffeine intake should be monitored during these times.

Rooibos tea

In South Africa, the leaves of the rooibos (pronounced roy-boss) plant (*Aspalathus linearis*) have been brewed as a refreshing beverage for centuries. Now, rooibos tea is becoming a popular drink all over the world as a result of its pleasant taste, caffeine-free content and, more important, the discovery of its remarkable antioxidant capacity; Therefore it may have the potential to improve general health and well-being as well as help in the treatment of many serious illnesses.

Opposite: Harvesting *Camellia sinensis* leaves for tea, one of the world's most popular beverages.

Golden camellia tea is prepared from a rare "living fossil" species found in China.

Tea tree

Melaleuca sp. Myrtaceae

In the 18th century, Aboriginal Australians taught Captain James Cook and his crew how to make poultices from the crushed leaves of tea tree to treat cuts and skin infections.

Parts used Leaves, branches

◼ Gardening

"Tea tree" is a misnomer, because that term also applies to *Leptospermum* species, while *Melaleuca* species are actually paperbarks. This has caused confusion and the widely held belief that the tea trialed by the Cook expedition was prepared from *Melaleuca*, which is not recommended.

Tea tree (*M. alternifolia*) is plantation-grown in Australia for high-quality essential oil. The species grows to about 23 ft. (7 m) and occurs naturally on the warm east coast of Australia, where it is often associated with swampy conditions.

M. leucadendron, a tall species, is the source of cajeput oil. Both *M. viridiflora* and *M. quinquenervia* are sources of niaouli oil, used in perfumery and as an antiseptic. All four species have whitish, layered, papery bark, stiff pointed narrow linear (*M. alternifolia*) or oval smooth leaves, and profuse, intensely honey-scented bottlebrush inflorescences, which are white, except in *M. viridiflora* where they are greenish white or, rarely, pink to red. Trees may literally drip nectar.

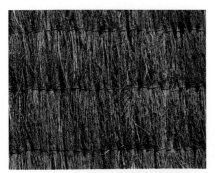

Tea tree makes an environmentally friendly fencing material that is also very attractive.

• **Position** The species of *Melaleuca* described require an acid, very moist soil, full sun and warm conditions.
• **Propagation** All species can be grown by seed, but trees with desirable chemotypes are raised by seed from selected trees or by cuttings.
• **Maintenance** Irrigation is important.
• **Pests and diseases** None of note.
• **Harvesting and storing** Trees are cut for foliage, which is water- or steam-distilled and cured for 6 weeks.

◼ Herbal medicine

Melaleuca alternifolia. Parts used: essential oil from leaves and branches. Scientific research has confirmed that the essential oil of the tea-tree plant possesses potent antimicrobial actions against many common bacterial, viral and fungal disease-causing organisms.

These days, tea-tree essential oil continues to be used extensively for its topical antiseptic actions. It is used to treat acne, gum infections and fungal infections of the foot, and clinical trials have shown that its effectiveness is comparable to some conventional treatments.

For the safe and appropriate external use of tea-tree oil, see First aid, *page 220*, Acne, *page 216*, and Athlete's foot, *page 218*. Tea-tree oil should not be used

Tea tree
(*Melaleuca alternifolia*)

internally. Do not use tea-tree oil if you are pregnant or breastfeeding.

◼ Around the home

Tea-tree oil is powerfully antiseptic, with antimicrobial and antibacterial properties.

• Wipe down surfaces with a disinfectant solution – mix tea-tree oil with either water or vinegar.
• Disinfect a shower and remove mold by mixing ¼ cup (60 g) borax, 2 cups very hot water and ¼ teaspoon tea-tree oil. Shake in a spray bottle until borax dissolves. Spray on surfaces, leave overnight, then rinse.
• Deodorize and disinfect garbage bins — wipe them out with a solution of ½ teaspoon tea-tree oil and a little detergent in hot water.

In World War II, soldiers in the tropics used tea-tree oil to treat infections, wounds and fungal infections.

Thyme

Thymus sp. Lamiaceae

There are an astonishing number of aromatic thyme species with a wide variety of fragrances, flavors and uses, from culinary and medicinal to mystical and magical. No wonder the highest praise in ancient Greece was the expression "To smell of thyme."

Common thyme
(*Thymus vulgaris*)

Part used Leaves

◾ Gardening

There are some 350 species of thyme. They share much in common, most being sun-loving, perennial woody subshrubs or creeping woody plants with a neat habit that are high in fragrant essential oils.

Garden or common thyme (*T. vulgaris*) is the principal culinary thyme. The leaves of all forms are tiny, narrow, elliptic, gray-green and aromatic. The tiny white or occasionally lavender flowers are borne terminally in many-layered whorls.

Selected forms include 'Silver Posie', with soft green and white variegated foliage; 'German Winter', a very hardy spreading form; 'Provence', a selected high-quality culinary variety from France; a hybrid called 'Fragrantissimus', or orange thyme, with very fine, erect, thyme- and citrus-scented gray foliage; and 'Erectus', with strong vertical growth.

Caraway or seedcake thyme (*T. herba-barona*) is a wiry carpeting thyme with a delicious caraway scent and lavender flowers. The neat foliage is deep green and the loose flower heads are mauve. Varieties include 'Lemon Caraway' and 'Nutmeg'.

Conehead thyme (*T. capitatus* syn. *Coridothymus capitatus*) is another very popular cooking thyme. It is an intensely scented, compact spreading subshrub with distinctive terminal conical clusters of deep pink flowers.

Spanish thyme (*T. mastichina*) forms a neat gray, upright subshrub. The scent is predominantly of common thyme with an element of eucalyptus leaf. This thyme is excellent for barbecues.

'Bush BBQ' thyme is very aromatic, perfect for adding flavor to barbecued meat.

Lemon thyme (*T. x citrodorus*) has neat, bushy, fresh green-leafed plants that are redolent of lemon and thyme, making them ideal for fish and chicken dishes. The plants have somewhat sparse heads of lilac flowers. 'Silver Queen', also known as 'Silver Strike', is a white-variegated form, and golden-variegated thyme was the old Elizabethan 'embroidered thyme'. 'Lime' is a low-growing fresh green variety with a tangy lime scent.

Broad-leafed thyme has broadly elliptical leaves with the true thyme fragrance and interrupted inflorescences with whorls of mauve flowers. Varieties include 'Oregano' or 'Pizza' thyme, which is often listed as *T. nummularium*; 'Pennsylvania Tea', with broad leaves and a gentle flavor that's ideal for tisanes; and 'Bertram Anderson' syn. 'Archer's Gold', with pink flowers and bright golden foliage in summer.

Winter-flowering thyme (*T. hyemalis*) forms a small, densely clothed gray bush and is harvested for commercial dried thyme and essential oil.

A number of thymes are popular as much for their profuse flowering and dense matting habit as for their fragrance. **Azores or orange peel thyme** (*T. micans* and *T. caespititius* syn. *T. azoricus*) resembles a dense, bitter orange-scented, mosslike carpet. The flowers are white or lavender.

Mother of thyme (*T. serpyllum*) has been divided taxonomically into two species, previously classified as subspecies — *T. serpyllum* and *T. quinquecostatus*, with reddish stems. Many popular varieties of carpeting thymes have been developed from the latter, including red-flowered 'Coccineus', 'Minimus', 'Pink Chintz', 'Russetings' and 'Snowdrift'.

Woolly thyme (*T. pseudolanuginosis*) has soft, gray, dense foliage. Hybrid carpeting varieties also include 'Coconut' and gold-speckled, lemon-scented 'Doone Valley'. 'Porlock' and 'Westmoreland' (Turkey) thyme are both robust culinary varieties.

Thymus vulgaris 'Silver Posie' bears pink-purple flowers in late spring to early summer.

Thyme *Continued*

- **Position** Thymes require good drainage and a sunny position.
- **Propagation** Raise thyme from seed in spring, but propagate varieties by cuttings and by division.
- **Maintenance** Weed the carpeting thymes regularly.
- **Pests and diseases** There are none of significance if grown in full sun. Substances leached from the leaves of thyme inhibit surrounding plant growth, reducing weed and grass competition.
- **Harvesting and storing** Thyme is low in moisture and easily air-dried out of direct sunlight. It retains its flavor.

▪ Herbal medicine

Thymus vulgaris. Parts used: leaves, flowering tops. Thyme has potent anti-microbial properties, attributed to the high content of essential oil found in the plant. Thyme also possesses a muscle-relaxant effect and an ability to thin mucus in the lungs, making it easier to expel. These combined effects make thyme a

Grow common thyme (*Thymus vulgaris*) in pots or as a border plant in the garden.

According to folklore, a garden full of thyme will attract fairies.

formidable remedy when it comes to treating respiratory conditions, such as colds and flus. Thyme can also be used as a gargle for sore throats and tonsillitis.

In addition, thyme alleviates the symptoms of indigestion, such as gas, bloating and cramps, and its antimicrobial action can also be helpful in treating gastrointestinal infections.

For the safe and appropriate medicinal use of thyme, see Sore throats, colds and flu, *page 200*. Do not use thyme in greater than culinary quantities and do not use the essential oil if you are pregnant or breastfeeding.

▪ Around the home

Thyme essential oil is a great addition to cleaning products and disinfectant sprays. For a powerful and fresh-smelling bath-room cleaning spray, mix ¼ teaspoon each of lemon, bergamot, pine, thyme, citronella and tea-tree essential oils with 2 teaspoons vinegar, 1 tablespoon cloudy ammonia and 4 cups (1 liter) water. Then, to this solution add 2 tablespoons club soda and shake until well combined.

Use thyme essential oil in an oil diffuser in a sick room for its antibacterial qualities and soothing aroma.

▪ Cooking

Various types — including lemon thyme and caraway thyme — have the flavor suggested by their names. Lemon thyme and common thyme, with their warm, pleasant aromas, are the ones commonly used in cooking, but it's well worth trying other varieties.

Thyme is a major culinary herb in Europe, where it shines in slow-cooked casseroles and dishes containing meat, poultry or game. It can be assertive and dominate other milder flavors, so robust companions, such as onions, red wine and

Lemon thyme (*Thymus* x *citrodorus*)

garlic work well. Use thyme in terrines, pâtés, meat pies, marinades (especially for olives), eggplant and tomato dishes and thick vegetable-based soups. Dried thyme is often used in the jambalayas and gumbos of Creole and Cajun cooking.

To see fairies

A recipe for a magical oil, allegedly enabling one to see fairies, was found in a 17th century manuscript in the Ashmolean Museum in Oxford, England. The recipe includes a rather oblique instruction for collecting wild thyme: "The thyme must be garnered near the side of a hill where fairies used to be."

Turmeric

Curcuma longa Zingiberaceae

Turmeric is a member of the ginger family and its rhizomes add a golden color to curries. It has long had medicinal herbal use, particularly in Ayurvedic medicine, and a rhizome constituent, curcumin, is currently exciting scientific interest for its potential in treating a range of diseases.

Part used Leaves

Turmeric (*Curcuma longa*)

The flowers are accompanied by pale green lower bracts and pink to purple upper bracts.

■ Gardening

Turmeric is an herbaceous perennial native to tropical Southeast Asia. It forms a dense clump of aromatic foliage to about 3.5 ft. (1 m), spreading by rhizomes that are brown with bright yellow flesh. The flowers are borne in dense spikes with yellow and white to orange tubular flowers. The leaves are simple and the lamina extends to the base of the stems. There are ornamental forms of *C. longa*, including 'Bright White', 'Jamaican Red' and 'Vietnamese Orange'.

• **Position** Turmeric requires a rich, moist soil and consistently warm temperatures in order to flourish. Plants die back underground each winter and will survive some frosts.

• **Propagation** Propagate from sections of rhizome.

• **Maintenance** Divide each year.

• **Pests and diseases** It repels ants.

• **Harvesting and storing** Boil the rhizomes for several hours before drying and powdering.

■ Herbal medicine

Curcuma longa. Part used: rhizome. Turmeric has a long history of use in both Ayurvedic and Chinese traditional medicinal systems, where it is regarded as an excellent tonic and blood purifier and an effective remedy for inflammatory conditions such as arthritis, skin conditions, including psoriasis, and digestive and liver disorders. Extensive scientific research and clinical trials are providing supportive evidence for its therapeutic effects.

Turmeric contains a compound called curcumin, which is responsible for the vivid yellow color and has also been shown to be involved in many of turmeric's medicinal effects. Potent antioxidant and anti-inflammatory properties have been identified, as well as a protective effect on the liver and an ability to increase bile secretion. Turmeric has also been shown to reduce harmful cholesterol levels in the blood and reduce the development of hardened and blocked arteries. Recent research has also led to the discovery of a remarkable range of potential anti-cancer effects.

Clinical trials have shown that turmeric is effective in reducing the symptoms of rheumatoid arthritis and post-operative inflammation. It has also been shown to be effective in the treatment of indigestion, stomach ulcers and inflammatory bowel conditions, such as Crohn's disease and ulcerative colitis.

In addition, studies on large populations have shown that the consumption of large quantities of turmeric is associated with a reduced risk of developing certain cancers.

For the safe and appropriate medicinal use of turmeric, see Liver support, *page 209*, High blood pressure and cholesterol, *page 228*, and Psoriasis, *page 217*. Do not use turmeric in doses greater than culinary quantities if you are pregnant or breastfeeding.

■ Cooking

Buy plump, firm, clean rhizomes. They should have a warm, mild aroma and an earthy, musky flavor. Turmeric can be used fresh or dried and ground, and adds a brilliant yellow color to foods. It is used in curry powders and pastes, pickles and chutneys, vegetable, rice and lentil dishes (especially in India, where it often partners potatoes and cauliflower), and with poultry, fish and shellfish. It is also an ingredient in the Moroccan spice blend chermoula (see *page 352*).

Followers of Jainism, a religion founded in India, rub wet turmeric over brides' faces.

Valerian

Valeriana officinalis Valerianaceae

Valerian root is believed to be the attractant used by the Pied Piper in the medieval German milling town of Hamelin in 1284. It certainly proved to be profitable knowledge for the rat catcher, at a time when the mayor was desperate to save the town's food supplies.

Part used Root

◾ Gardening

Once praised by Arab physicians, valerian (*V. officinalis*) is an herbaceous perennial forming a large basal rosette of compound, fern-like leaves. The tall flowering stem bears large, dense pale pink to pure white heads of sweetly scented flowers. The essential oil is used commercially for such purposes as flavoring tobacco and beer.

Chinese medicine has employed several additional species, such as *V. coreana*, *V. fauriei*, *V. amurensis* and *V. stubendorfi* for indications similar to those used in the West. Note that red valerian or kiss-me-quick is *Centranthus ruber*, which is of no value medicinally.

- **Position** Native to Western Europe, valerian prefers a cool root run, a sunny to lightly shaded position, and a moist, well-composted, well-drained loam.
- **Propagation** Valerian is propagated by seed sown in spring, scattered over the propagation mix and gently pressed down, because the seed requires light to germinate. Transplant 2 to 2.5 ft. (60 to 70 cm apart.

Valerian (*Valeriana officinalis*) bears clusters of white flowers, followed by tiny seeds.

- **Maintenance** Divide mature plants in autumn or early spring. Cats are as enchanted by valerian roots as rats, so you may need to provide protection for young plants.
- **Pests and diseases** There are none of significance.
- **Harvesting and storing** Lift the rhizomes in early spring, then rinse gently and dry them in a cool 200°F (100°C) fan-forced oven with the oven door left ajar. Grind if desired.

Valerian (*Valeriana officinalis*)

◾ Herbal medicine

Valeriana officinalis. Part used: root. Valerian has been used medicinally as a remedy for aiding sleep and relaxation for hundreds of years. Pharmacological studies on the plant have confirmed its sedative effects on the nervous system as well as its relaxant action on muscles.

A number of clinical trials have assessed the efficacy of valerian on its own or in combination with other relaxing herbs for insomnia, when there is difficulty falling asleep and/or sleep that is easily disturbed. The results of these trials are mixed and may be the result of large variations in the dose and preparation of valerian used as well as the length of time it was taken; however, they are strongly suggestive of positive effects on sleep, particularly if taken consistently for more than 2 weeks.

A small number of human trials have also shown a beneficial effect of valerian in alleviating the symptoms of anxiety and mental stress.

Valerian's calming effect on nerves and muscles explains the traditional use of the herb for gastrointestinal cramps, period pains and headaches as well, particularly when they are related to nervousness and tension.

For the safe and appropriate use of valerian, see Insomnia, *page 214*. Do not use valerian if you are pregnant or breastfeeding.

Vervain

Verbena officinalis Verbenaceae

Despite its lack of looks and scent, vervain was once considered the most magical of all herbs in Europe, the Middle East and China, and was used for purifying sacred spaces and in spells and potions for divination, immortality, crop fertility, prosperity, love and for protection from evil forces and lightning.

Other common names Devils' bane, enchanter's plant, herb of grace, herb of the cross, herb Venus, holy herb, pidgeonweed (it is a bird attractant), simpler's joy, tears of Isis
Parts used Aerial parts

Vervain (*Verbena officinalis*)

■ Gardening

Vervain is native to Europe, Asia and Africa, and is naturalized in North America. A slender erect herbaceous perennial growing to 4 ft. (1.2 m), It Is found on dry, stony ground such as roadsides. The leaves are coarsely and irregularly toothed, and the slender, branched, terminal flowering spikes bear small tubular lavender flowers. Blue vervain (*V. hastate*) finds similar uses. Pineapple verbena (*Nashia inaguensis*, family Verbenaceae) is used as an herbal tea.

• **Position** Grow plants 1 ft. (30 cm) apart, in full sun, in well-drained soil.

• **Propagation** Grow vervain from seed in spring. Germination is erratic and can take 4 weeks.
• **Maintenance** Keep plants weed-free.
• **Pests and diseases** Knot-like galls caused by insects can form in the stem.
• **Harvesting and storing** Harvest the green tops just before the flowers open, then air-dry them. Store under airtight conditions.

■ Herbal medicine

Verbena officinalis. Parts used: aerial parts. Vervain has both calming and restorative effects on the nervous system and an uplifting effect on mood. It can help to relieve nervous exhaustion and depression, and act as a supportive remedy during times of tension and stress. Vervain is particularly effective for those who feel miserable and fatigued during recovery from feverish illnesses such as flu. The plant's relaxing effects are also of benefit for any muscular tension in the body, reducing intestinal cramps and easing the discomfort of period pains.

Vervain is also traditionally prescribed during the early stages of fever. Further, it is regarded as a liver remedy and can be used to treat some conditions associated with this organ.

For the safe and appropriate use of vervain, consult your healthcare professional. Do not use vervain if you are pregnant or breastfeeding.

Devil's bane

Derived from the Celtic *ferfaen*, from *fer*, "to drive away" and *faen*, "a stone," vervain has a multitude of religious, cultural and magical associations. For instance, the names herb of the cross, holy herb and devil's bane derive from vervain's reputation for staunching Christ's wounds on the cross, and it was also used in sacrifice and purification ceremonies by the ancient Romans and Druids. In more recent times, the Iroquois people of North America used a concoction of smashed blue vervain (*Verbena hastate*) leaves to make an obnoxious person go away.

The Druids may have built Stonehenge, the standing stones on Salisbury Plain, England.

Vervain tea was once used to protect people from vampires.

Viburnum

Viburnum opulus, V. prunifolium Caprifoliaceae

Viburnum species are shrubs grown for their outstanding spring displays of usually fragrant flowers, colorful autumn leaves and berries. But the bark of two species has also found herbal use as a muscle relaxant in treating cramps, especially those associated with menstruation.

Other common names Cramp bark, European cranberry bush, guelder rose (*V. opulus*); American sloe, black haw, stagbush (*V. prunifolium*)
Parts used Stem bark (*V. opulus*); stem and root bark (*V. prunifolium*)

◼ Gardening

Cramp bark (*Viburnum opulus*) is a widely distributed deciduous shrub, with vine-shaped leaves that turn red in autumn and large lacy heads of white flowers borne in late spring.

Black haw (*V. prunifolium*) forms a spreading deciduous shrub to small tree that reaches to 16 ft. (5 m). It has fine and sharply toothed, rounded leaves and flat-topped lacy heads of reddish buds opening to white flowers in spring,

followed by lime green berries that ripen black in autumn. Do not eat the berries of either species.

Another species sometimes used is American highbush cranberry (*V. trilobum* syn. *V. americanum*).

• **Varieties** *V. opulus* varieties include 'Sterile' (the snowball tree); 'Notcutt's Variety', with excellent autumn foliage and large red fruits; and 'Xanthocarpum', with translucent golden berries.
• **Position** The species described above are all deciduous shrubs for cool to mild climates, and prefer an open position and well-drained soil. Once established, they have modest drought resistance.
• **Propagation** The species above are easy to grow from seed, while the varieties can be propagated by semi-hardwood cuttings.
• **Maintenance** Prune after flowering, if required.
• **Pests and diseases** There are none of significance.

The red berries of cramp bark (*Viburnum opulus*) are poisonous.

Viburnum (*Viburnum opulus*)

• **Harvesting and storing** Peel off the outer bark in strips and dry it.

◼ Herbal medicine

Viburnum opulus. Part used: bark. As its name suggests, cramp bark is effective for most types of muscular tension and can help to relax the muscles of the body after strenuous or ongoing physical activity. Cramp bark is also prescribed for tension and cramping in the digestive system, and it will ease the symptoms of indigestion, colic and gut cramps, including those brought on by nervous tension.

The medicinal properties of cramp bark are particularly useful in treating menstrual and menopausal symptoms. Its muscle relaxant properties help to ease the spasm and discomfort of period pains and, due to a slightly astringent or drying effect, cramp bark can reduce heavy bleeding during menstruation as well as irregular bleeding that can occur during menopause. Black haw (*V. prunifolium*) is used for similar indications.

For the safe and appropriate use of cramp bark, see Sports injuries, *page 223.* Do not use cramp bark if you are pregnant or breastfeeding, except under professional supervision.

Poisonous plants

The berries of *Viburnum opulus* are poisonous, while those of European cranberry bush can cause vomiting and diarrhea. And there are other species in the plant world that should not be grown in a garden that young children can access. Poisonous foxgloves (*Digitalis* sp.), for instance, produce tall spires of flowers that fit neatly over the fingers, tempting children to play with them. Monkshood (*Aconitum* sp.), which has a similar flowering habit, contains an extremely toxic compound that was once used to poison arrow tips. According to Greek mythology, aconite was created by the goddess of the Underworld, Hecate, from the mouths of Cerberus, a three-headed dog that guarded the gates of Hades.

Watercress and nasturtium

Nasturtium officinale, Tropaeolum majus Brassicaceae

Watercress is cultivated for its attractiveness as a garnish as well as the bite it gives to soups, pesto, trout, salads, sandwiches and vegetable juices. It is high in vitamin C, folic acid, beta-carotene and minerals, including potassium.

Parts used Leaves, young stems (watercress); aerial parts (nasturtium)

Watercress
(*Nasturtium
officinale*)

■ Gardening

Watercress is a semi-aquatic perennial herb found wild in streams passing through chalk soils. The cultivated form, now usually grown hydroponically, is preferred, because wild watercress is often a refuge for liver flukes (*Fasciola hepatica*) in areas where sheep graze. The plant has compound green leaves, a hollow stem and insignificant white flowers. The plant is notably more bitter when flowering.

Nasturtium or Indian cress (*Tropaeolum majus*) has large, shield-shaped, peppery leaves and cheerful, helmet-shaped flowers in yellow, orange and red.

• **Position** You can grow watercress in pots in a partially shaded position. It prefers a well-limed soil. The large seeds of nasturtium germinate easily in spring,

either planted directly into moist soil or germinated in pots and transplanted into a sunny position.

• **Propagation** To propagate, use tip cuttings grown in regularly changed water, rooted runners or seeds. Grow all other cresses by seed.

• **Maintenance** Water very regularly.

• **Pests and diseases** None of note.

• **Harvesting and storing** Harvest watercress fresh and only use before flowering. Store it at room temperature with its roots in water.

■ Herbal medicine

Tropaeolum majus. Parts used: aerial parts. Nasturtium and watercress belong to the same family as horseradish and, like their relative, contain pungent compounds known as mustard oil glycosides, which are responsible for the major medicinal effects of nasturtium. These compounds possess potent antibacterial and anti-fungal properties that have particular application in the treatment of infectious conditions of the respiratory and urinary tracts. They can help the body fight off colds, flus and other infections of the lungs as well as cystitis.

The fresh form of the herb is reputed to have a higher antimicrobial effect than the dried form, and is commonly prepared as an infusion. Applied externally as a poultice or compress, the fresh herb is also used as a local antibacterial agent for cuts and wounds. Interestingly, fresh

nasturtium juice rubbed onto the scalp is said to stimulate hair growth.

For the safe and appropriate use of nasturtium, consult your healthcare professional. Do not use nasturtium if you are pregnant or breastfeeding.

■ Cooking

The sharp, peppery taste of watercress makes it a good salad green. It goes well with a citrus dressing. Use watercress in soups (see recipe, *page 346*), sandwiches and sauces for fish (see Frankfurt green sauce, *page 338*). Nasturtium flowers make an attractive edible garnish.

Nasturtium flowers, leaves and seeds are edible.

Other cresses

A number of other species share the hot peppery flavor of watercress and find similar culinary uses. Upland or winter cress (*Barbarea verna*) is a cold-hardy dry-land cress. The cress sold in trays to be clipped for salads is garden cress (*Lepidium sativum*). The cucumber-flavored Lebanese cress (*Apium nodiflorum*) resembles watercress but is, in fact, a land plant that's related to celery.

White horehound

Marrubium vulgare Lamiaceae

Used as a cough and bronchitis medicine since Egyptian times, horehound is a member of the mint family and has attractive white furry foliage. It is also used in making horehound ale and flavoring liqueurs, and attracts bees to gardens.

Parts used Leaves, flowering tops

■ Gardening

White horehound is a perennial with attractive crinkled, downy, gray-white, toothed foliage. The small white flowers, borne in summer, are densely clustered in successive upper leaf axils. The plant yields an aromatic bitter juice with a distinctive and not unpleasant smell.

Black horehound (*Ballota nigra*), a member of the same family, was also used medicinally, but this use has largely fallen away now. Native to Mediterranean Europe and Asia, black horehound is a fully hardy perennial herb that is still widely grown in herb gardens.

White horehound (*Marrubium vulgare*)

• **Variety** A very attractive, heavily white-variegated form of *B. nigra*, 'Archer's Variety', has deep green, toothed leaves and small, hairy, tubular lilac (rarely white) flowers borne in whorls in the upper stem axils. The scent is rather disagreeable.
• **Position** Grow white horehound in a sunny, well-drained position, and black horehound in well-drained soil in sun to partial shade.
• **Propagation** Propagate both white and black horehound by seed. The latter's variegated form can only be reliably propagated by cuttings.
• **Maintenance** Both forms are hardy plants needing little care.
• **Pests and diseases** There are none of significance. White horehound has been used as a grasshopper repellent on various crops.
• **Harvesting and storing** Cut down the whole plant just as flowering begins and dry it for herbal use.

■ Herbal medicine

Marrubium vulgare. Parts used: leaves, flowering tops. Not to be confused with black horehound, which is used for quite different purposes, white horehound is best known as a remedy for respiratory conditions such as colds and bronchitis — especially when there is mucus that is difficult to expel by coughing. White

Passover plate

In late March or in April each year, Jews celebrate Passover with a meal that symbolizes the flight of the Jews from Egypt. Each of the six items on the plate, or *seder*, represents part of the story of their escape: Along with romaine lettuce or grated horseradish, white horehound is one of the bitter herbs eaten to symbolize the harshness of living as a slave in Egypt.

horehound relaxes the bronchial muscles while at the same time encouraging easier removal of mucus from the lungs.

As a result of its pronounced bitter taste, due to the presence of specific compounds, white horehound has an appreciable and somewhat stimulating effect on the digestive system. It can improve a poor appetite as well as ease symptoms of indigestion, particularly when there is gas and bloating.

It also has a positive effect on liver function and increases the secretion of bile, which can aid the digestive process as a whole.

For the safe and appropriate use of white horehound, see Sore throats, colds and flu, *page 200*. Do not use white or black horehound if you are pregnant or breastfeeding.

Fresh white horehound can be used to make syrup and candy to ease sore throats and coughs.

Yarrow

Achillea millefolium Asteraceae

Yarrow is one of our oldest herbs. In China, stripped and dried yarrow stalks were tossed to consult the *I Ching*, the *Book of Changes*, and, in the West, it has been widely used as an herb of powerful but neutral magic.

Other common names Achillea, allheal, bloodwort, carpenter's herb, milfoil
Parts used Leaves, flowers

Yarrow (*Achillea millefolium*)

■ Gardening

Yarrow is a tough, fully hardy perennial forming a rosette of very finely divided feathery leaves with a pungent, refreshing scent that is strangely uplifting to the senses. It multiplies via underground rhizomes. The small white flowers form dense, flat-headed, large inflorescences borne on wiry stems to about 2.5 ft. (70 cm).

There are some 85 species of *Achillea*, and many hybrids. Yarrows are among the toughest and prettiest modern ornamental perennials; many have been bred from *A. millefolium*.

• **Varieties** Some beautiful varieties include 'Lemon Queen', 'Paprika', 'Cerise Queen', 'Appleblossom', cream-flowered 'Credo', blackcurrant-colored 'Cassis', Damask rose-scented 'Fawncett Beauty', 'Lilac Beauty' and coppery 'Colorado'.

Other widely cultivated species include feathery, woolly yarrow (*A. tomentosa*); fern-leaf yarrow (*A. filipendulina*) and its golden-flowered hybrid 'Coronation Gold'; sneezewort (*A. ptarmica*); and *A. taygetea* and its famous hybrid 'Moonshine'.

• **Position** The yarrows described above all require a sunny, well-drained position. They are frost-hardy and have good drought resistance.

• **Propagation** Raise species by seed sown in pots and transplant about 6 to 8 weeks later. Propagate named varieties by division.

• **Maintenance** Divide clumps every 3 to 4 years in late autumn or, in cooler climates, early spring.

• **Pests and diseases** There are no pests or diseases of any consequence. Cold, wet winters may cause rotting if plants are poorly drained.

• **Harvesting and storing** Harvest the flowering stalks just as they fully open, and dry in small bunches hung upside down out of direct sunlight. Harvest leaves at any time.

■ Herbal medicine

Achillea millefolium. Parts used: aerial parts. Yarrow has been used since ancient times for its healing effects on wounds, quickly stopping bleeding and reducing inflammation. It is also well known for its application in any feverish condition where it encourages perspiration and reduces body temperature; for this purpose it is commonly taken with elderflowers.

Yarrow is a valuable digestive remedy, alleviating colic and indigestion and improving appetite while also having a stimulatory effect on bile flow and liver function. Traditionally regarded as a women's herb, yarrow was commonly used to treat menstrual complaints associated with particularly heavy and painful bleeding.

For the safe and appropriate use of yarrow, see Sore throats, colds and flu, *page 200*. Do not use yarrow if you are pregnant or breastfeeding.

Achilles the healer

Yarrow has been used on many battlefields, hence two of its common names, allheal and bloodwort. One of our oldest herbs, it was named for the ancient Greek hero Achilles who, according to Homer's *The Iliad*, used it to staunch the flow of blood from his troops' wounds in the Trojan War. Achilles had been taught how to use plants by Cheiron, a learned centaur. At one point, Eurypylus is wounded and begs Patroclus to 'put the right things on it.' 'Patroclus... crushed a bitter root...and put it on the wound. The root took away all the pain. The blood stopped and the wound dried.'

Trees

Admired for their flowers, nuts and fruit, or simply for their form, each of these trees is also the source of medicinal properties that have long been used as herbal remedies.

1 Magnolia *Magnolia officinalis*

Best known as an ornamental tree, the magnolia is a bitter tonic herb used to improve digestion, menstrual and liver problems.

2 Oak *Quercus robur*

Dried oak bark is an astringent herb used to reduce inflammation, control bleeding, and treat diarrhea and various skin conditions.

3 Walnut *Juglans nigra*

Black walnut hulls have traditionally been used for the treatment of worms and intestinal parasites.

4 Hawthorn *Crataegus sp.*

Hawthorn is an aromatic warming herb used to treat circulatory disorders and heart disease in both European and Chinese medicine.

5 White willow *Salix alba*

White willow bark's analgesic and anti-inflammatory properties make it a useful treatment for arthritis, back pain and headaches.

6 Olive *Olea europaea*

Not only does the olive produce wonderful fruit and oil, it is also a blood pressure–lowering herb with antioxidant properties.

7 Horse chestnut *Aesculus hippocastanum*

The seed, or 'conker', of the horse chestnut tree provides an important circulatory remedy, used to treat varicose veins, leg ulcers and other blood vessel problems.

8 Prickly ash *Zanthoxylum americanum*

This herb is prescribed by herbalists for circulatory problems such as varicose veins and Raynaud's disease.

9 Witch hazel *Hamamelis virginiana*

Soothing and anti-inflammatory, witch hazel is used topically for a range of skin and vascular problems. Its astringent nature means it is also prescribed for diarrhea and heavy menstrual bleeding.

Caution

With the exception of the topical use of witch hazel, do not use any of these herbs if you are pregnant or breastfeeding, except under the advice of a healthcare professional.

Berries

While some of these berries are delicious and safe to eat, either fresh or cooked, others are strictly for medicinal use only and should always be taken under the supervision of a professional herbalist.

1 Bilberry *Vaccinium myrtillus*

Compounds in bilberries called anthocyanosides have potent antioxidant properties, which contribute to the herb's many benefits, particularly for vision and eye health.

2 Saw palmetto *Serenoa repens*

The berry contains an oily extract that has been clinically proven to reduce symptoms of benign prostatic hyperplasia (BPH).

3 Chaste tree *Vitex agnus-castus*

Chaste tree helps to regulate the menstrual cycle and is used to treat a range of hormonal imbalances, including PMS symptoms.

4 Cranberry *Vaccinium macrocarpon*

Rich in antioxidants, including vitamin C, cranberries are an important remedy for preventing and treating cystitis.

5 Schisandra *Schisandra chinensis*

These berries are prescribed for a wide range of symptoms and conditions, including asthma, cough, insomnia and liver disorders.

6 Juniper *Juniperus communis*

Often taken in combination with other diuretic herbs, an infusion of berries is a traditional remedy for arthritis, gout and rheumatism.

7 Raspberry *Rubus idaeus*

Traditionally used to treat diarrhea, the leaves are also taken during the third trimester to prepare the uterus for childbirth.

8 Wild strawberry *Fragaria vesca*

Rarely used these days, an infusion of the leaves was once taken to relieve mild cases of diarrhea and soothe minor stomach problems.

9 Blackberry *Rubus fruticosus*

Strongly astringent due to large quantities of tannins, blackberry leaves have traditionally been used in the treatment of diarrhea.

Caution

Except for raspberry leaf, as directed on pages 236–7, do not use any of these herbs if you are pregnant or breastfeeding, except under the advice of a healthcare professional.

Spices

Bark, resin, seeds, seed pods, fruit, flower buds, even stigmas — various parts of these plants are used as culinary spices as well as in herbal medicinal preparations.

1 Asafetida *Ferula asafetida*

The resin is used as a remedy for flatulence, so it's worth adding it to dishes based on legumes and pulses that tend to cause wind.

2 Fenugreek *Trigonella foenum-graecum*

Fenugreek is used under professional supervision to help manage blood sugar in patients with diabetes, and to lower cholesterol.

3 Cinnamon *Cinnamomum verum, C. cassia*

The volatile essential oils of both cinnamon and cassia contain high quantities of a compound called cinnamaldehyde, which is believed responsible for most of the plants' medicinal activity.

4 Cumin *Cuminum cyminum*

A popular cooking spice, medicinally cumin can be used to reduce flatulence and colic; it has a reputation as an appetite tonic.

5 Cloves *Syzygium aromaticum*

The essential oil in the flower buds contains eugenol, responsible for its use as a local anaesthetic, antiseptic and anti-inflammatory.

6 Saffron *Crocus sativus*

Saffron threads with a vibrant orange-red color contain the highest concentrations of the carotenoid crocin, which may have the potential to help treat and prevent cancer.

7 Black pepper *Piper nigrum*

Black, green, white, pink and red peppercorns all come from *Piper nigrum*. The different appearance and taste characteristics of each type are created by different processing methods.

8 Nigella *Nigella sativa*

The peppery flavor of nigella seed is used in cooking and in Ayurvedic medicine to treat a variety of digestive problems.

9 Tamarind *Tamarindus indica*

The fruit is used widely in cooking, and various parts of the plant also have traditional medicinal uses. For example, in India the fruit is used as a laxative and also taken for nausea in pregnancy.

Caution

Do not use any of these herbs if you are pregnant or breastfeeding, except under the advice of a healthcare professional.

Gardening

Thriving herbs are a beautiful sight. Whether you grow them for cooking or for their health and beauty benefits, or simply to enjoy their appearance and aroma, this guide shows you how to grow herbs with great success.

Herb garden styles

Whether your herb garden is formal or informal, shape, texture and perfume all play an integral role in creating an inviting outdoor space.

The beauty of herbs

Herbs form such a diverse group of plants, from groundcovers to shrubs and trees, that there are herbs to suit any climate, soil type and position. Even if you live in an apartment with a small balcony or have no outdoor space at all, you can still grow culinary herbs in a window box.

And herbs are incredibly versatile. Take the elder, for example. A deciduous shrub or tree that grows to about 20 ft. (6 m), in summer it produces clusters of tiny, creamy white scented flowers that attract bees, followed by blue-black berries in autumn. Elders make a great hedge, and you can use the flowers and berries to make cordials, wines, jams and jellies. The leaves repel flies and mosquitoes while the flowers are used medicinally to treat coughs, colds, allergies and arthritis, and cosmetically as a skin toner. Note, however: In some locations it is a weed.

Herbs for a knot garden

Today, the most commonly used hedging plant is box, as it is compact, robust and long-lived, but you could use other traditional knot garden plants such as rosemary, lavender, santolina, germander and mugwort (at right). Variegated varieties can also look attractive. Pansies, groundcovering thymes and calendulas are ideal for filling these spaces, but avoid invasive herbs, such as mint, which produces runners.

Your herb garden

Depending on your lifestyle and on the amount of space you have, your herb garden can be anything from a showpiece to a personal retreat. Good garden design can seem deceptively simple, and some gardens often belie the creativity, skill and sheer hard work involved in their creation, while others leave visitors in no doubt of the financial commitment and years of effort invested in their planning, planting and presentation.

Fortunately, travel — whether by car, plane or armchair — can provide you with inspiration for ideas and styles that suit your personal preferences. Often, it's not until you consciously explore your own taste that you begin to build a mental catalogue of what you'd like to grow in your own garden.

To help make your "wish list" a reality, consult the expertise of garden designers and landscape architects.

You might prefer a potted herb garden so you can grow your favorite culinary herbs, or perhaps you have the space for a sprawling cottage garden, where shrubs and trees mingle with annuals, perennials and groundcovers. Or you could design a formal garden that's dedicated to herbs, like the grand knot gardens and parterres of Europe in the 16th and 17th centuries.

Formal herb gardens

Traditionally, plants were grown for their uses, not their beauty: herbs were highly valued for their culinary and medicinal qualities, and in great European medieval monasteries, monks grew a vast range of herbs in apothecary gardens.

Knot gardens

During the reign of Henry VIII, in the 16th century, decorative knot gardens became popular. These gardens were often complicated, designed to be viewed from above: low, evergreen hedges were planted in geometric or symmetric interlinking patterns, such as diamonds.

The knots or patterns could be quite intricate scrollworks, such as coats of arms or heraldic symbols. To distinguish the patterns, contrasting foliage textures or colors were planted together.

Originally, there was nothing inside the hedged areas except clipped grass, or gravel and stones, but later these compartments were filled with fragrant herbs, such as rosemary, lavender, sage and hyssop — perfect as drying 'racks' for linen (imagine sleeping on sheets scented with fresh lavender).

Hatfield House in Hertfordshire, in the U.K., is an excellent example of an intricate knot garden.

Repeating shapes, such as spheres, provides continuity and interest, at ground and eye level.

Parterre gardens

In 16th-century France, parterre gardens — intricate, complex beds spanning huge areas — developed from the English knot garden. Again, geometry and symmetry were intrinsic elements in these designs. Wide gravel paths separated beds, while flowers were used to balance the green hedging. These fine gardens were also designed to be viewed from above — perhaps from a terrace or upper floor.

Topiaries, a feature of parterres, provided focal points. They were crafted from small-leafed species, such as citrus, yew, bay, box or cypress, and punctuated corners and centerpieces in imaginative designs that ranged from spirals and spheres to cubes, symbols and animals.

While Versailles, outside Paris, showcases extravagant formal gardens fit for royalty, it took an army of workers to build them. You can still visit many stunning examples of these formal gardens, which have been re-created or restored; in the 18th century, many grand European gardens were destroyed and replaced by open, undulating landscapes, which were designed or greatly influenced by the great English landscape architect Lancelot "Capability" Brown.

Herbs for a parterre

In more recent times, the range of plants used for topiary in parterres has expanded to include those commonly referred to as "standards" — plants that can be grown and pruned into a lollipop shape. For their flowers, fragrance or compliant foliage, you could try duranta, roses, lillypilly, Chinese lanterns (*Abutilon* sp.) and muehlenbeckia.

Some grand restored gardens

Near London, Hampton Court Palace gardens is the home of the Privy Garden. Raised walks are lined with rows of yew cones and parterres on either side of a central walk leading to a circular pool and fountain. To the west of the Privy Garden is a small Knot Garden hedged with box.

A little farther north is Hatfield House, in Hertfordshire, where Elizabeth I spent part of her childhood. Included within the grounds are splendid examples of herb and scented gardens, kitchen and knot gardens.

A few hours from Paris, in the Loire Valley, is Château de Villandry, one of the most visited gardens in France. Designed to be viewed from above, the replicas of the 17th-century beds in the Love Garden have been planted in symbolic designs associated with love — for example, tragic love, represented by the shapes of blades, swords and daggers. Nearby are the Herb Gardens dedicated to about 30 aromatic, cooking and medicinal herbs.

Another fine European garden is in the grounds of the Dutch palace Het Loo, near Apeldoorn, in the Netherlands. It features restored parterre gardens, an axial layout, fountains and statues.

Designing a formal garden

In your own garden, you could plant out a simple knot garden in a small space of, say, 40 ft. (12 m) square, divided into four sections with low or dwarf hedges. Or you could design a circular garden by planting out a "wheel" and "spokes" with hedging material.

But be patient, because hedges grow best from immature plantings, and the gaps will take a few years to close up. Within the subdivisions, grow herbs for a variety of uses — for example, separate culinary herbs from medicinal ones.

Using a formal design is often the easiest way to start planning, especially if you think you lack imagination. Mirror images of garden beds are a good way to replicate patterns on either side of a path, lawn area or house. Use the continuity of low green hedges to balance color and reduce the possibility of overdoing the flower planting and parallel lines to give a sense of order and calm.

Maintenance

Pruning, clipping and general tidying are the main maintenance tasks for these formal gardens but, in spite of the work involved, there is a satisfying sense of purpose and achievement. The idea is to have no-nonsense clean lines and shapes.

Here, a formal layout, with raised beds and an arch, is softened by informal plantings of herbs.

Some herbs grow to over 6.5 ft. (2 m), forming a striking background planting in an informal border.

Informal gardens

If a softer, wilder cottage garden is more your style, set out beds and paths with sweeping curves, instead of rigid squares and rectangles, and plant herbs in round pots, rather than square ones. However, the principles of a formal garden can still be useful in providing structure.

Define planting areas with low hedging but, instead of traditional box, try a less regimented plant, such as catmint. This is a billowing flowering herb that softens lines, making it ideal for a more informal herb garden design.

Design informal herbal borders so that shrubs and trees form a high hedge to disguise the fence or an ugly shed, or to provide privacy from the neighbors.

In front of these, grow taller perennial herbs, such as cardoon and angelica (see *Herb Directory, page 13*), which can reach over 6½ ft. (2 m), then lower-growing herbs, such as salvias (see *page 108*).

Use trailing, groundcovering plants to blur garden lines and edges, and add self-seeding herbs, such as Californian poppy (see *page 93*) and pretty heartsease (see *page 62*), which pop up year after year.

You can even grow an herb lawn with a low-growing plant, such as chamomile (see *page 32*), or a compact groundcover, such as thyme (see *page 125*), between pavers. When walking on these herbs, you will crush them and release their scent.

Themed gardens

Sometimes, it's easier to design your herb garden according to a theme. Here are some suggestions.

■ **Sensory** Appeal to the senses of sight, sound, smell and touch. Grow herbs such as lavender and roses for their fragrant flowers, or others for the oils they release when you crush the stems or leaves — for example, citrus, lemon balm, thyme and aniseed. Contrast the gentle softness of lamb's ear with upright spikes of lavender or the roughness of lemon balm.

■ **Culinary** Choose a flavor theme for cooking. Try experimenting with different combinations of herbs, such as hot chilies, peppery rocket and spicy coriander. Or you could plant traditional French culinary herbs, such as tarragon, chervil and parsley. For information on cooking with herbs, see *page 328*.

■ **Picking** Create posies with flowers gathered from your garden. Peony, lavender, nasturtiums, geraniums, poppies, sage, calendula, feverfew and iris make lovely gifts or display plants. For projects on making herb and flower arrangements, see *Craft, pages 308–13*.

■ **Craft** Many decorative objects can be made with herbs. Use fragrant herbs in sleep pillows and moth-repelling sachets; press flowers for gift tags and cards; photograph herbs to create a mural; digitally print herbs onto napkins, or plant a hanging herb ball. For projects, see *Craft, pages 300–25*.

■ **Household use** Harvest roses, spearmint, marjoram and oregano for pot-pourri; make fragrant air fresheners and herbal cleaners; use flea-repellent plants, such as lavender, to protect your dog or cat. For recipes, see *Around the Home, pages 284–97*.

■ **Medicinal** Many medicines derive their healing properties from herbs. For the safe and appropriate use of herbal treatments you can prepare yourself to treat conditions ranging from sore throats to arthritis, see *Herbal Medicine, pages 200–39*.

■ **Cosmetic** With herbal essential oils, fresh herbs and some items from your pantry, you can make natural beauty products to tone your skin, condition your hair, and much more. For easy recipes, see *Natural Beauty, pages 242–81*.

Varieties of citrus, such as lemons, are grown for their fragrance and their culinary use.

Knowing your site

Before planting out an herb garden or starting a collection of herbs in pots, take the time to plan a little. By learning about your site and choosing the right herbs for your conditions, you'll be sure to create a thriving and productive garden.

Draw a plan

Once you've familiarized yourself with the main characteristics of your property, you can then decide how to utilize them. The easiest way to do this is to document your garden space.

First, measure your property carefully and sketch it onto a piece of grid paper. A scale of 1:100 or 1:50 is useful. Add the house, garage, driveway, shed and other existing structures, paths, paved areas, steps, fences, ponds or pools, power lines, underground services, trees and major shrubs. It doesn't have to be perfect, but a basic plan drawn to scale will help you to design your garden, even if all you are working with is a small courtyard area.

Next, use a compass to determine where north is and mark it on your plan. Now, use colored pencils to mark in any shady spots, the direction of prevailing winds, parts of the garden that slope or contain gullies, particularly damp or dry

Measure out new garden beds with a string line or rope, then mark them with lime or sand.

A formal herb garden

If you have a sunny, well-drained level area, consider planting a knot garden or parterre (see *pages 142–4*). Draw your plan to scale on a sheet of grid paper first, then transpose it to the bed itself by using sand, garden lime or landscape-marking paint, which is sold in a spray can.

Use stringlines to ensure straight lines, but for a circular bed, push a stake in the center of the bed and tie a length of string to another stake.

Then scribe a circle by walking around your central stake at the full length of the string.

Divide a knot garden into sections by planting hedges of low-growing compact herbs, such as rosemary, lavender or cotton lavender, then fill it with more herbs to create a color or foliage theme.

Finally, add a picket or wrought iron fence to add a touch of whimsy or a sense of discovery.

areas — in other words, any peculiarities or characteristics you need to consider before you start planting. Remember to include shade cast by neighboring trees or buildings: Although they aren't part of your property, they will certainly affect what you can grow.

As you record all this information, you'll gradually build a picture of the main elements of the garden and which favorite or difficult areas need some special consideration.

Experiment

Once you've created a basic template of your garden, photocopy it several times and use it as a basis for experimenting. You can either draw in existing garden beds or make a fresh start.

Mark any areas visible from inside the house that you want to enhance or disguise, and also note potential or existing seating, entertaining areas and play corners.

Planned areas

A garden area should be functional as well as visually stimulating, so the next step is to consider how you plan to use your outdoor area. Start by asking yourself some questions. Are there areas for

entertaining, or just for sitting? Do your children or the family pets need some play space? Do you have enough time, energy and interest to look after a high-maintenance garden, or do you just want a small section to tend? Are there some elements you'd like to enhance — such as views and wildlife sounds — or aspects you'd prefer to disguise — the utility area, for instance, or traffic noise? Is the space limited or unwieldy? Does the route you take to the washing line or compost heap follow the existing path, or do you traipse across the lawn? If you always take a shortcut to the utility area, think about redirecting the path, rather than wearing out the grass.

Research

Ponder the possibilities and look at the space from every angle. If you're making big changes, get others involved in the planning process; you may be surprised what a difference a new perspective can make. Talk to friends and other garden owners, read gardening magazines and books, watch gardening programs on the television, visit open gardens and shows, pick up color swatches from paint or fabric stores. In short, explore anything that will give you ideas and inspiration.

A design for a formal herb garden

olive

rosemary standard
bay in pot

box cone
in pot

nepeta

hollyhocks

golden
majoram

thyme

parsley

lavender

lemon
grass

dill

chives

passionfruit
on trellis

passionfruit
on trellis

chillies

water lilies

lemon
balm

lavender

lavender

parsley

hollyhocks

rocket

basil

echinacea

nepeta

nepeta

artemesia

rose

rose

artemesia

olive

olive

standard
bay in pot

rosemary

nepeta

echinacea

lavender

olive

- This formal herb garden has a classic symmetrical geometric layout, with the height elements provided by an olive tree in each corner and trellises on either side.

- The main color scheme is lavender and mauve flowers, with gray-green foliage provided by lavender, artemesia, nepeta, olive and rosemary, accented with pink, in the roses, hollyhocks and echinacea, and red, in the chillies.

- Bay and box topiaries draw the eye to the seating area, while the square pond provides the central focal point.

- The central herb garden is planted with culinary herbs, but you could also use the four quadrants to separate culinary from medicinal herbs, for instance. The brick paving radiating out from the pond makes each section easy to access for weeding and harvesting.

- The sandstone flagging and edging help to unify the garden. The peach-colored gravel, used to fill open areas between the beds, complements the overall color scheme of the main planting.

- The standard roses on either side of the entrance are reminders of how, in the Middle Ages, monks grew standard roses in their monastic gardens to represent themselves at work.

Aspect

One of the keys to growing successful herbs is plenty of sunlight, so the aspect of your property will determine what you can grow. A northerly aspect is ideal, because many herbs will struggle without daily exposure to the sun.

Remember that the amount of sunlight varies with the seasons: The sun is higher in the sky in summer than in winter, and deciduous trees will provide shade during warmer months but extra light during the cooler months of autumn and winter.

Climatic conditions

Climate types can be broadly broken down into tropical, subtropical, Mediterranean, temperate, semi-arid or cold.

Generally, planting is carried out in spring or autumn, with the determining factor being the timing of the first and last frosts.

Temperate locations with warm summers and cool winters can be divided further into "cool-temperate" climates, which are subject to frosts, and 'warm-temperate," which is frost-free. In tropical areas, the amount of rainfall and humidity can affect the suitability of some crops during particular months.

Microclimates

Within each climate zone are natural microclimates that create conditions outside the general climatic pattern,

A garden with a sunny aspect is ideal for a cottage garden featuring herbs. On the left side of the path, pale pink *Nicotiana* sp. towers over deep pink dahlias, orange nasturtiums and potted lilies.

thus affecting the growth and suitability of plants. You can also deliberately create microclimates to provide more suitable conditions by planting windbreaks for shelter or building brick walls to retain heat and warmth.

So, if you live in a cold location, and you really want to grow a frost-tender plant, such as citrus, you can try creating the protective environment it needs.

If you're unsure whether you're making an appropriate choice, just wander around your neighborhood and look at what's thriving in other people's gardens. Also, seek the advice of a horticulturalist at your local nursery.

Design tips

Before you start planting, always prepare new garden beds properly. Clear the area of weeds, rake it flat and improve the soil with organic matter (see *page 150*).

■ **Make** paths wide enough for a wheelbarrow or so that two people can comfortably walk side by side.

■ **Experiment** with plant placement. Sit rows of pots in position before planting, to ensure that the spacing

is correct, the height is accurate and your color, form and texture choices work well.

■ **Incorporate** surfaces and structures into the new design — for example, paint fences, lattice, gates or walls to contrast with or complement the garden color scheme. These features can provide interesting backdrops to garden beds and enhance or tone down flowers and foliage.

Use the vertical planes of your herb garden by installing pots of herbs on trellises.

The principles of plant selection

What you can grow will be determined by the amount of space and available sunlight you have, soil considerations and, of course, personal preferences. Think about where your new herbs will be positioned — at the front of a garden bed as a border, as a hedging or screening plant, near the kitchen door for culinary use, as companion plants or space fillers?

So, make a list of the characteristics your plants need to deliver — for instance, you might need plants that 'prefer full sun and grow to a height of less than 3.5 ft. (1 m), preferably with flowers.' Once you know what you want a plant to do and look like, it's much easier to choose.

And think about specific areas of the garden. If there is a spot that seems to collect water after rainfall or watering, grow thirsty plants there to improve the drainage. Any area that is hard to access is easily neglected, so plant it with resilient herbs, such as Greek sage (*Salvia fruticosa*) or other survivors.

Planting ideas

Herbs are extremely versatile plants, suitable for a range of garden designs, from formal to cottage gardens.

- Set aside a dedicated area for growing herbs, or consider interspersing them with vegetables, flowering perennials and annuals and shrubs.
- Grow herbs in containers, using them to create focal points or accents. For more impact, choose large containers, rather than small ones (see *page 167*).
- Think about color combinations throughout the year. For example, tone down summer's heat with soft, soothing blues, mauves and white.
- Plant tall herbs at the back of large beds, or in the center of circular beds, with other plants graduated in height in front of them.
- Use groundcover or spillover herbs to disguise borders or path edges.
- Position edible herbs where they're easy to access and can be monitored for growth, health and harvesting.

Aquatic herbs for ponds

An interesting twist on an herb garden is a pond or pool planted with aquatic herbs. Look for a low point in your garden that is consistently boggy or wet, perhaps at the bottom of a small slope where runoff collects. Instead of correcting the drainage problem, consider installing a pond.

You can either buy precast ponds, or simply dig a hole and line it with waterproofing membrane. But first check with your town to see if you need planning approval.

Think about the size and style of your pond. A larger pool will be less subject to changes in temperature; a small pond may freeze in winter in a cool-temperate zone. Make sure the pond is sited where it receives sunlight for about half a day, because too much sun will result in algal blooms.

Some aquatic herbs prefer to grow on the margins of a pond, while others thrive in the pond itself. When you dig the hole, you'll need to create a level shelf about 10 in. (25 cm) below the surface on which to position potted marginals, such as brahmi (*Bacopa monnieri*) and water iris (*Iris* sp.).

The water lily, an aquatic perennial, requires rich soil, still water and full sun.

In the pond itself, plant such herbs as yellow bladderwort (*Utricularia australis*) and water snowflake (*Nymphoides indica*). Both are native Australian herbs. To help shade the water and prevent algal blooms from developing, plant floating-leaf plants, such as water lily (*Nymphaea* sp.) and lotus (*Nelumbo nucifera*).

And if you don't have the space for a pond, you can always plant up a large decorative pot full of water.

The sacred lotus (*Nelumbo nucifera*) has large fragrant flowers with a seed cup that is reminiscent of a showerhead. It contains hard edible seeds that can be eaten raw or cooked.

Soils and organic matter

Good soil is the foundation for growing healthy plants. It provides access to nutrients, water and air, stabilizes roots and assists in plants' natural resistance to pests and diseases. Poor soils that are low in nutrients tend to result in weak, stunted plants, and although some of the tougher, more resilient herbs, such as St John's wort, thrive in these conditions, you should be aware that this resilience can turn such plants into weeds.

Soil types

There are three main types of soil: sandy, loamy or clay. Sandy soil is easy to dig, but it doesn't hold nutrients or moisture. Heavy clay soils tend to become waterlogged, are difficult to dig into and set hard when dry.

The ideal soil

Loam, on the other hand, is the ideal garden soil, a good balance of clay and sand. A rich brown color, it is slightly moist and crumbly, with a good earthy smell. It holds both air and water and releases the nutrients in the soil to the plant roots.

In a loamy soil, clay particles bind the soil together without making it sticky and impenetrable, while sand particles allow moisture penetration without letting the water run away. If a soil has too much clay, it will hold onto nutrients instead of releasing them.

A large component of loam is decomposed organic matter or humus. Soil microbes, such as bacteria, as well as fungi and earthworms help to break down dead plant material — leaves, branches, twigs, sawdust, kitchen scraps, manure and newspaper — in a process that can occur either naturally or in compost heaps and worm farms.

Improving your soil

Making nutrients available to plant roots is an important aspect of growing healthy plants, so if your soils are too sandy and porous, the best way to improve their structure is to add organic matter in the form of compost or manures.

In addition, to reduce compaction and improve aeration, apply gypsum (calcium sulphate), available from landscape suppliers, nurseries and garden centers, at the rate suggested by the manufacturer.

To grow healthy herbs, add plenty of organic matter to the soil, and mulch well.

Sweet or sour soil

To determine the levels of acidity ("sourness") or alkalinity ("sweetness") in your garden soils, use a pH soil-testing kit, available from nurseries and mail-order or online. On a scale of 0 to 14, 7 is neutral, while soils above 7 are alkaline and those below are acidic.

The acceptable range is between 5 and 7, with most plants enjoying a slightly acidic soil of 6.5. There are exceptions, of course — lavenders, for instance, grow naturally in alkaline, limestone soils while blueberries, rhododendrons and azaleas prefer to be in an acid soil.

Adjusting the pH level

If the pH of the soil is outside its normal range, this can mean the nutrients are either not available to plants or are too readily available. Either way, it can make them toxic. So, if your plants are showing signs of nutrient deficiency, but you know you have applied the correct amount of fertilizer, be sure to check the pH level of your soil.

If your garden soil is too acidic, raise the pH with an application of agricultural lime (calcium carbonate). This will also have a beneficial effect on the structure of clay soils. If your clay soil is also deficient in magnesium, apply dolomite (a combination of magnesium carbonate and calcium carbonate).

Where the soil is too alkaline, and you need to lower the pH level to make it more acidic, add some agricultural sulphur or sulphate of iron. Remember to check the pH again later, because you may need to make annual soil adjustments.

To make a comprehensive analysis, select at least five samples of soil from each garden bed or area.

Adding organic matter will improve soil and result in healthier plant growth.

Testing soil pH

You will need

☐ pH soil-testing kit
☐ samples of garden soil

1 Place a level teaspoon of soil onto the test card, and add drops of the indicator liquid. Repeat this process with different areas of the garden.

2 Stir the soil sample and keep adding more drops until you can stir it into a thick paste. Use the spoon or a small stick.

3 Dust the paste with the white powder provided, and wait about 1 minute until it changes color.

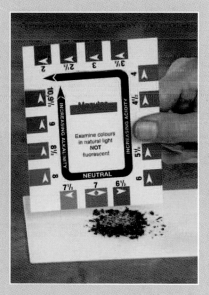

4 To determine if the sample is acidic, alkaline or neutral, match the color of the soil sample with the nearest pH value on the color card. Read the color chart in natural daylight, not fluorescent light. (Alternatively, send your samples to a laboratory for professional analysis.)

Compost heaps

Sometimes called "black gold," compost slowly releases nutrients to your soil and conserves moisture.

Successful compost heaps maintain a balance between carbon (dry, brown and woody material, such as dried leaves) and nitrogen (wet, fresh and green material, such as grass clippings). The ideal ratio is 25–30:1, so remember this easy rule: Loads of brown material, less green.

The pile should also be moist, not sodden. The moisture helps microbes to break down materials, but if you add too much water, you will create smelly anaerobic conditions — that is, without oxygen, and the pile needs oxygen in order to break down.

Making compost

Include kitchen scraps (excluding citrus, onions and meat), and a handful or two of blood and bone(see *Fertilizer types, page 156*)in your compost pile, and dig it over at least once a week. You can include cow, horse or chicken manure as well as mushroom compost — even natural carpet fibers from a vacuum cleaner. Add a compost activator to build up the heat in

To speed up the decomposition process in your compost heap, add comfrey leaves.

the pile and speed up the decomposition. Although you can buy powdered activators from nurseries, try a natural activator — comfrey, an herb.

Choose from free-standing compost bins or tumblers in a wide variety of shapes and sizes, or build your own frames, about 3.5 ft. (1 m) square. Have two or three compost bins or piles, so you have heaps in various stages of decomposition: by the time the third pile is full, the first will be ready for the garden.

Mulch

Mulch is a layer of material that's laid on top of the soil or potting mix, acting as a natural 'blanket' that has many beneficial functions. This layer can be made up of different types of materials, from bark and straw to pebbles and gravel.

The benefits of mulch

A thick layer of mulch shields the soil and plant roots from temperature fluctuations, keeping them cool and helping to retain moisture in the soil, reducing the need to water. This is particularly important for shallow-rooted plants.

Thick layers of mulch help to suppress weeds. Often there isn't enough light for weeds to successfully germinate or, if they do reach the seedling stage, they have to push their way up through thick mulch. This results in weak, exhausted specimens that are much easier to remove, so mulch saves you time, effort and energy.

If you use an organic material, such as lucerne, it will break down, adding organic matter to the soil. This provides the ideal environment for beneficial soil organisms, such as soil microbes, fungi and earthworms.

Worm farms

Worms are another great source of fertilizer, because their waste is rich in nutrients and a great way to recycle soft organic waste. You can purchase worm farms from most nurseries, garden centers and some specialized gardening businesses on the Internet.

Worm farms are actually a stack of 3 to 4 trays, each with holes in the bottom. The lowest tray collects the liquid waste that drains from the upper levels; this is then tapped and used as a liquid fertilizer.

The next tray initially houses the worms and their bedding material (such as coconut fiber); food scraps are then added to the layer above. The worms seek out food, wriggling their way up to the next layer. As the food is digested, it's turned into waste (worm castings), which can be dug into garden beds.

Only a few species of worms are suitable for this diet of food scraps, so buy compost worms with a worm farm, because earthworms prefer a more organic lifestyle in the garden.

Sweet violet thrives in a moist, humus-rich soil in sun or partial shade.

Aesthetically, mulch can add a "carpet," which puts the finishing touch to garden beds or container plantings. Choose the appropriate material and color to blend with your garden type, scale of plantings or the color scheme of your house and surrounds, and it will make a difference to the overall visual effect. While bright pebbles and mulches can look striking in rockeries and Japanese gardens, subtle, natural mulch complements any situation.

Mulch types

There are two types of mulch. Organic mulches — such as various wood or bark products, straw, pea straw and lucerne — break down, adding organic matter and nutrients to the soil.

On the other hand, inorganic mulches, such as gravel and pebbles, neither break down and provide soil with extra nutrients nor contribute to the soil structure and its water-holding capacity. However, they are very effective for a decorative look if the area isn't affected by fallen leaves and can be tidied easily.

It is worth noting that uncomposted bark products set off a chain reaction, stimulating bacterial and fungi activity in the soil, which uses nitrogen from the mulch. This process is known as "nitrogen drawdown," but you are able to combat it by applying a fertilizer that is high in nitrogen to the soil before mulching.

Applying mulch

Always apply mulch to a moist garden, preferably after rain; never apply it to a dry garden. Also, make sure the garden beds are weed-free, and that you leave a clear space around the trunks of tree and plant stems; otherwise rot can set in as a result of the moisture content.

How thickly you lay the mulch will depend on the type you use, but generally a good layer of 1 to 2.5 in. (2 to 6 cm) will be adequate. Finer mulches break down more quickly than the coarser ones and will need to be reapplied more frequently — perhaps once or twice each year.

Compost is best dug into the garden rather than applied as a mulch.

Mulches

There are many attractive types of organic and inorganic mulch to choose from.

1 **Leaf mulch** — a mixture of trunk and branch chips and leaves.
2 **Woodchip** — inexpensive and durable but not as attractive as fine pine bark.
3 **Lucerne** — available either in compressed layers of "mats" or as finely chopped pieces. (To avoid respiratory problems with the fine particles, wear a mask and also lightly dampen the mulch before applying it.)
4 **Pulverized cypress bark** — naturally termite-resistant with long-lasting color.
5 **Red woodchip** — woodchip colored with environmentally friendly dye.
6 **Tea-tree mulch** — attractive, fine, dark mulch, which is great for contrast in natural and native gardens.
7 **Fine pine bark** — an aesthetically pleasing, premium product that is slow to break down.
8 **River pebbles** (¾ in.)(20 mm) — come in a range of colors, from light gray to dark brown, and look good in native or natural gardens. Quartz pebbles are an alternative.
9 **Organic garden soil mix** — made up of mushroom compost, sand, soil, ash and chicken manure. Dig it into existing garden beds or use it to create new planting areas.

Cultivation

Choosing healthy plants, preparing the soil to suit their needs and giving them the appropriate care and maintenance will result in a thriving herb garden that will supply you with useful plants for cooking, natural beauty products, medicinal preparations and many uses around the home.

Kick-start a garden bed or potted display by purchasing maturing, flowering herbs in pots.

When to plant

The best time to plant depends on your climate. In general, planting times are divided into two seasons — warm and cool. The warmer months of spring and summer fall between September and February, while the cooler months of autumn and winter fall between March and October.

From year to year, these times may vary slightly, from a couple of weeks to a month, depending on the weather, with the limiting factor being the temperature — or more specifically, frost. In tropical locations, where many plants can be grown all year round in the hot and humid conditions, the overriding factor is rain. In such climates, the seasons are divided into wet or dry, and the best time for planting is during the wet season.

Plants themselves fall within two groups — frost-tender (including tropical and warm-temperate plants) and frost-hardy (cool-temperate and cold-hardy). If you live in a warm- or cool-temperate climate, you should determine when the first and last frosts are likely to occur and plant accordingly.

Plant frost-tender plants about two weeks after the last cold snap. In frost-prone areas, a good alternative planting method is to start seeds off indoors and then transplant the seedlings into the garden later.

Buying herbs at nurseries

At reputable nurseries and retail garden centers you'll find large display benches filled with lush, edible herbs of all shapes and sizes. You can select from annual or perennial seedlings in flats, or almost ready-to-eat plants in larger pots. It's good to see what's in season and check out other perennial herbs, shrubs and trees, such as salvias, lavender and bay trees — and companion plants.

You may be tempted to select young plants that look like they're maturing well, perhaps even flowering, but if this is the case, they have probably outgrown their pots. Smaller, immature seedlings will become healthier plants.

Before you buy, check that the herbs have healthy roots and are not pot-bound. Once the roots are tightly compressed, curled around the inside of a container and poking out the bottom, there is no guarantee they will grow well once you plant them in the garden.

And while you're at the garden center or nursery, ask for advice if you need to. Horticulturalists are employed to share

Once you've made your choice at the nursery, check for pests and even growth before buying.

Some of the taller-growing perennial herbs, such as some salvias, require pruning and staking, otherwise they become leggy and look unattractive.

their gardening knowledge with their customers and help them make the best choices, so don't hesitate to ask questions. You'll build a friendly, useful relationship with the staff in the process.

As soon as you get your purchases home, give them a good soak in a bucket of water for a couple of hours to ensure the rootball gets a thorough watering before planting.

Gently ease the herb out of its pot and check that the root system is healthy, not pot-bound.

Mail-order plants

Some herbs are hard to find at general nurseries, so you may have to buy them from specialist growers, who usually offer a mail-order service. The Internet is a great place to start your search.

Once you've placed your order, it's exciting to wait for the arrival of your precious package. Plants are packed in various ways, but they will usually be grown beyond seedling stage, but not to maturity, and will be sent in a sturdy cardboard box.

The roots and soil may be encased in plastic wrap or in tube stock pots, and secured with protective material to stop the potting mix from coming loose. Alternatively, you may receive only the roots — as with turmeric and ginger — or the cloves, as with elephant garlic.

They will survive for a day or two, but you'll need to unpack them soon after arrival and place them in a sheltered area that receives filtered light for several days until they acclimatize to your location.

To minimize transplant shock, water your plants with a weak solution of liquid fertilizer and a seaweed solution.

Preparing garden beds

Before transplanting or buying plants, prepare the areas in which they are going to be grown; these may be existing beds or newly created areas. To achieve the best results, remove any weeds and dig over the soil until it's loose, so the new roots can stretch out and grow unimpeded. It's also a good idea to improve the soil and its water retention and drainage with some organic matter.

Once you've prepared the site, start planting your herbs. Some herbs benefit from added nutrients in the soil, so give them a good start in their new environment by adding a slow-release fertilizer into your beds. Other herbs — such as anise, sweet basil and the various lavenders — like an application of lime.

For free plants, join a seed-swapping group, or exchange herbs with a friend.

Fertilizing

For healthy growth, plants need the right balance of nutrients, applied as fertilizers. These are sold on nursery shelves under a myriad of descriptions, and you'll probably find there's something for palms, herbs, roses, citrus trees, indoor plants and much more. You can add fertilizers to the soil so they're absorbed through the plant roots, or you can apply them as a foliar spray to the leaves.

Determine which plants you want to fertilize and find out a little about the chemical makeup of basic fertilizers to make sure you choose the right one.

Balancing the elements

The best fertilizer to choose is one that offers a bit of everything. This is known as a "balanced fertilizer," which you can use in various ways.

- Add it at the time of planting.
- Sprinkle it around garden beds as a seasonal top-up.
- Apply it as a weak, soluble solution to young seedlings or as a booster throughout the growing seasons.

Nutrient deficiencies

Well-balanced soils play an important role in ensuring that nutrients in the soil are being released and made available to plants. Adding more fertilizer will not necessarily resolve the long-term problem, but improving the soil will.

Nutrient deficiencies manifest themselves in various ways: distorted or stunted growth, yellow or mottled leaves, scorched leaf edges, premature maturity of fruit, dieback or poor root growth.

Some deficiencies are common to certain types of plants. For example, fruit trees with yellowing leaves and green veins benefit at times from chelated iron, while the older leaves of gardenias that are yellowing or browning around the outer part usually need the help of an old garden remedy — a combination of magnesium and Epsom salts (magnesium sulphate) dissolved in water.

Other symptoms might require more investigation. Take a cutting to your local nursery for horticultural advice, join a garden club, read gardening books or search the Internet.

Keep your herb cuttings out of direct sun until the roots have grown, then plant them out.

Avoid watering when it's windy, because the moisture will soon evaporate.

Fertilizer types

Some fertilizers are produced from manufactured chemicals (synthetics), others from natural products. The natural products, such as blood and bone, are based on ingredients that include animal by-products and manures, seaweed, rock minerals and fish, which tend to slowly feed plants over a period of several months. Other products combine both chemical and natural ingredients.

Fertilizers sold in a dry granular form are designed to release nutrients slowly. Faster-acting forms are liquid plant foods, which are dissolved in water to give plants a quick lift.

Whether you go synthetic, organic, dry or liquid, the important aspect is the N:P:K ratio (see box at left). Always read the label carefully and follow the manufacturer's directions.

Seaweed solutions

Strictly speaking, liquid seaweed-based products are soil conditioners that increase plants' resistance to drought, heat and frost. They also improve their

---

Chemical elements

Chemical elements — primary, secondary and trace — play a vital role in growing healthy plants. Look at the pack, where you'll find the symbols N:P:K, indicating the ratios of the three major elements — nitrogen, phosphorous and potassium.

Primary elements

- **Nitrogen (N)** — important for vegetative growth (leaves, stems and fruit), making leaves lush. Herbs grown for their foliage, such as mints, need a higher nitrogen value (for example, 12:1:5).
- **Phosphorous (P)** — for cell formation and chemical reactions involved in growth and reproduction. It promotes root development as well as seed, flower and fruit production.
- **Potassium (K)** — important for fruit-bearing trees and vegetable and flower crops, because it improves the quality of flowers and fruits. It aids plant health, stem and cell thickness and the movement of water within plants, providing resistance to pests, diseases, drought and heat. For a good flush of blooms, flowering plants need a fertilizer containing more potassium (6:14:17).

Secondary elements

- **Calcium (Ca)** — needed for healthy cell walls and root growth.
- **Magnesium (Mg)** — a key component in the green coloring of plants (that is, chlorophyll) and therefore vital for photosynthesis, a process whereby plants use the energy of sunlight to produce sugars.
- **Sulphur (S)** — part of the flavor and odor components (for example, onions and cabbages).

Trace elements

- These are iron (Fe), manganese (Mn), boron (B), copper (Cu), zinc (Zn) and molybdenum (Mo), which are needed in only minute quantities.

---

ability to take up nutrients and improve root and stem development as well as the water-holding capacity of the soil.

Typically, the ingredients include molasses and humic and fulvic acids, which increase soil microorganism and earthworm activity, making them a wholesome addition to the watering can. For larger garden-bed areas, use a "hose-on" application.

Watering

It's helpful to learn a few things about the logistics of watering. If you give your plants a good, long soak infrequently, they'll search downward for water. This in turn encourages strong root growth, so your plants will be better able to cope between waterings.

Regular surface waterings, however, tend to produce weaker plants that rely on moisture near the soil surface, so they have a hard time coping with drought.

Drought, or dry periods between rain, render soils hydrophobic: The soil repels water instead of absorbing it. But you can buy products to reduce or eliminate these effects.

These products include soil-wetting agents that help to reduce the amount of water that's repelled by the "waxy" coating that forms on dry soils. The agents are much more sophisticated versions of detergents, which reduce surface tension. Choose from granules that expand when watered and then retain the moisture, or a liquid form that's added to water and then soaks into the soil. Both are also suitable for dry potting mix.

Watering options

How you water your garden depends on its size, how much time you have and the local water restrictions. You can install a rainwater tank, a gray-water system or an appropriate timer-operated irrigation system. Check with your local council and consult a member of a quality-endorsed landscape association.

If you water by hand, stick to early mornings or late afternoons so the moisture won't evaporate immediately.

Planting

Once you've prepared your garden beds, it's time for planting. Soak the plant in a bucket of water beforehand, so that it will abosrb moisture more easily. We planted tarragon, a perennial herb that spreads by rhizomes and needs to be replanted every few years. Tarragon likes a well-drained soil that doesn't retain moisture too long; otherwise the rhizomes may rot.

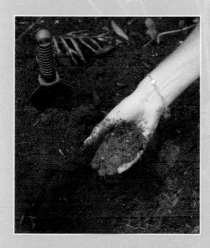

1 Ensure that your soil has plenty of organic matter, such as compost or well-rotted manure, then dig a hole that's larger than the root ball.

2 Tease out the roots and loosen the potting mix so that they will seek out nutrients and moisture from the soil around them.

3 Carefully position the plant in the hole, making sure it sits at the same level in the ground as it did in the pot. Don't cover the crown.

4 Backfill and firm down the soil around the plant. Tarragon can also be propagated by root division in spring.

5 Water the plant well, and then water regularly until established. Prune for culinary use and also to discourage woody stems.

Fillers and free plants

While you're waiting for other plants to mature and spread, plant some annuals as fillers. Although most annual herbs will need to be removed at the end of their life cycle, those that readily self-seed — such as catnip, nasturtiums and borage — will perpetuate themselves. With larger plants that self-seed, such as bay, remove any unwanted seedlings, then pot them and use them elsewhere.

When thinning out plants in the garden, think about giving those excess seedlings to a friend, novice gardener or school. Prunings from perennials can also be the start of newly propagated plants. For more information, see Stem cuttings, *page 163.*

Many herbs self-seed in the garden, popping up where you least expect them. Catnip, nasturtiums and borage, all shown above, keep appearing for years, as does heartsease.

Garden maintenance

Routine garden tasks, such as pruning and weeding, will not only keep your garden tidy but will also help prevent pest and disease attack, which often starts within decaying plant debris. So, employ good garden hygiene methods and you'll have less maintenance to do in the long run.

Pruning

Many herbs benefit from being cut back annually by up to one-third, because this not only makes them look more attractive but also promotes new growth in the following season.

Normally, gardeners are encouraged to prune back spent blooms on annuals and perennials after flowering, but that's not the case with herbs that are grown for their seeds, such as coriander, dill and fennel. Leave them to complete their life cycle. With herbs that are not grown for their flowers, pinch off their blooms to encourage leafy growth.

Removing spent flowers will prolong the flowering season.

You only need to prune trees if their branches are rubbing together, which can create open wounds that are prone to disease and insect attack, or if their limbs are congested, reducing light and air circulation. For low branches, use a small handsaw, but for larger ones, call in the professionals. Always protect your eyes from sawdust.

For regular stem pruning, invest in a good-quality pair of clippers, but for tougher stems and small branches, buy a pair of ergonomic ratchet or anvil pruners. If you regularly clean and oil them, they'll last a decade or more. On the other hand, if you habitually mislay things, buy the cheaper ones.

Always keep your herb garden weeded and well-mulched, and remove damaged foliage regularly.

Eliminating weeds

Garden weeds compete with other plants for nutrients, light and water, but you can eliminate or at least reduce them by following some basic garden practices.

If there is not enough room in the garden, weeds won't be able to grow, so plant groundcovers, such as thyme and mints, to fill in gaps and stop weeds jostling for position.

Hand weeding is still an effective way to remove plants, particularly those with rhizomatous roots. Dig up the whole root system, rather than pulling off the vegetative growth that's above the soil. And it's best not to put weeds with seed heads into the compost, or you could end up returning the problem to the garden.

It used to be considered good practice to smother weeds with sheets of ugly black plastic, but all this did was foster anaerobic conditions in the soil underneath, resulting in airless, slimy, smelly conditions. Weed mat is a much better alternative, because it allows air as well as moisture through.

Using herbicides

Use weedkillers, or herbicides, only as a last resort or if you're preparing a whole bed, but be careful, particularly if you're growing edible herbs or there are valuable or favorite plants nearby. Always read the label and follow the manufacturer's directions carefully.

When weeding, make sure you remove the whole root system, not just the foliage.

Be responsible and choose the type of herbicide that's appropriate, effective and safe, and always wear protective clothing, such as a mask, gloves, boots and goggles.

- **Selective herbicides** – kill only weeds.
- **Non-selective herbicides** – kill any plant they touch, so use them carefully on a still day so the spray drift doesn't land on your garden plants. The most commonly used non-selective herbicide is glyphosate.
- **Systemic herbicides** – travel through the entire plant, from the roots right up to the leaves.
- **Pre-emergent chemicals** – are applied to the soil before seedlings have emerged to eliminate weed seeds.
- **Post-emergent weed killers** – are applied after crops have emerged.

Topiary shears are ideal for shaping herbs with compact leaves, such as this variegated thyme.

What is a weed?

A weed is often a plant that's growing in the wrong place – and that includes herbs. Finding the right plant for the right place can be tricky: If you plant hardy plants to cope with drought or survive in difficult conditions or aspects, they're usually the resilient plants that end up taking over.

Chicory is a self-seeding herb that can become a weed in the garden.

■ **Check** whether your chosen herb has a reputation for being invasive, then decide whether to grow it. The staff at your local nursery should be able to advise you if a particular plant is a problem in your area. An herb that's invasive in one location may not be in another area with different climatic or soil conditions. In addition, not all plants of the same species may be rampant, so look for alternative varieties that may be bred as sterile (so the seed won't be viable and grow).

■ **Plant** garden escapees in pots, either as free-standing potted plants or in pots sunk into the ground, so their roots are restricted. Keep plants in check by removing the flowers before they set seed, which will be spread by wind and birds. Regularly prune those with invasive runners, such as mint, and dispose of the cuttings responsibly.

■ **Ask** your local council or weed authority if your herbs are on the noxious or invasive list. Some to be aware of include horseradish, St. John's wort, yarrow, chicory and mints.

Propagation

One of the most satisfying aspects of gardening is growing plants from seeds or cuttings and then watching them flourish. Although some herbs require particular treatments, there are several methods you can use, and it's always worth experimenting. Annual herbs are best planted each year from seed, while many perennial herbs are propagated by stem cuttings, layering or division.

Sowing seed

Source seeds through plants grown in the garden, or buy seed packets sold through nurseries or mail-order companies or websites. Collecting seed from the garden is the cheapest way, of course; however, there's very little guarantee that plants will come true from seed, because certain herbs may cross-pollinate or simply not represent the parent plant.

For ease of growing, particularly for new gardeners, packet seeds provide good value and instructions that indicate when, how and where to plant. In addition, the plants will be true to type, and are available in the right season.

The required depth of planting will vary, depending on seed size. In general, the finer the seed, the shallower it should be sown; sowing at a depth of about twice the diameter of the seed is a good gauge. It is easier to spread fine seeds, such as marjoram, savory and thyme, more evenly if you mix them with a little sand.

When to sow

When you plant your seeds will depend on your climate and the advice given on the seed packet. If your chosen seeds take 6 to 8 weeks to germinate, start them indoors or in a glasshouse about this far ahead, before the final frosts. Once the good spring weather starts, the seedlings will be ready to transplant. Some annual herbs can be sown successfully in autumn but, to achieve best results, follow the packet instructions.

Sow seeds in cell packs or seed trays, in individual pots or in situ. Herbs that don't transplant well, because disturbing

Carefully remove seedlings from punnets by gently squeezing the bottom of each cell.

their roots encourages them to "bolt" (flower prematurely), are best planted either directly in the garden or in large pots. These include borage, coriander, dill, chervil, fennel and summer savory.

To add interest and color to paved areas, paths or retaining walls, fill cracks, crevices or nooks with potting mix and sow seeds of compact or trailing plants, such as nasturtium, sweet violet and different varieties of thyme.

Sowing seeds under cover

Other seeds, such as coriander and verbena, need to be in the dark until they've germinated. Block out the light by covering the seed trays with sheets of newspaper and store in a dry, warm place. Soaking seeds in warm water overnight before planting will also help basil and parsley to germinate, while other seeds need to be stratified. For details on this process, see Echinacea, *page 44.*

Once seedlings appear, prick them out. See Pricking out, *page 162.*

Seed-raising mix

The growing medium plays a critical role in plant propagation. The tiny roots of new plants need to be able to grow in a lightweight material that provides support, air pockets, moisture and good drainage.

Potting mixes are developed especially for propagation and are usually sold as seed-raising mix or propagation mix. The ingredients may include:

- **SAND** Coarse river sand, not fine brickies sand, is best for good drainage.

- **VERMICULITE** This lightweight silicate material has been heated so it expands, soaks up water and attracts nutrients.

- **PERLITE** Derived from volcanic rock that has also been mined and heated, it is used to aerate soil and improve drainage.

- **COCONUT FIBER**, coco-peat or coir. This is a natural waste product with excellent water-holding capacities. It is used in gardening products instead of peat moss, which is a non-renewable natural resource.

To block out the light while seedlings germinate, cover the seed trays with newspaper.

It's easy to forget what you've planted. Write the names on labels and pop them into the pots or trays.

Using the Latin name to identify your plants is the professional way to go. It ensures that, should you wish to grow the same plant again, you will purchase exactly the right one.

Raising seeds

Keep seeds and seedlings moist but don't overwater them. Seeds, in particular, need to be kept damp but must not be soggy. Once plants dry out, their germination will be stunted, or may even stop.

It is important to water the seed tray gently. Either lightly mist the mix with a spray bottle, or dampen it before planting. Alternatively, you can water the tray from the bottom so the moisture can be drawn up into the mix.

Fertilizing

Once seedlings begin to emerge, give them just a half-strength solution of an all-purpose soluble fertilizer. Later, once you have transplanted them, increase the dosage, but remember: More is not better; plants can absorb only so much.

Heat

Warmth is also an important factor for germination and, depending on your location and the type of seed, you can provide artificial heat in a number of ways. Try heating trays from the base with purpose-built electrical heat packs or heat mats, even hot-water bottles.

You can also purchase portable glasshouses through nurseries and mail-order suppliers. These compact PVC greenhouses are lightweight and easy to assemble, and come in various sizes so you can position them against an outdoor wall or even on a balcony.

Propagators are portable trays, like a mini greenhouse, and are also sold by nurseries.

Alternatively, place seed trays by a sunny window, in a warm kitchen or outdoors in a warm, frost-free location.

Possible problems

At this stage, you could experience a couple of problems.

1 Damping off is a fungal disease that thrives in cool or cold, damp or overcast conditions. The best way to prevent this is to keep seed trays in a location with good air circulation, light and warmth, although you could also try watering the seedlings with chamomile tea, an old herbal remedy. If a white mold appears, in spite of your best efforts, discard the mix and transplant the seeds or seedlings into new sterilized containers.

2 Seedlings become leggy when there is not enough light or the conditions are overcrowded. Simply move the tray to a brighter spot and thin out the seedlings by cutting the unwanted seedlings at the base. If you pull them out, you run the risk of disturbing the roots of the others.

Seed sowing

You will need

- ☐ seed tray
- ☐ bag of propagating or seed-raising mix
- ☐ various seed packets or collected seed
- ☐ piece of dowel or pencil
- ☐ plant tag
- ☐ spray bottle
- ☐ plastic wrap (optional)

1 Fill the seed tray with quality seed-raising or propagating mix. (For best results, use clean sterilized trays and tools that have been washed in a weak solution of bleach.) Gently smooth the surface with a piece of dowel or a small block of wood, but do not compact the mix. Using a pencil or a piece of dowel, create a shallow channel. Gently shake the seeds evenly over the mix or, if they are large enough to handle, drop them one at a time, spacing them according to the packet instructions.

2 Smooth the mix so the seeds are just covered, or use a sieve to add a light covering. Very fine seeds may not need any covering. Select the fine spray setting on the spray bottle and water the tray thoroughly.

3 Place in a warm, dry location with natural indirect light (each plant type will have different light requirements). To retain moisture and humidity, cover trays with plastic wrap or a sheet of glass. Add a tag with the plant name and date of sowing. Remove the cover when the seeds begin to germinate.

Pricking out

Once the first few leaves have emerged, move the seedlings so they receive more indirect sunlight and heat, and they "harden off." Thin out the rows by transplanting individual seedlings into larger containers or single pots. Use a small wooden skewer to gently ease the delicate roots out, then carefully handle the seedlings by the leaves.

Minimizing transplant shock

Here are some tips for easing your plants into the garden.

- Gradually 'harden off' plants by moving them into stronger light while they are still seedlings and before transplanting them into the garden.
- If the plants don't like their roots being disturbed, grow them in small pots or individual cells so you won't need to thin them out from other seedlings.
- Don't transplant — simply grow plants directly in the garden bed.
- When watering, add a seaweed-based solution to increase the plants' resistance to drought, heat and frost. Seaweed-based liquid products improve the seedlings' ability to take up nutrients, and they also improve root and stem development as well as improve the water-holding capacity of the soil. The ingredients include molasses and humic and fulvic acids, which boost earthworm activity and the number of soil microorganisms.
- Apply an anti-transpirant foliar spray to protect against frost and reduce the effects of transplant shock, sudden climatic changes, drying winds, water loss and heat. These products are biodegradable, and the effects last for several months.

Runners

Strawberries, sweet violet, mint and Vietnamese mint all send out runners that will take root wherever they touch the soil. Carefully lift satellite plants that have developed roots and plant them in a new position. Consider planting them in a pot to keep them contained.

Layering

With this propagation method, the herb is still attached to the parent plant, but the stem is encouraged to take root before it is separated. Use this technique with perennial herbs, such as rosemary and sage, in late spring or early summer.

Bend a soft, flexible stem so it touches the soil, remove the leaves surrounding the bend, and using a sharp knife, nick the underside of the stem. Secure the stem to the ground or pot surface using hairpins or several pieces of soft wire, then cover with soil or potting mix.

Water and keep the soil moist until the roots develop in 4 to 8 weeks. You can then separate the new plant and plant it elsewhere.

Some seed heads explode as they dry. Hang stems upside down in a paper bag to capture seeds.

Division

Another way to multiply plants is by dividing them, which is best done with perennials, such as yarrow, bergamot, tarragon and chives, when they are dormant, or just before new growth appears in early spring or autumn.

Dig up the plant clump with a sharp spade. You may need to loosen the soil around the plant first, then cut away old stems and leaves to determine where the new shoots are appearing. Either use the back of two forks to separate the clump, or a spade or sharp knife, depending on the density of the roots and stems.

Clean up the clump by washing the roots and removing dead foliage, then gently divide it in two, ensuring there is new growth on each half. If the plant is a reasonable size, divide the two new plants in half again. Some plants are easy to pull apart by hand. Replant new plants into the garden or in pots.

Stem cuttings

You can take soft-stemmed cuttings, such as basil and mint, in spring (after the last frosts) until midsummer, and semi-hardwood cuttings, such as rosemary and myrtle, a bit later, from midsummer to mid-autumn.

■ **Use hormone powder** — Cut a piece of soft-stemmed plant about 1.5 to 2.5 in. (4 to 6 cm) long and remove the lower leaves. Dip the stem into a hormone powder, which will stimulate new root growth. Plant the stem in a small planting hole in a container filled with propagating mix. Using a spray bottle, water thoroughly, then place the cutting in a protected position with natural indirect light. Make a mini greenhouse by cutting a plastic soft-drink bottle in half and inverting it over the cuttings.

Dip the stems in some hormone powder.

Recycled plastic bottles create an ideal mini greenhouse.

■ **Use a glass of water** — Another method is to place stem cuttings in a glass of water in a position with indirect light, then wait for roots to form within 1 to 2 weeks. Change the water every few days and then transplant the cuttings into individual containers or into the garden. Herbs suitable for this treatment include mint and sage.

Container gardening

With residential areas expanding and more people setting up home in cities, living spaces appear to be getting smaller. But no matter where you live, you can always plant a selection of herbs, whether it's on a balcony, deck or veranda, or in a courtyard — any small garden space where they can thrive in hanging baskets, pots and other containers.

A potted herb garden

Herbs love growing in pots, and some herbs, such as mint and parsley, spread easily and will take over garden beds, so even if you have a huge garden, it's best to contain them. If you put containers in the right sunlit position, use good-quality potting mix and give your herbs the care they need, they will flourish.

The best position

Many herbs, such as marjoram, fennel and thyme, prefer to grow in full sun, while others, such as catmint, chamomile and coriander, are happiest in partial shade.

On the other hand, a few herbs, such as watercress and angelica, actually need the shade. So, determine how much sun your balcony, courtyard or window box will receive throughout the year, and choose your plants accordingly. Alternatively, choose the plants you want to grow and then find the most suitable spot in which to grow them.

In hot climates, it's best to give plants some shade protection, as the heat can be too intense, even if they enjoy full sun in cooler locations. Another important factor is good air circulation; humid conditions can create fungal problems. Also avoid positions open to strong winds; a barrier such as lattice, can diffuse the breeze.

The right pot for the job

Before you buy pots or containers, think about their different shapes, sizes and materials, as these will play an important part in the success of your herbs and the design of your display.

Don't use lots of little pots, particularly in different styles and colors, as these tend to make small spaces look cluttered. You can still grow a variety, but keep it simple: for example, select a single color to pull one area together.

Herbs such as parsley, peppermint and thyme enjoy being contained, and look attractive spilling exuberantly over pot rims, so consider the shape and form of what you're growing and select containers that suit their 'personality.'

Choose containers that complement the location and its surroundings, pick textures and colors to match the area's paintwork, paving or surface, and go for the biggest container that's practical.

A wide selection of herbs, including sage, chives and apple mint, highlights their different shapes, textures and colors.

Checklist for success

- **To reduce moisture loss**, apply a seal to porous pots. Or buy glazed ceramic pots, which are not as porous as untreated concrete, terracotta or limestone.

- **If moving pots** is a problem, buy fiberglass or polyethylene ones. They're lightweight and come in many different shapes, sizes and colors.

- **Sit your pots** on saucers to hold any excess water and to stop tile or surface staining. However, make sure you give the roots a chance to dry.

- **To raise pots**, and make moving or sweeping easier, use static or movable stands on casters. Make sure pots are secure and won't move around on windy days.

- **Heavy or large containers** are the best choice in areas regularly exposed to strong winds, such as rooftop gardens and balconies.

- **Consider the scale**: a very large pot will look totally out of place squeezed onto a tiny balcony.

Stagger the heights of complementary pots or containers and underplant tall herbs with trailing plants that will spill over the edge of the pot.

Shapes and sizes

Round, square or rectangular, squat or tall, with straight or tapered sides: any of these container types is perfect for growing herbs, as they all allow for good root growth and the display of foliage and flowers. Varying sizes of the same design will give an area a uniform look.

Although they look attractive, urns and 'oil jars' have narrow necks, making it extremely hard to remove plants without damaging them. You could also find yourself with many plant roots and very little foliage. If you favour bell-shaped pots, a cylindrical shape is best because ones that taper in sharply may not provide enough room for roots to space themselves out.

Troughs are generally long and narrow, like window boxes, and are perfect for formal or narrow areas. Team them with a square pot of similar material to create a right angle, then add a round pot to create a point of difference.

Materials

The type of pot material will also affect both the look and the portability of your herb garden. Terracotta pots are popular with gardeners because they're practical, affordable and look attractive in most situations. Limestone and concrete pots, with their lovely pale colorings, are also popular, while alternative materials, such as plastics, are worth exploring.

In fact, the new generation of plastic materials offers a range of good-looking, practical choices. Polyethylene and fiber-glass (including marine grade) are most commonly used, as they're long-lasting, lightweight, waterproof and available in a wide range of colors. They can also be frost-, UV- and scratch-resistant. And, because these materials are not porous, they'll hold moisture longer than concrete or terracotta.

Experiment with unusual containers, such as old colanders and wicker baskets.

If your chosen pot has no drainage holes (many pots are designed for indoor use and don't have them), just drill a few of them into the base.

Potting mix

One of the most important elements in growing herbs successfully is the right soil or planting mix. Potting mix is better than garden soil, as it's specially designed for container conditions and will provide just the right balance between holding water and providing good drainage. At your local nursery, you'll find various organic mixes that are tailored for different situations, such as hanging baskets.

The best products have a 'standards' mark to indicate the potting mix contains extra ingredients, such as a wetting agent to stop it drying out too fast, vermiculite to keep the mix lightweight, and a slow-release fertilizer that gradually feeds the roots. The old adage 'you get what you pay for' is true here: it is worth investing in a good quality mix as, over time, you'll have healthier, happier plants.

Feeding tips

There are many fertilizers on the market. A good all-rounder that will suit most herbs is a "balanced" or "all-purpose" one: it will contain all the necessary nutrients to promote strong, healthy roots, flowers and leaves as well as help herbs grow into vigorous, sturdy plants. A soluble fertilizer is ideal for container-grown herbs and also for seedlings, which need to be fertilized regularly so that they will flourish. Always follow the directions on the packet.

If you notice that white 'salt' deposits (fertilizer residues) are appearing on the outside of terracotta pots, you can easily wash them off.

Add a liquid seaweed product to your watering regimen, as this is an excellent tonic. Apply it when you are first planting up pots and containers to help minimise transplant shock (see *page 162*).

Watering

While most herbs like to be kept moist, they also need to be allowed to dry out in between waterings so they're not left standing with constantly damp roots.

A good potting mix provides good drainage, while holes in the base of the pots allow the excess moisture to escape. Buy a colorful watering can that's easy to find, fill and carry. Keep it out of direct sun so that it lasts longer.

Hanging gardens

You can also grow herbs in hanging baskets (see Hanging herb ball, *page 306*). Those that have a trailing habit, such as heartsease, thyme, mint and

Vibrant petunias add a splash of color to thyme, lovage, chamomile and erigeron.

pelargonium, are ideal for hanging at eye level where you can easily see your plants maturing and enjoy their fragrance. If you hang baskets higher than eye level, you'll tend to forget about them.

Baskets are commonly made of plastic or wire. Line wire baskets with sphagnum moss, a spongy fibrous material that will hold the potting mix and retain moisture, or use a ready-made basket liner made from coconut fiber. Hanging baskets are prone to drying out in winds, so keep an eye on their moisture levels — another reason to hang them at the right height.

Re-potting

About every 12 months or so, give your potted herb garden a boost by re-potting or replenishing it.

Discard annual herbs and start again. Remove perennial herbs carefully, compost the old potting mix, and re-fill the base of the pot with fresh mix. Then trim the roots of the plants if they look congested, and cut off any old stems to give the plant a tidier shape and to promote new growth. Replant them in the container and backfill with fresh mix, gently firming it as you go. Finally, water the herbs thoroughly.

Planting a strawberry pot

It's fun to plant up a strawberry pot with your favorite herbs and flowers.

Buy a few more herbs than you will actually need. Experiment with placement and combinations of herbs to get a look you like. Then get planting.

Always open bags of potting mix in a well-ventilated area. Avoid breathing in the dusty particles, and consider wearing a protective face mask.

You will need

- □ large terracotta strawberry pot
- □ selection of trailing herbs (we used variegated and common oregano, thyme and strawberry) and an upright plant (we used fan flower).
- □ bag of quality potting mix
- □ potting scoop or trowel
- □ small bag of coconut fiber (optional)

1　Fill the pot with potting mix until it comes to just beneath the level of the first hole.

2　Carefully remove the first herb from its container; tease the roots out so that the surrounding potting mix is loosened. Gently ease the roots into the lowest hole in the pot. Fill pot with more potting mix, gently firming the inside with your hand to ensure that the roots are covered. Add mix until you reach the level of the next hole. Plant until all holes are filled. To stop potting mix falling out the sides of the pot, tuck a small amount of coconut fiber around the edges of each hole.

3　Finish by creating an attractive centerpiece, tucking potting mix around its roots. This final plant doesn't have to be an herb. For a dash of color, you could use a flowering annual or perennial. We selected fan flower (*Scaevola aemula*), but any plant with an upright habit will help to balance the composition of the pot. Place your strawberry pot in a sunny spot, then water well.

Companion planting

For centuries, farmers, gardeners and herbalists believed there is a symbiotic, often beneficial relationship between certain plants that grow near each other. By growing certain herbs together for protection, and others to attract beneficial insects, you'll be harnessing nature to grow strong, healthy herbs without chemicals.

Types of companions

Farmers and gardeners have practiced companion planting for thousands of years, and there are several different types of companion plants. There are "nurse" plants, such as climbers, which shelter tender herbs from the wind or sun; "trap" plants, which lure pests away from your favorite plants like sacrificial lambs; and "barrier" crops, which exude a chemical or oil that deters pests. So, when you're choosing which herbs to grow, consider which ones enjoy each other's company or provide your garden with a particular benefit.

For instance, you can confuse the pests so they can't find the plants they're seeking. Mix non-flowering herbs, such as oregano, with flowering ones that attract chewing insects — such as geraniums or roses. Planting a companion that hides

or protects beneficial insects while they feed on the target pest is another worthwhile strategy.

Place plants with similar sunlight or watering requirements together, and grow heavy feeder crops, such as cabbages, which need high levels of calcium, with others that don't, such as sage or thyme.

Nitrogen "fixers"

Leguminous plants — including peas, beans, sweet peas and lupins — play an important role in the garden. Known as nitrogen-fixing plants, they can absorb nitrogen gas from the air and convert it into a nutrient form through their roots.

Once they've matured, add legumes and garden compost into the soil to replenish nitrogen sources. This is particularly beneficial before or after planting root crops or heavy feeders of nitrogen, such as

Plant cabbages with dill, because it attracts beneficial insects (see opposite), or with sage and thyme.

basil and parsley. In other words, rejuvenate the soil by rotating seasonal crops with varying needs.

Nematode repellers

In the Northern Hemisphere, gardeners believe that if you plant marigolds, a chemical exuded from their roots will prevent nematodes in the soil.

Some practices may be folklore, others based on scientific fact, and what works in one location may not work elsewhere, so experiment with various combinations.

These leguminous plants are nitrogen-fixers. From left: lupins, snow peas and sweet peas.

Insect types

Insects are an important part of a garden's natural ecosystem. As plant pollinators, they both bring life and sustain it, and may also defend your garden against unwanted predators and parasites.

For example, ladybirds love aphids, and some specific types also feed on scale insects and mites. The larvae of common lacewings eat caterpillars, aphids and other soft-bodied insects, while the assassin bug injects lethal saliva inside its prey before sucking out its insides.

Parasites often lay their eggs on or in the bodies of their prey where, once hatched, they will feed off their host, eating them from the inside; tachinid fly larvae are parasites of caterpillars.

So if you spray your susceptible herbs with insecticide, you're likely to kill all the beneficial insects as well. If you grow your herbs organically, essentially you're letting your garden — a balanced ecosystem — regulate itself.

Natural herbal insect repellents

Many herbs have aromatic oils containing chemical compounds that repel pests, but you need to brush against them before they release their scents, which are usually pleasantly aromatic. These herbs are good to grow in high traffic areas, such as alongside pathways. Here are some suggestions.

- **Wormwood** repels mosquitoes.
- **Tansy** banishes flies or ants.
- **Basil** wards off both flies and mosquitoes.
- **Fennel** and pennyroyal both repel fleas.
- **Rue** deters cats.

Dogbane, a plant that can become rampant, is said to repel dogs.

Trap crops or lures

Using natural decoys not only draws unwanted insects away from your plants but also makes pest control easier: Once they've congregated on the decoy plant, you can destroy the lure (and the pests). Find out when the peak pest times occur and decide whether one well-timed growing period is all that's required, or whether you need to plant trap crops successively throughout the season to keep the pests under control. It's also important to know the life cycle of various insects so you can successfully break their breeding cycle.

Nasturtiums, for instance, are ideal trap crops to grow near edibles and roses, because cabbage white caterpillars and aphids love them (aphids are often attracted to yellow flowers). You can also lure tomato fruit worms away from their intended target by planting borage or dill close to your tomato plants.

Beneficial insects

Not all insects are detrimental, so find out which ones you actually need to deter or destroy. For example, some caterpillars might chomp their way through a few leaves, but unless they're rampant, consider leaving them alone — after all, they might transform themselves into beautiful butterflies and adorn your garden. So establish which caterpillars are doing the damage and need to be stopped, and which ones you can ignore.

The bee pollinates millions of flowers to produce edible food crops and ornamental flowers. Butterflies are also attracted by scented flowers and foliage. In the herb garden, these include hyssop, oregano and woolly apple-mint, along with echinacea, bee balm and the yellow daisylike flowers of marigold and tansy.

Grow butterfly-attracting plants to draw insects, such as the Monarch butterfly, to your garden.

Other choices include borage, coriander, licorice, hops, lemon balm, lovage, sage, nasturtium, parsley, rosemary, rue, sweet violet and thyme. Many of these herbs repel pests, too. For example, tansy wards off aphids, fruit fly, cabbage moth and cabbage white butterfly.

You can also welcome other pollinating insects, such as some wasps and beetles, to your garden by planting flowering herbs, such as dill, chives and fennel.

Be careful when spraying your garden with pesticides, so you avoid kiling beneficial insects.

Pests and diseases

If there's a problem in your garden, note the symptoms before you pull out the offending plant or pick up the nearest all-purpose insecticide. The problem could be caused by a pest, bacterial disease or virus, even the environment, and each requires a different solution.

Common problems

Familiarize yourself with the plant's condition, or take a sample cutting to the horticulturalists at your local nursery or garden center and ask them to identify the problem for you. Here's a list of some symptoms and their possible causes.

Causes of pests and diseases

Pests and diseases are usually the symptoms of an underlying problem. Generally, healthy plants are insect- and disease-free, so look at the basics first.

Problem	Possible cause
Irregular holes, chewed leaves; black droppings	Caterpillars or loopers
Meandering silver lines across distorted leaves	Leafminers
Discolored or distorted leaves	Thrips; lack of nutrients
Speckled dots on leaves and "cobwebbing"	Two-spotted mite
Flowers dropping off before blooming; brownish marks on petals	Petal blight (fungus)
Stunted, wilted plant	Soil-borne fungus
Stunted plants; yellow, mottled leaves	Mosaic virus
Orange/brown powdery pustules underneath leaves	Rust, a fungal disease
Sticky leaves, black "soot" and ants	Sooty mold (a fungus) growing on a secretion produced by aphids, scale insects or mealybugs. The insects are the problem, the fungus is a by-product.
Buds not opening; leaves twisted and distorted	Aphids

- Does the herb have sufficient light? If not, you have three options: Thin out the surrounding plants, move the troubled herb or plant something more suitable. Herbs that have become leggy and straggly are often reaching for more light.

- Is it being overwatered? Many herbs like to dry out between waterings.
- Is underwatering the problem? Watering can require a fine balancing act. Stick a finger a few centimetres into the soil or potting mix to check on its moisture content.
- Is the herb being neglected? Move it to a more accessible position, remove it or write yourself reminder notes.
- How often is fertilizer applied? Giving plants access to the right nutrients will produce growth and vigour when and where it's needed. Check to see if the herbs need an all-purpose feed or one that is specifically for leaf or flower and fruit production and apply accordingly. Remember that more is not better, so overfertilizing won't produce faster-growing or healthier plants. Always remember to follow the manufacturer's recommendations.

Insecticides and fungicides

Basically, there are two major problems you can treat with chemicals — insect pests and fungal diseases. If you have any herbs affected by a virus, you'll have to destroy them.

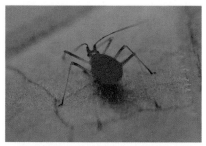
Leafhoppers are minute sapsuckers that damage plants and also spread plant pathogens.

Remove caterpillars by hand or plant "trap" crops to keep them under control (see *page 169*).

Female mealybugs are sapsuckers and protect themselves with an unsightly powdery wax.

To treat mildew, remove any affected foliage and also use a fungal spray.

Of course, it's much healthier to use natural remedies, particularly if you're growing edible herbs.

■ **Treat** insect pests such as mites, mealybugs, scale, whitefly and aphids with natural remedies made from low-toxic or potassium soap-based sprays. The soap coats the insect, which dies of suffocation and dehydration.

■ **Tackle** leaf-eating caterpillars of moths and butterflies with *Bacillus thuringiensis* (sold as Dipel). This naturally occurring bacteria will slowly kill most offenders.

■ **Pick** off larger pests, such as caterpillars and loopers, by hand.

■ **Control** various insects, including caterpillars, fruit fly, thrip, leafminer, sawfly and leaf beetle with spinosad, a natural product derived from a soil fungus.

A beer trap will attract slugs and snails. You can also recycle a margarine container.

■ **Try** plant-based oils (rather than petroleum-based) to smother insects such as mites, aphids, mealybugs, white fly and scale.

■ **Use** pyrethrum, a natural insecticide with a short residual life and low toxicity.

■ **Encase** an infested plant in a small plastic bag, tie it around the base, and pull the whole plant out (or just cut off the affected stem).

■ **Use** lures to detect thrips as soon as they appear in your garden.

Ladybirds devour aphids, scale insects and the two-spotted mite. This one feeds on mildew fungus and black mold on leaves. To attract them, plant some nettles: They'll harbor an aphid that doesn't attack other plants and that ladybirds like to eat. The ladybirds will then build up and attack other aphids.

Integrated pest management

An environmentally friendly alternative to pesticides is integrated pest management (IPM), which is usually available to home gardeners only by mail order. Certain insects are mass bred for their natural predatory habits and then released so they can seek out and attack their target prey. Some of the beneficial predators include predatory mites and lacewing.

Phytoseiulus persimilis is a predatory mite used to control two-spotted mites (or spider mites). These mites suck the sap from hop and rose leaves, causing them to mottle, yellow and die.

The Australian pear-shaped mite (*Typhlodromips montdorensis*) preys on most thrip larvae. Adult thrips create curling, deformed leaves or leave silvery-brown damage, deform fruit and leave pale feeding damage in flowers. This mite can be used for herbs that are susceptible to thrips, such as thyme and rosemary.

Green lacewing is employed to target thrips, mealybugs, greenhouse whitefly, small caterpillars and two-spotted mites and moth eggs.

It could be that insects such as aphids are carrying the virus, so perhaps you need to deal with the problem by using an appropriate chemical. It's also a good idea to go back to basics and check the plant's environment.

Insecticides

Formulated to kill only insects, insecticides fall into two broad categories: contact insecticides, which kill the pest after it makes direct contact with the chemical, and systemic insecticides where the insect ingests the chemical by chewing or sucking the plant, poisoning its nervous system.

However, the disadvantage of using insecticides is that they are very likely to kill beneficial insects (see *page 169*), not just the pests. Fortunately, over recent years, many changes have been made to the active ingredients used in insecticides,

and the more toxic chemicals have been removed from the marketplace.

At your local garden center you'll find low-toxic sprays that are less harmful to waterways, bees and other beneficial insects. Check with your local nursery so you can make an informed choice before tackling your specific problem.

Finally, take extra care when applying sprays to edible plants. Always follow the manufacturer's instructions.

Fungicides

These are added to water and used to drench the soil or saturate plants, thus treating a variety of air- or soil-borne fungal diseases. Add a wetting agent to help spread the fungicide, giving a better coverage. Using a seaweed-based product as a foliar spray or to drench the roots will also benefit the plant's health.

Harvesting, preserving and storing

Harvesting the flowers, leaves, seeds, roots and even bark of the herbs you've nurtured is one of gardening's true delights, and there's something just as special about gathering them in the wild. To make the most of your harvest, follow our tips for collecting, preserving and storing herbs as well as using them safely.

Safety

At best, mistaking the identity of a plant or using the wrong part could mean that your herbal remedy is ineffective, but at worst you could make yourself or someone else very ill by accidentally collecting a plant that's toxic.

Identification

From a safety standpoint, there's nothing more important than ensuring that you only harvest an herb if you are confident you know what it is. This is reasonably straightforward in your own garden, but can get tricky if you're collecting plants you haven't planted yourself.

Once plants are dried, it becomes even more difficult to tell them apart, so harvest and dry only one herb at a time to prevent different batches of plants getting mixed up, and always tag or label them immediately, so they're easy to identify.

Dried leaves should be brittle and easily snap in your fingers. Store them in an airtight glass jar.

Use the correct part

The chemical characteristics of different parts of each plant vary, and consequently have different effects on the body. For example, just as coriander leaves and seeds each bring different characteristics to a recipe, so too do the leaves and roots of the dandelion plant have different medicinal actions.

Before harvesting a plant for culinary or medicinal reasons, double-check which part of the plant you need to use. Once again, making a mistake could have dire consequences — for example, bark from the shrub called cramp bark (*Viburnum opulus*) is a very useful medicine, but the berries from the same plant are toxic and should not be eaten.

Harvesting and drying herbs

Freshly cut herbs add extra zing to your cooking and boost the refreshing flavor of herbal teas (see *Infusions, page 190*). But most of the time, you'll want to dry your herbal harvest so it's on hand to use when needed — regardless of the season.

Stored in labeled glass jars, in a cool dark spot, most dried herbs will keep for about a year. (Also see *Cooking, page 329*.)

For more information on the best time and way to harvest specific herbs, consult the *Herb Directory, pages 12–133*.

A cake rack is perfect for drying leaves, or you could stretch some mesh over a wooden frame.

Leaves

The best time to collect leaves is on a dry, sunny morning before flowering has started. Choose a time after the dew has evaporated, but before the sun gets too hot and starts causing the essential oils in the plant to evaporate.

Use gardening scissors or pruning shears to snip sprigs or stems of young, healthy leaves, or gently pluck individual leaves from the plant by hand. Remove any dirt by gently brushing the leaves, but don't wash them in water. Discard any leaves that look diseased or damaged.

If you've collected sprigs of leaves, strip the lower leaves from each stem, tie the stems together and hang the bunches upside down. Spread individual leaves out to dry — a cake rack covered with kitchen paper is ideal.

Keep the leaves in a warm, airy place away from sunlight, and check them every day or so until they have completely dried.

To ensure the best flavor in the dried product, begin the drying process as soon after harvesting as possible.

Hang bunches of flower stems, with their stems straight, where warm air can circulate around them.

Most of the equipment you'll need for harvesting herbs are everyday household items.

- **Sharp scissors, shears or garden knife** Help prevent damage to the plant by always using a sharp blade.

- **Gloves** Protect your hands from thorns, bristles and allergic reactions by wearing good-quality gardening gloves.

- **Basket** If possible, gather herbs in a tray or flat shallow basket, so you can spread out the samples, rather than pile them up. Avoid using bags or sacks that limit airflow or allow separate bunches of herbs to mingle.

- **Gardening fork** When digging up roots, use a gardening fork, not a spade or shovel, as it is less likely to damage the plant.

- **String** Tie bunches of herbs together with string.

- **Labels** The sooner you label your cut or dried herbs, the less likely you are to forget what they are.

- **Paper bags** Use paper bags for collecting seeds, and remember to label their contents as you go.

- **Rack or tray** Herbs dry best when there is good airflow around them, so a cake rack is perfect. You could also stretch mesh or netting over a frame.

- **Glass jars** Glass is airtight and moisture-proof, so it's perfect for storing dried herbs. If you notice condensation building up in the jar, the herbs may not be completely dry — remove them and allow them to dry further before storing.

Flowers

Collect flowers shortly after the buds have opened and well before they start losing their petals. Flowers that grow in clusters — for example, elder flowers, angelica and meadowsweet — and those with long stalks, such as lavender and roses, can be picked on the stem, but it's preferable to collect individual flower heads of others, such as calendula blooms.

To dry flowers, follow the instructions for leaves (see opposite) and hang bunches of flowers or spread individual flower heads in a place where there is plenty of warm air circulating over a period of a few weeks. Flowers contain high levels of moisture, so to prevent mold from forming, make sure the petals aren't overlapping on the tray. Once the flowers are completely dried, they should feel stiff, not limp.

Store dried flower heads in a dark glass jar, or use in a pot-pourri (see *Around the Home, page 284*). And once you remove flowers from dried stems, also store them in dark jars before they deteriorate.

Collecting wild herbs

Wandering fields, forests and footpaths as you collect wild herbs sounds rather romantic, but there are several important issues to be aware of before you start.

- **Identification** Identifying plants is a difficult skill, and even trained experts can make mistakes. Always carry a plant guide as a reference, and check both the photographs and the written description against each herb. If you are doubtful of a plant's identity, don't pick it. Prevent different plants from becoming jumbled or difficult to identify later by tying the samples into bundles and labeling them as you harvest. Make sure you collect the correct medicinal part of the plant, too.

- **Pollution** Many plants that seem to be growing in the clean, green countryside are actually exposed to large quantities of pollution, which can accumulate in their tissues and be passed on to those who consume them. Be aware that, in farming districts, agricultural chemicals are often sprayed on crops, and may drift to adjacent areas. Plants growing by the side of busy roads are constantly exposed to exhaust fumes. Even a patch of healthy-looking herbs that you discover in a country lane may have been sprayed with weedkiller just moments before you arrived. Wherever possible, gather information about any chemicals used in the area before you start collecting herbs, and always wash them thoroughly before using them.

- **Legalities** In some countries, it is illegal to collect plants without first seeking permission from the landowner. You'll also be in trouble if you harvest herbs in a national park, or if you gather plants that are endangered.

- **Ecology** Over-harvesting of wild crops of some medicinal herbs has resulted in them becoming endangered. The classic example is the North American herb golden seal, which has a deserved reputation as a potent antimicrobial remedy. Unfortunately, golden seal is a difficult plant to cultivate, but is one of the most popular medicinal herbs in America. Over many years, this has led to an extremely lucrative market for wild-harvested (or 'wildcrafted') golden seal root, and consequently the plant is far less prevalent now than it was in days gone by; its trade is now strictly controlled. You can play your part in protecting our herbal heritage by finding out which, if any, plants are endangered in your own local area, and leaving them behind. Even when plants are plentiful, it's good practice to harvest only what you can use immediately, and to leave at least a third of each plant behind to regenerate.

Harvest sweet-smelling elder flowers in spring, before the buds are fully open.

Seeds

When collecting seeds, the timing is vital. Harvest them in late summer in the short period between the ripening of the seed pod and the point when it bursts open to disperse the seeds into the air.

Keep a close eye on the plant, and when you judge that the seed pod is starting to ripen (its color will start changing from green to brown), cut the seed pods from the plant, taking plenty of the stem at the same time.

Gather the stems in a loose bunch, place the ends with the seed pods on them inside a brown paper bag, and use string to tie the opening of the bag around the stems. Hang the bag containing the herb in a warm, airy spot (see *page 163*). As the seed pods ripen over the following week or two, the seeds will be released into the bag for you to collect. When the stems are dry, scrape any seeds still attached to the seed pods into the paper bag.

If you're going to use the seeds for planting, you can keep them in the same bag, as long as you tape it shut and clearly label the bag with the plant name and the date on which it was harvested. If you're using seeds for culinary or medicinal purposes, they will have a stronger flavor if you store them in glass, but again, make sure you label each one appropriately. Avoid storing seeds in plastic bags, because they allow moisture to build up and can cause mold to develop.

Roots and rhizomes

Harvesting roots and rhizomes in autumn or winter maximizes the plant's ability to regenerate itself. Choose a time when the parts of the plant above the ground are starting to die back. That will also make it easier to identify them.

Using a gardening fork, dig out the whole plant and its roots. Carefully separate the portion of the root that you want to use, and replant the rest immediately.

Gently brush as much dirt as possible from the root. To clean more substantial

An Omani man taps a boswellia tree for the resin, better known as frankincense.

Freeze whole mint leaves or borage flowers in ice cubes and use them in fruit juices and cocktails.

roots and rhizomes, such as ginger and horseradish, scrub them with a vegetable brush; however, gently rinse finer and more delicate samples, such as valerian, under running water. Don't soak them, or they'll take up water and lose flavor, and perhaps develop rot.

Once the roots are clean, cut them into small pieces and dry them in the oven at a very low heat (120° to 140°F) (50° to 60°C). You may need to keep the oven door ajar to prevent the temperature from rising too much. Turn the root pieces regularly to ensure they dry out evenly; you'll know they're ready when they become brittle.

Allow the roots to cool before storing them in a dark glass jar.

Bark

It's easy to kill or injure a tree when collecting its bark, so in many cases it's better to use commercially harvested varieties of these herbs. If you do decide to collect bark yourself, choose a damp day, and use clean, sharp tools to remove it from the tree in vertical strips at least a metre above the ground. Never take a horizontal band of bark from trees or collect bark from saplings, or they will die.

Clean the bark to remove any dirt, and then flatten it out as much as you can before leaving it in a warm, airy place to dry for a few weeks.

Freezing herbs

Freezing herbs is a great way to retain their color and flavor. Although it isn't suitable for herbs you're going to use medicinally, it is ideal for culinary herbs with very fine leaves or a very high moisture content, and for those that lose their taste when dried. Good candidates include fennel and dill tips, tarragon, chives, parsley, chervil and basil.

For herbs you intend to use in small quantities or add to wet dishes, such as soups, casseroles and risotto, freezing herbs into ice cubes works perfectly. Rinse fresh herbs under cold running water before chopping them finely. Place a tablespoonful of the chopped herb into each segment of an ice-cube tray, add a little water, and then place the tray in the freezer. When the cubes are frozen, transfer them into a labeled plastic bag or container, and they'll keep for months.

Freeze whole bunches of herbs to use in larger quantities or in recipes that won't benefit from the extra water of the melted ice. After rinsing the herbs, pat them dry with a paper towel and tie them

Buying dried herbs

A wider variety of herbs than you could ever hope to dry or harvest yourself is available at your local health-food store. The more popular herbs are available in teabags, but while convenient, these sometimes contain a lower grade of herbal material, and tend to be more expensive by weight than loose herbs. Look for dried herbs that retain the color and shape of the plant and have a strong, pleasant scent. Reject those that are dusty, powdery or have little smell. See pages 328–9 for more information.

loosely together. Place the whole bunch inside a sealed and labelled plastic bag and store it in the freezer. The frozen herbs will become quite brittle, so before you use them, just scrunch the bag with your hand to break the leaves into pieces.

Another way to store chopped herbs is to freeze a large quantity in a small plastic container.

An ice-cube tray is ideal for freezing small quantities of herbs you tend to use sparingly.

Herbal medicine

Treating common ailments and conditions safely and effectively with herbs is an area of growing interest as well as the focus of research around the world. Find out which herbs have healing properties and learn the best ways to use them.

An herbal tradition

Humankind has been accumulating and utilizing herbal knowledge for at least 60,000 years.

The Ancients

Ancient Egypt, a center of advanced medical knowledge, borrowed knowledge from the Middle East and also imported many dried spices, herbs and fragrant oils from Mesopotamia. Its first recorded healer of genius was Imhotep, physician to the Pharaoh Zoser in about 2600 BCE. So great was Imhotep's reputation that he entered into Egyptian mythology.

As Ancient Greece rose to power, its medical knowledge was, in turn, built on that inherited from the Middle East and Egypt. Several famous schools of medicine evolved around its greatest healers. The earliest recorded Greek physician, Asclepius, was credited with performing miracles of healing; the rod of Asclepius, consisting of a snake wound around a staff, became the symbol of medicine that endures today.

Perhaps the greatest of all the Greek physicians was Hippocrates of Kos (b. 460 BCE), who deserves to be remembered as much for his sane medical advice on lifestyle as for his remarkable healing insights. Hippocrates developed a systematic approach to diagnosis and took a rational approach to healing, based on a profound knowledge of both herbs and human psychology.

While Hippocrates did not, to our knowledge, write an herbal, Theophrastus of Eresus (b. c. 379 BCE), who was a pupil of Aristotle, wrote two splendid herbals that encapsulated Greek herbal knowledge of the time. The herbals also included Aristotle's writings on botany, *Historia Plantarum* and *De Causis Plantarum*.

The Alexandrian School

The most influential of all the medical schools was the Alexandrian School, founded in Alexandria, on Egypt's Mediterranean coast, a great center of culture where Oriental and Greek influences met. The hybridization of the great medical traditions saw herbal medicine make many advances.

The knowledge contained within the Alexandrian School was largely encapsulated in the very influential herbal *De Materia Medica*, produced by Dioscorides, a 1st-century CE Greek physician. His herbal, containing some 600 precisely described medicinal plants, became the cornerstone of medicine for approximately 1400 years, as first the great Roman Empire contracted and then European learning stagnated.

Monastic gardens

During the medieval period, much of Europe's knowledge was guarded by monasteries and nunneries, which

In medieval monastery gardens, medicinal herbs and edibles were usually grown separately.

became medical centers not only for the religious but also for surrounding villages and travelers and pilgrims.

The gardens of the religious were usually constructed on a symbolic cross, created by intersecting paths. A number of specialized gardens were created within that layout, including cloister gardens; a physic garden full of healing herbs; productive gardens, each bed dedicated to a particular vegetable or herb; a picking garden to supply the church with flowers; and an orchard, where brothers and sisters were often laid to rest.

> *"Women with child that eat quinces will bear wise children."*
>
> Rembert Dodoens, 1517–1585

A surviving 820 CE plan for the model monastery, intended for St. Gall in Switzerland, reveals just such gardens together with plantings according to the list that was decreed by the Carolingian king, Charlemagne the Great.

Egyptian healers employed rhizomatists to supply their herbal needs from the wild.

The great herbals

The 10th-century *Glastonbury Herbal* revealed an extensive knowledge of herbs, while the *Leechdom*, produced in the same century, is an outstanding compilation of medical and veterinary herbal knowledge of the time. An extensive herbal was also produced by the preeminent medical school in Europe during this period, the Welsh Physicians of Myddfai.

The Norman invasion of England saw a refinement in the gardens of pleasure associated with castles and manor houses. Filled with fragrant herbs as well as flowers, they included plants such as the legendary *Rosa gallica* 'Officinalis', that found their way to Europe from the Crusader expeditions.

The greatest of the English herbals emerged from the 16th century onward. William Turner's *New Herbal* included no fewer than 238 British plants. But for charm as well as content, two others remain unsurpassed — that of John Gerard, physician, apothecary and knowledgeable gardener, who first published his *Herball* in 1597, basing it on that of the Flemish physician Dodoens; and also that of John

Parkinson, an apothecary and botanist who is remembered for *Paradisi in Sole Paradisus Terrestris* and *Theatrum Botanicum*.

Modern herbal medicine

The modern practice of herbal medicine, coupled with a fascination with culinary and fragrance herbs, has seen a great resurgence in herb usage and herb culture worldwide. At the same time, the complex interaction between body, mind and spirit is again being acknowledged in the field of holistic medicine.

An era of complementary medicine has come, and with it the acknowledgment that herbal medicine deserves respect in its own right.

Herbs in South Africa

In South Africa, 7 out of 10 black South Africans consult traditional healers. More than 700 species of indigenous herbs are harvested from the wild each year, and many are available in commercial preparations. Two popular examples are cancer bush (*Sutherlandia frutescens*), considered a good all-purpose tonic for HIV/AIDs sufferers who need to boost their appetite, and buchu (*Agathosma betulina*), taken for the treatment of mild urinary tract infections. Steps are now being taken to prevent the

Dried buchu leaves (*Agathosma betulina*)

commercial production of these herbs without any benefit accruing to the indigenous people (see feature box, Herbs in the future, *page 186*).

Herbs in Australia

The Australian continent includes a wide range of environments, from rain forests and cool-temperate moss forests to swampy coastal heathlands, eucalyptus scrub and vast deserts with sparse vegetation. Its ancient flora, descended from the great supercontinent of Gondwanaland, is quite possibly the richest in the world for both essential oils (a fire adaptation) and alkaloids.

Sadly, much of the knowledge passed on by the oral tradition of the Aboriginal Australians was lost before it could be recorded. Their techniques included antiseptic poultices, the inhalation of crushed leaves, sun-extracted teas and the chewing of various leaves.

At least 150 different species were employed in herbal medicine, including the hardened gum exudate of some *Eucalyptus* species. Known as kino, it became widely used by early settlers for diarrhea and the treatment of wounds. Pituri, a strain of *Duboisia hopwoodii*, was chewed and used similarly to coca leaves in South America, to dull hunger, overcome fatigue and numb pain, especially on long journeys.

Other species widely used included the antibacterial and antifungal *Melaleuca alternifolia* and some related species, and plumbush (*Santalum lanceolatum*).

Today, many aromatic herbs have become popular for culinary and perfumery use, including lemon myrtle (*Backhousia citriodora*) and mountain pepperberry (*Tasmannia lanceolata*).

Western herbal philosophy

The style of herbal medicine currently practiced in the Western world has its roots in the traditions of Europe and North America, but it has also adopted some key remedies from Africa and South America as well as from the practice of Chinese and Ayurvedic medicine.

Returning the body to balance

At its heart, Western herbal medicine retains some of the philosophies espoused by the Greek physician Hippocrates and his contemporaries more than 2,000 years ago. These teachings included the principle that a patient's diet, environment and mental state all contributed to his or her well-being.

Today's Western herbalists take a similar holistic approach to healthcare, prescribing dietary and other lifestyle changes as well as herbal remedies, based on the principle that the factors that contribute to ill health need to be removed in order for healing to occur.

This is an extension of their view that the body often repairs itself when provided with the optimal conditions in which to do so — another concept associated with the Hippocratic tradition, which taught the *vis medicatrix naturae*, or innate, self-healing capacity of the human body.

In many ways, this goal of returning the body to a state of balance is central to every decision the herbalist makes in treatment. Whereas the medical approach largely focuses on fighting disease and pathology, the Western herbalist mainly works toward optimizing the function of the organs and body systems so that the body can heal itself.

Of course, in all acute and serious conditions, medical intervention is entirely appropriate. The specific, targeted, disease-fighting approach is exactly what's required when dealing with dangerously high blood pressure, a life-threatening infection, a burst appendix or an anaphylactic allergic reaction — all of which require drastic and fast-acting treatment.

Gentle treatment for chronic health problems

On the other hand, herbs are often appropriate for chronic disease states, which develop over a longer period, and whose symptoms may be less well defined. These conditions are commonly linked with unhealthy dietary and lifestyle habits, and they often respond well to slower-acting, gentler herbal remedies — especially if healthier habits are adopted at the same time. By addressing these chronic states of ill-health, herbs may help prevent some conditions developing into more serious diseases that require acute intervention; in fact, disease prevention is often an important goal of treatment.

Digestive system

In order to restore the body to a state of balance, the Western herbalist considers the functioning of each of the body's major organs and body systems. Of central importance are the digestive system and the organs of elimination: optimizing their ability to assimilate nutrients and process the bodily wastes is a major focus of many treatment protocols.

The herbalist may also prescribe remedies that:
- help the patient cope better with stress by either building up or calming down the nervous system;
- enhance resistance to infection or allergy by supporting the patient's immune system;

"Cure sometimes, treat often, comfort always."

Hippocrates, c. 460–c. 370 BCE

Native American herbalism

It is said that when the Pilgrims arrived in North America, fewer than 90 diseases were known among Native American people, whose extraordinary fitness and vitality was noticed by European doctors in early Colonial days.

Native American healers were highly respected and played a valuable role in the physical and spiritual well-being of their society. They also had a rich herbal tradition on which to draw when treating illness or injury, and for midwifery and contraceptive purposes.

Today many of the remedies found in the Western herbalist's dispensary – including the very popular herbs echinacea, golden seal (below) and black cohosh – were first introduced to settlers by the Native Americans.

- normalize hormonal balance, relieving the symptoms of menopause or premenstrual syndrome and, where it is appropriate, priming the body for conception;
- relieve pain and inflammation; and
- support heart and blood vessel function.

Individualized care

Before determining an appropriate treatment, the herbalist considers each patient's individual circumstances and constitution. For example, in formulating a prescription for supporting weight loss, the herbalist may take into account factors such as the patient's bowel habits, energy levels, hormonal status and ability to cope with stress. This individualised approach to treatment — "treating the person, not the disease" — is the opposite of the "one size fits all" approach that can be characteristic of the medical or pharmaceutical model.

Combining science and tradition

To achieve these aims, the modern practice of Western herbal medicine, which is mainly based on the traditional practices of Europe and North America, has adopted an eclectic group of key remedies from Africa and South America as well as from traditional Chinese and Ayurvedic medicine.

Clinical trials

However, unlike Chinese and Ayurvedic herbalism (or, for that matter, the Hippocratic approach to medicine — see the box at right), modern Western herbalism does not incorporate a humoral or "elemental" approach to disease. For that reason, the herbal remedies the Western herbalist borrows from other traditions are rarely used in their original context.

The Western herbalist prescribing dan shen (*Salvia miltiorrhiza*), for example, is likely to be thinking of its clinically proven actions in angina and other heart problems, rather than its traditional Chinese attributes as a cooling herb.

In fact, Western herbalists are increasingly turning to scientific evidence such as this to validate their traditional knowledge. Notwithstanding that the scientific study of herbal medicines has to overcome a unique set of challenges (see Herbs in the future, *page 186*), the double-blind, placebo-controlled, randomized clinical trial has become the gold standard of herbal medicine research — just as it is in medical science.

Given that relatively few herbs have been subjected to any scientific scrutiny,

a prescription from your Western medical herbalist is likely to combine remedies that have been clinically proven with others whose use is based on traditional experience. In many cases, five or six different herbs — or more — are blended in one prescription.

Synergy

The prescription of combinations of remedies demonstrates the herbalists' belief in synergy — the concept that different botanical medicines work together to produce an effect that

is greater than any of the individual remedies acting alone.

Synergy also applies to the compounds within a plant, with Western herbalists believing that the whole remedy provides a safer, more effective medicine than its individual active constituents.

For example, aspirin, a salicylic acid compound originally derived from meadowsweet, sometimes causes side-effects of gastric bleeding, whereas the herb in its entirety does not, and even seems to offer some protection from the gastric irritation caused by salicylates.

The humors of Hippocrates

The Hippocratic school of medicine theorized that the world and everything in it — including the human body — was influenced by the four elements of fire, water, earth and air. In human, the elements ruled four fluids referred to as the humors, and these, in turn, influenced each individual's constitution and personality. Sickness was also blamed on an imbalance of the humors, and the particular imbalance involved helped to dictate the appropriate remedies to be used in treatment.

Element	Fire	Water	Earth	Air
Humor	Yellow bile	Phlegm	Black bile	Blood
Personality	Choleric (quick to anger)	Phlegmatic (lazy, slow-thinking and slow-moving)	Melancholic (prone to depression and sorrow)	Sanguine (relaxed and cheerful)
Health issues	Hot, dry conditions, eg. liver problems	Cold, damp conditions, eg. respiratory infection and other catarrhal conditions	Cold, dry conditions, eg. constipation	Hot, damp conditions, eg. diarrhea and other conditions associated with over-indulgence

Eastern herbal philosophy

The ancient practices of traditional Chinese and Ayurvedic herbal medicine, both holistic approaches to healing, are based on the principle of humors or elements and focus on creating internal harmony or balance in the body.

An ancient tradition with spiritual roots

Chinese herbalism has a history that can be traced back thousands of years. The most famous of Chinese herb books, *The Yellow Emperor's Inner Classic* (or *Huang Di Nei Jing*), may have been written in about 100 BCE, but its origins are even older: the emperor for whom it was named ruled from 2,698 to 2,596 BCE.

Since then, Chinese scholars have continued to document this complex and sophisticated method of healing, and traditional Chinese medicine continues to thrive today in mainland China, in other Chinese communities throughout Asia, and increasingly in the Western world.

The philosophy of traditional Chinese medicine (TCM) has its basis in the spiritual practice of Taoism (sometimes spelt Daoism), which teaches that human

1. Boxthorn (*Lycium barbarum*) 2. Ginkgo (*Ginkgo biloba*) 3. Chinese haw (*Crataegus pinnatifida*) 4. Ginseng (*Panax ginseng*) 5. Schisandra (*Schisandra chinensis*) 6. Dan shen (*Salvia miltiorrhiza*) 7. Bitter orange (*Citrus aurantium*) 8. Dong quai (*Angelica polymorpha* var. *sinensis*) 9. Qing hao (*Artemesia annua*) 10. Chinese date (*Ziziphus jujuba*)

beings should strive to live in accordance with the rules of nature and emphasise the importance of balance and harmony. In keeping with the Tao teachings, the goal of all healing in TCM is to restore internal harmony.

This philosophy of returning the body

> *"He who takes medicine and neglects to diet wastes the skill of his doctors."*
>
> Chinese proverb

to a state of balance in order to bring about healing is not unique to TCM — in fact, it is also central to the philosophies of Western herbalism and Ayurveda. But the methods used to achieve this aim in TCM are unique, and the concepts and practices involved can be quite difficult for Westerners to grasp, especially as they encompass not only herbal medicine, but also acupuncture, massage, diet therapy and healing exercises, such as qi gong.

The life force

The Chinese use the word *qi* (sometimes westernized as chi or ki) to refer to the life force that inhabits not only the human body, but also all aspects of the environment and everything in it. *Qi* is a moving energy, sometimes defined as 'breath' or 'air', which also has many characteristics of fluids.

In the human body, *qi* is believed to flow along channels called meridians. These are not physical anatomical structures like the blood vessels, but nevertheless TCM practitioners can identify their locations with pinpoint accuracy so they can insert acupuncture needles in any one of over 500 individual points, affecting the flow of *qi* through the body.

Yin and yang

Another important concept in TCM is that of yin and yang, two opposite but complementary qualities that can be attributed to all things. The familiar circular symbol made up of black and white tear-drop shapes, each containing a small piece of the opposing color, is called the *taijitu*. It represents the dichotomy of yin and yang by illustrating that any two opposites are dependent on each other, and cannot exist in isolation — each requires the other in order to make up the whole.

Yin is represented by the black segments of the *taijitu*. It is characterised as feminine, passive, dark, cooling and associated with night. Yang is depicted in white in the *taijitu*, and has active, masculine qualities associated with heat, lightness and daytime.

A state of harmony exists in the body when yin and yang are balanced, but a relative excess of one quality (and the consequent deficiency of the other) causes an imbalance that can lead to illness and disease. Herbs and foods are classified according to how yin or yang they are, and the effects they have on

the body, and these qualities are an important consideration in helping to restore harmony and health.

The five elements

Like several other ancient systems of medicine, TCM is based on a theory of elements or humors. Each of TCM's five elements or 'phases' — in reference to their cyclical nature — has different qualities, governs different bodily functions and can be influenced by different medicines and foods, with the taste of each medicine giving insight into which element or elements it affects. In addition, each of the elements — fire, earth, metal, water and wood — interacts with and influences the others in many ways.

Visiting a TCM practitioner

A TCM practitioner uses tongue, facial and pulse diagnosis, as well as your description of your symptoms, to determine whether there is an imbalance in the five elements, in the yin and yang of the body, or the flow of *qi*. The terms used can be quite bewildering to a Westerner, who might be puzzled to hear their practitioner make a diagnosis of spleen *qi* deficiency when they came for a consultation about their persistent headaches!

Depending on your individual needs, your practitioner is likely to prescribe herbs for you, and sometimes also a course of acupuncture. Chinese herbal formulas often contain numerous herbs, which are boiled together for up to an hour to make a traditional decoction that concentrates the herbs' flavors and medicinal actions. The full course of your treatment may be dispensed to you in a series of paper packets, each containing your daily dose.

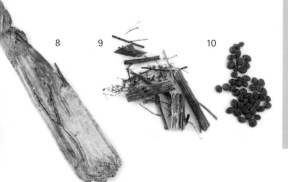

Ayurvedic medicine

1. Fenugreek (*Trigonella foenum-graecum*)
2. *Gymnema sylvestre* 3. Nigella (*Nigella sativa*)
4. Winter cherry (*Withania somnifera*)
5. Turmeric (*Curcuma longa*) 6. Brahmi (*Bacopa monnieri*) 7. Gotu kola (*Centella asiatica*) 8. Tamarind (*Tamarindus indica*)

Ayurveda, a traditional healing system from India, is an ancient holistic health practice with many similarities to traditional Chinese medicine (TCM). As with TCM, the aim of Ayurvedic medicine is to bring the body into balance. This is achieved through dietary change, the prescription of herbal medicines and also through meditation and yoga. "Ayurveda" is a Sanskrit word that literally means "the science of living," reflecting the principle that an individual's health is their own responsibility and that the physician can only guide their patients.

Again, like TCM, Ayurveda is based on a humoral philosophy, but there are three elements, called doshas, rather than five. You have all three of them in different proportions, and your constitution partly determines the ratio of each, but they are also affected by diet, climate and other lifestyle factors. Your doshas dictate your personality, the nature of the illnesses you experience and the types of food, herbal medicine and exercise that are best suited to you.

As with TCM, each of the doshas can be influenced by the tastes of the food and medicines you consume.

■ **Vata** governs movement of the body and mind, and the functioning of the circulation, nerves, muscles and bones. It is associated with dryness, cold and wind. When vata is low, it can be stimulated by bitter, astringent and pungent tastes, while sour, sweet and salty tastes help bring it into balance.

■ **Pitta** governs the power of transformation, such as the conversion of food into energy, and has moist, hot qualities. Associated with focus and concentration, it is stimulated by salty, sour, pungent tastes; sweet, bitter, astringent tastes reduce excess pitta.

■ **Kapha** is binding, provides structure to the body and governs lubrication — for example, keeping the joints from getting stiff. Its qualities are earthy, watery and cold. Kapha is stimulated by sweet, salty and sour tastes, and suppressed by pungent, bitter and astringent flavors.

Science of herbal medicine

Herbal medicine is both an art and a science, combining centuries of tradition with modern research methods and analytical techniques. Where herbalists were once self taught or learned their craft by apprenticing themselves to a more experienced practitioner, many are now university trained, and their study includes elements of a wide range of scientific disciplines.

The study of chemicals in plants

Despite still being regarded as unproven and old-fashioned in some quarters, the modern practice of herbal medicine is increasingly underpinned by scientific rigor and academic research, and gaining credibility as a result. Herbalists now study elements of botany, chemistry, biochemistry, pharmacology, toxicology and medicine.

Much of what we know about herbal medicine has been handed down through the ages. However, plants are complex chemical entities, and the herbalists of yesteryear could only observe their effects; they lacked the tools to work out why a certain herb works the way it does, or how it achieves its actions.

Today, the science of phytochemistry, the study of the chemicals in plants, reveals a much deeper level of information, which helps us understand how medicinal plants work.

Synergistic effects

It's quite likely that the combinations of active constituents in many herbs work together to create synergistic effects that are more powerful than any of the individual components acting alone. Even so, understanding the actions of the individual compounds helps researchers to make herbal medicine safer, more effective and more reliable.

In some cases, this type of research has identified new uses for existing remedies as well as potential adverse interactions between herbal medicines and pharmaceutical drugs.

Standardized herbal preparations

Unlike the production of pharmaceuticals, where manufacturing processes ensure each batch of medicine is exactly the same, the compounds in herbal medicines are subject to natural variation. Weather and soil conditions, the age of the plant and even the time of day the herbal remedy is harvested can all affect the levels of active constituents in a batch of herbal medicine.

To guarantee that each patient in a clinical trial receives a medicine of the same potency, many clinical studies are now performed using herbal remedies that are standardized to contain consistent levels of one or two key marker constituents.

High-quality tablets, capsules and liquid extracts for commercial sale are also made the same way — and this can be one advantage of purchasing commercial products rather than harvesting remedies at home or using dried herbs for infusions or decoctions. In many cases, but not always, the marker used is one of the compounds that plays an important role in the medicinal actions of the plant.

"The art of healing comes from nature and not from the physicians."

Paracelsus, 1493–1541

Major classes of phytochemicals

Thousands of different chemicals with physiological activity have been identified in plants, and no doubt there are many more yet to be discovered. Interestingly, many of the plants that have traditionally been prescribed for similar indications also share similar groups of active constituents. Some of the most important classes of phytochemicals are summarized below.

■ **Alkaloids** are potent compounds with very strong physiological effects, so herbs that contain them tend to be used in low doses or not at all. Alkaloids tend to affect the central nervous system, and some well-known examples include morphine and codeine from the opium poppy, which are central nervous system depressants, and caffeine from coffee, a nervous system stimulant.

■ **Anthraquinones** are a group of compounds with potent laxative action. Found in herbs such as senna and Chinese rhubarb, they stimulate peristaltic movements in the colon and trigger a bowel movement some hours later. These effects are magnified if the herbs are taken in overdose, and excessive use may cause diarrhea and the loss of important electrolytes. Anthraquinone-containing herbs should only be used occasionally, and only at the recommended doses, as excessive or long-term reliance on laxative herbs may render the bowel unable to function normally.

■ **Bitter principles** are substances that stimulate the bitter taste receptors at the back of the tongue. This is believed to trigger a reflex response in the vagus nerve, which in turn stimulates the production of various gastric secretions. Herbs that taste bitter have had a long history of use in stimulating digestive function in this way, and in many

traditional systems of medicine they are taken as tonics for the stomach, liver, gallbladder and pancreas. With its extremely bitter taste, gentian is one of the most potent bitter tonics, but even herbs with a milder bitter flavor – such as dandelion root – can act as digestive stimulants.

■ **Essential oils**, largely responsible for the aroma of herbs such as lavender, peppermint and basil, are often retained as one of many constituents of an herbal medicine. They can also be extracted from plants by processes that concentrate the essential oil, making it more potent, and enabling it to be used in aromatherapy, perfumes and foodstuffs. They commonly have anti-spasmodic and antimicrobial actions, and a number of mental and emotional effects have also been documented with their use.

■ **Flavonoids**, an extensive class of compounds found in many plant foods as well as in herbs, are responsible for a large number of beneficial effects. They have anti-oxidant properties and also a strong affinity with the blood vessels. Among their many actions, key flavonoids strengthen and maintain the integrity of the capillaries, stimulate circulation to the peripheral areas of the body and protect cholesterol molecules from harmful oxidative processes. Specific groups of flavonoids are responsible for the medicinal effects of ginkgo, hawthorn and horse chestnut, among other herbs.

■ **Glucosinolates** are sulphur compounds that are converted in the body into substances called isothiocyanates. The glucosinolates in horseradish and nasturtium are responsible for the anti-infective and mucous-liquefying properties of these herbs, while those in vegetables such as cabbage, broccoli and brussels sprouts are credited with helping to prevent cancer.

■ **Mucilage** is a type of fibre that binds with water to form an indigestible gel. Mucilage-rich plants such as psyllium have numerous benefits for the digestive system, including the ability to enhance bowel function and promote the removal of cholesterol from the body. Other mucilage-containing herbs, such as marsh mallow and slippery elm, are predominantly used for their soothing topical effect on inflamed mucous membranes.

■ **Phytoestrogens** are plant compounds with estrogen-like activity. The two main classes are the isoflavones found in red clover and soy, and the lignans found in flaxseed, some grains and other foods. Phytoestrogen-containing plants have been used in many herbal traditions for the treatment of female reproductive problems. In addition, the dietary intake of phytoestrogens has been associated with a number of health-protecting effects, including a possible reduction in the risk of breast cancer. On the other hand, consumption in excessive doses (above those normally consumed in the diet) is considered controversial by some authorities.

■ **Tannins** interact with proteins with which they come into contact, making the tissue tougher and less permeable. They are used to turn animal hides into leather in a process known as tanning. These astringent effects are utilized in herbal medicine to tighten mucous membranes and make them less easily penetrated by infective organisms, and also to reduce diarrhea, bleeding and other excessive secretions. Tea is the most widely used tannin-containing plant in the world, and its astringent nature can easily be felt by drinking a cup of tea that's been allowed to steep for too long and noting its drying, tightening effects on the mouth, gums and tongue.

These three scanning electron micrographs show: 1. Caffeine, an alkaloid. 2. Morphine crystals, another alkaloid. 3. Oil glands on the surface of corolla petal of peppermint (Mentha x piperita).

Herbs in the future

In the past, herbal medicine has sometimes been referred to as an art, practiced by people with a knowledge of plants and their qualities, but in the future, science, technology and economics will all have more and more influence on how it is practiced. Research is uncovering exciting developments in the applications of herbal medicines, which could lead to ground-breaking improvements in worldwide health problems.

Morphine, an addictive drug, is derived from the white latex that weeps from the opium poppy's capsule when it is wounded (see also *page 93*).

Unlocking nature's treasure chest

Scientists have long recognized the plant kingdom as a rich and bountiful source of potential medicines, and around the world researchers are systematically reviewing the chemistry of herbs in an attempt to reveal their therapeutic secrets. In some cases, laboratory studies will identify new compounds that have potential benefits for human health, and researchers will work to either isolate and purify the compound, or replicate it in a synthetic form to be used as a medicine.

This kind of research may seem rather speculative, but pharmaceutical companies have good reason to devote a portion of their research budgets to this kind of work, as many drugs already in use are produced in this way. For example, aspirin is a synthetic compound based on the salicylic acids found in meadowsweet and other herbs.

And there are exciting discoveries to be made: stevioside, found in a sweet herb called *Stevia rebaudiana*, is 300 times sweeter than sugar, minus the fattening or glucose-altering effects (see *page 75*).

Endorsing local traditions

Approaching the same goal from a different but equally rigorous angle, ethnobotanists explore the role that herbs and other plants play in different societies and cultures. The World Health Organization (WHO) recognizes that many people around the world rely on local traditional remedies for their healthcare, and that — particularly in developing countries — these are often more affordable than pharmaceuticals. In the future, ethnobotany will continue to play an important role in documenting these traditional practices so that their safety and efficacy can be evaluated and, where appropriate, endorsed by local healthcare providers.

Validating herbal medicines

The double-blind, placebo-controlled clinical trial is regarded as the gold standard for medicinal research, enabling unbiased statistical analysis of the safety and efficacy of medicines. As more and more herbs are subjected to clinical trials and proven to have therapeutic benefit, their credibility in the medical world increases, and doctors become more open to the idea of prescribing them for their

Appetite suppressant of the future

A medicine that successfully treats or prevents weight-related problems has enormous potential. The succulent plant hoodia (*Hoodia gordonii*), which has excited researchers, has a long history of use by the San people of the Kalahari Desert, who use it to help stave off hunger during long hunting trips. After preliminary research indicated that hoodia has significant appetite-reducing effects, scientific study into the plant and its safety is ongoing. It will be some years before hoodia's potential is fully understood, but if it does turn out to be the wonder weight-loss drug of the future,

the San people will benefit through a groundbreaking royalty agreement with the medicine developers. In the meantime, the herb is in danger of extinction due to unscrupulous overharvesting, and some of the products on sale in the United States and Europe are alleged to be counterfeit, containing little or no hoodia.

Each year, more than 500 million people become seriously ill with malaria; every 30 seconds, a child dies of it.

patients. Of course, clinical trials sometimes produce negative results, bringing the use of particular remedies into question.

Using clinical trials to verify herbal therapeutics provides researchers and clinicians alike with a great deal of valuable information, but there are some unique challenges involved in testing herbal medicines in this way.

The first hurdle to be overcome is that all the patients in the study should take exactly the same medicine; however, as they are natural substances, herbs can contain chemical variations from batch to batch.

Thus, the herbal products used in many studies are standardized, and we now possess a significant body of evidence supporting the use of standardized herbal products (commonly single herbs dispensed as tablets or capsules), but far less evidence of the effectiveness of more traditional preparations, such as homemade infusions and decoctions and compound medicines made up of several herbs.

The processes involved in creating standardized herbal products provide companies with a level of ownership of the research results, giving them more leeway to recoup their investment funds by claiming that their specific product has been clinically proven, while other non-standardized products have not.

These issues have major implications for the way herbal medicine is practiced in the future, and have already strongly influenced the prescribing habits of many doctors and herbalists, who prefer

Qing hao – changing the future of malaria

The story of qing hao (*Artemisia annua*), or Chinese wormwood, provides a snapshot of the way medicines derived from herbs may have a dramatic impact on the future of healthcare. In the 1970s, Chinese researchers seeking herbal remedies against malaria rediscovered its potential. Subsequent research revealed that the active constituent artemesinin is extremely effective against the malaria parasite, which is spread from person to person by mosquitoes, killing millions every year.

Today, malaria treatment has been revolutionised by artemesinin-based combination therapy (ACT), which pairs artemesinin derivatives with pharmaceutical agents into a single drug. As ACT safely treats malaria in just three days, WHO has endorsed it as the preferred approach for malaria treatment; thus far, it has saved millions of lives around the world. However, it is expensive, costing as much as 15 times more than the previous generation of anti-malarial drugs.

But economically, artemesinin has also proved revolutionary. In 2003, the medical charity Médecins Sans Frontières teamed with research institutes from Africa, Asia, Europe and South America to form the Drugs for Neglected Diseases Initiative, known as DNDi.

To date, this collaboration has developed two forms of ACT that are now in use in Asia, Africa and South and Central America, where, as the world's first patent-free medicines, they are changing not only the health outlook of communities affected by malaria, but also their economic prognosis.

A Chinese farmer carries stalks of qing hao, which contains the constituent artemisinin.

to focus on prescribing standardized remedies that have been clinically trialed.

It's also worth pointing out that the economics of scientific research are such that the herbs most likely to be investigated and "proven" to be effective are those for which there is the largest potential market. We therefore have a good understanding of the way the most

popular herbs work, and the roles that herbs can play in extremely common conditions, such as arthritis and heart disease. However, this focus on financially lucrative remedies may mean that our knowledge of more obscure herbs, and the herbal methods for treating less prevalent conditions, could languish in the future.

Using herbs safely

It's easy to fall into the trap of thinking that because herbs are natural they're also safe, but there are some important cautions you should be aware of. Always seek professional help if you suffer from a serious illness or severe symptoms, or if you are pregnant or breastfeeding, and if you're harvesting plants yourself, make sure you indentify the plant correctly. Finally, take care to choose a reputable professional herbalist.

Take the correct dose

The active constituents in herbs have the power to affect the physiological functioning of your body — some have a gentle impact while others are extremely potent medicines. As a rule of thumb, the stronger the action of the herb, the lower the dose required to cause a physical effect: Some herbs are so potent they are prescribed only in infinitesimal doses, because higher intakes are likely to cause serious adverse effects.

Our understanding of an appropriate dose for each herb is largely based on traditional and historical knowledge accumulated over hundreds of years and supplemented over recent times with a growing body of scientific study.

Always follow the dosage instructions, and do not exceed recommended doses or take a particular herb if there is a caution against its use in your circumstances. Seek professional advice before taking any herb over an extended period of time. In the majority of cases it is wise to seek professional advice before treating children or babies with herbs, because different doses may be required, depending on the child's age or condition. It is also important to keep herbal medicines safely out of the reach of children.

Identify the plant correctly

Identifying the correct herb to take as a medicine is not always easy, especially if you are harvesting plants yourself rather than buying commercially produced remedies. Plants that look alike sometimes have very different chemical makeups, and some plants from the same family have vastly different medicinal effects.

There are also many instances where the same common name is applied to several different species — for example, at least five different plants are referred to by the common name of balm of Gilead, making it very confusing, as well as potentially dangerous, for the amateur herbalist.

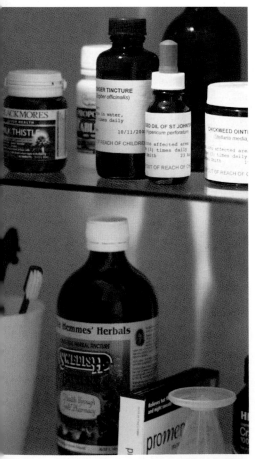

Like pharmaceutical medicines, herbal medicines should always be kept out of children's reach.

Herbalists overcome these problems by referring to plants by their botanical (Latin) names. This system of naming was developed by Linnaeus, the 18th-century Swedish botanist. The first word of a plant's botanical name refers to its genus — for example, all mint plants fall into the *Mentha* genus. The second word of the name refers to the plant's species, so the plant we commonly refer to as spearmint is named *Mentha spicata*.

Don't harvest or consume a plant if you have any doubt at all about its identity. Check which part of the plant to use before you harvest it, too — there is absolutely no point in collecting the leaves of a particular herb if the medicinal constituents are only present in the roots!

Avoid any adverse effects

Even when they're taken at appropriate doses, both herbal and pharmaceutical medicines can sometimes cause adverse effects, which generally fall into one of three categories.

• **Side effects** are symptoms or physiological changes that can be predicted to occur in a percentage of all users of a particular medicine. For example, herbalists can anticipate that a small number of patients who take valerian will report having vivid dreams, and similarly that some patients who take licorice will experience an increase in blood pressure. (Important side effects are listed on the relevant pages of this book.)

• **Drug interactions** may occur when a patient is taking two or more medicines simultaneously. For example, it is well-documented that the herb St. John's wort interacts with numerous pharmaceuticals, reducing the efficacy of the drugs. Given the vast number of potential interactions between herbs and drugs, and between herbs and other herbs, not all of these types of adverse effects are predictable, while others are well documented. The Conditions section of this book, *pages 200–39*, details major potential drug interactions where appropriate, but should not be considered an exhaustive reference on this important issue. If you are taking pharmaceutical medications, talk to your pharmacist or doctor before adding herbs to your treatment regimen, even if you are using them to treat a different condition.

• **Allergies** occur when the immune system overreacts to a substance that is otherwise innocuous, and can range from minor inconveniences to severe, life-threatening problems. Some herbs are more likely to cause allergies than others; however, the real reason that allergies are unpredictable is that the underlying issue is in the patient's immune system, rather than the plant itself. If you are an allergic person, take care with herbal medicines just as you would with other substances, and always patch test topical remedies before using them.

Deadly herbs

Hemlock (*Conium maculatum*)

■ **Hemlock** The Greek philosopher Socrates (c. 469–399 BCE) was found guilty of corrupting the youth of Athens and sentenced to death, so, according to Athenian law, he drank a cup of the poison hemlock. His student Plato recorded the effects of the poison, which started as a heavy sensation in Socrates's legs, gradually turning into a paralysis that crept up his body until his heart stopped beating.

■ **Mandrake** The root of the hallucinogenic poisonous plant mandrake (*Mandragora officinarum*) is shaped like a crude impression of a person, and has been associated with magical qualities since biblical times. As Harry Potter and friends learned in J. K. Rowling's *Harry Potter and the Chamber of Secrets*, legend has it that, when the root is unearthed, it emits such an ear-piercing shriek that anyone hearing it dies instantly.

■ **Belladonna** In spite of its attractive, glossy black berries, belladonna is both poisonous and hallucinogenic. Also known as deadly nightshade, its common name (*bella donna*, or "beautiful woman" in Italian) derives from its former cosmetic use, dilating women's pupils to make them more attractive; however, prolonged use led to blindness. It was also believed to be used by witches in "flying ointments."

Belladonna (*Atropa belladonna*)

If you develop any symptoms that could be due to an herb you are taking, stop using it immediately and, if necessary, seek medical treatment.

Choose a trained herbalist

Make sure you consult an herbalist who is appropriately trained. Do not be afraid to ask about their qualifications, whether they are a member of any professional associations, how long they've been practicing, or about the type of public liability insurance they carry. The answers to these questions may depend to a certain extent on the legal status of herbal medicine in your country, but should give you an indication of the professionalism and experience of the practitioner.

It is also important to have a good rapport with your herbalist, just as you have with your doctor, so assess whether you feel comfortable and confident with them. For this reason, many people prefer to seek a referral to an herbalist. If no one you know and trust can recommend a local practitioner, ask your local health food store proprietor or pharmacist.

Medicinal preparations

It's rewarding to make your own herbal medicines. Follow these step-by-step instructions to ensure you achieve the best results.

Infusions, decoctions, tinctures and syrups can all be prepared for internal use, while infused oils, compresses or poultices are more appropriate for topical applications. Some active constituents in herbs are readily soluble in water, while others require a more vigorous extraction process that involves alcohol.

Infusions

The word "infusion" is used to describe an herbal tea or tisane that is made by pouring boiling water over a quantity of fresh or dried herbal material. Every time you make a cup of tea with a tea bag, you are, in fact, making an infusion.

An infusion is an effective preparation method for delicate or fine plant parts, such as petals, leaves and other aerial parts. It is ideally suited to extracting water-soluble components from the plant and is often used for aromatic herbs that contain essential oils (such as peppermint, fennel and chamomile).

1 Place the recommended quantity of loose dried herb (dried chamomile is used here) or finely chopped fresh herb into a pre-warmed glass or china teapot or coffee plunger.

2 Pour about 1 cup freshly boiled water over the herb and stir. Place the lid on the teapot to trap the steam and prevent the essential oil evaporating. Allow the mixture to steep for 10 to 15 minutes.

3 Stir again before pouring through a strainer into your teacup.

Usage Drink one cup of tea three times a day over several weeks for chronic (long-standing) problems, or up to six cups a day in the shorter term for acute problems.

Storage Infusions do not store well, so it's always best to prepare a fresh pot of tea for each cup.

Decoctions

A decoction is an herbal tea made by boiling an herb in water. This method is most suitable for the woodier parts of a plant — such as the bark, roots, twigs and seeds — and is used to extract as many of the water-soluble active constituents as possible.

1 Grind the required quantity of dried herb (dried dandelion root is used here) into a coarse powder.

2 In a saucepan, cover the powder with about 2 cups (500 ml) cold (not hot) water; stir. Bring water slowly to the boil. Reduce heat to low and, with the lid still on, simmer for 10 to 15 minutes. (If your stovetop doesn't have a sufficiently low heat setting, use a double boiler.)

3 Stir again before pouring through a strainer into a teacup.

Usage Drink one cup three times a day over several weeks for chronic (long-standing) problems, or up to six cups a day in the shorter term for acute ones.

Storage Decoctions keep for a maximum of 3 days in the refrigerator. If you have the time, it's preferable to make a fresh decoction for each dose.

Chinese decoctions

Decoctions are revered by Chinese herbalists for their therapeutic effects and their versatility. They enable the herbalist to tailor remedies to the patient's needs, and allow the treatment to be amended as the patient's condition changes in response to the medicine.

The Chinese herbalist or pharmacist consults with the patient and determines the appropriate remedies to include in the prescription — the number of herbal ingredients (and their doses) is often larger than those used by Western herbalists.

Each daily dose of herbs is dispensed into a separate bag for the patient to prepare at home. The amount of water required, the boiling time and the quantity and frequency of medicine to be consumed may all vary.

Traditionally, ceramic clay pots with lids are used for Chinese decoctions, because chemical interactions can occur when herbs are exposed to metals such as iron, aluminium or copper.

Tinctures

Many of the active constituents in herbal medicines are readily soluble in alcohol, which is also an effective preservative. For this reason, professional herbalists use alcohol-based liquid herbal medicines to prescribe and dispense individualized herbal medicines for their patients.

For professional use, liquid extracts of herbs are made with a high concentration of pharmaceutical-grade alcohol (ethanol). Typically, 1 part of the herb is extracted in either 1 or 2 parts of alcohol.

Less concentrated preparations called tinctures are used for herbs that have a stronger taste (such as ginger or cayenne), and for those that are safest in very low doses (such as wormwood).

The recipes featured here use vodka in place of ethanol and a standard ratio of 1 part herb to 4 parts vodka. Note that while homemade remedies are often not as potent as the professional-strength remedies dispensed by an herbalist, they are still strong medicines and contain alcohol. Always store tinctures in a safe place, out of reach of children, and always observe the dosage guidelines, taking care that they are not consumed in situations where alcohol intake is ill advised.

Herbal tinctures are suitable for nearly every plant and every plant part, with the exception of mucilage-containing herbs (such as marsh mallow root and slippery elm bark), which are better extracted in cold water.

Different methods are used to make tinctures from dried or woody herbs, or more delicate fresh herbs.

Fresh plant tincture

Use a kitchen scale to measure out 1.5 oz. (40 g) fresh herb (thyme is used here), then wash it carefully to remove any dirt. Chop the herb into small pieces, then blend to a pulp using a stick blender (add some water to aid the blending, if necessary). If you don't have a stick blender, chop the herb very finely.

1 Add ⅔ cup (160 ml) vodka to the pulped herb, and then blend again before pouring the mixture into a glass jar with a screw-top lid. Seal the bottle tightly and shake vigorously.

2 Store the bottle in a cool, dark place for 10 to 14 days, shaking it once or twice a day. Strain the mixture through a piece of fine muslin.

3 Squeeze as much moisture as possible from the remaining pulp. Pour into a dark glass bottle, seal and label with the name of the herb and the date on which you prepared the tincture. Makes about ¾ cup (200 ml).

Usage Using a dropper, dispense the required dose into ¼ cup (60 ml) water before drinking (this is usually taken three times daily).

Storage Refrigerate and store for 6 to 12 months. Make sure it is stored safely out of reach of children.

Dried herb tincture

1 Weigh 1.5 oz. (40 g) dried herb. Chop or grind into a coarse powder to create a larger surface area; this allows for greater penetration of the liquid. (Cinnamon quills, used here, have a large surface area so do not need chopping.) Place the herb in a large glass jar with a secure lid and pour ²⁄₃ cup (160 ml) vodka over it, ensuring that the herb is completely submerged. Stand the bottle in a warm place for 10 to 14 days, shaking it once or twice a day.

2 Strain the mixture through a piece of fine muslin. Squeeze as much moisture as possible from the remaining pulp.

3 Pour the tincture into a dark glass bottle. Seal and label with the name of the herb and the date you prepared the tincture. Makes about ³⁄₄ cup (200 ml).

Usage Using a dropper, dispense the required dose into ¹⁄₄ cup (60 ml) water before drinking (usually three times daily).

Storage Refrigerate and store for 6 to 12 months. Make sure it is stored safely out of reach of children.

Herbal creams

Herbal creams help to relieve itchy skin, soothe burns and irritations, relax tense muscles, encourage wound healing and treat infection.

To make medicated herbal creams at home, start with an unscented non-greasy cream base, such as sorbolene or vitamin E cream. Add some herbal tincture, using a ratio of 1 part tincture to 10 parts cream, or essential oil at 1 to 2 percent the weight of your base cream. Stir until your cream has an even consistency. (Some essential oils are unsuitable for topical use, so seek professional advice if you are not sure.)

Homemade herbal creams have a short life span, so make a small quantity as you need it and use it up quickly. To help extend the shelf-life, add a few drops of lavender essential oil or the contents of some vitamin E capsules.

Syrups

Syrups are mostly used to ease coughs and sore throats, because the thick, sweet liquid has a very soothing effect. Commonly used herbs include marsh mallow, licorice, thyme and white horehound. Although syrups can also be made using an infusion or decoction, this recipe uses a tincture, so the result is a syrup with a stronger medicinal action.

Cough syrup from tincture

1 Stir together ¹⁄₂ cup (100 g) sugar (or honey) and ¹⁄₄ cup (50 ml) water in a small saucepan over a low heat until the sugar is dissolved and the mixture is thick but still runny. Remove from the heat and leave to cool. Add ¹⁄₄ cup (50 ml) of the appropriate tincture; stir.

2 Pour the cough syrup into a dark glass jar and seal with a cork. Makes about ³⁄₄ cup (200 ml).

Usage Take the appropriate dose directly from the spoon without diluting it.

Storage Refrigerate the syrup for up to 3 months. The sugar may crystallize as a result of the refrigeration, but the syrup will easily become liquid again if the bottle is allowed to stand in a bowl of hot water for a few minutes.

Caution

Occasionally, when syrups are stored, fermentation occurs, so it's best to make a small quantity at a time and to use it quickly. Syrups are traditionally stored in bottles with a cork stopper so that the bottle will not explode if fermentation does take place.

Compresses

A compress is a cloth that has been soaked in an infusion (or a diluted tincture) and applied to the skin. Compresses are used to relieve headaches and pain, disinfect wounds and soothe tired eyes. Make a fresh one each time.

Make a strong infusion of dried herb (lavender flowers are used here), using 2 to 3 teaspoons of dried herb per 1 cup (250 ml) water. Cover and steep for 10 to 15 minutes. Remove the cover and leave the infusion to cool to a temperature that is comfortable to the skin. Soak a face washer or flannel in the infusion and wring out the excess water.

Usage Apply to the affected part. As the compress dries out, it can be resoaked and reapplied.

Poultices

A poultice is a topical application of a fresh herb, which is most commonly used to encourage healing of injured muscles and bones (for example, strains, sprains and fractures), or to draw matter out of the skin (for example, to help remove a splinter or bring a boil to a head).

1 Chop sufficient fresh herb (comfrey leaves are used here) to cover the affected body part. Place in a container and blend using a stick blender, adding a little water to aid the blending, if necessary. The finished mixture should be of a mushy consistency.

2 Place the mixture on a piece of folded muslin. Use a spatula or the back of a spoon to spread the mixture thinly so that the surface area will cover the whole area of the affected body part.

3 Rub a little body oil onto the affected body part to prevent the poultice sticking to the skin. Apply the poultice, covering the muslin with plastic wrap to keep it in place. To make it more secure, if necessary, place a bandage around the poultice.

Usage Change the poultice about every couple of hours, or, if possible, leave it in place overnight.

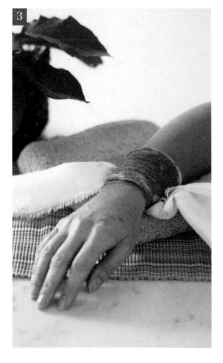

Infused oils

Oil-soluble components can be extracted by infusing an herb in oil over an extended period of hours or days. The pure infused oil is then used for topical applications or added to a cream or ointment. Medicated infused oils are similar to (although much stronger than) culinary infused oils. They are quite different to the essential oils used in aromatherapy, which are commonly extracted from plants by distillation.

Cold infused oils

A cold infusion process (shown below) is used for fragile or delicate plant parts such as flowers, petals and leaves. Among the most popular cold infusions are calendula flowers (for eczema and other skin complaints), St. John's wort flowers (for the relief of nerve pain) and lavender flowers and rosemary leaves (both to help relieve muscle soreness).

1 Pack a wide-necked, clear glass jar with fresh or dried herb (fresh calendula flowers are used here), leaving about ½ in. (1 cm) space at the top of the jar. Pour vegetable oil (such as olive oil) over the herb until it is covered to a depth of about ¼ in. (5 mm). Stir gently.

2 Fold some fine muslin and place on top of the oil. Seal the lid tightly and give the bottle a good shake. Store in a warm, sunny place for 3 to 10 days. Shake the bottle several times a day.

Filter the oil through fine muslin into a clean jug. Squeeze as much oil as possible through the remaining pulp. If any sediment remains in the oil, cover the jug and leave the oil to stand for a day or two until the sediment settles to the bottom.

3 Gently pour the oil into a dark glass bottle, taking care to leave the sediment layer behind. Seal; label with the name of the herb and the date on which you prepared the oil.

Usage Apply topically as is or add it to a cream or ointment.

Storage Store in a cool, dark place for up to 6 months, but discard at the first sign of rancidity or fermentation.

Hot infused oils

Hot infused oils are used for woodier, denser plant parts, and are used for plants with "heating" characteristics. Popular examples are hot infused oils of cayenne (chili pepper), black pepper and ginger, all of which are used to warm stiff, painful muscles and joints.

For dried herbs, use a ratio of 1 part herb to 3 parts oil. For fresh herb, the ratio is 1 part herb to 1.5 parts oil.

1 Coarsely chop or grind the herb (fresh bird's-eye chilies are used here). Add to a saucepan or glass bowl and stir in the required quantity of oil. Place the covered saucepan in a frying pan half-filled with water (or use a double boiler). Simmer over very low heat for 2 to 3 hours. Do not allow oil to boil.

2 Allow to cool before straining through fine muslin into a clean jug. Squeeze as much oil as possible through the remaining pulp. Gently pour the oil into a dark glass bottle. Seal; label with the name of the herb and the date you prepared the oil.

Usage Apply topically or add to a cream or ointment. Do not use oils from hot-flavored plants on inflamed or sensitive skin. Do not get them in your eyes.

Storage Store in a cool, dark place for up to 6 months, but discard at the first sign of rancidity or fermentation.

Flower essences

A cross between herbal medicine and homeopathy, flower essences are subtle remedies that gently help resolve emotional problems.

Bach Flower Essences

Dr. Edward Bach was an eminent researcher in the fledgling science of immunology when he gave up medicine in 1930. A firm believer that mental and emotional issues were behind every illness, from then on he devoted his life to identifying gentle natural remedies to bring the heart and mind back to a state of balance.

Bach spent much of his time in the British countryside, where he "tuned in" to the healing properties of flowers, and where he developed a system of preparing his remedies — or flower essences — that is still in use today. He believed the subtle energetic qualities of the plant could be captured by floating freshly picked flowers in bowls of pure spring water, which were then allowed to sit in a sunny place for several hours before he used brandy to preserve and stabilize the essence.

This concentrated flower essence, called the "stock" remedy, can be further diluted with spring water and brandy for dispensing to patients, animals or plants. The stock is also sometimes added to creams and ointments.

Dr. Bach identified 38 flower essences that are still used throughout the world, and their indications are summarized below. Rescue Remedy, the most popular of his creations, is indicated during any emergency, large or small. This combination of the five flower essences — cherry plum, clematis, impatiens, rock rose and star of Bethlehem — helps to relieve fear, panic, stress and shock, and is mostly taken by mouth, but it can also be added to a bathtub, applied to the wrists or forehead, or administered in a cream.

Building on Bach's work, researchers have developed ranges of essences from flowering plants that are found in other parts of the world, including Australia, New Zealand, South Africa, Hawaii and even far-flung places such as Alaska, the Himalayan mountains and the Amazon jungle.

Introducing the remedies

Here's a list of the Bach Flower Remedies and their main indications.

Agrimony helps cheerful people who are secretly troubled to deal with their underlying problems.

Aspen supports those who are anxious or worried, but are unable to identify what frightens them.

Beech fosters a spirit of compassion in those who are intolerant of people who are different to them.

Centaury helps people who over-extend themselves helping others to learn to say no so they don't wear themselves out.

Cerato boosts self-confidence, teaching you to listen to your own counsel instead of others' opinions.

Clematis (*Clematis vitalba*) may also encourage great creativity and make you more alert.

Cherry plum is for people who fear for their sanity, who feel they are heading for a nervous breakdown, or who are frightened they will harm themselves or others.

Chestnut bud teaches you to learn from your experiences, so you don't repeat the same mistakes again.

Chicory is for people who risk stifling their relationships by clinging too tightly to their loved ones.

Clematis brings those who are always dreaming about the future back down to earth to focus on the present.

Crab apple helps you to heal yourself of any feelings of unworthiness and uncleanliness.

Elm helps people who are overwhelmed by their responsibilities to feel able to cope again.

Gentian provides energy and enthusiasm after discouraging setbacks.

Gorse renews optimism in those who feel hopeless, and enables them to see the positive steps they can take.

Star of Bethlehem (*Ornithogalum umbellatum*) is a perennial bulbous plant with a delicate flower.

Cherry plum (*Prunus cerasifera*) in blossom

Heather helps self-centered people who constantly seek attention from others to become less needy.

Holly helps release feelings of anger, aggression, jealousy and hatred, and encourages a positive, open outlook.

Honeysuckle is for people who are stuck in the past, reliving either their past mistakes or past happiness.

Hornbeam supports people who procrastinate because they are so overwhelmed by the tasks before them that they feel exhausted before they begin.

Impatiens is for critical, irritable or impulsive people who are easily frustrated by the slowness of others.

Larch builds self-confidence in those people who consider themselves inferior to others, and helps overcome an expectation of failure.

Mimulus helps heal fears and phobias, ranging from anxiety about public speaking to fear of illness or death.

Mustard brings clarity and light during times of despair and despondency.

Oak helps determined, driven people to realize when it is time to sit back and take a rest, or perhaps to realize that their goal is neither achievable nor worth striving for.

Olive brings renewed energy to those who are exhausted by struggle and ready to give up.

Pine is for those who feel guilty about their own perceived past failings, and always feel they could have done better.

Red chestnut releases excessive anxiety or fear for the well-being of others.

Rock rose brings calm during times of terror, panic or extreme fear.

Rock water is for those who deny themselves pleasure in favor of some higher goal and feel a failure when they cannot maintain their own impossibly high standards.

Scleranthus helps people who question themselves when making decisions to instead feel confident in their convictions.

Star of Bethlehem heals feelings of shock, regardless of whether the unpleasant event occurred recently or in the distant past.

Australian and South African flower essences

More than 65 essences are made from the flora of the Australian wilderness. Many Australian plants are unique in the world, and according to the manufacturers of the Australian Bush Flower Essences, these remedies draw on the wisdom of this ancient landscape to promote lasting emotional change.

The extensive range includes Sturt Desert pea for sadness and deep emotional pain, sunshine wattle to help people who are struggling with negativity to return to a positive outlook, and old man banksia to reenergize those who have become lethargic due to frustrations and setbacks.

Like the Bach Flower Remedies, the Australian Bush Flower Essences are created by "tuning in" to each plant's energetic qualities in its natural bushland setting. These energies are then captured and transferred to a liquid remedy that can be taken orally or added to creams.

Also available is a range of South African flower essences, which include agapanthus, blushing bride, keurtjie, nicotiana, sour fig and silverleaf.

Sturt Desert pea (*Swainsona formosa*) has been proven to help alleviate deep emotional pain.

Sweet chestnut strengthens those who feel they are in a hopeless situation and cannot go on.

Vervain brings flexibility and detachment to people who zealously try to convert others to their own beliefs, and who can become quite worked up by their own efforts.

Vine eases the need to dominate and control, and is for those who are prone to aggression and the abuse of power.

Walnut eases you through times of change and helps you confidently stand your ground when those around you have different opinions.

Water violet helps isolated or aloof people to reconnect with others.

White chestnut calms an overly busy mind, helping to settle circular or repetitive thoughts and allowing concentration and focus to return.

Wild oat helps those who can't decide their direction in life to identify their path.

Wild rose rekindles motivation in people who no longer strive for change because they have become resigned to their particular lot in life.

Willow helps people who feel overly sorry for themselves and resent the success and happiness of others to return to a more positive outlook.

Medicinal herbs

Modern botanical medicine has become truly international, and herbalists now have access to the most effective herbs from all corners of the globe.

Dang shen is the Chinese name for the herb known in English as bonnet bellflower.

Albizia
Albizia lebbeck
Part used Stem bark

The traditional Ayurvedic applications for albizia include a range of inflammatory and allergic skin and respiratory conditions, and laboratory research indicates that it does indeed have anti-allergic properties. It appears to have particular benefits for mast cells, which play a major role in allergic reactions, so it may help some people become less sensitive to substances to which they are allergic.

Andrographis
Andrographis paniculata
Parts used Leaves, aerial parts

Andrographis features in the traditional medicine of China, Thailand, India and Korea. An extremely bitter herb, it is used as a digestive tonic in Ayurvedic medicine, while in traditional Chinese medicine, its cooling properties mean that it is indicated for dispelling heat and treating infections and toxins. Andrographis also has immune-stimulating properties, and is used to help prevent colds and flu and to treat their symptoms.

Astragalus
Astragalus membranaceus
Part used Roots

One of the most important *qi* tonics in traditional Chinese medicine, astragalus is taken to enhance vitality and increase energy. It has potent immune-boosting properties, so it may be prescribed to build resistance against infections as well as for more serious problems, such as helping the body's defenses cope with the trauma of chemo- and radiotherapy. Herbalists also prescribe astragalus for a wide range of other conditions, including liver and kidney dysfunction, heart problems and for aiding recovery from blood loss (especially after childbirth).

Buchu
Agathosma betulina
Part used Leaves

The South African herb buchu is mainly regarded as a remedy for the urinary tract, although traditionally it was also used to treat digestion and joint problems. Its volatile essential oil has antiseptic properties and is considered responsible for the herb's benefits in treating infections of the kidneys, bladder, urethra and prostate. Buchu also has diuretic actions, so it is indicated for fluid retention.

Cat's claw
Uncaria tomentosa, U. guaianensis
Part used Vine bark

Cat's claw grows in tropical South and Central America and takes its name from the shape of the long thorns that help it to climb over other plants in the jungle. It has been used for hundreds of years by Peruvians to treat inflammatory conditions, such as arthritis, asthma and skin problems, and is also a traditional remedy for infections, fatigue and cancer. Laboratory studies attribute it with a number of immune-stimulating and anti-inflammatory properties, which may be behind many traditional applications; little research has been conducted in humans.

Dang shen
Codonopsis pilosula
Part used Roots

Chinese herbalists regard dang shen as a gentler version of the more famous stress and energy tonic, Korean ginseng. This distinction means that it can be prescribed for patients who are frail or debilitated, for whom ginseng is considered too stimulating. Dang shen is also traditionally used for treating digestive, respiratory and cardiac problems (especially when caused by stress) and as a nourishing blood tonic for nursing mothers and other anemic patients.

Cat's claw has hook-like thorns, which enable it to climb other plants rather voraciously.

Devil's claw

Harpagophytum procumbens
Part used Tubers

Devil's claw grows in the grasslands of southern Africa and has been used there as a topical treatment for ulcers and wounds, and taken internally for fevers, allergies, digestive problems and as a pain reliever. Numerous scientific studies confirm its benefits, most notably as an effective analgesic and anti-inflammatory for arthritis pain and backache. Some studies have shown devil's claw to be as effective as pharmaceutical painkillers and anti-inflammatory drugs.

Golden seal

Hydrastis canadensis
Part used Rhizomes

Golden seal is named for its rhizome's characteristic yellow color, and it was used as both a dye and a medicine by Native Americans. It is still beloved by herbalists today, who regard it as a bitter digestive stimulant, an astringent tonic for the mucous membranes and a potent broad-spectrum antimicrobial remedy. Some of its most medically important alkaloids are also present in other plants (such as barberry and Indian barberry), and these are now largely used in its place, because golden seal has become endangered by over-harvesting.

The Cherokees pounded golden seal rhizomes with bear fat to make an insect repellent.

Each seed in the milk thistle bears a tuft of white hairs that help it to become airborne.

Milk thistle

Silybum marianum
Part used Seeds

Milk thistle has such a remarkable ability to prevent and repair liver damage that certain constituents are sometimes used intravenously to treat death cap mushroom poisoning. It is also employed against more frequently encountered toxins, such as alcohol and environmental pollutants, and can help digestive and cholesterol problems, thanks to its effects as a liver and gallbladder tonic. The best-quality products are standardized for their silymarin content, which is considered to be responsible for most of the herb's medicinal benefits.

Pau d'arco

Tabebuia impetiginosa
Part used Inner bark

In the 1960s, pau d'arco developed an international reputation as a cancer cure, but it had been used as a traditional medicine in Brazil for hundreds of years before that. Some of the herb's constituents have been shown in a laboratory setting to inhibit the growth and activity of tumor cells. An immuno-stimulant action that may further help the body fight cancer (as well as fungal diseases and other infections) has also been documented. However, extensive research will be required before its potential is fully understood.

Senna

Senna alexandrina syn. *Cassia angustifolia*
Parts used Leaves, pods

Senna's purgative action is due to its content of anthraquinone glycosides, which stimulate intestinal peristalsis, triggering a bowel movement some 12 hours later. Probably the most popular laxative herb, senna has an effect that is strong and reliable, if a little drastic. Habitual use may lead to "lazy bowel syndrome," in which the colon becomes unable to function without the laxative.

You can use dried senna pods, available at health-food stores, to make an infusion.

Uva-ursi

Arctostaphylos uva-ursi
Part used Leaves

Uva-ursi's antimicrobial properties are specifically indicated for urinary tract infections, and seem to be more effective when the urine is alkaline. Since many urinary tract infections acidify the urine, the herb is sometimes prescribed with an alkalizing substance (such as bicarbonate of soda) to maximize its effects. The compounds that are responsible for the antibiotic action are not present in uva-ursi itself, but are formed from its content of phenolic glycosides after the herb is ingested.

Caution

• Do not take the herbs on these pages if you are pregnant or breastfeeding, except under the advice of a healthcare professional.

Sore throats, colds and flu

The choice of an appropriate remedy to relieve a cold or a bout of flu is determined by the symptoms you're experiencing.

Sage
Salvia officinalis
Sore throat soother

Certain compounds in sage have been documented as having antimicrobial properties, which may help to explain the herb's traditional use as a gargle for sore throats and tonsillitis.

DOSAGE Make a strong infusion of dried sage; use as a gargle several times per day, as required.

Yarrow
Achillea millefolium
Fever remedy

Native Americans traditionally used yarrow to treat feverish conditions, and modern herbalists still follow their lead. It is often called for in the early stages of cold or flu, and is commonly combined with elder flower, which is also considered helpful in lowering high temperatures.

DOSAGE Infuse 1 teaspoon (4 g) dried yarrow (the flowers, seeds and leaves) in boiling water; drink 3 cups per day.

Elder
Sambucus nigra
Fever and flu relief

Elder flowers are used to treat upper respiratory infections with fevers or sinus congestion. The berries have long been used to make cordials and wines, but more recent research in Israel has established that a commercial preparation of elderberries, standardized for its content of anthocyanins — the purple compounds that give the berries their color — helps relieve the symptoms of flu and shorten the duration of the

infection. The researchers in Israel hypothesize that the extract works by altering the surface of the virus, preventing it from taking hold in the body.

DOSAGE Infuse 1 to 2 teaspoons (2 to 5 g) dried elder flowers in boiling water; drink 3 cups per day. Alternatively, look for a commercial preparation made from elderberries and follow the manufacturer's instructions.

Andrographis
Andrographis paniculata
Clinically proven to reduce symptoms of respiratory infection

Used in many parts of Asia for the treatment of infectious and feverish conditions, andrographis has been investigated in several clinical trials. These studies document improvements in symptoms of cold, flu and pharyngo-tonsillitis, such as fatigue, sore throat, muscle aches, shivering, excessive nasal secretions, sinusitis and headache, and suggest that andrographis may also reduce the amount of sick leave patients need in order to recover. Like echinacea, astragalus and garlic, andrographis also appears to have some preventative action and, when taken over several months, may help reduce the incidence of colds.

DOSAGE For the best results, take andrographis as soon as possible after the onset of cold or flu symptoms. Look for commercial preparations standardized for their content of andrographolides, which are considered responsible for much of the herb's activity, and follow the manufacturers' instructions. Doses of up to 6 g dried herb per day are normally used to treat infection, while lower doses are taken for prevention.

The main active constituent of garlic is allicin, which is released when you crush fresh cloves.

Garlic
Allium sativum
Broad-spectrum infection fighter

In vitro research has shown that garlic and several of its constituents have broad-spectrum activity against a wide variety of disease-causing organisms, including strains of the virus that causes flu. Garlic also helps fight colds and flu by enhancing the activity of immune cells and, when taken prophylactically — that is, as a preventative medicine — may help protect you from catching a cold.

DOSAGE To treat infection, take up to 2 cloves fresh garlic per day. Chop them and leave them to sit for 5 to 10 minutes before cooking with them. This will allow the medicinally active component allicin to form. For prevention, aim for a dose of up to 3 cloves per week, or buy a commercial preparation that provides a standardized quantity of either alliin or allicin, and follow the manufacturer's instructions.

Thyme
Thymus vulgaris
Antimicrobial and antispasmodic

The essential oil of thyme is regarded as one of nature's most potent antimicrobial substances, so herbalists commonly prescribe the plant to help resolve respiratory tract infections, such as colds, flu, tonsillitis and laryngitis. It also has antispasmodic properties, so it can be used to help reduce coughing.

⬭ DOSAGE Infuse up to 1 teaspoon (4 g) dried thyme leaves or 2 teaspoons fresh leaves in boiling water; drink 3 cups per day.

White horehound

Marrubium vulgare
Loosens the mucus in
unproductive coughs

White horehound has expectorant properties, helping to break up thickened phlegm and encouraging you to cough to remove it from the respiratory tract. It is particularly favored by herbalists when coughs are dry, hacking and unproductive.
⬭ DOSAGE Infuse up to 1 teaspoon (2 g) dried flowering tops of horehound in boiling water; drink 3 cups per day.

Marsh mallow

Althaea officinalis
Soothing expectorant
for irritated airways

Both the roots and leaves of the marsh mallow plant can be used to treat coughs. However, herbalists prefer the root for its higher mucilage content, which is responsible for the herb's soothing actions on the respiratory mucous membranes. Marsh mallow is traditionally indicated to relieve irritated and inflamed throats and airways, and to help expel mucus when lungs are congested.
⬭ DOSAGE Infuse 2 to 5 g dried marsh mallow root in cold (not hot) water, and steep for 8 hours to release mucilage; drink up to 3 cups per day.

Cautions
- Exceeding the recommended doses of yarrow, andrographis or white horehound may cause side effects and should be avoided.
- If you are taking blood-thinning or blood pressure medications, don't take garlic, andrographis or yarrow. Stop taking any of these herbs at least 2 weeks before undergoing surgery.
- Marsh mallow may interfere with the absorption of other medicines, so separate doses by 2 hours.

- Marsh mallow and andrographis may affect blood sugar levels, so they should not be taken by people with diabetes, except under professional supervision.
- Don't use yarrow if you are allergic to members of the Asteraceae family of plants (for example, chicory, daisies, echinacea and chrysanthemums).
- Do not consume the isolated essential oil of thyme. Use only the fresh or dried herb.
- Uncooked fresh elderberries may cause diarrhea and vomiting. Use only the dried or cooked berries.
- Andrographis may exacerbate pre-existing cases of heartburn and gastric ulcer. Garlic may cause minor gastric upset in some people, but these symptoms are less likely when the herb is cooked.

- Yarrow may very occasionally increase sensitivity to sunlight. If you develop this symptom, stop using it immediately and seek medical advice.
- Do not use large doses of elder flower over long periods of time.
- Black horehound (*Ballota nigra*) should not be used as a substitute for white horehound (*Marrubium vulgare*).
- With the exception of normal culinary quantities of sage, garlic and thyme, do not take the herbs on these two pages if you are pregnant or breastfeeding, except under professional advice.

Elder flowers and berries have many applications in natural beauty preparations and in cooking.

Immune support

Help boost your body's defenses against disease-causing bacteria and viruses by taking immune-stimulating herbs.

Echinacea
Echinacea sp.
Strengthens resistance to infection

Laboratory studies into several different echinacea species and constituents isolated from the plant have identified a variety of immunological effects, and seem to validate the herb's usage to support immunity. The results of human clinical trials have not always demonstrated the anticipated effects, however, causing the popular use of echinacea as a preventative against colds and flu to become controversial.

But a meta-analysis published in 2007 may go some way in clarifying the situation. In this study, researchers pooled the results of 14 clinical studies and estimated that taking echinacea decreased the likelihood of developing a cold by 58 percent, and when a cold did occur, its duration was shortened by about 30 hours.

DOSAGE The most appropriate dose of echinacea depends on both the plant part and the species used, but it is important to start taking the herb as soon as possible after symptoms develop. Preparations made from the root of *Echinacea angustifolia* or *E. pallida* are generally taken at doses of about 1 g taken 3 times daily to treat colds or, in lower doses, as a preventative. For *E. purpurea*, either the whole plant (including roots) or the aerial parts may be used. The dose is up to 2 g taken 3 times daily as an infusion of dried herb, or 3 ml juice made from the fresh plant and taken 3 times daily.

To make the juice, liquefy fresh aerial parts of *E. purpurea* with a little water in a home juicer or blender. The juice doesn't store well, so make only as much as you need to use immediately.

Three species of echinacea are cultivated for medicinal purposes — *Echinacea angustifolia*, *E. pallida* and *E. purpurea* (shown above). They also make very attractive additions to the garden.

Astragalus
Astragalus membranaceus
Improves immunity in chronic conditions

In traditional Chinese medicine, the herb astragalus is attributed with warming properties and is regarded as a lung tonic. It is indicated for patients with longstanding illnesses and for those who are susceptible to recurrent infection, and appears to improve the functioning of the immune system so that the body can better defend itself against pathogens — especially viruses. Astragalus is a good herb to try if you're run-down and tired and repeatedly catch colds or flu since, in addition to its immune-boosting properties, it is also traditionally used to raise overall vitality and energy.

DOSAGE Boil 3 to 10 g dried astragalus root in 3/4 cup (180 ml) water for 10 minutes before straining; drink the decoction in 2 doses during the day. Alternatively, take tablets or capsules according to the manufacturer's instructions, up to a maximum dose of 7.5 g dried root per day.

Cautions
- Do not use echinacea if you are allergic to members of the Asteraceae family of plants (for example, daisies, chrysanthemums, chicory and chamomile); people with pollen allergies should also take care, as some preparations may contain pollen. Cases of contact dermatitis have also occasionally been reported.
- Talk to your doctor before taking echinacea if you have an autoimmune condition, such as lupus, or a progressive disease, such as multiple sclerosis or HIV/AIDS. Echinacea should not be used by patients taking immunosuppressive medications.
- Note that astragalus is recommended for chronic (longstanding) rather than acute infections; discontinue use if you develop an infection while taking it.
- The resistance-boosting effects of astragalus may help reduce the side effects of some immunosuppressive cancer treatments, such as radio- and chemotherapy, but should only be used in this way in consultation with your doctor.
- Do not use the herbs on this page if you are pregnant or breastfeeding, except under the advice of a healthcare professional.

Hay fever and sinusitis

Herbs can help provide relief from, and may even prevent, the debilitating pain of sinusitis and the symptoms of hay fever.

Horseradish
Armoracia rusticana
Relieves congested sinuses

If you've ever tasted horseradish (or its Japanese cousin wasabi), you'll know that it is a rapid decongestant, clearing the sinuses and easing breathing almost immediately after ingestion. This effect is due to the ability of compounds called glucosinolates to liquefy thickened mucus, making it easier to clear and relieving the pressure and head pain associated with sinus congestion. These are the same compounds that give horseradish its spicy taste. They also have antimicrobial properties, so horseradish helps fight sinus infections, too. In clinical trials in Europe, researchers found that a combination of horseradish and nasturtium (which also contains glucosinolates) was just as effective in treating sinus infection as antibiotics but produced fewer side effects.
✎ **DOSAGE** Use horseradish paste or wasabi as a condiment. Alternatively, take commercially prepared tablets or capsules (with or without nasturtium) at a dose of up to 3 g per day.

Eyebright
Euphrasia officinalis
Traditional remedy for catarrh

Eyebright is traditionally used for respiratory conditions with watery discharges, so it's an ideal herb to take when you are suffering from hay fever symptoms, such as constant sneezing, a runny nose and watery or irritated eyes. It can also be used for colds and flu with similar symptoms.
✎ **DOSAGE** Infuse up to 1 teaspoon (1 to 4 g) dried aerial parts of eyebright in boiling water; drink 3 cups per day.

Albizia
Albizia lebbeck
Ayurvedic anti-allergy herb

Albizia lebbeck has a long history of use in Ayurvedic medicine, where it is prescribed for allergies and inflammatory conditions, including hay fever, asthma, hives and allergic conjunctivitis. Studies suggest that albizia works by stabilising the cells that release histamine and other allergic mediators, thereby relieving allergic tendencies and helping to manage allergy symptoms.
✎ **DOSAGE** Look for commercial preparations providing the equivalent of 3 to 6 g per day of the dried stem bark, and take it according to the manufacturer's instructions.

Perilla
Perilla frutescens
May prevent hay fever symptoms

Also known as shiso or beefsteak plant, perilla is a common ingredient in the traditional diet of Japan. Scientists there have also been integral in identifying its potential for preventing hay fever symptoms. Both the leaf and the seed of perilla contain compounds that help reduce allergy symptoms, such as sneezing, itchiness of the nose and scratchy, watery eyes. Preliminary research suggests that the herb (and particularly the constituent rosmarinic acid) may help seasonal allergy sufferers experience fewer hay fever symptoms during periods of high-pollen exposure.
✎ **DOSAGE** Take up to 9 g of dried leaf per day in tablet or capsule form. For the treatment of seasonal allergies, it may help to start taking perilla about a month before the hay fever season.

Horseradish root is rich in vitamin C, and sailors once ate it on long voyages to prevent scurvy.

Cautions
- Horseradish may irritate the digestive tract in some people and should be avoided by those with gastric ulcers; it may also cause irritation and burning if it comes into contact with the skin or eyes.
- If you suffer from thyroid disease or are taking blood-thinning medications, do not take horseradish at doses higher than normal culinary intake, except under professional supervision.
- Albizia and perilla should not be taken at the same time as pharmaceutical anti-allergy medications (such as antihistamines) except under professional supervision, as the effects of the drugs may be enhanced.
- Except for normal culinary quantities of horseradish, do not use the herbs on this page if you are pregnant or breastfeeding, except under the advice of a healthcare professional.

Indigestion

The enjoyment of a meal quickly dissipates if the burning pain and discomfort of indigestion or dyspepsia follow.

Slippery elm
Ulmus rubra
Soothing and healing

The mucilage in slippery elm bark forms a gel that lines the gastrointestinal tract, acting as an anti-inflammatory and encouraging healing. Slippery elm is an ideal herb for indigestion sufferers, because the gel helps protect the stomach lining from the effects of excess acid.

DOSAGE Stir 1 teaspoon powdered slippery elm bark into water and drink 15 to 30 minutes before meals. (As slippery elm trees are becoming increasingly rare, it's preferable to buy bark in powdered form rather than collect it yourself.)

Meadowsweet
Filipendula ulmaria
Acid balance

Meadowsweet relieves indigestion, reflux and other problems of over-acidity. Taken over a period of several weeks, it helps to normalize stomach acid production while soothing inflamed gastric tissues and promoting healing.

In the Middle Ages, meadowsweet flowers were a popular flavoring for wine and beer.

DOSAGE Infuse 4 to 6 g dried leaves and flowering tops of meadowsweet in boiling water; drink 3 cups per day.

Gentian
Gentiana lutea
Stimulates digestion

Bitter-flavored gentian improves digestion by stimulating the bitter taste receptors on the tongue, triggering the release of saliva, gastric acid and other digestive fluids. Gentian aids many of the symptoms that can occur due to poor digestion, including heartburn, flatulence, nausea and poor appetite. It is best taken before meals over several weeks, but a single dose after a heavy meal can also be beneficial.

DOSAGE Take 2 to 5 drops gentian root tincture in water, or infuse 1 g dried root and rhizome in boiling water. Take gentian 3 times per day, preferably 15 to 30 minutes before meals.

Anise
Pimpinella anisum
Relieves fullness and bloating

Anise helps to relieve the discomfort and pain of indigestion, and is particularly beneficial when wind or bloating are also present. Other aromatic herbs — such as caraway, fennel and dill — can be used in the same way.

DOSAGE Grind up to 1 teaspoon (2 g) ripe anise seeds to release the essential oil before infusing them in boiling water. Drink up to 3 cups per day.

Cautions
- See your doctor if you experience indigestion or heartburn frequently, or if vomiting occurs.

Herbal aperitifs

Many popular aperitifs are based on traditionally used bitter herbal medicines, such as wormwood, which not only stimulate stomach secretions but also act as tonics for the liver and gallbladder. Many other aperitifs, including ouzo from Greece and pastis from France, are dominated by the licorice-like aroma of anise or star anise. Taking a dose of one of the many bitter or aromatic herbs before your meal can have the same benefits; try peppermint, fennel, ginger or globe artichoke.

- A heart attack sometimes mimics the symptoms of indigestion. Call for an ambulance immediately if your symptoms are accompanied by a pain that radiates down the arm or up the neck, or by dizziness, weakness or shortness of breath.
- Slippery elm may interfere with the absorption of other medicines, so separate doses by 2 hours.
- Do not take meadowsweet if you are taking blood-thinning or anticoagulant medications (including aspirin), or if you are allergic to salicylates.
- Do not confuse anise and star anise.
- Do not take gentian if you suffer from peptic or duodenal ulcer.
- With the exception of normal culinary quantities of anise, do not use the herbs on this page if you are pregnant or breastfeeding, except under the advice of a healthcare professional.

Nausea

Whether it's a 24-hour stomach bug, a case of food poisoning or a bout of seasickness, nausea makes you feel miserable.

Ginger
Zingiber officinale
Settles the stomach

If you're feeling queasy, reach for ginger first. Several clinical trials support its traditional reputation as an effective treatment and preventative for nausea from a variety of sources, including morning sickness, motion sickness and post-operative vomiting and nausea. For more information on ginger and morning sickness, see Pregnancy, *page 236*.

🍃 DOSAGE Add 20 to 30 drops ginger tincture to water, or infuse ½ teaspoon powdered ginger or 1 to 2 teaspoons grated fresh ginger root in boiling water; take 3 times per day. For children over the age of 4, add 10 to 15 drops of ginger tincture to lemonade or ginger beer.

To prevent seasickness and travel sickness, take 1 g dried ginger 30 minutes before the trip starts and every few hours during the journey. The same dose can be taken before surgery to reduce post-operative nausea (but discuss this with your surgeon first — see *Cautions*).

Peppermint
Mentha x *piperita*
Antispasmodic

Peppermint is specifically indicated when nausea is accompanied by churning sensations in the stomach or gripping pains in the bowel. Its antispasmodic actions in the gastrointestinal tract are due to its content of a menthol-rich essential oil.

🍃 DOSAGE Add 10 to 15 drops peppermint tincture to water, or infuse 1 teaspoon fresh or dried aerial parts in boiling water; take 3 to 4 times per day. Children over 4 years can take a third to a half of the adult dose.

German chamomile
Matricaria recutita
Eases anxiety

The essential oil that gives chamomile its characteristic smell also imparts antispasmodic and anti-inflammatory properties, while its bitter principles help stimulate the secretion of gastric juices. This combination of actions, along with its renowned calming effects, make chamomile a very useful herb for the treatment of nausea, especially when it is due to, or accompanied by, anxiety and emotional upset.

🍃 DOSAGE Infuse 1 to 2 teaspoons dried chamomile flowers in boiling water; drink 3 to 4 cups per day. Children over the age of 4 years can take a third to a half of the adult dose.

Cautions

- In some cases, nausea and vomiting may be symptomatic of underlying disease. See your doctor if symptoms are severe, prolonged or occur frequently.
- Medical attention is also warranted if nausea is accompanied by severe abdominal pain, confusion, headache or a stiff neck, or is triggered by a head injury.
- Dehydration can occur as a consequence of vomiting. Watch out for symptoms such as dry lips and mouth, decreased urination and rapid pulse, especially in children. Rehydrate using an electrolyte replacement supplement (available from pharmacies), and seek medical advice immediately.
- Ginger should not be taken for 2 weeks prior to undergoing surgery. However, in consultation with your physician, a single dose can be taken just prior to surgery to reduce post-operative nausea.
- Don't use peppermint if you suffer from gastro-oesophageal reflux disease (GORD) or hiatus hernia, because its antispasmodic effect may worsen your symptoms by relaxing the esophageal sphincter and allowing reflux to occur more readily. Ginger is also contraindicated in reflux and should not be used medicinally if you suffer from gastric ulcer or gallstones.
- Don't use chamomile if you are allergic to members of the Asteraceae family of plants (for example daisies, chicory, chrysanthemums and echinacea).
- With the exception of normal culinary quantities of peppermint and German chamomile, do not use any of the herbs on this page if you are pregnant or breastfeeding, except under the advice of a healthcare professional.

German chamomile grows wild throughout Europe where it has long been used medicinally.

Wind, bloating and flatulence

A certain amount of wind every day is normal, but it can be uncomfortable and embarrassing if it occurs to excess.

Peppermint
Mentha x piperita
Irritable bowel relief

Long known to relieve wind and gastro-intestinal spasm, peppermint is an ideal remedy for people with irritable bowel syndrome (IBS), a condition characterized by abdominal pain, bloating and excessive flatulence. Several clinical trials support the use of peppermint to relieve IBS symptoms, especially when taken as enteric-coated peppermint oil capsules that break down in the bowel, where their antispasmodic effects are most needed.

DOSAGE Add 10 to 15 drops peppermint tincture to water, or infuse 1 teaspoon fresh or dried aerial parts in boiling water; take 3 to 4 times per day. Alternatively, use commercial peppermint oil capsules and follow the manufacturer's instructions.

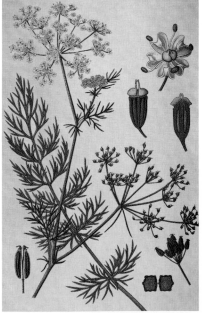

Caraway is combined with fennel and dill to make an infusion for treating intestinal problems.

Caraway
Carum carvi
Aromatic antispasmodic

Caraway is another herbal medicine that has been traditionally used to relieve wind, bloating and flatulence. Like peppermint, it helps to decrease spasm in the muscles of the digestive tract, and the essential oils of the two herbs are sometimes combined in commercial products.

DOSAGE Grind up to 1 teaspoon (2 g) caraway seeds to release the essential oil before infusing them in boiling water. Drink up to 3 cups per day. Alternatively, use commercial caraway oil capsules (often combined with peppermint) and follow the manufacturer's instructions.

Dill
Anethum graveolens
Soothes colic

Of the many herbs with calming actions on the digestive system, dill is the preferred remedy for the treatment of colic in babies and is equally beneficial for adults suffering from uncomfortable wind pain. As with other digestive remedies, it is the herb's essential oil that is responsible for its actions as a gastrointestinal antispasmodic, with the effect of releasing wind and reducing pain and discomfort.

DOSAGE Grind up to 2 teaspoons (4 g) dill seeds to release the essential oil before infusing them in boiling water. Drink up to 3 cups per day to relieve bloating and flatulence in yourself or colic in a breastfed baby. For babies over the age of 3 months, allow the infusion to cool and give 1 to 3 teaspoons at a time up to 4 times a day.

Star anise and colic

Chinese star anise (*Illicium verum*) has a long history of use in Spain, Latin America and the Caribbean as a treatment for colic, but following a number of severe adverse reactions in infants and young children, this practice should now be avoided. Some of these cases have been attributed to contamination by the related herb Japanese star anise (*Illicium anisatum*), which is toxic. However, Chinese star anise is also considered responsible for at least some of the reactions and even in low doses may cause severe reactions in young children.

Cautions
- Products containing the essential oils of peppermint and/or caraway are not recommended for infants, children, pregnant or breastfeeding women, or for people with gallbladder, kidney or gastro-oesophageal disease. Do not exceed the dose recommended by the manufacturer.
- If you are already taking prescribed medicines, talk to your doctor before taking peppermint oil capsules, because they may interact with some drugs.
- Caraway may cause an allergic reaction in some people. Stop using it if you experience any adverse effects, such as diarrhea or a runny nose.
- Do not use the herbs on this page in greater than culinary quantities if you are pregnant or breastfeeding, except under the advice of a healthcare professional.

Constipation and hemorrhoids

Ongoing problems with constipation can lead to hemorrhoids and an increased risk of diverticular disease and bowel cancer.

Psyllium
Plantago ovata, P. psyllium
Soluble fiber supplement

Mucilage-rich psyllium husks are a valuable source of soluble fiber, often lacking in the Western diet. In fact, psyllium is one of the few types of fiber supplement that have been proven to aid the management of chronic constipation problems.

DOSAGE Psyllium husks are available in tablets, capsules and soluble powders, and should be taken according to the manufacturer's instructions. A teaspoon of the powdered husks can also be sprinkled on fruit or breakfast cereal once a day. Every dose of psyllium should be taken with a large glass of water.

Chinese rhubarb
Rheum palmatum
Strong laxative

Chinese rhubarb root is a strong laxative with a potent content of anthraquinone glycosides. In traditional Chinese medicine it is prescribed for constipation and is considered to promote bile secretion, improve appetite and act as a liver and gallbladder tonic.

DOSAGE Boil ¾ oz. (20 g) dried or 1½ oz. (40 g) fresh Chinese rhubarb rhizome in 3 cups (750 ml) water. Simmer until reduced to 2 cups (500 ml). Take ¼ to ½ cup (50 to 100 ml) of the decoction with your evening meal.

Yellow dock
Rumex crispus
Gentle cleanser

Yellow dock is a gentle digestive stimulant that is specifically indicated for sluggish liver or bowel function. While it does contain anthraquinone glycosides, its laxative action is less marked than that of Chinese rhubarb or other herbal laxatives such as senna and cascara.

DOSAGE Boil 1 to 4 g dried yellow dock root in a cup of water for 10 minutes; drink the decoction up to 3 times daily.

Witch hazel
Hamamelis virginiana
Hemorrhoid healer

In clinical trials, topical applications of witch hazel have been demonstrated to be as effective as other medications (including corticosteroids) for the relief of the pain, itching and bleeding of hemorrhoids. The herb is also traditionally taken internally for the treatment of hemorrhoids, but its astringent nature makes it unsuitable for people with a tendency to be constipated.

DOSAGE Rub witch hazel gel, ointment or tincture into the affected area once a day. Talk to a professionally trained herbalist, who can help determine whether internal use of witch hazel is appropriate for your circumstances.

A natural trigger

Laxative herbs tend to contain varying quantities of compounds called anthraquinone glycosides, which travel through the digestive system to the intestine, where they stimulate peristalsis and trigger a bowel movement. Since this effect usually occurs about 8 hours after the herbs are consumed, they are traditionally taken in the evening, with the objective of developing a regular bowel habit in the mornings.

Witch hazel is native to North America, where it was used medicinally by Native American tribes.

Cautions
- Anthraquinone-containing herbs should not be taken in excessive doses, or for more than 10 days at a time.
- Do not use herbs to treat constipation in children, or if you are pregnant, breast-feeding, have undiagnosed abdominal pain or an intestinal or gallbladder blockage. Chinese rhubarb is also contraindicated in persons suffering from arthritis or kidney or urinary tract disease.
- Persons diagnosed with an intestinal illness should only use herbal medicines (including psyllium) on medical advice.
- Psyllium may interfere with the absorption of other medicines, so separate doses by 2 hours.
- Always drink lots of water when using psyllium, because cases of choking have occasionally been reported in people who have taken psyllium powders without adequate fluids.
- Rhubarb leaves are toxic and should not be consumed.
- Topical applications of witch hazel occasionally cause contact allergy. Stop using it immediately if you are concerned.
- With the exception of topical applications of witch hazel, do not use the herbs on this page if you are pregnant or breast-feeding, except under the advice of a healthcare professional.

Liver and gallbladder support

Your liver and gallbladder are vital for your digestive and detoxification processes. Look after them, so they can look after you.

Milk thistle
Silybum marianum
Liver protection and repair

The seeds of milk thistle (also known as St Mary's thistle) contain a group of antioxidant compounds collectively referred to by the name silymarin.

Studies show silymarin helps protect liver cells from damage and aids the repair or replacement of injured cells. Under professional supervision, milk thistle and silymarin aid the management of a wide range of serious liver problems, including non-alcoholic and alcoholic liver disease and some forms of hepatitis.

Milk thistle can also be used to prevent or treat the effects of overindulgence in alcohol and fatty foods, to prevent liver damage from toxic exposure, and for headaches and skin problems associated with poor liver function.

DOSAGE Look for tablets or capsules that are standardized for their silymarin content (sometimes labelled as flavanolignans or silybin), and follow the manufacturer's instructions.

Schisandra
Schisandra chinensis
Liver support

Although there is less scientific evidence to support its use, schisandra may have similar liver-protecting properties to milk thistle. Laboratory studies demonstrate a number of antioxidant effects and suggest that it, too, has the ability to prevent cell damage by harmful substances and to reduce some of the symptoms associated with liver disease.

DOSAGE Take the equivalent of 500 to 1500 mg of the dried fruit 3 times per day, in either tablet or tincture form.

The white veins on the leaves of milk thistle were said to be milk from the Virgin's breast.

Dandelion root
Taraxacum officinale
Traditional hepatic tonic

As a bitter herb, dandelion root stimulates gastrointestinal function and is traditionally used for minor digestive ailments, especially sluggish liver and gallbladder function, indigestion and mild cases of constipation. An infusion of the roasted root is a popular caffeine-free alternative to coffee and a pleasant way to stimulate digestion before or after a heavy meal.

DOSAGE Infuse ½ to 2 teaspoons (2 to 8 g) dried or roasted dandelion root in boiling water; drink 3 cups per day. If using the roasted root, add milk or soy milk to taste, but avoid sweeteners, because they may diminish the herb's effective-ness. Tablets, capsules and a tincture are also available.

Turmeric
Curcuma longa
Stimulates gallbladder function

Among its many other medicinal actions, turmeric helps to stimulate bile secretion and may offer some protection against the development of gall stones. Its effects on the liver and gallbladder may also be responsible for the herb's ability to help lower blood cholesterol levels.

DOSAGE Mix ½ teaspoon powdered turmeric with cold water and drink 2 to 3 times per day for up to 4 weeks at a time. Alternatively, take turmeric capsules, standardized for their content of curcumin.

Cautions
- If you suffer from liver or gallbladder disease (including gall stones), do not attempt to treat yourself using these or any other herbal medicines. Instead, seek the care of an appropriately trained healthcare professional.
- Minor gastrointestinal symptoms, such as nausea, diarrhea and flatulence are sometimes experienced when these remedies are taken. If you experience any discomfort, discontinue use.
- Don't use milk thistle or dandelion root if you are allergic to members of the Asteraceae family of plants (for example, daisies, chrysanthemums and echinacea).
- If you have a gastric or duodenal ulcer, or are taking blood-thinning medications, do not take turmeric at doses higher than normal culinary intake.
- In traditional Chinese medicine, schisandra is contraindicated in the early stages of coughs and colds.
- With the exception of normal culinary quantities of turmeric, do not use the herbs on this page if you are pregnant or breastfeeding, except under the advice of a healthcare professional.

Detox

Feeling sluggish and run-down? Maybe it's time to detox, especially if you've been overindulging or neglecting your diet.

Dandelion leaf

Taraxacum officinale
Herbal diuretic

Dandelion leaves have powerful diuretic activity: They promote the production and excretion of urine. They also have liver- and gallbladder-stimulating properties (although, traditionally, these actions are considered to be milder than the actions of the dandelion root).

DOSAGE Infuse 1 to 2 teaspoons (4 to 10 g) dried dandelion leaves in boiling water; drink 3 cups per day.

Cleavers

Galium aparine
Lymphatic cleanser

Cleavers is traditionally regarded as a gentle yet effective tonic for the lymphatic system, which collects wastes and foreign

material from the body and returns them to the bloodstream for disposal. It is specifically indicated when the lymph glands are chronically enlarged or congested, and when skin problems, such as acne or eczema, are present.

DOSAGE Infuse 1 teaspoon (4 g) dried aerial parts of cleavers in boiling water; drink 3 cups per day. Alternatively, juice the fresh herb and drink 5 to 15 ml 3 times daily.

Psyllium

Plantago ovata, P. psyllium
Facilitates excretion of toxins

Soluble fiber of the type found in psyllium husks is especially beneficial when you're detoxing because it forms a gel-like substance in the intestines, trapping toxic compounds so they can be excreted.

DOSAGE Psyllium husks are available in tablets, capsules and soluble powders, and should be taken according to the manufacturer's instructions. A teaspoon of powdered husks can also be sprinkled on fruit or breakfast cereal once a day. Take every dose of psyllium with a large glass of water.

Cautions

- Most people can safely undergo a gentle detox program by adopting a diet of fresh fruit and vegetables, drinking plenty of water, and avoiding caffeine, cigarettes, alcohol and processed foods for a few days. However, transient side effects do sometimes occur during a detox. These include gastrointestinal disturbances, headaches, joint and muscle pain, fatigue and skin rashes.
- The following people should not undergo detox regimens or take the herbs listed on this page except under the supervision of an appropriately qualified healthcare

The roots of dandelion are dried and roasted to make a caffeine-free coffee substitute.

professional: children, teenagers, pregnant and breastfeeding women; people with chronic illness, diabetes, diagnosed intestine, kidney, liver or gallbladder disease; cancer patients; people taking prescribed medications; people with a history of eating disorders or alcohol or drug abuse; people who have had a higher than normal exposure to toxins (for example, through occupational exposure).
- Don't use dandelion leaf if you are allergic to members of the Asteraceae family of plants (for example, daisies, echinacea and chrysanthemums) or are taking potassium-sparing diuretics or ACE inhibitors.
- Psyllium may interfere with the absorption of other medicines, so separate doses by 2 hours.
- Always drink lots of water when using psyllium, because cases of choking have occasionally been reported in people taking psyllium powders without adequate fluids.
- Do not use any of these herbs if you are pregnant or breastfeeding, except under the advice of a healthcare professional.

Eliminating toxins

Herbalists believe that it's difficult for the body to function at its best if the organs of elimination are overloaded. In the philosophies of many traditional healing systems, the resulting buildup of toxins can lead to symptoms as diverse as headaches, fatigue and skin problems. The liver and gallbladder play a major role in the formation and excretion of the feces, so remedies such as the ones detailed on this page tend to be central to any detox prescription, often with the support of herbs for the urinary and lymphatic systems.

Tension and stress

If you are feeling the pressure of too much to do
in too little time, these herbs may help you to cope.

Korean ginseng
Panax ginseng
Improves performance under stress

The most highly valued of all Chinese
herbs, Korean ginseng has a long-held
reputation for helping the body and mind
cope with stress. It has been the subject
of numerous clinical trials, which have
documented (among other effects)
improvements in alertness, relaxation,
mood and performance on various tests.
Not all clinical trials have supported
Korean ginseng's traditional reputation.
DOSAGE Take commercially prepared
Korean ginseng tablets according to
the manufacturer's instructions (up to a
maximum of 1000 mg of dried root per
day). Look for products standardized for
their content of ginsenosides. Note that
Korean ginseng is traditionally taken for
8 to 12 weeks at a time, followed by a
break of several weeks; it is not appropriate
for frail or anxious patients.

Oats
Avena sativa
Traditional restorative
for the nervous system

The leaves, stems and other green parts
(sometimes called "oat straw") of the oat
plant are used to help restore a depleted
or debilitated nervous system and aid
with coping in times of stress or nervous
exhaustion. Herbalists consider this herb
a gentle and reliable nervous system tonic,
capable of calming or energizing as
required. Even the very frail or anxious
patient can take this herb.
DOSAGE Infuse 1 to 1½ teaspoons
(3 g) dried oats greens in boiling water;
drink 3 cups per day. Children over 4 years
can take up to half the adult dose.

Lemon balm
Melissa officinalis
Calming and relaxing

Lemon balm is traditionally used during
times of tension, restlessness and anxiety,
and is ideal when you are feeling uptight,
agitated or overwrought. In clinical trials,
people affected by stress have reported
feeling increased levels of calmness and
improved mood after just a single dose of
lemon balm, but it can also be taken over
a longer period when stress is ongoing.
DOSAGE Infuse 1 to 2 teaspoons of
fresh aerial parts of lemon balm in boiling
water; drink 1 cup 2 to 3 times per day.
The herb has a mild sedative action, so
if you are suffering from fatigue, take
it only in the evening.

Cautions
- Do not take Korean ginseng if you have
  diabetes, cardiovascular disease (including
  high and low blood pressure), depression,
  anxiety, hyperactivity, mental illness
  (including bipolar disorder and similar
  conditions), insomnia, blood clots or
  bleeding disorders.
- Korean ginseng is known or suspected
  to interact with many pharmaceutical
  medications — including antidepressants,
  antipsychotic medications, anticoagulants,
  insulin and hormonal therapy — so consult
  with your physician or pharmacist before
  taking it. Do not take it at the same time
  as stimulants such as caffeine.
- Korean ginseng is traditionally contraindicated during acute infections.
- Side effects are occasionally reported
  with the use of Korean ginseng. These may
  include headache, disturbed sleep and skin
  problems. If this occurs, stop taking the herb.
- Do not use oats if you have celiac disease
  or gluten intolerance.
- Lemon balm may interact with some
  pharmaceutical medications, including

An infusion of oats seed is used topically to
soothe itchy skin.

certain sedatives, and a group of medicines
referred to as cholinergic (or parasympa-
thomimetic) drugs, which are prescribed
for Alzheimer's disease and a range
of other conditions — if you are taking
prescribed medicines, talk to your doctor
before using lemon balm.
- Do not take any of these herbs if you are
  pregnant or breastfeeding, except under
  the advice of a healthcare professional.

Depression and anxiety

Used appropriately, herbs can help lift your mood or calm your nerves when you find things difficult to deal with.

St. John's wort

Hypericum perforatum
Herbal antidepressant

Clinical research has proven the anti-depressant effects of St. John's wort, with some studies demonstrating a level of efficacy in mild to moderate depression that is similar to that of important pharmaceutical anti-depressants, but with a better safety profile. Interestingly, the way the herb works in the body is also similar to the mechanisms of action of some of these pharmaceutical medicines.

DOSAGE Look for supplements that are standardized for their contents of hypericin and hyperforin (considered to be the main active constituents) and with a daily dose of 900 mg per day of the concentrated (6:1) extract, equivalent to 5.4 g of dried herb.

Lavender

Lavandula angustifolia
Aromatherapy to relieve anxiety

The scent of lavender has long been attributed to promoting relaxation, and there is a growing body of evidence to support this traditional practice. Studies indicate that inhaling lavender essential oil helps ease anxiety and improves feelings of calmness and well-being in a range of stressful situations, including dental waiting rooms and intensive-care units. Research also shows that lavender inhalation has the effect of reducing the body's production of the stress hormone cortisol.

DOSAGE To enjoy the anti-anxiety effects of lavender, use a ratio of 4 drops lavender essential oil for every 10 ml carrier oil and massage into the shoulders

Soothing and aromatic, lavender flowers are cultivated commercially. For instructions on how to make an herb pillow that will help you to relax and sleep, see *page 300*.

and temples. Or, inhale the steam from 4 drops essential oil diluted in 20 ml hot water (for example, in an oil burner). You can also drink an infusion made from ½ teaspoon (1 to 1.5 g) of the dried flowers twice a day, and again at bedtime.

Cautions

- St. John's wort is known or suspected to interact with many pharmaceutical medications (including antidepressants, cardiovascular medicines and contra-ceptives), so consult your physician or pharmacist before taking it.
- Depression is a serious condition and is not suitable for self-treatment. Do not stop taking prescribed antidepressants except under the advice and supervision of your doctor. A 2-week wash-out period is advised if you are switching from pharmaceutical antidepressants to St. John's wort.
- Research into the use of St. John's wort in severe depression has not yet demonstrated safety or efficacy and so should be avoided unless medically prescribed. It should not be used by people with bipolar disorder.

- The effects of St. John's wort take 2 to 4 weeks to develop. If there is no noticeable improvement after 6 weeks, this herb may not be suitable for you; consult your doctor.
- St. John's wort occasionally causes minor side effects (for example, gastrointestinal upset, headache). The most common of these is photosensitivity, a condition in which the skin becomes more prone to sunburn. Avoid sunbathing or prolonged sun exposure while taking St. John's wort and consult your doctor if you develop this symptom.
- Stop taking St. John's wort at least 2 weeks prior to undergoing surgery.
- Unless advised to do so by your doctor, do not take St. John's wort if you are pregnant or breastfeeding, and do not give it to children.
- Do not ingest lavender essential oil and do not use it during pregnancy or breast-feeding, except under the advice of a healthcare professional.

Tiredness and fatigue

If your energy levels are flagging, a stimulating herbal pick-me-up may be all that you need.

Siberian ginseng
Eleutherococcus senticosus
Extra energy during stressful times

Herbalists recommend Siberian ginseng as a stimulating herb for people who are tired and run-down, especially those affected by stress. It is traditionally used to help rebuild energy levels during the recovery period following an illness, and may be beneficial for some sufferers of chronic fatigue syndrome when professionally prescribed.

DOSAGE Take commercially prepared Siberian ginseng tablets according to the manufacturer's instructions (up to a maximum of 3 g per day) for a period of up to 6 weeks, followed by a 2-week break.

Withania
Withania somnifera
Blood-building herb

In Ayurvedic medicine, withania (also known as ashwagandha or Indian ginseng) is used to enhance energy and stamina and to help the body cope with stress, so it's considered especially beneficial for patients who are physically or emotionally exhausted. Withania contains iron, so it can also be helpful for fatigue caused by anemia or low iron levels. A small number of studies indicate that it helps to promote blood-cell formation and raise the level of hemoglobin in the blood.

Native to Mongolia and parts of China, astragalus is also called milk vetch.

DOSAGE Take commercial withania tablets according to the manufacturer's instructions. Look for a product providing the equivalent of 3 to 6 g of the dried root per day.

Astragalus
Astragalus membranaceus
Energy tonic with immune support

Astragalus is one of the most important energy tonics in traditional Chinese medicine. It is used to help increase the vitality of patients who are debilitated, and is specifically indicated for cases of fatigue accompanied by poor appetite. Astragalus is particularly useful if you are constantly feeling run-down as well as tired, since it also supports the immune system, helping the body to fight off infections, such as colds and flu.

DOSAGE Boil 3 to 10 g dried astragalus root in ¼ cup (60 ml) of water for 10 minutes before straining; drink the decoction in 2 doses during the day. Alternatively, take tablets or capsules according to the manufacturer's instructions, up to a maximum dose equivalent to 7.5 g dried root per day.

Cautions
- Do not exceed the recommended dose of Siberian ginseng.
- Siberian ginseng is unsuitable for people with hyperactivity disorders, bipolar disorder or similar conditions. If you have cardiovascular disease (including high and low blood pressure), or if you are taking anticoagulant medication, only use it under professional supervision.
- Siberian ginseng and astragalus are contraindicated during acute infections.
- Stop using Siberian ginseng at least 2 weeks before undergoing surgery.

Why am I so tired?

Fatigue is your body's way of telling you that it's time to rest. However, if your energy levels seem to be much lower than usual, or you are too tired to participate in normal everyday activities, then it's time to see a healthcare professional, who can help determine the underlying issue behind your fatigue. Although most causes of fatigue are related to lifestyle factors, such as the amount of sleep, exercise and healthy food you are getting each day, tiredness can also present as a symptom of an underlying health problem, such as anemia, underactive thyroid conditions or glandular fever. As well as the herbs detailed on this page, the remedies for Tension and stress (see *page 210*) and Insomnia (see *page 214*) may also be useful.

- If you are diabetic, do not use Siberian ginseng, except under medical supervision.
- If you are taking tranquillizers, sedatives, antidepressants, thyroid medication, chemotherapy or immunosuppressant medication, do not take withania, except under professional supervision.
- Resistance-boosting astragalus may help reduce the side effects of some immuno-suppressive cancer treatments, but should only be used in this way in consultation with your doctor. Siberian ginseng may also interact with chemotherapy.
- Do not take withania if you are sensitive to plants belonging to the Solanaceae family (for example, potato, tomato, eggplant).
- Do not use these herbs if you are pregnant or breastfeeding, except under the advice of a healthcare professional.

Memory and concentration

If you keep forgetting where you put the car keys or your glasses, it could be time to mix up a memory tonic.

Ginkgo

Ginkgo biloba
May delay the progression of dementia

Ginkgo is the world's most popular memory tonic, and is believed to work via a number of mechanisms, including improving blood flow to the brain, acting as an antioxidant and helping to prevent injury to blood vessels. It may help delay the progression of Alzheimer's disease and other forms of dementia, so has the ability to improve the quality of life for sufferers of these debilitating conditions. Ginkgo can also be taken for more minor memory problems or as a supportive tonic during study periods. However, there is little scientific evidence available to help us understand whether the herb is also beneficial in healthy people.

DOSAGE Look for supplements standardized for their content of the important active constituents ginkgo flavone glycosides, ginkgolides and bilobalides, with a daily dose of 120 mg of a concentrated (50:1) extract, providing the equivalent of 6 g of the dried herb. Ginkgo takes a month or two to reach its maximum effect, so use it for 6 to 12 weeks before assessing whether or not it is helping you.

Brahmi

Bacopa monnieri
Aid for learning

Brahmi appears to enhance the way the brain processes new information, which makes it a perfect herbal tonic for students. It also helps relieve anxiety, so it can be of real benefit at exam time — but it does take up to 3 months to start working, so don't leave it too late!

DOSAGE Infuse 1 to 2 g dried brahmi in boiling water; drink 3 cups each day. Alternatively, take commercial preparations, up to a maximum of 6 g per day, according to the manufacturer's instructions.

Rosemary

Rosmarinus officinalis
Traditional memory tonic

Rosemary has had a reputation as a memory tonic since the time of the ancient Greeks, and it can help increase alertness, reduce anxiety and encourage a calm mind.

DOSAGE Add a few drops of rosemary essential oil to an oil burner in the room or area where you are studying or working.

Cautions

- If your memory problems worsen or become serious, it is essential to discuss your concerns with a doctor.
- If you have been diagnosed with Alzheimer's disease or any other form of dementia, do not take ginkgo or brahmi without first talking to your doctor.
- Ginkgo is known or suspected to interact with many pharmaceutical medications (including antipsychotic medications, anticonvulsants, anticoagulants and anticholinergic medications), so consult your doctor or pharmacist before taking it. Stop taking ginkgo at least 2 weeks before undergoing surgery.
- Always use commercially prepared ginkgo products from a reputable company. Do not consume unprocessed ginkgo leaves, as they may cause an adverse reaction. Do not eat large quantities of the seeds or allow children to do so.
- Ginkgo sometimes causes mild adverse reactions, which may include dizziness, gastrointestinal upset, headache and allergic skin reactions. More severe

Ginkgo trees, which date back to the Jurassic period, can live for more than a thousand years.

reactions have occasionally been recorded, including bleeding problems and seizures. If symptoms occur, stop taking the herb and seek medical advice.
- Brahmi occasionally causes gastrointestinal irritation (for example, reflux). It should not be taken with anticholinergic medications.
- Do not take ginkgo if you suffer from a bleeding disorder.
- Do not take brahmi if you suffer from celiac disease, malabsorption syndromes, gallbladder blockage or gastric reflux problems.
- Both brahmi (*Bacopa monnieri*) and gotu kola (*Centella asiatica*) are sometimes referred to by the name "brahmi" in Ayurvedic herbal texts, so make sure you don't confuse the two.
- Do not take ginkgo or brahmi, or apply rosemary essential oil to the skin, if you are pregnant or breastfeeding, except under the advice of a healthcare professional.

Insomnia

Missing out on a good night's sleep can be enough to ruin your whole day. The right herb may prevent that from happening.

Valerian
Valeriana officinalis
Clinically proven herbal sedative

A number of clinical studies support valerian's traditional reputation as a sedative herb. It helps insomnia sufferers to fall asleep more quickly, wake less often during the night and generally experience a better night's sleep. In contrast to some pharmaceutical sedatives, it is very rarely associated with side effects, and doesn't tend to cause sleepiness and difficulty waking in the morning.

DOSAGE Infuse 3 g dried valerian rhizome in boiling water and drink 1 cup an hour before bedtime. Alternatively, take commercial preparations according to the manufacturer's instructions. Valerian works best when it is taken every night over a period of several weeks, rather than when taken occasionally.

Hops
Humulus lupulus
Traditional sleep inducer

Although more famous as an ingredient in beer, hops has a long history of being used to help treat insomnia and sleep disorders. This herb is also traditionally regarded as helpful in treating anxiety and restlessness, although there is conflicting evidence about its effects on depression. In many cases, hops is taken in combination with other sedative herbs, such as valerian and passionflower.

DOSAGE Infuse up to 1 g dried hops in boiling water and drink 1 cup an hour before bedtime. Dried hops can also be used to make pillows to aid restful sleep in the same way that lavender is sometimes used. To make an herbal sleep pillow, see *page 300.*

The aerial parts of passionflower are collected at the end of summer and then dried.

Passionflower
Passiflora incarnata
Sleep problems with anxiety

Passionflower is traditionally taken to aid insomnia — especially when sleep troubles are accompanied by nervousness or anxiety — so it is ideally suited to those whose insomnia has an emotional basis. Although there hasn't been much scientific research into passionflower's actions, there is some preliminary data to support its traditional applications.

Herbalists commonly prescribe passion-flower in combination with other relaxing herbs, such as valerian.

DOSAGE To treat insomnia, infuse 2 g dried passionflower leaves in boiling water and drink 1 cup an hour before bedtime. For anxiety, take the same dose twice more during the day. Like valerian, passionflower may take several weeks to achieve optimal effect.

Cautions
- Do not exceed the recommended dose of the herbs listed here.
- If you are taking pharmaceutical tranquillizers, sedatives or antidepressants, do not take the herbs listed here, except under professional supervision. If you are taking anticoagulant medication, do not use passionflower except under professional supervision.
- If valerian worsens insomnia and/or causes exceptionally vivid dreams, discontinue it and try an alternative herb.
- If you suffer from depression, do not use hops, except on professional advice.
- Allergic symptoms sometimes occur from contact with hops, and may include dermatitis and respiratory symptoms.
- Do not use hops if you have a history of hormone-sensitive tumors or are taking anti-estrogenic medication.
- Do not use these herbs if you are pregnant or breastfeeding, except under the advice of a healthcare professional.

Headache and migraine

Whether you suffer from headache or migraine frequently or occasionally, an herbal alternative may bring welcome relief.

Feverfew
Tanacetum parthenium
Reduces migraine
frequency and symptoms

Feverfew is the most famous of all herbs for treating headache, and is one that migraine sufferers find particularly effective. If taken over several months, it lowers the frequency of migraines and reduces symptoms, such as headache, nausea and vomiting, as well as decreases the duration of the attacks.

DOSAGE You can take feverfew either by eating 2½ fresh leaves every day (with or after food) or by using commercial preparations according to the manufacturer's instructions. It may take from 1 to 4 months before the effects become evident — perhaps even longer if you are taking the fresh leaves.

White willow bark
Salix alba
Herbal aspirin

White willow bark contains compounds called salicylates, which are similar to the active ingredient in aspirin. It has traditionally been used to relieve headaches of all types, especially those accompanied by fever. In one small-scale preliminary study, white willow bark was also combined with feverfew for the prevention of migraine, producing highly significant improvements in the frequency, intensity and duration of the attacks.

DOSAGE Boil 1 to 3 g dried white willow bark in a cup of water for 5 to 10 minutes; drink the decoction up to 3 times daily. Alternatively, take commercially prepared products according to the manufacturer's instructions.

Peppermint oil
Mentha x *piperita*
Rapid relief for tension headaches

Applying peppermint essential oil to the forehead and temples has been scientifically proven to be as effective as paracetamol (acetaminophen) for the relief of tension headaches. This effect occurs very quickly — a significant reduction in the headache's intensity may be noted as quickly as 15 minutes after the oil has been applied.

DOSAGE Apply a solution containing 1 part peppermint oil diluted in 9 parts alcohol (or water if alcohol is not available) to the forehead and temples every 15 to 30 minutes after the onset of symptoms. Take care not to allow the solution to come into contact with the

White willow bark is harvested from young branches in late winter and spring.

eyes. Using both peppermint oil and paracetamol simultaneously may enhance the effects of both treatments.

Cautions
- Severe or frequent headaches may require medical investigation — always consult your doctor.
- Feverfew sometimes causes allergic side effects, most commonly mouth symptoms, such as mouth ulcers and soreness of the tongue. These symptoms are more likely to occur in people chewing fresh leaves (as opposed to taking tablets or capsules).
- Do not take feverfew if you develop a rash after coming into contact with the plant or if you are allergic to other members of the Asteraceae family of plants (for example, chicory, daisies, chrysanthemums, sunflower and echinacea).
- Do not take white willow bark if you are allergic to salicylates (including aspirin).
- Do not take feverfew or white willow bark with antiplatelet or anticoagulant medication, or if you suffer from a blood disorder.
- Peppermint oil should always be diluted before application. It should not be used on or near the face of children and babies (even in its diluted form).
- Do not take feverfew or white willow bark, or apply peppermint oil to the skin, if you are pregnant or breastfeeding, except under the advice of a healthcare professional.

Is it really a migraine?

Although we often use the word "migraine" to describe a particularly severe headache, in medical terms a migraine is a specific type of debilitating headache that may be accompanied by other symptoms, such as nausea and vomiting, blurred vision or other visual disturbances, and tingling or numbness of the limbs. Sufferers may also be particularly sensitive to noise or light during an attack, and may retreat into a dark, quiet room until the episode has passed.

Acne

Breaking the cycle of skin eruptions can be a living hell.
Try these herbal solutions for treating problem skin.

Tea-tree oil

Melaleuca alternifolia
Nature's powerful pimple healer

With a combination of broad-spectrum antimicrobial properties and anti-inflammatory activity, tea-tree oil is an ideal topical treatment for acne. In a recent study, people with mild-to-moderate acne experienced reductions of more than 40 percent in both the number of acne lesions and the severity of their acne when they used a tea-tree oil gel over a 6-week period. A previous study had already shown that tea-tree gel had a similar level of efficacy to benzoyl peroxide (also used topically for the treatment of acne), but with a much lower incidence of side effects.

🌿 DOSAGE In these scientific studies, a gel containing 5 percent tea-tree essential oil was used — a more concentrated preparation may have yielded even more impressive results, but may also have increased the risk of side effects (see *Cautions*). To replicate the study conditions at home, apply tea-tree gel to the affected area twice a day, washing it off with water after 20 minutes.

Chaste tree

Vitex agnus-castus
Herbal hormone balancer

Hormonal imbalance can be an important factor in the development of acne — not just in teenagers, but also for many adults. To restore hormonal balance and help resolve problem skin, herbalists often prescribe chaste tree. This herb, *Vitex agnus-castus*, is more widely known for its role in the treatment of premenstrual syndrome (PMS) and female reproductive issues, but can also be taken by both males and females for treating acne. It is especially useful for premenstrual acne flare-ups.

🌿 DOSAGE Take tablets, capsules or tincture according to the manufacturer's instructions. Look for products that are standardized for their content of the compounds casticin and/or agnuside. Results may take up to 12 weeks or longer to become noticeable.

The chaste tree is also called monks' pepper because it was once used to suppress libido.

Cleavers

Galium aparine
Skin and lymphatic detoxifier

In the Western herbal tradition, skin problems, such as acne, are considered an indication that toxins in the bloodstream are being excreted via the skin. Cleavers is one of a wide range of blood-cleansing herbs that are used to detoxify the blood and lymph and support the body's organs of elimination, thus improving skin health.

🌿 DOSAGE Infuse 4 g (1 teaspoon) of dried aerial parts of cleavers in boiling water; drink 3 cups per day. Alternatively, juice the fresh herb (excluding the root) using a stick blender, and drink 5 to 15 ml 3 times daily.

Cautions

- Tea-tree oil sometimes causes reactions, such as contact dermatitis, itching, burning or scaling of the skin, especially if used in high concentrations or on inflamed or eczematous skin. Use diluted preparations to reduce the likelihood of these reactions occurring, and patch test on an unaffected area of skin 24 hours before applying to any infected or inflamed area.
- Do not ingest tea-tree oil.
- Chaste tree occasionally causes mild, reversible side effects, such as headache, nausea and gastrointestinal upset. Stop taking it if you experience these symptoms.
- Do not take chaste tree at the same time as the oral contraceptive pill, hormone-replacement therapy (HRT) or drugs containing progesterone, except under professional advice. People with a history of hormone-sensitive tumors should not take chaste tree, because safety in people with these conditions has not been established.
- Do not take chaste tree or cleavers, or apply undiluted tea-tree oil to the skin, if you are pregnant or breastfeeding, except under the advice of a healthcare professional.

Eczema and psoriasis

Herbalists use a combination of internal and topical treatments to relieve itchy, inflammatory skin conditions.

Chickweed
Stellaria media
Soothing relief from the garden

You probably have some chickweed growing in your garden — it's one of the most common weeds in the world. Chickweed is traditionally used to relieve itchy and inflamed skin conditions, including eczema, dermatitis and psoriasis. It's gentle enough to use on the most delicate and inflamed skin, and is even suitable for use on babies (see *Cautions* before using).

DOSAGE Juice the fresh aerial parts of the chickweed plant, then mix into a cream or ointment base using a ratio of 1 part chickweed to 5 parts base cream. Apply to the affected area as required. Alternatively, use a commercially prepared cream in the same way.

Flaxseed oil
Linum usitatissimum
Herbal source of
omega-3 fatty acids

Without fats and oils in your diet, your skin can become dry, flaky, scaly and itchy, so the quality and type of fats you eat is very important. The omega-6 group of fatty acids (found in safflower, sunflower, corn and grapeseed oils) can exacerbate inflammation. On the other hand, omega-3 fatty acids, such as those found in flaxseed (as well as other seeds, nuts and seafood), enhance the body's production of anti-inflammatory compounds, and can be beneficial in the treatment of psoriasis, eczema and other inflammatory skin conditions.

DOSAGE Take flaxseed oil in either capsules or liquid form, according to the manufacturer's instructions. Alternatively,

grind fresh whole seeds and serve them with breakfast cereal, smoothies or yogurt. Note that the oil is more unstable than other culinary oils, so keep it refrigerated to ensure its freshness.

Turmeric
Curcuma longa
Ayurvedic anti-inflammatory

In Ayurvedic medicine, turmeric has been used for centuries as a topical treatment for psoriasis and other inflammatory skin disorders. Modern Western herbalists sometimes also prescribe it internally for the well-documented antioxidant, anti-inflammatory and immune-stimulating properties of both turmeric and a yellow pigment it contains, called curcumin. As the herb is also a liver and gallbladder tonic, this use reflects the traditional view that cleansing the body of toxins can help to resolve chronic skin problems.

DOSAGE Mix ½ teaspoon powdered turmeric with cold water and drink it 2 to 3 times per day for up to 4 weeks at a time. For topical use, mix ½ cup (50 g) turmeric powder with 1 teaspoon baking soda and some hot water and apply as a poultice. For more detailed instructions, see *page 194*.

Cautions
- Chickweed and turmeric occasionally cause allergic skin reactions. Patch test on an unaffected area of skin 24 hours before applying to inflamed skin or before using either herb on infants or children.
- Although they are made from the same plant, flaxseed oil is a different preparation from the refined oil sold as "linseed oil" and used for industrial purposes (for example, in paints), which should not be consumed.
- If you are taking anticoagulant or blood-thinning medications, talk to your doctor

before taking high dosages of flaxseed oil or other omega-3 fatty acids.
- Turmeric is a safe herb, although high doses can cause minor gastrointestinal symptoms. Do not use it at higher than culinary doses if you have liver and gallbladder disease (including gall stones), gastric or duodenal ulcer, or take blood-thinning medication, except under professional advice.
- Do not use flaxseed oil or turmeric in greater than culinary quantities if you are pregnant or breastfeeding, except under the advice of a healthcare professional.

The stalks of the flax are used to make linen, while its seed oil is used in herbal medicine.

Athlete's foot and fungal infections

Once a fungal infection takes hold, it can be hard to get rid of.
Try these herbal options, but be prepared to wait for results.

Tea-tree oil
Melaleuca alternifolia
Proven tinea treatment

Tea-tree oil is effective against a vast number of disease-causing fungi. Clinical trials also support its use, especially in foot conditions, such as tinea pedis (athlete's foot) and onchomycosis, a fungal infection of the toenail that is very difficult to treat and can lead to destruction of the nail.

In order to be effective, the tea-tree oil needs to be used at just the right concentration — in one study, a solution containing 50 percent tea-tree oil killed the fungal infection in 64 percent of tinea sufferers after 4 weeks. However, in another study that used tea-tree at a concentration of only 10 percent, the tinea symptoms improved but the infection remained present.

With fungal nail infections, applying 100 percent tea-tree oil for a minimum of 3 months has been shown to achieve similar results to pharmaceutical topical agents, with about half of all people experiencing improvements in symptoms and the appearance of the affected nails.

DOSAGE To treat athlete's foot (tinea), make a solution containing 25 to 50 percent tea-tree oil in water, and apply to the affected area twice daily for several weeks. Alternatively, add 15 drops of pure tea-tree oil and some salt to an electronic foot bath (the heat and salt may enhance the antifungal activity of the essential oil), and use for 20 minutes twice a day. For onchomycosis, apply 100 percent tea-tree oil to the affected area twice daily for at least 3 months. Specially formulated tea-tree oil products can also be useful for some other types of fungal infections — talk to your medical herbalist.

Native to mountainous regions of South America, pau d'arco prefers a tropical to subtropical climate.

Pau d'arco
Tabebuia impetiginosa
Antifungal remedy
from the Amazon

The wood of the South American tree pau d'arco is famously resistant to fungi. In the traditional medicine of Brazil, a poultice or decoction made from the tree's inner bark is applied to the skin to treat fungal infections as well as conditions such as eczema, psoriasis and skin cancer. Laboratory studies support a number of pau d'arco's traditional uses, including fungicidal activity.

DOSAGE Add 10 g inner bark of pau d'arco to 2½ cups (600 ml) water and simmer gently for 15 minutes. Cool it to a comfortable temperature and then use the decoction as a compress or poultice on the affected area twice daily. For more detailed instructions, see *page 194*.

Cautions

- Tea-tree oil may cause reactions, such as contact dermatitis, itching, burning or scaling of the skin in as many as 1 in 25 people with tinea, especially if used at high concentration or on inflamed or eczematous skin. Use diluted preparations to reduce the likelihood of these reactions occurring, and patch test on an unaffected area of skin 24 hours before applying to any infection or inflammation.

- Pau d'arco can be taken internally to support the immune system during systemic fungal infection. However, such conditions are not suited to self-treatment, especially because certain components of pau d'arco may be toxic if taken in excessive amounts. Consult a professionally trained herbalist for more information before using.

- Do not use any of the herbs listed on this page if you are pregnant or breastfeeding, except under the advice of a healthcare professional.

Cold sores, gums and mouth health

Whether you're suffering from the pain of cold sores, toothache or bleeding gums, herbs can help keep your mouth healthy.

Lemon balm
Melissa officinalis
Cold-sore treatment

Clinical studies show that lemon balm is an effective topical remedy for cold sores, helping to decrease healing time, prevent lesions from spreading and relieve symptoms. Symptomatic relief is particularly impressive on the second day of the outbreak, which is usually the time when symptoms are at their most acute. These effects aren't surprising, since laboratory tests show that the herb, and particularly its fragrant essential oil, has the ability to quickly kill the herpes simplex viruses 1 and 2.

🍃 DOSAGE The lemon balm cream used in the clinical studies mentioned was extremely concentrated (containing the equivalent of 700 mg of lemon balm extract per gram). Look for commercial preparations of the same strength, or

ask a medical herbalist to make some for you. Alternatively, try making a strong infusion of lemon balm and use the liquid in a compress. For more detailed instructions, see *page 194*.

Clove oil
Syzygium aromaticum
Rapid toothache relief

Clove oil is a remarkably effective painkiller and anaesthetic. When applied to toothache or inflamed gums, it reduces pain within minutes — although only for a relatively short time. It works by decreasing the affected tissue's perception of pain, and also has anti-inflammatory and antibacterial properties.

🍃 DOSAGE Dab a small quantity of clove essential oil directly onto the site of the pain. If the essential oil is not available, gently rub powdered cloves or clove buds on the affected area, but take note that they may not be as effective as the essential oil, which is rich in eugenol, the most important active constituent.

Myrrh
Commiphora myrrha
Traditional antiseptic for gums

The gum (or resin) of the myrrh tree is used for the treatment of mouth and gum problems in many of the world's traditional healing systems. It's a useful, fast-acting treatment for mouth ulcers, gingivitis, periodontitis and bleeding gums because it is an effective antiseptic, helps reduce swelling and inflammation, has a local anaesthetic action and encourages wound healing.

🍃 DOSAGE Myrrh is normally used as a tincture, which is available from an herbalist. It can be painted onto mouth

If you brush past lemon balm, the leaves release a delicious lemon-and-mint scent.

A biblical herb

Myrrh has long been a valuable trading commodity, and was used in Ancient times in both incense and cosmetics. It was often worth more than its weight in gold, hence its status as a suitable gift for the infant Jesus. According to the Bible, myrrh was also used to anoint Jesus's body after the crucifixion. Uses throughout the ages include: mummification; the preservation of wine; a treatment for snake bite, intestinal worms and scurvy; and as an aphrodisiac. It is known to kill various pests that carry human parasites, including mosquitoes and ticks; pellets of myrrh were burned in ancient Egyptian homes to help rid them of fleas.

ulcers and infections without being diluted, or added to water (30 to 60 drops at a time) for use as a mouthwash or gargle for more generalized gum problems. See also the mouthwash recipe for bleeding gums, *page 257*.

Cautions
- Only apply clove oil as a topical treatment to teeth and gums. Do not take it internally.
- Clove oil sometimes causes contact dermatitis or worsens irritation of the gums and mucous membranes. If this occurs, stop using it and rinse your mouth thoroughly with water.
- Use clove oil only as an emergency or short-term remedy until you are able to access professional dental care. Avoid using it repeatedly or for long periods of time, as it may damage gum tissue.
- Do not confuse myrrh (*Commiphora myrrha*) with *Myrrhis odorata* (sweet cicely).
- Do not use any of the herbs listed on this page if you are pregnant or breastfeeding, except under the advice of a healthcare professional.

First aid

Stock your herb garden and medicine cabinet with the right remedies and you'll be ready to handle all life's little mishaps.

Aloe vera
Aloe vera, A. ferox
Speedy burn repair

Keep an aloe vera plant (*Aloe* sp., including *Aloe vera* and *A. ferox*) on your kitchen windowsill so that it's handy if you accidentally burn yourself while cooking. Not only does the cooling aloe vera gel soothe the pain of burns, it also reduces inflammation. And if the skin is broken, aloe vera helps protect the burn site from infection as well as encourages the skin's collagen to repair itself. The result is that burns (and other kinds of wounds) heal more rapidly when aloe vera is used; in fact, researchers estimate that using aloe vera gel speeds up burn healing time by more than 8 days.

✎ **DOSAGE** Apply the mucilaginous gel from the center of the aloe vera leaf to the affected area 3 times per day, or use a commercially prepared gel that contains a high percentage of aloe vera. Avoid using small, young leaves, as the active constituents are most prevalent at about 3 years old. When shopping for commercial products, choose those certified by the International Aloe Science Council (IASC), which ensures that the product is of high quality.

Arnica
Arnica montana
Bumps and bruises

Arnica has a long history of use as a topical treatment for bruises and for helping them to heal quickly. Users often report that their bruises change color more quickly and consider this an indication that the healing process is enhanced. It is also traditionally indicated for the treatment of swollen or sprained tissue. Homoeopathic preparations of arnica can be taken internally for the same conditions.

✎ **DOSAGE** Apply arnica cream, ointment or infused oil to the affected area 3 times per day. Choose a product that contains 10 to 20 percent arnica tincture or oil.

Calendula
Calendula officinalis
Skin healer

A traditional remedy for burns, wounds, grazes and rashes, calendula has been documented as encouraging skin healing in a range of circumstances, and may also be useful in helping stop bleeding.

✎ **DOSAGE** For broken skin, first cleanse the wound with an antiseptic solution to ensure that it's clean, then apply calendula tincture to the affected area 3 times per day. For closed wounds, grazes, rashes and burns, apply calendula cream, ointment or infused oil to the affected area 3 times per day.

Chickweed
Stellaria media
Soothes itches and relieves rashes

Cooling chickweed is a traditional remedy for all manner of itchy skin conditions, so it's useful to have on hand to relieve rashes and bites. It may also be useful in soothing the irritation and itch of urticaria or hives.

✎ **DOSAGE** Juice the fresh aerial parts of the chickweed plant, and mix into a cream or ointment base using a ratio of 1 part chickweed to 5 parts base cream. Apply to the affected area as required. Alternatively, use a commercially prepared cream in the same way.

New Zealand tea tree

The essential oil of the New Zealand tea tree or manuka (*Leptospermum scoparium*) is strongly antimicrobial and can be diluted and used to disinfect wounds. A particularly important remedy is honey from bees that graze on manuka. Manuka honey contains a compound called Unique Manuka Factor (UMF), which super-charges its ability to heal infections. Extensive research at the University of Waikato in New Zealand has demonstrated that high-UMF honey disinfects wounds and also encourages them to heal, making it an ideal dressing for leg ulcers and other slow-healing skin infections. High-UMF honey is labeled as "active manuka" honey. Other manuka honeys without the "active" label (or a UMF rating of at least 10) are not likely to be as potent.

Lavender oil
Lavandula angustifolia
Takes the sting out of insect bites

Lavender essential oil can quickly relieve inflammation and swelling when applied to insect bites and stings. It also has antimicrobial activity to help prevent wounds from becoming infected. Its use in burns is reputed to have started when the French scientist Gattefosse (one of the pioneers of aromatherapy) stuck his hand in a nearby bowl of lavender oil after burning himself in his laboratory, and was intrigued by how quickly his skin healed.

✎ **DOSAGE** Dab undiluted lavender oil onto insect bites or stings as quickly as possible after they occur. For wounds and burns, first cleanse the wound with an antiseptic solution to ensure that it's clean, then apply undiluted lavender oil to the affected area 3 times a day.

Slippery elm

Ulmus rubra
Drawing agent for
splinters and boils

In the same way that slippery elm is used internally to reduce inflammation in the gastrointestinal tract, its soothing properties can also be applied to irritated and inflamed skin. Mixed with water, it forms a gel-like layer that protects the wound and allows it to heal. Slippery elm poultices can also be used to draw splinters and other foreign bodies from the skin, and to encourage boils and abscesses to come to a head.

DOSAGE Mix slippery elm bark powder with hot water until it has a pastelike consistency, and use it as a poultice on wounds, to draw foreign bodies out of the skin or to hasten the resolution of boils and abscesses. For more detailed instructions, see *page 194*.

Tea-tree oil

Melaleuca alternifolia
Nature's potent antiseptic

Tea-tree oil is one of nature's most important antiseptics, and its activity against an extensive variety of bacteria, viruses and fungi is well documented. Since it also has anti-inflammatory properties, it's very useful for cuts, grazes and deeper wounds, and can help prevent them from becoming infected.

DOSAGE Tea-tree oil can be used undiluted to help cleanse wounds at risk of infection or on tougher skin surfaces (for example, the soles of the feet), but will often make an open wound sting and smart, so in most cases a solution containing 15 percent tea-tree oil is more appropriate. Creams and lotions containing tea-tree oil are also available.

Cautions

- Do not consume essential oils of tea-tree or lavender.
- Do not consume aloe vera gel unless in a commercial form that is specifically intended for internal use.

ALOË VERA VULGARIS.

Aloe vera gel is reputed to have been used by Cleopatra as a beauty preparation.

- Do not take arnica internally, except in its very dilute homoeopathic form. Do not apply it to broken skin or near the eyes or mouth. Do not use topical applications of arnica for more than 10 days at a time.
- Topical applications of any herb can sometimes cause reactions, such as dermatitis, or itching and burning sensations, so perform a patch test at least 24 hours before use. Discontinue use if a reaction develops. Take particular care with arnica and calendula if you are allergic to the Asteraceae family (for example, daisies, chrysanthemum and echinacea) and with arnica if you are allergic to the Lauraceae family (for example, sassafras, avocado, camphor laurel). Take note that topical use of essential oils may also irritate the skin, especially if it is already inflamed.
- With the exception of topical applications of calendula and aloe vera, do not use the herbs listed on these pages if you are pregnant or breastfeeding, except under the advice of a healthcare professional.

Sports injuries, sprains and strains

Taken a nasty knock? These herbs can help you get up and about and back on the playing field.

Arnica

Arnica montana
Reduces bruising and repairs swollen or injured tissue

Topical applications of arnica have traditionally been used to reduce bruising and stimulate the healing of muscles and other soft tissues after trauma. As long as the skin is not broken, arnica can be rubbed into sprains, strains, swollen joints, fractures and dislocations. It is also used internally in extremely dilute homoeopathic preparations, and although this use is controversial in the medical world, several clinical trials have been published that suggest arnica may have a beneficial effect. For example, marathon runners have been documented to experience less muscle soreness when they take homoeopathic arnica pills in the days before and after a race.

🍃 DOSAGE Apply arnica cream, ointment or infused oil to the affected area 3 times per day. For internal use, take commercially prepared homoeopathic arnica pills or liquid in the strength 30x (sometimes labeled 30D) according to the manufacturer's instructions.

Comfrey

Symphytum officinale
Traditionally used to heal strains, sprains and fractures

Comfrey was once widely used internally as well as externally to encourage broken bones to heal, and was so highly regarded for this use that it was also known by the names "knitbone" and 'boneset." However, following the revelation that some of its compounds (known as pyrrolizidine alkaloids) are potentially toxic, these days its use is restricted to topical applications.

As well as being used for fractures, comfrey helps soothe and take the swelling out of strains and sprains.

🍃 DOSAGE Juice the fresh aerial parts of the comfrey plant, and mix into a cream or ointment base using a ratio of 1 part comfrey to 5 parts base cream. Apply to the affected area as required. Alternatively, blend a few fresh leaves from a comfrey plant into a pulp and make a poultice from them. For detailed instructions, see *page 194*. If you don't have access to a comfrey plant, commercial cream and ointments are also available.

Witch hazel

Hamamelis virginiana
Stems bleeding and reduces swelling

With its high concentration of tannins, witch hazel is highly regarded as an astringent remedy with the ability to stop bleeding and reduce inflammation — especially the localised swelling caused by sprains and other injuries. It is also used to encourage the healing of bruises.

🍃 DOSAGE Apply commercially prepared witch hazel cream or ointment to strains, sprains, grazes or bruises 2 to 3 times per day. Alternatively, prepare a decoction using 1 to 2 teaspoons of the dried leaves or bark, and use the liquid to make a compress for the affected part. For detailed instructions, see *page 194*.

With the help of a witch hazel wand, a witch performs a curative spell on a man's swollen foot. The word "witch" in witch hazel comes from the Old English *wice*, meaning "bendable."

White willow bark

Salix alba
Aspirin-like pain relief

Studies show that white willow bark preparations, standardized for their content of salicin, provide effective relief of lower back pain, with up to 40 percent of volunteers becoming pain-free after taking the herb for 4 weeks. These results are not surprising, since salicin (which has aspirin-like properties), has well-documented anti-inflammatory and analgesic effects.

🍃 DOSAGE Take commercially prepared white willow bark tablets or capsules (standardized to contain 240 mg of salicin per day), according to the manufacturer's instructions.

The hairy foliage of the comfrey plant may cause skin irritation in some people.

Devil's claw

Harpagophytum procumbens
Highly effective anti-inflammatory

This African herb has a long history of use to reduce pain and inflammation in muscles and joints, and is traditionally prescribed for joint, back and tendon pain caused by injury and overuse. These traditional applications are supported by scientific studies in which devil's claw reduced muscle stiffness when taken for 4 weeks, and reduced back pain and increased mobility in 4 to 8 weeks.

DOSAGE The most important active constituent of devil's claw is a compound called harpagoside, and according to researchers, preparations standardized for their content of harpagoside are more effective than non-standardized preparations. Look for commercial tablets or capsules providing at least 50 mg harpagoside per day, and take according to the manufacturer's instructions.

Cramp bark

Viburnum opulus
Muscle relaxant and anti-spasmodic

If you're prone to tension or spasms in your muscles, cramp bark may be just the herb you're looking for. Native Americans used it to relieve cramps and other types of muscle pain, and herbalists still prescribe it today. With an ability to reduce both long- and short-term muscle tension, it is considered particularly effective for overuse injuries and backache.

DOSAGE Take commercially prepared cramp bark tablets or tincture, up to a maximum dose of 1 g, 3 times per day.

St. John's wort

Hypericum perforatum
Topical treatment for nerve pain

Topical applications of St. John's wort have historically been used to treat nerve pain of various kinds, but especially the pain of sciatica. This traditional use is supported by laboratory tests that demonstrate both anti-inflammatory and painkilling properties.

DOSAGE Rub the infused oil of St. John's wort flowers into the affected part, 2 to 3 times per day. For instructions on how to make infused oils, see *page 195*. Alternatively, buy a commercial product.

Cautions

- Arnica and comfrey should not be taken internally (except in their very dilute homoeopathic forms), and should not be applied to broken skin or near the eyes. Avoid using comfrey for more than 10 days at a time.
- Topical applications of any herb can sometimes cause reactions, such as dermatitis or itching and burning sensations, and ideally a patch test should be performed at least 24 hours prior to use; discontinue if a reaction develops. Take particular care with arnica if you are allergic to the Asteraceae (for example, daisies, chrysanthemum, echinacea) or Lauraceae families of plants (for example, sassafras, avocado, camphor laurel).
- Cramp bark berries are poisonous and should not be ingested.
- Do not take white willow bark if you are allergic to salicylates (including aspirin). If you are taking antiplatelet or anti-coagulant medication, or if you suffer from a blood disorder, only take it under professional supervision.
- Devil's claw may occasionally cause digestive problems, such as diarrhea, and should not be used by people with pre-existing gastrointestinal complaints, such as ulcers, gall stones or diarrhea, except under professional advice.
- Do not take devil's claw if you are taking warfarin or antiarrhythmic drugs, except under professional advice. Stop taking devil's claw at least 2 weeks before undergoing surgery.
- Devil's claw does not appear to be effective for back pain that radiates down the legs, a symptom that may indicate nerve involvement. It should be investigated by a healthcare professional.
- With the exception of topical applications of St. John's wort and witch hazel, do not use any of these herbs if you are pregnant or breastfeeding, except under the advice of a healthcare professional.

Take action

The actions you take immediately after a soft tissue injury have a direct influence on how quickly the problem heals.

- **Reduce** blood flow and slow both swelling and bleeding by resting the injured part as quickly as you can.

- **Apply** an ice pack to the injured area to reduce inflammation, pain and tissue damage, but always make sure you protect your skin from ice burn by placing a wet towel or cloth beneath the ice and your skin.

- **Apply** a firm, wide bandage, known as a compression bandage, over the injured area to help reduce bleeding and swelling.

- **Raise** the injured part so it is higher than the heart, further reducing blood flow to the area.

- **Consult** your physiotherapist or doctor as soon as possible, because many soft tissue injuries require professional treatment.

Arthritis and gout

Don't let the stiffness, debilitating pain and inflammation of arthritis cramp your style. Try some herbal remedies.

Boswellia
Boswellia serrata
Relief from rheumatoid and osteoarthritis

The resin from the boswellia tree has been used in Ayurvedic medicine for the treatment of inflammatory and rheumatic conditions for centuries. With a combination of anti-inflammatory, analgesic and immune system-modifying effects, it is particularly relevant for rheumatoid arthritis, an auto-immune form of arthritis that is both debilitating and difficult to treat.

In a review collating the results from 12 rheumatoid arthritis studies, researchers concluded that boswellia was just as effective as some medicinal treatments (for example, gold therapy), and could be particularly useful for sufferers whose arthritis responds poorly

to more conventional medication, for those who have had the disease for a long time, and for children with juvenile chronic arthritis. Boswellia also offers improvements in osteoarthritis, and is documented to help decrease pain and swelling, improve range of motion and increase walking distance in people with osteoarthritis of the knee.

DOSAGE Look for commercial preparations standardized for their content of the active constituents boswellic acids, and take according to manufacturer's instructions or as professionally prescribed. The research into osteoarthritis used the equivalent of 1000 mg of boswellia resin (sometimes referred to as oleo-gum or gum resin) per day, standardized to contain 40 percent (400 mg) boswellic acids. Research indicates that it may take up to 2 months for significant effects to be felt, but that

The rhizomes of the leafy ginger plant are harvested at least a year after planting.

they persist for some time after the herb is stopped. Rheumatoid arthritis is a complex condition that is not well suited to self-treatment — ask your healthcare professional to assess whether boswellia is an appropriate treatment for you, and only take it according to the prescribed dosage.

Devil's claw
Harpagophytum procumbens
Clinically proven for arthritis pain

Devil's claw has anti-inflammatory and analgesic properties, and is a proven treatment for osteoarthritis, with several studies demonstrating its benefits — particularly for osteoarthritis of the knee and/or hip. In some of these studies, devil's claw was compared to pharmaceutical analgesics, with researchers concluding that the herb was just as effective as the drug, but with a lower incidence of side effects. Laboratory tests suggest that devil's claw may provide more than just symptomatic relief — it also appears to inhibit some of the

Devil's claw, a creeping perennial, gets its name from the hooks on its strange-looking fruits.

processes that both damage cartilage and trigger the joint changes characteristic of osteoarthritis. Clinical trials indicate that pain and other symptoms of osteoarthritis start to abate after about 2 months of taking the herb.

DOSAGE The most important active constituent of devil's claw is a compound called harpagoside, and according to researchers, preparations standardized for their content of harpagoside are more effective than non-standardized preparations. Look for commercially prepared tablets or capsules providing at least 50 mg harpagoside per day, and take according to the manufacturer's instructions.

Ginger

Zingiber officinale
The spicy anti-inflammatory

The humble spice ginger is also a potent medicine with impressive anti-inflammatory capabilities. Laboratory tests show that ginger inhibits a number of the compounds that promote inflammation in the body — including several of the enzymes that are targeted by pharmaceutical anti-arthritis medications. As a result, it provides relief from arthritis pain, and some studies have even found it to be as effective as the non-steroidal anti-inflammatory drug ibuprofen.

DOSAGE Add 20 to 30 drops of ginger tincture to water, or infuse 1/2 teaspoon powdered ginger or 1 to 2 teaspoons of grated fresh ginger root in boiling water; take 3 times per day. Concentrated ginger tablets may also be useful.

White willow bark

Salix alba
Herbal pain reliever

The bark of the white willow tree is believed to have been used as an herbal painkiller since at least the time of Hippocrates. Laboratory tests have demonstrated the anti-inflammatory

and analgesic properties of its aspirin-like substances. Most (but not all) clinical trials also support its role in relieving the pain of osteoarthritis, but there has not been enough research to confirm its effectiveness in the treatment of rheumatoid arthritis.

DOSAGE Take commercial white willow tablets or capsules standardized to contain 240 mg of salicin per day according to the manufacturer's instructions.

Celery seed

Apium graveolens
Handy gout remedy

Celery seed is a traditional remedy for all kinds of arthritis, but it is considered particularly effective for the treatment of gout. This extremely painful form of arthritis classically affects a single joint, such as the big toe, which rapidly becomes hot, swollen and inflamed.

DOSAGE Boil 0.5 to 2 g dried celery seed in a cup of water for 10 minutes; drink the decoction up to 3 times daily. Alternatively, take a commercially prepared tincture, tablet or capsule according to the manufacturer's instructions.

Cautions

- Boswellia occasionally causes mild adverse effects, such as diarrhea or hives. If this happens, discontinue its use. Little is known about potential interactions between boswellia and other medications, so if you are taking prescription drugs, talk to your doctor or pharmacist before using it.
- Devil's claw may occasionally cause digestive problems such as diarrhea, so should not be used by people with pre-existing gastrointestinal complaints, such as ulcers, gall stones or diarrhea, except under professional advice.
- Do not take devil's claw if you are taking warfarin or anti-arrhythmic drugs, except under professional advice. Stop taking devil's claw at least 2 weeks before undergoing surgery.
- Do not take white willow bark if you are allergic to salicylates, including aspirin. If you are taking antiplatelet or anticoagulant medication, or suffer from a blood disorder, take it only under professional supervision.

White willow grows in damp places and was introduced to the eastern U.S. from Europe during the Colonial times.

- Ginger should not be taken in medicinal doses by people suffering from gastric ulcer or gall stones, or those taking warfarin or antiplatelet medication, except under professional advice. Stop taking it at least 2 weeks prior to undergoing surgery.
- Celery seed may interact with medications, including warfarin and thyroxine. It may also increase the risk of side effects associated with some forms of ultraviolet light therapy. Consult your doctor before use.
- Do not use celery seed if you have a kidney disorder, or if you have low blood pressure.
- Celery occasionally causes allergic reactions. Do not take the seed if you are allergic to the plant or vegetable, and exercise caution if you are allergic to dandelion or wild carrot.
- With the exception of ginger, do not take these herbs if you are pregnant or breastfeeding, except under the advice of a healthcare professional.

Circulation problems and varicose veins

Inadequate circulation – particularly in the legs – can become a persistent and debilitating problem as you age.

Horse chestnut

Aesculus hippocastanum
Relieves symptoms of
chronic venous insufficiency

The term "chronic venous insufficiency" is used medically to describe leg veins that are having trouble pumping blood back up to the heart. In time, and with the effects of gravity, the legs become heavy and swollen, and can feel itchy, tense and painful. Varicose veins may also develop. At least 17 clinical trials have examined the effects of horse chestnut seed extract (HCSE), standardized for its content of escin, on the symptoms of chronic venous insufficiency. Collectively, this research demonstrates that HCSE can help to relieve the pain, swelling and itchiness associated with chronic venous insufficiency. It appears to do this by helping to maintain the integrity of the blood vessel walls.

DOSAGE Take commercial tablets or capsules of HCSE that are standardized for their content of escin (sometimes spelt aescin). Look for a product that provides 100 to 200 mg of escin per day, and always take it with food.

Grapeseed

Vitis vinifera
Antioxidant support
for blood vessels

Grapeseed extract is rich in a potent group of antioxidants collectively referred to as oligomeric proanthocyanidins (OPCs). OPCs help to maintain the integrity of the blood vessels and stabilise the capillary walls, so they may be beneficial for a wide range of circulatory problems. In people with chronic venous insufficiency, grapeseed extract has been shown to relieve symptoms such as itchiness and leg pain in as little as 10 days,

and it's likely to have even more benefits for the circulatory system when taken over a longer period of time.

DOSAGE Look for commercial grapeseed tablets, or capsules that are standardized to provide 150 to 300 mg OPCs per day, and take them according to the manufacturer's instructions.

Ginkgo

Ginkgo biloba
Tonic for peripheral circulation

Although most famous for its action as a memory tonic, ginkgo is also an important circulatory tonic. For example, it helps relieve symptoms of both Raynaud's syndrome and intermittent claudication — two conditions associated with peripheral circulation issues. Raynaud's syndrome is characterized by coldness of the extremities and intermittent claudication by severe cramping pain in the legs that is triggered or exacerbated by walking.

DOSAGE Look for supplements standardized for their content of the active constituents ginkgo flavone glycosides, ginkgolides and bilobalides, with a daily dose of 120 mg of a concentrated (50:1) extract, providing the equivalent of 6 g
of the dried herb. Higher doses may be required for intermittent claudication — for more information, talk to your healthcare professional.

Cautions

- Horse chestnut, ginkgo and grapeseed are known or suspected to interact with some prescription medications, so consult your doctor or pharmacist before taking them. Stop taking ginkgo and grapeseed at least 2 weeks before undergoing surgery.
- HCSE occasionally causes side effects including gastrointestinal symptoms,

The abundant qualities of grapes are exemplified in an 1870s wallpaper design by William Morris.

nausea, headaches and itchy or irritated skin. If this occurs, stop taking the herb and seek medical advice.
- Do not take homemade horse chestnut or ginkgo preparations, as they may contain toxic compounds and/or cause adverse reactions.
- Do not use horse chestnut if you are allergic to latex, as cross-reactivity may occur.
- Do not take HCSE if you have diabetes, liver or kidney problems, or celiac or other intestinal diseases, or if you are taking anti-platelet or anticoagulant medication, except under professional supervision.
- Grapeseed may reduce iron absorption, so separate doses by 2 hours.
- Ginkgo may cause mild adverse reactions, including dizziness, gastrointestinal upset, headache and allergic skin reactions. More severe reactions, including bleeding problems and seizures, have occasionally been recorded. If symptoms occur, stop taking the herb and seek medical advice.
- Do not take ginkgo if you have any kind of bleeding disorder.
- Do not use any of the herbs listed on this page if you are pregnant or breast-feeding, except under the advice of a healthcare professional.

Leg ulcers

A leg ulcer that won't heal can have a negative impact on your quality of life. Use herbs to aid the healing process.

Horse chestnut
Aesculus hippocastanum
Helps heal ulcers from the inside

According to a small clinical trial, a standardized extract of horse chestnut seed (HCSE) has been demonstrated to enhance the standard medical treatment of leg ulcers. Australian researchers found that compared to those taking a placebo, the wound dressings on the legs of people taking HCSE could be changed less frequently, resulting in a significantly lower cost of treatment. These effects are probably an extension of the actions of horse chestnut on peripheral circulation (see opposite), as about half of all leg ulcers occur as a result of chronic venous insufficiency.

DOSAGE Take commercial tablets or capsules of HCSE that are standardized for their content of escin. Look for a product that provides 100 to 200 mg of escin per day, and always take it with food.

Gotu kola
Centella asiatica
Nature's tissue healer

Gotu kola contains compounds that encourage wounds, ulcers and scars to heal, and can be used both internally and externally for this purpose. Taken internally, it can also aid symptoms of chronic venous insufficiency so, like horse chestnut, it may encourage the healing of ulcers.

DOSAGE Take commercially prepared tablets or capsules of gotu kola extract according to the manufacturer's instructions. For topical use, add gotu kola tincture to a cream or ointment base (for detailed instructions, see *page 193*), and apply to the affected area 2 to 3 times per day.

Calendula
Calendula officinalis
Accelerates ulcer healing

Calendula ointment was recently the subject of a small-scale clinical trial that suggests it may play a valuable role in helping to heal leg ulcers. In this study, ulcers were treated with either calendula ointment or saline solution dressings for 3 weeks. At the end of the trial, the ulcers treated with calendula ointment had shrunk in size by more than 40 percent, while those treated with saline had only decreased by about 15 percent.

DOSAGE Apply calendula ointment to the affected area 2 to 3 times per day, or soak dressings with calendula tincture and then apply to the affected area. You can also use fresh calendula flowers to make a poultice (see *page 194*). If the skin is broken, disinfect the wound by washing it with an antiseptic before using calendula.

Cautions
- Ulcers are not well-suited to self-treatment, as they may be symptomatic of underlying vascular problems. Always seek medical advice before commencing any self-prescribed treatment, including topical applications.
- HCSE occasionally causes side effects, including gastrointestinal symptoms, nausea, headaches and itchy or irritated skin. It should not be taken by people with a latex allergy.
- Do not consume homemade horse chestnut preparations, as they may contain toxic compounds.
- Do not take HCSE if you have diabetes, liver or kidney problems, or celiac or other intestinal diseases, or if you are taking anti-platelet or anticoagulant medication, except under the supervision of a healthcare professional.
- The skin around leg ulcers is particularly prone to dermatitis and rashes. Ideally, a patch test should be performed at least 24 hours before any topical application. If a reaction develops, discontinue use and seek medical advice. Take particular care with calendula if you are allergic to the Asteraceae family of plants (for example, daisies, chrysanthemum and echinacea).
- With the exception of topical applications of calendula, do not use any of the herbs listed on this page if you are pregnant or breastfeeding, except under the advice of a healthcare professional.

Horse chestnut is also known as buckeye, because the seeds resemble the eyes of deer.

High blood pressure and high cholesterol

Blood pressure and cholesterol levels are important indicators of heart health, as well as your risk of cardiovascular disease.

Hawthorn

Crataegus laevigata, C. monogyna,
C. pinnatifida
Classic heart tonic

Herbalists regard hawthorn as the most important of all cardiovascular remedies, with a protective action on the heart and its function. It is prescribed for a range of cardiovascular problems, including high blood pressure, high cholesterol, angina, irregular heartbeat and heart failure. Numerous clinical trials support the use of hawthorn as an adjunctive treatment for heart failure, and in this context it is documented to help reduce blood pressure as well as improve other symptoms, such as tiredness and shortness of breath. Some of hawthorn's active constituents have potent antioxidant activity, and these compounds may be responsible for the herb's cholesterol-lowering effects, helping to prevent the oxidation of LDL-cholesterol (so-called "bad" cholesterol), and decreasing both the production and absorption of cholesterol.

DOSAGE Ask your healthcare professional to assess whether hawthorn is an appropriate treatment for you, and take it according to the dosage prescribed. To ensure you receive a guaranteed dose of the herb's key active constituents, your practitioner may stipulate a standardized hawthorn preparation. Take it for at least 2 months before assessing whether it's working effectively. Western herbalists have long used *Crataegus laevigata* and *C. monogyna* to treat cardiovascular problems. In traditional Chinese medicine, *C. pinnatifida* has an extensive history of use as a digestive tonic, but its application has extended to heart complaints, in line with the promising results attributed to the European species.

Garlic

Allium sativum
Protects the heart and blood vessels

There's good evidence to suggest that the more garlic you include in your diet, the less likely you are to suffer from cardiovascular disease. And when taken as an herbal medicine, it's been shown to lower blood pressure, reduce total cholesterol levels and the development of plaque in the arteries, and inhibit the formation of blood clots. Some of these actions in the body are only mild, temporary or applicable to certain groups of people, but because it works via several pathways, the collective effect is a degree of protection for overall cardiovascular health.

DOSAGE The scientific research into garlic's potential as a treatment for high blood pressure and cholesterol is controversial — not least because different commercial garlic preparations have different chemical characteristics, and some may not retain the medicinally effective compounds, which can degrade quickly after the garlic bulb is cut or crushed. If you decide to take garlic tablets or capsules, opt for those that are enteric-coated and labeled with a guaranteed yield of the compound allicin, or standardized for their content of alliin. Other high-quality supplements may be standardized for their content of S-allyl-L-cysteine (SAC). Follow the dosage recommendations of the manufacturer. If you prefer to consume garlic as a food, aim to eat at least 3 cloves per week, or even more if you are at particular risk of cardiovascular disease. Chop or mince the cloves, then leave them to stand at room temperature for 5 to 10 minutes, so that enzymatic reaction allows the biologically active compounds to develop.

With its bushy habit and white flowers followed by red berries, the hawthorn makes a pretty hedge.

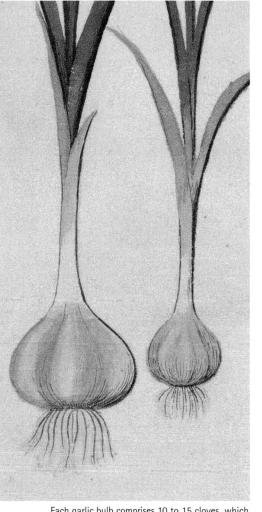

Each garlic bulb comprises 10 to 15 cloves, which form the plant's underground storage system.

Turmeric

Curcuma longa
Cholesterol-clearing spice

Turmeric is another culinary spice that supports heart and blood vessel health. It contains a yellow-colored pigment called curcumin — the compound that is credited with most of the herb's medicinal activity. For example, curcumin has been shown to lower levels of total cholesterol, increase levels of HDL-cholesterol ("good" cholesterol), and protect both HDL- and LDL-cholesterol from the damaging effects of free radical activity. In laboratory and animal studies, it has also been shown to help lower blood pressure and reduce the ability of cholesterol to form plaque on artery walls.

DOSAGE Add up to 3 g of grated or powdered turmeric root to your cooking each day. Alternatively, look for a commercial preparation that has been standardized to contain 95 percent curcumin, and take it according to the manufacturer's instructions, up to a maximum of 300 mg per day.

Psyllium

Plantago ovata, P. psyllium
Lowers cholesterol levels

Psyllium is an important source of water-soluble fiber, which forms an absorbent gel in the bowel, trapping cholesterol and facilitating its excretion from the body. Combining psyllium with a low-fat diet for as little as 8 weeks has been shown to reduce LDL-cholesterol without adversely affecting HDL-cholesterol levels. Under professional supervision, psyllium may be particularly beneficial for patients with type 2 diabetes, because it can also help control their blood glucose and insulin responses after meals.

DOSAGE Psyllium husks are available in tablet, capsule and soluble powder form, and should be taken according to the manufacturer's instructions (note that the dose of psyllium used in cholesterol research is generally about 10 g per day). Every dose of psyllium should be taken with a large glass of water.

Lime flowers

Tilia cordata, T. platyphyllos, T. x europaea
Calming blood pressure remedy

Lime flowers are a traditional European medicine for high blood pressure, especially when it is accompanied by heart palpitations or hardening of the arteries. They are also a gently calming remedy for anxiety and restlessness, so are particularly useful when high blood pressure is caused or worsened by worry.

DOSAGE Infuse 1 teaspoon of dried lime flowers in boiling water and drink up to 3 cups per day.

Cautions

- Heart disease and other cardiovascular conditions are potentially serious issues, and should not be self-treated. Always follow the advice of your doctor, and if you experience any symptoms that may indicate a heart attack, such as chest pain (which may radiate to the jaw, back or arms), shortness of breath, or a general feeling of discomfort in the upper body, call for an ambulance without delay.
- Hawthorn, garlic and turmeric are known or suspected to interact with many prescription medications (including heart, blood pressure, cholesterol and blood-thinning drugs), and may alter the dosage requirements of your existing medication, so consult your doctor or pharmacist before taking these particular herbal remedies.
- Occasionally, adverse effects of hawthorn have been reported in clinical trials, but they tend to be mild and transient. The symptoms may include digestive problems, headache, dizziness, sleepiness and palpitations. If you experience any of these symptoms, consult your healthcare professional.
- Garlic sometimes causes side effects, including gastrointestinal discomfort, nausea, indigestion, offensive breath and body odor. Some of these effects can be minimized by eating cooked rather than raw garlic.
- Turmeric sometimes causes side effects of gastrointestinal upset when taken in large doses. Except under professional advice, it should not be used at higher than culinary doses by people with liver and gallbladder disease (including gall stones), gastric or duodenal ulcer, or people taking blood-thinning medication.
- Persons with diagnosed intestinal illness should only use psyllium on medical advice.
- Psyllium may interfere with the absorption of other medicines, so separate doses by at least 2 hours.
- Always drink plenty of water when using psyllium, as occasionally cases of choking have been reported when psyllium powders have been taken without adequate fluids.
- Lime flowers may reduce the absorption of iron, so separate doses by at least 2 hours.
- Contact allergies to lime flowers have occasionally been reported.
- If you are pregnant or breastfeeding, do not take hawthorn, lime flowers or psyllium, except under professional supervision. Do not take garlic or turmeric in greater than culinary quantities.

Premenstrual syndrome

There is gentle herbal help available for treating hormonal imbalances, period pain, mood swings and cravings.

Chaste tree
Vitex agnus-castus
Clinically proven to reduce PMS symptoms

In clinical trials, chaste tree extracts have shown a remarkable ability to relieve many of the symptoms of premenstrual syndrome (PMS), including depression, anger and irritability, mood swings, food cravings, bowel problems, and headaches. It achieves these effects by helping to normalize the complex hormonal fluctuations that govern the female menstrual cycle, and can help set up a regular pattern of menstruation. In clinical practice, herbalists also prescribe chaste tree (often in combination with other herbs) for women who are experiencing difficulties conceiving.

🍃 DOSAGE To relieve the symptoms of premenstrual syndrome, take tablets, capsules or tincture throughout the month, according to the manufacturer's instructions. Look for products that are standardized for their content of the compounds casticin and/or agnuside. Results may take 12 weeks or longer to become noticeable. If you're experiencing difficulty conceiving, consult a medical herbalist who has been professionally trained and who can help to determine whether chaste tree is appropriate for you.

The fruits of the chaste tree are used as a pepper substitute and in Middle Eastern spice mixes.

White peony
Paeonia lactiflora
Hormone balancer

In the traditional medicine of China and Japan, white peony root is combined with other herbs to treat period pain, heavy bleeding, uterine fibroids and other issues that, in Chinese medical philosophy, are associated with pelvic congestion. It is commonly prescribed with licorice for conditions such as polycystic ovarian syndrome (PCOS) and endometriosis and, like chaste tree, is thought to exert its effects via a balancing influence on hormone levels.

🍃 DOSAGE Talk to a professionally trained herbalist, who can help to determine whether white peony is appropriate for your individual needs.

Dong quai
Angelica polymorpha var. *sinensis*
Chinese tonic for female problems

Dong quai is another herb prescribed in traditional Chinese medicine for female reproductive disorders. Among other indications, and generally in combination with other herbs, it is prescribed for a range of gynaecological conditions, including painful, irregular, scanty or absent periods. To date there has been little clinical research to confirm whether the high regard in which it is held in China is justified.

DOSAGE Boil 1 to 3 g dried dong quai root in a cup of water for 10 minutes; drink the decoction 3 times daily. Alternatively, take commercial tablets or capsules, according to the manufacturer's instructions.

St. John's wort
Hypericum perforatum
Proven antidepressant

PMS causes many women to experience depression, increased anxiety and also difficulty in relating to family and friends. Since its efficacy for the treatment of depression from other causes is well established, it's likely that St. John's wort is also an effective treatment for these PMS symptoms. In a small pilot study published in 2000, women taking St. John's wort reported that the severity of their mental and emotional PMS symptoms had improved by more than 50 percent after just two menstrual cycles. Further investigation is required to determine whether longer-term use has additional health benefits.

DOSAGE Look for supplements that are standardized for their content of hypericin and hyperforin, which are considered the main active constituents, and with a daily dose of 900 mg per day of the concentrated (6:1) extract, which is equivalent to 5.4 g of the dried herb. Take the supplements throughout the month.

Cramp bark
Viburnum opulus
Pain relief for cramps and spasms

Women who experience period pain of any kind will find cramp bark invaluable because, as its name suggests, it has a long history of use for the relief of cramps. It is traditionally used for any type of spasmodic or cramping pain, including uterine, ovarian, abdominal,

back and leg pains that occur during the premenstrual phase of the monthly cycle.

DOSAGE Take commercially prepared cramp bark tablets or tincture, up to a maximum dose of 1 g, 3 times daily, as required for symptomatic relief.

Clary sage
Salvia sclarea
For period pain
and emotional upsets

The essential oil of clary sage is one of the most popular aromatherapy treatments for PMS, especially as it is also considered to have antidepressant, anti-fatigue and stress-relieving properties. Laboratory research supports the oil's use by demonstrating an antispasmodic action on uterine tissue, but the efficacy of this treatment has only recently been tested in human studies. In 2006, researchers conducted a clinical trial in which college students who suffered from period pain and menstrual cramps used either aromatherapy massage oil containing clary sage, lavender and rose essential oils; massage without aromatherapy; or no treatment at all. The symptoms of the women who received the aromatherapy massage were significantly less severe during the first 2 days of their period than the women in either of the other treatment groups.

DOSAGE To relieve period pain, make a massage oil using 1 drop of clary sage, 1 drop of rose and 2 drops of lavender essential oil per 5 ml of almond oil, and rub into the abdomen or lower back as required. For premenstrual mood swings or emotional problems, clary sage can also be added to an oil vaporizer.

Cautions
- The herbs featured on this page have known or suspected hormonal activity and should not be taken at the same time as the oral contraceptive pill, hormone replacement therapy or other medications that affect hormonal balance, except under professional supervision. People who have a history of hormone-sensitive tumors should only take these herbs under professional advice.

Revered in traditional Chinese medicine, the peony is an inspiration to many Chinese artists.

- Chaste tree occasionally causes mild, reversible side effects, such as headache, nausea and gastrointestinal upset. If you experience any of these symptoms, stop taking it.
- Do not take white peony or dong quai if you are taking warfarin or other blood-thinning or anticoagulant medicines.
- Dong quai is traditionally contraindicated in women with bleeding disorders, heavy periods or a history of recurrent miscarriage. It should not be used during bouts of diarrhea or acute viral infection.
- Cramp bark berries are poisonous and should not be ingested.
- Clary sage essential oil is very potent and should always be diluted and used sparingly. It may cause headaches or sedation in some people, and may also cause contact dermatitis or skin irritation. Do not apply it to inflamed skin or open wounds, and do not use it topically if you are prone to dermatitis.
- For the safe and appropriate use of St. John's wort, see Depression and anxiety, *page 211*.
- Do not use any of the herbs listed on this page if you are pregnant or breastfeeding, except under the advice of a healthcare professional.

Fluid retention and cystitis

Try using these herbs to keep your waterworks in good order and to prevent inflammations and infections such as cystitis.

Cranberry
Vaccinium macrocarpon
Prevents cystitis

Cranberry is famous for its ability to help prevent cystitis, a bladder infection that causes burning pain on urination. It works by preventing the bacteria *E. coli* (which causes the vast majority of cystitis cases) from taking hold on the bladder wall and setting up an infection. This herb is particularly useful for women who experience recurrent urinary tract infections (UTIs), as clinical trials indicate that, over a 12-month period, the frequency of UTIs in women taking cranberry is significantly reduced. Other people who are prone to recurrent UTIs — such as the elderly and people with spinal cord injuries — may also benefit from taking cranberry as a prophylactic against cystitis, but there is not as much scientific data available to confirm its efficacy in these groups of people.

The fruit of the cranberry, shown here at harvest time, follow bell-shaped pink flowers.

🖊 DOSAGE Cranberry can be taken in juice, tablet or capsule form. Many people prefer to take the tablets or capsules, as up to 1¼ cups (300 ml) per day of pure juice may be required in order to reach therapeutic levels. Few commercial juice products contain 100 percent cranberry juice, so if you do decide to take the juice for medicinal purposes, you'll need to calculate how many glasses of juice you require, depending on the percentage of cranberry that's present in the product. Alternatively, cranberry tablets and capsules are made from concentrated juice, and are generally taken at doses of approximately 30 g (30,000 mg) per day, in divided doses.

Marsh mallow
Althaea officinalis
Soothes inflamed mucous membranes

With its rich content of mucilage, marsh mallow provides soothing relief to irritated mucous membranes of the urinary tract. Herbalists often prescribe it to ease the pain and discomfort of infections or inflammation of the bladder and kidneys.
🖊 DOSAGE Infuse 2 to 5 g of dried marsh mallow root in cold (not hot) water, and steep for 8 hours to release the mucilage; drink up to 3 cups per day.

Self-help for cystitis

Cranberry is an effective preventative medicine for cystitis, but once an infection takes hold, you may need to take stronger medicine. Your doctor may prescribe antibiotics, or your professionally trained medical herbalist may treat you with urinary antiseptics, such as the herb uva-ursi. Meanwhile, these steps can help.

- **Act quickly** While cystitis is generally a relatively mild and self-limiting condition, if it is left untreated, the infection can spread to the kidneys – with much more serious consequences.

- **Increase your fluid intake** Although the intense pain during urination may discourage you from drinking more, it's vital that you do. At the first sign of symptoms, increase your fluids to about 1 liter per hour, if possible. This helps flush bacteria from the bladder, and can help prevent infections from becoming more serious. Choose water or soothing herbal teas (such as marsh mallow), and avoid alcohol, caffeine and fizzy soft drinks, which may aggravate the problem.

- **Make sure your bladder is completely empty** every time you go to the toilet. Wait a few moments after urinating, and then try again to expel the last few milliliters of urine from the bladder. Afterwards, women should take care to wipe from front to back to ensure that bacteria from the anus aren't accidentally transferred to the urinary tract.

- **Alkalize your urine** Reducing urinary acidity may help to relieve burning symptoms, and can also make it more difficult for bacteria to survive. Avoid acidic foods, such as citrus and tomatoes, and consider taking a commercial urinary alkalizer (available from pharmacies). A home remedy of a teaspoon of baking soda in water is also an effective urinary alkalizer.

Dandelion leaf

Taraxacum officinale
Nature's diuretic with
plenty of potassium

Dandelion leaf is traditionally regarded
as one of the most important herbal
remedies for the elimination of excess
fluid, regardless of its cause. Although
there is little data available to confirm
its efficacy in humans, a small number
of animal studies suggest that it may be
as effective as some commonly prescribed
pharmaceutical drugs. Dandelion leaf is a
natural source of potassium; therefore, it
doesn't tend to cause the adverse effects
associated with potassium depletion that
are sometimes observed with the use of
pharmaceutical diuretics.

✒ DOSAGE Infuse 1 to 2 teaspoons
of dried dandelion leaf in boiling water;
drink 3 cups per day.

Grapeseed

Vitis vinifera
Relieves premenstrual
fluid retention

Hormonal fluctuations during the
menstrual cycle can cause troublesome
fluid retention in some women. Although
predominantly considered a remedy for
the blood vessels, grapeseed extract has
also been documented to effectively
reduce premenstrual fluid retention and
associated symptoms, including weight
gain and abdominal pain and swelling.

✒ DOSAGE Look for grapeseed
tablets or capsules that are standardized
to provide 150 to 300 mg oligomeric
proanthocyanidins (OPCs) per day, and
take them during the second half of the
menstrual cycle. You may need to take
them for several months before
experiencing the full benefits.

Cautions

- UTIs are potentially serious — consult
  your doctor at the first sign of symptoms
  or if your symptoms worsen during
  treatment. Always investigate UTIs
  in children immediately.

- Fluid retention is sometimes a symptom
  of heart problems or other serious health
  conditions, in which case medical treatment
  is required. Always talk to your doctor
  before commencing self-treatment.

- High doses of cranberry juice may cause
  diarrhea and other gastrointestinal
  symptoms — if this occurs, discontinue
  use immediately.

- If you are taking warfarin or have a history
  of kidney stones, do not take medicinal
  quantities of cranberry except under
  professional supervision.

- If you have diabetes, avoid drinking high
  quantities of sugar-sweetened cranberry
  juice and do not take marsh mallow except
  under professional supervision, as it may
  affect blood sugar levels.

- Marsh mallow may interfere with the
  absorption of other medication, and
  grapeseed may reduce iron absorption, so
  separate doses by at least 2 hours.

- Don't use dandelion leaf if you are allergic
  to members of the Asteraceae family
  of plants (for example, daisies, echinacea).

- Grapeseed and dandelion leaf (and,
  particularly, the potassium found in
  dandelion) may interact with some
  medications, so check with your doctor
  or pharmacist before taking them.

- Do not use dandelion if you suffer from
  liver or gallbladder disease (including
  gall stones).

- Stop taking grapeseed at least 2 weeks
  before undergoing surgery.

- With the exception of normal culinary
  quantities of cranberry, do not take the
  herbs on this page if you are pregnant or
  breastfeeding, except under the advice of
  a healthcare professional.

There are hundreds of cultivars of the grape vine, grown for fruit (fresh and dried) as well as wine.

Menopause

There are natural herbal remedies that will help support your body through the demands of menopause or the change.

Black cohosh

Actaea racemosa
Proven treatment for hot flushes

An extract of the North American herb black cohosh has been used to relieve menopause symptoms for more than 50 years. As the subject of numerous clinical trials, black cohosh extract has demonstrated significant improvements in symptoms such as hot flushes, night sweats, insomnia, depression and anxiety. Of these, it is probably most effective against hot flushes, which many women consider the most troublesome aspect of menopause. Some research indicates that hot flushes may be reduced by more than 50 percent after just 4 weeks of therapy with standardized black cohosh extract. When taken under medical supervision, this extract may also be beneficial for some women who, for medical reasons, are unable to use menopause treatments that are estrogen-based, or who prefer to use natural alternatives.

🖋 DOSAGE Take black cohosh tablets standardized for their content of triterpene glycosides according to the manufacturer's instructions, or as prescribed by your doctor. You may need to take black cohosh for up to 3 months before your symptoms start to improve.

St. John's wort

Hypericum perforatum
Relieves anxiety and depression

While black cohosh is very effective for the treatment of hot flushes, night sweats and insomnia, its effects against the anxiety and depression that sometimes come with menopause are less marked. Consequently, herbalists often prescribe it with St. John's wort for women whose menopausal symptoms include emotional upset. When the two herbs were taken together during a 2006 study, significant improvements were noted in both the psychological and physical symptoms. In other research, St. John's wort alone demonstrated a significant ability to reduce menopausal symptoms in women whose primary concerns were mood-related.

🖋 DOSAGE Buy supplements that are standardized for their content of hypericin and hyperforin, which are considered to be the main active constituents, and with a daily dose of 900 mg per day of the concentrated (6:1) extract, equivalent to 5.4 g of the dried herb. Take supplements throughout the month.

Many sages flower for long periods and make an ornamental addition to the garden.

Menopause and soy products

Soy foods are a major dietary source of phytestrogens, plant compounds that have mild estrogen-like effects in the body. Soy phytestrogens can help to reduce menopausal symptoms and appear to have protective effects against some of its associated health problems.

Soybeans, soy flour, miso, tofu and tempeh can all help to top up the small quantities of phytestrogens you obtain from other dietary sources.

Alternatively, supplements that contain concentrated phyto-estrogens (also referred to as isoflavones) are now widely available, and most (but not all) research indicates that they are an effective strategy for reducing hot flushes and night sweats.

Consuming soy phytestrogens at levels higher than normal culinary intake may cause problems for women with some health conditions or who are taking certain types of medications, so talk to your doctor before taking a soy supplement.

Red clover

Trifolium pratense
Herbal phytestrogens

Red clover is an interesting example of an herb whose modern application is largely different to its historical uses. While the flower heads have long been regarded as a detoxifying remedy for skin problems, the relatively recent discovery that the leaves contain phytestrogens similar to those found in soybeans means that red clover is now predominantly thought of as a treatment for menopause. Clinical trials investigating the effects of phyto-estrogens from red clover have yielded ambiguous results, so more research is needed to clarify their effects, but there are some indications that they may help to prevent the decline in cardiovascular and bone health that many women experience after menopause.

🌿 DOSAGE Take commercially prepared red clover isoflavones in doses of 40 to 86 mg per day, or as prescribed by your doctor.

The old French name for sage was *toute bonne*, meaning "all is well."

Sage

Salvia officinalis
Traditionally used to reduce hot flushes

Sage is not only a popular culinary herb, but also a widely used traditional remedy for the relief of hot flushes. The plant is rich in tannins, giving it astringent properties and supporting its use to reduce excessive bodily secretions. In addition to hot flushes, these drying properties may benefit other menopausal symptoms such as night sweats and heavy periods. Laboratory studies have demonstrated that some compounds in sage possess estrogenic effects, which may further help to explain its traditional use in menopause.

🌿 DOSAGE Infuse 1 to 4 g of dried sage in boiling water; drink 3 cups per day.

Lemon balm

Melissa officinalis
Helps anxiety, insomnia and concentration

As a traditional remedy for restlessness and anxiety, lemon balm is ideal for women who find themselves worrying more or becoming more sensitive to stress during and after menopause. Its relaxing properties can also help with sleep disturbances. Lemon balm helps promote feelings of calmness and can be beneficial as a mood lifter when you're feeling emotionally flat. It has also been used to promote mental function, and preliminary research indicates that it may help memory and concentration.

🌿 DOSAGE Infuse 1 to 2 teaspoons of fresh aerial parts of lemon balm in boiling water; drink 1 cup 2 to 3 times per day, with the last cup 30 to 60 minutes before bed.

Cautions

- Do not take any of the herbs listed on these pages if you have a history of hormone-sensitive tumors, endometriosis or uterine fibroids, except under the supervision of a healthcare professional.
- Do not take black cohosh if you are taking any prescription medication, except under medical supervision.
- Do not take black cohosh except under medical supervision if you have a history of liver disease, as some authorities believe that black cohosh may occasionally cause severe liver damage. These instances are extremely rare, but potentially very serious. If you experience minor side effects, such as mild, reversible stomach upset and skin problems, stop using the herb and seek medical advice.
- Do not confuse black cohosh with blue cohosh (*Caulophyllum thalictroides*), which you should only take under medical supervision.
- Do not take red clover isoflavones if you are taking warfarin or anticoagulant medication, except under medical supervision.
- Due to its astringent nature, sage tea has sometimes been reported to cause dryness and irritation of the mouth. If this occurs, try reducing the dose of sage relative to the amount of water used, and make sure you drink plenty of water throughout the day.

- Sage may reduce the absorption of minerals such as calcium and iron, so separate doses by at least 2 hours.
- Lemon balm may interact with some pharmaceutical medications, so consult your doctor or pharmacist before taking it.
- For the safe and appropriate use of St. John's wort, see Depression and anxiety, *page 211*.
- Do not use the herbs on this page if you are pregnant or breastfeeding, except under the advice of a healthcare professional.

Popular in dried form for teas, lemon balm was called the "elixir of life" by Paracelsus (*page 49*).

Pregnancy

Only the safest of herbal medicines are recommended for women to use during pregnancy and breastfeeding.

Ginger
Zingiber officinale
Reduces morning sickness

Many women are understandably reluctant to take drugs to help deal with the nausea and vomiting of morning sickness, so it's reassuring to know that ginger, which has been used medicinally for thousands of years, is both safe and effective to use. Ginger has been compared to other drugs and placebos in a number of clinical trials, with overwhelmingly positive results. It does occasionally cause minor, self-limiting side effects in some women, but the results of these scientific studies indicate that ginger doesn't have any negative effects on the baby's health.

DOSAGE Clinical trials for morning sickness have generally used doses of 1 to 2 g of ginger in tablet or capsule form, in divided doses throughout the day. Ginger tea made from freshly chopped or powdered ginger may also be effective, but different preparations of ginger have different chemical characteristics, so if your homemade ginger remedy doesn't work, try a commercial preparation.

Witch hazel
Hamamelis virginiana
**Relieves hemorrhoids
and varicose veins**

Bowel habits can become less regular during pregnancy — yet another effect of the hormonal changes your body is going through. Aside from being uncomfortable, constipation sometimes leads to hemorrhoids, or piles, which are actually varicose veins in the blood vessels supplying the anus and rectum. Swollen, itchy and painful varicose veins can also

appear in the legs or around the genitals. Topical applications of witch hazel may help relieve the pain and itchiness of both varicose veins and hemorrhoids, and can also stop hemorrhoids from bleeding.

DOSAGE Rub witch hazel gel, ointment or tincture into the affected area once a day. It may take up to 3 weeks before you notice any improvements.

Calendula
Calendula officinalis
Great all-round healer

Calendula has many uses during pregnancy. If your gums become prone to bleeding, try a strong infusion of the flowers as an antiseptic mouthwash. Calendula cream, ointment or infused oil are traditionally rubbed into aching or itchy hemorrhoids and varicose veins, and bring relief to cracked nipples. Occasionally, herbalists and midwives even use the tincture to encourage the healing of vaginal tears or caesarean section scars after delivery.

DOSAGE For hemorrhoids, varicose veins and cracked nipples, apply calendula cream, ointment or infused oil to the affected area 3 times a day; the infused oil is preferred for use on the nipples if you are breastfeeding, as it is safe for your baby to consume in small quantities. For bleeding gums, prepare a strong infusion of dried calendula, and use it as a mouthwash after brushing your teeth. Don't use calendula tincture on surgical wounds or vaginal tears without talking to your doctor or midwife first, as it's vital to ensure that the wound is clean and free of infection before you start. Tissue treated with calendula heals remarkably quickly, so, it is important to check that no infection remains beneath the treated wound.

Gather calendula flowers from early summer onwards, then dry them in a cool, dark place.

Rosehip oil
Rosa canina
May help prevent stretch marks

Rosehip oil is growing in popularity as a remedy for the prevention of stretch marks — including those of pregnancy. The herb has a rich content of anti-inflammatory compounds, including vitamins A and C and essential fatty acids, all of which are important for skin health. So, although its efficacy hasn't yet been scientifically confirmed, there may be some substance to its reputation.

DOSAGE Massage commercially prepared rosehip oil into the abdomen twice daily.

Raspberry leaf
Rubus idaeus
Prepares the uterus for childbirth

The traditional use of raspberry leaf to help the body prepare for labor is supported by laboratory studies indicating that the herb has a range of effects on the pregnant uterus. Although very little clinical research has been conducted, in one small study, researchers concluded that raspberry leaf may help to shorten labor time and decrease the likelihood of babies being born either prematurely or after their due date. This study also suggested that taking raspberry leaf may help to reduce the risk of forceps or vacuum delivery, or caesarean section. In a second study, 192 women with low-risk pregnancies took either raspberry leaf or a placebo from the 32nd week of pregnancy. In this trial, the second stage of labor was about 10 minutes shorter in those women who took raspberry leaf, and fewer forceps deliveries were required. At 1.2 g of raspberry leaf twice daily, the dose used in this study is only 10 percent of that recommended by herbal authorities, so it's possible that more remarkable results could be obtained with higher doses.

DOSAGE Infuse 4 to 8 g dried raspberry leaf in boiling water; drink 3 cups per day from the 32nd week of pregnancy. Alternatively, take raspberry leaf tablets or capsules according to the manufacturer's instructions, at a dose equivalent to 4 to 8 g of dried herb, 3 times daily.

Cautions

- Self-treatment with herbal medicine is only appropriate for women whose pregnancies have been assessed as low-risk. Use of any herbal medicine during pregnancy and breastfeeding, including those on this page, is best carried out under professional supervision. Seek immediate professional care for any but the most minor problems during pregnancy, or if you are concerned

Breech babies and Chinese medicine

Towards the end of pregnancy, most babies position themselves so that they'll exit the birth canal head first. The term "breech" is used to describe those babies that are not in this position, and who are therefore at increased risk of complications during labor. If your baby is breech, your doctor will probably suggest that he or she manually adjust the baby into a more appropriate position – a procedure that's both very safe and highly effective.

Alternatively, you could consider traditional Chinese medicine, which has a good success record for turning breech babies. Your acupuncturist will use an acupuncture needle on a specific point on your little toe

and simultaneously burn the herb mugwort (*Artemisia vulgaris*) near the skin in the same place. While this process, called moxibustion, may seem peculiar if you haven't experienced acupuncture before, research in both Asia and Europe suggests that it is quite effective at encouraging breech babies to turn. In one trial conducted in Japan, 92.5 percent of babies whose mothers had acupuncture and moxibustion subsequently rotated into the head-first position, compared to only 73.7 percent of those whose mothers did not. Other researchers have monitored unborn babies' reactions to this procedure and reported that it does not appear to cause any foetal distress.

about the health or well-being of your baby. Always inform your doctor or midwife of any herbal medicines you are taking.
- Ginger occasionally causes minor, self-limiting symptoms, such as heartburn and gastrointestinal discomfort. If this occurs, stop taking the herb, or try taking it in a different form.
- Ginger has documented blood-thinning effects, and should not be taken concurrently with anticoagulant or

anti-platelet medication, except under professional supervision. Women who are at risk of hemorrhage should not take ginger in greater than culinary quantities.
- Ginger should not be taken for 2 weeks prior to undergoing surgery. However, in consultation with your physician, a single dose can be taken just prior to surgery to reduce post-operative nausea.
- Topical applications of any herb can sometimes cause reactions, such as dermatitis or itching and burning sensations, and ideally a patch test should be performed at least 24 hours before use. Discontinue use if a reaction develops. Take particular care with calendula if you are allergic to the Asteraceae family of plants (for example, daisies and echinacea).
- Like ginger, raspberry leaf has traditionally been used as a treatment for morning sickness. However, it is best avoided during the first trimester of pregnancy, as there is no research to confirm its safety at this time.
- Raspberry leaf may reduce the absorption of minerals, such as calcium and iron, so separate doses by at least 2 hours.
- Do not use raspberry leaf if you are suffering from constipation, peptic ulcer, or any inflammatory disease of the digestive system.

Superlative Raspberry
ELLWANGER & BARRY,
Mt Hope Nurseries.
ROCHESTER, N.Y.

An American advertisement from the 1890s captures the beauty of the raspberry.

Sexual and prostate health

The traditional use of herbs to support male reproductive health is being increasingly backed up by medical science.

Saw palmetto

Serenoa repens
**Clinically proven for
prostate problems**

With prostate problems affecting about half of all men aged 50 and over, saw palmetto is one of the world's most popular herbs for male health. It's been the subject of numerous clinical studies, the majority of which show it to be an effective treatment for mild cases of benign prostatic hyperplasia (BPH), and specifically for symptoms such as reduced or hesitant urinary flow and the need to urinate overnight. It has been compared with several of the key pharmaceutical treatments for the same condition and shown to have a similar level of efficacy, but with fewer side effects. Research also suggests that, unlike some pharmaceutical medications, saw palmetto does not interfere with the measurement of a marker called prostate-specific antigen (PSA), the levels of which are used by

doctors to predict the presence of prostate cancer.

DOSAGE Most research has used a special extract from saw palmetto berries that is standardized for its content of free fatty acids and other oily compounds, referred to as a liposterolic extract. Take 160 mg of the concentrated liposterolic extract in capsule form, twice daily with meals. You may need to take saw palmetto for 1 to 2 months before your symptoms improve.

Nettle root

Urtica dioica
**Support for mild
prostate conditions**

Like saw palmetto, nettle root has been clinically trialled for the relief of mild BPH, and the two herbs are often taken in combination. Nettle is documented to improve a range of BPH symptoms, including nighttime urination, frequent urination and incomplete emptying of the

The berries of the saw palmetto were used by both Native Americans and European settlers.

bladder. In a study of over 2000 patients taking a formula containing nettle root and saw palmetto, improvements were noted in both symptoms and pathological changes — an indication that the herbal combination helps treat the disease, rather than simply suppresses the symptoms.

DOSAGE Look for tablets or capsules that provide the equivalent of up to 6 g of dried nettle root per day, and take them according to the manufacturer's instructions.

Korean ginseng

Panax ginseng
Potent male tonic

In traditional Chinese medicine, Korean ginseng is regarded as the most important herbal medicine for men, and ginseng roots with a shape resembling a man's body are highly prized. Its traditional indications include replenishing vital energy (referred to in Chinese as *qi*), helping the body and mind to cope with stress, and as a tonic to promote general health and longevity. Ginseng is also widely used to enhance men's sexual performance, and has been shown in a few clinical trials to have a beneficial

Tomatoes for a healthy prostate

Tomatoes — along with other red- and pink-colored fruit and vegetables, such as guava, watermelon and pink grapefruit — contain a pigment called lycopene, which has important benefits for men's health. Population studies suggest that men whose diets are highest in tomatoes have up to 40 percent less chance of developing prostate cancer than those men whose tomato consumption is low. As a potent antioxidant, lycopene also supports the heart and blood vessels and may help to reduce the risk of cardiovascular disease. For optimal absorption, lycopene needs to be consumed at the same time as a little oil, so tomato-based products such as pasta sauces and tomato paste are valuable inclusions in your diet.

effect on erectile dysfunction. Results of these trials, as well as animal studies, suggest that the effects on sexual performance cannot be attributed to a purely hormonal effect, but may be caused at least in part by the herb's impact on the central nervous system and on the blood supply to the penis.

🌿 DOSAGE Take Korean ginseng tablets up to a maximum of 1000 mg of the dried root per day, according to the manufacturer's instructions. (Higher doses may sometimes be appropriate under professional supervision.) Look for products that are standardized for their content of ginsenosides. Traditionally, Korean ginseng is taken for 8 to 12 weeks, followed by a break of several weeks. This herb is not appropriate for frail or anxious people.

Ginkgo

Ginkgo biloba
Stimulates circulation

With its documented ability to improve circulation, ginkgo can be a useful remedy for cases of male sexual dysfunction that are known or suspected to be due to reduced blood flow to the penis.

Problems with both libido and sexual performance are fairly common side effects of some groups of pharmaceutical medicines, and there is a small amount of evidence that treatment with ginkgo can help to resolve these issues in some patients when taken under the supervision of a professional.

🌿 DOSAGE Look for supplements standardized for their content of the important active constituents ginkgo flavone glycosides, ginkgolides and bilobalides, with a daily dose of 120 mg of a concentrated (50:1) extract, providing the equivalent of 6 g of the dried herb.

Ginkgo takes a month or two to reach its maximum effect, so use it for 6 to 12 weeks before assessing whether or not it has helped you. If you suspect you are experiencing any adverse effects of your prescribed medication, talk to your doctor before taking ginkgo, and refer also to the Cautions section that follows.

Cautions

- The symptoms of BPH and prostate cancer can be very similar, so it's important to see your doctor for a diagnosis before commencing self-treatment. Only mild cases of BPH are suitable for self-treatment. All men over 50 years of age should consider regular screening for prostate cancer, which can easily go undetected without testing.
- Do not take saw palmetto or nettle root if you are taking pharmaceutical medication for BPH or prostate cancer, except on professional advice.
- Saw palmetto occasionally causes mild adverse effects, such as digestive upsets and headaches. Nettle root infrequently causes mild adverse effects; if this occurs, stop taking the herb.
- Nettle plants cause urticaria, or hives, if they touch the skin, so if you choose to harvest nettle root, take appropriate precautions. Do not take nettle root if you have had an allergic reaction to the nettle plant.
- Do not take Korean ginseng if you have diabetes, cardiovascular disease (including high and low blood pressure), depression, anxiety, hyperactivity, mental illness (including bipolar disorder and similar conditions), insomnia, blood clots or bleeding disorders, except under the advice of a healthcare professional.
- Korean ginseng and ginkgo are known or suspected to interact with many pharmaceutical medications (including antidepressants, antipsychotics, digoxin, anticoagulants, anticonvulsants, insulin and hormonal therapy), so consult your physician or pharmacist before taking them.
- Do not take Korean ginseng at the same time as stimulants such as caffeine.
- Korean ginseng is traditionally contraindicated in people suffering from acute infections.
- If you have been diagnosed with Alzheimer's disease or any other form of dementia, do not take ginkgo without first talking to your doctor.
- Stop taking ginkgo at least 2 weeks before undergoing surgery, and do not take it if you have a bleeding disorder.
- Always use commercially prepared ginkgo products from a reputable company. Do not consume unprocessed ginkgo leaves as they may cause adverse reactions. Do not eat large quantities of the seeds or allow children to do so.

In World War I, German soldiers wore uniforms of nettle fabric, made from the plant's stalks.

- Ginkgo sometimes causes mild adverse reactions, which may include dizziness, gastrointestinal upset, headache and allergic skin reactions. More severe reactions have occasionally been recorded, and have included bleeding problems and seizures. If symptoms occur, stop taking the herb and seek medical advice.
- Do not use any of the herbs on this page if you are pregnant or breastfeeding, except under the advice of a healthcare professional.

Natural beauty

Using aromatic herbs and essential oils to make your own natural body-care and beauty treatments brings many rewards. These easy and inexpensive recipes will cleanse, detoxify, soothe and energize.

Herbs for beauty and well-being

Nourish your body with natural homemade herbal preparations that will exfoliate, cleanse, tone, condition, heal and soothe.

We drink herbal tea, add fresh herbs to recipes for extra flavor and take medicinal herbs to ward off colds and other common ailments. So it makes sense to use herbs in skin and hair-care products. Effective for fighting the signs of aging, such as wrinkles and dark spots, herbs also cleanse, tone, moisturize and exfoliate your skin and add condition and color to your hair.

Herbs contain thousands of active biochemicals and, thanks to the principle of synergy, they provide various benefits: your skin and hair recognize these substances as biocompatible and absorb them more readily than mineral oils or petrochemicals. Herbs can mitigate a vast array of skin and hair problems, ranging from facial lines to dandruff.

These healing botanicals, which contain minerals that calm and fatty acids that soothe, are among the most effective of cosmetic and personal care ingredients. Herbs also enhance each other. The right combination — such as antiseptic pine and cooling sage — makes a homemade recipe even more effective.

Make your own products

Making your own herbal skin and hair-care products is easy and rewarding. It's also a very practical way of avoiding exposure to undesirable and potentially harmful solvents, surfactants, silicone, artificial fragrances and other synthetic additives found in conventional products. And it's a means of contributing to a healthier environment and saving some money at the same time.

On the following pages, there are dozens of simple, effective step-by-step recipes for herbal moisturizing lotions and creams, toners and astringents, powders, oils, scrubs, soaps and masks, plus special treatments to solve specific problems such as acne. Some recipes have been inspired by centuries-old texts from Western herbalism and Ayurveda, India's traditional medical system. Others are tried-and-true remedies handed down by generations of European "herb-wifes" who knew the healing secrets of wild plants. The rest are recommendations from natural health practitioners who continue to use herbs as a primary healing method.

Nutrients for skin

What you eat affects how you look and how your skin ages. That's why it's smart to consume an anti-inflammatory diet that includes whole grains; fruits and vegetables of different hues; omega-3 fatty acids from cold-water fish; walnuts; extra-virgin olive oil and flaxseed; and antioxidant-rich herbs and spices, such as green tea, ginger and cumin. To keep skin hydrated, it's also smart to drink a minimum of eight glasses of water a day.

It's important, too, to avoid partially hydrogenated oils, trans fats and polyunsaturated vegetable oils, which are all pro-inflammatory. Also, steer clear of foods that cause a rapid rise in blood sugar and insulin — such as sugary or starchy processed foods — and trigger inflammation. This occurs in a process called glycation: sugar binds to collagen fibers in the skin, which makes it stiff and inflexible and can lead to wrinkles. Premature aging of the skin is also caused by sun damage, stress, pollution and lack of exercise, so be sure to avoid these factors, too, where possible.

Super skin supplements

A good multivitamin and mineral supplement helps to provide your complexion with all the nutrients it needs. Extra amounts of certain vitamins may be indicated in particular conditions: notably A (which rebuilds tissue and balances sebum production), C (which your body uses to produce collagen, the connective tissue that keeps skin firm) and E (which reduces wrinkle formation, protects skin cells and prevents UV-light damage). These five supplements combat the aging process because they are antioxidants or natural anti-inflammatory agents.

- **Alpha lipoic acid** is a powerful antioxidant that helps defend against damage caused by free radicals (damaging metabolic by-products that accelerate aging).

- **Coenzyme Q10** is an antioxidant with anti-inflammatory properties. It is helpful for gum health.

- **Fish oil** contains essential fatty acids docosahexaenoic acid (DHA) and eicosapentaenoic acid (EPA), which plump skin, keeping it supple.

- **Grapeseed** contains antioxidant oligomeric proanthocyanins (OPCs) that strengthen blood vessels and slow signs of aging.

- **Zinc** balances oil-gland function, encourages wound healing and regenerates skin cells.

Essential oils starter kit

These five essential oils will form a useful foundation for your collection.

GERANIUM Astringent and refreshing, this oil has a balancing effect on the skin, making it a great choice for homemade massage oils and footbaths. Invaluable for female reproductive health, it helps overcome irritability and bloating caused by premenstrual syndrome (PMS).

LAVENDER Helpful for cramps, headaches, nervous disorders and insomnia. Healing and antiseptic, this oil helps heal burns and other skin disorders, and prevents scarring. It's also a great insect repellent.

PEPPERMINT Stimulating, digestive and anti-inflammatory. Use in an inhalation to relieve nausea and respiratory problems, or in a bath to soothe muscle aches.

ROSEMARY For mental fatigue, headaches, colds and flu.

TEA-TREE Renowned as an antifungal and antiseptic, this oil can be used for clearing yeast infections, athlete's foot and acne, and also as first aid for minor wounds.

Take care

- Do not take essential oils internally. Except for lavender oil, they should be diluted before being applied to the skin.

- Pregnant and breastfeeding women should avoid essential oils, unless on the advice of a qualified aromatherapist.

- Certain essential oils, such as bitter orange and grapefruit, can cause skin photosensitivity.

- Some oils, such as lemongrass, can also irritate sensitive skin.

Tools of the trade

The basic tools for making your own herbal skin and hair-care products are very simple. It is a good idea to keep them separate from the ones you use for everyday cooking, though — plastic and wood absorb flavors and smells; metallic bowls and spoons can oxidize (react) with fruit and vegetable juices; and substances such as vegetable wax and beeswax are difficult to clean thoroughly from surfaces. Here's what you need.

- measuring cups and spoons
- kitchen scales
- non-aluminium saucepans, including a double boiler
- heat-resistant, non-metallic mixing bowls, such as Pyrex

- non-metallic strainers — for example, cheesecloth or muslin squares and coffee-filter papers
- funnels, in different sizes
- glass dropper
- wooden spoons
- spatulas, in different sizes
- chopping boards
- airtight glass jars and bottles with non-metallic caps; pump, squeeze and spray bottles
- food processor
- handheld mixer
- kitchen thermometers
- electric coffee grinder or mortar and pestle

Aromatherapy

Essential oils are very versatile and add a wide variety of benefits to homemade skin and hair-care products. They offer potent protection against a range of common ailments and help improve skin and hair health. Their small molecular size means that they can penetrate deep into the dermis to provide a profound healing effect. Their wonderful scents also help balance your emotions.

Depending on the essential oil you select, you can add antiseptic, rejuvenating, tonic or relaxing properties to a cleanser, moisturizer, ointment or body splash. Different oils can help prevent or clear skin problems; stimulate the generation of new cells; improve muscle tone; stimulate circulation of blood and lymph; eliminate waste; counter inflammation; balance sebum (oil) production; and reduce stress.

Hydrotherapy at home

Considered the life-giver in just about every culture, water is included in all manner of spiritual and religious ceremonies to cleanse the skin and replenish the mind.

Spa-goers can enlist the benefits of hydrotherapy: a dip in a hot jacuzzi, followed by a dunk in a cool pool, a hot sauna and then a cold shower all get your systems flowing and working in harmony, and your body works more efficiently afterwards. You can easily replicate this effect with some herbal hydrotherapy treatments at home.

Herbal hydrotherapy

Start by massaging your body with a homemade scrub, such as Orange body polish (see *page 279*). Take a hot shower for about 5 minutes, then turn the water temperature down (as cold as your body can tolerate) for 1 to 2 minutes. Repeat 2 to 3 times, depending on the amount of time you have. When you step out of the shower and pat yourself dry, follow with an all-over spritz of Citrus zinger (see *page 279*). This will give your skin an instant refresh.

The essential oils used in aromatherapy massage have profound healing effects.

Body brushing

Skin is the body's largest detoxification organ. Sluggish elimination via the skin places a greater load on other organs, especially the liver. To boost circulation and stimulate the lymphatic system to release toxins, naturopaths and herbalists recommend dry body brushing with either a soft body brush or a loofah.

Body brushing also improves muscle tone and reduces puffiness and cellulite. It sloughs off the dead skin cells that clog pores and encourages cellular renewal, giving your skin a youthful glow. Here's what you need to do.

- Buy a natural (not synthetic) brush with a firm bristle. Soft bristles won't do the job. Make sure it has a long handle, so you can get at hard-to-reach spots.
- Do your dry brushing on alternate days, first thing in the morning before showering.
- Always brush towards your heart, using gentle, circular movements. Start with the soles of your feet and work your way up your legs, then hands and arms. Reach over and brush your back from the buttocks up the back and around to the stomach. Brush your stomach in an anti-clockwise direction. Avoid tender areas, such as the nipples, or wherever your skin is thin, irritated or damaged.

- Wash your brush regularly in warm water and mild soap. Rinse and leave to air-dry.

Before you start...

You will find the majority of the ingredients used in these recipes at your local pharmacy, supermarket or health food store, even in your kitchen cupboard. Others, such as cosmetic clays and soap moulds, are available from specialty distributors or craft shops and websites. When a recipe calls for fruit, vegetables, fresh herbs or eggs, wherever possible opt for organic to avoid exposure to pesticides.

If a vegetable oil is required (for example, olive, almond or avocado), make sure that you choose an unrefined, cold-pressed variety that has not undergone heat or chemical extraction. In between uses, store these oils in the refrigerator. Use filtered or distilled water wherever water is listed as an ingredient; failing this, cooled, boiled water is acceptable.

Make allowances

Homemade herbal skin and hair-care products are free from the emulsifiers, thickeners and colorings found in conventional ones. As a result, they may not look like the creams and lotions you're used to buying in the shops. You will also need to make allowances for differences in the texture and quality of some raw materials — for example, oatmeal, oils, waxes and the herbs themselves. Feel free to adjust the quantities.

Storage and keeping properties

Adding a small amount of vitamin E oil, citrus seed extract or benzoin (from pharmacies) to your products will extend their life and reduce the risk of rancidity. As a general rule, the herbal creams, oils and balms described here will last up to 12 weeks in the refrigerator; dry scrubs and powder mixes will last up to 6 months in the refrigerator; infusions made with fresh herbs and masks or pastes made with fruit should be refrigerated and used within 2 days.

Hygiene

Adopting a commonsense approach to hygiene when preparing herbal skin and hair-care products will keep them as safe and pure as possible. Before commencing, tie your hair back, wear an apron and wash your hands thoroughly.

Sterilize glass or plastic bottles and jars for storing your products by placing them in boiling water for 15 minutes, then allowing them to air-dry, upside down, on a rack. Ensure all utensils are clean and dry when you finish.

Patch testing

Finally, always patch-test products and ingredients first, especially if you have sensitive skin or a history of allergies. Natural products are less likely to cause an allergic reaction, but it can happen.

To test, place a small amount of one of the ingredients — for example, 2 drops of essential oil diluted in 1/2 teaspoon of vegetable oil — on a cotton-wool ball and tape it to the inside of your elbow; leave it for 24 hours. If the area becomes red or sore, do not use this ingredient in your beauty products.

Turn your bathroom into a haven where you can experience your own salon-style treatments.

Normal skin

Normal skin is soft, evenly textured with medium-sized pores and not too oily or dry. Wash with a gentle cleanser and follow with a toner containing balancing herbs such as elderflower or chamomile. Moisturize with a lightweight face serum or a cream moisturizer made with vitamins and plant oils. Exfoliate regularly with a natural fruit peel or mask. Treat your skin with the respect it deserves and it will stay looking its best.

Cinnamon scrub

A gentle scrub that leaves your skin exceptionally smooth and soft, this will brighten and refine all skin types. Almond meal soothes the skin while sugar buffs away dead skin cells. The cinnamon has a mildly antibacterial effect.

> 2 tablespoons fine-ground almond meal
> 1 tablespoon rice flour
> 2 teaspoons caster sugar
> 1/2 teaspoon ground cinnamon
> plain yogurt

1 Combine almond meal, rice flour, sugar and cinnamon in a bowl. Add enough yogurt to form a gritty paste.
2 To use, gently massage the scrub into dampened skin, then rinse off.

Green-tea toner

This herbal blend is healing and mildly astringent. Vinegar restores the skin's pH balance, the antioxidant-rich green tea is calming and hydrating, and the fennel adds a light licorice-like scent. Elderflower is mild enough to suit the most sensitive skin and helps to reduce redness and inflammation.

> 1 tablespoon green tea
> 1 teaspoon crushed fennel seeds
> 1 teaspoon dried elderflower
> 1/2 cup (125 ml) boiling water
> 2 tablespoons apple cider vinegar
> 1 teaspoon vegetable glycerine

1 Place herbs in a bowl and cover with the boiling water. Cover bowl and leave herbs to steep until water cools. Strain. Combine herbal water, vinegar and glycerine in a bottle.
2 To use, shake well. Saturate a cotton ball with the liquid and wipe over skin after cleansing. Store toner in the refrigerator. Use within 10 days.

Get steamy

An herbal steam is simple and inexpensive. It gives a healthy glow naturally by improving micro-circulation to the surface of the skin and flushing out the toxins and debris. A steam also helps to open pores, making it easier for your skin to absorb the essential oils and aromatic herbs in the water.

Floral milk

Milk, nature's own skin softener, contains lactic acid. This mild exfoliant gently lifts dead cells and tones your skin. Milk's fat content acts as a moisturizer and soothes any irritation.

> 2 tablespoons dried rose petals
> 1 tablespoon dried lavender
> 1 tablespoon dried chamomile
> 1/3 cup (90 ml) whole milk
> 1 tablespoon vegetable glycerine

1 Place herbs in a glass jar. Add milk and glycerine and seal securely. Chill overnight in the refrigerator. Strain and pour into an airtight bottle.
2 To use, shake bottle well and upend onto a cotton ball. Wipe gently over skin 2 to 3 times, then rinse. Store floral milk in the refrigerator. Use within 1 week.

Three roses moisturizer

Rosehip oil is used in this lovely, light-textured cream for its anti-inflammatory and anti-allergenic properties. Completing the rose trio, rose geranium oil is used to tone while rose oil is used to soothe, heal and slow the aging process.

> 2 tablespoons jojoba oil
> 2 tablespoons rosehip oil
> 1 tablespoon grated beeswax
> 1000-mg evening primrose oil capsule
> 250-IU vitamin E capsule
> 1 tablespoon Rescue Remedy (from health food stores)
> 2 tablespoons rosewater
> 5 drops rose geranium essential oil
> 5 drops rose essential oil

1 Place jojoba oil, rosehip oil, beeswax and the contents of both capsules in the top of a double boiler, set over simmering water. Stir until melted. Warm Rescue Remedy and rosewater together in a separate saucepan.
2 Remove oil mixture from heat and add warmed Rescue Remedy mixture, beating vigorously with a small whisk or electric mixer set on low speed until cream thickens. Add essential oils and mix again. Allow to cool slightly before

When faced with stress, allergens and other environmental factors, even normal skin can change temporarily. Support your skin with these strategies.

■ **Massage** your face fortnightly to improve circulation and create a glow.

■ **Follow** a sleep routine of 8 hours each night. To calm overstimulated adrenal glands, take 200 mg *Panax ginseng* daily. To ease tension, add 10 to 20 drops of an essential oil — such as lavender, lemon verbena or clary sage — to a bath.

■ **Install** water filters in your sink and shower and place air purifiers in rooms that are used frequently. Take a skin-clearing herb such as nettle (right) in tincture form. Drink 2 cups of green tea daily to scavenge free radicals and keep skin vibrant.

■ **Use** a humidifier in your bedroom to help your skin stay hydrated at night. Clean the filter regularly; add essential oils such as jasmine to help you relax.

spooning into a shallow tub or jar. To use, massage a small amount into skin. Store in a cool place.

Cucumber and chamomile steam

Cucumber has a cooling, mildly astringent effect, while chamomile softens skin.

> 2 chamomile teabags
> boiling water
> 2 or 3 drops chamomile essential oil
> 1 small cucumber, thinly sliced
> almond or apricot kernel oil, or moisturizer

1 Place teabags in a sink or bowl and cover with boiling water. Add essential oil and cucumber.
2 Drape a towel over your head and shoulders to create a tent and lean over the steaming bowl, keeping your face about 4 in. (10 cm) above the water. Close your eyes and stay leaning over the bowl for 5 to 10 minutes.
3 Splash your face and neck with cool water; pat dry. Using a small amount of the nut oil or another moisturizer, finish with a soothing massage.

Pawpaw mask

This mask exfoliates and stimulates micro-circulation to the skin's surface, resulting in a warm, rosy glow. Pawpaw contains papain, an enzyme that helps dissolve dead skin cells. Honey helps skin to retain moisture. Yogurt is a source of lactic acid, which helps to dissolve dead skin cells, while lemon juice has a mild bleaching effect, reducing discoloration and evening out skin tone.

> 1/2 cup (90 g) ripe pawpaw, diced
> 1 tablespoon plain yogurt
> 2 teaspoons honey
> 2 drops orange essential oil
> 1 teaspoon lemon juice
> rice flour

1 Mash pawpaw in a bowl. Add yogurt, honey, oil and juice; mix until smooth. Add sufficient rice flour to form a paste. Cover; chill in the refrigerator for 30 minutes.
2 Lightly remix and apply a thick layer to clean, dry skin, covering the face and neck but avoiding the eye area. Lie still for 15 minutes. Rinse off and pat dry. Apply a light moisturizer.

Dry skin

Skin that tends to be dry not only feels rough, tight and itchy, but also reflects light poorly, resulting in a dull-looking complexion. This problem is worse in winter or if you live or work in a dehydrated environment, such as an air-conditioned office. Untreated, dry skin can lead to severe chapping and cracking, or even fissures. The solution is to avoid harsh detergent-based skin-care products and to use herbal hydrating agents such as marsh mallow, which lubricate and moisturize the skin.

Softening rice bran scrub

Finely ground oats and powdered rice bran are gentle exfoliants that are suitable to use on dry skin, providing moisture as well as safely sloughing off any dead skin cells. Green tea provides additional antioxidant protection while gently tightening the pores.

>   1 tablespoon green tea
>   1 tablespoon dried calendula
>   1 tablespoon dried rose petals
>   ¼ cup (35 g) finely ground oats
>   ¼ cup (35 g) powdered rice bran
>   ¼ cup (25 g) almond meal
>   cream or almond oil

1 Grind green tea, calendula and rose petals to a fine powder.
2 Combine the powder with oats, rice bran and almond meal, and mix thoroughly. Store the mixture in an airtight jar.
3 To use, mix 1 to 2 tablespoons of scrub with sufficient cream or almond oil to make a paste.
4 Let it thicken for 1 to 2 minutes, then massage it into damp skin with your fingertips; rinse off.

Avocado-cream mask

Nourish dry skin and protect it from the effects of the sun, wind and air-conditioning with this rehydrating mask. The recipe contains cooling cream, to restore skin's moisture levels, and a swirl of soothing and healing honey.

>   half a ripe avocado, peeled
>   and stoned
>   1 tablespoon thick fresh cream
>   1 tablespoon honey
>   1000-mg evening primrose
>   oil capsule
>   5 drops sandalwood essential oil
>   rice flour, sufficient to form a paste

1 Mash avocado in a bowl. Add cream, honey, the contents of the capsule and the essential oil. Mix until smooth.

2 Add enough rice flour to form a paste. Cover and refrigerate for 30 minutes.

3 Lightly remix and apply a thick layer to clean, dry skin over face and neck, avoiding eye area. Lie still for 15 minutes. Rinse skin with lukewarm water and pat dry. Apply a light moisturizer.

Mother Nature's moisturizer

Honey is a time-honored treat for dry skin. Its unique texture holds the key to its many benefits. The high sugar content makes it a natural humectant, meaning it pulls moisture from the air into the skin, helping to keep it hydrated and plump, and because it's so thick, it's occlusive, which means it locks moisture in. In addition, its antioxidant properties fight free radicals from the sun and pollution that age skin. Its low pH makes it acidic and provides a mild antibacterial effect.

Dos and don'ts

- **Do** drink at least eight 8-oz. (250-ml) glasses of water a day to provide your skin with the moisture it needs from within.

- **Do** use lukewarm water. It's less likely to strip skin of moisture.

- **Do** use regular massage and dry-skin brushing (see *page 245*) to stimulate sebum (oil) production and circulation. Use light, gentle pressure to avoid irritation.

- **Don't** use soap on your skin.

Marsh mallow cleanser

The herbs marsh mallow and soapwort grow in swampy, watery areas, where their roots soak up moisture to create a slippery sap that can both cleanse and relieve dry skin. The glycerine in this soothing formula binds water to thirsty skin.

    1 tablespoon chopped
       dried marsh mallow
    1 tablespoon chopped dried soapwort
    1/4 cup (60 ml) water
    1/4 cup (60 ml) rosewater
    1/4 cup (60 ml) vegetable glycerine
    1 tablespoon sunflower seed oil
    1 tablespoon aloe vera gel
    5 drops chamomile essential oil

1 Place herbs and water in a small saucepan; bring to boil. Reduce heat, cover and simmer 15 minutes. Cool and strain, pressing down on herbs to extract as much liquid as possible.
2 Combine herbal liquid with rosewater, glycerine, sunflower seed oil and aloe vera gel in a bottle. Add chamomile oil.
3 To use, dampen skin with warm water and massage a little cleanser into skin; rinse off. Store in the refrigerator but use it within 10 days. Follow with a mild toner, such as Flower balm (see right), then moisturize.

Flower balm

This ultra-mild herbal blend helps keep moisture close to the pores of dry skin. Elderflower eases irritation, fennel restores skin pH levels, while comfrey produces soothing mucilage with excellent hydrating properties.

    1 tablespoon chopped dried
       comfrey root
    1 tablespoon dried fennel
    1 tablespoon dried elderflower
    3/4 cup (180 ml) rosewater
    1/4 cup (60 ml) witch hazel
    1 teaspoon vegetable glycerine
    5 drops rose essential oil

1 Place herbs in a dark glass jar with a tight-fitting cap. Add rosewater and witch hazel. Steep mixture in a dark place for 2 weeks, gently shaking once a day. Strain.
2 Add glycerine and rose oil to herbal mixture. Pour into a pump-spray bottle.
3 To use, mist onto clean skin before applying moisturizer. Store in the refrigerator. Use within 10 days.

Rich repair elixir

This hydrating serum is especially designed for the needs of dry or sensitive skin. Sandalwood and calendula essential oils are anti-inflammatory and regenerative, while the rosehip and macadamia nut oils are rich in skin-supportive essential fatty acids.

    2 tablespoons jojoba oil
    2 tablespoons rosehip oil
    1 tablespoon apricot kernel oil
    1 teaspoon macadamia nut oil
    1 teaspoon carrot seed oil
    4 drops palmarosa essential oil
    3 drops calendula essential oil
    3 drops sandalwood essential oil

1 Combine the first five oils in a small dark-colored glass bottle. Add essential oils.
2 To use, shake well and massage a few drops of elixir into damp skin.

Oily skin

All skin needs some oil — in moderation. But too much oil, the result of overactive sebaceous glands, can contribute to clogged pores, a tendency to develop pimples and blackheads, and an unwelcome shine. To control oil, opt for a toning cleanser; a hard-working scrub; an oil-absorbing mask with soothing minerals; and a light lotion or serum with aromatherapy oils and herbal essences that remove oil without drying the skin.

Lemony whip cleanser

This quick and easy cleanser removes makeup and grime, and has powerful skin-balancing properties. Yogurt tones skin, honey is naturally antiseptic, while lemon juice controls oiliness and tightens the pores.

> 2 tablespoons plain low-fat yogurt
> 1 teaspoon honey, warmed
> juice of half a lemon
> 2 drops lemon essential oil

1 Place yogurt, honey and juice in a bowl and mix well. Add the lemon essential oil and mix again.
2 To use, massage mixture into face and throat, avoiding eye area. Rinse off.

Mint astringent

Barley water is a good source of zinc and sulphur, two minerals that help balance oil production. Peppermint is a refreshing, stimulating and cooling herb, which also calms inflammation.

> 1 tablespoon fresh peppermint leaves
> 1 tablespoon fresh lemon
>   balm leaves
> 1 tablespoon fresh rosemary leaves
> 1/2 cup (125 ml) witch hazel
> 1 tablespoon vodka
> 1 tablespoon pearl barley
> 1/2 cup (125 ml) water
> 5 drops peppermint essential oil

1 Crush herbs with a mortar and pestle. Transfer to a jar with a tight-fitting lid.
2 Add witch hazel and vodka and steep for 10 days. Strain.
3 Place barley in a saucepan with water. Bring to the boil then simmer, covered, for 15 minutes. Cool, then strain.
4 Combine barley water and herbal liquid in a bottle. Add oil.
5 Shake well before use. Store in the refrigerator, but make sure you use it within 2 weeks.

Fruity scrub

This scrub is great for problem areas on the shoulders, chest and back. Papain, an enzyme found in pawpaw, dissolves dead cells; the oats and almonds buff skin; white willow bark is anti-inflammatory; and the clay absorbs excess oil. Lemon essential oil adds a fresh, zingy fragrance and also helps to tone and refine the skin.

> quarter of a small pawpaw
> 1/4 cup (25 g) almond meal
> 1/4 cup (35 g) coarse-ground oats
> 1 tablespoon white cosmetic clay
> 1 white willow bark tablet, crushed
> 2 drops lemon essential oil

1 Peel, seed and chop pawpaw. Mash to form approximately 1/2 cup pulp.
2 Add almond meal, ground oats, clay, white willow powder and oil. Mix well.
3 Apply to clean skin using firm, circular movements. Rinse off.

Peppermint power

Peppermint (*Mentha* x *piperita*) is a versatile herb. It has been used for everything from easing indigestion and clearing sinuses to relieving headaches and improving memory. Peppermint's main component is menthol. When applied to the skin, menthol rapidly produces a cooling sensation, which the body reacts to by increasing blood flow to the area. This in turn results in improved oxygenation of skin tissue, speedier removal of toxins and a pleasant tingling sensation.

Aromatherapy skin spritz

Use this instant refresher to remove cleanser residue and excess perspiration and oil, especially during hot weather. Grapefruit and lemon have gentle astringent and bleaching properties, while apple cider vinegar balances the skin's pH.

1/2 cup (125 ml) carbonated mineral water
1/2 cup (125 ml) witch hazel
1 tablespoon apple cider vinegar
5 drops lavender essential oil
5 drops grapefruit essential oil
3 drops lemon essential oil

1 Place water, witch hazel and vinegar in a pump-spray bottle with a fine mist head. Add oils.
2 To use, shake and lightly spritz over face and neck, avoiding eyes. Store in the refrigerator for up to 1 month.

Brewer's yeast mask

Brewer's yeast absorbs excess oil from the skin's surface and stimulates a sluggish complexion. Egg white shrinks pores, while spirulina is an aquatic herb that is full of skin-supportive nutrients such as vitamin A and trace minerals.

1 tablespoon powdered brewer's yeast
1 teaspoon powdered spirulina
1 tablespoon plain yogurt
1 egg white
cornflour

1 Place yeast, spirulina and yogurt in a bowl. Mix well.
2 In a separate bowl, beat egg white with a whisk until foamy. Add to yeast mixture and stir to combine. Add a little cornflour to make a workable paste.
3 To use, apply to clean, slightly damp skin, avoiding eyes and lips. Leave for 15 minutes, then rinse off. Follow with a light moisturizer.

Eat herbs from the sea

If your skin produces excess oil, especially in the face's T-zone (forehead, nose and chin), these delicious seaweeds can make a difference by working from within.

- **Kelp** (*Laminaria* sp.) This source of vitamins C and A is a blood purifier, while its natural iodine content normalises the lymph system.

- **Kombu** (*L. setchelli*) Also known as horsetail kelp, kombu is a staple ingredient in Japanese cooking that is rich in skin-balancing minerals such as silica and zinc as well as the healing trace element germanium.

- **Arame** (*Eisenia bycyclis*) High in protein and iodine, arame contains compounds that help to detoxify the body, improve metabolism and tone the skin.

Herbal serum

Even oily skin needs a light moisturizer to put a barrier between your skin and environmental pollutants. Jojoba oil is compatible with skin and leaves little residue; the cinnamon and essential oils counteract the bacteria and toxins on the skin's surface.

1 small cinnamon stick
3 tablespoons jojoba oil
2 drops tea-tree essential oil
2 drops cypress essential oil
2 drops grapefruit essential oil

1 Lightly crush cinnamon and place in a small container with a lid. Add jojoba oil and steep for 10 days. Strain. Add essential oils.
2 Pour serum into a small bottle with a dropper opening. To use, warm a few drops between your fingertips and lightly massage into clean, slightly damp skin.

Sensitive skin

Sensitive skin is characterized by a thin epidermis and small surface veins. It can be easily irritated by artificial ingredients and even hot water. To soothe sensitive skin, avoid harsh exfoliants and toners containing alcohol. Use gentle, non-irritating skincare products formulated with naturally calming herbal extracts and essential oils.

Aromatherapy face wash

Use this light cleanser whenever your skin feels tight and dry. The glycerine draws moisture from the air to the skin.

- 1/2 cup (125 ml) rosewater
- 1/4 cup (60 ml) vegetable glycerine
- 10 drops rose essential oil
- 5 drops chamomile essential oil

1 Combine all the ingredients in a bottle.
2 To use, shake well. Massage a small amount into damp skin, then rinse. Store in a cool, dry place away from direct sunlight.

Toning mist

Chamomile and elderflower eliminate redness and blotchiness, marsh mallow and aloe vera are hydrating, and the vinegar restores the skin's pH balance.

- 1 teaspoon dried chamomile
- 1 teaspoon dried elderflowers
- 1 teaspoon dried marsh mallow root, chopped
- 1/4 cup (60 ml) water
- 1/4 cup (60 ml) rosewater
- 1 teaspoon aloe vera gel
- 1 teaspoon apple cider vinegar

1 Place herbs and water in a saucepan. Bring to the boil, remove from heat, cover and steep for 15 minutes. Strain.
2 Pour liquid into a pump-spray bottle. Add rosewater, aloe vera and vinegar. To use, shake well and mist face before applying moisturizer.

Calendula cream

Calendula is excellent for irritated skin, and it is included in many baby products for just this reason. This moisturizer soothes sensitive skin and helps it to manage environmental stress.

- 4 tablespoons jojoba oil
- 4 teaspoons rosehip oil
- 3 teaspoons grated beeswax
- 4 tablespoons rosewater
- 250–IU vitamin E capsule
- 1000–mg evening primrose oil capsule
- 7 drops calendula essential oil
- 3 drops chamomile essential oil

1 Place jojoba oil, rosehip oil and beeswax in a double boiler. Place over a low heat and allow to melt. Warm rosewater in another saucepan.
2 Remove pans from heat. When the contents of both are lukewarm, whisk rosewater into oil mixture. Using an electric mixer set on low, beat for 2 to 3 minutes.
3 Add contents of capsules and the essential oils; whisk until cool. Spoon mixture into a small, wide-mouthed jar. To use, warm a little cream in your palms, then massage into skin.

Soothing secret

There's a good reason why herbalists have dubbed chamomile 'nature's own cortisone': according to a study in the *European Journal of Medical Research*, chamomile cream worked better than 0.5 percent hydrocortisone in treating the inflammation and irritation associated with eczema.

Pear hydrating mask

A luscious treat for sensitive or reactive skin, the pear in this mask is cooling and emollient, while the cream is rich with skin-nutritive fats.

- 1 tablespoon peeled and grated pear
- 1 tablespoon fresh heavy cream
- 5 drops rose essential oil
- 2 drops sandalwood essential oil
- rice flour

1 Combine pear, cream and oils in a bowl. Mix in sufficient rice flour to thicken into a paste.
2 Smooth mask over face and neck, and leave for 10 minutes. Rinse off.

Calendula flowers stimulate the growth of new, healthy skin.

Mature skin

As you get older, your skin's dead surface cells don't slough off efficiently, which can make your complexion look dull. Regular use of a natural skin peel will keep cell turnover high and make your skin glow. In addition, mature skin will benefit greatly from rich moisturizing treatments and rejuvenating essential oils.

Strawberry skin peel

Strawberries boast high levels of skin-brightening alpha-hydroxy acids, while white willow bark contains salicylic acid, which removes dead surface cells and cleans pores.

- 4 large fresh strawberries
- 1 white willow bark tablet
- 1 egg yolk
- 1 teaspoon honey
- 2 drops frankincense essential oil
- cornflour

1. Mash strawberries in a bowl. Grind tablet to a powder and add to bowl. Add egg yolk, honey and oil and mix to combine. Mix in sufficient cornflour to thicken.
2. Smooth mask onto damp skin and leave for 10 minutes. Rinse off.

Green-tea skin polish

Refine the skin's surface and boost its radiance with regular exfoliation. As a bonus, sloughing off dead cells primes skin for a rich moisturizing treatment.

- 1 tablespoon ground adzuki beans
- 1 teaspoon white cosmetic clay
- 1 tablespoon almond meal
- 1 teaspoon green tea
- 1 teaspoon lemon juice
- 1 teaspoon honey
- about 2 tablespoons mashed
    fresh pineapple

1. Combine ground beans, clay, almond meal and tea in a bowl. Add juice, honey and enough pineapple to make a gritty paste.
2. To use, massage mixture into damp skin. Rinse off.

Immortelle nourishing oil

The immortelle (everlasting) flower has impressive anti-aging properties, while carrot seed and rosehip oils plump up the epidermis, so skin looks more youthful.

- 1½ tablespoons jojoba oil
- 1 teaspoon carrot seed oil
- 1 teaspoon rosehip oil
- 500-IU vitamin E capsule
- 10 drops immortelle
    essential oil
- 5 drops rose essential oil
- 3 drops frankincense essential oil
- 2 drops palmarosa essential oil

Place all the ingredients in a bottle. To use, massage a small amount into face and neck.

Age spot lightener

Licorice blocks tyrosine, an enzyme that controls melanin (pigment that colors skin) production. Here, it's paired with fruit acid from apples and vitamin C, a mild bleach.

- 1 tablespoon dried licorice root
- ¼ cup (60 ml) boiling water
- 1000-mg vitamin C tablet
- 1 tablespoon apple pulp
- 5 drops lemon essential oil
- rice flour

1. Place dried licorice root in a bowl with boiling water. Cover bowl and leave licorice to steep for 15 minutes. Strain into a clean bowl.
2. Grind tablet to a powder. Add powder, pulp and oil to herbal liquid; thicken with sufficient flour to make a paste.
3. To use, paint paste over spots and leave to dry. Rinse off. Store remaining paste, covered, in the refrigerator. Repeat daily for 2 weeks.

Rosehip oil softens dry skin, fades scarring and eases sun damage.

Blemished skin

Use these natural topical treatments to tackle acne and pimples, and cleansing herbal tonics to detoxify your system from within. Herbal remedies are less likely to cause sensitivity and irritation than conventional medications.

Citrus steam

Steam opens the pores while adding herbs and essential oils enhances the detoxifying effect: lemon tones skin; lemongrass is healing; and rosemary stimulates circulation.

> 1 lemon, sliced
> 6 fresh rosemary sprigs
> 5 drops lemongrass essential oil

1 Fill a bowl with boiling water. Add lemon, rosemary and oil.
2 Drape a towel over your head and shoulders to create a tent and lean over bowl, keeping your face about 4 in. (10 cm) above the water. Steam your face for 10 minutes. Splash with water; pat dry.

Healing green mask

This deep-cleansing mask helps remove impurities and heal blemishes. The clay absorbs excess oil, tea tree is antibacterial and parsley is a skin-clarifying herb. Oat flour helps bind the mixture and also has a softening effect on skin.

> 1 tablespoon green cosmetic clay
> 1 tablespoon chopped fresh parsley
> 1 teaspoon oat flour
> 2 tablespoons aloe vera gel
> 5 drops tea-tree essential oil

1 Combine clay, parsley, flour and gel in a bowl. Add oil and mix to a paste.
2 Spread paste over face, avoiding eye and lip areas. Leave for 10 minutes. Rinse off.

Herbal antiseptic lotion

Thyme is antibacterial and antimicrobial while witch hazel is a natural astringent. Yarrow and comfrey are both superb skin healers.

> 2 teaspoons dried thyme
> 1 teaspoon dried yarrow
> 1 teaspoon dried comfrey
> ½ cup (100 ml) boiling water
> ¼ cup (60 ml) witch hazel

1 Put herbs in a bowl and cover with boiling water. Cover bowl and steep for 15 minutes. Strain.
2 Pour liquid into a bottle. Add the witch hazel.
3 To use, shake bottle well and upend onto a cotton ball. Wipe gently over skin. Store in the refrigerator. Use within 10 days.

Detox tea

The humble dandelion is a powerful detoxification agent, helping rid the body of waste. Red clover and alfalfa are traditional digestive and kidney tonics.

> 2 teaspoons dried dandelion
> 1 teaspoon dried red clover
> 1 teaspoon dried alfalfa
> 1 teaspoon lemon zest
> 2 cups (500 ml) boiling water

Place herbs in a teapot and pour on boiling water. Cover pot and steep for 15 minutes. Strain. Drink 2 to 3 cups daily.

Lemongrass skin saver

In an Indian study, researchers found lemongrass essential oil was effective in discouraging 22 types of bacteria that can cause skin infections. It is also high in tannins, natural vaso-constrictors (constrictors of blood vessels), which reduce inflammation. Add a couple of drops to a homemade toner, or sprinkle 5 drops in boiling water for a clarifying steam treatment.

Red clover belongs to a class of herbs that purify the blood. Regular use of red clover, both as a wash and a tea, benefits acne.

Sunburn and sun damage

While some sun exposure is healthy, helping to strengthen bones and balance hormones, too much damages skin. Observe common sun-sense, and wear sunscreen and protective clothing from 10 AM to 2 PM. Whenever sunburn does occur, these herbal remedies will ease the pain and speed healing.

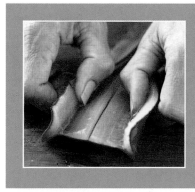

Aloe vera wrap

Slice open a fresh aloe leaf as shown (see also *page 258*) and wrap it around the problem area like a bandage, so the gel sits against your skin. Leave it for 10 minutes, or until skin feels better, then rinse off. Aloe vera has a long history as a first aid treatment.

Cooling calendula bath

Rice bran is an effective remedy for heat rash and sunburn. Antiseptic calendula is an all-around healer, while milk soothes.

- ¼ cup (35 g) dried calendula flowers
- ¼ cup (35 g) rice bran
- 10-in. (25-cm) square piece of muslin string

1 Pile all the ingredients in the middle of the muslin square. Gather up sides and tie securely with string to make a bag.
2 Toss into the bath as it is filling. To use, squeeze herbal liquid over skin and use bag as a compress on sore spots.

Green tea body spray

Green tea contains powerful polyphenols that protect skin and slow inflammation triggered by sun exposure. Feverfew reduces redness and lavender is healing.

- 4 teaspoons green tea
- 2 teaspoons dried feverfew
- ½ cup (125 ml) boiling water
- ¼ cup (60 ml) rosewater
- 10 drops lavender essential oil

1 Place tea and feverfew in a pot and pour on boiling water. Cover the pot and steep for 15 minutes, then strain and refrigerate.
2 Stir in rosewater and oil. Pour into a spray bottle.
3 To use, shake and lightly mist over skin. Store in the refrigerator. Use the spray within 10 days.

Native Americans called aloe vera "the wand of heaven" and used it to heal desert sunburns and treat scorpion bites.

Kitchen sunburn cures

- **Dab** with cold, wet teabags.

- **Snip** open 2 to 3 vitamin E 500-IU capsules and massage the oil into skin.

- **Swirl** 1 cup apple cider vinegar or baking soda into lukewarm bath water and soak.

- **Taking** antioxidant nutrients may offer some limited protection against sun damage. A Munich University study found that people who supplemented with 1000 IU vitamin E and 2000 mg vitamin C daily demonstrated 34 percent greater resistance to sunburn.

Eyes and lips

The skin around the eyes is very sensitive, the first part of your face to show the strain of stress and tiredness. Lips are also very susceptible to drying out because they are simply a thin layer of skin that is constantly exposed to the elements.

Chamomile–milk soother

Chamomile contains anti-inflammatory azulene, which reduces redness, while milk fats calm irritated skin. Using very cold milk constricts the blood vessels, reducing puffiness.

> **2 chamomile teabags**
> **¼ cup (60 ml) ice-cold milk**

1 Soak teabags in milk for 5 minutes. Squeeze out excess liquid.
2 Place teabags over eyes. Rest for 10 minutes.

Eyebright compress

This recipe refreshes eyes that are tired and aggravated by dust, allergies or computer use. The tannins in the herbs tighten tissue and stimulate lymphatic drainage around the eyes.

> **1 tablespoon dried eyebright**
> **1 teaspoon crushed fennel seeds**
> **1 teaspoon dried elderflower**
> **1 cup (250 ml) boiling water**

1 Place herbs in a bowl and cover with boiling water. Cover and refrigerate until cold.
2 Strain through muslin or a coffee filter.
3 Dip a clean cloth into the liquid and place over eyes. Rest for 10 minutes.

Gift of the Magi

Frankincense is an aromatic gum resin obtained from trees of the genus *Boswellia*, primarily *B. sacra*. The bark of the tree is incised and a milky resinous liquid oozes out, hardening to droplets, or 'tears.' Used since ancient times by various cultures, including the Greeks, Romans, Egyptians, Assyrians and Babylonians, frankincense is familiar to many Westerners through the Christian story of the Magi, who brought gifts of gold, frankincense and myrrh to the baby Jesus. The name comes from the Old French *franc encens*, or 'pure incense'; that was, and remains, one of its principle uses. In China, *fanhunxiang*, as it is known, is categorised as an herb for vitalising the blood, and is used to

The three Magi presented the baby Jesus with gifts of gold, frankincense and myrrh.

treat painful swellings and other ailments. Steam distillation of the dry resin produces an essential oil valued in modern aromatherapy to treat wounds, scars, acne and bacterial and fungal infections. The oil is also an ingredient in cosmetics, soaps and perfumes.

Herbal eye oil

This fine-textured eye oil uses vitamin E to moisturize lashes and jojoba to reduce the appearance of fine lines. As a bonus, vitamin E also helps to slow down the aging process.

> **1½ tablespoons jojoba oil**
> **3 drops rose essential oil**
> **2 drops frankincense essential oil**
> **500-IU vitamin E capsule**

1 Combine oil, essential oils and the contents of the capsule in a dark glass bottle.
2 To use, upend bottle onto your ring finger. Pat a small amount of the oil around your eyes.

Honey lip balm

Conventional lip balms generally contain petroleum derivatives, fake fragrances and potential carcinogens, and are best avoided. Try this plant-derived balm.

> **1 tablespoon grated beeswax**
> **2 tablespoons almond oil**
> **2 tablespoons castor oil**
> **1 tablespoon cocoa butter**
> **1 teaspoon honey**
> **500-IU vitamin E capsule**
> **10 drops rose essential oil**

1 Place beeswax, almond and castor oils, butter and honey in the top of a double boiler. Melt over low heat, whisking constantly.
2 Remove from heat. Add contents of the capsule and rose oil. Place pan in a shallow ice-water bath and whisk until mixture becomes creamy.
3 Spoon mixture into small jars. Store in a cool place for up to 6 months.

Use almond oil as a gentle cleanser for the delicate eye area.

Teeth and gums

Using herbal toothpastes and mouthwashes heals gums, freshens breath and even whitens teeth. Avoid conventional toothpastes that may contain chemicals such as sodium lauryl sulphate (a harsh detergent), as well as alcohol (which can be drying) and artificial colors and flavors.

Cinnamon tooth powder

This inexpensive recipe polishes and whitens teeth, leaving your mouth feeling super-clean. Cinnamon has antibacterial properties, while clove is both antiseptic and healing.

- 2 tablespoons baking soda
- 1 teaspoon fine sea salt
- ½ teaspoon powdered cinnamon
- 5 drops clove essential oil
- 3 drops peppermint essential oil

1 Sift soda, salt and cinnamon together to remove lumps. Add essential oils, then sift again. Store powder in an airtight container.
2 To use, dampen your toothbrush and then dip it in the powder.

Herbal breath fresheners

Try these natural alternatives to artificially colored and flavored breath mints.

- **Chew** ½ teaspoon fennel seeds or aniseed, which will leave your breath smelling of licorice.

- **Nibble** on fresh parsley. It fights bacteria and plaque.

- **Gargle** a solution of liquid chlorophyll and water to fight odor-causing bacteria. Dilute 1 teaspoon chlorophyll in a small glass of water.

Double-mint mouthwash

Cooling peppermint and spearmint are effective in banishing odor and making your mouth sweet and fresh. Tea-tree essential oil fights gum disease and aloe vera soothes oral tissue.

- 1 tablespoon dried spearmint
- 1 tablespoon dried peppermint
- ³/4 cup (180 ml) boiling water
- 1 tablespoon aloe vera juice
- 5 drops tea-tree essential oil
- 3 drops peppermint essential oil

1 Place herbs in a bowl and cover with boiling water. Cover bowl and steep for 30 minutes. Strain.
2 Add aloe vera and essential oils. Mix well. Store in a dark glass container.
3 Shake well, then swish 1 to 2 tablespoons around your mouth. Do not swallow. Store in a cool place. Use within 1 week.

Mouthwash for bleeding gums

Black tea and witch hazel are rich in tannins, which have a tightening effect. Green tea is an antioxidant, and goldenseal is a natural antibiotic. Myrrh has antiseptic and astringent properties.

- 1 tablespoon black tea
- 1 tablespoon green tea
- ³/4 cup (180 ml) boiling water
- 1 tablespoon witch hazel
- ½ teaspoon powdered goldenseal (from capsules)
- 5 drops myrrh tincture
- 3 drops lemon essential oil

1 Place black and green teas in a bowl and cover with boiling water. Cover bowl and steep for 30 minutes. Strain.
2 Add other ingredients. Mix well. Store in a dark glass bottle.
3 To use, shake well and swish 1 to 2 tablespoons around mouth. Do not swallow. Store in a cool place. Use within 1 week.

Strawberry tooth whitener

For a brilliant polish that will give your teeth a silky feel, mash a ripe strawberry and dip a toothbrush in it to clean your teeth. Rinse thoroughly, as strawberries are very acidic. Use every 1 to 2 months.

Hands and nails

We work our hands hard, soak them in detergents and expose them to sun, wind, cold and heat. Hands reveal our health and character and, more than any other feature, betray our age. They contain only a few oil-producing glands, so they are very prone to dryness. Give yourself a weekly manicure to prevent problems such as split nails and chapped skin.

Peppermint hand gel

This scented formula has a restorative effect on dry, work-roughened hands.

- 1 teaspoon honey
- 2 tablespoons glycerine
- 2 tablespoons powdered arrowroot
- ¹/₄ cup (60 ml) cooled, strained peppermint tea
- 5 drops peppermint essential oil
- 5 drops frankincense essential oil

1 Place honey and glycerine in a small saucepan over low heat and slowly warm through, stirring constantly. Add arrowroot powder and whisk together. Remove from heat and stir in tea and oils.

2 Let mixture cool slightly, then pour into a clean glass jar with a non-aluminium lid. To apply, massage a small amount into your hands.

Anti-aging hand mask

Masks aren't just for your face. This softening and moisturizing recipe also helps to even out skin tone and fade age spots.

- 1 tablespoon honey
- 3 tablespoons aloe vera gel (see below)
- 1 teaspoon lemon juice
- 10 drops lemon essential oil
- almond meal, sufficient to make a paste

1 Melt honey over low heat. In a small bowl, combine the aloe vera gel with the honey and lemon juice. Add the essential oil and mix thoroughly.

2 Add sufficient almond meal to make a soft, workable paste; it should not be too sloppy. Smooth mask over clean hands, paying particular attention to the backs of hands and knuckles. Leave for 20 minutes. Rinse off with warm water and apply moisturizer.

Harvesting aloe vera gel

At their center, aloe vera leaves contain a thick, colorless gel. This soothing gel is useful for treating burns and dry skin conditions. Use it fresh, as soon as you have harvested it, because it is unstable and quickly loses its consistency. Do not use any gel that has a green tinge. The gel is available from health food stores.

1 Cut off a healthy large leaf close to its base.

2 Slice carefully along the center of the leaf, along its entire length. Gently peel back the two cut edges. Use a blunt-edged knife to scrape the clear gel from the center of the leaf, then place it in a bowl.

Aromatherapy cuticle oil

The essential oils in this fine-textured blend help to counter cracked and ragged cuticles. Calendula and myrrh essential oils both have antiseptic properties to help prevent common nail infections, while lavender is anti-inflammatory and healing.

1 tablespoon jojoba oil

1 tablespoon avocado oil

5 drops myrrh essential oil

5 drops lavender essential oil

10 drops calendula essential oil

1 Pour the jojoba and avocado oils into a small, dark-colored glass bottle, which will help preserve the oil.

2 Add essential oils, screw on cap and shake to combine.

3 Before using the cuticle oil, shake the bottle well, then massage a few drops into your nails and cuticles daily to soften your cuticles and prevent them from splitting.

Healthy nails

- **Maximize** nail health with herbal products. Tea-tree oil, for instance, can clear up fungal infections of the nails, while a daily application of vitamin A-rich cod liver oil rubbed into nails and cuticles helps strengthen them.

- **Eat** a healthy, varied diet rich in whole foods and essential fatty acids (EFAs), and make sure you get adequate hydration — a much better insurance policy for nail health than using commercial nail potions that promise to increase nail growth and strength.

- **Wear** rubber gloves to protect your hands whenever you are washing the dishes or using cleaning products.

Honey and almond balm

To moisturize your nails, rub a little rosehip essential oil into them, using small, circular movements. Then massage your hands with this balm, which is ideal for soothing rough hands and is also a good all-purpose skin salve for minor cuts and abrasions.

2 x 1000-mg lecithin capsules

1 tablespoon rosewater

1 teaspoon honey

1/3 cup (90 ml) almond oil

1 tablespoon cocoa butter

2 teaspoons beeswax granules

10 drops lavender essential oil

10 drops rose essential oil

1 Pierce lecithin capsules and combine contents with rosewater. Set aside. Combine almond oil, cocoa butter and beeswax granules in the top of a double boiler over simmering water.

2 Heat, stirring with a small whisk until the beeswax has melted. Whisk in lecithin and rosewater mixture and remove from heat. Stir in essential oils.

3 Let mixture cool slightly before pouring into a clean glass jar with a non-aluminium lid. To use, massage a small amount into your nails and cuticles every night before bed. Store in a cool, dry place away from direct sunlight for up to 6 months.

If you do not have a double boiler, use a pan that sits in the top of another saucepan. The base of the upper pan should be well clear of the simmering water in the base of the lower pan.

Years ago, Japanese women who splashed their faces with the water used for rinsing rice were called "rice bran beauties."

Foot care

Give yourself a regular pedicure and care for your feet with soothing natural products. Let your feet breathe and exercise naturally by walking barefoot whenever you can. Being vigilant about foot care helps prevent problems such as corns and keeps your feet feeling smooth and soft.

Keep feet sweet

Your feet have more sweat glands than any other part of your body, but they're usually trapped inside shoes for most of the day. Here are ways to keep them odor-free.

- **Wash** feet daily with Tea-tree antiseptic soap (see *page 273*). Tea-tree oil is excellent for inhibiting bacterial growth and odor. Dry feet thoroughly.

- **Apply** an astringent herbal foot spray. Make strong sage tea by steeping 2 tablespoons dried sage in ½ cup (100 ml) boiling water; allow to cool. Add ¼ cup (50 ml) witch hazel and 10 drops lavender essential oil. Pour into a pump bottle. Refrigerate. Shake well before use. Use within 10 days.

- **Wear** cotton socks, which absorb moisture better than synthetic ones, and rotate your shoes. Dust the inside of shoes with baking soda.

Peppermint foot scrub

Peppermint cools and deodorises the skin and sugar buffs away dead skin cells. Your feet will feel soft and refreshed with this easy and effective scrub.

> 1 tablespoon coarse-ground oatmeal
> 1 tablespoon polenta (cornmeal)
> 1 tablespoon sugar
> 2 teaspoons dried peppermint leaves
> 1 tablespoon natural yogurt
> juice of 1 lemon
> 5 drops peppermint essential oil

1 Combine oatmeal, polenta, sugar and peppermint in a bowl.
2 Add yogurt, lemon juice and oil; mix to form a gritty paste.
3 To use, sit on the edge of the bathtub and massage mixture into feet, paying particular attention to heels and soles. Rinse and dry thoroughly and follow with a rich moisturizer, such as Rose geranium foot balm (see below).

Rose geranium foot balm

This fragrant balm is perfect for softening leathery or dry feet. For best results, leave it on overnight, wearing socks to seal in moisture and protect the sheets.

> 2 tablespoons cocoa butter
> 2 tablespoons apricot kernel oil
> 1 tablespoon beeswax granules
> 1 tablespoon vegetable glycerine
> 1 teaspoon honey
> 10 drops rose geranium essential oil
> 10 drops lemon essential oil

1 Put the cocoa butter, apricot kernel oil and beeswax in the top of a double boiler over low heat, and stir until melted together.
2 Remove from heat and whisk in glycerine and honey. Add essential oils and stir.
3 Pour into a glass jar and cool before sealing. The finished formula has a waxy consistency that softens when applied to skin.

Horsetail tablets contain keratin-producing silica, which strengthens nails.

Fragrant foot soak

The herbs and essential oils in this aromatic blend are astringent and antibacterial, helping to reduce sweatiness, fight odor and leave feet fresh and clean. Both rosemary and ginger are warming herbs and stimulate circulation of blood; their uplifting scents raise the spirits.

> 2 tablespoons fresh rosemary
> 2 tablespoons fresh sage
> 1 tablespoon fresh ginger root, finely grated
> 4 cups (1 liter) water
> 1 tablespoon baking soda
> 1 tablespoon Epsom salts
> 10 drops eucalyptus oil
> 10 drops lavender essential oil
> extra water
> small ice cubes or crushed ice

1 Place rosemary, sage and ginger root in a large saucepan with water. (If you have no fresh herbs to hand, use 1 tablespoon of each herb in dried form instead.) Bring to the boil. Remove from heat, cover bowl and steep for 10 minutes. Strain.
2 Add baking soda, Epsom salts and essential oils. Mix well. Pour into a foot spa or shallow dish big enough for both feet. Top up with extra water and add ice.
3 Soak feet for 15 minutes; pat dry. Finish with a light dusting of Orange-blossom powder (see *page 274*).

Super-soft powder

Cornflour and arrowroot add a silken texture while the clay absorbs more than 200 times its weight in moisture. In addition, the essential oils eliminate odor-causing bacteria. To boost this powder's ability to stop sweatiness, try adding 1 tablespoon zinc oxide powder (available from your chemist).

½ cup (60 g) baking soda
½ cup (60 g) cornflour
2 tablespoons powdered
   arrowroot
2 tablespoons white
   cosmetic clay
15 drops lemon essential oil
15 drops neroli essential oil
10 drops lemongrass essential oil

1 Sift baking soda, cornflour and arrowroot to remove lumps. Add clay and mix well. Add the oils and sift again.
2 Store powder in an airtight, lidded container in a cool, dark place.
3 To use, dip a powder puff into the mixture and apply after bathing, or decant mixture into a small shaker.

Try flower power

Bunions are painful, bony bumps that protrude from the side of the big or little toe joint, usually courtesy of wearing high-heeled or ill-fitting shoes. Custom-made orthotics can strengthen the arch and surgically shaving the bone will realign the toe, but it would be better to avoid these methods. Why not try marigolds? A study in *The Journal of Pharmacy and Pharmacology* found that applying a paste of alcohol and crushed marigolds (*Tagetes* sp.), then covering it with a pad can reduce the size and pain of a bunion. The researchers concluded that flavonoids in the marigold reduce inflammation in the joint.

Treat your feet

This therapeutic and relaxing home pedicure avoids the toxic polishes and potentially dangerous fungal infections associated with nail salons.

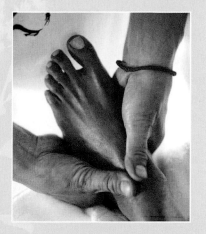

1 Use an acetone-free product to remove old nail polish. Remove stains by rubbing nails with a few drops of lemon essential oil. Buff with a fine emery board. Fill a large flat-bottomed bowl with warm water and add 1 cup (250 ml) apple cider vinegar and 1 cup (250 ml) strong lavender tea (steep 4 teaspoons dried lavender in 1 cup (250 ml) boiling water for 10 minutes; strain). The acetic acid in the vinegar softens the skin, while lavender heals any minor infections.

2 While skin is still damp, massage with Peppermint foot scrub (opposite) or make a simple foot scrub with equal parts sea salt and Castile soap (available from health food stores). Buff heels and soles with a pumice stone or loofah.

Rinse off residue and pat dry. Cut nails straight across with nail clippers. Smooth with an emery board, remembering to always file in one direction. Gently push back cuticles with a cuticle stick. Never cut cuticles, as they protect nails from bacteria.

3 Massage your feet with Rose geranium foot balm (opposite). Wipe over nails with acetone-free remover, then paint with a toluene-free polish.

Normal hair

Blow-drying, straightening, curling and using harsh shampoos all take a toll on your hair. So do a poor diet and other lifestyle factors, such as stress, illness, hormonal fluctuations, alcohol and smoking, and inadequate exercise or sleep. Coax your hair into healthier shape with a nutrient-rich diet and hair-care products that are based on herbs and essential oils specific to your hair type.

Nutrients for healthy hair

Boost your intake of the following and start seeing results in weeks.

Protein fortifies hair and promotes growth. Food sources: beans, dairy products, eggs, fish, meat and poultry.

Iron oxygenates blood and boosts circulation in the scalp. Food sources: dried fruit, egg yolks, legumes, meat, leafy greens and whole grains.

Omega-3s (essential fatty acids) prevent dryness and add moisture. Food sources: flax seeds, sardines, soybeans, walnuts and wild salmon.

Silica strengthens the hair cuticle, boosting strands' elasticity. Food sources: cabbage, celery and oats.

Vitamin A supports the health of the scalp. Food sources: leafy greens, pumpkins, carrots, capsicums and sweet potatoes.

Biotin (vitamin B_7) maintains hair growth and may be beneficial for hair loss. Food sources: eggs, organ meats, dried fruit and molasses.

Zinc is essential for skin and hair health and for balancing hormones. Food sources: meat, eggs, poultry, crab, oysters, brazil nuts and soybeans.

Steps to success

- Wash hair gently with a mild shampoo. Vigorous scrubbing can damage hair and cause the sebaceous glands to produce too much oil.
- Unless you use a lot of hairspray, one lathering with a small amount of shampoo should be sufficient; too much strips the scalp's naturally protective sebum (oil).
- To stimulate your circulation and enhance shine, rinse out shampoo and conditioner with cool water.
- If you use a hair dryer, turn down the heat setting. Ideally, let your hair air-dry naturally.
- Wear a hat to protect hair from drying and color-fading sunlight (especially if you have color-treated hair). Always remember to wear a cap when you swim in chlorinated pools.
- Stress and depressed spirits can cause dull, lifeless hair and, sometimes, hair loss. Learn to meditate, or take up yoga or another calming pursuit.

Do-it-yourself scalp massage

A regular scalp massage encourages fresh blood supplies to flow to the scalp and feed the hair follicles. Tip your head forward and, using small, circular movements, massage your scalp gently with your fingertips for 3 to 5 minutes. Pay particular attention to the crown and hair line. If hair is very dry, rub a few drops of Rosemary hot oil intensive (see *page 265*) onto your fingers first.

Lavender shampoo

This mild, lightly fragranced shampoo is suitable for all hair types. Lavender calms and tones the scalp and rosemary boosts shine.

- 2 tablespoons dried lavender
- 1 tablespoon dried rosemary
- 1 teaspoon orange zest
- 1 cup (250 ml) water
- ½ cup (125 ml) Castile shampoo
- 20 drops lavender essential oil
- 10 drops orange essential oil

1 Place dried herbs, zest and water in a saucepan. Bring to the boil, then reduce heat and simmer until liquid is reduced to ¼ cup (60 ml). Strain.
2 Combine herbal liquid and shampoo. Add essential oils. Store in a plastic squeeze-bottle.
3 To use, shake well and massage a tablespoonful into the scalp. Leave for 2 to 3 minutes before rinsing.

Aromatherapy detangling spray

This detangling spray keeps hair shiny and manageable during cold, dry weather or high humidity. The oils stimulate circulation to the scalp and balance sebum production.

- 10 drops rosemary essential oil
- 10 drops chamomile essential oil
- 10 drops ylang ylang essential oil
- 1 teaspoon jojoba oil
- ½ cup (125 ml) water

Keep the balance

If your hair is normal, you'll want to keep it that way. Use a gentle SLS (sodium lauryl sulphate)-free shampoo. SLS is the detergent ingredient in most shampoos and dishwashing liquids and it can irritate the scalp. Reduce static with a fragrant herbal rinse and keep hair manageable and smooth with Aromatherapy detangling spray (below).

1 Add oils to water and pour into a pump-spray bottle. Store in a cool, dark place.
2 To use, shake well and mist hair 2 to 3 times, then use a comb or fingers to style.

Fragrant hair rinse

Nettle is restorative, horsetail is a rich natural source of silica, and sandalwood and clary sage add a lingering fragrance. Apple cider vinegar restores the scalp's natural pH balance.

- 1 tablespoon dried burdock
- 1 tablespoon dried nettle
- 1 tablespoon dried horsetail
- 10 drops sandalwood essential oil
- 5 drops clary sage essential oil
- 1½ cups (375 ml) boiling water
- ½ cup (125 ml) apple cider vinegar

1 Place herbs, oils and water in a bowl. Cover and steep till cool. Strain. Stir in vinegar.
2 To use, pour through hair as a final rinse after shampooing.

Color boost

Herbal hair rinses accentuate your hair's natural color and make any highlights appear brighter. If your hair is permed, chemically colored or very dry, patch-test a small amount of hair first.

For blond hair
- 1 cup (250 ml) water
- 4 tablespoons dried chamomile
- 1 tablespoon lemon zest
- 2 tablespoons lemon juice

For red hair
- 1 cup (250 ml) water
- 3 tablespoons dried calendula
- 1 tablespoon dried hibiscus
- 2 tablespoons red wine

For dark hair
- 1 cup (250 ml) water
- 3 tablespoons dried sage
- 1 tablespoon dried rosemary
- 2 tablespoons apple cider vinegar

1 Place water and dried herbs of your choice in a saucepan. Bring to the boil; remove from heat. Cover and steep for 1 hour. Strain. Add juice, wine or vinegar. Pour into a plastic spray bottle.
2 To use, spray through hair after shampooing. Comb through, squeeze out excess, but do not rinse.

Save the whale

Jojoba is a shrub that's native to parts of California, Arizona and Mexico. After the banning of the importation of whale oil into the United States in the 1970s, jojoba oil (a liquid wax from the seeds of the plant) was discovered as a replacement. As a result of its very fine texture and skin nutrients, its application in skin and hair-care products was subsequently considered superior to that of whale oil.

Oily hair

Cleanse oily hair with a refreshing, herbal-scented shampoo and use essential oils to encourage blood flow to the scalp. Natural vinegar rinses will help to reduce oiliness, especially if they are combined with astringent herbs.

Cleansing clay shampoo

Clay is useful for deep-cleansing the scalp, absorbing excess oil and removing dead skin. Peppermint produces a tingling effect, while the citrus oils and zest counter oiliness and stimulate circulation.

- 1 tablespoon dried lemon balm
- 1 tablespoon dried peppermint
- 1 teaspoon lemon zest
- 1 cup water
- ½ cup (125 ml) Castile shampoo
- 3 teaspoons green cosmetic clay
- 10 drops lemon essential oil
- 10 drops orange essential oil
- 10 drops peppermint essential oil

1 Place herbs, zest and water in a saucepan. Bring to the boil, then reduce heat and simmer until liquid has reduced to ¼ cup (60 ml). Strain.
2 Combine herbal liquid and shampoo. Add clay and oils. Store in a plastic squeeze-bottle in the refrigerator.
3 To use, shake well and massage a tablespoonful into the scalp. Leave for 2 to 3 minutes before rinsing.

Give hair luster and help reduce oiliness by adding a few drops of rosemary essential oil to your hairbrush before brushing.

Bee business

Melissa, the botanical name for lemon balm, comes from the Greek word for honey bee. Lemon balm was once planted around hives to help guide bees back home: '…when they are strayed away, they do find their way home by it,' observed Pliny, a Roman writer on natural history.

Aromatherapy dry shampoo

Banish that greasy look in just a few seconds. Neem and sandalwood have a tonic effect on hair follicles, and orris root absorbs oil and impurities and also leaves behind a light floral scent.

- 1½ tablespoons powdered orris root
- 1 tablespoon semolina
- 10 drops lavender essential oil
- 10 drops sandalwood essential oil
- 5 drops neem oil

1 Place orris root and semolina in a bowl and mix well; sift to remove lumps. Add oils and mix thoroughly.
2 To use, hang head upside down and lightly massage small pinches of the mixture into scalp and hair, moving forwards from the neck. Throw head back and brush hair lightly to distribute mixture.

Scarborough Fair rinse

This refreshing rinse tones an oily scalp and stimulates hair growth. The four herbs in the classic folk song "Scarborough Fair" are perfect for correcting the pH balance of the hair and scalp, and they boost shine.

- 1 tablespoon fresh parsley
- 1 tablespoon fresh sage
- 1 tablespoon fresh rosemary
- 1 tablespoon fresh thyme
- 1½ cups (375 ml) boiling water
- juice of 1 lemon

1 Place herbs in a bowl and pour boiling water over. Cover and steep until cool. Strain. Stir in lemon juice.
2 To use, pour through hair as a final rinse after shampooing.

Dry hair

Many culprits conspire to damage the hair shaft and turn hair dull and dry as straw: sun, surf, chlorine, overzealous styling and even air-conditioning. To repair hair and restore sheen, try these recipes.

Rosemary hot oil intensive

The molecular structure of apricot kernel oil is small enough to penetrate the hair shaft, where it nourishes, strengthens, protects and repairs, and also brings a sheen to dull or damaged hair.

> ½ cup (125 ml) apricot kernel oil
> 20 drops rosemary essential oil

1 Combine oils and mix well. Drape a towel around your shoulders.
2 Massage oil into hair and scalp, starting at the ends and working towards your scalp. Continue until all your hair is coated in oil. Cover with a shower cap. Warm another towel, then wrap it around and over the cap. Leave until cool.
3 Wash out, using a small amount of shampoo. Finish by adding ½ cup (125 ml) apple cider vinegar to a sink of tepid water and dunking your hair into it. Let hair dry naturally.

Leave-in conditioner

This treatment coats and protects hair even after blow-drying and styling. It also helps to seal the hair cuticle, which causes light to reflect off the hair's surface. This conditioner makes an excellent styling wax, especially for curly or unruly hair.

> 1 tablespoon beeswax
> 2 tablespoons cocoa butter
> 1 tablespoon almond oil
> 1 tablespoon wheatgerm oil
> 1 teaspoon honey
> 2 tablespoons rosewater
> 10 drops lime essential oil
> 10 drops lavender essential oil

1 Combine beeswax, cocoa butter, almond and wheatgerm oils with honey in the top of a double boiler over low heat, until melted. Remove from heat.
2 Gently heat rosewater. When both oil mixture and rosewater are lukewarm, whisk together. Using a mixer set on low speed, add the essential oils and continue to beat until creamy. Spoon into a wide-mouthed jar and store in a cool, dark place.
3 To use, take a small pinch and warm between palms, then work through dry or freshly washed hair.

Too much sun?

Unlike the skin, which undergoes continuous renewal, UV-damaged hair cannot spontaneously repair itself. Too much UV exposure weakens the hair's keratin (protein) and also causes discoloration, known as melanin oxidation, resulting in brassiness as well as dryness. Use a sun hat or a nourishing hair pomade such as the Leave-in conditioner (see left) to protect your hair.

Tropical hair mask

Eggs have a high protein content that helps improve hair's resilience and luster. Banana is hydrating and moisturizing, and avocado is a rich source of natural oils that help soften and condition dry hair.

> 1 egg yolk
> 1 small banana
> 1 large avocado, peeled and stoned
> 1 tablespoon mayonnaise
> 1 tablespoon rum

1 Combine all ingredients in a bowl; mash to form a creamy paste.
2 Massage the mixture through dry hair and wrap hair in a hot, moist towel. Leave for 10 minutes. Rinse out mixture, then shampoo as usual.

Dandruff

Dandruff can be triggered by a poor diet, emotional stress, fungal infection or conventional hair products that are too alkaline. A mild herbal shampoo and aromatherapy scalp treatments can relieve itchiness and flakiness and restore your hair's pH balance.

Anti-dandruff shampoo

Unlike conventional shampoos, Castile soap is free from potentially irritating sodium lauryl sulphate. It will keep hair clean and soft and is also completely biodegradable. Tea-tree essential oil is a powerful antifungal and antiseptic.

> 3/4 cup (180 ml) liquid Castile soap
> 25 drops tea-tree essential oil
> 20 drops rosemary essential oil
> 15 drops cedarwood essential oil

1 Place all the ingredients in a bowl and stir to combine. Pour into a plastic squeeze-bottle.
2 To use, massage shampoo into wet hair, then rinse several times, finishing with the Herbal vinegar rinse (see the next recipe).

Reach for birch

Used since Roman times to treat hair and scalp disorders, birch leaves are a rich source of salicylate, which is used in many conventional dandruff treatments to lift and break down dead skin cells, encourage new ones and keep hair follicles healthy.

Natural medicine chest

- **Clean** up your diet by limiting sugar and refined carbohydrates. Avoid deep-fried foods, excess alcohol, red meat and chocolate. Eat more fresh fruit and vegetables. Drink 8 glasses of water daily.

- **Eliminate** allergens if you suspect you're sensitive to dairy or wheat. Try eliminating them for a month to see if your dandruff clears.

- **Take** out nutritional insurance. The B-group vitamins, vitamin A, zinc and selenium are all important for hair and scalp health.

- **Catch** some rays. While too much sunshine damages hair, some exposure is beneficial for scaly skin conditions. Spend 30 minutes outdoors every day.

Herbal vinegar rinse

Apple cider vinegar normalises the scalp's delicate pH balance and aids in toning the scalp. It also successfully removes oil and shampoo residue from the hair. Nettle is a traditional hair tonic, used for its stimulating effect on the scalp. It also has anti-allergenic properties, making it useful for itchy scalp conditions.

> 4 tablespoons dried nettle
> 1 tablespoon dried rosemary
> 1 tablespoon dried sage
> 1 cup (250 ml) boiling water
> 1/4 cup (60 ml) apple cider vinegar
> 5 drops eucalyptus oil

1 Place herbs in a saucepan with water and vinegar, and bring to a simmer. Remove from heat, cover bowl and steep overnight.
2 Strain liquid and add oil; stir. To use, pour through freshly washed hair; do not rinse out.

Warm oil treatment

With its slightly medicinal scent, this treatment eases a flaky, dry, irritated scalp. It also gives hair lustre and body. Warming the oil increases absorption and promotes circulation to the scalp.

> 4 tablespoons jojoba oil
> 10 drops rosemary essential oil
> 10 drops birch essential oil
> 5 drops cedarwood essential oil
> 5 drops tea-tree essential oil

1 Place ingredients in a saucepan and warm gently over a low heat.
2 Massage mixture into clean, damp hair, paying particular attention to scalp and hair roots. Cover with an old shower cap, then wrap head in a warm towel. Leave for 1 hour.
3 Rinse, then shampoo. Finish with Herbal vinegar rinse (see left).

Hair loss

It's normal to lose about 100 hairs a day, but if you're losing more, check with your doctor. Hair loss that is not linked to hereditary conditions can be due to hormonal imbalance, the contraceptive pill and other drugs, stress, illness and nutrient deficiencies.

Stimulating scalp oil

Rosemary oil increases peripheral circulation and brings nutrients and oxygen to the tiny blood vessels where hair follicles are located.

1½ tablespoons sesame oil
15 drops rosemary essential oil
10 drops cedarwood essential oil
5 drops clary sage essential oil

1 Combine all ingredients in a small bottle. Store in a cool, dark place.
2 To use, pour a teaspoonful into your palm and rub hands together briskly before massaging into the scalp, using small circular movements. This treatment is best done just before bedtime, because most hair growth occurs while you are asleep. Shampoo in the morning.

Hair scare

Thinning hair is likely to make you panic, but you should stay calm and help minimize the loss.

- **Feed** your follicles. Hair that breaks easily or looks dull may need nutrients. For example, insufficient vitamin A leaves hair dry; B vitamins strengthen the hair shaft and help your body handle stress, which can cause or worsen hair loss. Zinc is needed for strong hair and normal growth; iron deficiency causes hair loss. Hair also requires good-quality protein to grow. Good sources include cold-water fish, free-range and organic eggs and chicken, and soy foods such as tofu.

- **Add** flaxseed oil, which provides alpha linolenic acid, an omega-3 fat that makes hair shiny and strong. Take 1 tablespoon daily.

- **Eat** sushi. If an iodine deficiency is causing hair loss, eat sea vegetables such as kelp and dulse, which are naturally high in iodine.

- **Get** herbal help. Grapeseed extract contains powerful antioxidants that stimulate hair growth. Horsetail, alfalfa and oats are all rich in silica, which helps thinning hair and hair that splits easily and is slow to grow. Ginkgo, cayenne (from chillies) and ginger help micro-circulation.

Aromatherapy hair tonic

Neem oil has long been used in Ayurveda, India's centuries-old healing tradition, to treat hair thinning and scalp problems. Aloe vera relieves dryness and has a mildly antifungal effect. It is also useful for any scalp conditions that require soothing and astringency.

¼ cup (60 ml) witch hazel
1 tablespoon aloe vera gel
1 tablespoon vodka
1 tablespoon orange flower water
30 drops neem oil
15 drops rosemary essential oil
15 drops lemongrass essential oil

1 Combine all ingredients in a small bottle. Store in a cool, dark place.
2 To use, massage a small amount vigorously into scalp once a day.

Herbs prevent hair loss in women by balancing hormones.

Hang your head in hope

An easy way to increase the flow of blood to the scalp — which is known to help hair growth — is to lie across a bed and hang your head over the side each day for 10 minutes. Certain yoga poses, notably headstands, are also thought useful for hair health.

Herbal and aromatherapy baths

Depending on which herbs or essential oils you use, a bath can soothe your nerves, ease aching limbs, soften your skin, lull you to sleep or stimulate you into action. Enjoy one of these spa-style soaks at home.

Cooling green-tea bath bags

Oats ease itchy skin and the fat in whole-milk powder moisturizes as its lactic acid gently exfoliates. Green tea soothes skin, while spearmint and peppermint add a refreshing scent and tingly sensation.

> 1/2 cup (70 g) fine-ground oats
> 1/2 cup (50 g) whole-milk powder
> 6 teaspoons dried green tea
> 6 teaspoons dried spearmint
> 20 drops peppermint essential oil
> 6 x 6-in. (15-cm) square pieces of
>   muslin or fine cotton

1 Place oats, milk powder and dried herbs in a bowl; mix well. Add essential oil, several drops at a time, mixing well after each addition.
2 Place 1 to 2 spoonfuls of oat mixture in the center of a muslin square, then gather up the sides and secure with ribbon or twine. Store bath bags in an airtight container until ready to use.

3 To use, run a bath and drop a bath bag in the water. Allow to steep for 5 to 10 minutes before getting into the tub. Use the wet bath bag as a soothing compress for skin, squeezing it to release the milky oat essence. Soak for 15 minutes.

Stimulating ginger bath bags

Ginger is the perfect pick-me-up. The warming, spicy blend in this bath bag helps relieve lethargy, settle the nerves and ease muscle aches and soreness.

> 1/2 cup (60 g) sunflower seeds
> 1/2 cup (70 g) Epsom salts
> 6 teaspoons dried rosemary
> 6 teaspoons dried chopped orange rind
> 1 tablespoon powdered dried ginger
> 10 drops sandalwood essential oil
> 10 drops orange essential oil
> 6 x 6-in. (15-cm) square pieces of
>   muslin or fine cotton

1 Grind sunflower seeds in a food processor to a fine meal. Place Epsom salts, sunflower meal, rosemary, orange rind and powdered ginger in a bowl; mix well. Add essential oils, several drops at a time, mixing well after each addition.
2 Place 1 to 2 spoonfuls of mixture in the center of a muslin square, then gather up the sides and secure with ribbon or twine. Store bath bags in an airtight container until ready to use. Use as for Rose petal bath bags (see below).

Rose petal bath bags

This sensuous blend transforms an ordinary bath into an indulgence. Marsh mallow root and chamomile both soften the skin, while the delicate fragrances of lavender and rose balance the emotions and soothe the psyche.

> 1 cup (150 g) fine-ground oats
> 4 teaspoons dried chamomile
> 4 teaspoons dried rose petals
> 4 teaspoons dried lavender
> 1 tablespoon powdered dried
>   marsh mallow root
> 10 drops rose essential oil
> 5 drops frankincense essential oil
> 5 drops ylang ylang essential oil
> 6 x 6-in. (15-cm) square pieces of
>   muslin or fine cotton

1 Place oats, dried herbs and powdered marsh mallow root in a bowl; mix well. Add essential oils, several drops at a time, mixing well after each addition.
2 Place 1 to 2 spoonfuls of mixture in the center of a muslin square, then gather up the sides and secure with ribbon or twine. Store bath bags in an airtight container until ready to use.
3 To use, hang bag from the hot water tap so the water runs through it as you fill the bath. Then untie the bag and let it float in the water. Soak for 15 minutes.

Turn your shower into a spa

This treatment will strengthen your immune and lymphatic systems.

- **Sprinkle** a few drops of lavender and rosemary essential oils onto the bristles of a long-handled body brush. Starting with the soles of your feet and working upwards, briskly brush your body, using firm, circular movements.

- **Add** a few extra drops of each oil onto the shower floor and run the water as hot as you can tolerate it for 2 minutes.

- **Turn** off the hot water and stand under the cold water for a few seconds. It will close your skin's pores, stimulate the circulation and smooth hair follicles, leaving skin glowing and hair shiny.

Herb-filled bath bags

For a bath bag that's a little more special than herbs wrapped in muslin, embroider a ready-made organza bag.

What you need

This bag is 6 in. (15 cm) high.

☐ purchased ready-made 6-in. (15-cm) high organza drawstring gift bags (from craft stores)

☐ fine lead pencil

☐ Anchor Stranded Embroidery Cotton. Rosemary: 855 Ultra V. Light Tan, 858 V. Light Fern Green, 861 Dark Avocado Green, 939 Baby Blue. Lavender: 101 Very Dark Violet, 1030 Dark Blue-Violet, 860 Fern Green. Chamomile: 291 Dark Lemon, White

☐ crewel embroidery needle

☐ 4 small yellow buttons (for Chamomile bag)

☐ herbs and spices for filling (the Lavender bag is filled with a mixture of lavender, rolled oats, dried orange peel and bay leaves; the Chamomile bag is filled with a mixture of dried chamomile, bay leaves and rose petals; the Rosemary bag is filled with a mixture of dried rosemary, lavender, sage and bay leaves)

1 Draw the motif of your choice (see the Rosemary motif at right). For both the Rosemary and Lavender, you only need to draw the stalk positions.

2 Slip the traced motif inside the organza bag and very lightly trace over the stalks, using a fine lead pencil.

3 To embroider Rosemary, using 1 strand of each of 855, 858 and 861 in the needle (3 strands in all), embroider the stalks by working several long straight stitches along the traced line for each stalk, taking a tiny back stitch to anchor each straight stitch. To work the leaves, thread the needle with 2 strands of 858 and 4 strands of 861 (6 strands in total) and work a series of straight stitches on an angle down each side of each stalk.

Work neatly and do not drag the thread for any great distance, as the work on the back is visible on the front. Using 2 strands of 939, work random small flowers among the leaves, working 3 straight stitches per flower.

4 To embroider Lavender, using 2 strands of 860, embroider the stalks by working 2 or 3 long straight stitches along the traced line for each stalk, taking a tiny back stitch to anchor each straight stitch. Thread the needle with 2 strands of each color (6 strands in total) and work the flowers in small straight stitches on each side of the stalks, using your diagram as a guide.

5 To embroider the Chamomile bag, place the buttons on the front of the bag in a pleasing arrangement and mark their positions lightly with a pencilled cross. Using 2 strands of White, work lazy daisies around the pencilled crosses, leaving room for the button centers.

6 Stitch a button to the center of each flower, using 2 or 3 strands of 291.

7 Loosely fill the bag with the herb combination of your choice and pull the drawstring.

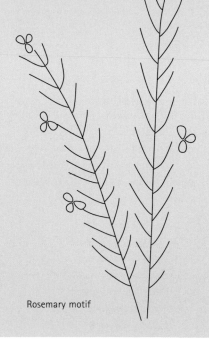

Rosemary motif

Bath salts and oils

Waters from natural hot springs and the sea have long been credited with impressive healing powers. The mineral salts and trace elements they contain help to stimulate the body's own natural detoxification process, relax muscles and soften skin. Adding salts, moisturizing oils and other natural active ingredients such as milk, vinegar or even seaweed to a bath will restore the skin's natural pH balance, improve circulation and help a wide range of ailments, from colds to arthritis.

Do-it-yourself home beauty treatments are inexpensive and easy to make.

Lavender bath salts

Epsom salts are rich in magnesium, which eases muscle aches and tension. Borax and baking soda leave skin silky smooth, while lavender's relaxing aroma will lull you to sleep.

- 1 cup (140 g) Epsom salts
- ¼ cup (30 g) baking soda
- ¼ cup (30 g) borax
- 20 drops lavender essential oil
- 10 drops clary sage essential oil
- 10 drops chamomile essential oil

1. Place dry ingredients in a bowl; mix well. Add essential oils, several drops at a time, mixing well after each addition.
2. Store mixture in an airtight jar in a cool, dark place.
3. To use, sprinkle 2 to 3 tablespoons of mixture into warm bath water. Swish water with your hands to disperse evenly. Soak for 10 to 15 minutes.

Mermaid bath

Sea salt and seaweed help ease irritating skin disorders such as psoriasis, while iodine-rich kelp is a natural antiseptic and tonic. Calendula oil is an excellent calming remedy for red or inflamed skin. Do not use this if skin is broken or very inflamed.

- 1 cup (130 g) sea salt
- ½ cup (60 g) baking soda
- 20 drops calendula essential oil
- 10 drops pine essential oil
- 1 tablespoon kelp powder
- 2 to 3 strips wakame (dried culinary seaweed)

1. Place sea salt and baking soda in a bowl; mix well. Add essential oils, several drops at a time, mixing well after each addition.
2. Store mixture in an airtight jar in a cool, dark place.
3. To use, sprinkle 2 to 3 tablespoons of the mixture and 1 tablespoon of kelp powder (available from health food stores) into warm bath water; swish with your hands to disperse evenly. Drop the wakame strips (available from health food stores or Asian supermarkets) into the water, and swish again. Soak for 15 minutes.

Rich vanilla bath oil

This bath oil is a luxurious blend with a warm, sensual aroma that lingers on the skin; it is also ideal for massage. The cold-pressed nut and seed oils are rich in essential fatty acids that nourish and moisturize your skin. Take care when stepping in and out of the tub, as the oils will make the bath slippery.

- 4 vanilla beans
- 1 tablespoon jojoba oil
- ½ cup (125 ml) almond oil
- ¼ cup (60 ml) macadamia oil
- ¼ cup (60 ml) avocado oil
- 15 drops rose essential oil
- 5 drops ylang ylang essential oil
- 5 drops sandalwood essential oil
- 2 x 500–IU natural vitamin E capsules

1. Slit beans lengthwise and scrape out seed paste. Snip pods into short lengths. Place paste and pods in a glass jar or bottle and add oils, essential oils and contents of capsules. Seal securely; set aside in a cool, dark place for 1 month.
2. Strain oil through a fine-mesh sieve; strain again through a coffee filter to remove residue. Pour into a glass bottle.
3. To use, add 1 to 2 tablespoons to bath water; swish to disperse evenly. Soak for 10 to 15 minutes.

Chamomile essential oil contains strong anti-spasmodic ingredients that reduce muscle aches and pains.

Herbal vinegar bath

If your skin's natural pH balance has been disrupted, perhaps through the use of harsh deodorant soaps, you may have dry, itchy skin. The apple cider vinegar helps restore the correct acid/alkaline ratio; it also relieves the sting of sunburn.

> 2 cups (500 ml) apple cider vinegar
> ½ cup (50 g) dried chamomile flowers
> ¼ cup (30 g) dried comfrey root powder
> ¼ cup (60 ml) aloe vera juice

1 Place apple cider vinegar and chamomile in a non-aluminium saucepan over medium heat. When mixture comes to a simmer, remove from heat. Cover; let stand 3 hours, or overnight.
2 Strain off herbs. Add powder and juice to vinegar, stirring well. Pour into a glass bottle with a non-metallic cap. Store in a cool, dark place.
3 To use, shake well and add ½ cup (125 ml) to bath while tap is running. Soak for 10 to 15 minutes.

What works, and why

Each mineral salt possesses specific health properties. These useful tools can be harnessed in many natural beauty treatments.

- **Sulphur** stimulates the mucous membranes and helps relieve the symptoms of colds and other respiratory problems; it may also benefit acne and eczema.

- **Calcium and potassium** may improve the symptoms of arthritis as well as some disorders of the central nervous system.

- **Magnesium** is essential for strong bones and a healthy heart. It also promotes the proper functioning of the nerves and muscles.

Citrus bath bombs

These bath bombs have a zingy, uplifting scent that refreshes the senses and clears the mind. Neroli and lemon create an energizing and stimulating atmosphere, while grapefruit has a detoxifying effect. To prevent the scent fading too fast, store the bath bombs in an airtight container in a dry, dark place; they will keep for 3 to 6 months.

> 1 cup (125 g) baking soda
> ½ cup (60 g) citric acid
> ½ cup (60 g) cornflour
> 2½ tablespoons almond oil
> 1 tablespoon water
> 10 drops neroli essential oil
> 10 drops lemon essential oil
> 10 drops grapefruit essential oil
> 1 teaspoon borax
> spray bottle filled with witch hazel

1 Place baking soda, citric acid and cornflour in a bowl; mix well. In another bowl, combine almond oil, water, essential oils and borax. Drizzle wet ingredients into dry ingredients, pouring with one hand and squishing mixture together with the other.

2 Pack firmly into soap molds or flexible silicone muffin pans; leave overnight.

3 To remove, flip over and tap out onto baking paper. Lightly mist the bombs with witch hazel; this forms a crust to reduce cracking.

After bathing, almond oil leaves a fine film on the skin, helping to "lock in" moisture.

Aromatherapy soaps and gels

All soap will get you clean, but adding pure, natural ingredients such as herbal extracts and essential oils will leave your skin feeling silkier. However, even the mildest soap is strongly alkaline, which means that it temporarily disrupts the skin's delicate pH balance and natural oils. To prevent dryness and irritation, use all soaps sparingly and wash with warm, not hot, water.

Peppermint shower soap

An aromatic, pick-me-up cleanser for the entire body, this contains calendula essential oil to soothe the skin, peppermint to provide a cooling, refreshing effect and comfrey to heal skin problems. Glycerine is an excellent moisturizer often recommended for delicate skin.

> about ¼ cup (60 ml) boiling water
> 2 tablespoons chopped dried
>   comfrey root
> ½ cup (125 ml) liquid Castile soap
> 1 tablespoon vegetable glycerine
> 15 drops peppermint essential oil
> 10 drops calendula essential oil
> 10 drops lemon balm essential oil

1 Pour boiling water over comfrey root. Steep for 15 minutes. Strain off through muslin.

2 Measure ¼ cup (60 ml) comfrey mixture and add to soap. Add glycerine and essential oils. Stir thoroughly to combine.

3 Pour into a plastic pump dispenser. To use, apply 1 to 2 teaspoons and work into a gentle lather. Rinse off. Pat skin dry with a soft towel and apply a body lotion or oil.

Grapefruit and white clay soap

Perfect for washing oily skin, this soap uses white clay and orange zest to exfoliate and extract surface dirt from pores. Pink grapefruit essential oil is refreshing, while orange essential oil is toning and invigorating. The finely milled oatmeal increases the soap's scrubbing power and also helps to smooth and soften your skin.

The science of suds

All soaps are derived from two basic ingredients: a fat (animal or vegetable) and an alkali (usually lye or sodium hydroxide). Soap is made by combining the two in a process called saponification, which creates a molecule that attracts both water and the dirt or oils on the surface of your skin. Some conventional soaps are made with tallow (animal fat), while others are made primarily from glycerine, a by-product of soap production that helps moisturize.

> 5½ oz. (150 g) vegetable glycerine soap
> 1 tablespoon fine-ground oats
> 1 teaspoon white cosmetic clay
> 1 tablespoon almond oil
> 1 teaspoon finely grated orange zest
> 10 drops pink grapefruit essential oil
> 10 drops orange essential oil

1 Lightly grease soap molds, as for Rosehip soap balls (see opposite). Chop or grate soap and place in the top of a double boiler over simmering water. Stir until melted.

2 Remove the liquefied soap from the heat and add oats, clay (available in pharmacies, or online), almond oil, zest and essential oils. Stir the mixture to thoroughly combine.

3 Pour soap mixture into greased molds and leave in a cool, dark place to harden for 1 week.

4 To remove soaps from molds, run the tip of a sharp knife around the edge. Wrap soaps in tissue paper.

Castile soap facts

- **Castile** soap is thought to have originated in the Castile region of Spain. Originally made from olive oil, it is now made with olive, hemp, coconut and palm oils.

- **Unlike** conventional soap, which is made from tallow (from beef fat) or glycerine (a by-product of soap production) and a small amount of coconut or palm kernel oil, Castile is less likely to strip the skin of its natural oils.

- **To meet** government standards, organic Castile soap must support sustainable farming methods, farm worker health and ecological processing methods.

- **Castile** is the only soap that camping authorities approve for use in the wilderness, because it has no impact on the environment.

Tea-tree antiseptic soap

This invigorating body wash for oily skin is also an effective antibacterial hand soap.

    ½ cup (125 ml) unscented liquid
      Castile soap
    1 teaspoon jojoba oil
    10 drops tea-tree essential oil
    10 drops lavender essential oil
    10 drops sage essential oil

1 Place all ingredients in a bowl and stir well to combine.
2 Pour into a plastic or glass pump dispenser. To use, apply about 1 to 2 teaspoons and work into a gentle lather. Rinse off.

Rosehip soap balls

Olive oil soap's rich lather helps calm irritated skin, while the natural rosehip oil imparts a sweet but subtle scent. Aloe vera and honey are added to maximize moisture, while sandalwood and vitamin E both have anti-aging properties. Buy olive oil soap and aloe vera gel at health food stores or online.

    5½ oz. (150 g) soft olive oil soap
    1 tablespoon aloe vera gel
    1 tablespoon honey
    1 teaspoon rosehip oil
    10 drops sandalwood essential oil
    10 drops patchouli essential oil
    1 x 500-IU vitamin E capsule

1 Lightly grease small silicone soap molds with canola or peanut oil. Chop or grate soap and place in a double boiler over simmering water. Stir until melted.

2 Remove liquefied soap from heat and stir through aloe vera gel, honey, rosehip oil and essential oils, and the contents of vitamin E capsule. Mix thoroughly. Pour soap mixture into molds. (Decorative soap molds are available from craft suppliers. Alternatively, use silicone mini muffin or friand tins. Do not use metal, because it's too difficult to pop out the soap.)

3 Leave in a cool, dark place to harden for 1 week.

4 To remove soaps from molds, run the tip of a sharp knife around the edge. Wrap soaps in tissue paper. Note that this type of soap will remain slightly soft.

Deodorants

These natural deodorants contain herbs and essential oils that keep you feeling dry and smelling fresh by controlling surface bacterial growth — the main trigger for underarm odor — without the addition of worrisome chemicals.

Orange blossom powder

This silky, fine powder is gentle enough to use on the most delicate parts of the body. The three citrus-derived essential oils (neroli comes from orange blossoms, petit grain from the leaves and sweet orange from the peel) are uplifting.

- 3 tablespoons white cosmetic clay
- 1/4 cup (30 g) baking soda
- 1/4 cup (30 g) cornflour
- 20 drops neroli essential oil
- 10 drops petit grain essential oil
- 10 drops sweet orange essential oil

1 Sift dry ingredients to remove lumps. Place in a bowl. Add essential oils and stir. Sift again.
2 Store in an airtight tin or jar. Apply with a powder puff or fingers.

Lavender fresh deodorant

This lightly scented deodorant spray uses lavender, patchouli and clary sage to control odor, and antibacterial citrus seed extract and aloe vera to soothe skin that may be irritated by shaving.

- 3/4 cup (180 ml) witch hazel
- 1 tablespoon vodka
- 2 teaspoons aloe vera juice
- 15 drops patchouli essential oil
- 15 drops citrus seed extract
- 10 drops lavender essential oil
- 10 drops clary sage essential oil
- 5 drops bergamot essential oil

1 Place all ingredients in a glass spray bottle. Store in a cool, dry place.
2 Shake well before using.

Aromatherapy body powder

Absorbent baking soda, cornflour and arrowroot protect against wetness, while sage and thyme fight the bacteria that cause body odor. Lavender is strongly antiseptic and also provides a fresh scent.

- 1/2 cup (60 g) cornflour
- 2 tablespoons baking soda
- 2 tablespoons arrowroot
- 1 tablespoon powdered thyme
- 1 tablespoon powdered sage
- 20 drops lavender essential oil
- 10 drops rosemary essential oil
- 10 drops patchouli essential oil

1 Sift dry ingredients into a bowl to remove any lumps and grit.
2 Stir in essential oils. Sift again.
3 Store in an airtight jar or tin. Apply with a powder puff, or sprinkle on with your fingers.

Rosemary and thyme deodorant

Coriander and hempseed essential oils both neutralize odor-causing bacteria, while sage, rosemary and thyme essential oils are high in chlorophyll and have strong, clean fragrances that effectively mask odors.

- 2 tablespoons dried rosemary
- 2 tablespoons dried thyme
- 2 tablespoons dried sage
- 3/4 cup (180 ml) witch hazel
- 1/4 cup (60 ml) apple cider vinegar
- 1 tablespoon hempseed essential oil
- 15 drops coriander essential oil
- 15 drops citrus seed extract
- 10 drops lavender essential oil

1 Place dried herbs in a glass jar; add witch hazel and vinegar. Seal securely. Store in a cool, dark place for 2 weeks, shaking daily.
2 Strain liquid and pour into a glass spray bottle. Add oils. Shake well before using.

Unlike conventional antiperspirants, natural deodorants don't block sweat — they simply absorb it.

Men's grooming

Take care what you choose to place between your skin and a piece of sharpened steel. The average man shaves 21,900 times in his life, so finding a soothing shaving cream and calming aftershave balm is a must. And for an easier shave, shave right after (or during) a steamy shower. This removes excess oil, opens pores and softens your beard.

Dream shaving cream

This super-shave solution softens bristles and keeps your skin smooth and nick-free. Olive, jojoba and grapeseed oils are all emollient and replenish moisture; glycerine facilitates blade glide over your skin; witch hazel is useful for inflamed and tender skin; and comforting aloe vera moisturizes and heals. Try to avoid conventional aftershaves based on alcohol: not only can they burn and dry out skin, they can also stimulate oil production and upset the skin's acid balance.

> 6 tablespoons coconut oil
> 2 tablespoons witch hazel
> 1 tablespoon olive oil
> 1 tablespoon jojoba oil
> 1 tablespoon grapeseed oil
> 2 tablespoons aloe vera juice
> 10 drops sandalwood essential oil
> 10 drops lavender essential oil

1 Place coconut oil in a double boiler over low heat and liquefy.
2 Remove from heat and stir in witch hazel and also the olive, jojoba and grapeseed oils.
3 Add aloe vera juice and the essential oils. Using an electric mixer, beat on low speed for 2 to 3 minutes. Spoon into a wide-mouthed jar.
4 To use, scoop up about 1 tablespoon of the shaving cream, warm it between your palms, then smooth it over your face and neck. After shaving, remove any traces of shaving cream with a warm, damp face flannel.

Herbal balm

Comfrey is a natural soother that helps to regenerate the thin layer of skin that has just been removed with shaving. Chamomile contains azulene, a powerful anti-inflammatory, while vitamin E softens and heals.

> 2 tablespoons dried comfrey
> 2 tablespoons dried chamomile
> 2 tablespoons dried calendula
> 3/4 cup (180 ml) witch hazel
> 1 tablespoon vegetable glycerine
> 1000-IU vitamin E capsule

1 Place dried herbs in a jar; add witch hazel. Seal securely. Store in a cool, dry place for 2 weeks, shaking daily.
2 Strain liquid; pour into a bottle. Add glycerine and contents of capsule. To use, shake well and pat onto skin after shaving.

Brush up

Try lathering with a shaving brush, which lifts the hair away from your face more effectively than your fingers. But don't skimp on cost by buying a synthetic model. A brush made from badger hair or another natural bristle is softer and absorbs cream and water more efficiently.

Sandalwood aftershave

Sandalwood is antiseptic and also provides a calming, earthy, masculine scent. Tea tree fights inflammation, spearmint is cooling and rosemary stimulates circulation.

> 3/4 cup (180 ml) witch hazel
> 1 tablespoon apple cider vinegar
> 10 drops sandalwood essential oil
> 5 drops spearmint essential oil
> 3 drops rosemary essential oil
> 2 drops tea-tree essential oil

Place all ingredients in a bottle. To use, shake well and pat onto skin after shaving.

Body lotions and moisturizers

Body creams and lotions help to improve the skin's barrier function by locking in moisture and preventing dehydration. For maximum impact, apply a moisturizer when your skin is still slightly damp from bathing; this will help to seal in the moisture. Using long strokes to work in the product, gently massage your arms and legs.

Spicy body oil

This is a silky, exotically scented oil that provides luxurious, long-lasting moisture. Vitamin E revives your skin and fights free radicals, while manuka honey helps to heal any minor skin abrasions. The fragrance of sandalwood and orange calms the senses.

3½ fl. oz. (100 ml) grapeseed oil
1 tablespoon manuka honey
¼ cup (60 ml) jojoba oil
2 x 500–IU vitamin E capsules
10 drops sandalwood essential oil
10 drops sweet orange essential oil
10 drops frankincense essential oil

1 Place grapeseed oil and honey in a small saucepan over low heat. Warm gently until honey has liquefied. Remove from heat.
2 Stir in jojoba oil and the contents of the vitamin E capsules. Add essential oils, several drops at a time, mixing well after each addition. Pour into a dark-colored glass bottle. To use, massage a small amount into the skin and rub in well.

Rich body butter

For winter-worn cracked, scaly skin, this luscious body butter delivers peerless relief. Rose, calendula and chamomile are all naturally soothing, while the plant fats in avocado oil and shea butter sink in quickly to keep skin soft and elastic.

¼ cup (60 g) grated shea butter
1 tablespoon grated beeswax
½ cup (125 ml) avocado oil
2 tablespoons coconut oil
3 tablespoons vegetable glycerine
10 drops rose essential oil
10 drops calendula essential oil
10 drops chamomile essential oil

1 Place shea butter, beeswax and avocado and coconut oils in the top of a double boiler over simmering water. Heat gently until beeswax and shea butter have liquefied. Remove from heat and cool slightly.
2 Whisk in vegetable glycerine, then add essential oils, several drops at a time, whisking after each addition. Pour into an airtight, wide-mouthed glass jar, and store in a cool, dark place.

Spotlight on shea

Shea nut butter is made from the fruit of the shea (or karite) tree (*Butyrospermum parkii*), which is indigenous to West Central Africa. It is rich in antioxidants such as vitamins A and E, plus countless nutrients that combine to provide your skin with deeply hydrating effects. A versatile product, it has been used for centuries for culinary, medicinal and cosmetic purposes. Traditionally, it has been regarded as sacred to women. In Africa, only village women may harvest the nuts and extract the butter, and profits from the enterprise are returned to them. Shea trees are an important resource for West Africa, where they are grown wild, without the use of chemical pesticides.

Rose essential oil

The rose is the mystical symbol of love and romance and its essential oil, made from the petals of damask roses, is thought to be an aphrodisiac. Often included in beauty preparations for its refreshing and mild tonic effect, rose essential oil is particularly recommended for sensitive skin.

The world is a rose. Smell it and pass it to your friends.

Persian proverb

Rosemary and mint body lotion

A lighter-textured blend, this is a very effective moisturizer that helps heal and nourish dry skin. It is scented with a refreshing blend of rosemary and peppermint essential oils.

    1 tablespoon grated beeswax
    1/4 cup (60 ml) almond oil
    1/4 cup (60 ml) grapeseed oil
    1/4 cup (60 ml) rosewater
    1/4 cup (60 ml) vegetable glycerine
    1/2 teaspoon borax
    10 drops rosemary essential oil
    10 drops peppermint essential oil
    10 drops lavender essential oil

1 Place beeswax, almond oil and grapeseed oil in the top of a double boiler over simmering water. Heat gently until beeswax has liquefied. Remove from heat.

2 Meanwhile, place rosewater, glycerine and borax in another small saucepan and heat gently until borax has dissolved. When both liquids are lukewarm, stir rosewater mixture into oil mixture; whisk to combine.

3 Add essential oils, several drops at a time, and whisk again until cool, using either a small wire whisk or a blender set on low. Pour into an airtight jar or bottle. Shake well before using.

Orange flower body cream

Use this cream on rough spots such as elbows, knees and heels. It is very effective on mature skin. The cocoa butter and carrot seed oil are both ultra-hydrating, while the neroli provides a light, citrus fragrance.

    2 tablespoons cocoa butter
    1/4 cup (60 ml) apricot kernel oil
    1/4 cup (60 ml) soybean oil
    1 tablespoon vegetable glycerine
    1 teaspoon carrot seed oil
    10 drops neroli essential oil
    10 drops lemon essential oil
    10 drops jasmine essential oil

1 Place cocoa butter and apricot kernel and soybean oils in the top of a double boiler over simmering water. Heat gently until cocoa butter has melted. Remove from heat.

2 Add vegetable glycerine and carrot seed oil; mix well. Add essential oils, several drops at a time; mix well after each addition. Pour into an airtight, wide-mouthed jar.

Sandalwood, the rescuer

■ **Sandalwood** (*Santalum album*) grows in India, and the best quality is found in the province of Mysore. The dried bark and essential oil have been used for centuries, both in traditional Ayurvedic herbal medicine and as a perfume and incense.

■ **Soothing**, relaxing and toning, sandalwood essential oil is renowned for its rejuvenating effects, especially for dry, mature or weather-beaten skin. It is used to soften wrinkles, replenish moisture, help reduce puffiness, and stimulate the body's lymphatic system to speed the removal of toxins.

■ **Its sultry**, sensuous aroma is soothing and harmonizing, helping to promote restful sleep.

Body scrubs and splashes

Body scrubs and polishes work wonders on rough, dehydrated skin. Scrubbing whisks dead, dull cells away, resulting in brighter, more radiant skin. It also improves the skin's absorption of other products, such as moisturizers and oils, so that they can produce more noticeable results. Many conventional products harbor artificial and unappealing ingredients; fortunately, natural formulas containing herbal essences, crushed nuts, sugar and even coffee grounds work just as well.

Smooth and glow

Every day the epidermis (the outermost layer of the skin) sheds millions of dead cells. The rate at which your body renews its skin slows as you get older, however, so exfoliation (scrubbing) becomes increasingly important for maintaining healthy, youthful skin. Scrubbing also helps loosen ingrown hairs, stimulate circulation and lift away dirt and sebum without the use of potentially drying soaps. Get the most benefit out of your homemade herbal body scrub or polish by following these steps.

- Cleanse your body as usual before scrubbing, but hold off on shaving until another time, as scrubs may aggravate newly shaved skin.
- Linger in the bath or shower to soften your skin before attacking tough spots with your scrub. Use more scrub on your knees, heels and elbows.
- Massage scrub into damp skin with circular motions, working your way up from your feet to your heart; avoid your genitals and nipples.
- These scrub recipes contain essential oils, each with a different purpose and scent: chamomile, for instance, calms sensitive skin. Leave scrub on your skin for 2 to 3 minutes to let oils penetrate.

Splish, splash!

Body splashes are lightly scented toners that help hydrate the skin, balance the pH level and remove excess perspiration and oil. Depending on the essential oils and herbs you use, body splashes have the power to heal skin and to energize you or calm you down. To use, spray all over body after bathing; let skin air-dry. Store in the refrigerator between uses.

- If you have delicate or acne-prone skin, use scrubs with caution, as scrubbing can actually spread breakouts and irritate sensitive skin. Start with gentle pressure, avoid scrubbing if you experience any discomfort, and exfoliate just once a week.
- These recipes contain oil, so they can make the floor of the shower slippery, so always stand on a rubber mat.

Spicy body scrub

This skin-softening blend combines coffee, known for its toning and stimulating properties, with the sweet, uplifting scent of cinnamon. The coffee grounds exfoliate skin, while the oil from the peanut butter moisturizes it.

> 1 tablespoon used coffee grounds
> 3 tablespoons crunchy peanut butter
> 1 teaspoon wheatgerm oil
> 1/2 teaspoon powdered cinnamon
> 1/4 teaspoon powdered nutmeg
> 1/4 teaspoon powdered ginger
> 5 drops cedarwood essential oil

1 Place all ingredients in a bowl; mix to form a gritty paste.
2 To use, stand in the shower and massage handfuls of paste into wet skin. Rinse off and pat dry.

Orange body polish

The fruit acids in the orange juice and the lactic acid in the yogurt remove dead cells. These acids gradually stimulate growth of collagen and possibly elastin (proteins and fibers in the skin that tend to break down over time). Sea salt is healing to the skin when used with care, but it can sting and irritate sensitive, fair, mature or sunburned skin. If you have any concerns, substitute raw sugar for the sea salt.

> 1 orange
> 2 tablespoons fine sea salt
> 3 tablespoons plain yogurt
> 1 teaspoon almond oil
> 5 drops lemon essential oil
> rice flour, sufficient to make a paste

1 Cut the orange in half; juice one half, and set the other aside.
2 Combine orange juice, salt, yogurt, oil and essential oil; mix well. Add a little rice flour to thicken and form a workable paste.
3 To apply treatment, first rub the exposed side of the cut half of the orange over knees, elbows, heels and other rough spots. Then massage in the salt mixture to remove dead skin. Rinse off and pat dry.

Swathed in patchouli

Patchouli essential oil is distilled from the dried branches of the bushy patchouli tree, a member of the lavender family. In Victorian England, there was a craze for wearing Bengali cashmere shawls that were packed in chests with patchouli leaves to deter moths. The patchouli-scented shawls eventually created a demand for the perfume itself.

Gentle walnut scrub

Rich in skin-softening essential fatty acids, walnut is an extra-gentle exfoliant, while oats contain beta-glucan, a soluble fiber that creates a moisture-retaining film on the skin's surface.

> 1/2 cup (60 g) shelled walnut pieces
> 2 tablespoons rolled oats
> 1 small avocado, stoned, peeled and chopped
> 1 teaspoon avocado oil
> 2 tablespoons honey
> 5 drops geranium essential oil
> 5 drops chamomile essential oil

1 Place walnuts and oats in the bowl of a food processor; blend at slow speed to create a fine-textured powder.
2 Add avocado, avocado oil and honey; process again briefly to form a workable paste. Add the essential oils, and mix well.
3 To use, stand in the shower and gently massage the mixture into skin. Rinse off and pat dry.

Citrus zinger

A refreshing, clean blend that is wonderful to use chilled in the warmer months.

> juice of 1/2 lemon, strained
> 1/2 cup (125 ml) witch hazel
> 1/2 cup (125 ml) distilled water
> 10 drops neroli essential oil
> 5 drops lemon essential oil
> 5 drops grapefruit essential oil

Combine all ingredients in glass spritzer bottle. Shake well before use.

Softly, softly splash

The soothing, relaxing aroma and the softening properties of aloe vera and marsh mallow make this perfect for skin that tends to be dry.

> 1 tablespoon dried marsh mallow root
> 1/4 cup (60 ml) apple cider vinegar
> 1/2 cup (125 ml) distilled water
> 2 tablespoons aloe vera juice
> 1 tablespoon vegetable glycerine
> 10 drops rose essential oil
> 5 drops sandalwood essential oil
> 5 drops patchouli essential oil

1 Chop marsh mallow root and place in a glass jar with vinegar; seal securely. Steep for 10 days.
2 Strain liquid through muslin into a glass spritzer bottle
3 Add water, aloe vera juice, glycerine and the essential oils. Shake well before use.

The pelargonium produces an essential oil that helps balance oil production in the skin.

Massage oils

Massage is one of the great pleasures in life — and it's good for you. It relaxes tight muscles, stimulates blood and lymph flow, and speeds the elimination of toxins. It also calms the nervous system, reduces stress hormones, alleviates depression, boosts immunity and diminishes pain. Effective massages don't have to be given by massage therapists. Simple massages, such as the Instant energizer shown here, can be exchanged at home between friends and family, or can even be self-administered.

Instant energizer

Whether they're tapping at a keyboard, cleaning, lifting or driving, your arms, shoulders and hands work hard. Look after them by taking regular breaks from repetitive work and trying this self-massage sequence, using the Stimulating massage oil (see right).

■ **Support** your left elbow with your right hand. Make a loose fist of your left hand and gently pound across your right shoulder. Using your thumb and fingertips, make small circular movements to work muscles, moving from the back of your neck down your right shoulder. Repeat, using your right hand on the left-hand side of your body.

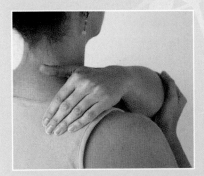

■ **Straighten** your right arm, open your palm and tap down the inside from the shoulder to the open hand with your left hand. Turn your arm over and tap up the back of your arm, from the hand to the shoulders. Repeat this sequence 5 times, then do the same again on your left arm.

■ **Use** your left thumb to work your right hand, gently massaging the palm, then the mound at the base of the thumb, pressing deep with your knuckles to release tension. Search out sore spots and press with the thumb, holding for a count of 5. Squeeze and massage the joints of each finger, using your index finger and thumb. Pull out the fingers and briskly rub your fingertips to release stress and tension in your hands. Repeat on the left hand.

Stimulating massage oil

This invigorating, skin-conditioning oil blend is an effective pick-me-up for when your energy levels are sagging. Eucalyptus and peppermint have a warming, head-clearing effect, making this recipe ideal for anyone with respiratory congestion.

> ½ cup (125 ml) almond oil
> 2 tablespoons grapeseed oil
> 10 drops eucalyptus oil
> 10 drops peppermint essential oil
> 10 drops rosemary essential oil
> 5 drops lemon essential oil
> 5 drops basil essential oil

1 Combine all ingredients in a dark-colored glass bottle and seal securely.
2 Store in a cool place away from direct sunlight. Shake well before using.

Creamy massage blend

An exceptionally rich and nourishing oil, this is an excellent restorative for dry, mature, sensitive, inflamed or weather-beaten skin. Use this blend to soothe period pain or ease cramps.

> 1 tablespoon shea butter
> ½ cup (125 ml) macadamia nut oil
> 1 tablespoon soybean oil
> 2 x 500–IU vitamin E capsules
> 10 drops geranium essential oil
> 10 drops sweet orange essential oil
> 10 drops chamomile essential oil
> 5 drops rose essential oil
> 5 drops clary sage essential oil

1 Place shea butter, macadamia nut oil and soybean oil in a small saucepan over low heat; stir until melted and well combined.
2 Remove from heat and stir through contents of vitamin E capsules and essential oils. Pour into a wide-mouthed, dark-colored glass jar and seal securely.
3 This blend will thicken in cool weather. To liquefy, simply place the jar in a pan of hot water for 5 to 10 minutes.

Floral massage oil

With its fine, silky texture and sensuous, luscious vanilla aroma, this is the perfect choice for a loving and relaxing partner massage. Jojoba oil is chemically quite similar to human sebum, so it is more readily absorbed than other oils.

> 4 vanilla pods
> 1/2 cup (125 ml) jojoba oil
> 2 tablespoons grapeseed oil
> 10 drops ylang ylang
>   essential oil
> 10 drops rose essential oil
> 10 drops lavender essential oil
> 5 drops geranium essential oil
> 5 drops jasmine essential oil

1 Split pods in half lengthwise; scrape out the seeds. Chop pods into small pieces and place in a glass jar with seeds, jojoba oil and grapeseed oil. Seal securely.
2 Store in a dark place for 1 month. Strain off oil, then strain again through muslin to remove fine vanilla particles.
3 Pour oil into a dark-colored glass bottle. Add essential oils and seal securely. Shake before use.

Warming massage oil

Mustard is the secret ingredient in this recipe. Its pronounced warming and reviving effect helps to relax tight, cramped muscles. Ginger is also a highly effective ingredient because it stimulates circulation, helping blood flow to the skin's surface, making this recipe ideal for people with arthritis.

> 1/2 cup (125 ml) olive oil
> 2 tablespoons avocado oil
> 10 drops wintergreen
>   essential oil
> 10 drops rosemary essential oil
> 10 drops ginger essential oil
> 5 drops sandalwood essential oil
> 5 drops frankincense essential oil
> good pinch of dry mustard

1 Combine all ingredients in a dark-colored glass bottle; seal securely.
2 Store in a cool place away from direct sunlight. Shake well before using.

Different strokes

There are several different types of massage movements, and each has a specific effect on the body.

GLIDING This involves the use of the whole hand in long, slow, smooth, broad movements. The first and last strokes of a massage usually consist of gliding strokes.

CIRCLING With circling, the hands move over large areas in a circular motion, typically along or across the length of muscle fibers in the back, shoulders, legs or arms. This helps to release tension before deeper strokes are used.

KNEADING After the recipient has been relaxed by the steady gliding movements, kneading (or petrissage) helps to loosen any cramped muscles and knots. These movements involve a firm, squeezing action to encourage the elimination of waste matter and to allow the free flow of fresh, oxygenated blood.

PRESSURE Deeper massage involves using your thumbs, knuckles or the flat heel of your hand to apply strong, focused pressure on a particular trouble spot.

PERCUSSION Also known as tapotement, these percussive strokes are performed quickly to stimulate the circulation under the skin and to tone the associated muscles. An example is hacking, whereby the sides of the fingers are used to tap rhythmically up and down.

Around the home

For a healthier home the natural way, use air fresheners, cleaning agents, pest repellents and pet-care items made from herbs, essential oils and other non-toxic products. They're kind to you and your family and all your belongings.

Air fresheners

A home that smells clean and fresh is a pleasant place to be, but there's no need to reach for a commercial air freshener when you want to sweeten your surroundings. Homemade herbal solutions are not only much cheaper than their artificial counterparts, they also smell beautiful, do not rely on an arsenal of possibly harmful chemicals and do their job rather better, working to neutralize unpleasant odors rather than simply masking them.

Potpourri

As far back as the 12th century, sweetly perfumed herbs and flowers were salted and left to ferment or rot into potently perfumed mixtures, which were then used to disguise household odors and, it was believed, help prevent the spread of disease.

The dry potpourri mixtures on these pages still have a heavenly scent but they are somewhat easier to prepare. They also have the advantage of looking much more attractive than their mediaeval counterparts. Display them in decorative bowls and stir them gently once in a while to release their scent.

Rose and lavender potpourri

This is a classic potpourri recipe — fragrant, spiced and pretty to look at.

> 1 cup (10 g) dried rosebuds
>   and/or petals
> 1 cup (30 g) dried lavender flowers
> 1 cup (10 g) dried rose geranium leaves
> peel of 1 orange, cut into thin strips
>   before drying
> 2 tablespoons whole cloves,
>   lightly crushed
> 1 tablespoon whole allspice
>   (pimento), lightly crushed
> 5 cinnamon sticks, broken into pieces
> 2 tablespoons orris root powder
> 6 to 10 drops lavender essential oil
> ½ teaspoon rose geranium
>   essential oil

1 Combine all the ingredients and mix well. Put in a sealed container and leave for a few weeks to mature.
2 To use, transfer to open bowls and stir gently to release the scent.

Lemon-scented potpourri

If you like a citrus scent, you'll love the fresh perfume of this colorful mixture. If you have other lemon-scented leaves, such as lemon-scented geranium, lemon-scented tea-tree or lemon-scented gum, feel free to add them.

> 1 cup (15 g) dried calendula flowers
> 1 cup (20 g) dried chamomile flowers
> ½ cup (10 g) dried lemon balm
> ½ cup (10 g) dried lemon verbena
> ½ cup (15 g) dried lemon thyme
> ½ cup (10 g) dried basil
> ½ cup (80 g) finely diced dried
>   lemon peel
> 2 tablespoons orris root powder
> ½ teaspoon lemon verbena essential oil
> 6 drops chamomile essential oil

Mix and use as for Rose and lavender potpourri. This mixture makes a lovely, scented filler for placing inside cushions on chairs and sofas.

Smell busters

Mix a few drops of antibacterial essential oil (such as lavender, tea-tree, rosemary or peppermint) into some baking soda. Pack the mixture into a sock or stocking, and stuff it into your sneakers. Leave in overnight to deodorize them. When re-using the mixture, add extra oil.

Air freshener spray

Lightly mist this delicious-smelling air freshener in a room whenever you feel the need.

> 1.5 oz. (50 ml) vodka
> 1/4 teaspoon bergamot essential oil
> 8 drops clove essential oil
> 5 drops lemon essential oil
> 6 fl. oz. (200 ml) distilled water

1 Put the vodka and oils in a spray bottle and shake to disperse the oils. Add distilled water and shake again to thoroughly combine.
2 Leave for a few days to mature. Spray briefly to refresh a room.

Rosemary potpourri

This combination of fresh peppermint and aromatic rosemary is a good mix for bathrooms or sick rooms.

> 1 1/2 cups (100 g) dried rosemary leaves
> 1/4 cup (5 g) dried peppermint leaves
> 1/4 cup (30 g) whole cloves, lightly crushed
> 1/4 cup (20 g) crumbled cinnamon sticks
> 1/4 cup (60 g) orris root powder
> 1/4 teaspoon rosemary essential oil

Mix the ingredients together and use as for Rose and lavender potpourri.

Simmering or steaming potpourri deodorizer

As its name suggests, a simmering potpourri is simmered gently on the stove in order to release a sweet fragrance that will pervade the whole house. Vary the spices to suit your taste. Simply keep topping up the water until the fragrance has disappeared, or allow the spices to dry out on a tray between uses.

> 1/4 cup (40 g) dried or fresh lemon peel
> 1/2 cup (80 g) dried or fresh orange peel
> 1 cup (120 g) whole cloves, lightly crushed
> 1 cup (100 g) whole allspice (pimento)
> 1 cup (75 g) coriander seeds, crushed
> handful of dried or fresh bay leaves, roughly crushed (optional)
> 5 cinnamon sticks, roughly broken
> 1 cup (250 ml) boiling water

1 Mix all the ingredients together in a bowl and store in an airtight container until needed.

2 Simmer the spices in a small saucepan of water on the stove, topping up the water as needed.
Alternatively, place 2 tablespoons of the potpourri mixture in a heatproof container, cover with boiling water and leave in the room that needs deodorizing until the spicy fragrance released by the steaming potpourri replaces the unpleasant smell.

The word potpourri literally means "rotten pot" — an unattractive name for a sweet substance.

Room fresheners

HANG sachets of aromatic potpourri from door handles or sunny windows.

PUSH herb or spice sachets down the sides and backs of lounge cushions or inside cushion covers.

PLACE a container of potpourri in the lounge room or bedroom. Whenever you spend time in this room, remove the lid and stir the potpourri.

KEEP a small porous pottery bottle filled with a favorite essential oil near a sunny window so that the heat will cause the oils to evaporate.

DAB a little essential oil on a light bulb before turning it on.

PUT a couple of drops of spicy essential oil on a cotton ball; wipe this over your heater in wintertime for a comforting fragrance.

Caring for clothing

If you believe the marketing hype, your laundry is the forum for a vicious battle between dirt and the arsenal of toxic weapons that are clearly required to stop it in its tracks. But do you ever get the feeling that you might be aiming a machine gun at an ant? You bought a power gel with optical brighteners, oxy action and improved grease cutting — but, hey, you only wore the T-shirt once. Go back to some basic principles. Soap and water are the time-honored enemies of dirt, and nothing beats the delicious fresh scent and non-toxic disinfectant qualities of simple herbs.

Herbal pre-wash stain remover

Ammonia is a strong cleaning agent with fumes that can irritate, but it quickly breaks down in the environment and is safer than many commercial products.

> ½ cup (125 ml) water
> ½ cup (125 ml) phosphate-free laundry or dishwashing detergent
> ½ cup (125 ml) cloudy ammonia
> 10 drops lavender or lemon essential oil or eucalyptus oil

1 Combine all the liquids in a spray bottle, then shake.
2 Spray onto stains before washing, then wash immediately. (Do not leave clothes that have been sprayed with this solution unwashed because it can have a bleaching effect.) Do not use it with chlorine bleach.

Powerful stain remover

Eucalyptus oil is one of the most powerful natural antiseptic oils, but is also invaluable for removing stains — particularly grease and perspiration — from clothing and other fabric. Moisten a clean rag with a little oil and dab the stain from the edge to the middle, then launder as usual.

Lemon laundry soap powder

Borax is a mildly toxic disinfectant, stain remover, deodorizer and water softener that is considered environmentally safe. Both borax and washing soda can irritate sensitive skin, so wear rubber gloves whenever you use this powder to hand wash garments.

> ½ cup (125 g) washing soda
> 1 cup (200 g) finely grated pure soap
> ½ cup (120 g) salt
> ½ cup (120 g) borax
> ½ cup (125 g) baking soda
> ¼ teaspoon or more lemon, lavender or peppermint essential oil or eucalyptus oil

1 Put the washing soda crystals in a clean plastic bag and crush them finely with a rolling pin.
2 Mix the crushed washing soda with the rest of the dry ingredients.
3 Add the essential oil and, wearing rubber gloves, distribute it through the powder. Store in an airtight box or jar.
4 Use 1 tablespoon for a small load, 1½ tablespoons for a medium load and 2 tablespoons for a large load. Dissolve in a jug of hot water before adding to a top-loading machine. For a front-loader, dissolve powder in a small amount of hot water and add to the dispenser.

To whiten sheets, add 3 tablespoons of lemon juice to the washing cycle, then dry them in the sun.

Lavender liquid laundry soap

This simple liquid soap is gentle on both septic systems and the environment. Costing much less than commercial laundry detergent, it leaves clothes smelling wonderful and feeling soft.

- ½ cup (125 ml) liquid Castile soap
- ½ cup (125 g) washing soda
- ½ cup (120 g) borax
- 2 to 3 teaspoons lavender or lemon verbena essential oil
- 7.5 qt. (7 ls) hot water

1 Mix all the ingredients in a 9.5-qt. (9-l) bucket and stir well until soda crystals and borax are dissolved.
2 Decant into clean plastic detergent containers (recycle your old ones).
3 Shake the mixture before using. Use about ¼ cup (60 ml) per load.

Rose geranium fabric softener

This simple treatment will leave fabrics soft and fluffy without the cloying scent of artificial perfumes.

- 1 cup (250 ml) white distilled vinegar
- 1 cup (250 g) baking soda
- 2 cups (500 ml) water
- 10 drops rose geranium, lavender or lemon essential oil or eucalyptus oil (or a combination of your favorite oils)

1 Combine ingredients slowly and carefully over the sink, because the mixture will fizz. Pour into a plastic bottle and replace the lid.
2 Add ¼ cup (60 ml) to the final rinse or place it in the fabric softener dispenser of your washing machine.

Easy being green

Add your favorite scent to perfume-free, environmentally friendly laundry powder (from organic or health food shops).
Just add a few drops of herbal essential oil to the powder as you put it into the machine.

Eucalyptus wool wash

For generations this recipe has been used to wash woolen garments. It's ideal for blankets, quilts and pillows, too. The eucalyptus helps to keep the wool soft and repels moths. There is no need to rinse it out unless you are washing white items, in which case rinsing will prevent yellowing.

- 2 cups (500 ml) water
- 2 cups (200 g) pure soap flakes
- ½ cup (125 ml) methylated spirits
- 2½ teaspoons eucalyptus oil

1 Bring the water to the boil and stir in the soap flakes. Remove the pan from the heat and continue to stir until the soap has dissolved and the mixture is smooth.
2 Add the methylated spirits and the eucalyptus oil and mix well.
3 Spoon the mixture into a wide-mouthed jar, where it will set fairly solid.
4 To use the wool wash, dissolve 1 to 2 tablespoons in a bucket of warm water. Keep the unused mixture tightly sealed.

Moth-repellent herbs

When you need to repel moths, choose from any or all of the following herbs.

- Lavender
- Cotton lavender
- Rosemary
- Wormwood
- Sweet woodruff
- Feverfew (right)
- Tansy
- Patchouli

Lavender linen water

Known in France as *eau de linge*, this spray imparts a beautiful fresh lavender scent when used to dampen clothes and linen before ironing. It can also be used directly in some steam irons, if the manufacturer says it is safe to do so.

    ¼ teaspoon lavender essential oil
    1.5 fl. oz. (40 ml) vodka
    2 cups (500 ml) demineralised
        water (from the laundry section
        of supermarkets)

1 Combine the lavender essential oil and vodka in a clean, dry glass bottle. Replace the lid and leave for 24 hours.
2 Add the water, shake to combine and cap tightly. Transfer to a spray bottle when ironing and use as required.

Fragrant clothes drying

Put several drops of your favorite essential oil — a combination of lavender, rosemary, lemon and pine is lovely — on a damp wash cloth and throw it into the tumble dryer with a load of damp clothes.

Herbs for your clothes

If you've taken the trouble to wash, iron and fold your clothes and household linen, you want them to remain in pristine condition after you put them away. There's nothing more disappointing than pulling out a favorite shirt or sheet set to discover that it's full of tiny moth holes.

Banish clothes moths and keep your closet smelling fresh and sweet with the following easy herb projects. Few everyday pleasures are more delightful than sleeping in herb-scented sheets.

Queen Victoria had all the rooms of her residences perfumed with lavender.

Moth-repellent sachets

Take advantage of the natural moth-repellent qualities of many common herbs and spices and tuck these sachets into drawers or hang them from coat hangers in your closet. To make moth-repellent sachets, see *page 302*.

Quick moth repellent

Combine equal amounts of lavender, rosemary, clove and lemon essential oils in a small bottle. Take everything out of your cupboards and wipe the interior and shelves with a damp cloth that's been sprinkled with a few drops of the oil blend. You can also sprinkle it onto cotton balls, then place them in the closet when you replace the clothing.

Pomanders

Pomanders are small balls of perfumes and fragrant spices which, from the 14th to the 17th centuries, were used to mask unpleasant odors and ward off disease in times of pestilence. They could be hung in rooms or worn on chains, rings or girdles. The name comes from the French *pomme d'ambre*, or "apple of amber," and refers to both the round shape and ambergris, one of the ingredients. The term also refers to the small filigree metal, ivory or china container that housed the ball. In the late Middle Ages, these were often lavishly embellished with gems and enamels and carried as fashion accessories.

What you need

- ☐ 1 medium to large thin-skinned orange
- ☐ 1 oz. (25 to 30 g) whole cloves
- ☐ 1 teaspoon orris root powder (from health food shops and craft stores)
- ☐ 1 teaspoon each ground cinnamon, nutmeg and cloves
- ☐ enough ribbon to tie twice around the orange, and to make a hanging loop, if desired
- ☐ tape of the same diameter as the ribbon
- ☐ pins
- ☐ toothpicks or cocktail sticks

1   Use the tape to mark the orange into quarters. (Once the pomander has dried, the tape will be replaced with ribbon.)

2   Insert the cloves at intervals of ⅛ to ¼ in. (3 to 6 mm). If you have difficulty pushing them in, use a cocktail stick, toothpick or darning needle to make a small hole before you insert each clove. You can place the cloves randomly or in a pattern. As the pomander dries, it will shrink to fill up the spaces between the cloves.

3   Carefully remove the tape when all the segments are covered in cloves.

4   Combine the orris root and spices in a small bowl or paper bag. Roll the orange in the spice mixture, thoroughly coating it. (Complete each pomander to this stage within 24 hours to prevent mold from forming.)

5   Leave the pomander in the spice bath in a warm, dry place for 2 to 4 weeks, until dry and hard.

6   Turn the pomander daily and make sure it is evenly coated with spices. The pomander will be ready when it feels light in weight and sounds hollow when tapped.

7   When cured, shake or brush off any spice powder. Wrap ribbon around the pomander in the tape tracks. Finish with a hanging loop.

Drawer liners

These drawer liners, lightly filled with lavender or a mixture of moth-repellent herbs, can also be placed between layers of bed or table linen. Unryushi paper is a strong and fibrous but porous Japanese paper, available from paper specialists and gift stores.

What you need

☐ sheets of unryushi paper

☐ sewing thread

☐ dried herbs and spices for filling

1 Cut 2 sheets of unryushi paper a bit smaller than the size of the drawer bottom, or just cut 1-ft. (30-cm) squares, a good workable size. Machine stitch the 2 pieces together about ½ in. (1 cm) from the edge, leaving an opening for the filling.

2 Fill the liner with dried herbs and spices and stitch the opening closed.

Scented coat hangers

Padded coat hangers keep your clothes and shirts in better shape than the wire variety, and these ones have the added advantage of both smelling nice and keeping moths at bay.

What you need

☐ wooden coat hanger with screw-in hook

☐ herbal essential oil of your choice, such as lavender

☐ bias binding or ribbon, for covering hook (optional)

☐ quilt wadding

☐ craft glue

☐ two 6 x 18-in. (45 x 16-cm) rectangles fabric

☐ sewing thread

☐ dried lavender (or other herbs/spices)

☐ 50 cm decorative braid (optional)

Lavender wands

Place these charming 'wands' among your clothes and linen. When the scent begins to fade, add a few drops of lavender essential oil to refresh them.

What you need

☐ 7 or 9 long stems of young lavender (it must be an odd number and the stems must be as pliable as possible)

☐ sewing thread

☐ ½-in. (5-mm) wide ribbon

1 Remove all the leaves and arrange the stems around a 20- to 24-in. (50- to 60-cm) length of ribbon so the ribbon extends about 6 in. (15 cm) above the flowers and the rest of the ribbon hangs down with the stems. Wind a piece of cotton around the stems just below the flower heads and tie off securely.

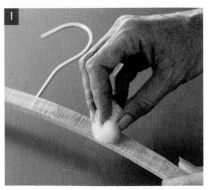

1 Use a small cloth or cotton ball to rub a little essential oil over the wooden hanger. If you want to cover the hook, make a narrow bias tube, or wind ribbon or bias binding tightly around it. Secure the end by taking a stitch or two around the hanger to hold it in place.

2 Cut 2-in. (5-cm) wide strips of quilt wadding and glue them end to end, if necessary, to make one long strip. (The length will depend on how tightly padded you like your hanger.) Glue a couple of small pieces of wadding over the ends of the hanger, then

2 Gently bend the stems back over the flower heads to enclose them in a sort of cage, evenly distributing them around the heads.

3 Take the longer length of ribbon (which is now at the top, extending beyond the flower heads) and weave it alternately over and under the stems, working around the flower heads. Continue weaving in this manner, pushing each

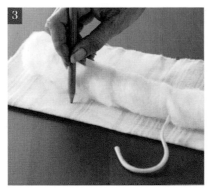

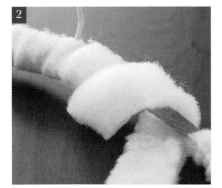

evenly wind the long strip around the hanger from end to end until it is evenly padded. Secure the ends in place with a dab of glue or a stitch.

3 Center the hanger on the wrong side of the fabric rectangles and trace around the top to give you the curved outline. Also mark the center point of the hook.

4 Stitch around the sides and top of the cover, leaving a tiny opening in the center top edge for the hook. Trim the seam allowance, clip the curves and turn the cover right side out.

Press under the raw edges on the lower edge. Fit the cover over the hook and onto the padded hanger. Topstitch the pressed edges together, leaving an opening for the filling.

5 Fill with a couple of handfuls of dried herb, then stitch the opening closed. Stitch a piece of decorative braid along the bottom edge, if desired.

row of ribbon up close to the previous row. When you get to the bottom of the flower heads, having enclosed them completely in a woven cage, you will meet the piece of ribbon that you left extended at the beginning. Wrap the weaving end firmly around the stems a couple of times, then tie the two ends of ribbon into a neat bow and trim.

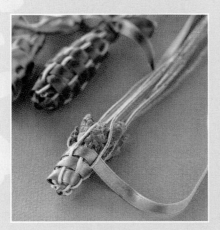

Cleaning with herbs

The beauty of homemade herbal cleaning products is that they're mostly composed of just one main substance — the cleaning agent — which means that you're not paying for bulking additives, artificial colors or perfumes. You can also choose the type and strength of the scent you want; fresh herbs or essential oils almost invariably leave a delightfully fresh, clean smell. So, whether you're already committed to a greener way of cleaning or you just want to save money and simplify your life a little, herbal cleaning makes a lot of sense.

All-purpose herb vinegar spray

This all-purpose, environmentally friendly, non-toxic spray is great to have on hand for wiping, cleaning and deodorizing almost every surface (except marble). If you don't have any fresh herbs, add drops of essential oil instead.

fresh or dried herbs (you can also use herbal tea bags)
distilled white vinegar

1 Roughly chop 1 to 2 large handfuls of fresh or dried herbs (such as lemon verbena, peppermint, rosemary, lemon balm or lavender), or place 5 to 10 tea bags in the bottom of a wide-mouthed glass jar.

2 Add vinegar to fill the jar. Replace the lid, leave for a few days to infuse, then strain out the herbs. (If you are using tea bags, you can gently warm the vinegar before pouring to ensure maximum diffusion.)

3 Pour into a plastic spray bottle. This spray is perfectly safe and very effective to use at full-strength, but it can also be diluted half-and-half with water for lighter jobs.

How to use herb vinegar spray

- **Keep** your dishwasher clean and fresh: Add ½ cup (125 ml) Herb vinegar to the rinse cycle.

- **Cut** grease and make glasses sparkle: Add 3 tablespoons Herb vinegar to the sink with the dishwashing detergent.

- **Dissolve** mineral build-up on clogged shower heads: Soak overnight in diluted Herb vinegar.

- **Clean** soap scum from a glass shower screen: Mix 2 parts salt with 1 part Herb vinegar. Rub onto the screen with a cloth or fine steel wool. Rinse and dry.

- **Stop** mold: Mix 2 teaspoons borax and 1 cup (250 ml) Herb vinegar. Apply with a cloth, leave for 30 minutes then wipe off.

- **Clean** the refrigerator: Wipe out the fridge with Herb vinegar, then rub over with a sponge dipped in vanilla essence.

- **Remove** mold from refrigerator door seals: Scrub the mold from the folds with an old toothbrush dipped in Herb vinegar.

- **Keep** kitchen cloths fresh: Soak overnight in a solution of boiling water with a good dash of Herb vinegar and a few drops of eucalyptus oil. Rinse well.

- **Steam-clean** the microwave: Place 1 cup (250 ml) water and ¼ cup (60 ml) Herb vinegar in a bowl in the microwave and zap on High for 5 minutes. When it cools a little, use it to wipe the walls of the oven with a damp cloth.

All-purpose non-vinegar herbal cleanser

If you don't want to use vinegar in your herbal cleanser — perhaps because you have marble countertops that the acid in vinegar can damage — you can still make an all-purpose spray with water and a little extra cleaning power from borax.

> fresh or dried herbs
>   (or herbal tea bags)
> 2 tablespoons borax
> herbal essential oil (optional)

1 Prepare the herbs as for the All-purpose herb vinegar spray (opposite).
2 Pour over hot water to cover and allow to steep for a few days. Strain, then add the borax and a few drops of essential oil, if using.
3 Shake to mix well and decant into spray bottles.

Lemon-grapefruit dishwashing liquid

When washing dishes use a tablespoonful of this dishwashing liquid in hot water. You could also use lavender or rosemary essential oil: both are good at cutting grease. As this is a soap, it does not produce as many suds as detergent, but it is still very effective.

> 3 tablespoons liquid Castile soap
> 2 cups (500 ml) warm water
> 2 teaspoons vegetable glycerine
> 2 tablespoons distilled
>   white vinegar
> 10 drops lemon essential oil
> 10 drops grapefruit essential oil

Mix all ingredients in a jar, cover and shake well to blend. Store in a plastic squeeze bottle.

Many herbs are antibacterial, making them natural disinfectants.

Rosemary handwash

This foamy gel is ideal for keeping your hands clean while cooking, and the rosemary essential oil is antibacterial.

> ¼ to ½ cup (50 to 100 g) pure
>   soap flakes
> 2 cups (500 ml) very hot water
> ¼ cup (60 ml) glycerine
> ½ teaspoon rosemary essential oil
>   (or the herbal essential oil of
>   your choice)

1 Put the soap flakes and the water in a bowl and whisk vigorously until the flakes have dissolved and you have a foam that is rather like whipped egg white. Cool to lukewarm.
2 Stir in the glycerine and the essential oil, whisk again and leave to cool. As the mixture cools, it becomes more

solid, but if you have whisked enough, it should remain foamy. If it is too thick for a pump bottle, beat in more water.
3 To use, squirt a little into the palms of your hands, lather and rinse off.

Your green cleaning kit

BAKING SODA Gentle, moderately alkaline, non-toxic abrasive; cuts through grease and oil; absorbs odors.

BORAX Disinfecting, stain-removing, deodorizing, mold-inhibiting, strongly alkaline salt that breaks down easily in the environment; softens water and kills ants and cockroaches.

DISTILLED WHITE VINEGAR Moderately strong acid that is grease-cutting, mold-inhibiting, deodorizing and a disinfectant.

HERBAL ESSENTIAL OILS Many oils are disinfectant, antibacterial and anti-fungal as well as sweet-smelling; use 100 percent pure essential oils.

LEMON JUICE Mold-inhibitor, deodorizer, stain remover and mild bleach.

PURE SOAP FLAKES OR LIQUID CASTILE SOAP 100 percent bio-degradable, low-toxic, phosphate-free.

Castile soap is available from health food or organic stores. For more information about this product, see Castile soap facts, *page 273*.

SALT Mild abrasive and disinfectant.

VEGETABLE GLYCERINE Non-toxic, useful cleaning product that helps mix oil with water and dissolves many forms of dirt.

WASHING SODA Moderately alkaline crystals; softens water, cuts grease and removes stains.

Citrus and tea-tree disinfectant

Spray this disinfectant in the kitchen or bathroom, or into a smelly garbage bin. Increase its cleaning properties by adding 1 teaspoon liquid Castile soap to the solution. For extra disinfectant power, choose vinegar rather than water.

> 3½ fl. oz. (50 ml) vodka or methylated spirits
> ¼ teaspoon tea-tree oil
> ¼ teaspoon lemon essential oil
> ¼ teaspoon grapefruit essential oil
> 1 cup (250 ml) water or white distilled vinegar

1 Pour the vodka or methylated spirits and essential oils into a spray bottle and shake to combine.
2 Add the water or vinegar and shake for several minutes.

White goods cleaner

Regular wiping with this cleaner will remove grubby fingermarks and leave the surfaces of freezers, refrigerators and washing machines looking like new without scratching them.

> 2 tablespoons phosphate-free dishwashing liquid
> 1 tablespoon cornflour
> 1 cup (250 ml) water
> 1 cup (250 ml) distilled white vinegar
> a few drops of herbal essential oil of your choice

1 Put the ingredients in a plastic spray bottle and shake gently to combine.
2 Spray a fine film of the mixture over the grubby surface and wipe clean with a soft cloth.

Lemon creme cleanser

This slightly abrasive cleaner is great for cleaning baths, basins and stainless steel appliances, sinks and countertops, but do not use it on fiberglass bathroom fixtures. You can substitute a different essential oil if you prefer.

> ½ cup (125 g) baking soda
> 5 to 6 teaspoons liquid Castile soap or phosphate-free liquid detergent
> ½ teaspoon lemon essential oil
> 1 teaspoon glycerine

1 Combine all the ingredients and mix well. Store in a sealed glass jar.
2 To use, scoop the mixture onto a cloth or sponge, rub over the surface, then wipe off with a rinsed cloth.

Disinfectant scouring powder

Use this simple cleaner as you would a commercial powdered cleanser. To use it in a toilet, sprinkle the powder into the bowl, then spritz with All-purpose herb vinegar spray (see *page 292*) and allow it to fizz before brushing the toilet bowl and flushing.

> 1 cup (250 g) baking soda
> 10 drops each of grapefruit, cinnamon, thyme and rosemary essential oil

1 Blend the ingredients well and store in a sealed glass jar. Leave for a couple of days before using.
2 Apply the powder with a damp cloth and rinse well.

Pure and simple dishwashing liquid

If you don't want to make your own dishwashing liquid from scratch, buy an unscented, undyed, phosphate-free detergent from your local health food or organic store. Add your own essential oil plus a couple of sprigs of matching herb, decant into a pretty bottle and enjoy your washing up!

To clean mold from canvas

Scrub the canvas with very salty water (2 lb./1 kg salt in a bucket of water) and allow the solution to dry on the canvas in the sun. Brush away any salt crystals, then spray with Tea-tree anti-mold spray (see below) and allow to dry. This is good for canvas awnings and director's chairs.

Tea-tree anti-mold spray

Tea-tree, cloves and borax are powerful mold inhibitors. Keep this spray in the bathroom to use on the shower recess or for wiping the shower curtain.

> 2 teaspoons borax
> 1 cup (250 ml) warm water
> 10 drops clove essential oil
> 1 tablespoon tea-tree oil

1 In a spray bottle, dissolve the borax in the warm water.
2 Add the clove and tea-tree oils and shake well.
3 To use, spray onto areas susceptible to mold and mildew, then leave to dry.

Peppermint–lemon glass cleaner

This fresh-smelling cleaner leaves glass sparkling clean. When used on windows, it will also help to deter flies.

> juice of 1 lemon
> 2 cups (500 ml) club soda
> 1/2 teaspoon peppermint essential oil
> 1 teaspoon cornflour

1 Combine all ingredients in a bowl and stir until blended.
2 Pour into a plastic spray bottle. Shake well before using.

Use eucalyptus oil to remove scuff marks and sticky spills from all types of hard floor.

Spicy carpet deodorizer

Banish pet smells and other stale odors from your carpet with this sweet-smelling mixture. Before measuring the dried herbs, you need to grind them very finely in a spice or coffee grinder.

> 2 cups (500 g) baking soda
> 4 tablespoons borax
> 4 teaspoons ground cloves
> 4 teaspoons ground cinnamon
> 4 tablespoons each of finely ground dried mint, rosemary, lavender and thyme

1 Combine all the ingredients in a bowl and mix thoroughly.
2 To use, sprinkle the powder over the carpet and leave for an hour or more (even overnight) before vacuuming the carpet thoroughly.

Eucalyptus stain foam

Use this fresh-smelling foam as a stain remover for both carpets and upholstery. For extra-tough stains, add 1/4 cup washing soda to the hot water and Eucalyptus wool wash, and whisk until the crystals have completely dissolved.

> 3 tablespoons Eucalyptus wool wash (see page 287)
> 1 qt. (1 l) hot water

1 Vigorously whisk the Eucalyptus wool wash in the hot water until suds form.
2 Rub just the foam over the carpet stain and leave for 10 minutes.
3 Wipe the foam away with a damp sponge dipped in distilled white vinegar (this neutralizes the alkalinity).
4 Blot thoroughly with a clean pad.

Eucalyptus floor wash

This simple solution can be used on both timber and lino floors. When washing a timber floor, remember not to saturate it. Your mop should be damp, not dripping wet, and the floor should be well-swept or vacuumed before mopping.

> 1 teaspoon eucalyptus oil
> 2 tablespoons methylated spirits
> 5 1/4 qt. (5 l) hot water (about half a bucket)

1 Combine all the ingredients in a bucket.
2 Wring out a mop in the solution and use it to damp mop the floor. Leave to dry; you don't need to rinse.

Peppermint floor wash

This is a great fresh-smelling rinse for tiled floors. If you use it on tiled areas outdoors, it will help to keep flies away.

> 1 cup (250 ml) distilled white vinegar
> 1 cup (250 ml) methylated spirits
> 1 cup (250 ml) strong peppermint tea (from tea bags or leaves)
> 5 to 10 drops peppermint essential oil
> 5 drops dishwashing liquid

1 Combine all the ingredients in a large plastic bottle, shake thoroughly and then decant into a spray bottle.
2 Spray onto the floor and damp mop.

Rosemary beeswax furniture polish

This is a thick liquid polish. If you like more of a paste, increase the amount of beeswax and decrease the turpentine to about half-and-half. Gum turpentine is highly flammable, so take care when making this.

> 2 oz. (60 g) pure beeswax pellets
>   (or grated beeswax)
> 1 cup (250 ml) pure gum turpentine
> 1½ teaspoons rosemary essential oil

1 Put the beeswax and turpentine into a heatproof bowl.
2 Carefully sit the bowl over a saucepan of barely simmering water and stir until the beeswax melts and the solution is smooth. Take great care not to spill the liquid as you stir. Alternatively, to avoid exposing the mixture to a naked flame, sit the bowl in an electric frying pan on a low heat.
3 Remove from the heat and allow to cool before adding the rosemary oil. Store in a sealable glass bottle.
4 To use, pour a little onto a soft cloth and apply to wooden surfaces. Polish off with a second cloth until the surface shines.

Quick lavender furniture polish

Make up this polish in small quantities, as you need it. The vinegar cleans, the oil nourishes and the lavender disinfects, leaving that incomparable scent.

> ½ cup (125 ml) distilled white vinegar
>   (or better still, Herb vinegar on
>   page 292 made with lavender)
> 2 teaspoons olive oil
> 5 to 10 drops lavender essential oil

1 Combine all the ingredients in a jar or bottle.
2 To use, pour a little onto a soft cloth and rub the surface until you achieve a soft shine.

Lavender dusting cloth

Keep this lightly scented cloth for general dusting. Being slightly oily, it works much better than a plain cloth and will hold the dust as you pick it up.

> 1 cup (250 ml) hot water
> 2 tablespoons olive oil
> 10 drops lavender essential oil

1 Whisk all the ingredients in a bowl.
2 Dip clean soft rags into the solution, wring them out and hang them to dry. Store them in a sealed container and use them for dusting as required.
3 When the cloth is grubby, simply wash and re-dip it.

Quick vacuum deodorizer

For a clean fresh scent as you vacuum, sprinkle a few drops of a disinfectant essential oil, such as rosemary, or a mix of your favorites, onto a cotton ball and drop it into the dust bag or canister of your vacuum cleaner.

Herbal pet care

Just as you can use herbs to treat human ailments, you can also use them effectively for those minor ailments that sometimes trouble your cat or dog. But remember, if any symptoms persist, you must seek veterinary help. You can also use herbs to keep your pet's bedding or sleeping quarters clean and fresh-smelling.

Arthritis infusion

The pain and debilitating effects of arthritis can affect elderly cats or dogs as well as particular breeds. Try these two herbal remedies.

- Add a little chopped fresh parsley or grated ginger to your pet's diet.
- Pour 1 cup (250 ml) boiling water over 1 teaspoon fresh rosemary leaves. Stir and cover for 15 minutes. Strain and store in the refrigerator for up to 3 days. Over several weeks, mix a little into your pet's food.

To deter fleas, scatter dried wormwood beneath bedding.

Scald, sunburn or hotspot salve

Aloe vera gel takes the sting out of scalds and sunburn and soothes an itch with its moisturizing properties. Cut an aloe vera leaf and apply the gel directly onto scalds, sunburn or hotspots caused by excessive scratching. Make sure you always break off the more mature leaves from the aloe vera plant.

Fight-the-fleas spray

Fleas can drive cats and dogs quite crazy, and the incessant scratching can make owners pretty edgy, too. To keep fleas at bay, spray this mixture onto your pet's bedding and directly onto your pet.

1 cup (250 ml) water
4 to 6 drops tea-tree oil
4 to 6 drops lavender essential oil

1 Mix ingredients together and pour into a spray bottle.
2 Keep spray by the door and spritz your dog or cat each time it goes outside, taking care to avoid the eyes.

Sunburn soother

Relieve the discomfort and sting of sunburn by spraying the affected area with cool water mixed with witch hazel. It has a numbing effect. Be sure to keep it away from your pet's eyes.

Winter paw moisturiser

In cold weather, your dog's paws can become dry, particularly if they spend a lot of time out in the snow. Rub a daily smear of calendula ointment over the affected areas.

Peppermint kennel cleaner

Keep your dog's sleeping quarters flea-free and smelling fresh with this easy herbal spray.

2 cups (500 ml) boiling water
2 to 3 peppermint
(or spearmint) tea bags
¼ teaspoon clove essential oil

1 Make a strong tea with the water and tea bags.
2 Allow to cool and add the essential oil. Transfer to a spray bottle.
3 To use, spray onto the inside surfaces of the kennel and wipe clean. Spray again and allow to dry on the walls without rinsing. Be sure to wash the bedding regularly, too.

Crafts

Embroidery, flower pressing and arranging, photography, woodworking — whatever your favorite craft or hobby, herbs have a part to play. Choose from these easy, stylish projects that feature both fresh and dried herbs.

Herbal sleep pillows

Rest your head on a pillow filled with aromatic herbs and you'll quickly find yourself relaxing and drifting into an untroubled sleep.

Fill your sleep pillow with a single herb or with a combination of herbs. Take care to choose ones that will help to ease your mental and physical fatigue and also complement each other. Herbs known for their calming properties include lavender and roses. Avoid herbs such as eucalyptus and cinnamon, as their more insistent aromas tend to energize rather than relax.

What you need

The pillows vary in size from about 10 in. (25 cm) square to 9½ to 12½ in. (32 x 24 cm). These instructions are for a 10-in. (25-cm) square pillow.

☐ 12 x 20 in. (30 x 50 cm) cotton print

☐ 12 in. (30 cm) square contrast cotton print

☐ 4½ ft. (1.3 m) ric-rac or bobble braid

☐ matching sewing thread

☐ 1 x 2 ft. (30 x 60 cm) calico, or other fine material

☐ dried herbs of your choice, for filling

To make your pillow

1 For pillow front, cut one 10½-in. (27-cm) square (finished measurement + ½-in./1-cm seam allowance on all sides). From the same fabric, cut one rectangle, 10½ x 6 in. (27 x 15 cm), for the Flap (same height as front x 4¾-in./12-cm flap + ½-in./1-cm seam allowance + 1-in./2-cm hem). From the contrast fabric, cut one Back, 10½ x 11¾ in. (27 x 30 cm) (same height as front x finished width + ½-in./1-cm seam allowance + 2-in./4-cm hem).

2 Starting and finishing in the center of one side and with right sides together, baste ric-rac to edge of the pillow front, remembering to allow for ease around the corners.

3 Press under and stitch a ½-in. (1-cm) double hem (1 in./2 cm in all) on one long edge of the flap.

4 With right sides together and allowing a ½-in. (1-cm) seam, stitch flap to one side of the pillow along the 10½-in. (27-cm) edge. Press seam open.

5 Press under ½ in. (1 cm) on one side of Back. Press under another 1½ in.

(3 cm). Stitch hem in place. (Back now measures 10 x 10½ in./26 x 27 cm.)

6 Place pillow front, right side up, on your work surface, with the flap extended. Place the back on top, right side down, so that raw edges match the front and the hemmed edge of the back aligns with the seam line of the Flap.

Fold the flap back over the back, so that the right side of the flap is against the wrong side of the back.

7 Allowing ½-in. (1-cm) seams, stitch around the three edges, through all layers. (If you have used a very bulky braid, you might need to use a zipper foot.) Trim corners, fold flap back over and turn the cover right side out.

8 From calico, cut and stitch an inner pillow the same finished size as the finished cover measurements (in this case, 10 in./25 cm square). You will need to leave an opening for filling and turning.

9 Turn the calico pillow to the right side out, and use a greaseproof paper cone to loosely fill it with the herb of your choice. Stitch opening closed, then insert the pillow into the cover, using the Flap to hold it in place.

Moth-repellent sachets

Keep your clothing in good condition with pretty sachets filled with herbs that deter would-be marauding insects.

Herbs with properties that repel insects are generally very aromatic. Wormwood, whole cloves, bay leaves, eucalyptus, lavender, chamomile, crushed cinnamon sticks, peppermint and feverfew are useful weapons in the fight against moths and other insects that can damage fabrics such as wool, mohair and other animal fibers. These herbs also help purify stale air, while rue is useful for keeping pesky flies at bay. For the best effect, give the sachets an occasional quick squeeze or shake to release more scent.

Not only are insects keen to make a meal of particular fabrics, they will also target ones stained with perspiration or food. Be sure to launder your household linen and clothes before you store them.

What you need

Each finished sachet measures 5 in. (13 cm) approximately in diameter.

☐ 2 x 6-in. (15-cm) squares plain or embroidered organza, lawn or pretty brocade

☐ sharp pencil

☐ machine thread

☐ dried moth–repellent herbs and spices (use a mixture of any, or all, of the herbs mentioned above)

☐ pinking shears

☐ length of ribbon, for the hanging loop

☐ small or decorative button (optional)

☐ scraps of felt in two toning colors (optional)

☐ stranded embroidery cotton (optional)

To make your sachet

1 Using an appropriately sized cup or saucer, lightly trace a 4-in. (10-cm) diameter circle in the center of one square. If using embroidered organza or brocade, try to center motif or embroidery in the circle.

2 Place second square beneath the first, wrong sides together. Carefully machine-stitch around traced line, leaving an opening) of about 2 in. (4 cm for the filling. Tie off threads neatly on the back (remember you're working on the right side of the fabric).

3 Trim around edge of circle with pinking shears, cutting about ¾ in.(1.5 cm) from stitched line.

4 Carefully fill the sachet with moth-repellent herbs, using a funnel or cone of paper. Don't fill too tightly.

5 Stitch opening closed, trying to be as accurate as possible. If you want to add a hanging loop, insert the ends of the ribbon into the opening and secure them in the seam. Tie off thread ends.

6 To add a felt flower, use the templates (see opposite) to trace and cut a Small flower and a Large flower from two different-colored scraps of felt.

7 Place the Small flower on top of the Large one and center a button on top. Place the flower unit in the center of the sachet and stitch it in place through all the layers with two or three strands of embroidery cotton in a complementary color. Tie off the thread securely at the back of the sachet.

felt flower template

Use several sachets. The stronger the fragrance, the greater the protection against destructive insects.

Lavender heart sachets

Tuck one of these sachets under a pile of linen or clothing, and the gentle, aromatic fragrance will permeate the fabric.

Lavender has a fresh scent associated with cleanliness, which isn't surprising when you consider that the name is derived from the Latin word for "to wash." The sachets work best in small, enclosed areas and their fragrance should last for about three months. After this time, they can be opened and refilled with some newly dried lavender.

Alternatively, you could try a filling of cotton lavender. A moth-deterrent, it also has a fresh, aromatic scent.

What you need

Finished sachets are approximately 5 x 5 in. (12 x 12 cm).

- ☐ thin cardboard or template plastic
- ☐ 2 x 8-in. (20-cm) squares cotton print (or 1 square print and 1 square embroidery linen)
- ☐ fine lead pencil
- ☐ matching machine thread
- ☐ narrow ribbon, for hanging (optional)
- ☐ dried lavender
- ☐ small button (optional)
- ☐ Anchor Stranded Cotton: 101 Very Dark Violet; 1030 Dark Blue-Violet; 860 Fern Green (optional)
- ☐ crewel embroidery needle (optional)

You can easily make other simple shapes by drawing your own cardboard templates.

To make your sachet

1 Trace heart outline onto thin cardboard or template plastic and cut out. (Using template plastic makes it easier to center the embroidered design and the center back seam on the fabric.)

2 To make the cotton print sachet, cut one fabric square in half, then stitch the halves back together again, allowing a 1/4-in. (6-mm) seam and leaving a small opening in the center of the seam for turning and filling. (This will be the center back seam.) Press seam open.

3 Making sure the back seam is centered, trace around the heart template onto the wrong side of the joined fabric square, but do not cut out.

4 Place the two fabric squares right sides together. If you are using a hanging loop, insert the ends into the seam at the dip in the top of the heart shape. Stitch around the traced outline, taking care not to catch the ribbon loop in the seam. Trim away excess fabric about ¼ in. (6 mm) outside the stitching. Trim

the point, clip the curves and turn the sachet right side out through the center back seam.

5 Using a paper funnel, loosely fill the sachet with lavender and slipstitch the opening closed.

6 Stitch a small button to the center of the heart, through all layers, using a double strand of machine thread or embroidery cotton. Tie off securely at the back.

7 To make the embroidered sachet, construct the back from a cotton print fabric, as described above. For the embroidered front, trace the stalk positions on the diagram very lightly onto the center of the embroidery linen. (You don't need to trace the flowers.)

8 Using two strands of 860, embroider the stalks by working two or three long straight stitches along the traced line for each stalk, making a tiny back stitch to anchor each straight stitch. Thread the needle with two strands of each color (six strands in total) and work flowers in small straight stitches on each side of the stalks, using the diagram as a guide.

9 Making sure the embroidered motif is centered on the heart shape, trace around the template on the wrong side.

10 Join the back and front together, stitching around the traced outline and making sure the back seam is centered. Finish as for the cotton print sachet, above (step 6), but omit the button.

Use this heart-shaped template to trace the sachet outline.

Hanging herb ball

Form and function go hand in hand in this mini hanging garden. Change the contents with the seasons and pop in a few flowers for added color.

When you choose your herbs, think about their leaf shapes, colors and growing habit. We selected wild creeping thyme as a groundcover and oregano to cascade over the sides, then contrasted the broad-leafed herb comfrey with the feathery foliage of the curry plant. Then we selected lime-scented geranium for its delicious fragrance, yellow-flowered marigolds for a color burst, and basil, parsley, chives and Vietnamese mint for their versatile culinary value.

To care for your ball

- Select a secure position to hang the finished herb ball, as it is heavy when watered. Choose hooks and brackets that are designed to withstand the weight. Never attach brackets to crumbling brickwork or rotting wood.
- Until the roots are established, hang the ball in a position that receives only morning sun for one to two weeks. Herbs love the sun, so move it to a sunny spot, away from drying winds.
- Feed the ball fortnightly with water-soluble fertilizer.
- Water daily through the holes on top.
- Use a spray bottle to water the foliage so the herb ball gets a good drink.

Always wear garden gloves to protect your fingers from the sharp edges of cut wire.

What you need

- [ ] 2 metal hanging baskets
- [ ] 2 coconut fiber basket liners (or bark liner or sphagnum moss)
- [ ] small bag of perlite and vermiculite mix
- [ ] good-quality potting mix containing both a slow-release fertilizer and a wetting agent
- [ ] plastic wrap
- [ ] wire
- [ ] corrugated cardboard
- [ ] selection of herbs (see opposite)
- [ ] wire-cutting pliers
- [ ] scissors
- [ ] garden gloves
- [ ] florist's watering can
- [ ] spray bottle
- [ ] water-soluble fertilizer (see To care for your ball opposite)

To make your herb ball

1 Support one of the wire baskets on a suitable stand (we used a small rubbish bin) with the basket liner in place. Decide which basket is to be the upper one. Thoroughly wet the liner so it expands, making it easier to create insertion points. Create a series of holes in the liner so you can plant the herbs (we used a cutting/piercing tool and forced the fiber outwards with your fingers). Protect individual herbs with plastic wrap. Carefully push them into holes in prepared liner. Repeat for second basket.

2 For a lightweight growing medium, blend potting mix with perlite and vermiculite mix and partially fill baskets. Gently press potting mix into place to ensure all the air pockets are filled around the roots, planting comfrey through the bottom of the upper basket. Once you have put the ball together, the comfrey will be growing out of the top of the upper basket.

3 Cut out a circle of corrugated cardboard to cover the top of the upper basket. Pierce with holes to allow water to drain through. Wire into place.

4 Align the baskets to create the ball. Wire together (we used wire fencing clips, but twisted wire will do the same job). For maximum security, attach the hanging chains on the wire baskets to the rim of both baskets.

If you like cooking Asian dishes, plant a range of spicy or strongly flavored herbs, such as coriander, perilla, Thai basil and chilies. Or, if you're fond of Mediterranean recipes, plant oregano, sage, thyme and savory, all of which thrive in the same conditions.

Herb and flower wreath

Use wreaths to decorate your home, just as you would potted plants or flowers. Quick and easy to create, they make a delightful welcome.

A wreath can be rich in meaning. The circular shape is a symbol of infinity, without beginning or end. It represents unity, perfection and the cycles of both nature and time. A laurel wreath was used as a symbol of excellence by the ancient Greeks, who awarded it to great scholars, artists, soldiers and athletes. The ancient Romans also crowned their successful military commanders with wreaths.

Today, a wreath can be either purely decorative or significant in some way. You can choose flowers and herbs that symbolise a religious festival or a personal event, such as a birthday or wedding. Or you can simply make wreaths that feature what's in season in your garden — for example, in autumn, berries and rose hips can look stunning.

Obviously, an herb and flower wreath is not designed to last, but most frames can be reused many times and each one is simple to make. Once one wreath begins to fade, start planning the next one.

Frames

You can buy ready-made frames made of raffia, styrofoam, wire, dried grasses or some form of pliable timber. You can also make a timber frame from wisteria twigs or olive branches (you will need to strip them of leaves). The important thing to remember is that whatever you use, the material must bend smoothly into a circle but be sufficiently sturdy to hold the flowers and foliage without pulling out of shape. Finally, it should be easy to attach foliage and flowers to your frame.

Decorating the frame

How you decorate your frame is a matter of individual taste. You can keep things simple, as we have here, or build up more layers with some supplementary flowers and herbs. Try using a combination of fresh and dried herbs and flowers, bearing in mind that, once cut, some will have a shorter lifespan than others. With the flowers, experiment with a single color, several tones of one color or several contrasting colors.

Plant meanings

Olive branches Peace, fruitfulness, purification, strength, victory and reward.
Bay leaves Victory and excellence. Bay is an aromatic, broad-leafed evergreen.
Evergreens Eternal life and resurrection.
Violets Faithfulness.

Evergreen wreaths can be just as attractive as floral ones. Try different combinations of leaf shapes and colors. We used bay and olive.

Don't over-engineer your wreath by making it too neat and tidy. A relaxed, natural look is far more appealing.

What you need

- ☐ wreath frame (the one used here is 1 ft. (30 cm) in diameter and made of wisteria), from florist supply shops and craft shops
- ☐ green florist's wire (18 or 22 gauge), cut into short lengths
- ☐ clippers
- ☐ ribbon for hanging or for decoration (optional)
- ☐ olive branches
- ☐ bay sprigs
- ☐ violets

To make your wreath

If you are using a ribbon, tie this onto the base first, as it is difficult to add it later without squashing or hiding the foliage. Attach a length of florist wire to make a loop for hanging. At the end of each step, place the wreath in an upright position to check the coverage and balance. It is hard to judge if something is lopsided or overworked when it is lying flat on a bench.

1 Lay the frame on a work surface. Using the wire, attach short lengths of olive branch to the whole circle, allowing them to overlap.

2 Add short lengths of bay sprigs, tying them on securely with the wire. Keep them small; the result should not be too bushy.

3 Add small bunches of violets or other flowers, such as lavender, roses (trimmed of thorns), clove pinks or jasmine. If your chosen flower has particularly attractive leaves that are worth featuring, include them, too. Here, the broad leaves of the violets contrast with the narrow olive and bay leaves.

Table centerpiece

Balance the colors, shapes and textures of your chosen flowers and herbs to give your centerpiece a unique look.

Exploit the natural characteristics of each plant: floppier, softer plants look good gently overhanging the sides of a container, while stiffer, bolder ones act as focal points and accents as well as provide support for the softer plants. Also work out how the flowers are best viewed. For example, the hellebore flowers that we used do not look their best if seen from above; ensure that such flowers are cupped by other foliage so that their faces can be seen. Sweet peas, in contrast, have stiff stems and a ruffled profile, so feature them in the center of the arrangement. Choose plants with a gentle perfume and make your centerpiece a reasonable height so that guests can easily see one another across the table.

Suggested plants

Pieris *Pieris japonica, P. formosa* and *P. floribunda* Pieris is also known as lily of the valley shrub, andromeda or pearl bush. The small bell-like flowers form elegant sprays, and range in color from ivory white to a deep pinky red. The leathery, oval leaves grow in attractive spiral whorls. Young spring leaves are sometimes bright pink or red.

Sweet peas *Lathyrus odoratus* These old-fashioned, sweetly scented flowers come in

Pieris, sweet peas, flat-leaf parsley, sea holly and hellebores.

many colors, from white to pink, mauve and red through to velvety purple-black. The seeds are poisonous (they contain a neurotoxin) and should not be eaten.

Flat-leaf parsley *Petroselinum crispum* The bright green, serrated leaves of this herb act as both a filler and a background for showier flowers. Parsley is the least hardy of all the plants used here, so replace it with fresh cuttings as needed

during the life of the centerpiece, or experiment with other sturdier herbs, such as rosemary and lavender.

Sea holly *Eryngium planum, E. alpinum* and *E. maritimum* These plants bear thistle-like flowers in various shades of blue or green, and have a metallic sheen. They are surrounded by spiky white, silver, blue, green or violet bracts. The flowers dry well and are attractive in dried arrangements. In the 17th and 18th centuries, the candied roots were considered an aphrodisiac.

Hellebores *Helleborus niger, H. orientalis* If you pick these beautiful cup-shaped flowers when they're mature, they will last for weeks as they slowly fade and change color. They are lovely in float bowls. All parts of the plant are toxic. Use gloves when using this plant, as bruised foliage can cause skin irritation.

What you need

☐ container (we used a low, rectangular metallic container)

☐ clippers

☐ florist's foam (optional)

☐ large pebbles or glass marbles, to anchor the flowers

☐ flowers and herbs of your choice

To make your centerpiece

1 Trim the flowers and herbs to an appropriate height and remove spent blooms or yellowing leaves.

2 Before you start making the centerpiece, soak the stems in water for at least an hour.

3 If you are using florist's foam, cut it to the shape of the container, making sure it sits about 1 in. (2 cm) below the top, otherwise it will be visible once the arrangement is finished.

4 Soak the foam in a bucket of water, allowing it to sink naturally. The foam should be completely sodden before you use it. Place it in the

container. If you are not using foam, half fill the container with pebbles or marbles, then add water.

5 Starting from the outside in, poke the stems of the flowers or herbs into the foam, pebbles or marbles to hold them in place.

6 Turn the container around as you work, checking for visual balance and filling in any sparse patches. Where necessary, intertwine some pieces of foliage to provide more support. Finish with a light misting of water from a spray bottle to refresh the flowers and give them a dewy look.

Tussie-mussies

These pretty little bouquets are a nostalgic way to combine flowers and herbs with a personalized message.

Tussie-mussies are small posies of flowers and aromatic herbs. They were used in medieval and Elizabethan times to mask unpleasant odors and also because their scent was believed to protect the holder from diseases, such as the plague, that were thought to be spread by "bad air." This use led to their other name, "nosegays." They were also credited with refreshing the mind and sharpening the memory.

Tussie-mussies reached the peak of their popularity with floriography, or the art of sending messages by flowers, in the Victorian era. Various plants were considered to represent certain qualities or emotions. Some meanings were adapted from classical mythology, others from ancient lore and religious symbolism.

Young ladies and their suitors were well-versed in the meanings of various flowers and herbs. At the start of a courtship, it was common for a man to express his feelings for his intended with a tussie-mussie, known as a "word-posy." There were risks attached to this method of courtship, however: a slight mistake in shade or pattern could significantly alter the intended meaning. Also, some flowers have ambiguous or contradictory meanings: for example, hydrangeas can signify both "thank you for understanding" and "heartlessness."

Among the most common meanings were those relating to love and fidelity, making tussie-mussies most suitable for wedding bouquets. Some appropriate plants for such a bouquet might include bluebell (constancy), chervil (sincerity), forget-me-not (true love), holly (domestic happiness), honeysuckle or violet (fidelity), ivy or lime blossom (wedded love) and mint (warmth of feeling).

What you need

☐ prominent flower(s) for the center (traditional tussie-mussies had a single central flower, generally a rose, but ours uses several roses)

☐ 1 or 2 types of smaller complementary flowers

☐ a variety of herbs and leaves

☐ wax florist's tape

☐ about five large, broad leaves to frame the bouquet (optional)

☐ ribbon or strips of leftover wedding-dress fabric

☐ pearl pins

☐ gift card

To make your tussie-mussie

1 Soak the stems in water for at least an hour, or overnight if possible.

2 When ready to begin, remove from the water and wipe the stems dry.

3 Cut the stems on the diagonal to about 5 in. (12 cm).

4 Strip any thorns and all the lower leaves from the stems.

5 If using one central flower, hold it in one hand and use the other to surround it with the first ring of smaller flowers and herbs. If replicating the pictured tussie-mussie, start with a small handful of greenery and build a circle of roses and filler flowers around this. Rotate the posy as you go to ensure a balanced shape. Tightly wrap the stems of each layer with florist's tape, pressing so the tape will adhere to itself (the ribbon will disguise any untidiness).

6 Continue adding concentric layers until all the flowers and herbs are used. Lastly, frame the bouquet with large leaves.

Use a thorn remover (right, available from florist suppliers) to strip thorns from stems.

7 Wrap the stems tightly from top to bottom with florist's tape.

8 Wrap the stems with ribbon or fabric, securing it with pearl pins inserted into the stems (at the top) and up the stems (at the bottom).

9 Tie matching or contrasting ribbon near the top of the stems, leaving the ends to trail decoratively.

10 If your tussie-mussie is a gift, include a small card on which you have written the names of the plants and their meanings.

Tussie-mussies for other occasions

- The posy pictured uses white roses (innocence and purity), sweet peas (tender memory), lily of the valley (purity of heart, sweetness), rosemary (remembrance) and parsley (festivity).

- For a bouquet of condolence, you could choose from red poppies (consolation), rosemary (remembrance), wormwood (grief), weeping willow (sorrow), lemon balm (sympathy), fennel (strength) and borage (courage).

- To wish someone luck for an exam or job interview, consider basil (good wishes), four-leaf clover (happiness), juniper (protection), buttercup (promise of riches), hawthorn or snowdrop (hope), lavender (luck), sage (wisdom) or dandelion (wishes come true).

- It's not only traditional occasions that can be enhanced by a little floriography. For a racier message, try your luck with gardenia (ecstasy), tuberose (dangerous pleasure or voluptuousness), coriander (lust), forsythia (anticipation), chickweed (rendezvous) or red camellia (you're a flame in my heart)!

Herb pot trio

Customized pots are a pretty and practical way of displaying and labeling your herbs. Choose from blackboard paint, stencils and felt.

Stencilled herb pot

This simple and bold treatment uses a stencil of the herb's initial letter. It can be applied to a plain galvanized metal pot, or one that has been painted a contrast color first. This style of pot is useful if you always have a crop of the same herb on the go.

We used a laser printer to create the stencil, but you can use hand lettering if you prefer. Whichever method you choose, pick a style of lettering that is not too complicated and that does not have very thin areas, as these will weaken the stencil and are less likely to transfer well. Plain, rather blocky lettering will give the most reliable results. Use spray paint in a well-ventilated area, preferably outdoors.

What you need

- ☐ galvanized metal flower pot
- ☐ vinegar or methylated spirits (denatured alcohol)
- ☐ commercial stencil (optional)
- ☐ thin cardboard or stencil film (from craft stores)
- ☐ fine craft knife and cutting mat
- ☐ spray adhesive
- ☐ spray paint (or paint of your choice and a stencil brush)
- ☐ cotton buds
- ☐ mineral turpentine
- ☐ newspaper or other waste paper

1 Wash the pot in warm soapy water, then rinse. Wipe over with vinegar or methylated spirits and allow to dry.

2 Trace your chosen letter onto thin cardboard or stencil film, and cut out the stencil with a fine craft knife.

3 Lay down some newspaper to protect the work surface. Use spray adhesive to stick the stencil to the surface of your flower pot.

4 Spray the newspaper until the spray is fine and even, then spray lightly and evenly over the cutout area of the stencil. To avoid seepage and drips, spray two or three very thin coats rather than one thick one. Allow the paint to become touch-dry between coats, then peel off the stencil.

5 Remove any oversprays or seepages with a cotton bud dipped in turpentine.

6 Allow to dry completely, painted side up, to prevent the paint from running. Plant with herbs.

Pot with blackboard paint

If you change your herb plantings frequently, try this great option. When one herb is finished, you can wipe off its name with a damp cloth, wait for it to dry, then write the new name on with chalk.

What you need

- ☐ terra-cotta pots
- ☐ small can of blackboard paint
- ☐ straight-edged paintbrush
- ☐ chalk

1 Clean the surface of the pot as directed on the paint can (the paint will not adhere properly to a greasy or dusty surface). Allow the pot to dry thoroughly.

2 Carefully paint the rim of the pot with the blackboard paint. Allow it to dry, then plant with herbs.

3 Use chalk to write the name of the herb on the pot. For fun, use both the common and Latin or botanical names; if you bought the herbs at a nursery, both names should be given on the label.

Felt pot

This unusual pot stands about 5 in. (13 cm) high. Fill it with herbs and either leave it above ground or plant it in the garden — the herbs' roots will eventually grow right through the fabric.

What you need

- ☐ 12 x 16 in. (30 x 40 cm) industrial felt, 3 to 4 mm thick
- ☐ sewing thread and needle
- ☐ stranded embroidery cotton
- ☐ terra-cotta, galvanized iron or plastic flower pot to use as a template
- ☐ brown paper or newspaper
- ☐ 2 pins or toothpicks
- ☐ sticky tape
- ☐ pencil
- ☐ paper scissors

1 To make the template, tape a pin or toothpick to the top and bottom edges of the pot, aligning them, and letting them protrude a little beyond the edge; these will act as markers for the start and finish point of the template.

2 Lay the pot on the paper, pins down. Mark this point, which will be the left edge of the template. Starting at the pins, slowly roll the pot across the paper, tracing along both top and bottom edges as you go. Stop when you reach the pins again.

3 Remove the pot, then draw vertical lines at each end of the template to join the two curved lines. This forms the template for the body of the pot.

4 Draw around the base of the pot.

5 Cut out the paper pieces along the marked lines. Note that you do not need a seam allowance. When you have finished, you should have one pot piece and one base piece.

6 Pin the paper pieces to the felt and cut carefully around them.

7 Butt the straight edges of the pot and oversew them together with a sewing thread in a matching color. With stranded embroidery cotton, work a line of cross stitch along the seam, from side to side. This decorative stitch strengthens the join. Using sewing thread, oversew the circular base into the bottom of the pot.

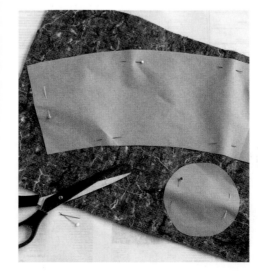

Digital print transfers

The digital camera and print shop put a contemporary spin on craft, so being creative has never been easier.

This is the simplest of projects, requiring no more than a photograph or other image, a hand towel or napkin to apply it to, and a trip to the nearest digital print shop. Many craft projects require weeks of work, but if patience isn't your strong point, this is the project for you. Whether you make it for your home, or as a gift for someone else, the results are impressive.

Choosing an image

You'll get the best results from an image that has a simple shape and not too many complicated areas, such as the bay sprigs used on the napkins here (see opposite). Avoid using dark images, as they tend to become darker during the transfer process. Images with a good contrast between light and dark will work best.

If photographing your own image, place your chosen herb on a white background and shoot from straight overhead. If using a digital camera, set it to the highest resolution you can. This will ensure a crisp, clear image.

Remember that white does not print; the fabric will show through any parts of the design that are white, so you will not, for example, be able to print white flowers onto a colored fabric. Images will show up best on white, cream or pastel fabrics; dark colors and busy prints, on the other hand, are both unsuitable.

Because the image will be printed facedown, it will be a mirror image of the original photo. This means that you may need to ask the print shop to flip the image if you want it to be facing a particular way.

Preparing the fabric

Choose the article on which you want the print. We used hand towels and napkins, but other options are T-shirts or tablecloths. For the clearest print, choose a smooth, closely woven fabric in a

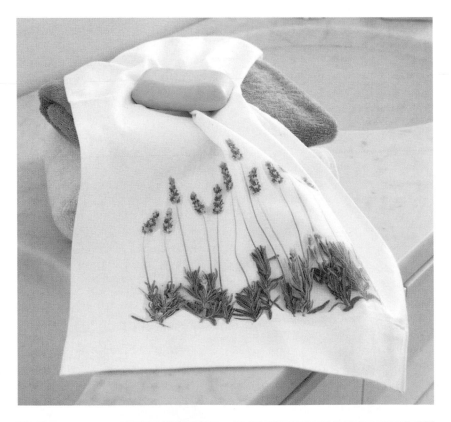

At the digital print shop, a transfer print is made from the image on your disk.

Cut around the image and place it facedown on the fabric.

What you need

- ☐ a good-quality image (see right)
- ☐ fabric item such as a hand towel to which to transfer the image
- ☐ small, sharp scissors
- ☐ masking tape

natural fiber, such as cotton or linen. Fine-knit fabrics work well, too, but textured fabrics, such as toweling or waffle weave, will result in an unclear image, while synthetic fibers may melt under the high heat that is needed for the transfer process. If you are transferring the image to an item of clothing, put a piece of brown paper inside the garment so that the transfer does not go through to both the front and the back.

Next, wash the fabric to eliminate the possibility of shrinkage, which can cause the transferred image to crack, then iron the fabric smooth.

If you want the image centered but don't trust yourself to do this by eye, mark a crease by folding the fabric item in half in both directions. Using cotton thread and long stitches, baste along this crease. The point at which the stitches intersect is the center. On the back of the transfer, draw horizontal and vertical lines through the center of the design, then match these with the basting stitches. Once the image has been transferred and allowed to cool, remove the basting stitches.

Creating the transfer

Take the photograph or an image on disk to a digital print shop. If your image needs touching up or cropping, the print shop will be able to do this for you. They can also digitally manipulate your image and, if it is small enough, repeat it so that you get some spare images on the transfer sheet, thus saving money (transfer paper is expensive).

Ask for the image to be photocopied onto transfer paper at a size that fits your chosen item. Avoid handling the transfer paper while the ink is drying.

Carefully cut out the image around the outline (do this at home in an unhurried manner, then bring the project back to the print shop for the next step). Using masking tape, position the transfer print onto the fabric, facedown, ensuring it is in the desired position. Then get the print shop to transfer the image (they will use a high-pressure heat press).

Allow the item to cool for a few minutes, then remove the backing from the transfer paper. Embellish the item with ribbon, beads or embroidery, if desired.

Laundering

Using mild detergent, wash and dry the finished item on a cool setting only. Do not use bleach. Don't iron the image, as this can cause the transfer to move.

A note on copyright

If you take your own photograph, you own the copyright to it and can use it as you wish. However, if you use someone else's image, you may risk infringing their copyright; you cannot copy such an image for articles that you will sell.

Make sure you photograph your herb or flower on a white background.

Kitchen print triptych

Take your favorite herb photographs from camera to canvas and decorate your walls with beautiful images that won't cost a fortune.

Making your own masterpiece has never been easier. Many home stores, photographic shops and online digital photography companies now offer a service that enables you to transfer your photographs onto canvas, to a size and format that suits your setting.

What you need

☐ 3 good-quality images of herbs (we used flowering rosemary, heartsease and flowering sage)

☐ dimensions of finished print (ideally, discuss this first with your chosen supplier; see step 1)

To make your triptych

1 Check out suppliers of photographic prints on canvas, and find out what sizes are available and how best to supply your image.

2 Think about where you want to hang your prints. Bear in mind that prints are made with pigment ink, which is extremely fade-resistant. However, they should not be exposed to direct sunlight for long periods of time.

3 Consider whether to have your print laminated. Unlaminated prints can be cleaned by dusting them lightly with a soft cloth, while laminated prints can be wiped down very gently with a damp cloth. Remember, the image is water-resistant, not waterproof.

4 Take your photographs. Today, many of even the most basic digital cameras do much of the hard technical work for you. What you need to concentrate on is creating a good composition. To do this, think about your viewpoint and the angle at which you are photographing the plant, taking time to mentally arrange the shot before you take it.

5 Decide if you want to have the whole image in focus or whether you want to concentrate on just one particular area, such as the flowers. Experiment with scale. A small flower such as heartsease takes on a dramatic look when it occupies the entire frame.

While placing the subject directly in the center of the frame may work at times, zooming in a little or shifting your angle can turn an ordinary image into something dynamic.

Digital photography gives you immediate control over what you are doing in a way that conventional photography does not. If you don't like the preview image, delete it and shoot another. Experiment until you get the picture you want to live with.

Herb candleholders

Candlelight generates a special aura that's both romantic and flattering. This simple project adds a decorative touch.

Creating a relaxed atmosphere is easy with candles, particularly if they are scented with herbs, such as roses, lemon verbena or lavender. With a few herbs, some vellum paper and a photocopier, you can customize your candles to suit your décor, setting and the fragrance of your candles. Vellum paper (from the French *vélin* for calfskin) was originally used for scrolls and handwritten manuscripts bound into books. Today's vellum is made from cotton, comes in a wide range of colors and is suitable for many papercrafts. It is available from specialist stationery suppliers.

To make your candleholder

1 Work out the size of vellum you will need to wrap around your glass, remembering to add a small overlap. Cut out as many pieces as you need.

2 Lay a few appropriately sized herb sprigs or leaves on the paper to get an idea of the arrangement you like best. Try spiky leaves (rosemary); simple, bold leaves (bay); or feathery foliage (fennel). Arrange the herbs on the copy plate of a photocopier and print an image onto ordinary paper until you are happy with the arrangement. Then insert the vellum into the paper tray and print your design onto it.

3 Wrap the printed vellum around the glass, then fix the edges together with double-sided tape. Place a candle in each glass.

Experiment with sprigs and leaves to get the effect you want.

What you need

These can be made to fit a glass of any size.

☐ fresh herb leaves or sprigs, such as bay, fennel or rosemary

☐ color photocopier

☐ pale green translucent vellum paper

☐ straight-sided high-ball glass

☐ double-sided tape

☐ tea light or small herb-scented candle

Herb cards and tags

A personalised handmade card is something to treasure, and pressed and dried flowers and herbs are perfect for decorating them.

If you want the cards to last a long time, use acid-free paper, cardboard and cardstock. There is a vast range of beautiful papers and cardstocks available, and many of them are handmade. For example, unryushi paper, handmade in Thailand, is semi-transparent and contains short and long fibers. Mulberry paper comes in a range of textures and thicknesses. It is meant to be torn, not cut, producing a pretty frayed edge. We have given finished measurements but you can adapt them to any size you wish.

Microwave it!

The traditional method of pressing flowers is to place them between layers of absorbent materials in a book or flower press. While this is an enjoyable way to go about things, it is quite time-consuming. You can now buy flower presses that enable you to press and dry flowers in the microwave in a process that takes only a few minutes or less. Presses are available from craft shops and via the Internet.

For best results, pick flowers and leaves in the morning when they are fresh but free of moisture. Give some thought to how they'll look once they are flattened: heartsease will flatten much better than a rose, for instance.

Lavender card

What you need

This card measures 4½ x 6 in. (15 x 11 cm).

- ☐ 6 x 9 in. (22 x 15 cm) purple cardstock
- ☐ 4 x 5½ in. (9.5 x 13.5 cm) purple spot scrapbook paper
- ☐ 3 x 4½ in. (8 x 12 cm) textured mauve decorative paper
- ☐ purple sewing thread
- ☐ sewing machine
- ☐ dried lavender sprigs and leaves
- ☐ tacky craft glue

Pressed flower wreath card

What you need

This card measures 5 in. (12 cm) square.

- ☐ 5 x 10 in. (12 x 24 cm) pale green cardstock
- ☐ 5 in. (12 cm) square pale green unryushi or mulberry paper
- ☐ spray adhesive
- ☐ deckle-edge scissors
- ☐ dried herbs and flowers (we used chervil, heartsease and chamomile)
- ☐ PVA glue

1 Score the pale green cardstock in half crosswise and fold it in half to make a single-fold card.

1 Score the purple cardstock in half crosswise, then fold it in half to form a single-fold card.

2 Secure the mauve decorative paper to the center of the scrapbook paper with just a dab of glue.

3 Using purple machine thread, work a line of zigzag around the edges of the decorative paper to hold it in place. (It's a good idea to test your stitch width and tension on scraps of paper before you start.)

4 Glue the stitched unit to the center of the cardstock card.

5 Carefully glue lavender sprigs and leaves in place on the front.

2 Using deckle-edge scissors, trim the square of unryushi paper to 4½ in. (11 cm).

3 Use spray adhesive to glue the unryushi square to the center of the card.

4 Arrange dried herbs and flowers into a wreath shape and carefully glue each piece in place.

Orange blossom wedding card, Scented Valentine card in front (instructions overleaf), Lavender card and Pressed flower wreath card.

Scented Valentine card

What you need

This card measures 4 x 5½ in. (10.5 x 14 cm).

- [ ] purchased trifold card with heart cutout (or make your own)
- [ ] gingham-patterned scrapbook paper
- [ ] fine craft knife and cutting mat
- [ ] spray adhesive
- [ ] small amount organza or other sheer fabric
- [ ] tacky craft glue
- [ ] dried rose petals and lavender

1 Cut a rectangle of scrapbook paper ¼ in. (5 mm) smaller all round than the size of the card front.

2 Using the card as a template, trace the heart outline onto the wrong side of the paper rectangle. Now add 3 to 5 mm all round the traced outline and cut out carefully with a craft knife.

3 Using spray adhesive, glue the paper rectangle to the front of the card, taking care to position it accurately.

4 Glue a small piece of organza behind the heart-shaped opening by running a thin line of glue around the edge of the heart. Don't stretch the fabric too

tightly across the opening – it needs some give to contain the herbs.

5 Place a small amount of dried lavender and rose petals on the organza, and use tacky craft glue to secure the card flap, enclosing the herbs.

Orange blossom wedding card

What you need

This card measures 5½ in. (13.5 cm) square.

- [ ] 5½ x 11 in. (13.5 x 27 cm) cream cardstock
- [ ] 3½ in. (9 cm) square firm cardboard
- [ ] 4½ in. (11 cm) square pale green silk dupion
- [ ] spray adhesive
- [ ] tacky craft glue
- [ ] 4 in. (10 cm) square olive green cardstock
- [ ] small amount white cardstock
- [ ] daisy punch (from craft and scrapbooking stores)
- [ ] yellow stranded embroidery cotton
- [ ] large embroidery needle
- [ ] small pressed leaf sprays (we used new shoots from murraya)
- [ ] craft glue
- [ ] orange essential oil (optional)
- [ ] cotton bud (optional)

1 Score the cream cardstock in half crosswise and fold in half to make a single-fold card.

2 Lightly spray the front of the 3½-in. (9-cm) cardboard square with spray adhesive and place it facedown in the center of the wrong side of the silk dupion square. Fold the edges of silk to the back, folding the corners neatly, and secure in place with tacky craft glue.

3 Glue the silk-covered square to the center of the olive green cardstock square. Glue this unit to the front of the cream card.

4 To make the orange blossoms, punch as many as you desire from white cardstock with a small daisy punch. Lightly score each petal from the edge of the center to the tip. (This will make the petals curve slightly, giving them a three-dimensional appearance.)

5 Using all six strands of yellow embroidery thread in a large needle, push the needle through the center of a daisy from the front. Bring the needle back to the front, close to the original entry point (as though you were sewing on a button), leaving a tail of thread on the front (above). Insert it again into the first hole, then back to the front again. Unthread the needle and trim the loops and ends of thread to about ½ in. (1 cm) long, creating a set of stamens. (They will be held in place when you glue the blossom to the background.)

6 Fold up the edges of the petals around the center and along the score lines.

7 Arrange and glue the dried leaf sprays on the silk background in the desired pattern. (This can be quite fiddly — you might find it easier to use spray adhesive.) Add the orange blossoms and glue in place with craft glue to hold them securely.

8 If you wish to add fragrance, dab the center and stamens of each blossom with a cotton ball dipped in orange essential oil or one of your choice.

Herb tags

What you need

This card measures 3½ in. (9 cm) square.

- ☐ 2 x 2¾ in. (5.5 x 7 cm) fine corrugated board
- ☐ 3½ in. (9 cm) square cardstock
- ☐ 2¼ x 2¾ in. (6 x 7 cm) plain calico
- ☐ tacky craft glue
- ☐ herb sprigs (we used chervil, rosemary, parsley and sage)
- ☐ hole punch
- ☐ natural string

1   Glue the corrugated board to the cardboard square on an angle.

2   Fray the edges of the calico a little, then glue it to the center of the corrugated board, off-setting it again.

3   Glue a sprig of dried herb to the calico background.

4   Punch a hole in one corner and add a string tie.

Bay in myth

In Greek mythology, the bay tree was considered sacred to Apollo, the sun god, and later to his son Aesculapius, the god of medicine. Apollo became infatuated with a lovely nymph called Daphne. She spurned him and begged the gods to rescue her. Their solution was to turn her into a bay tree.

While victors at the first Olympic games were crowned with olive leaves, later they were replaced with bay and dedicated to Apollo. The tradition is still retained in terms such as "poet laureate" and the important French secondary school examination, the "baccalaureate."

Herb pot window box

Create a garden on your windowsill, outdoors or in, and enjoy the fragrance, taste and color of herbs through the seasons. Only basic carpentry skills are required.

To create an interesting paint finish, use a sponge to stipple on a contrasting color of gloss acrylic.

A window box is a miniature portable garden. Whether you sit it on a windowsill or attach it to brackets to cheer up an outside wall, this simple container is both decorative and practical. The design neatly accommodates three pots of herbs. Trailing herbs, such as evening primrose or nasturtiums look good when contrasted with upright ones, such as chives or dill. Try grouping herbs with different textures — for example, position velvety, furry sage alongside shiny basil and tightly curled parsley.

Customize your window box to suit your culinary requirements, teaming spicy Vietnamese mint with citrus-flavored lemon balm and pungent, peppery thyme. Color can play a part, too. Purplish-red perilla, cream-and-green variegated apple mint and bright red chilies all make a visually striking splash.

If you position your window box outdoors, it will be constantly exposed to the vagaries of the weather, so make sure you choose quality materials. If you decide to hang it on brackets, check that they are strong enough to support the weight of the pots and that the surface on which you place them and the box is not cracked or crumbling.

As for your chosen herbs, keep an eye on the moisture content of the soil in the pots. Wind and sun can quickly dry it out.

Other ideas

- Try color theming your window box with flowering herbs. A mauve and purple theme could include herbs that enjoy a sunny position, such as sage, hyssop and lavender.

- Or plant a variety of the same herb. Try common mint, peppermint and spearmint, or sweet basil, Thai basil, holy basil and 'Red Rubin.'

- Choose a color theme that will complement your house's exterior paint scheme. For example, white-flowering herbs such as valerian and Roman chamomile look fresh with a blue color scheme.

To make your window box

What you need

Finished box is 19½ x 9 x 6¾ in. (488 x 228 x 170 mm).

- ☐ 40 x 2-mm galvanized twist nails
- ☐ drill and ¹/₁₆-in. (1.5-mm) twist bit
- ☐ 35½ x 7½ x ¾ in. (900 x 190 x 19 mm) radiata pine
- ☐ 82 x 1½ x ¾ in. (2100 x 42 x 19 mm) radiata pine
- ☐ external undercoat paint
- ☐ external gloss acrylic paint for top coat
- ☐ sandpaper, handsaw
- ☐ pencil, tape/square measure
- ☐ small paintbrush
- ☐ hammer, putty

1 Cut a piece of 7½ x ¾ in. (190 x 19 mm) pine into a 1 x 17¾ in. (450 mm) length for the base and

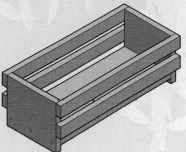

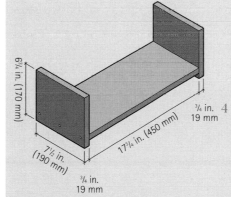

6¾ in. (170 mm)
7½ in. (190 mm)
17¾ in. (450 mm)
¾ in. 19 mm
¾ in. 19 mm

2 x 6¾ in. (170 mm) lengths for the ends. Cut the 42 x 19 mm pine into 1½ x ¾ in. (4 x 488 mm) lengths. Sand all edges and corners.

2 Drill 3 holes in each of the end pieces 1¼ in. (30 mm) up from the bottom: two holes ½ in. (10 mm) in from each side and one in the center. Nail the ends to the base, one end at a time.

3 Position a 19¼-in. (488-mm) length on each side of the box, level with the tops of the ends. Drill 2 holes at each end of these lengths. Hammer in nails. Repeat on the other side. Position remaining 2 x 19¼-in. (488-mm) lengths 1¼ in. (30 mm) below the top rung and repeat drilling and hammering.

4 Sand timber all over. Punch nail heads and putty over them. Seal with one coat of undercoat. Sand again. Apply two top coats of your chosen color. Allow each coat to dry before sanding. Sanding the final coat will give the box a rustic, distressed look.

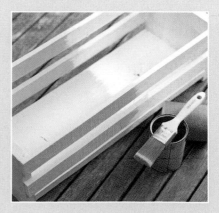

Cooking

Cuisines around the world derive much of their distinctive character from the addition of herbs and spices. Go globetrotting with this collection of recipes, from pasta and pickles to meat and fish, from oils and breads to cakes and drinks.

A world of herbs and spices

The extraordinary range of herbs and spices available to us today continues to expand, driven by consumer demand.

A multitude of flavors

Can you imagine pasta sauces with no basil, Japanese food without wasabi or Mexican food minus the chilies? Creating authentic dishes from around the world has never been easier.

Asian herbs, in particular, have enjoyed a huge surge in popularity in recent years, and Thai basil, coriander, Vietnamese mint, perilla, kaffir lime leaves, lemongrass and turmeric are becoming easier to source. Also, the seasonings used in Africa, the Middle East, the Caribbean islands and Latin America are more readily available, and in Australia, native plants such as lemon myrtle and other "bush" herbs are being added to the cook's repertoire.

And it's not just the leaves that are used in recipes: flowers, seeds, stems and roots are also often included.

Balancing act

The recipes in this book give measures for the amount of herbs and spices to use, but you can vary them to suit your taste. One of the great bonuses of using

"Garlic is as good as 10 mothers."

Traditional proverb

herbs is that you'll find you can cut back on the amount of salt you add to your food. The herbs will be flavor enough!

One golden rule is to avoid allowing one flavor to dominate the others. Herb and spice mixes such as garam masala and ras el hanout are a delicate exercise in balancing a wide range of flavors. Even if you like a bit of heat, too much fresh chili can overwhelm the more subtle herbs and spices accompanying it. Similarly, very pungent herbs, such as fresh coriander, are not to everyone's taste, so a light hand is recommended.

You can always add more fresh herbs at the table. In Iranian and Vietnamese cooking, a bowl of fresh herbs is a standard appetiser or accompaniment. Similarly, the Lebanese offer a platter of fresh herbs and vegetables as part of a mezze table.

Bouquet garni, an herb mix used in classic French cuisine, includes parsley, bay and thyme.

As a general rule, when cooking with herbs, the soft-leafed ones, such as coriander, are best added late in the cooking process to preserve their flavor. The coarser ones, such as rosemary, are ideal for dishes that require long, slow cooking. Dried herbs are usually more concentrated in flavor than fresh ones, so you will need less of them.

Fresh herbs

- Select vibrant, aromatic leaves with no signs of wilting or yellowing.
- Ideally, buy fresh herbs as and when you need them. However well you store them, they quickly deteriorate in flavor and appearance, particularly the soft-leafed varieties such as flat-leaf parsley, coriander and lovage. The coarser herbs, such as thyme and rosemary, are a little hardier.
- Store fresh herbs for no more than 3 or 4 days. Loosely wrap unwashed bunches in damp paper towels and store in an airtight container or sealed plastic bag in a cool place.
- Alternatively, stand the stems in a jug with a little water and loosely cover the leaves with a plastic bag. Store in the refrigerator, changing the water daily.
- Or store the herbs in plastic bags and place them in the vegetable crisper of the refrigerator.

Get chopping!

Chop herbs with a mezzaluna (half-moon-shaped blade), a sharp knife or scissors. You can use a food processor for large bunches, but don't over-process them. Fine-leafed herbs can also be shredded by hand, but coarse herbs, such as rosemary, need fine chopping unless whole sprigs are appropriate for the recipe. Herbs such as basil, coriander and sage discolor if they are chopped too early before use.

- Buy herbs sold in plastic boxes or cellophane bags — they keep well if stored in the refrigerator.
- Preserve chopped fresh herbs by freezing them in a little water in ice-cube trays.
- For more detailed information, see Harvesting, preserving and storing, *pages 172–5*. Delicate herbs such as basil do not dry well, but more robust herbs such as thyme and rosemary retain their flavor well and are a convenient alternative to fresh.
- When you are ready to use them, wash herbs in a bowl of cold water rather than running water, which can bruise them. Pat them dry with paper towels.

The must-haves

This selection of herbs and spices that you can grow yourself or buy is a useful culinary starting point. (If you enjoy making herbal teas, add chamomile, dandelion and lemon verbena.)

Basil, bay, chilies, chives, coriander, dill, garlic, ginger, lemongrass, lemon tree (it's an herb, too), lovage, marjoram or oregano, mint, parsley, rosemary, sage, tarragon, thyme and Vietnamese mint.

Dried herbs and spices

While you may prefer the taste of herbs picked fresh from the garden, there is always a place for dried or frozen ones as well as for dried spices. In Greek cooking, for example, dried oregano (rigani) is used extensively in preference to fresh, while paprika, rather than fresh chilies, is an important ingredient in Hungarian food.

- Buy dried herbs and spices in small quantities to avoid waste, and store in airtight containers in a cool, dark place.
- Ignore the use-by date on commercial products, as the dried herb or spice may deteriorate long before the given date. The best way to check for freshness is by smell, taste and appearance — for example, color fading is a good indicator of flavor loss.

- Whole spices, such as coriander and cumin seeds, retain their flavor and aroma longer than ground. Grind them in a spice grinder, or in a coffee-grinder kept specifically for the purpose, or use a mortar and pestle.
- Spices add color as well as flavor. Paprika adds a glorious red color, while saffron and turmeric transform a dish into a golden yellow.

Herb oils

Quality ingredients make great-tasting oils that enhance dips, marinades, sauces and dressings. Change herbs with the season.

Basil oil

3 tablespoons fresh basil leaves
1 cup (250 ml) boiling water
2 cups (500 ml) olive oil

1 Place basil leaves in medium bowl and cover with boiling water. Stand 2 minutes. Drain; pat leaves dry. Process basil and oil in food processor until combined. Alternatively, finely chop basil leaves, add 2 tablespoons oil and mash basil into oil with a fork. Add remaining oil.

2 Leave 2 to 3 days to allow flavors to develop. Strain oil through muslin; pour into clean 17 fl. oz. (500 ml) bottle. Store in a cool, dark place. Use with tomatoes and salad greens.

MAKES 2 CUPS (500 ml)
Preparation 15 minutes plus 2 to 3 days for infusing

Rosemary oil

2 or 3 large sprigs fresh rosemary
3 cloves garlic
3 fresh bay leaves
2 cups (500 ml) olive oil

1 Lightly bruise rosemary, garlic and bay leaves by hitting them with the flat of a knife. Place herbs in clean 17 fl. oz. (500 ml) bottle; pour in olive oil.

2 Leave for 2 to 3 days to allow flavors to develop. Store in a cool, dark place. Use with pork and lamb.

MAKES 2 CUPS (500 ml)
Preparation 10 minutes plus 2 to 3 days for infusing

Cook's tip

To sterilize jars, wash jars and lids thoroughly in warm, soapy water, using a bottle brush. Rinse well in cold water to remove all traces of soap. Stand jars on baking tray and place in oven. Heat oven to 200°F (100°C). Leave oven on for 45 minutes; turn off. Remove jars when cool enough to handle. Or, wash jars and lids in dishwasher on the hottest cycle. Cool before handling.

Lemongrass oil

2 to 3 fresh lime leaves
1 stalk fresh lemongrass
2 cloves garlic
3 x ¼-in. (5-mm) slices fresh ginger
2 cups (500 ml) peanut oil

1 Lightly bruise lime leaves, lemongrass, garlic and ginger by hitting them with the flat of a knife. Place herbs in clean 17 fl. oz. (500 ml) bottle; pour in peanut oil.

2 Leave 3 to 4 days to allow flavors to develop. Store in a cool, dark place. Use with fish and seafood.

MAKES 2 CUPS (500 ml)
Preparation 10 minutes plus 3 to 4 days for infusing

Herb guide

The more robust the herb, the better the finished oil. Experiment with marjoram or oregano, chilies, garlic, chervil, coriander, chives or mint. Clean the leaves very carefully to remove all traces of dirt or pesticides.

Tools of the trade

Muslin is a type of very finely woven cotton fabric. It is used in the same way as a sieve, allowing liquid to pass through while retaining any unwanted sediment. Look for it in kitchen supply or fabric shops.

Rosemary oil, lemongrass oil and Basil oil

Herb vinegars

As with oils, wine vinegars vary greatly in price and quality, so buy the best you can afford. Experiment with different types of vinegar.

Tarragon and red wine vinegar

15 fresh tarragon leaves
10 juniper berries
2 cups (500 ml) red wine vinegar

1 Lightly bruise leaves and berries by hitting them with the flat of a knife. Place bruised leaves and berries in clean 17 fl. oz. (500 ml) bottle; pour in vinegar.

2 Leave 3 to 4 days to allow flavors to develop.

MAKES 2 CUPS (500 ml)
Preparation 10 minutes plus 3 to 4 days for infusing

Rice vinegar with coriander

3 fresh lime leaves
4 x ¼-in. (5-mm) slices galangal
2 cloves garlic
15 to 20 fresh coriander leaves
1 cup (250 ml) rice wine vinegar

1 Lightly bruise lime leaves, galangal and garlic by hitting them with the flat of a knife. Place herbs, including coriander leaves, in clean 8 fl. oz. (250 ml) bottle; pour in vinegar.

2 Leave 3 to 4 days to allow flavors to develop.

MAKES 1 CUP (250 ml)
Preparation 10 minutes plus 3 to 4 days for infusing

Cook's tip

The seeds of herbs, such as dill, fennel, celery and coriander, can be used to make seed vinegars. Prepare in the same way as herb vinegars. To retain their flavor, store herb vinegars and oils in a cool, dark place.

Fennel and saffron vinegar

4 sprigs fresh fennel leaves
2 to 3 whole dried chilies
2 cloves garlic
¼ teaspoon fennel seeds
pinch of saffron
2 cups (500 ml) white wine vinegar

1 Place fennel leaves, chilies, garlic, fennel seeds and saffron in clean 17 fl. oz. (500 ml) bottle; pour in vinegar.

2 Leave 3 to 4 days to allow flavors to develop.

MAKES 2 CUPS (500 ml)
Preparation 10 minutes plus 3 to 4 days for infusing

Try these, too...

Red chili vinegar
Cut 1 long red chili in half lengthwise and place in clean 25 fl. oz. (750 ml) bottle with 2 whole long red chilies. Pour in 3 cups (750 ml) white wine vinegar. Seal and store.

Berry vinegar
Combine 1 lb. (500 g) berries (such as a mixture of raspberries, strawberries and blueberries) and 3 cups (750 ml) white wine vinegar in a large ceramic or glass bowl and stir well to lightly bruise fruit. Cover mixture and leave in a cool place for a few days to infuse. Pour mixture into saucepan, bring to the boil and remove from heat. Allow to cool. Strain mixture through a double layer of muslin into clean jars. Seal and store. Makes 3 cups (750 ml).

Rice vinegar with coriander, Tarragon and red wine vinegar, and Fennel and saffron vinegar

Herb and spice pickles

Many pickles rely on spices for their assertive flavor. The fresher the spice, the better the result, so it's best to buy little and often.

Chili jam

1½ cups (250 g) char-grilled capsicums, seeded and skin removed

2 long red chilies, roughly chopped

1 small red chili, roughly chopped

¼ cup (60 ml) olive oil

1 small brown onion, finely chopped

2 cloves garlic, finely chopped

1 tablespoon palm sugar

1 tablespoon fish sauce

2 teaspoons tamarind paste

1 tablespoon finely chopped fresh coriander leaves

1 tablespoon finely chopped fresh mint leaves

1 Process capsicums and chilies in food processor until smooth.

2 Heat oil in small saucepan over medium heat. Cook onion 1 to 2 minutes, until softened. Add garlic; cook 30 seconds.

3 Add capsicum mixture, sugar, fish sauce and tamarind; cook 10 minutes on low heat, stirring occasionally. Stir through herbs; bottle until needed. Serve with barbecued food.

MAKES APPROXIMATELY 1 CUP (250 ML)
Preparation 5 minutes
Cooking 15 minutes

Spicy eggplant relish

2 tablespoons vegetable oil

1 large red chili, finely chopped

1 clove garlic, finely chopped

1 tablespoon finely grated fresh ginger

1 teaspoon turmeric powder

1 teaspoon mustard seeds

1 medium eggplant, cut into ½-in. (1-cm) cubes

1 teaspoon salt

¼ cup (60 ml) white wine vinegar

1 tablespoon sugar

½ cup (125 ml) water

3 tablespoons roughly chopped fresh coriander leaves

Date, lime and mint chutney; Chili jam and Spicy eggplant relish

1 Heat oil in medium saucepan over medium heat. Add chili, garlic, ginger, turmeric and mustard seeds; cook, stirring, 1 minute.

2 Add eggplant, salt, vinegar, sugar and water. Cook 10 to 12 minutes over low heat, adding extra tablespoons of water if mixture gets dry.

3 Remove from heat, stir through coriander. Refrigerate until required. Serve with eggs, chicken or fish.

MAKES APPROXIMATELY 2 CUPS (500 ML)
Preparation 5 minutes
Cooking 12 minutes

Date, lime and mint chutney

1 tablespoon vegetable oil

2 teaspoons finely grated fresh ginger

¼ teaspoon ground cloves

½ teaspoon ground cinnamon

½ teaspoon ground cumin

½ teaspoon chili flakes

2 cups (350 g) roughly chopped pitted dates

1 cup (125 g) raisins

1 tablespoon sugar

¼ cup (60 ml) white wine vinegar

½ cup (125 ml) fresh lime juice

zest of 1 lime

1 cup (250 ml) water

2 tablespoons finely chopped fresh mint leaves

1 Heat oil in small saucepan over medium heat. Add ginger, cloves, cinnamon, cumin and chili flakes; cook, stirring, 1 minute.

2 Add dates, raisins, sugar, vinegar, lime juice, zest and water; cook over low heat, stirring regularly, until fruit is soft.

3 Remove from heat, stir through mint. Refrigerate until required. Serve with meat or cheese.

MAKES APPROXIMATELY 2 CUPS (500 ML)
Preparation 5 minutes
Cooking 12 minutes

Herb butters

Spread these flavor-packed butters on crusty bread, or
use them to dress up cooked vegetables and barbecued meat.

Coriander and chili butter

¼ cup (40 g) macadamia nuts, roughly chopped
2¼ sticks (250 g) butter, softened
3 tablespoons roughly chopped fresh coriander leaves
2 fresh lime leaves, finely chopped
1 large red chili, finely diced
1 tablespoon lime juice

1 Toast chopped macadamia nuts in dry frying pan on
  medium heat, tossing until smallest pieces are just
  golden. Transfer to small bowl; cool before use.

2 Place softened butter in medium bowl. Add toasted
  nuts and remaining ingredients; mix until well combined.

3 Place mixture on a piece of plastic wrap about 8 in. (20 cm)
  long. Roll mixture into a log about 2 in. (5 cm) in diameter;
  wrap tightly. Chill until required.

  Preparation 10 minutes
  Cooking 2 minutes

Sage butter

2¼ sticks (250 g) butter, softened
1 tablespoon finely chopped fresh sage leaves
3 tablespoons finely chopped fresh flat-leaf parsley leaves
10 pitted medium green olives (¼ cup/30 g), roughly chopped
2 anchovy fillets, finely chopped

1 Place softened butter in medium bowl. Add remaining
  ingredients; mix until well combined.

2 Place butter mixture on a piece of plastic wrap about
  8 in. (20 cm) long. Roll mixture into a log about 2 in. (5 cm)
  in diameter; wrap tightly. Chill until required.

  Preparation 10 minutes

Try these, too...

Parsley and lemon butter
Combine 2¼ sticks (250 g) softened butter, 3 tablespoons
finely chopped fresh parsley, 2 teaspoons grated lemon zest,
3 teaspoons lemon juice, and salt and freshly ground black
pepper.

Blue cheese and herb butter
Combine 2¼ sticks (250 g) softened butter and 4.5 oz. (125 g)
blue vein cheese, chopped. Add 1 tablespoon each chopped
fresh chives, mint and dill. Add 1 tablespoon white wine.

Horseradish and mustard butter
Combine 2¼ sticks (250 g) softened butter, 2 tablespoons
horseradish cream, 1 tablespoon Dijon mustard and
2 tablespoons finely chopped fresh parsley.

Ginger and spice butter
Combine 2¼ sticks (250 g) softened butter, 2 teaspoons
finely grated fresh ginger, 1 teaspoon mild chili powder and
1 tablespoon Worcestershire sauce.

Cook's tip

All herb butters are prepared in the same way and are very
versatile. Fresh or dried herbs, ground spices, sun-dried
tomatoes, chopped nuts, mustards, wine, lemon or lime juice
and many other ingredients can be incorporated. Formed into
a log and wrapped in plastic wrap, butters will keep for up
to 1 month in the freezer and up to 5 days in the refrigerator.
Allow to soften slightly at room temperature before slicing into
rounds. You can halve the quantities given here, if preferred.

Coriander and chili butter and Sage butter

Herb and spice sauces

Featured in many cuisines, these delicious sauces can be used as
dips, served on the side or incorporated into a wide variety of dishes.

Harissa

8 dried chilies

2 cloves garlic, peeled

½ teaspoon salt

2 tablespoons olive oil

1 teaspoon ground caraway seeds

1 teaspoon ground coriander

½ teaspoon ground cumin

1   Soak dried chilies in very hot water 30 minutes. Drain.
    Remove stems and seeds. Place chilies, garlic, salt and
    olive oil in a food processor; blend to a paste.

2   Add the remaining spices and blend. Pack into an airtight
    container and top with a thin layer of olive oil. Keeps for
    a month in the refrigerator. Thin with a little oil and lemon
    juice or hot stock before use. Use as a condiment with eggs
    and couscous-based dishes.

This fiercely fiery, chili-based sauce is a feature of North
African cooking. If using fresh chilies, omit the soaking step.

Sorrel sauce

7 oz. (200 g) sorrel leaves, chopped

1¼ cups (310 ml) fish or chicken stock

1½ tablespoons (20 g) unsalted butter

1 tablespoon plain flour

4 tablespoons cream

salt and freshly ground black pepper

1   Simmer leaves in stock 5 minutes. Allow to cool slightly.
    Purée in blender or food processor.

2   Melt butter in saucepan, add flour and stir over gentle
    heat until blended. Add purée to the pan; simmer about
    4 minutes, stirring.

3   Add cream and season to taste. Serve with poached white
    fish or salmon. It also goes well with pasta. Serves 4.

A classic in French cuisine, fresh sorrel gives this sauce
a sharp, lemony taste. When preparing sorrel, cut out the
central stalk, which can be rather tough.

Frankfurt green sauce

½ oz. (15 g) each fresh borage, salad burnet, parsley and sorrel

¾ oz. (20 g) each fresh chives and cress or watercress

¼ oz. (10 g) each fresh tarragon and chervil

½ cup (125 g) mayonnaise

1 teaspoon German mustard

2 hard-boiled eggs, chopped

1 small pickled gherkin, with dill, chopped

1 small onion or shallot, chopped

1 clove garlic, chopped

salt and pepper

grated rind and juice of 1 lemon

2 tablespoons sour cream or yogurt (optional)

1 egg yolk

1   Chop all the herbs finely.

2   Add ingredients in given order, seasoning to taste and
    beating in egg yolk last of all. Serves 4.

You can vary the herbs used in this German sauce, but be
sure to always use 7 or 8 different ones. Serve with fried or
poached fish or cold fish with hard-boiled eggs, cold meat,
or use as a sandwich filler.

Nuoc cham

2 (or more, to taste) small red chilies, seeds removed

2 cloves garlic

1 teaspoon sugar

2 limes, peeled and chopped

1 tablespoon hot water

1 tablespoon vinegar

5 tablespoons fish sauce

1   Pound chilies and garlic to a fine paste. Add sugar and
    limes; pound to a pulp.

2   Add water, vinegar and fish sauce. Serves 2.

An indispensable seasoning in Vietnamese cooking, this spicy
mixture can be served with mixed salad greens and herbs or
used as a dipping sauce or marinade.

Herb and yogurt sauce

4 tablespoons fresh chopped mixed herbs such as
    chives, coriander, dill, lemon balm or parsley
1 clove garlic, crushed
2 tablespoons lemon juice
1 cup (250 g) yogurt
salt and freshly ground black pepper
pinch of paprika

1 Combine herbs, garlic, lemon juice and yogurt.

2 Season to taste with salt, pepper and paprika.

A light alternative to egg-based or creamy sauces, this recipe
can be varied according to what herbs you have to hand, but
use at least three types. Serve with salads, curries or as a dip.

Béarnaise sauce

¼ cup (60 ml) white wine vinegar
6 black peppercorns
1 fresh bay leaf
1 spring onion, roughly chopped
1 tablespoon each finely chopped fresh
    tarragon and chervil leaves
2 egg yolks
pinch each salt and white pepper
¼ cup (110 g) unsalted butter, softened
1 teaspoon each finely chopped fresh tarragon
    and chervil leaves, extra

1 Combine vinegar, peppercorns, bay leaf, spring
   onion, tarragon and chervil in small saucepan.

2 Bring to the boil, then leave to boil,
   uncovered, until liquid is reduced to
   about 1 tablespoon. Remove from
   heat; set aside.

3 Place egg yolks in medium
   heatproof bowl; add salt,
   pepper and 1½ tablespoons
   (20 g) softened butter. Strain
   reduced vinegar mixture into
   same bowl.

4 Place bowl over saucepan of simmering water, ensuring
   water doesn't touch bowl. Keep stirring until the butter
   has melted.

5 Repeat with remaining butter, adding small amounts at
   a time; stir after each addition until melted.

6 Remove sauce from heat, stir through extran herbs and
   serve. Serves 6.

Tarragon is synonymous with this French classic, a relation
of hollandaise sauce, which uses a reduction of lemon juice.
One of the most versatile of sauces, it goes well with meat,
chicken or fish.

Pesto bread

Pesto is a showcase for fresh basil. Pistou, the French variation of this Italian sauce, is made without pine nuts.

2½ cups (310 g) plain flour

3 teaspoons baking powder

1 large egg

1½ cups (375 ml) buttermilk

5 tablespoons basil pesto

4 tablespoons sun-dried tomato pesto

¼ cup (40 g) chopped sun-dried tomatoes packed in oil

¼ cup (30 g) freshly grated parmesan

extra basil pesto, to serve

1 Preheat oven to 400ºF (200ºC). Sift flour and baking powder into large bowl.

2 Add egg, buttermilk and basil pesto; mix until well combined.

3 Line a 4in. x 8 in. (10.5 cm x 21 cm) loaf tin with baking paper. Spoon loaf mixture into tin. Swirl tomato pesto through top of loaf; sprinkle with sun-dried tomatoes and parmesan.

4 Bake 40 to 45 minutes, or until cooked. Turn out onto a rack to cool. Serve warm, spread with extra basil pesto.

MAKES 1 LOAF
Preparation 15 minutes
Cooking 45 minutes

Try this, too...

Sweet basil has a spicy aroma with a mild aniseed flavor. Basil is synonymous with pesto, but other soft-leaf herbs such as fresh coriander or rocket can also be used. For another variation, try a mixture of equal quantities of a strong-tasting herb such as purple (opal) basil or lemon basil and a milder one, such as flat-leaf parsley or mint.

Making pesto

Use 2 fat cloves garlic, peeled, 1 oz. (30 g) pine nuts, ¼ cup (30 g) freshly grated parmesan or pecorino cheese, 4 heaped tablespoons fresh basil leaves (tough stalks removed) and 3 tablespoons good-quality olive oil.

Process dry ingredients roughly. Add oil in a steady stream; mixture should be slightly grainy. Add more oil, if needed. Pack in a jar; top with a film of olive oil. Seal; refrigerate. Use within 2 weeks.

Rosemary focaccia

The dough for this Italian flatbread is enriched with olive oil.
Brush with olive oil and top with herbs, olives or salt before baking.

7 g (1 packet) dried yeast

pinch of sugar

5 fl. oz. (150 ml) lukewarm water

1½ cups (185 g) plain flour

½ teaspoon salt

3 tablespoons olive oil

1 tablespoon finely chopped fresh
rosemary leaves

1 tablespoon olive oil, extra

1 tablespoon finely chopped fresh rosemary
leaves, extra

1 teaspoon sea salt

1 Mix yeast and sugar with 2 tablespoons
   lukewarm water. Stir in remaining water;
   stand 10 minutes.

2 In large bowl, mix flour, salt, olive oil,
   rosemary and yeast until well combined.

3 Turn out dough onto lightly floured
   surface; knead lightly, about 5 minutes.

4 Replace dough into lightly greased bowl.
   Cover with clean tea towel and leave to
   rise in warm place about 45 minutes, or
   until doubled in size.

5 Preheat oven to 400°F (200°C). Turn out
   dough onto lightly floured surface; knead
   lightly a further 2 minutes. Shape dough
   into a ball; lightly press down to make
   disk about 1 in. (2 cm) thick.

6 Place disk on oven tray; brush with extra
   oil and sprinkle with extra rosemary and
   sea salt. Bake about 20 minutes, or until
   well risen and golden.

MAKES 1 LOAF
Preparation 15 minutes plus
55 minutes standing
Cooking 20 minutes

Try this, too...

Eat focaccia just as it is, or split it and toast or grill it for sandwiches. For a quick
pizza, pan-fry on the cut side, then top with hot roasted or barbecued vegetables and
grated cheddar or parmesan, or thin slices of mozzarella. Sprinkle with fresh basil.

Sage and prosciutto damper

Traditionally, this basic bread was cooked in the hot ashes of an open fire in outback Australia. Our modern version has gourmet touches.

2 oz. (50 g) prosciutto, roughly chopped

2 cups (250 g) self-raising flour

2 teaspoons baking powder

1 teaspoon salt

2 oz. (50 g) fetta, crumbled

1 tablespoon finely chopped fresh sage leaves

1 cup (250 ml) milk

1 tablespoon milk, extra

1 Preheat oven to 425°F (220°C). Cook prosciutto in dry frying pan on medium heat, stirring until browned and slightly crisp. Drain on paper towel; cool.

2 Sift flour, baking powder and salt into large bowl. Add cooked prosciutto and remaining ingredients; mix together until well combined.

3 Turn out dough onto lightly floured surface; knead lightly about 1 minute. Shape dough into ball and flatten slightly. Using sharp knife, cut a cross on surface of dough, about 1 in. (2 cm) deep.

4 Place dough on oven tray; brush with extra milk. Bake 25 to 30 minutes, or until golden.

MAKES 1 LOAF
Preparation 15 minutes
Cooking 30 minutes

Ingredient guide

Prosciutto is a type of Italian ham that has been seasoned, salt-cured and air-dried. You can buy it thinly sliced from delicatessens and supermarkets. As an alternative, use thinly sliced pancetta, ham or bacon.

Scones and muffins

Chive and cheesy bacon muffins

5 oz. (150 g) bacon, finely chopped

1³/₄ cups (215 g) plain flour

2 teaspoons baking powder

½ teaspoon salt

2 tablespoons chopped fresh chives

2 tablespoons freshly grated parmesan

1 large egg

¾ cup (185 ml) buttermilk

¼ cup (60 g) butter, melted

1 Preheat oven to 356ºF (180ºC). Cook bacon in dry frying pan on medium heat, stirring until crisp. Drain on paper towel; cool.

2 Sift flour, baking powder and salt into large bowl. Add bacon and remaining ingredients; mix until well combined.

3 Spoon into lightly oiled muffin pan. Bake 12 to 15 minutes, or until cooked. Turn out onto wire rack to cool.

   MAKES 10
   Preparation 10 minutes
   Cooking 15 minutes

Tarragon and pumpkin scones

2 cups (250 g) self-raising flour

½ teaspoon salt

3 tablespoons (40 g) chilled butter

1 cup (250 g) mashed cooked pumpkin, cold

2 tablespoons finely chopped fresh tarragon leaves

½ cup (60 g) freshly grated parmesan

1 large egg

2 tablespoons milk

1 Preheat oven to 400ºF (200ºC). Sift flour and salt into medium bowl; using fingertips, rub butter into flour until mixture resembles breadcrumbs.

2 Using a plastic spatula or wooden spoon, fold in remaining ingredients until combined. Turn out dough onto lightly floured surface; knead lightly until smooth.

3 Press or roll out dough evenly to about 1-in. (2-cm) thickness. Cut out scones, using 2-in. (5-cm) round cutter.

4 Place scones on tray lined with baking paper. Bake 18 to 20 minutes, or until scones look evenly browned and sound hollow when tapped. Turn scones onto wire rack to cool.

   MAKES 12
   Preparation 15 minutes
   Cooking 20 minutes

Thyme and goat cheese muffins

2 cups (250 g) plain flour

1½ teaspoons baking powder

1 tablespoon sugar

½ teaspoon baking soda

1 tablespoon finely chopped fresh thyme leaves

3 tablespoons finely chopped fresh flat-leaf parsley leaves

3½ oz. (100 g) goat cheese, crumbled

1 large egg

1¼ cups (310 ml) buttermilk

3 tablespoons (50 g) butter, melted

1 Preheat oven to 400°F (200°C). Sift flour, baking powder, sugar and baking soda into large bowl. Add remaining ingredients; mix until well combined.

2 Spoon mixture into lightly oiled muffin pan. Bake 15 to 18 minutes, or until muffins are cooked. Turn out onto wire rack to cool.

MAKES 12
Preparation 10 minutes
Cooking 18 minutes

Watercress soup

Rich in antioxidants, peppery watercress is one of the most nutritious of salad greens. Cook only briefly to preserve its vitamins.

1 tablespoon olive oil

6 spring onions, thinly sliced

25 oz. (700 g) washed potatoes, peeled and diced

6 cups (1½ l) chicken stock

2 bunches fresh watercress (about 7 oz./200 g in total), tough stalks removed

2 teaspoons bottled horseradish sauce

½ cup (125 g) crème fraîche or sour cream

2 tablespoons fresh chives, cut into 1-in. (2-cm) lengths

1 Heat oil in large saucepan; sauté spring onions until softened. Add potatoes and stock. Bring to the boil. Reduce heat; simmer 15 to 20 minutes, or until potatoes are tender.

2 Add watercress and horseradish sauce. Add crème fraîche, reserving a little. Stir until watercress wilts. Do not overcook.

3 Using food processor or handheld blender, process soup until smooth. Divide among 6 serving bowls, add a swirl of the remaining crème fraîche and sprinkle with chives.

SERVES 6
Preparation 10 minutes
Cooking 30 minutes

Try these, too...

Spicy-style watercress soup

In place of horseradish sauce, stir in 2 teaspoons very finely chopped fresh ginger. Omit crème fraîche. Sprinkle with chopped fresh Thai basil and coriander leaves. Serve with lime wedges.

Summer chilled soup

Use a mixture of half potatoes and half leeks. Season cooked soup with salt to taste. Refrigerate 3 to 4 hours before serving. Sprinkle with chopped fresh dill.

Seafood coconut soup

Tangy kaffir lime leaves are a traditional flavoring in Thai cooking. Shred leaves needle-thin for this recipe.

3½ oz. (100 g) flat rice noodles or noodles of your choice

1 tablespoon peanut oil

3 stalks fresh lemon grass, inner white part finely sliced (about 3 tablespoons)

2-in. (5-cm) piece galangal, cut into thin slices

1 tablespoon chili paste

4 cups (1 l) chicken stock

2 cups (500 ml) coconut milk

2 tablespoons shredded fresh kaffir lime leaves

1 tablespoon palm sugar, finely chopped

¼ cup (60 ml) fish sauce

14 oz. (400 g) firm white fish fillets, cut into 1-in. (2-cm) cubes

8 large shrimp, shelled and deveined, leaving tails intact

2 tablespoons fresh lime juice

1 tablespoon roughly chopped fresh coriander leaves, to serve

1 tablespoon roughly chopped fresh Thai basil leaves, to serve

lime wedges, to serve

1 Place noodles in heatproof medium bowl and cover with boiling water. Stand 10 to 15 minutes, or until soft; drain and set aside.

2 Heat oil in large saucepan. Add lemon grass, galangal and chili paste; cook, stirring, 1 minute. Add stock and coconut milk. Bring to the boil. Reduce heat; simmer 5 minutes.

3 Add kaffir lime leaves, palm sugar, fish sauce and noodles; simmer a further 3 minutes. Add fish; cook 2 minutes. Add shrimp; cook 1 minute, or until shrimp turn pink.

4 Remove from heat. Stir through lime juice, coriander and basil. Place noodles in serving bowl. Add soup and serve with lime wedges.

SERVES 6
Preparation 20 minutes
Cooking 12 minutes

Ingredient guide

Palm sugar is a dense, sticky sugar made from sap from the palmyra, or sugar palm. It is sold in rounded cakes, cylinders, blocks or jars. If unavailable, use equal parts maple syrup and soft brown sugar.

Soup with herb dumplings

Herb dumplings turn a soup into a substantial meal. For a bold celery flavor, use leaves of fresh lovage in place of parsley.

35 oz. (1 kg) roma tomatoes, halved

4 cloves garlic, unpeeled

1 red onion, peeled and quartered

1 teaspoon sea salt

2 tablespoons olive oil

18 oz. (500 g) blade beef steak, cut into 1-in. (2-cm) cubes

4 cups (1 l) vegetable stock

Herb dumplings

6½ oz. (190 g) self-raising flour

¼ cup (60 g) butter, chilled and cut into cubes

2 tablespoons grated parmesan

1 tablespoon finely chopped fresh chives

1 tablespoon finely chopped fresh parsley

½ cup (125 ml) milk

Herb guide

In France, lovage is called céleri bâtard, or false celery. It has a much stronger flavor than parsley when used raw but its pungency diminishes in cooking. Try the leaves and stems in salads.

----

1 Preheat oven to 350°F (180°C). Place tomatoes (cut-side up), garlic and onion on baking tray, sprinkle with salt and drizzle with 1 tablespoon oil.

2 Roast vegetables 30 minutes. Remove from oven, cool slightly; roughly peel tomatoes and peel garlic.

3 Using food processor or handheld blender, process vegetables in medium bowl until smooth.

4 Heat remaining 1 tablespoon oil in large saucepan; brown meat in batches. Return meat to saucepan with tomato mixture and stock; simmer 45 minutes before adding dumplings.

5 To make dumplings, place flour in medium bowl. Using fingertips, rub butter into flour until mixture resembles breadcrumbs. Using a wooden spoon or plastic spatula, fold in parmesan and herbs. Add milk, using flat-bladed knife; mix until just combined. Knead briefly.

6 Using a teaspoon, scoop dough roughly into balls. Shape with floured hands. Drop balls into soup, and simmer, covered, 15 minutes. Divide soup among serving bowls.

SERVES 6
Preparation 20 minutes
Cooking 1 hour 30 minutes

Preparing the dumplings

Rub butter and flour together until mixture resembles breadcrumbs.

Use a wooden spoon to fold in parmesan and herbs. Add milk to form dough.

Scoop mixture roughly into balls. Shape quickly with floured hands.

Potato and horseradish salad

This crunchy salad goes well with barbecued meats. Fresh horseradish roots can be grated and frozen. Grating releases their pungent volatile oil.

35 oz. (1 kg) small kipfler or baby potatoes, halved
2 small heads of chicory
½ cup (20 g) chopped fresh flat-leaf
   parsley leaves
2 tablespoons roughly chopped fresh
   tarragon leaves
½ cup (60 g) roughly chopped walnuts
juice of 1 lemon
1 tablespoon grated fresh horseradish root
7 oz. (200 g) crème fraîche or sour cream
pinch of sea salt

1 Cook potatoes in large saucepan
   of boiling water until tender. Drain;
   cool briefly.

2 Place potatoes in large bowl. Add
   chicory leaves, parsley, tarragon and
   walnuts; toss to combine.

3 Combine lemon juice, horseradish
   and crème fraîche in a small bowl;
   season with sea salt. Pour dressing
   over potatoes; toss to combine.

SERVES 6
Preparation 15 minutes
Cooking 10 minutes

Cook's tip

Potatoes are used warm in this salad
because they will better absorb the
flavors of the dressing. A dressing
added to cold potatoes tends to coat
them rather than soak in.

Fattoush

Sumac is a dark purplish-red ground spice with a slightly sour, lemon taste. It's used in Lebanese dishes such as this bread salad.

4 pita breads
1 tablespoon olive oil
1 tablespoon sumac
18 oz. (500 g) small roma tomatoes, halved
2 Lebanese cucumbers, quartered and cut
into 1-in. (2-cm) lengths
1 red onion, halved and finely sliced
5 tablespoons finely chopped fresh
coriander leaves
5 tablespoons finely chopped fresh mint leaves
5 tablespoons finely chopped fresh flat-leaf
parsley leaves
12 butter lettuce leaves, torn in half
5 oz. (150 g) fetta, crumbled
2½ oz. (75 g) kalamata olives

Sumac dressing

1 clove garlic, crushed
¼ cup (60 ml) lemon juice
½ cup (125 ml) olive oil
¼ teaspoon sumac
pinch of sea salt

1 Preheat oven to 350°F (180°C). Cut each pita into quarters; lightly brush with oil and sprinkle with sumac. Place pita on oven tray; bake 10 to 15 minutes, or until golden and crisp.

2 Combine remaining salad ingredients in large bowl. Tear pita quarters into small pieces; add to salad.

3 To make dressing, whisk all ingredients in small bowl. Pour over salad; toss gently and serve.

SERVES 4 TO 6
Preparation 15 minutes
Cooking 15 minutes

Try this, too...
Instead of baking, try frying pita bread in a little olive oil until crisp. This salad is one of many such frugal peasant dishes around the world that use bread (often stale bread) to add bulk and texture.

Tabbouleh beef wraps

Parsley is a key ingredient in tabbouleh, a traditional
Middle Eastern salad, and in other garnishes and herb mixes.

4 large pita breads, halved

8 thin slices rare roast beef

4 slices (90 g) Swiss-style cheese, halved

8 cherry tomatoes, quartered

1 medium avocado, peeled and sliced

2 tablespoons hummus

Tabbouleh

7 oz. (200 g) burghul or cracked wheat

2 medium tomatoes, peeled, seeded and
   finely chopped

1 Lebanese or small cucumber, finely diced

5 tablespoons finely chopped fresh mint leaves

¾ cup (30 g) finely chopped fresh
   flat leaf parsley leaves

2 spring onions, finely chopped

2 tablespoons olive oil

juice of 1 lemon

Herb guide

*When eaten in portions of at least 1 oz. (30 g), fresh
parsley contains useful amounts of vitamin C,
iron and calcium.*

---

1 To make tabbouleh, soak burghul in hot water 15 minutes. Drain; squeeze
   out excess water. Combine with remaining ingredients in medium bowl,
   and season to taste.

2 Fill pita bread halves with tabbouleh, beef, cheese, tomato, avocado
   and hummus.

SERVES 4
Preparation 10 minutes plus 15 minutes soaking

Try these, too...

Persillade

This combination of chopped fresh parsley and garlic gives a great flavor boost
to a dish if it is added just at the very end of the cooking process. It can also be
used as a garnish. Vary it with the addition of lemon zest or anchovies. Tarragon
or thyme can be used in place of parsley. Use ½ cup parsley to 2 cloves garlic.

Chermoula

A Moroccan herb and spice mixture, chermoula is used as a marinade for meat,
poultry and fish. It can also be applied as a paste, which forms a crust during
cooking. Chermoula traditionally includes a mixture of fresh coriander and
parsley but the combination of spices can vary. For this version, combine ½ cup
each finely chopped fresh coriander and parsley with 1 small finely chopped red
onion, 2 cloves crushed garlic, 1 teaspoon each ground cumin, paprika, turmeric
and chili powder, ½ cup (125 ml) olive oil and 2 tablespoons lemon juice.

Tabbouleh

Persillade

Chermoula

Vegetarian spring rolls

This is a light, healthy alternative to deep-fried spring rolls. You can add shrimp or chicken to this basic version.

1¾ oz. (50 g) vermicelli

12 medium round rice paper wrappers

2 Lebanese or small cucumbers, seeded and cut into thin strips

4 spring onions

1 red pepper, cut into strips

12 snow peas, cut into strips

1 carrot, cut into strips

12 fresh mint leaves

12 fresh coriander leaves

12 fresh basil leaves

Dipping sauce

2 tablespoons lime juice

1 tablespoon fish sauce

1 teaspoon sugar

1 small red chili, seeded and finely sliced

1 Place vermicelli in heatproof medium bowl and cover with boiling water. Stand 10 to 15 minutes, or until soft; drain and set aside.

2 Place rice paper rounds in medium bowl of warm water until just softened (about 30 seconds). Carefully lay out each one flat on work surface or cutting board and gently pat dry with paper towel.

3 Divide vermicelli, vegetables and herbs among rounds, placing them in the center of each one. Fold in one edge of the round to partly enclose vegetables, then fold in the two opposing sides. Fold in remaining side, then roll into cigar shape to completely enclose filling.

4 To make dipping sauce, combine all ingredients in medium bowl; stir to dissolve sugar. Serve in a small bowl with rolls.

SERVES 4
Preparation 30 minutes

Folding the rolls

Place vegetable mixture in center of rice paper wrapper.

Fold in one side of the round and then two opposing sides.

Roll into a compact cigar shape to enclose filling.

Chervil, pea and fetta quiche

For a touch of heat, try adding a little finely chopped red chili to the mixture. Use a combination of half cream and half milk, if preferred.

4 large eggs

1¼ cups (300 ml) cream

½ teaspoon salt

3 tablespoons roughly chopped fresh chervil

1 tablespoon finely chopped fresh chives

1 to 2 sheets ready-made shortcrust pastry

1 cup (155 g) fresh shelled peas

4 oz. (120 g) soft fetta, crumbled

½ cup (60 g) grated cheddar

1 Preheat oven to 350°F (180°C). In medium bowl, whisk together eggs and cream; season with salt and stir through herbs.

2 Lightly oil 5-in. x 13-in. (35 cm x 12 cm) rectangular or 9-in. (23-cm) round tin. Gently place pastry into tin, using 2 sheets if required; mould pastry into sides and trim any excess.

3 Sprinkle top of pastry with peas and fetta. Pour over egg and herb mixture; sprinkle with cheddar.

4 Place quiche on bottom shelf in oven; cook 30 to 35 minutes, or until quiche is set. Serve with salad.

SERVES 4
Preparation 20 minutes
Cooking 35 minutes

Herb guide

Chervil belongs to the parsley family, but is much more aromatic than parsley. One of the staples of classic French cooking, it is used with tarragon, chives and parsley in the seasoning blend fines herbes.

Lovage and fennel omelettes

An omelette is fast food at its best. Use spicy Vietnamese mint, perilla or Thai basil in place of the celery-flavored lovage.

8 large eggs

⅓ cup (80 ml) milk

1 teaspoon salt

½ cup (25 g) roughly chopped fresh chives, sliced into 2–cm lengths

3 tablespoons roughly chopped fresh lovage

2 tablespoons roughly chopped fresh fennel leaves

1 tablespoon butter

½ cup (60 g) grated full-flavored cheese such as gruyère

1 Whisk eggs and milk in a large bowl. Season with salt; stir in herbs.

2 Melt butter in small non-stick frying pan over high heat. Pour one quarter of egg mixture into pan. Cook about 1 minute, stirring gently. Egg will begin to set around edge of pan almost immediately. Using fork or wooden spoon, gently pull back cooked egg from edge of pan, allowing any uncooked egg mixture to run underneath.

3 Cook a further 45 seconds to 1 minute, or until egg is just set. Sprinkle over cheese. Fold over one half of omelette and slide onto serving plate. Cover with aluminium foil to keep warm. Continue with remaining mixture. Serve at once with a crisp mixed salad.

SERVES 4
Preparation 10 minutes
Cooking 10 minutes

Cook's tip

Work quickly when making omelettes and do not overcook them. Remove from the pan when just set or they will continue cooking. Sprinkle on all the herbs at the end of cooking, if preferred, rather than adding them to the eggs and milk.

Thyme and oregano soufflés

Individual soufflés never fail to impress. The fruit chutney base
is a surprise extra that complements the flavors of the herbs.

¼ cup (60 g) butter

2 tablespoons plain flour

1⅓ cups (330 ml) milk

1 cup (100 g) grated strong cheddar

¼ teaspoon cayenne pepper

4 large eggs, separated

2 teaspoons finely chopped fresh thyme leaves

2 teaspoons finely chopped fresh oregano leaves

2 tablespoons finely chopped fresh
parsley leaves

2 tablespoons fruit chutney

1 Preheat oven to 400°F (200°C). Lightly oil 4 x 1-cup (250-ml) ramekins. Melt butter in small saucepan over low heat. Using wooden spoon, fold in flour; stir mixture continuously, about 1 minute. Remove from heat.

2 Gradually add milk to mixture, stirring until smooth. Return pan to medium heat, stirring until mixture thickens and thickly coats back of spoon. Fold in cheese and cayenne pepper. Transfer mixture to large bowl, cover with plastic wrap; cool. When mixture is cool, stir through egg yolks and herbs.

3 In clean, small bowl, beat egg whites until soft peaks form. Lightly fold egg white into soufflé mixture, just until white streaks are not visible. Do not overmix.

4 Place ½ tablespoon chutney in each ramekin. Divide soufflé mixture among ramekins, taking care not to mix in chutney. Run small spatula around rim to shape the top of soufflés. Place ramekins on oven tray.

5 Bake soufflés 20 minutes, or until risen and golden. Serve at once.

SERVES 4
Preparation 30 minutes
Cooking 20 minutes

Making the soufflés

Carefully fold egg whites into soufflé mixture. Do not overmix.

Place fruit chutney in the bottom of each ramekin.

Run spatula around rim of ramekin to shape top of soufflés.

Pumpkin pancakes with sage

The warm, musky, spicy taste of sage teams well with pumpkin.
Bruise sage leaves lightly with a rolling pin to maximize the flavor.

1½ cups (310 g) plain flour

pinch each of salt and pepper

2 large eggs

2 teaspoons olive oil

2 cups (500 ml) chilled water

4½ lb. (2 kg) pumpkin, peeled, seeded and coarsely chopped

2 tablespoons olive oil, extra

7 oz. (200 g) fresh ricotta

1½ cups (180 g) grated parmesan

half a small red chili, finely chopped

1 teaspoon dijon mustard

1 tablespoon finely chopped fresh chives

1 tablespoon finely chopped fresh parsley leaves

1 clove garlic, finely chopped

½ cup (60 g) grated parmesan, extra

Burned butter and sage sauce

2¼ sticks (250 g) salted butter

20 fresh sage leaves

1 Combine flour, salt and pepper, eggs, oil and water in large bowl. Whisk until smooth; mixture should be consistency of single cream. Stand 30 minutes before cooking.

2 Heat lightly oiled non-stick frying pan; pour ¼ cup batter into pan, tilting pan to coat base with batter. Cook 1 minute, or until underside is golden. Using plastic spatula, loosen pancake; turn and cook other side for a further 30 seconds. Repeat with remaining batter to make 6 pancakes.

3 Meanwhile, preheat oven to 350°F (180°C). Toss pumpkin and extra oil in roasting dish; bake 30 minutes, or until pumpkin is cooked and golden.

4 Combine cooked pumpkin, ricotta, parmesan, chili, mustard, chives, parsley and garlic in large bowl; mash mixture with fork, then cool.

5 Preheat oven to 350°F (180°C). Lightly oil 8-in. (20-cm) springform tin. Place one pancake flat on bottom of tin, then top with some pumpkin mixture; repeat layers, finishing with pancake. Press down lightly and sprinkle with extra parmesan. Bake 15 minutes, or until golden.

6 To make sauce, melt butter in small saucepan over medium heat until butter foams and turns dark golden brown. Remove from heat; add sage leaves.

7 Carefully remove pancake stack from tin onto cutting board; cut into wedges. Serve drizzled with burned butter.

SERVES 6
Preparation 40 minutes
Cooking 40 minutes

Cook's tip

The term "burned butter" or "beurre noir" is misleading. The butter should be heated until it is a rich golden brown, not black. It will taste nutty and sweet with a hint of richness. Keep a watchful eye on it while it is cooking.

Chive and ricotta gnocchi

A few chopped fresh basil or sage leaves can be added to the chives.
Try fontina cheese in place of blue cheese. It has a buttery, nutty taste.

26 oz. (750 g) fresh ricotta

¾ cup (185 g) grated parmesan

2 small eggs

¾ cup (115 g) plain flour

1 cup (60 g) finely chopped fresh chives

1 tablespoon butter, melted

1 cup (250 ml) cream

3½ oz. (100 g) blue cheese, crumbled

6 slices prosciutto (about 60 g),
    torn into strips

3 tablespoons chopped fresh chives

1   Preheat oven to 350°F (180°C). Place ricotta, parmesan, eggs, flour and chives in medium bowl; season to taste. Using wooden spoon, mix until well combined.

2   Bring large saucepan of water to the boil then reduce heat to simmer. Using two spoons, shape spoonfuls of mixture into ovals and drop into simmering water; cook 4 to 5 minutes, or until gnocchi float to surface. Remove gnocchi; place on absorbent paper. Repeat with remaining mixture, in batches, avoiding overfilling saucepan.

3   Lightly grease shallow ovenproof dish with melted butter; place gnocchi in dish.

4   Combine cream, blue cheese and prosciutto in medium bowl. Pour over gnocchi, then bake 10 to 12 minutes, or until gnocchi is lightly browned. Serve gnocchi warm, with green salad.

SERVES 6
Preparation 30 minutes
Cooking 30 minutes

Making gnocchi

Shape the gnocchi mixture between two spoons.

Scoop gnocchi from pan with a slotted spoon; drain on paper towels.

Combine cream, blue cheese and prosciutto and pour over gnocchi.

Rubs and marinades

Homemade rubs and marinades enrich the flavor and aroma of meat, chicken, fish or vegetables, particularly when barbecuing or roasting.

Cajun rub

2 tablespoons paprika
1 tablespoon chilli flakes
1 tablespoon celery salt
1 teaspoon allspice
2 cloves garlic
2 tablespoons dried onion flakes
2 tablespoons dried oregano
2 tablespoons dried thyme
1 teaspoon peppercorns

Using a pestle, pound the ingredients in a mortar until fine and well combined. Store in an airtight container in the refrigerator for up to 1 month.

Jamaican jerk seasoning

1/2 cup (about 50 g) ground allspice berries
1 cup (155 g) brown sugar
6 cloves garlic
4 Scotch bonnet chillies (a variety of habañero and very hot)
1 tablespoon dried thyme or 2 tablespoons fresh thyme leaves
8 spring onions, chopped
1 teaspoon cinnamon
1/2 teaspoon ground nutmeg
salt and pepper, to taste
2 tablespoons soy sauce

Place all the ingredients in a food processor and blend to a paste. Store in an airtight container in the refrigerator up to 1 month.

Ingredient guide

"Jerk" is the term given to the process of spicing and grilling meats. It is also used as a noun to describe the dry or wet seasoning mix used to jerk particular foods. In Caribbean cooking, pork and chicken are the most popular. Roadside jerk shacks are part of the local fast-food industry in Jamaica.

Spicy barbecue rub

2 tablespoons salt
2 tablespoons brown sugar
2 tablespoons ground cumin
2 tablespoons chilli powder
2 tablespoons freshly ground black pepper
1 tablespoon cayenne pepper
3 tablespoons paprika

Combine all ingredients. Use on a large piece of beef, chicken, lamb or pork when barbecuing or spit-roasting. Store in an airtight container in the refrigerator up to 1 month.

Moroccan rub

1 teaspoon saffron
1 teaspoon harissa (see page 338)
1 teaspoon ground cardamom
4 cloves
1 teaspoon cumin seeds
2 cloves garlic
3 tablespoons fresh mint leaves
3 tablespoons fresh coriander leaves

Pound ingredients in a mortar until fine and well combined. Store in airtight container in refrigerator up to 1 month.

Mediterranean rub

1 tablespoon dried oregano
1 tablespoon dried marjoram
1 tablespoon dried parsley
1 tablespoon dried basil
1 teaspoon sea salt
1/2 teaspoon black peppercorns
2 cloves garlic, roughly chopped
1 tablespoon lemon zest

Using a pestle, pound all the ingredients in a mortar until fine and well combined. Store in an airtight container in the refrigerator up to 1 month.

Lemon and marjoram baste

1 tablespoon freshly squeezed lemon juice

1 teaspoon finely chopped fresh marjoram

2 teaspoons olive oil

Combine all the ingredients. Use as a baste for barbecued chicken kebabs in the last few minutes of cooking.

Madras curry blend

2 dried chillies

4 tablespoons coriander seeds

2 tablespoons cumin seeds

1 teaspoon mustard seeds

1 tablespoon black peppercorns

6 curry leaves

1 teaspoon ground ginger

1 teaspoon turmeric

Dry roast chillies, coriander, cumin, mustard and pepper in a frying pan until aromatic. Leave to cool. Dry curry leaves briefly in pan and add to spices. Grind to a powder, sieve and stir in ginger and turmeric. Store in airtight container in the refrigerator for up to 2 months.

Classic herb marinade

½ cup (125 ml) balsamic vinegar

½ cup (125 ml) olive oil

3 tablespoons chopped fresh parsley or fresh coriander

1 tablespoon sugar (optional)

2 tablespoons finely chopped fresh dill

½ teaspoon salt

pinch of freshly ground black pepper

Place all ingredients in screw-top jar and shake well to combine. Use to marinate raw or briefly blanched vegetables such as yellow squash or zucchini and carrot. Serve as a side salad. Make marinade on day of using.

Lamb with herb and garlic rub

Lamb is best teamed with herbs that pack a punch, as this trio
does. Also try a combination of oregano, thyme and mint or coriander.

4½ lb. (2 kg) leg of lamb
1 lemon, halved and seeded

Herb and garlic rub
3 tablespoons finely chopped fresh thyme
2 tablespoons finely chopped fresh rosemary
2 tablespoons finely chopped fresh parsley
8 cloves garlic, finely chopped
1 tablespoon sea salt flakes
½ teaspoon ground black pepper
¼ cup (60 ml) olive oil

1 To make rub, mix herbs, garlic, salt and pepper in medium bowl. Pour in
   the oil and mix until well combined.

2 Using a sharp knife, make several slits about ¼ in. (5 mm) long all over lamb.
   Rub herb mixture all over meat, pushing it into slits; leave lamb 1 hour
   at room temperature to marinate.

3 Preheat oven to 350ºF (180ºC). Place lamb on baking tray, fat side up, and cook
   about 2 hours (30 minutes per 1lb./500 g). Cover with aluminium foil after 1 hour.

4 Transfer lamb to cutting board. Squeeze lemon juice over lamb; rest 10 to
   15 minutes before cutting and serving. Serve with roasted vegetables.

SERVES 6
Preparation 20 minutes plus 1 hour marinating
Cooking 2 hours

Cook's tip

It's important to rest a joint of meat for
at least 10 minutes before carving and
serving. When rested, the internal and
external temperatures even out and the
juices are redistributed, making the meat
more succulent and easier to carve.

Using the rub

Combine herbs, garlic and seasoning.
Pour in olive oil and mix well.

Make slits in the meat. Rub mixture all
over it, pushing it into the slits.

When cooked, the flavors of the herb
rub will have fully permeated the meat.

Moroccan lamb with couscous

Ras el hanout is a Moroccan mixture of 20 or more spices and herbs that typically includes cinnamon, cloves, lavender, orris root, cloves and turmeric.

1/3 cup (40 g) almond slivers
3 tablespoons (40 g) butter
2 cloves garlic, finely chopped
2 cups (500 ml) chicken stock
pinch of saffron threads
2 cups (370 g) quick-cook couscous
2 tablespoons ras el hanout
1 tablespoon olive oil
2 lb. (1 kg) lamb backstraps or fillets
2 red peppers, cut into strips
3 zucchini, cut into long ribbons
14 oz. (400 g) can chickpeas, drained
4 tablespoons roughly chopped fresh mint leaves
4 tablespoons fresh coriander leaves

1 Toast almond slivers in dry frying pan on medium heat, tossing until just golden. Transfer to small bowl; cool before use.

2 Melt butter in large saucepan; sauté garlic until softened. Add stock and saffron; bring to the boil.

3 Stir couscous through boiling stock. Remove saucepan from heat; cover and stand 5 minutes, or until couscous has absorbed stock. Using a fork, separate couscous grains.

4 Meanwhile, preheat grill to medium. Rub seasoning and oil into lamb; grill 3 to 4 minutes each side, or until cooked to your liking. Remove lamb from grill; set aside to rest, keeping meat warm until required.

5 Cook red peppers and zucchini on grill 2 to 3 minutes each side.

6 Toss red peppers, zucchini, chickpeas and herbs through warm couscous; top with sliced lamb and sprinkle with almonds.

SERVES 6
Preparation 20 minutes
Cooking 30 minutes

Ingredient guide

A traditional ingredient in North African cooking, couscous is coarse-ground wheat made into tiny balls and pre-cooked. Preparing traditional couscous is time-consuming, but good-quality, quick-cook (or instant) varieties produce an excellent result.

Tandoori chicken pizza

The lemon-and-ginger flavor of fresh coriander is a good partner for spicy tandoori paste. Fresh oregano can be used as an alternative.

7 g (1 packet) dried yeast

pinch of sugar

²/₃ cup (150 ml) lukewarm water

1³/₄ cups (220 g) plain flour

¹/₂ teaspoon salt

¹/₄ cup (60 ml) olive oil

2 x ¹/₂ lb. (250 g)skinless chicken breasts, sliced into ¹/₂-in. (2-cm) slices

3 tablespoons tandoori paste

2 tablespoons plain yogurt

¹/₂ cup (75 g) roughly chopped cashew nuts

1 cup (250 ml) Italian tomato sauce

4 spring onions, thinly sliced

2 tablespoons finely chopped fresh coriander

¹/₂ cup (125 g) plain yogurt, extra

2 tablespoons finely chopped fresh mint leaves

lime wedges, to serve

1 Mix yeast and sugar with 2 tablespoons lukewarm water. Stir in remaining water; stand 10 minutes.

2 Mix flour, salt, oil and yeast mixture in a large bowl until well combined.

3 Turn out dough onto lightly floured surface; knead lightly, about 5 minutes.

4 Return dough to lightly oiled bowl. Cover with clean tea towel and leave to rise in warm place for about 45 minutes, or until dough has doubled in size.

5 Turn dough onto lightly floured surface; knead lightly 2 minutes. Divide dough in half; shape into two balls. Roll out each ball into circle 10 in. (25 cm) in diameter. Place on pizza tray; set aside until required.

6 Combine chicken, tandoori paste and yogurt in large bowl; refrigerate 1 to 2 hours to allow flavors to develop.

7 Preheat oven to 450°F (230°C). Toast cashew nuts in dry frying pan on medium heat, tossing until just golden. Transfer to small bowl; cool before use.

8 Spread tomato sauce evenly on each pizza; top with chicken slices, spring onions, coriander and cashews. Bake 5 minutes near bottom of oven. Reduce heat to 400°F (200°C); cook further 15 minutes.

9 Combine extra yogurt and mint in small bowl. Drizzle over each pizza. Serve with lime wedges.

SERVES 4

Preparation 30 minutes plus 1 to 2 hours for marinating
Cooking 20 minutes

Cook's tip

Lightly oil your hands before mixing or kneading dough so that the dough doesn't stick to them. Pizza bases require cooking at a high heat, so use heavy-gauge tins and baking trays to avoid warping.

Mexican chicken with green rice

Arroz verde (green rice) is delicious with grilled or barbecued poultry or meat. A garnish of sliced avocado complements the robust flavors of the dish.

4 cloves garlic, finely chopped

2 teaspoons finely chopped fresh oregano leaves

½ teaspoon ground cinnamon

½ small red chilli, finely diced

1 teaspoon ground cumin

½ teaspoon ground coriander

½ teaspoon ground allspice

½ cup (125 ml) red wine

4 x 250 g skinless chicken breasts

Green rice

2 cups (400 g) long-grain rice

5 oz. (150 g) English spinach or baby spinach

5 tablespoons roughly chopped fresh flat leaf parsley

5 tablespoons roughly chopped fresh coriander

2 spring onions, roughly chopped

1 clove garlic, finely chopped

½ cup (125 ml) water

¼ cup (60 ml) peanut or safflower oil

3 cups (750 ml) chicken stock

¼ teaspoon salt

2 long green chillies, finely sliced

1 Using a food processor or handheld blender, process garlic, oregano, cinnamon, chilli, cumin, coriander, allspice and wine. Coat chicken breasts with mixture; refrigerate 30 minutes.

2 Preheat oiled grill plate or frying pan to medium heat. Cook chicken 10 minutes, turning once, or until cooked through.

3 Pour boiling water over rice in heatproof medium bowl. Soak 10 minutes; drain.

4 Rinse spinach. Cook undrained, in small saucepan uncovered on medium heat, 1 to 2 minutes or until just wilted.

5 Process spinach, parsley, coriander, spring onions, garlic and water until smooth.

6 Heat oil in large saucepan. Add rice, stir uncovered on medium heat, until golden.

7 Add stock and spinach purée; cook, stirring occasionally, until rice is tender (about 15 minutes). Stir through chilli. Serve chicken on a bed of green rice.

SERVES 4

Preparation 10 minutes plus 30 minutes refrigeration

Cooking 25 minutes

Cook's tip

Keep fresh garlic in a dry, dark, cool place. It will last longer and retain its flavor. Store it in a terra-cotta pot made especially for the purpose, or in something as simple as a brown paper bag. Never store garlic in the refrigerator because it is likely to sprout and become bitter.

Tarragon chicken

This is a time-saving version of a French dish that traditionally uses a whole chicken, with tarragon butter inserted under the skin.

¼ cup (60 g) unsalted butter

1 tablespoon olive oil

4 x ½ lb. (250 g) skinless chicken breasts

2 spring onions, finely chopped

1 clove garlic, finely chopped

¼ cup (60 ml) dry white wine

½ cup (125 ml) cream

1 tablespoon roughly chopped fresh tarragon

1 Melt butter and oil in large frying pan on medium heat. Add chicken; cook, turning occasionally, until browned and cooked through.

2 Add spring onion and garlic; cook until garlic softens. Add wine, cream and tarragon; cook a further 2 minutes, stirring to coat chicken.

3 Serve chicken with steamed vegetables.

SERVES 4
Preparation 10 minutes
Cooking 15 minutes

Herb guide

A bouquet garni comprising fresh tarragon, parsley, bay and bruised lemongrass adds a beautiful flavor to slow-cooked poultry dishes. The slightly aniseed, spicy taste of tarragon can overwhelm the flavor of other herbs, so use it with a light hand.

BBQ swordfish kebabs

Swordfish steaks are perfect for the barbecue, and cooking them on bay and rosemary skewers infuses the meat with a delicious flavor.

3 swordfish steaks (about 21 oz./600 g in total), cut into 1-in. (3-cm) pieces

2 tablespoons lemon juice

1 tablespoon finely chopped fresh oregano

2 bay leaves (preferably fresh), shredded

1 clove garlic

2 tablespoons olive oil

4 fresh rosemary sprigs

4 large fresh bay sprigs

4 large flour tortillas

3½ oz. (100 g) baby spinach leaves

2 small tomatoes, halved and thinly sliced

1 Lebanese cucumber, thinly sliced diagonally

4 tablespoons baba ganoush (eggplant dip)

1 Strip all but the top leaves from rosemary and bay sprigs to make skewers.

2 Combine swordfish in large bowl with lemon juice, oregano, shredded bay leaves, garlic and oil; marinate 30 minutes.

3 Preheat barbecue grill on medium. Thread swordfish pieces onto skewers.

4 Cook skewers 2 minutes each side, or until cooked to your liking.

5 Place tortillas on a work surface or cutting board; top with baby spinach, tomato, cucumber and skewers. Remove fish from skewers. Roll up tortillas; cut crosswise to serve. Serve baba ganoush on the side.

SERVES 4
Preparation 10 minutes plus 30 minutes marinating
Cooking 4 minutes

Try this, too...

Use any type of pliable, soft flatbread to make these wraps. Flatbreads such as mountain bread, lavosh and focaccia are available at supermarkets. Alternatively, split open small pita breads and use them as pockets for the fish and salad.

Pad Thai

The Thai word 'pad' is used to describe stir-fried food.
Tamarind paste gives this dish a fruity, sweet-and-sour flavor.

6⅓ oz. (180 g) dried flat Thai rice noodles

⅓ cup (80 ml) peanut oil

2 spring onions, finely chopped

2 cloves garlic, finely chopped

2 large eggs, beaten

2 tablespoons fish sauce

2 tablespoons tamarind paste

2 teaspoons sugar

2 tablespoons fresh lime juice

2 tablespoons tomato sauce

16 large shrimp, shelled and deveined, leaving
   tails intact

¼ cup (40 g) roughly chopped roasted peanuts

3½ oz. (100 g) bean sprouts

3 tablespoons fresh coriander leaves

3 tablespoons fresh Thai basil leaves

lime wedges, to serve

1　Place noodles in heatproof medium bowl
　 and cover with boiling water. Stand 10 to
　 15 minutes, or until soft; drain.

2　Heat peanut oil in wok or large frying
　 pan. Cook spring onion 1 minute until
　 softened. Add garlic; cook 30 seconds.
　 Add eggs, stirring, until lightly cooked.
　 Add fish sauce, tamarind paste, sugar,
　 lime juice and tomato sauce; mix until
　 well combined.

3　Toss drained noodles through sauce.
　 Add shrimp; cook 2 to 3 minutes, or
　 until shrimp turn pink. Remove from
　 heat; add peanuts, sprouts, coriander
　 and basil. Serve with lime wedges.

SERVES 4
Preparation 15 minutes
Cooking 10 minutes

Ingredient guide

Rice noodles are available dried, frozen and fresh. They vary in width from very fine
vermicelli to sheets of dough. Rice noodles are a common ingredient in East and
Southeast Asian cooking. They are transparent and have a gelatinous, chewy texture.

Coriander salmon parcels

Cooking delicately flavored fish such as salmon in aluminium foil
or baking paper is an ideal way to retain its flavor and nutrients.

5 oz. (150 g) baby spinach leaves

4 x 7 oz. (200 g) salmon fillets

2 limes, cut into ½-in. (1-cm) rounds

4 fresh kaffir lime leaves, cut into slivers

1 large red chilli, finely sliced (optional)

5 tablespoons fresh coriander leaves

5 tablespoons fresh Thai basil leaves

2 spring onions, finely sliced

½ cup coconut milk

1 tablespoon fish sauce

1 teaspoon sesame oil

½ cup (70 g) roughly chopped
cashew nuts, toasted

1 Preheat oven to 350°F (180°C). Lay 4 x 12-in. (30-cm) squares of aluminium foil on a work surface. Divide spinach among foil squares. Place salmon fillet in center of each square; top each fillet with lime rounds, lime leaves, chilli, coriander, basil and spring onion.

2 Combine coconut milk, fish sauce and oil in a small bowl.

3 Fold in two opposite sides of foil square, forming seam down middle. Fold over bottom end several times to secure. At open end of each parcel, pour in 2 tablespoons coconut milk mixture; fold and secure top ends.

4 Place fish parcels on oven tray. Cook in oven about 12 minutes (for medium-rare salmon), or until cooked to your liking. Serve fish in the parcels, with steamed vegetables and rice. Garnish with cashew nuts, if desired.

SERVES 4
Preparation 20 minutes
Cooking 12 minutes

Herb guide

Thai basil has a warm, peppery taste and a lingering aniseed flavor. Fennel fronds have an aniseed taste and can be used instead.

Assembling the parcels

Layer spinach, fish, lime and herbs and spices on a square of aluminium foil.

Wrap and seal the fish at one end. Pour in coconut milk mixture.

Completely seal the parcel, ready for cooking in the oven.

Rose petal jelly

For a special celebration, this pretty dessert is a winner. Other edible flower petals that could be used include borage and scented geraniums.

4 gelatin leaves (or 2 heaped teaspoons gelatin crystals)

2 cups (500 ml) sparkling wine

²/₃ cup (145 g) caster sugar

1 tablespoon rosewater

18 small rose petals, carefully washed

raspberries and cream, to serve

1 Soak gelatin leaves in cold water to soften (about 2 to 3 minutes).

2 Heat ½ cup sparkling wine and sugar in large saucepan over medium heat, stirring until sugar dissolves.

3 Add gelatin leaves to sugar mixture, stirring to melt gelatin. Remove from heat to cool. Stir through remaining sparkling wine, rosewater and rose petals.

4 Pour mixture into individual glasses or lightly oiled mold; refrigerate at least 8 hours, or until set. Serve jelly with raspberries and cream.

SERVES 2
Preparation 20 minutes
Cooking 5 minutes

Herb guide

There are many varieties of scented geranium, ranging in aroma from apple to nutmeg and mint to pine. Rose- and lemon-scented plants are the best for cooking.

Basil sorbet and minted melon

Sorbet and herbs make a refreshing dessert. Try mango or a mixture of raspberries and alpine strawberries instead of the honeydew or rockmelon.

1½ cups (375 ml) water

¾ cup (170 g) sugar

½ cup (125 ml) fresh lime juice

20 fresh basil leaves, roughly chopped

1 honeydew melon or rockmelon

2 tablespoons roughly chopped fresh mint leaves

2 tablespoons lime juice, extra

1 tablespoon sugar, extra

1 Combine water and sugar in medium saucepan, stirring until sugar is dissolved. Bring to the boil then reduce heat; simmer a further 5 minutes. Remove from heat to cool.

2 Using food processor or handheld blender, process sugar syrup, lime juice and basil leaves until well combined.

3 Pour mixture into shallow dish. Freeze for at least 3 hours, or until firm. Process mixture again; return to dish and freeze several hours.

4 Meanwhile, peel melon and remove seeds. Slice thickly. Combine mint leaves, extra lime juice and extra sugar in small bowl. Pour over prepared melon. Chill until required. Serve chilled melon topped with sorbet.

SERVES 6
Preparation 20 minutes plus 6 hours freezing
Cooking 7 minutes

Try this, too...

Mixed herb sorbet

Bring ½ cup (115 g) caster sugar and 1 cup (250 ml) water to a boil, stirring until sugar dissolves. Add 4 tablespoons finely chopped mixed fresh herbs, such as a combination of apple mint leaves, lemon balm and scented geranium or rosemary. Cover, remove from heat; let mixture infuse about 20 to 30 minutes. Test for flavor; add more herbs, if preferred. Strain; add juice of 1 lemon. Pour mixture into shallow dish and freeze at least 3 hours, or until firm. Process in food processor or use handheld blender. Freeze again for several hours.

Bay-scented panna cotta

Panna cotta is a wobbly Italian dessert that translates as 'cooked cream'.
Flavor with a little ground cinnamon or cardamom, in place of the vanilla.

⅓ oz. (10 g) gelatin leaves

2 cups (500 ml) full-cream milk

1 vanilla bean, split lengthwise, seeds
scraped out

2½ oz. (70 g) caster sugar

2 fresh bay leaves

1½ cups (350 ml) crème fraîche

2 cups fresh berries

1 teaspoon sugar

2 teaspoons chopped fresh mint leaves

juice of half a lime

1 Soak gelatin leaves in cold water to
soften (about 2 to 3 minutes).

2 Heat milk, vanilla, sugar and bruised bay
leaves in large saucepan, stirring until
sugar dissolves. Add gelatin leaves,
stirring to melt gelatin; remove from
heat to cool slightly. Add crème fraîche,
stirring until well combined.

3 Remove bay leaves and vanilla. Pour
mixture into 4 lightly oiled 5-oz. (150-ml)
molds; refrigerate at least 4 hours,
or until set.

4 In medium bowl, toss berries with sugar,
mint and lime juice; stand 5 minutes.

5 To remove panna cotta from molds,
carefully slide thin knife around the
circumference and invert onto serving
plates. Serve with berries.

MAKES 8
Preparation 20 minutes
Chilling 4 hours

Cook's tip

Turning desserts out of molds can be a little traumatic. For a successful result,
always lightly coat the molds with an oil, such as peanut or almond oil. Instead of
running a knife around the edge, dip the mold very briefly into a bowl of hot water.

Chocolate mint cake

This cake sinks slightly in the center during cooling, providing a perfect space for a topping of soft fruit.

9 tablespoons (125 g) unsalted butter

5½ oz. (150 g) dark chocolate (at least 70 percent cocoa), broken into pieces

handful finely chopped fresh mint or chocolate mint leaves (or 1 teaspoon peppermint extract)

6 large eggs, separated

pinch of salt

⅓ cup (80 g) caster sugar

1½ cups (150 g) ground almonds

1 lb. (450 g) soft berries (strawberries, blackberries, blueberries or raspberries)

confectioner's sugar, for dusting

whipped cream, to serve

1 Preheat oven to 340°F (170°C). Grease 8-in. (20-cm) springform cake tin; line base with baking paper.

2 Melt butter and chocolate in heatproof medium bowl over saucepan of just simmering water, stirring occasionally. Remove from heat; cool slightly. Stir through mint leaves.

3 In medium bowl, whisk egg whites with pinch of salt until soft peaks form. Gradually add sugar, whisking well after each addition until just dissolved.

4 Beat egg yolks in large bowl, and stir through ground almonds. Pour in cooled chocolate mixture; mix well. Using metal spoon, fold in 2 large spoonfuls of egg white to lighten mixture, then carefully and quickly fold in the remainder. Do not overwork.

5 Pour mixture into prepared tin. Bake 35 to 40 minutes until cake is well risen and just firm to the touch. Cool in tin 15 minutes before turning out onto wire rack. Cake will sink slightly in the center.

6 Decorate cooled cake with fresh berries; dust with sifted confectioner's sugar. Serve with whipped cream.

SERVES 8
Preparation 25 minutes
Cooking 35 minutes

Herb guide

Chocolate mint has the taste and aroma of an after-dinner chocolate mint. Use in chocolate desserts such as mousse and ice cream. With its dark green to purple leaves, it also makes an attractive garnish.

Cupcakes with crystallized flowers

Crystallized flowers are available from shops that sell cake-decorating supplies. Alternatively, it's easy to make your own.

1/2 lb. (225 g) butter, softened
1 cup (230 g) sugar
1 teaspoon vanilla extract
4 large eggs
2 cups (235 g) self-rising flour
1 tablespoon milk
12 to 24 crystallized flowers (see below)

Icing
9 tablespoons (125 g) butter, softened
2 cups (230 g) confectioner's sugar
2 tablespoons milk
food coloring

1 Preheat oven to 350°F (180°C). In a large bowl and using an electric mixer, beat butter and sugar until thoroughly combined and light and creamy.

2 Add vanilla and eggs, one at a time, mixing after each addition until well combined.

3 Sift flour into mixture. Using a plastic spatula or wooden spoon, fold in flour and milk until combined.

4 Divide mixture to make 12 cupcakes, filling each until two-thirds full; bake 15 minutes, or until golden. Turn out onto a wire rack to cool.

5 To make icing, mix butter and confectioner's sugar until creamy (about 2 minutes), using electric mixer. Add milk and food coloring, mixing until combined.

6 Ice cooled cakes and decorate with crystallized flowers.

MAKES 12
Preparation 30 minutes plus 1 to 3 days for flowers (if making your own)
Cooking 15 minutes

Crystallized flowers

12 to 24 rose or violet petals, or other edible flower petals
1 egg white, at room temperature
few drops of water
1 cup (230 g) sugar

1 Combine egg white with water; using a fork, beat lightly until white just shows bubbles. Place sugar in shallow dish.

2 Hold flower or petal in one hand; with other hand, dip a small paintbrush into egg white and gently paint flower or petal, covering flower or petal completely but not excessively. Gently sprinkle sugar over flower or petal.

3 Place flower or petal on wire rack covered with baking paper to dry. Repeat with remaining flowers or petals.

4 Allow flowers or petals to dry completely before use (about 12 to 36 hours, depending on humidity). Store crystallized flowers or petals in airtight container until required.

Drinks with herbs

Take the heat out of long, hot summers with refreshing drinks made simply and easily with fresh herbs and fruit.

Coriander and lime juice

4 tablespoons fresh coriander leaves

2 stalks celery

1 lime, peeled

2 medium green apples, cored and quartered

1 cup (250 ml) cranberry juice

ice cubes

1 Put coriander, celery, lime and apples through juicer. Pour juice into large jug; add cranberry juice and ice. Serve chilled.

MAKES APPROXIMATELY 3 CUPS (750 ml)
Preparation 5 minutes

Lemonade with mint

1 cup (230 g) sugar

1 cup (250 ml) water

1 cup (250 ml) lemon juice

4 cups (1 l) soda or mineral water

½ cup fresh mint leaves

lemon slices, to serve

1 Place sugar and water in small saucepan. Bring to the boil over a high heat, stirring until sugar is dissolved; cool.

2 Mix sugar syrup with lemon juice, soda or mineral water and mint leaves. Serve with lemon slices and ice.

MAKES APPROXIMATELY 6 CUPS (1.5 L)
Preparation 15 minutes

Try these, too...

Lassi

For a traditional Indian drink, place ½ cup (125 ml) plain yogurt, 1¼ cups (310 ml) cold water, ½ teaspoon dry-roasted cumin seeds, ¼ teaspoon salt and 1 teaspoon chopped fresh mint leaves in a blender. Process to combine. Serve chilled, garnished with mint sprigs.

Mulled wine

To beat the winter chills, place 3 cups (750 ml) dry red wine, 1 cup (225 g) white sugar, ½ cup (125 ml) brandy, ½ cup (125 ml) water, 2 thinly sliced oranges and 1 thinly sliced lemon, 2 small lightly crushed cinnamon sticks, 9 whole cloves and a pinch of grated nutmeg in a large saucepan over low heat. Bring to simmering point. Simmer, stirring occasionally, 5 to 10 minutes, or until sugar has dissolved and mixture is aromatic. Remove from heat. Strain into a large jug. Serve while still warm.

Heartsease flowers are edible and can be scattered through salads or crystallized for cake decoration. Freeze them in water in ice-cube trays and then pop a few cubes into a jug of lemonade.

Lemonade with mint and Coriander and lime juice

Index

malaria treatment 187
male reproductive health 65, 238–9
mallow 79
    gardening 79
    herbal medicine 79
    see also marsh mallow
Malva moschata 79
Malva sylvestris
    herbal medicine 79
Manchurian licorice 76
Mandragora officinarum 189
mandrake 189
manganese 156
manuka 220
manuka honey 220
manures 150
manzanilla 32
marigolds 28, 168, 261
marinades *364–5*
marjoram 80, 81
    cooking 81, *365*
    herbal medicine 81
Marjoram and sausage pasta *81*
Marjorana hortensis 80, 81
Marrubium vulgare 132, **132**
    herbal medicine 132, 201
    respiratory system 201
marsh mallow 79
    herbal medicine 185, 201,
       232, 233
Marsh mallow cleanser *249*
Mary's mantle 104
massage 280, 281
massage movements 281
massage oils 280–1
Matricaria matricarioides 32
Matricaria parthenium 51
Matricaria recutita 32, **32, 205**
    digestive system 205
    herbal medicine 32
mature skin, beauty products 253
maypops 88
meadow honeysuckle 97
meadow queen 82
meadow trefoil 97
meadowsweet 82, **82**, 181, 186, **204**
    cooking 82
    gardening 82
    herbal medicine 82, 204
mealybugs 170
Medicago sativa 97
medicinal herbs 198–9
medicinal preparations 190–5
medicinal theme (herb garden) 145
Mediterranean rocket 98
Mediterranean rub *364*
Melaleuca sp. 124
Melaleuca alternifolia 124, **124**, 179
    herbal medicine 124, 216,
       218, 221
    skin conditions 216, 218, 221
Melaleuca leucadendron 124

Melaleuca quinquenervia 124
Melaleuca viridiflora 124
melissa 73
Melissa sp. 264
Melissa officinalis 73, **73,**
    219, 235
    herbal medicine 73, 210,
       219, 235
    nervous system 210
    skin conditions 219
    women's health 235
memory tonics 20, 26, 61, 90, 105,
    110, 213
menopause 63, 90, 97, 107,
    130, 234–5
    and soy products 234
men's grooming 275
men's health, sexual and prostate
    health 238–9
menstrual cramps 32, 231
menstrual problems 17, 63, 87, 90,
    130, 133, 134, 136
Mentha sp. 83–4
Mentha aquatica 83
Mentha arvensis 83
Mentha canadensis 83
Mentha x *gentialis* 83
Mentha x *piperita* 83, **84**
    to cool the skin 250
    digestive system 205, 206
    herbal medicine 84, 205,
       206, 215
    nervous system 215
    var. *officinalis* 83
    var. *piperita* 83
Mentha pulegium 83, 84
Mentha requinii 83
Mentha spicata 83, **83**, 84, 188
    var. *crispa* 83
Mentha suaveolens 83
Mentha x *villosa* var.
    alopecuroides 83
menthol 250
Mermaid bath *270*
Mexican chicken with green rice
    370, **370**
Mexican coriander 40
Mexican mint marigold 121
Mexican tarragon 121
microclimates 148
Micromeria biflora 112
middle ear infections 45, 49
migraine treatment and prevention
    51, 215
mildew 170
milfoil 133
milk thistle 199, **199, 208**
    herbal medicine 208
mimulus (flower essence) 197
mineral salts 271
mint 83–4, 250
    around the home 84

    cooking 84, *335, 379, 383*
    gardening 83–4, 159
    herbal medicine 84, 205, 206, 215
    See also peppermint;
       peppermint oil
Mint astringent *250*
Mint jelly *84*, **84**
mitsuba 86, 87
Mixed herb sorbet *377*
modern herbal medicine 179
moisturizers 276–7
mold, removal from canvas 295
mole poblano 377
molybdenum 156
monarda 23
Monarda sp. 23
Monarda citriodora 23
Monarda didyma 23
    herbal medicine 23
Monarda fistulosa 23, **23**
    herbal medicine 23
Monarda x *media* 23
Monarda menthifolia 23
Monarda punctata 23
monastic gardens 178
Mongolian licorice 76
monk's pepper 216
monkshood 130
morning sickness 138, 205, 236
Moroccan lamb with couscous
    368, **368**
Moroccan rub *364*
morphine 93, 94, 185, 186
mosaic virus 170
moth-repellent herbs 288
Moth-repellent sachets 288,
    302–3, **303**
mother of thyme 125
motion sickness 205
mountain laurel 21
mountain tobacco 16
mouth ulcers 27, 79, 92, 110, 219
Mouthwash for bleeding
    gums *257*
mouthwashes 79, 110, 257
moxibustion 238
mucilage 185
mucolytics 201
muffins 344–5
mugwort 17, 237
mulch 152
    applying 153
    benefits of 152–3
    types of 153
mulled wine *383*
Murraya koenigii 41
muscatel sage 108
muscle aches 46, 81, 82
muscle cramps 59, 90, 106
muscle relaxants 51, 72, 90, 126,
    128, 130, 223
muscle tension 72, 130

musculoskeletal system
    arthritis and gout 31, 58, 61, 65,
       85, 87, 106, 127, 134, 136,
       198, 199, 224–5
    sports injuries, sprains and
       strains 24, 39, 220, 222–3
musk mallow 79
mustard (flower essence) 197
mustard oil glycosides 131
myoga ginger 58
Myrica gale 117
Myrica pensylvanica 21
myrrh
    herbal medicine 219
Myrrhis odorata 116, **116**, 219
Myrtus communis 117, **117**

N

N:P:K ratio 156
nail-care products 259, 260
nail health 259
nail infections (fungal) 218
Nardus italica 70
narrowleaf echinacea 44
narrow-leafed peppermint 46
nasal decongestants 84, 203
Nashia inaguensis 129
nasturtium 131, **158**, 203
    gardening 158, 169
    herbal medicine 185
Nasturtium officinale 131,
    131, 185
Native American herbalism 180
native wormwood 17
natural beauty products *see*
    beauty products
nausea 13, 30, 32, 51, 53, 58, 73, 84,
    91, 138, 205
Nelumbo nucifera 149, **149**
nematode repellers 168
Nepeta cataria 30, **30**
    herbal medicine 30
    var. *citriodora* 30
Nepeta x *faassenii* 30
Nepeta mussinii 30
nepetalactones 30
nerve pain 93, 107, 223
nerve tonics 61, 105
nervous exhaustion 129
nervous system
    anxiety 26, 61, 63, 66, 73, 77, 87,
       93, 107, 128, 205, 211, 213,
       214, 234, 235
    depression 72, 73, 105, 107, 108,
       129, 211, 231
    headache and migraine 25, 72,
       73, 74, 215
    insomnia 63, 124, 214, 235
    memory and concentration 20,
       26, 61, 213
    tension and stress 20, 60, 66, 73,

Photography credits

12 *tr* RD-owned; 12 *bl* RD-owned; 13 *tr* RD-owned; 13 *br* RD-owned; 14 *tr* Shutterstock; 14 *bl* RD-owned; 15 *tr* RD-owned; 15 *bl* RD-owned; 16 *tr* istockphoto; 16 *bl* Tafel; 17 *tr* RD-owned; 17 *b* RD-owned; 18 *tr* RD-owned; 18 *bl* RD-owned; 19 *tl* RD-owned; 19 *tr* RD-owned; 19 *br* RD-owned; 19 *bl* RD-owned; 20 *t* Biblioteca Nazionale Marciana Venice/The Art Archive; 20 *r* RD-owned; 20 *b* RD-owned; 21 *r* National Gallery Collection/Corbis; 21 *bl* RD-owned; 22 *t* RD-owned; 22 *bl* RD-owned; 22 *br* The Bridgeman Art Library/Photolibrary.com; 23 *tr* RD-owned; 23 *bl* Anna Watson/Corbis; 24 *tl* RD-owned; 24 *tr* RD-owned; 24 *br* The Gallery Collection/Corbis; 25 *t* Shutterstock; 25 *b* RD-owned; 26 *tr* RD-owned; 26 *bl* Shutterstock; 27 *tr* Keith A. McLeod; 27 *b* RD-owned; 28 *t* Keith A. McLeod; 28 *b* RD-owned; 29 *tr* RD-owned; 29 *bl* RD-owned; 30 *tr* RD-owned; 30 *bl* RD-owned; 31 *tr* RD-owned; 31 *bl* RD-owned; 32 *tr* RD-owned; 32 *bl* RD-owned; 33 *tr* RD-owned; 33 *bl* RD-owned; 34 *tr* RD-owned; 34 *bl* RD-owned; 35 *tl* RD-owned; 35 *tr* RD-owned; 35 *b* RD-owned; 36 istockphoto; 37 *t* RD-owned; 37 *bl* RD-owned; 37 *r* RD-owned; 38 *t* RD-owned; 38 *bl* Keith A. McLeod; 39 *tr* RD-owned; 39 *br* Dorling Kindersley/Getty Images; 39 *bl* Shutterstock; 40 *tr* RD-owned; 40 *br* RD-owned; 41 *tr* Shutterstock; 42 *tr* RD-owned; 42 *bl* istockphoto; 43 *tr* RD-owned; 43 *br* RD-owned; 44 *l* RD-owned; 44 *r* RD-owned; 45 *tr* RD-owned; 45 *b* Photolibrary.com; 46 *tr* RD-owned; 46 *l* RD-owned; 46 *b* RD-owned; 47 Brian Carter/Photolibrary.com; 48 *t* Keith A. McLeod; 48 *b* RD-owned; 49 *b* Irene Windridge/Photolibrary.com 50 *tr* Carole Orbell; 50 *bl* RD-owned; 51 *tl* RD-owned; 51 *br* RD-owned; 52 *tr* Dave Reede/Corbis; 52 *l* The Bridgeman Art Library/Photolibrary.com; 52 *b* istockphoto; 53 *tr* RD-owned; 53 *bl* RD-owned; 54 *tr* RD-owned; 54 *bl* Keith A. McLeod; 55 *tr* RD-owned; 55 *br* RD-owned; 55 *bl* RD-owned; 56 *tr* RD-owned; 56 *bl* RD-owned; 57 Reza/Corbis; 58 *tr* RD-owned; 58 *br* RD-owned; 59 *tr* istockphoto; 59 *br* Jim Zuckerman/Corbis; 60 *tr* RD-owned; 60 *bl* RD-owned; 61 *tr* RD-owned; 62 *tr* P.Lippmann/Corbis; 62 *bl* RD-owned; 63 *tr* RD-owned; 63 *bl* Bettmann/Corbis; 64 *tr* RD-owned; 64 *bl* RD-owned; 65 *tr* RD-owned; 65 *br* Keith A. McLeod; 66 *tr* RD-owned; 66 *b* RD-owned; 67 *tr* Carole Orbell; 67 *bl* istockphoto; 67 *br* RD-owned; 68 *tr* Keith A. McLeod; 68 *l* RD-owned; 69 Robb Kendrick/Getty Images; 70 *tr* Richard Bloom/Photolibrary.com; 70 *bl* RD-owned; 71 *t* istockphoto; 71 *bl* RD-owned; 71 *br* RD-owned; 72 *t* istockphoto; 72 *b* Keith A. McLeod; 73 *tr* RD-owned; 73 *b* istockphoto; 74 *t* RD-owned; 74 *r* RD-owned; 74 *bl* RD-owned; 75 *tr* RD-owned; 75 *bl* Carol Sharp/Photolibrary.com; 76 *tr* Wildlife/Alamy 76 *tl* RD-owned; 76 *b* RD-owned; 77 *tr* Photolibrary.com; 77 *bl* Clay Perry/Corbis; 78 *tr* RD-owned; 78 *b* RD-owned; 79 *tr* RD-owned; 79 *br* Keith A. McLeod; 80 *tr* RD-owned; 80 *bl* RD-owned; 81 *t* Keith A. McLeod; 81 *b* RD-owned; 82 *tr* RD-owned; 82 *br* Mary Evans Picture Library/Photolibrary.com; 83 *tr* RD-owned; 83 *bl* RD-owned; 83 *br* RD-owned; 84 *tr* Gilbert S Grant/Photolibrary.com; 84 *tl* RD-owned; 84 *b* RD-owned; 85 *tr* RD-owned; 85 *br* Lynher Dairies UK; 86 *tr* RD-owned; 86 *b* RD-owned; 87 *bl* StockFood Getty Images; 88 *tr* RD-owned; 88 *b* RD-owned; 89 Tony Arruza/Corbis; 90 *tr* RD-owned; 90 *bl* Demetrio Carrasco/Corbis; 91 *tr* RD-owned; 91 *bl* RD-owned; 92 *tr* RD-owned; 92 *br* RD-owned; 93 *tr* istockphoto; 93 *bl* Stefano Bianchetti/Corbis; 94 *tr* istockphoto; 94 *l* Carole Orbell; 95 *tr* Carole Orbell; 95 *br* Maria & Bruno Petriglia/Photolibrary.com; 96 *tr* Howard Rice/Photolibrary.com; 96 *br* Forest & Kim Starr; 97 *tr* RD-owned; 97 *bl* Widmann Widmann/Photolibrary.com; 97 *br* istockphoto; 98 *tr* RD-owned; 98 *tl* RD-owned; 98 *b* Timothy Hearsum/Getty Images; 99 *tl* RD-owned; 99 *tr* RD-owned; 99 *br* RD-owned; 99 *bl* RD-owned; 100 *tr* Keith A. McLeod; 100 *bl* Shutterstock; 101 *tl* Keith A. McLeod; 101 *br* Stapleton Collection/Corbis; 101 *bl* Keith A. McLeod; 102 *t* Keith A. McLeod; 102 *b* RD-owned; 103 Janet Seaton/Photolibrary.com; 104 *tr* RD-owned; 104 *bl* RD-owned; 105 *tl* Torsten Blackwood/AFP/AAP Image; 105 *tr* RD-owned; 105 *b* RD-owned; 106 *t* Howard Rice/Photolibrary.com; 106 *bl* RD-owned; 106 *br* RD-owned; 107 *b* Keith A. McLeod; 108 *tr* RD-owned; 108 *br* RD-owned; 108 *bl* RD-owned; 109 *t* Keith A. McLeod; 109 *br* RD-owned; 109 *bl* RD-owned; 110 *tr* RD-owned; 110 *bl* RD-owned; 111 *tl* RD-owned; 111 *br* RD-owned; 112 *tr* RD-owned; 112 *bl* RD-owned; 113 *tr* RD-owned; 113 *tl* Keith A. McLeod; 113 *br* Keith A. McLeod; 114 *bl* RD-owned; 115 *tr* RD-owned; 115 *b* RD-owned; 116 *tr* RD-owned; 116 *bl* The Bridgeman Art Library/Getty Images; 117 *bl* Keith A. McLeod; 117 *br* The Bridgeman Art Library/Photolibrary.com; 118 *tr* The Gallery Collection/Corbis; 118 *bl* Keith A. McLeod; 119 *tr* RD-owned; 119 *br* Keith A. McLeod; 120 *tl* Shutterstock; 120 *tl* Keith A. McLeod; 120 *br* RD-owned; 121 *tr* Dave G. Houser/Corbis; 121 *bl* Keith A. McLeod; 121 *bl* RD-owned; 122 China Photos/Getty Images; 123 *tr* De Agostini Picture Library/Getty Images; 124 *tr* RD-owned; 124 *bl* istockphoto; 125 *t* RD-owned; 125 *c* RD-owned; 125 *b* RD-owned; 126 *tr* RD-owned; 126 *br* Blue Lantern Studio/Corbis; 126 *bl* RD-owned; 127 *tr* RD-owned; 127 *br* EPA Corbis; 127 *tl* RD-owned; 128 *t* RD-owned; 128 *b* RD-owned; 129 *tr* Photolibrary.com;

129 *bl* Adam Woolfitt Corbis; 130 *tr* Pat Tuson/Alamy; 130 *bl* Keith A. McLeod; 131 *tr* RD-owned; 131 *br* RD-owned; 132 *tr* RD-owned; 132 *bl* RD-owned; 133 *tr* RD-owned; 133 *b* Mary Evans Picture Library/Photolibrary.com; 134 *tl* RD-owned; 134 *tc* istockphoto; 134 *tr* Photolibrary.com; 134 *cl* istockphoto; 134 *cc* Jose B. Ruiz/Nature Picture Library; 134 *cr* istockphoto; 134 *bl* Shutterstock; 134 *bc* Corbis; 134 *br* RD-owned; 136 *tl* Mike Grandmaison/Corbis; 136 *tc* Shutterstock; 136 *tr* RD-owned; 136 *cl* Michael P Gadomski/Photolibrary.com; 136 *cc* Science Photo Library/Photolibrary.com; 136 *cr* RD-owned; 136 *bl* Dreamstime; 136 *bc* RD-owned; 136 *br* RD-owned; 138 *tl* Henriette Kress 138 *tc* TH Foto-BSIP/Auscape; 138 *tr* Shutterstock; 138 *cl* Shutterstock; 138 *cc* Owen Franken/Corbis; 138 *cr* AFP/Getty Images; 138 *bl* Photolibrary.com; 138 *bc* Mark Bolton/Corbis; 138 *br* Forest & Kim Starr; 142 *bl* Keran Barrett; 142 *tr* RD-owned; 143 Clay Perry/Corbis; 144 *bl* RD-owned; 145 *br* Shutterstock; 145 *tl* RD-owned; 146 *br* RD-owned; 147 RD-owned; 148 *tr* RD-owned; 148 *br* RD-owned; 149 *tr* RD-owned; 149 *br* RD-owned; 150 RD-owned; 151 RD-owned; 152 *t* RD-owned; 152 *bl* RD-owned; 152 *br* RD-owned; 153 *tl* RD-owned; 153 *br* RD-owned; 154 *tr* Carole Orbell; 154 *bl* RD-owned; 155 *t* RD-owned; 155 *bl* RD-owned; 156 RD-owned; 157 RD-owned; 158 *t* RD-owned; 158 *b* RD-owned; 159 *tr* RD-owned; 159 *br* RD-owned; 159 *bl* RD-owned; 160 *t* RD-owned; 160 *br* RD-owned; 161 RD-owned; 162 RD-owned; 163 *t* RD-owned; 163 *b* RD-owned; 164 *bl* RD-owned; 164 *br* RD-owned; 165 RD-owned; 166 *tr* RD-owned; 166 *bl* RD-owned; 167 RD-owned; 168 *bl* istockphoto; 168 *bc* istockphoto; 168 *br* istockphoto; 168 *tr* istockphoto; 169 *tr* RD-owned; 169 *b* istockphoto; 170 *tl* RD-owned; 170 *tr* RD-owned; 170 *bl* Denis Crawford/Graphic Science; 170 *br* Denis Crawford/Graphic Science; 171 *tl* RD-owned; 171 *tr* RD-owned; 172 *tr* RD-owned; 172 *bl* RD-owned; 173 RD-owned; 174 Fresh Food Images/Photolibrary.com; 175 *tl* Mike Nelson/EPA/Corbis; 175 *bl* RD-owned; 176 *br* istockphoto; 178 *tr* Photolibrary.com; 178 *bl* Gianni Dagli Orti/Corbis; 179 *tr* Geoff Kidd/Photolibrary.com; 179 *br* Lycett Joseph ca. 1775-1828 National Library of Australia; 180 *t* Science Photo Library/Photolibrary.com; 180 *c* Science Photo Library/Photolibrary.com; 180 *b* Science Photo Library/Photolibrary.com; 182 *tr* Dreamstime; 182 *bl* Louise Gubb/Corbis; 183 Michael Reynolds/Corbis; 184 Gail Jankus/Photolibrary.com; 185 Science Photo Library/Photolibrary.com; 186 *b* RD-owned; 187 RD-owned; 188 RD-owned; 189 *tl* istockphoto; 189 *tr* Photolibrary.com; 189 *br* Klaus Honal/Corbis; 190 RD-owned; 191 *t* RD-owned; 191 *bl* RD-owned; 192 RD-owned; 193 *t* RD-owned; 193 *b* RD-owned; 194 *t* RD-owned; 194 *b* RD-owned; 195 *l* RD-owned; 195 *r* RD-owned; 196 *tr* istockphoto; 196 *br* DeAgostini/Getty Images; 196 *b* Panoramic Images;/Getty Images; 197 Patricia Fogden/Corbis; 198 *tr* Botanica/Photolibrary.com; 199 *t* Shutterstock; 199 *r* Ken Lucas/Getty Images; 199 *bl* James Worrell/Time & Life Pictures/Getty Images; 200 istockphoto; 201 Tafel; 202 RD-owned; 203 Elizabeth Blackwell/Stapleton Collection/Corbis; 204 *bl* istockphoto; 204 *tr* RD-owned; 205 Tafel; 206 *l* Tafel; 206 *r* RD-owned; 207 RD-owned; 208 Tafel; 209 istockphoto; 210 Tafel; 211 istockphoto; 212 Shutterstock; 213 istockphoto; 214 Michael Maslan/Corbis; 215 istockphoto; 216 RD-owned; 217 Tafel; 218 Forest & Kim Starr; 219 Tafel; 221 Philip de Bay/Historical Picture Archive/Corbis; 222 Time Life Pictures/Getty Images; 223 RD-owned; 224 *tr* RD-owned; 224 *bl* Martin Harvey/Gallo Images/Corbis; 225 *tr* Jose B. Ruiz/Nature Picture Library 226 Stapleton Collection/Corbis; 227 *br* Tafel; 228 *bl* istockphoto; 229 The Bridgeman Art Library/Photolibrary.com; 230 Tafel; 231 *tr* Artkey/Corbis; 232 Preston Schlebusch/Imagebank,/Getty Images; 233 Tafel; 234 The Bridgeman Art Library/Photolibrary.com; 235 *tr* RD-owned; 235 *br* RD-owned; 236 *tr* Keith A. McLeod; 237 *bl* Cynthia Hart/Corbis; 238 *tr* istockphoto; 238 *bl* istockphoto; 239 The Bridgeman Art Library/Photolibrary.com; 243 RD-owned; 244 *tl* RD-owned; 245 *t* istockphoto; 245 *bl* istockphoto; 246 RD-owned; 247 RD-owned; 248 *tr* RD-owned; 248 *b* RD-owned; 249 RD-owned; 250 *b* RD-owned; 251 *tr* istockphoto; 251 *br* RD-owned; 252 *tr* RD-owned; 252-253 RD-owned; 254 RD-owned; 254-255 RD-owned; 255 *t* RD-owned; 256 *tr* The Bridgeman Art Library/Photolibrary.com; 257 RD-owned; 258 *tr* RD-owned; 258 *b* RD-owned; 259 RD-owned; 260 *bl* RD-owned; 261 *tr* istockphoto; 261 *br* RD-owned; 262 RD-owned; 263 *tr* istockphoto; 263 Shutterstock; 264 *t* istockphoto; 264-265 RD-owned; 265 *r* istockphoto; 266 *bl* RD-owned; 266-277 RD-owned; 267 *tr* RD-owned; 268 *bl* istockphoto; 269 *tr* RD-owned; 270 *tr* RD-owned; 271 RD-owned; 272 *tr* RD-owned; 272 *tl* RD-owned; 273 *tl* istockphoto; 273 *br* RD-owned; 274 *tr* RD-owned; 275 *br* RD-owned; 276 *tr* David Pluth/Getty Images; 276 *b* RD-owned; 277 RD-owned; 278 RD-owned; 279 *tr* RD-owned; 279 *b* RD-owned; 280 RD-owned; 281 *tr* istockphoto; 281 *b* RD-owned; 295 *t* istockphoto; 296 *br* istockphoto

Acknowledgments

The publishers wish to thank the following individuals,
companies and organizations for their help during the preparation of
The Complete Book of Herbs.

Alex Jordan. Ambiance Interiors. Australia Post. Australia's Open Garden Scheme. Baytree. Beclau.
Blooms the Chemist. British Sweets & Treats.
Buds and Bowers Florist. Bulb. Bunnings. Chee Soon and Fitzgerald.
Chinese Ginseng & Herb Co. Coles Supermarkets Australia. Darling Street Health Centre. Domayne.
Dong Nam A & Co. Doug Up on Bourke. Dulux.
Feed Ya Face. Flower Power Nursery. Freedom Furniture. Fruitique. Funkis Swedish Forms.
Gardens R Us. Glebe Newsagency. Glenmore House. Gold's World of Judaica. Gundabluey.
Herb Herbert. House of Herbs and Roses.
Julie Pilcher Flowers. Mint Condition. Moss River. Mr Copy.
Mrs Red and Sons. New Directions Australia. No Chintz. Oishi. Oxford Art Supplies.
Paper Couture. Paper2. Pet City. Price War. Reln Plastics. Rococo Flowers.
Ros Andrews. Royal Botanic Gardens, Sydney. Sally Stobo. Spotlight Australia.
St. Vincent de Paul Society. Stark's Kosher Supermarket. Summers Floral Woollahra.
Swadlings Timber and Hardware. The Barn Café and Grocery.
The Floral Decorator. The Nut Shop. The Tegal Garden. Urban Balcony. Vicino.
Wholefoods House. Yarrow's Pharmacy.

Special thanks to Fratelli Fresh for the supply of fresh herbs for photography.
Herbie's Spices. Ici et La.

Craft project makers Irene Barnes – hanging herb ball.
Georgina Bitcon – sewing and embroidery projects.
Margaret Cox – garden dibbers.
Julie Pilcher – herb and flower wreath; table centrepiece; tussie-mussie.
Stephen Prodes – window boxes.

Locations and animals Finckh/Talako house and Akira (the cat).
Gibson/Chamberlain house and Pinky (the cat). Martin/Barnes house
and Maxie and Saffron (the dogs). Ladkin house. Sarsfield house.